Children's
Literature
Review

Guide to Gale Literary Criticism Series

When you need to review criticism of literary works, these are the Gale series to use:

If the author's death date is: **You should turn to:**

After Dec. 31, 1959
(or author is still living)

CONTEMPORARY LITERARY CRITICISM

for example: Jorge Luis Borges, Anthony Burgess,
William Faulkner, Mary Gordon,
Ernest Hemingway, Iris Murdoch

1900 through 1959

TWENTIETH-CENTURY LITERARY CRITICISM

for example: Willa Cather, F. Scott Fitzgerald,
Henry James, Mark Twain, Virginia Woolf

1800 through 1899

NINETEENTH-CENTURY LITERATURE CRITICISM

for example: Fedor Dostoevski, Nathaniel Hawthorne,
George Sand, William Wordsworth

1400 through 1799

LITERATURE CRITICISM FROM 1400 TO 1800
(excluding Shakespeare)

for example: Anne Bradstreet, Daniel Defoe,
Alexander Pope, François Rabelais,
Jonathan Swift, Phillis Wheatley

SHAKESPEAREAN CRITICISM

Shakespeare's plays and poetry

Antiquity through 1399

CLASSICAL AND MEDIEVAL LITERATURE CRITICISM

for example: Dante, Homer, Plato, Sophocles, Vergil,
the Beowulf Poet

Gale also publishes related criticism series:

CHILDREN'S LITERATURE REVIEW

This series covers authors of all eras who write for the preschool
through high school audience.

SHORT STORY CRITICISM

This series covers the major short fiction writers of all nationalities
and periods of literary history.

volume 17

Children's Literature Review

Excerpts from Reviews,
Criticism, and Commentary
on Books for Children
and Young People

Gerard J. Senick
Editor

Melissa Reiff Hug
Associate Editor

Gale Research Inc.
Book Tower
Detroit, Michigan 48226

STAFF

Gerard J. Senick, *Editor*

Melissa Reiff Hug, *Associate Editor*

Susan Miller Harig, *Senior Assistant Editor*

Motoko Fujishiro Huthwaite, *Assistant Editor*

Sharon R. Gunton, *Contributing Editor*

Debra A. Wells, *Contributing Assistant Editor*

Jeanne A. Gough, *Permissions & Production Manager*

Lizbeth A. Purdy, *Production Supervisor*
Kathleen M. Cook, *Production Coordinator*
Christine A. Galbraith, David G. Oblender, Suzanne Powers, Linda M. Ross,
Lee Ann Welsh, *Editorial Assistants*

Linda M. Pugliese, *Manuscript Coordinator*
Maureen A. Puhl, *Senior Manuscript Assistant*
Donna Craft, Jennifer E. Gale, *Manuscript Assistants*

Victoria B. Cariappa, *Research Supervisor*
Maureen R. Richards, *Research Coordinator*
Mary D. Wise, *Senior Research Assistant*
Joyce E. Doyle, Rogene M. Fisher, Kevin B. Hillstrom, Karen D. Kaus, Eric Priehs, Filomena Sgambati, *Research Assistants*

Janice M. Mach, *Text Permissions Supervisor*
Kathy Grell, *Text Permissions Coordinator*
Josephine M. Keene, *Senior Permissions Assistant*
H. Diane Cooper, Kimberly F. Smilay, *Permissions Assistants*
Melissa Ann Brantley, Denise M. Singleton, Lisa M. Wimmer, *Permissions Clerks*

Patricia A. Seefelt, *Picture Permissions Supervisor*
Margaret A. Chamberlain, *Picture Permissions Coordinator*
Pamela A. Hayes, Lillian Quickly, *Permissions Clerks*

Mary Beth Trimper, *Production Manager*
Darlene K. Maxey, *External Production Associate*

Arthur Chartow, *Art Director*
Linda A. Davis, *Production Assistant*

Laura Bryant, *Production Supervisor*
Louise Gagné, *Internal Production Associate*

CONTENTS

PREFACE

As children's literature has evolved into both a respected branch of creative writing and a successful industry, literary criticism has documented and influenced each stage of its growth. Critics have recorded the literary development of individual authors as well as the trends and controversies that resulted from changes in values and attitudes, especially as they concerned children. While defining a philosophy of children's literature, critics developed a scholarship that balances an appreciation of children and an awareness of their needs with standards for literary quality much like those required by critics of adult literature. *Children's Literature Review (CLR)* is designed to provide a permanent, accessible record of this ongoing scholarship. Those responsible for bringing children and books together can now make informed choices when selecting reading materials for the young.

Scope of the Series

Each volume of *CLR* contains excerpts from published criticism on the works of authors and illustrators who create books for children from preschool through high school. The author list for each volume is international in scope and represents the variety of genres covered by children's literature—picture books, fiction, folklore, nonfiction, poetry, and drama. The works of approximately fifteen authors of all eras are represented in each volume. Although earlier volumes of *CLR* emphasized critical material published after 1960, successive volumes have expanded their coverage to encompass criticism written before 1960. Since many of the authors included in *CLR* are living and continue to write, it is necessary to update their entries periodically. Thus, future volumes will supplement the entries of selected authors covered in earlier volumes as well as include criticism on the works of authors new to the series.

Organization of the Book

An author section consists of the following elements: author heading, author portrait, author introduction, excerpts of criticism (each followed by a bibliographical citation), and illustrations, when available.

- The **author heading** consists of the author's full name followed by birth and death dates. The portion of the name outside the parentheses denotes the form under which the author is most frequently published. If the majority of the author's works for children were written under a pseudonym, the pseudonym will be listed in the author heading and the real name given on the first line of the author introduction. Also located at the beginning of the introduction are any other pseudonyms used by the author in writing for children and any name variations, including transliterated forms for authors whose languages use nonroman alphabets. Uncertainty as to a birth or death date is indicated by question marks.

- An **author portrait** is included when available.

- The **author introduction** contains information designed to introduce an author to *CLR* users by presenting an overview of the author's themes and styles, occasional biographical facts that relate to the author's literary career, a summary of critical response to the author's works, and information about major awards and prizes the author has received. Where applicable, introductions conclude with references to additional entries in biographical and critical reference series published by Gale Research Inc. These sources include past volumes of *CLR* as well as *Authors in the News, Contemporary Authors, Contemporary Literary Criticism, Dictionary of Literary Biography, Nineteenth-Century Literature Criticism, Something about the Author, Something about the Author Autobiography Series, Twentieth-Century Literary Criticism,* and *Yesterday's Authors of Books for Children.*

- **Criticism** is located in three sections: **author's commentary** and **general commentary** (when available) and within individual **title entries,** which are preceded by **title entry headings.** Criticism is arranged chronologically within each section. Titles by authors being profiled are highlighted in boldface type within the text for easier access by readers.

The **author's commentary** presents background material written by the author or by an interviewer. This commentary may cover a specific work or several works. Author's commentary on more than one work appears after the author introduction, while commentary on an individual book follows the title entry heading.

The **general commentary** consists of critical excerpts that consider more than one work by the author being profiled. General commentary is preceded by the critic's name in boldface type or, in the case of unsigned criticism, by the title of the journal.

Title entry headings precede the criticism on a title and cite publication information on the work being reviewed. Title headings list the title of the work as it appeared in its country of origin; titles in languages using nonroman alphabets are transliterated. If the original title is in a language other than English, the title of the first English-language translation follows in brackets. The first available publication date of each work is listed in parentheses following the title. Differing U.S. and British titles of works originally published in English follow the publication date within the parentheses.

Title entries consist of critical excerpts on the author's individual works, arranged chronologically by publication date. The entries generally contain two to six reviews per title, depending on the stature of the book and the amount of criticism it has generated. The editors select titles that reflect the entire scope of the author's literary contribution, covering each genre and subject. An effort is made to reprint criticism that represents the full range of each title's reception—from the year of its initial publication to current assessments. Thus, the reader is provided with a record of the author's critical history. Publication information (such as publisher names and book prices) and parenthetical numerical references (such as footnotes or page and line references to specific editions of works) have been deleted at the editor's discretion to provide smoother reading of the text.

Entries on authors who are also illustrators will occasionally feature commentary on selected works illustrated but not written by the author being profiled. These works are strongly associated with the illustrator and have received critical acclaim for their art. By including critical comment on works of this type, the editors wish to provide a more complete representation of the author's total career. Criticism on these works has been chosen to stress artistic, rather than literary, contributions. Title entry headings for works illustrated by the author being profiled are arranged chronologically within the entry by date of publication and include notes identifying the author of the illustrated work. In order to provide easier access for users, all titles illustrated by the subject of the entry will be boldfaced.

CLR also includes entries on prominent illustrators who have contributed to the field of children's literature. These entries are designed to represent the development of the illustrator as an artist rather than as a literary stylist. The illustrator's section is organized like that of an author, with two exceptions: the introduction presents an overview of the illustrator's styles and techniques rather than outlining his or her literary background, and the commentary written by the illustrator on his or her works is called illustrator's commentary rather than author's commentary. Title entry headings are followed by explanatory notes identifying the author of the illustrated work. All titles of books containing illustrations by the artist being profiled as well as individual illustrations from these books are highlighted in boldface type.

• Selected excerpts are preceded by **explanatory notes,** which provide information on the critic or work of criticism to enhance the reader's understanding of the excerpt.

• A complete **bibliographical citation** designed to facilitate the location of the original book or article follows each piece of criticism.

• Numerous **illustrations** are featured in *CLR*. For entries on illustrators, an effort has been made to include illustrations that reflect the characteristics discussed in the criticism. Entries on major authors who do not illustrate their own works may also include photographs and other illustrative material pertinent to the authors' careers.

Other Features

• A list of **authors to appear in future volumes** follows the preface.

• An **appendix** lists the sources from which material has been reprinted in the volume. It does not, however, list every book or periodical consulted for the volume.

• The **cumulative index to authors** lists authors who have appeared in *CLR* and includes cross-references to *Authors in the News, Contemporary Authors, Contemporary Literary Criticism, Dictionary of Literary Biography, Nineteenth-Century Literature Criticism, Something about the Author, Something about the Author Autobiography Series, Twentieth-Century Literary Criticism,* and *Yesterday's Authors of Books for Children.*

- The **cumulative nationality index** lists authors alphabetically under their respective nationalities. Author names are followed by the volume number(s) in which they appear. Authors who have changed citizenship or whose current citizenship is not reflected in biographical sources appear under both their original nationality and that of their current residence.

- The **cumulative title index** lists titles covered in *CLR* followed by the volume and page number where criticism begins.

Acknowledgments

No work of this scope can be accomplished without the cooperation of many people. The editors especially wish to thank the copyright holders of the criticism included in this volume, the permissions managers of many book and magazine publishing companies for assisting us in securing reprint rights, and the staffs of the Kresge Library at Wayne State University, the University of Michigan Library, the Detroit Public Library, and the Wayne Oakland Library Federation (WOLF) for making their resources available to us. We are also grateful to Anthony J. Bogucki for his assistance with copyright research.

Suggestions Are Welcome

In response to various suggestions, several features have been added to *CLR* since the series began, including author entries on retellers of traditional literature as well as those who have been the first to record oral tales and other folklore; entries on prominent illustrators featuring commentary on their styles and techniques; entries on authors whose works are considered controversial or have been challenged; occasional entries devoted to criticism on a single work by a major author; explanatory notes that provide information on the critic or work of criticism to enhance the usefulness of the excerpt; more extensive illustrative material, such as holographs of manuscript pages and photographs of people and places pertinent to the authors' careers; a cumulative nationality index for easy access to authors by nationality; and occasional guest essays written specifically for *CLR* by prominent critics on subjects of their choice.

Readers are cordially invited to write the editor with comments and suggestions for further enhancing the usefulness of the *CLR* series.

AUTHORS TO APPEAR IN FUTURE VOLUMES

Adams, Harriet S(tratemeyer)
 1893?-1982
Adams, Richard 1920-
Adler, Irving 1913-
Ahlberg, Janet 1944- and Allan 1938-
Anderson, C(larence) W(illiam)
 1891-1971
Arrick, Fran
Arundel, Honor (Morfydd) 1919-1973
Asbjörnsen, Peter Christen 1812-1885
 and Jörgen Moe 1813?-1882
Asch, Frank 1946-
Atwater, Richard Tupper 1892-1948
 and Florence (Hasseltine Carroll)
Avery, Gillian 1926-
Avi 1937-
Aymé, Marcel 1902-1967
Bailey, Carolyn Sherwin 1875-1961
Ballantyne, R(obert) M(ichael)
 1825-1894
Banner, Angela 1923-
Bannerman, Helen 1863-1946
Barrett, Judi(th) 1941-
Baumann, Hans 1914-1985
Beatty, Patricia Robbins 1922-
 and John 1922-1975
Beckman, Gunnel 1910-
Behn, Harry 1898-1973
Belaney, Archibald
 Stansfield 1888-1938
Belloc, Hilaire 1870-1953
Berenstain, Stan(ley) 1923- and
 Jan(ice) 1923-
Berger, Melvin H. 1927-
Berna, Paul 1910-
Bianco, Margery Williams 1881-1944
Bishop, Claire Huchet
Blake, Quentin 1932-
Blos, Joan W(insor) 1928-
Blumberg, Rhoda 1917-
Blyton, Enid 1897-1968
Bodecker, N(iels) M(ogens) 1922-1988
Bodker, Cecil 1927-
Bonham, Frank 1914-
Boutet De Monvel, (Louis)
 M(aurice) 1850(?)-1913
Brancato, Robin F(idler) 1936-
Branscum, Robbie 1937-
Breinburg, Petronella 1927-
Bridgers, Sue Ellen 1942-
Bright, Robert 1902-
Brink, Carol Ryrie 1895-1981
Brinsmead, H(esba) F(ay) 1922-
Brooke, L(eonard) Leslie 1862-1940
Brooks, Bruce
Brown, Marc Tolon 1946-

Browne, Anthony (Edward Tudor)
 1946-
Bryan, Ashley F. 1923-
Buff, Mary 1890-1970 and Conrad
 1886-1975
Bulla, Clyde Robert 1914-
Burch, Robert (Joseph) 1925-
Burgess, Gelett 1866-1951
Burgess, Thornton W(aldo) 1874-1965
Burkert, Nancy Ekholm 1933-
Burnett, Frances Hodgson 1849-1924
Butterworth, Oliver 1915-
Caines, Jeannette (Franklin)
Carlson, Natalie Savage 1906-
Carrick, Carol 1935- and Donald 1929-
Chambers, Aidan 1934-
Chönz, Selina
Christopher, Matt(hew F.) 1917-
Ciardi, John (Anthony) 1916-1986
Clapp, Patricia 1912-
Clarke, Pauline 1921-
Cohen, Barbara 1932-
Colby, C(arroll) B(urleigh) 1904-1977
Cole, Brock 1938-
Colman, Hila
Colum, Padraic 1881-1972
Cone, Molly 1918-
Conrad, Pam 1947-
Coolidge, Olivia E(nsor) 1908-
Coolidge, Susan 1835-1905
Cooney, Barbara 1917-
Corbett, W(illiam) J(esse) 1938-
Courlander, Harold 1908-
Cox, Palmer 1840-1924
Crane, Walter 1845-1915
Cresswell, Helen 1934-
Crompton, Richmal 1890-1969
Crutcher, Chris(topher C.) 1946-
Cunningham, Julia (Woolfolk) 1916-
Curry, Jane L(ouise) 1932-
Dalgliesh, Alice 1893-1979
Daly, Maureen 1921-
Danziger, Paula 1944-
Daugherty, James 1889-1974
D'Aulaire, Ingri 1904-1980 and Edgar
 Parin 1898-1986
DeClements, Barthe 1920-
De la Mare, Walter 1873-1956
De Regniers, Beatrice Schenk 1914-
Dickinson, Peter 1927-
Dillon, Eilís 1920-
Dillon, Leo 1933- and Diane 1933-
Disch, Thomas M(ichael) 1940-
Dodge, Mary Mapes 1831-1905
Domanska, Janina
Drescher, Henrik

Duncan, Lois S(teinmetz) 1934-
Duvoisin, Roger 1904-1980
Eager, Edward 1911-1964
Edgeworth, Maria 1767-1849
Edmonds, Walter D(umaux) 1903-
Epstein, Sam(uel) 1909- and Beryl
 1910-
Ets, Marie Hall 1893-
Ewing, Juliana Horatia 1841-1885
Farber, Norma 1909-1984
Farjeon, Eleanor 1881-1965
Field, Eugene 1850-1895
Field, Rachel 1894-1942
Fisher, Dorothy Canfield 1879-1958
Fisher, Leonard Everett 1924-
Flack, Marjorie 1897-1958
Forbes, Esther 1891-1967
Forman, James D(ouglas) 1932-
Freedman, Russell 1929-
Freeman, Don 1908-1978
Fujikawa, Gyo 1908-
Fyleman, Rose 1877-1957
Gantos, Jack 1951-
Garfield, Leon 1921-
Garis, Howard R(oger) 1873-1962
Garner, Alan 1935-
Gates, Doris 1901-1988
Gerrard, Roy 1935-
Giblin, James Cross 1933-
Giff, Patricia Reilly 1935-
Ginsburg, Mirra 1919-
Goble, Paul 1933-
Godden, Rumer 1907-
Goodall, John S(trickland) 1908-
Goodrich, Samuel G(riswold)
 1793-1860
Gorey, Edward (St. John) 1925-
Gramatky, Hardie 1907-1979
Greene, Constance C(larke) 1924-
Grimm, Jacob 1785-1863 and Wilhelm
 1786-1859
Gruelle, Johnny 1880-1938
Guillot, René 1900-1969
Hader, Elmer 1889-1973 and Berta
 1891?-1976
Hague, Michael 1948-
Hale, Lucretia Peabody 1820-1900
Haley, Gail E(inhart) 1939-
Hall, Lynn 1937-
Harnett, Cynthia 1893-1981
Harris, Christie (Lucy Irwin) 1907-
Harris, Joel Chandler 1848-1908
Harris, Rosemary (Jeanne) 1923-
Hayes, Sheila 1937-
Haywood, Carolyn 1898-
Head, Ann 1915-

Heide, Florence Parry 1919-
Heine, Helme
Heinlein, Robert A(nson) 1907-1988
Henkes, Kevin 1960-
Hoberman, Mary Ann 1930-
Hoff, Syd(ney) 1912-
Hoffman, Heinrich 1809-1894
Holland, Isabelle 1920-
Holling, Holling C(lancy) 1900-1973
Hunter, Mollie 1922-
Hurd, Edith Thacher 1910-
    and Clement 1908-1988
Hutchins, Pat 1942-
Hyman, Trina Schart 1939-
Ipcar, Dahlov (Zorach) 1917-
Iwasaki, Chihiro 1918-1974
Jackson, Jesse 1908-1983
Janosch 1931-
Johnson, Crockett 1906-1975
Johnson, James Weldon 1871-1938
Jones, Diana Wynne 1934-
Judson, Clara Ingram 1879-1960
Juster, Norton 1929-
Kelly, Eric P(hilbrook) 1884-1960
Kennedy, (Jerome) Richard 1932-
Kent, Jack 1920-1985
Kerr, (Anne-)Judith 1923-
Kerr, M. E. 1927-
Kettelkamp, Larry (Dale) 1933-
Kherdian, David 1931-
King, (David) Clive 1924-
Kipling, Rudyard 1865-1936
Kjelgaard, Jim 1910-1959
Klein, Robin 1936-
Kraus, Robert 1925-
Krauss, Ruth (Ida) 1911-
Krumgold, Joseph 1908-1980
La Fontaine, Jean de 1621-1695
Lang, Andrew 1844-1912
Langton, Jane (Gillson) 1922-
Latham, Jean Lee 1902-
Lattimore, Eleanor Frances 1904-1986
Lavine, Sigmund A(rnold) 1908-
Leaf, Munro 1905-1976
Lenski, Lois 1893-1974
Levy, Elizabeth 1942-
Lightner, A(lice) M. 1904-
Lindgren, Barbro 1937-
Lipsyte, Robert 1938-
Lofting, Hugh (John) 1866-1947
Lunn, Janet 1928-
MacDonald, George 1824-1905
MacGregor, Ellen 1906-1954
Mann, Peggy
Marshall, James 1942-
Martin, Patricia Miles 1899-1986
Maruki, Toshi 19??-
Masefield, John 1878-1967
Mattingley, Christobel
    (Rosemary) 1931-
Mayer, Marianna 1945-

Mayne, William (James Carter) 1928-
Mazer, Norma Fox 1931-
McCaffrey, Anne (Inez) 1926-
McGovern, Ann
McKee, David (John)
McKillip, Patricia A(nne) 1948-
McNeer, May 1902-
Meader, Stephen W(arren) 1892-1977
Means, Florence Crannell 1891-1980
Meigs, Cornelia 1884-1973
Merrill, Jean (Fairbanks) 1923-
Miles, Betty 1928-
Milne, Lorus 1912- and Margery 1915-
Minarik, Else Holmelund 1920-
Mizumura, Kazue
Mohr, Nicholasa 1935-
Molesworth, Mary Louisa 1842-1921
Morey, Walt(er Nelson) 1907-
Mowat, Farley (McGill) 1921-
Munsch, Robert N. 1945-
Neufeld, John (Arthur) 1938-
Neville, Emily Cheney 1919-
Nic Leodhas, Sorche 1898-1969
North, Sterling 1906-1974
Norton, Andre 1912-
Ofek, Uriel 1926-
Ormerod, Jan(ette Louise) 1946-
Ormondroyd, Edward 1925-
Oxenbury, Helen 1938-
Parish, Peggy 1927-1988
Patent, Dorothy Hinshaw 1940-
Paulsen, Gary 1939-
Peck, Robert Newton 1928-
Perl, Lila
Perrault, Charles 1628-1703
Petersen, P(eter) J(ames) 1941-
Petersham, Maud 1890-1971 and
    Miska 1888-1960
Picard, Barbara Leonie 1917-
Pierce, Meredith Ann 1958-
Platt, Kin 1911-
Politi, Leo 1908-
Price, Christine 1928-1980
Pyle, Howard 1853-1911
Rackham, Arthur 1867-1939
Rawls, Wilson 1919-
Reiss, Johanna 1932-
Reeves, James 1909-1978
Richards, Laura E(lizabeth) 1850-1943
Richter, Hans Peter 1925-
Robertson, Keith (Carlton) 1914-
Rockwell, Anne 1934- and Harlow
    19??-1988
Rodgers, Mary 1931-
Rollins, Charlemae Hill 1897-1979
Ross, Tony 1938-
Rounds, Glen H(arold) 1906-
Salinger, J(erome) D(avid) 1919-
Sanchez, Sonia 1934-
Sandburg, Carl 1878-1967
Sandoz, Mari 1896-1966

Sawyer, Ruth 1880-1970
Scarry, Huck 1953-
Scoppettone, Sandra 1936-
Scott, Jack Denton 1915-
Seton, Ernest Thompson 1860-1946
Sharmat, Marjorie Weinman 1928-
Sharp, Margery 1905-
Shepard, Ernest H(oward) 1879-1976
Shotwell, Louisa R(ossiter) 1902-
Sidney, Margaret 1844-1924
Silverstein, Alvin 1933- and Virginia
    B(arbara Opshelor) 1937-
Sinclair, Catherine 1800-1864
Skurzynski, Gloria (Joan) 1930-
Sleator, William (Warner) 1945-
Slobodkin, Louis 1903-1975
Smith, Jessie Willcox 1863-1935
Snyder, Zilpha Keatley 1927-
Spence, Eleanor (Rachel) 1928-
Sperry, Armstrong W. 1897-1976
Spykman, E(lizabeth) C. 1896-1965
Starbird, Kaye 1916-
Steele, William O(wen) 1917-1979
Stolz, Mary (Slattery) 1920-
Stratemeyer, Edward L. 1862-1930
Taylor, Sydney 1904?-1978
Taylor, Theodore 1924-
Tenniel, Sir John 1820-1914
Thiele, Colin 1920-
Thomas, Joyce Carol 1938-
Thompson, Julian F(rancis) 1927-
Thompson, Kay 1912-
Titus, Eve 1922-
Tolkien, J(ohn) R(onald) R(euel)
    1892-1973
Trease, (Robert) Geoffrey 1909-
Tresselt, Alvin 1916-
Treviño, Elizabeth Borton de 1904-
Turkle, Brinton 1915-
Twain, Mark 1835-1910
Udry, Janice May 1928-
Unnerstad, Edith (Totterman) 1900-
Uttley, Alison 1884-1976
Vining, Elizabeth Gray 1902-
Waber, Bernard 1924-
Wahl, Jan 1933-
Ward, Lynd 1905-1985
White, T(erence) H(anbury) 1906-1964
Wiese, Kurt 1887-1974
Wilkinson, Brenda 1946-
Wood, Audrey and Don 1945-
Worth, Valerie 1933-
Wyeth, N(ewell) C(onvers) 1882-1945
Yates, Elizabeth 1905-
Yonge, Charlotte M(ary) 1823-1901
Yorinks, Arthur 1953-
Zelinsky, Paul O. 1953-
Zemach, Harve 1933-1974 and Margot
    1931-
Zion, Gene 1913-1975

Readers are cordially invited to suggest additional authors to the editors.

Children's
Literature
Review

Verna (Norberg) Aardema (Vugteveen)

1911-

American reteller.

One of the most highly regarded adapters of African folktales for children, Aardema is noted for creating authentic interpretations which skillfully incorporate the outstanding features of the oral tradition with wit, charm, and vitality. Best known for the cumulative pourquoi tale *Why Mosquitoes Buzz in People's Ears: A West African Tale* (1975) and for *Who's in Rabbit's House? A Masai Tale* (1977), the story of an outwitted caterpillar, she is also popular for her first collection of African folklore, *Tales from the Story Hat* (1960), in which listeners choose an object dangling from the storyteller's hat to represent their requests. Aardema's stories, which are published both in collections and individually, introduce children to exotic characters from well-researched sources covering a broad range of geographic and cultural backgrounds—East, Central, West, and South Africa as well as Mexico. She expresses observations of human behavior and the universal values inherent in the morals of her tales through the inclusion of such elements as animal trickery, magic, adventure, and romance. Formerly a primary teacher, Aardema brings her singular use of unusual names, African ideophones, repetition, rhythmic verses, onomatopoeia, and surprise endings to her works, which are often considered ideal for reading aloud and for audience participation. In addition to her stories and fables, Aardema has also written *Ji- Nongo-Nongo Means Riddles* (1978), a book of riddles from eleven African tribes.

Praised as a master of the storyteller's art, Aardema is also celebrated for her apt selections, simplicity, and humor. Although some reviewers find her writing style too austere, most agree that Aardema has made stories of diverse cultures available to children in books that are understandable, enjoyable, and memorable.

Aardema has won several awards for her books. In 1976 *Why Mosquitoes Buzz in People's Ears,* illustrated by Leo and Diane Dillon, won the Caldecott Medal. In 1978 *Who's in Rabbit's House* received the Lewis Carroll Shelf Award.

(See also *Something about the Author,* Vol. 4; *Contemporary Authors New Revision Series,* Vols. 3, 18; and *Contemporary Authors,* Vols. 5-8, rev. ed.)

GENERAL COMMENTARY

ROY TOOTHAKER

Verna Aardema is an author of children's books who tells stories as skillfully as she writes them. So far, she is the author of nine books for children; some of the books are collections of African folktales and some are single folktales in picture-book format.

Mrs. Aardema takes a folktale from its source and applies rules for adaption she has discovered through years of practicing her craft. She fixes the title, cuts out unnecessary words, and strengthens the plot; she tightens the tales by emphasizing cause and effect relationships, making one episode cause the next to happen; then she gives the story a bang-up climax, and rounds

out the ending. She says, "I always strive for brevity, sometimes eliminating unimportant episodes to achieve it. Like the African storyteller, I retell a tale to make it more satisfying and more understandable to my audience, my readers."

Consequently, she comes up with stories which are highly enjoyable, easily read by children, and are especially suited for storytelling and dramatizing. In fact, when she was a primary teacher, she had the children in her various classes act out many of her stories.

She traces her "beginnings" as an author to the day she returned from school with an "A" on a poem she had written. Her mother recognized for the first time that her dreamy daughter who dallied over housework had a special talent. "Mama read it and said, 'Why, Verna, you're going to be a writer like my grandpa!' And that was the first time I had been noticed for any good reason. Right then and there, I decided to make a career of being like my ancestor who had published frequently in religious magazines."

From then on, little Verna was encouraged to write. At the edge of her favorite spot—a solitary, cedar swamp—she made up stories and told them to her young friends.

Mrs. Aardema recalls, "Years later, it was my little daughter who got me started writing children's stories. She wouldn't eat without a story. And she could make a scrambled egg last all the way through 'Little Red Riding Hood.'''

After a time, Mrs. Aardema began to make up little feeding stories, to which the child did not know the ending. Mrs. Aardema says, ''That way she didn't know how far off the ending would be.'' And because Mrs. Aardema was usually reading about Africa, the feeding stories were apt to be set in Ashantiland or the Kalahari Desert.

It was one of those feeding stories that Mrs. Aardema sold to the *Instructor* magazine that got her into the Coward-McCann stable of authors. The editor, Alice Torrey, asked her to use it as chapter one of a juvenile novel. Mrs. Aardema countered with the suggestion of a collection of African folk tales which had not been done for children.

Mrs. Aardema recalls, ''She told me to go ahead. Then I set to work. I was like Ekoi the mouse who listens to the tales people tell. When Ekoi hears one she likes, she takes it home with her, makes a new garment for it, and it becomes her story child.''

Mrs. Aardema had to burrow into old library books, many obtained through inter-library loan, to find her stories. Then, she had to make new garments for them. She says

> For although the African storyteller embellishes his tales with plenty of songs, descriptions, and explanations when he is performing for an audience, he's apt to clam up for an anthropologist with a pencil. So the versions available to me are likely to be incomplete.
>
> In order to place a story in its proper setting, I have to read other books about the area from which it comes. Often a song is mentioned, but not given. And I have to make one up out of the whole cloth. Sometimes I have to change episodes because the original action is taboo in our culture.

Mrs. Aardema has an open ear to all the tales people told. She discovered the African storyteller, who kept track of the many stories in his head by attaching small carvings representing each story to his hat. Whoever wanted a story asked for it by picking an object on the hat. She says, ''The storyteller had the stories IN his head and the Table of Contents ON his head!'' These stories were collected and adapted for *Tales from the Story Hat* and *More Tales from the Story Hat*.

''When I learned that the publishers had accepted this book,'' she says, ''I couldn't breathe; I had to get out of the house and walk. When I returned to my teacher's desk that afternoon, I was so nervous I had broken out in hives.''

She laughs, ''You see, I can't stand success!''

Success has come many times to her. The book, *Why Mosquitoes Buzz in People's Ears*, a West African pourquoi tale, has been awarded the Caldecott Medal for [Leo and Diane Dillon's] distinguished illustrations. The book is scheduled for translation and publication into Afrikaans. *Who's in Rabbit's House?* is scheduled for translation and publication into Japanese. (pp. 190-91, 193)

> *Roy Toothaker, "Verna Aardema: Her Wondrous Tales Fall on Willing Ears,"* in Language Arts, *Vol. 56, No. 2, February, 1979, pp. 190-93.*

ALETHEA K. HELBIG

[*The Riddle of the Drum* is] not quite successful at meeting the challenge of creating cultural identity . . . ; [It is] a picture book

edition of the amusing Mexican counterpart of the drolly humorous Spanish tale, ''The Flea.'' . . . Because he loves his beautiful daughter very much, the proud king of Tizapan decrees that he will give her in marriage only to the man who can guess from what kind of leather a certain drum that gives off a sound like thunder has been made. The aspiring suitor is a handsome, young prince from a nearby land, not a humble shepherd from the hills, as in the Spanish tale. The prince is assisted, not by several lowly animals, but by five peasants he meets along the way to the palace, a swift runner, a sure archer, a keen hearer, a mighty blower, and a tremendous eater. Each of them agrees to accompany the prince and eventually proves helpful to him in winning the girl because of his peculiar ability. Then, in another interesting deviation from the Spanish story, the prince and princess are married and live happily for many years in the palace along with their remarkable helpers.

The narrative flows smoothly and lovingly, revealing Verna Aardema's characteristically keen sense of the storytelling situation. Although she might have employed more description in order to localize the story better, the language she has chosen falls felicitously upon the ear and tastes good on the tongue. Occasional internal rhymes and chimes give the prose portions of the story a poetic quality, while, as in the Spanish counterpart of this tale, verses extend a provocative invitation to listeners to join in the story. Not only do the verses help to move the plot along, they build atmosphere and add greatly to the charm of the story. (p. 48)

While Aardema's text is strong enough to stand by itself, it is really Tony Chen's magnificent illustrations that lift up this book and make it a memorable work of art. . . . The illustrations add details where the story needs fleshing out and strengthen the text by picturing a distinctively Mexican setting, bolstering the text where it can most use propping. . . . Taken together, Chen's art and Aardema's tale telling produce a highly attractive book that should wear well and make a graceful addition to any picture book collection.

Aardema, who handled African tales so successfully in *Who's in Rabbit's House?* and *Why Mosquitoes Buzz in People's Ears*, has created a picture book version of an Ashanti tale in *Half-a-Ball-of-Kenki*. This light and amusing explanatory story has two friends, Fly and Leopard, set out to find wives for themselves. Everywhere the two of them go, the villagers welcome gentle, courteous, little Fly, but they drive away vain and crafty Leopard. After this has happened several times, Leopard turns on Fly, captures him, and binds him to palm tree. He is certain that without Fly along he will soon find a bride. Because they are afraid Leopard will kill them if they release Fly, no one dares to set him free except Half-a-Ball-of-Kenki, a small ball of cornmeal mush. In anger, Leopard attacks her, and the two then engage in a violent wrestling match, until Kenki gets the upper hand and tosses Leopard into the fire. When he comes out, his previously yellow coat is spotted black and white from the charred wood and the ashes. Ever since that time, leopards have had black-and-white spotted coats.

Aardema manages to convey a stronger sense of culture in *Kenki* than she does in *Drum*. One way she does this is by employing the African tale teller's method of making the sounds of words suggest ideas. When a villager turns his dog on Leopard to drive him away, ''Leopard went flying *kuputu, kuputu, kuputu, kuputu* out the gate.'' These words, which have no meaning in themselves, more effectively put across the manner and mood of Leopard's frantic and hasty departure than would a prosaic phrase like, ''he got out of there as fast as he could.''

And besides, the repetition is rhythmically very appealing and adds much to the charm of the story. When Leopard grabs Fly and binds him to the palm tree, "winding the creeper *kpong, kpong, kpong,*" we can see and hear him slap the vine violently about the tree, confident that he is putting an end to what he perceives as rivalry. Again, the situation is described, the mood is set, and a pleasing rhythm is created by one word very felicitously chosen and repeated three times. Here and there Aardema casts a few speeches into verse, another device the old tale tellers employed. By preserving these African conventions, Aardema produces a sense of the original culture in which the storytellers actually used such phrases and verses to embellish their tales. At the same time, she provides the material by which those reading and hearing her story can join in the telling and so can experience something of the African shared storytelling situation. (pp. 49-50)

> *Alethea K. Helbig, "The Wheat and the Chaff: Separating Some Retellings," in* The World of Children's Books, *Vol. VI, 1981, pp. 46-52.*

TALES FROM THE STORY HAT   (1960)

[Nine] African stories, charmingly told, appear in this collection illustrated by Elton Fox. Dealing with animals and men of the jungle, the stories possess humor and shrewd observation. In most cases they either dramatize a characteristic trait or explain the origin of a particular tendency, either physical or emotional. Engrossing, often humorous, and refreshingly uncluttered, these stories should appeal to children of reading and pre-reading age.

> *A review of "Tales from the Story Hat," in* Virginia Kirkus' Service, *Vol. XXVIII, No. 7, April 1, 1960, p. 288.*

Skillful retellings of nine African folk tales—tales of animals and men, of the origins of things, of the wise and the foolish, of tricksters and the tricked. The entertaining collection is illustrated with striking illustrations which capture the spirit of the stories. The simplicity of the plots, straightforward style, and the humor make the tales particularly suitable for storytelling. Notes, sources, and a glossary are appended.

> *A review of "Tales from the Story Hat," in* The Booklist and Subscription Books Bulletin, *Vol. 56, No. 21, July 1, 1960, p. 663.*

Nine folktales . . . , most of them to do with animals rather than people; all are suitable for storytelling. The writing is rather dry, and there are occasional abrupt breaks in the narrative flow that are most apparent when the tales are read aloud.

> *A review of "Tales from the Story Hat," in* Bulletin of the Center for Children's Books, *Vol. XIV, No. 1, September, 1960, p. 1.*

THE NA OF WA; OTWE; THE SKY-GOD STORIES   (1960)

In each of these easy-to-read books, an African folk tale has been retold with simplicity and humor. *The Na of Wa* is the old story of the foolish son who proves to be really very wise. Otwe laughed all the time because he could understand the language of the animals. What happens when he shares this secret with his wife makes a humorous tale. *The Sky-God Stories* is a version of how Ananse, the spiderman, wins the right to have the African stories called Ananse or Spider Stories. . . .

Worthy additions to the author's *Tales from the Story Hat.* Recommended as additional African folklore for younger children.

> *Augusta Baker, in a review of "The Na of Wa," "Otwe," and "The Sky-God Stories," in* Junior Libraries, *an appendix to* Library Journal, *Vol. 7, No. 6, February 15, 1961, p. 50.*

[*Otwe* is a] simplified retelling of an African folk tale, based on a story called "The Man and the Snake" in *Nuer Customs and Folklore.* Writing style is rather pedestrian. . . . Otwe has the power of hearing animals talk, a power given him by a snake whom he had befriended, but his habit of laughing whenever he heard this led Otwe into trouble. After confessing his secret, he fell dead, but the snake brought Otwe back to life and laughter. The motivation of the tale is not apparent: Otwe makes no use of his power, and it is not made clear why he reacts with laughter.

> *Zena Sutherland, in a review of "Otwe," in* Bulletin of the Center for Children's Books, *Vol. XIV, No. 7, March, 1961, p. 104.*

[*The Na of Wa* is an] African folktale about Kojo, a boy who liked spending money rather than working. Each time his mother gave him gold dust, he made a foolish trade—but his last trade, a dove, turned out to be king of the doves. To redeem their king, the doves gave Kojo a magic ring; with it he obtained a village and became the chief, or Na. The tale has a typical folk pattern, but the writing style is abrupt in places and quite dull.

> *Zena Sutherland, in a review of "The Na of Wa," in* Bulletin of the Center for Children's Books, *Vol. XV, No. 2, October, 1961, p. 21.*

TALES FOR THE THIRD EAR, FROM EQUATORIAL AFRICA (1969)

Nine stories adapted from early (c. 1900) ethnic collections are presented in the simple, spacious format of *Tales from the Story Hat* and similarly geared to younger readers. In content, however, they are somewhat less intriguing. Two involve rather distasteful episodes (a greedy spider removing too much fat from around a cow's heart; much fetching and carrying of a lion cub's corpse); another hinges on an implausibility (a spider consuming one hundred crocodile eggs without a bulge); still another, the familiar attempt to disprove a liar, succeeds in wresting an admission from him only under duress. Most, however, turn on trickery of one sort or another—a practical joke in the case of the caterpillar who holds on to Tricksy Rabbit's house by faking a big scary voice (in **"The Long One,"** a funny episodic tale). Equally a fraud is the lioness who gets to keep four kidnapped ostrich chicks because the other animals are afraid to say they're not her own. . . . An up-and-down collection then, replete with incident, and authentic if not appetizing in its grislier moments.

> *A review of "Tales for the Third Ear from Equatorial Africa," in* Kirkus Reviews, *Vol. XXXVII, No. 9, May 1, 1969, p. 508.*

Hausa storytellers, according to the author, often preface tale telling with "How many ears have you?" To answers of "We have two ears!" the storytellers reply "Add a third, and listen to what I have to tell you!" Hence the title of this very good book, in which Mrs. Aardema presents nine central African stories, retold from earlier publications . . . and rewritten for children. Ananse, the crafty spider, is featured, as are other appealing, sometimes dishonorable, animals—a hoax-perpetrating, egotistical caterpillar, the crafty jackal Engojine, etc. The well chosen, skillfully rewritten tales are accompanied by humorous drawings in mustard, orange, and olive [by Ib Ohlsson], and by concluding notes which list sources of the stories and include definitions of unfamiliar words and terms.

> *Harold Lancour, in a review of "Tales for the Third Ear from Equatorial Africa," in* School Library Journal, *an appendix to* Library Journal, *Vol. 16, No. 2, October, 1969, p. 135.*

Nine folktales retold from original sources that gave verbatim versions of African storytelling. Several are about the familiar character Ananse the spider, three about humans, and the rest about other animals. All are concerned with trickery, the prankster sometimes suffering retribution, sometimes emerging in triumph from danger. The style is occasionally awkward, but the tales are full of action and humor, and are an excellent source for storytelling.

> *Zena Sutherland, in a review of "Tales for the Third Ear; from Equatorial Africa," in* Bulletin of the Center for Children's Books, *Vol. 23, No. 3, November, 1969, p. 37.*

BEHIND THE BACK OF THE MOUNTAIN: BLACK FOLKTALES FROM SOUTHERN AFRICA (1973)

As in her earlier African collections, the reteller and adapter of these ten short tales admirably indicates the sources of the stories (English-language volumes published from 1868 to 1938). Thus one can compare her work with earlier translations of Zulu, Bantu, Tshindao, Thonga, Bushman, and Hottentot texts. Told in a pleasing, clear manner, the stories should be interesting to children since they often detail the trickery of animals in their dealings with human beings or amongst themselves. A few stories—about people—contain universal motifs, such as that of maidens from heaven who take off their wings when bathing in a pool (Tshindao) and that of the King's faithful daughter and the beast (Zulu).

> *Virginia Haviland, in a review of "Behind the Back of the Mountain: Black Folktales from Southern Africa," in* The Horn Book Magazine, *Vol. XLIX, No. 6, December, 1973, p. 587.*

A tricky crocodile, some heavenly maidens, an extremely stupid jackal, and a gluttonous farmer are among the many characters in this diverse collection of tales from various tribes. Some of the stories are fables, with a definite moral, while others are based on such familiar themes as winning the hand of a beautiful princess or outwitting a monster. The author of *Tales for the third ear, from Equatorial Africa* has maintained the atmosphere of the stories' origins in her spirited, entertaining retelling....

> *Denise Murcko Wilms, in a review of "Behind the Back of the Mountain: Black Folktales from Southern Africa," in* The Booklist, *Vol. 70, No. 7, December 1, 1973, p. 384.*

Skillful retellings of Zulu, Bantu, Bushman, Tshindao, and Thonga folk tales adapted from late 19th- and early 20th Century English versions. These stories have more fantastic and eerie elements than do the author's *Tales from the Story Hat* and *More Tales from the Story Hat*; they contain less sly satire

than is found in the animal folk tales in such anthologies as Heady's *Safiri the Singer: East African Tales;* and, they are better suited to oral presentation than Fuja's *Fourteen Hundred Cowries.* Aardema makes good use of chants and details of South African culture (e.g., brass pillows, winged-ant food, the *ungongo* or marriage hut); [and] glossary gives background information.... Successfully blending the sophistication and naïveté characteristic of African folklore, these tales should appeal to a wide audience.

> *Dorothy de Wit, in a review of "Behind the Back of the Mountain: Black Folktales from Southern Africa," in* School Library Journal, *an appendix to* Library Journal, *Vol. 20, No. 8, April, 1974, p. 54.*

WHY MOSQUITOES BUZZ IN PEOPLE'S EARS: A WEST AFRICAN TALE (1975)

A "why" story from Africa is retold with verve in a picture book that should delight young listeners and adult readers—especially those who may use it for storytelling—equally. A mosquito tells a whopping lie to an iguana who, muttering, fails to respond to the greeting of a friendly snake. The snake goes into a rabbit hole and frightens a rabbit . . . and this chain of events leads to an owlet accidentally killed and its mother failing to hoot and wake the sun. No sun? The lion calls a meeting of all animals, the chain is unraveled, and the mosquito is condemned. The cumulation will appeal to listeners, and the youngest children especially will enjoy the descriptions of sound (the snake moves "wasawusu, wasawusu . . .") and the surprise ending.

> *Zena Sutherland, in a review of "Why Mosquitoes Buzz in People's Ears: A West African Folk Tale," in* Bulletin of the Center for Children's Books, *Vol. 29, No. 3, November, 1975, p. 37.*

This charming narrative of cause and effect is an African legend retold, one of the nicest of many such adaptations of African folklore. It begins with a mosquito teasing an iguana.... [The] chain of events is unraveled in a singsong, this-is-the-house-that-Jack-built rhythm that traces all the trouble right back to the lowly mosquito.

Children will enjoy the tattle-tale quality of the denouement. It is so satisfying to see the blame being passed along the line, and at the end to find the real culprit....

The repetitive patterns of feathers, leaves and scales [in Leo and Diane Dillon's illustrations] complement the lilting rhythms of the text—the snake slithers "wasawusu, wasawusu, wasawusu," and the monkey leaps "kili wili" and the iguana's head nods "badamin, badamin." I would never have imagined that a lion laughed "nge, nge, nge," but mosquitoes, it is certain, speak the same language all over the world.

> *Carol Stevens Kner, in a review of "Why Mosquitoes Buzz in People's Ears," in* The New York Times Book Review, *November 9, 1975, p. 48.*

Ms. Aardema has given us an excellent African story explaining why mosquitoes buzz in people's ears which by itself would be good, but the illustrations by Leo and Diane Dillon transform the text into a most superior work of art.... A superior book recommended for every media center serving children grades K-4.

James Norsworthy, in a review of "Why Mosquitoes Buzz in People's Ears," in Catholic Library World, *Vol. 47, No. 9, April, 1976, p. 409.*

WHO'S IN RABBIT'S HOUSE? A MASAI TALE   (1977)

[The] African Masai tale, interpreted by Verna Aardema is intriguing with its use of mystery and surprise. . . .

[Children] should thoroughly enjoy the scary dilemma of little Rabbit trying to deal with the villainous assertions of The Long One who has taken over his house. The moral of the story is not too heavily hammered and has the kind of toothsome twist that delights young readers.

Guernsey Le Pelley, "Goofy, Growing Monster Eats Its Way to Fame," in The Christian Science Monitor, *May 3, 1978, p. B6.*

An African legend re-told in a way both unexpected and thrilling. . . . It has a clear development and the repetitions so beloved of small children. The joke ending is a complete surprise and the text hums with marvellous sound-effects. . . . Don't be put off by the scholarly introductions. It is a genuine children's book, a marvellous read aloud.

Ann Pilling, in a review of "Who's in Rabbit's House?" in Books for Your Children, *Vol. 16, No. 1, Spring, 1981, p. 15.*

The writer and artists have achieved a really fine adaptation of a Masai tale for European children. The language used in the text is attractive with wonderful rhythms. . . . There is much humour in the story which highlights many facets of human behaviour.

Eileen A. Archer, in a review of "Who's in Rabbit's House?" in Book Window, *Vol. 8, No. 3, Summer, 1981, p. 18.*

JI-NONGO-NONGO MEANS RIDDLES   (1978)

Aardema has collected a number of riddles from 11 African tribes, among them the Hausa, the Masai and the Wolof. Unlike Western riddles, which often are simple puns, these tend to be more philosophical, more puzzlelike. They are humorous, instructive and, once you know the answer, so full of common sense that it's hard to believe you didn't guess it immediately. (p. E4)

Lawanda Randall, "Folktales of Fabled Africa," in Book World—The Washington Post, *November 12, 1978, pp. E1, E4.*

The idea in this riddle collection, gathered from eleven tribes, is rather good, but once again we have the African heritage bit. The riddles, however, are very corny and almost appear to be American ones set in a pseudo-African locale. Most African jokes and riddles have morals; these do not.

James S. Haskins, in a review of "Ji-Nongo-Nongo Means Riddle," in Children's Book Review Service, *Vol. 7, No. 4, December, 1978, p. 33.*

Fifty-odd African riddles, mostly of indifferent interest to children, are given added weight by being identified with particular "tribes"—and herein lies the rub. Even if it made sense to present a riddle (as distinct from a folktale) as the product of a particular tribal culture, several of these eleven designations

do not refer to tribes at all, and in the worst case, that of "Kafir," what is being put forth, unthinkingly, is a derogatory term once used in southern Africa to refer to all black Africans. (Other instances of mislabeling involve "Accra," a city not a group, and "Congo," a region occupied by several groups, among them the Bakongo.) What Aardema apparently has done is to carry over the designation from her source—hence the riddles culled from a 1904 English work, *The Essential Kafir,* are identified as "riddles from the Kafir" (though how anyone familiar with the terrain can speak of "riddles from the Accra" defies understanding). . . . [This] is egregious pseudo-Africana of the most dispensable sort. (pp. 7-8)

A review of "Ji-Nongo-Nongo Means Riddles," in Kirkus Reviews, *Vol. 47, No. 1, January 1, 1979, pp. 7-8.*

THE RIDDLE OF THE DRUM: A TALE FROM TIZAPÁN, MEXICO   (1979)

Renowned folklorist Aardema moves far from the African settings of *Why Mosquitoes Buzz in People's Ears* and other books to produce this fast, exciting version of a favorite Mexican legend. [Tony] Chen's paintings and drawings evoke the color and vigor in events south of the border, described in the rhythmic narrative. The king of Tizapán vows that his daughter Fruela shall marry no ordinary prince. Her suitors must guess what the king's magic drum is made of or forfeit their lives. Prince Tuzán is lucky. On the way to ask for Fruela's hand, he meets several super-humans who agree to help him in return for rich rewards. The suspense is terrific as the king pits his allies against Tuzán and the finale is a surprise. As a bonus, readers get phonetic pronunciations for the Mexican words.

A review of "The Riddle of the Drum: A Tale," in Publishers Weekly, *Vol. 215, No. 10, March 5, 1979, p. 105.*

Tum-te-dum!
The head of the drum-te-dum!
Guess what it's from-te-dum!
And marry the Princess Fruela!

So goes the riddle that handsome Prince Tuzán must solve if he is to win the hand of the daughter of the king of Tizapán. . . .

[Verna Aardema] repeats the insistent riddle throughout the book in an effort to mimic the sound of the drumbeat, and repeats other rhymes to move the narrative along.

Is this a good idea?

No. The reason soon will become obvious to the parent who a) unwisely spends $7.95 on this slender version of a familiar fable . . . , b) must then read the book aloud to a 6-year-old, who will c) march around chanting this relentless little rhyme *ad naus-e-am.*

The problem is that the story is complex enough that it must be read aloud to a 6-year-old but is hardly worth the effort for a 10-year-old, who won't learn much more than a few Spanish words and their etymology. Spare us the te-di-um.

Randolph Hogan, in a review of "The Riddle of the Drum," in The New York Times Book Review, *May 6, 1979, p. 20.*

Some of the best features of Bishop's *Five Chinese Brothers* and all the do-this-and-win-the-hand-of-my-daughter stories are combined in this retelling of a Mexican folktale. Prince Tuzan wins the Princess Fruela in marriage because his five companions have superhuman skills which allow them to complete the impossible tasks set by Fruela's father, the King. The principle task (guessing the material of a magic drumhead) is unfortunately first instead of last so that the monarch's imposition of further tests not part of the original bargain seems both unjust and anti-climactic. . . . Young children will enjoy hearing the story read aloud, both for the plot itself, which is certainly not destroyed by its inverted order, and for the rhythmical and cumulative verse lines which recur effectively. The illustrations . . . are as fine as the text.

> *Paula Bondurant, in a review of "The Riddle of the Drum: A Tale from Tizapán," in* School Library Journal, *Vol. 26, No. 2, October, 1979, p. 132.*

HALF-A-BALL-OF-KENKI: AN ASHANTI TALE RETOLD (1979)

"Kuputu, kuputu, kuputu," Leopard dashes off from the village where the chief sets the dogs on the big cat. "Tih! Tih!" the nubile maidens chortle admiringly to Fly, Leopard's rival, as the improbable companions travel in search of brides. Throughout her effervescent retelling, folklorist Aardema makes shrewd use of onomatopoeia to emphasize the far-out doings. Jealous Leopard immobilizes Fly by tying the insect to a tree. Half-a-Ball-of-Kenki (cold cornmeal mush) rescues Fly, and the hero then has to fight enraged Leopard. Readers will learn that the outcome gave Leopard his spots. . . .

> *A review of "Half-a-Ball-of-Kenki: An Ashanti Tale," in* Publishers Weekly, *Vol. 215, No. 13, March 26, 1979, p. 81.*

The translation is not smooth . . . and the engaging rhymes throughout do not help enough to make this curious tale more appealing. There is also no explanation of the expressions (tribal words?) used in the text, e.g., "Leopard went flying *kuputu, kuputu, kuputu* out the gate!" The audience for this book will not be as wide as for Aardema's *Why Mosquitos Buzz in People's Ears,* but for collections with a demand for African folktales, the odd story does have humor and the unusual characters are engagingly portrayed.

> *Jane Bickel, in a review of "Half-a-Ball-of-Kenki," in* School Library Journal, *Vol. 25, No. 9, May, 1979, p. 48.*

This is a double why-story, since it ends with Dokonfa throwing Leopard into a fire, producing his spots, and also explains that flies always sit on leaves in which kenki has been wrapped because they are saying thank you on behalf of their ancestor. Nice to read aloud or use for storytelling, the tale has representations of sounds ("Leopard leaped *harrr* out of the bushes . . . she unwound the creeper kpung, kpung, kpung . . . She was stepping daintily pip, pip, pip . . ."), repetition, and the victory of the weak over the strong as appeals, and it's told with verve and humor.

> *Zena Sutherland, in a review of "Half-a-Ball-of-Kenki: An Ashanti Tale," in* Bulletin of the Center for Children's Books, *Vol. 33, No. 2, October, 1979, p. 21.*

BRINGING THE RAIN TO KAPITI PLAIN (1981)

Based on a tale heard in Kenya and adapted by British anthropologist Sir Claud Hollis, this has been brought closer to the format of "The House That Jack Built" by the [reteller].

The story, which comes from the Nandi people, was first published in 1909. Here it has the appeals of rhyme, rhythm, and cumulation as well as the satisfaction of achievement as it describes the herdsman Ki-Pat's ingenious solution to the drought that threatened the lives of his animals.

> *Zena Sutherland, in a review of "Bringing the Rain to Kapiti Plain: A Nandi Tale," in* Bulletin of the Center for Children's Books, *Vol. 34, No. 9, May, 1981, p. 165.*

As a note acknowledges, Aardema has taken a folk tale from Kenya, one which reminded its original British collector of "The House That Jack Built," and brought it even closer to the cumulative structure and rhythm of that English nursery rhyme. Her rhymed version begins with a drought on Kapiti Plain: ". . . This is the grass / all brown and dead, / That needed the rain / from the cloud overhead. . . . The Africans never told it this way to be sure, but the borrowed form gives this version a brisk, easy lilt, and the graphic, cut-out-like pictures are similarly crisp and direct.

> *A review of "Bringing the Rain to Kapiti Plain," in* Kirkus Reviews, *Vol. XLIX, No. 13, July 1, 1981, p. 795.*

WHAT'S SO FUNNY, KETU? A NUER TALE (1982)

Aardema excels again with the fable in her new book. . . . Set in Africa near the Mountains of the Moon, the story gains impetus from the author's echoic phrases: a dog slinking off, "prada, prada, prada," Nyaloti's baby crying, "ke-yaa, ke-yaa" and father Ketu's laughing, "ge-e, ge-e, ge-e." It's that laugh that gives Ketu trouble. A snake he has helped gives the man a magic gift that allows him to understand what animals are saying, and Ketu thinks their remarks are hilarious. Nyaloti thinks he's laughing at her and brings him before the tribe's wise men who insist that he disclose the cause of his mirth. The problem is that the snake has warned Ketu that he will die if he reveals his secret, and, on that suspenseful note, the snake takes charge again, bringing events to a happy conclusion.

> *A review of "What's So Funny, Ketu?" in* Publishers Weekly, *Vol. 222, No. 12, September 17, 1982, p. 114.*

[*What's So Funny, Ketu?* is] adapted from the author's *Otwe,* which was a retelling of "The Man and the Snake," a tale in Ray Huffman's *Nuer Customs and Folklore.* . . . While children may enjoy the action, the humor, and the happy ending, the story seems weak in two respects: one is Ketu's laughing at such things as reading a rat's mind (it is wondering where Ketu's wife keeps her butter) and the other is that the cause and effect (tell and die) are nullified for no apparent reason.

> *Zena Sutherland, in a review of "What's So Funny, Ketu?" in* Bulletin of the Center for Children's Books, *Vol. 36, No. 3, November, 1982, p. 41.*

A secret joke leads to fun and near disaster in this comic Sudanese folk tale, vigorously retold in the African tradition. . . . The vitality of the telling lies in the precise choice of words (the dog "yelps" and "slinks," the rat "scurries") as much as in the action sounds and rhythms ("the cow sent the bowl rolling, denki, denki, denki, in the dirt"). . . . [This funny story] demands reading aloud.

Hazel Rochman, in a review of "What's So Funny, Ketu?" in School Library Journal, *Vol. 29, No. 5, January, 1983, p. 56.*

THE VINGANANEE AND THE TREE TOAD: A LIBERIAN TALE (1983)

A capable retelling of a folktale in which a small creature succeeds where large beasts fail (always appealing to young children). . . . The use of rhyme, repetition, and onomatopoeia adds appeal . . . to the story of the monstrous (humanoid) creature, the Vingananee, whose ferocious appetite leaves Spider's household with no food. Not even Lion can best the Vingananee; it is little Tree Toad who finally saves the day. This should be useful for storytelling as well as for reading aloud.

Zena Sutherland, in a review of "The Vingananee and the Tree Toad," in Bulletin of the Center for Children's Books, *Vol. 37, No. 2, October, 1983, p. 21.*

Aardema has admirably retold this finely-crafted story by replicating in her text the vitality and nuance of the oral tradition as well as the strong moral backbone of folk humor. Storytellers will be thrilled by her use of sound in the text: the "fras fras fras" of the sweeping broom or the "pusu pusu pusu" of the strange and monstrous Vingananee coming up the bush path followed by the "kpong kpong kpong" of the rope as he ties up his victim. The hidden strength of the smallest animal, the frog, to triumph over the oppressive Vingananee after bigger animals have failed is both an important and an appealing theme. Then there is the internal building; the magic in the repetition of events like the ritual bedtime song of the tree frog in the story as each day closes, the sweeping with which each day begins and the ongoing battle with the Vingananee, who steals the animal's supper. . . . To capture the fullness of the story, this book, like most folk tales, would be best shared, although many children (and adults) will enjoy reading it on their own.

Gale P. Jackson, in a review of "The Vingananee and the Tree Toad: A Liberian Tale," in School Library Journal, *Vol. 30, No. 4, December, 1983, p. 51.*

The direct retelling is cleverly made more musical by the astute use of repeated phrases and the inclusion of sound effects. . . . The short pat ending may be traditional but it has a jolting effect as it interrupts the expectations set during the tale. It gives the reader an uncomfortable sense that the writer simply ran out of pages!

The tale lends itself to being retold by a narrator accompanied by mime and the chanting of the repetitive phrases. Children will also want to draw the REAL Vingananee!

Ronald A. Jobe, in a review of "The Vingananee and the Tree Toad: A Liberian Tale," in Language Arts, *Vol. 61, No. 1, January, 1984, pp. 74-5.*

OH, KOJO! HOW COULD YOU! AN ASHANTI TALE (1984)

In *Oh, Kojo! How Could You!* Verna Aardema—a highly regarded storyteller—and award-winning illustrator Marc Brown have teamed together to bring a most humorous Sudanese folk tale spectacularly to life. Children (aged 4 to 8) will also be enchanted with the various human characters: the evil and dis-

honest Ananse, symbolizing all that will deceive the unwary; the long-suffering mother, Tutuola; and the lazy, gullible son, Kojo.

The easily beguiled Kojo does indeed give all his mother's gold to the clever Ananse. Tutuola is certainly not enchanted by a dog Kojo buys from Ananse because he can supposedly fetch firewood all by himself. Nor is she taken with the cat who is said to be able to clear an entire compound of rats singlepaw-edly. Still, the cat and dog provide much more than just no work for Kojo: It's their rescue mission in pursuit of a most powerful magic ring that forms the basic excitement of the tale. And what comes to light at the end is a lazy boy's innate sense of well-meaning and, ironically, a kingly sense of right judgment.

The prose begs to be read aloud. It is melodious and rhythmic, and the frequent interspersion of thrice-repeated Sudanese words invites listeners into an oral "join-in." Brown's . . . illustrations contribute to the overall feeling of authenticity. . . . Thus this unusual and absorbing book offers an original ethnic experience.

Darian J. Scott, "Mice and Monkeys, Dogs and Cats," in The Christian Science Monitor, *October 5, 1984, p. B9.*

Verna Aardema has found an excellent Ashanti variant of the familiar folk-theme of the bad bargain, best known perhaps in the German 'Lucky Hans'. The unfamiliar twists come from characteristic Ashanti details, such as the unconventional birth and growth of the hero and the antisocial activities of Ananse. The amusing and suspenseful story is told with much liveliness and with the injection of many onomatopoeic phrases which are a gift to the oral story-teller. For once the text of a picture-book, if a trifle long, is of greater interest than the illustrations.

M. Crouch, in a review of "Oh, Kojo! How Could You!" in The Junior Bookshelf, *Vol. 49, No. 2, April, 1985, p. 69.*

[This] picture book really demands to be read aloud. The gently meandering pace of this Ananse tale, combined with the opportunity for voice effects and for audience participation, make it a gift for the expert storyteller. Although it is not one of the more tightly plotted of the Ananse stories, the narrative . . . provides sufficient variation to attract the attention of the younger listener. . . . It is perhaps disappointing that so much effort, both in the writing and in the pictures, has gone into a book which will, of necessity, have only a limited use.

Keith Barker, in a review of "Oh, Kojo! How Could You!" in The School Librarian, *Vol. 33, No. 2, June, 1985, p. 125.*

BIMWILI AND THE ZIMWI: A TALE FROM ZANZIBAR (1985)

In a fluid style, Aardema retells a folk tale from Zanzibar that was first published in 1896. As in some of her previous books, she creates words to express various sounds throughout the text. Whether it's the *t-lopping* of a wave, the *che, che, che* of laughter or a crab making a *guga, guga, guga* sound as it skitters along, young and old alike will enjoy vocalizing the interpretations of these unique words. A little girl, Bimwili, is captured by an ugly troll-like character known as a Zimwi. The Zimwi forces the child to stay inside his drum and sing for the inhabitants of various villages. Bimwili is saved when she sings in her own village and her mother recognizes her voice. . . . Coming from a culture so steeped in oral tradition, it is no surprise that this tale makes for lively fun whether read independently or aloud.

> *Tom S. Hurlburt, in a review of "Bimwili and the Zimwi," in* School Library Journal, *Vol. 32, No. 3, November, 1985, p. 64.*

Based on an African story previously retold in *Tales for the Third Ear,* this picture-book version makes the folktale all the more appealing. . . . A tightly written, slightly scary story with a heroine who uses her wits and courage to overcome a powerful enemy, this could become a favorite for reading aloud to children in the primary grades.

> *Carolyn Phelan, in a review of "Bimwili and the Zimwi: A Tale from Zanzibar," in* Booklist, *Vol. 82, No. 7, December 1, 1985, p. 564.*

Introducing a folk tale to an alien culture is a challenging task, especially when it is for a picture-book audience. Verna Aardema has often met that challenge with her elegant, authentic-sounding versions of traditional African tales, including *Why Mosquitoes Buzz in People's Ears* and *Bringing the Rain to Kapiti Plain.* Her latest venture is a curious tale from Zanzibar (now part of Tanzania).

The intriguing narrative is in polished prose that is a pleasure to read aloud. Yet for a story of childhood terror and triumph, this one is oddly restrained. The original dramatic emphasis seems obscured by the writer's fascination with the intricacies of the tale. Bimwili's sisters, her pleasure in the seashell, her song, the trials of her kidnapping, the tender moments of her rescue, the absurd transformations of the Zimwi—all these details are given equal place. None are made to bear the emotional weight that shapes a story.

Without a sense of what is significant, and why, Bimwili's world, like Wonderland, seems curiouser and curiouser. What sort of evil is this lurking Zimwi who, by Western standards, behaves so strangely for a monster? Why is the seashell so special to Bimwili and later to the villagers? After all, they live near the shore. Is this tale, for the people of Zanzibar, the harrowing story of Bimwili's kidnapping, or merely the amusing account of her passage (only implied here) from a tag-along baby sister to a voice among her people?

Unfortunately the watercolor-and-colored-pencil illustrations do not supply what is lacking in the text. Though Susan Med-

daugh has made her best effort, her static, literal, cartoonlike style . . . is sadly mismatched to a story with a heritage and a place of its own.

> *Janice Prindle, in a review of "Bimwili and the Zimwi," in* The New York Times Book Review, *February 16, 1986, p. 22.*

PRINCESS GORILLA AND A NEW KIND OF WATER (1988)

[This] tale originated in Africa with the Mpongwe people. When King Gorilla finds a barrel of vinegar, he decides that his daughter will marry whatever animal can drink it. Several, from elephant to warthog, fail; by pretending to be just one monkey and each taking a sip, a crowd of Talapoin monkeys succeeds, but is disqualified for cheating and banished to the treetops forever. Fortunately, now that the barrel is empty, Princess Gorilla is free to marry her original choice, a young male gorilla who plays tag with her—and loves her.

Embellished with engaging animal noises and dialogue that varies entertainingly as each animal takes its turn, this funny-wise story should make good telling.

> *A review of "Princess Gorilla and a New Kind of Water," in* Kirkus Reviews, *Vol. LVI, No. 3, February 1, 1988, p. 197.*

Artist [Victoria Chess] and author, displaying the considerable wit and style for which each is known, turn an age-old idea on its side: the events surrounding a contest for the hand of a princess. . . . Aardema has created a high-spirited, infectiously funny story, and the language of the tale is jaunty, playful and sure—perfect for reading aloud.

> *A review of "Princess Gorilla and a New Kind of Water," in* Publishers Weekly, *Vol. 233, No. 8, February 26, 1988, p. 196.*

Romance abruptly turns into pourquoi story. . . . Despite the shaky structure, children will respond favorably to Aardema's trademark descriptions of sounds (Hog moves "naka, naka, naka") gentle humor, and simple rhymes. . . . While this story lacks the spirit of Aardema's best work, it is adequately retold and suitable for reading aloud and storytelling.

> *Julia Corsaro, in a review of "Princess Gorilla and a New Kind of Water, in* School Library Journal, *Vol. 35, No. 9, June-July, 1988, p. 96.*

Elsa (Maartman) Beskow

1874-1953

Swedish author and illustrator of picture books, fiction, and nonfiction; reteller; playwright; and illustrator.

One of Sweden's most beloved and consistently popular picture book creators, Beskow is appreciated internationally for the fresh and happy tone of her works and for her sensitivity to the things that delight young children. Influenced by such illustrators as Walter Crane and Kate Greenaway, she was a major contributor to the development of a Swedish picture book tradition which concentrated on naturalistic depictions of the countryside. The success of Beskow's illustrations—detailed pictures in bright watercolors which incorporate such subjects as country settings, changing seasons, wildlife, farmlands, insects, fruit, and flowers—have caused her to be called the Swedish Beatrix Potter. Beskow wrote both fantasy and nonfiction, occasionally combining elements of both to create works characterized by their warmth, insight, and regard for nature. Many of her books focus on woodland creatures, fairies, spirits, and the magical worlds they inhabit. One of her most popular fantasies, *The Elf Children of the Woods* (1910), centers on the lifestyle of a tiny family who are hidden from the outside world by their mushroom caps. Beskow's most well-known realistic stories include *Pelle's New Suit* (1912), the story of a farm boy who has a suit made from the wool of his pet lamb, and a series of adventures about Aunt Green, Aunt Brown, and Aunt Lavender, their two adopted children, and their neighbor Uncle Blue. *Pelle's New Suit* presents young readers with a step-by-step process that stresses cooperation and the value of community: Pelle does chores in exchange for the help of several skilled adults who each bring his suit nearer to completion. Gaining attention in the early 1920s by adding to the trend of realism endorsed by New York's Bank Street College, *Pelle* is now considered a classic of its genre. In addition to her works of fantasy and realistic fiction, Beskow created an ABC, a calendar book of monthly verses, an activity workbook, grade school readers, and works which encourage children to fill in the color or to complete the verses. In Sweden, Beskow is also recognized as a reteller and illustrator of fairy tales and nursery rhyme collections, as well as an illustrator of songs and poems. Although only a few of Beskow's approximately fifty works have been translated into English, several of her works were reissued beginning in the mid-1970s as examples of excellent period art.

Beskow is considered an expert colorist who combined accuracy with quiet beauty and produced books which capture the imagination and interest of children. While a few reviewers find some of her works boring or outdated, most say that Beskow's simple stories and charming pictures have contributed both to Swedish children's literature and to the enjoyment of young readers around the world.

Beskow received the Nils Holgersson Plaque for her body of work in 1952. The Elsa Beskow Award for the best Swedish picture book illustrator was established by the Swedish Library Association in 1958.

(See also *Something about the Author*, Vol. 20.)

Courtesy of Swedish Information Service

AUTHOR'S COMMENTARY

As far back as I can remember I loved to draw and sketch. I have been told that I also began to make up stories at a very early age which I told to my brother, one year older than I. I was allowed to go to my aunts' small kindergarten at the age of four. My grandmother lived with us, taught me to crochet, and told me many amusing stories. As soon as I learned to read, I spent all my time reading fairy tales, especially those of Hans Christian Andersen. When I was fifteen, my father died, and I went to Technical School in order to be able to earn and help the family as quickly as possible. In spite of economic difficulties we were a very happy family with lots of fun. My first picture book, *The Wee Little Old Woman,* was published in 1892. The same year I was married and went to live in Djursholm, a charming suburb of Stockholm. There my husband, a minister and headmaster of a school, was from the beginning an interested adviser in my work. He himself liked to paint. My five sons, now all grown up, were models and critics for me in their young years. My grandchildren serve me now in the same way.

Elsa Beskow, in an extract in Illustrators of Children's Books: 1744-1945, *Bertha E. Mahony, Louise Payson Latimer, Beulah Folmsbee, eds., The Horn Book Inc., 1947, p. 278.*

GENERAL COMMENTARY

MARION BROMLEY NEWTON

In Djursholm, a beautiful, residential suburb of Stockholm, Sweden, lives Elsa Beskow, the much loved artist and author of beautiful books for children. She is the wife of Dr. Nathaniel Beskow, an eminent clergyman, writer, and pioneer social worker, and the mother of six boys.

Not long ago, a writer in a Swedish magazine said of her,

> If one asks himself, What is the secret of Elsa Beskow's art as an author, a pencil artist, and a colorist for the youngest of humanity, one need not be long in doubt about the answer. She possesses the gift of understanding the soul of the child. She has the power, in using this understanding, to play upon their chords of fancy in a way which tunes them with the innermost feelings of her own heart. She possesses the right love for children and the world peculiar to them. With good reason has it been said of her that her own fine and rich inspiration has a natural connection with the child's mind and his expressive life. The glowing charm, the smiling purity, the idealistic beauty in her art reflect in a splendor as fresh as the dew the paradise of childhood, which her eyes behold, and in artistic expression have portrayed.

It was my pleasure in the winter of 1926 to visit Djursholm as the guest of Mrs. Beskow. . . . The warmth and friendliness of her manner instantly put me at ease, and I felt as if I had come under the protecting care of that love which has endeared her to the hearts of her host of readers.

There is a light of kindness and understanding in her clear, blue eyes, a smile plays readily upon her face, her manner is gracious and sincere, with a certain shyness and modesty when her work is mentioned. (pp. 21-2)

It is not difficult to weave romance and saga around the individuality of Elsa Beskow. Her father, Bernt Maartman, was born in Flekkefjord, on the picturesque southwestern coast of Norway. Her mother, Augusta Fahlstedt, bore a name honored in the history of Finland. From her mother she inherited her artistic talent, which began to express itself in early years as she told stories to her young brothers and sisters, and, to their great delight, illustrated them with her own drawings.

Her schooling was received at the Anna Whitlock School for girls, to which she later returned as instructor in drawing, having completed the course at the so-called high industrial art school, in preparation for such work as a teacher. Her appreciation of the practical, artistic needs of children found expression at this time in her well-known **"Will you paint?"** books. These consisted of outline drawings to be filled in in color by the children, were carefully graded, appealing to the imagination and active interests of the child, and became a valuable educational medium in art expression.

Her course at the Art Academy was interrupted by her meeting with Dr. Nathaniel Beskow, and their marriage four years later, in 1897. Meanwhile her sketches appeared in Christmas magazines, which have attained a remarkable standard of excellence in Sweden, and are often veritable treasures of art.

In the year of her marriage Mrs. Beskow's first picture book was published—*The Story of the Little, Little Old Woman*. For more than thirty years this quaint, colorful tale for very little people has withstood the test of time, and today is no less in demand than when it first appeared. Successors have followed each year. These have attained a ripeness and a depth without losing any of the qualities that make them attractive to the mind of the child. In their own way her six sturdy boys came to have part in their mother's work, by serving as models for her drawings, and receiving, it is said, the hourly wage of about a half a penny, which sum they added happily to the contents of their Christmas savings boxes.

It is in her association with her children, no doubt, that Mrs. Beskow has conceived many of the ideas in her most popular stories. Certainly in her own boys these tales have had a first attentive public, whose criticisms, as frank as they were innocent, have contributed largely toward giving them their finishing touches.

Putte's Adventure in the Blueberrywood, which appeared in 1901, marked the beginning of her conquest of the larger child world, outside of her own home. Today her books are known and loved in every Swedish home, and have penetrated far beyond the borders of Sweden, translated into French, Finnish, Polish, German, Czech, Russian, Danish, Norwegian, Dutch and English. An evidence of the educational value attributed to them is the fact that Jan Ligtharts of Holland, a renowned educator, himself translated *Tomtebo Children* and *Pelle's New Clothes* into his native tongue.

Some one has said of her illustrations, "They are just what they ought to be for children." In Europe, to enumerate the titles of the picture and story books which bear the name of Elsa Beskow on the cover would be quite unnecessary, so well known are they. *Mother's Little Ole, Festival of the Flowers, Tummelisa, Little Lasse in the Garden, Bubblemuck, Little Brother's Sailing Trip, Aunt Green, Aunt Brown, and Aunt Purple, Journey to the Land of Long Ago* will recall to many, older as well as young, happy childhood memories intertwined with the creations of Elsa Beskow's pencil and pen. It has been said that her great gift is, without doubt, to be able, even among grown-ups, to waken the child to life.

To quote further from the article in Swedish—

> Spontaneity and at the same time clearness give her descriptions in word and in picture a peculiar charm. Perhaps quite the most captivating are her presentations of the transformations in nature's forms—illusions, in which, to the gratifying of the child's imagination, different subjects are interwoven one with another; elves and maidens dissolve into buds and blossoms, out of tree stumps glimpses can be caught of mysterious, but never frightening sprites—the whole of nature is made to throb with life under the touch of her fairy wand. Her text for the pictures flows equally lightly, clearly, and quickly, like a spring brooklet murmuring in the sunshine. It is never without an undercurrent of useful philosophy of life, which is intended to set its mark permanently in the heart of the child—permanently, as only the child appropriates it, but never is it that which can be impressed merely on the outside. Her children's books are moral without moralizing. This is one of the reasons, not the least, why many small readers of Elsa Beskow, both boys and girls, of generations of children in our own and in other lands, have received a wealth of happiness, beauty, and goodness moulded into their lives, often without a consciousness of the source from which they originally came.

We in America have yet to come under the spell and enriching influence of this charming writer for children. Her motherliness, which once caused her to be titled "the Swedish children's best friend,'' spreads far over the world, and has already embraced the children of our country in its arms. (pp. 25-30)

Marion Bromley Newton, "Elsa Beskow," in The Horn Book Magazine, *Vol. IV, No. 1, February, 1928, pp. 21-30.*

ANNE THAXTER EATON

Few picture books are more satisfying to very little children than those of Elsa Beskow, because of their bright colors, their simple outlines, and this artist's faculty of seeing the same fun in a situation that a child sees. *The Tale of the Wee Little Old Woman* should be among the first picture books shown to the youngest children. Two-year-olds can grasp the story and from two years on to five it is a favorite. *Pelle's New Suit* pleases the two- and three-year-olds because of its pictures; four- to seven-year-olds enjoy as well the story of how the wool from the lamb became Pelle's new suit of clothes. The pictures in *Olle's Ski Trip* have vigorous lively action as they describe six-year-old Olle's visit to King Winter. *Aunt Green, Aunt Brown, and Aunt Lavender* and *The Adventures of Peter and Lotta* are popular a little later, with seven- and eight-year-olds. (pp. 295-96)

Anne Thaxter Eaton, "Artists at Work for Children," in her Reading with Children, *The Viking Press, 1940, pp. 281-309.*

MAY HILL ARBUTHNOT

[After *The Poppy Seed Cakes* by Margery Clark was published in 1924, the] next good realism for the youngest came from the Swedish. It was a translation of *Pelle's New Suit*, told and illustrated by Elsa Beskow.

The little boy, Pelle, needs a new suit. He raises his own lamb and then, for each person who helps him with his suit, he performs some useful service. He also watches the shearing of the sheep and sees the wool washed, carded, and spun into yarn. He helps with the dyeing and weaving and watches anxiously the important process of cutting the beautiful blue cloth into a suit to his measure. He follows the tailoring even as he assists the tailor. Finally, for his Sunday best he triumphantly wears his beautiful blue suit.

Here is a plot reduced to its lowest denominator, but what the story lacks in conflict and excitement it makes up in the intensity of its realism and the significance of the whole story. This is what [Lucy Sprague Mitchell of the Bank Street College of Education] was moving toward. A plot for small children need not have elaborate complications if it has enough meaning and significance as an explanation of the world in which they find themselves. Here is a story as spare of ornamentation as a loaf of bread, but, like bread, it is good to the taste, plain, wholesome, and nourishing. No pitter-patting, no furbelows, no meaningless action! Every episode is honestly chosen to tell an important story as clearly as possible. It is addressed to thinking children who love new clothes, for themselves, to be sure, but who are also reasonably interested in how things come to be. Pelle had the good luck to be right there at the source of supplies. Children follow his experiences with sensible and satisfied absorption, and the story gives them new insight. Mrs. Beskow's bright pictures are as clear and fresh and interesting as her text. The whole book commands adult respect and the child's devotion. This honest bit of realism is already a children's classic.

Pelle's New Suit was both preceded and followed by other realistic picture-stories by Elsa Beskow—stories of great charm but lacking the significance of *Pelle*. Her *Aunt Green, Aunt Brown, and Aunt Lavender, The Tale of the Wee Little Old Woman, Aunt Brown's Birthday*, and other stories are all well liked, and the pictures are a delight to the eye.

A word more needs to be said about Mrs. Beskow, the artist. The pictures in *Pelle* are clear, graphic, and explanatory. No needful detail is missing to make the action understandable; no unnecessary embellishments clutter up the page. Everywhere there is simplicity, order, and strength—the Swedish countryside in cool blues and greens, the little houses with fresh curtains and pots of flowers, the people in substantial clothes with bright touches of color illuminating the strong, plain faces. Pictures of *The Wee Little Old Woman* are enclosed in cozy circles with gay red geraniums blooming throughout the pages. No picture book since Kate Greenaway's has more of the precise and delicate decorative quality of this one. The series of books about the Aunts are in pastel colors, fresh and delicate. The latter books have a rare combination of the fanciful and the realistic that is unusually appealing. About all of her books there is a sincerity and strength particularly good for small children. (pp. 363-64)

May Hill Arbuthnot, "Here and Now: 'Pelle's New Suit'," in her Children and Books, *Scott, Foresman and Company, 1947, pp. 363-64.*

MARIA CIMINO

Elsa Beskow's picture books have good design and color, and the warmth, simplicity and storytelling qualities which appeal especially to a small child's imagination. In each of her books are experiences a child may share—the wonderful adventures of a small boy's ski trip in *Olle's skidfärd*, the making of a new suit for Pelle, or the joys of acquaintance with three old aunts.

Maria Cimino, "Foreign Picture Books in a Children's Library," in Illustrators of Children's Books: 1744-1945, *Bertha E. Mahony, Louise Payson Latimer, Beulah Folmsbee, eds., The Horn Book Inc., 1947, pp. 123-156.*

MARY ØRVIG

Around Christmas-time in 1897, a picture book by Elsa Maartman was lying on the bookshop counters throughout Sweden. It was called *The Tale of the Wee Little Old Woman*, and in ten pages of gay colors an old nursery rhyme of a little old woman and her somewhat naughty cat was retold.

This first picture book already shows with what precision the future picture book artist drew trees, flowers, and leaves and those parts of the Swedish countryside that were alternately the background and center of her illustrating art. Here the country of Idyllia opens before us, and it continued to do so throughout all her work. Generations of Swedish children have, through Elsa Beskow's picture books, enjoyed blossom and berrying time, spring and summer tide, and have kept the impressions thus made upon them all their lives.

During berry and mushroom picking—for which there is still time and feeling in the industrialized and modern Sweden of today—one often stops at some moss-covered tussock, a drooping blueberry bush or the cheerful yellow mushrooms of the *Cantharellus* family, and smiles, reminiscently thinking: "Look, a real Elsa Beskow wood," or, "Putte and the Elf Children of the Wood can't be far away!" From the turn of the century and the beginning of her long picture book production, Elsa Beskow has made her place in the Swedish childhood land, and there, today, she still is. (pp. 240-41)

During Elsa's very early childhood the life at her home was free from the material worries of which she would later, as a young girl, have her share. Between her fourth and fifteenth years, Elsa spent her summers with her family in an attractive, old-fashioned house at Skärfsta in an untouched Swedish countryside of woods, mountains, and wild flowers, and in these surroundings the themes of several of her picture books began to grow. The following summers were spent at Drottningholm outside Stockholm, together with her mother, uncle, and aunts, whose gay daily life she later immortalized in the books about Aunt Green, Aunt Brown, and Aunt Lavender. It is said that the atmosphere of Elsa's home during the years she grew up was singularly harmonic and optimistic in spite of many worries. Brightness and merriment were also characteristic for her, and shadows seldom crept into the children's world she created in her books.

The age in which she grew up was characterized by new pedagogical theories, and Elsa Maartman was sent to Anna Whitlock's Stockholm's New Co-Educational School. Ellen Key was a teacher at this school—at that time she had not yet published her important work *The Child's Century* (1900)—but there is no doubt that the young pupil gathered many impressions from her views on life and, above all, from her dislike of conformity in education.

Elsa's interest in drawing was early awakened, and it was therefore obvious that she wanted an art education. . . . [She] studied at the Stockholm Technical School, later on renamed The Swedish State School of Arts, Crafts, and Design. . . .

It so happened that a young student at the Royal Academy of Arts, Natanael Beskow, was looking for a girl to serve as a model for a head of Psyche he was planning to do for a contest, and so he became acquainted with Elsa Maartman. . . . (p. 241)

In 1897 Elsa Maartman and Natanael Beskow were married, and after a while they moved to their house, Ekeliden, in Djursholm. It was a great house with many rooms and an infinite number of crooks and crannies, a paradise for the six sons who would be born there. . . . It is said that [Elsa Beskow's] picture books followed her life's pattern during the early years of marriage: every second year a book, every second year a boy. Each child got a picture book of his own. (p. 242)

Elsa Maartman Beskow made her entrance into the Swedish picture book field with *The Tale of the Wee Little Old Woman* (1897) and she had come to stay. The year before, the Swedish Artists' Association in Stockholm had arranged an exhibition of selected works by Walter Crane. In an excellent biography on Elsa Beskow, Stina Hammar . . . says that, while walking around this exhibition, she discovered how she wanted to make her first picture book. She received deep inspiration from the

From Pelle's New Suit, *written and illustrated by Elsa Beskow. Translated by Marion Letcher Woodburn. Harper and Brothers, 1912.*

work of Walter Crane, while, at the same time, she discovered her own style. When *The Flower Feast in the Garden* was published several years later (1914), it was evident how important "Flora's Feast" had been to her. It was not only Walter Crane's way of expressing himself that Elsa Beskow felt sympathy for, but also his social pathos—that one should express art so as to be understood by the people.

The Children of Sunny Hill was published in 1898 and *Putte's Adventures in the Blueberry Patch* in 1901. In the years between, Elsa illustrated old Swedish nursery rhymes, which are now classics, and also a famous edition of *Swedish Folk Tales*, selected and retold by Fridtjuv Berg, who played an important role in the re-organization of the Swedish school system.

In *Putte's Adventures in the Blueberry Patch*, flowers and berries have human guise, as they do in most of her picture books. However, all details are correct, and everyday life and fantasy are woven together by invisible threads. Flowers, berries, and trees are characters to Elsa Beskow, characters that she can both talk to and be in many-sided contact with. The story about Putte, who went to the wood to pick blueberries and lingonberries, has without doubt made a profound impression on children for several generations. The pictures are gay and vivid and the story has all the qualities that appeal to a child. She gave everything the right proportions, so that the tall trees do not any longer seem so frightening, while the small blueberry bush, on the contrary, grows like a tree, covered with ripe berries and within easy reach of the child. Spellbound, one sees that the boat carrying Putte and the three Blueberry boys has been made of bark. Every detail is correctly and lovingly depicted. In this book is clearly seen how deeply Elsa Beskow understood children and with what genuine simplicity she talked to them. (pp. 243-44)

Weeping Willie was published in 1904. The book, which has the subtitle, "As a warning to all crybabies and a help to all their mothers," is one of Elsa Beskow's most didactic ones and tells about a boy at his most tiresome with tears always streaming. There are even tears dripping beneath the title on the title page. Everything around Weeping Willie participates emotionally in his escapades: the ginger-biscuit pig is crying, the daisy raises its eyebrows in surprise. There is a moralizing tone in this book which is rather unusual in Elsa Beskow's works, but the warmth is still evident and so is the laughter in her voice.

Olle's Ski Trip is really the only book which she has devoted entirely to the long Swedish winter. Of course, the winter is found in most of her books, which are so often about the different Swedish seasons, but usually only for contrast, or in a short, pleasant little glimpse: a white Christmas or a friendly evening round the fire with snow outside the window. But, above all, Elsa Beskow describes the northern summer, so short and so beloved. Her picture books are full of sunshine; rain and wind pass quickly by. Even *Olle's Ski Trip*, with its beautiful winter landscape, Father Frost, and King Winter, ends with spring and blue anemones peeping out of the earth under the warming sun.

Elsa Beskow was often criticized by her contemporaries for her love of sunshine. But she was acquainted with both shadows and cold winds and was, therefore, often a little perturbed herself by the atmosphere of flowers and unconcern that had been created around her. There were indeed many shadows in her life's pattern.

When she painted *The Elf Children of the Woods*, so loved by Swedish children, she lived in Liljendal not far from the Dalecarlian border. Here she found powerful Nordic scenery, woods dark with secrets, hills, water, flowers, and animals. Her little people belong to nature; it is their home. The loving pictures she has drawn also show a great knowledge of nature. The various mushrooms are drawn in such detail that they could be used for an elementary lesson in fungology. In this book she tells about a family of elves throughout the year. There are some winter pictures with skiing and fairy tales told round the blazing fire, but the last scene is, of course, of the spring. (pp. 244-45)

Pelle's New Suit is, for some reason, the most well-known book by Elsa Beskow in the United States. Probably this book is the one that is most influenced by Swedish traditionalism, and it also has many didactic features. Elsa Beskow probably wanted to show that little can be done alone in this world and that cooperation is necessary, even for such a small thing as a suit of new clothes.

Next came *The Flower Feast in the Garden* (1914), the story of little Lisa who was invited to the flowers' midsummer feast. A few drops of poppy juice on her eyelids make Lisa invisible, and so she discovers that even the flower world has its problems and its sorrows. There is imperiousness, class difference, and despair, as there was in the Swedish society which had, before World War I, experienced social conflicts, strikes, and depression. Still, everything turns out right as always in Elsa Beskow's children's world and in the end even the weeds, at first snubbed and despised, are allowed to go to the feast. The style is decorative, but the book gives the feeling of flowers and sun, movement and life. Elsa Beskow's great knowledge of botany is ever-present; flowers and plants are, even in their human guise, drawn with love and accuracy.

After *Goran's Book* (1916) Elsa Beskow published *Aunt Green, Aunt Brown, and Aunt Lavender* in the same year as World War I came to an end (1918). The picture book about the three aunts, Uncle Blue, Peter and Lotta, little Spot the dog, and Esmeralda the cat, was to be followed by *Aunt Brown's Birthday* (1925), *The Adventures of Peter and Lotta* (1929), *Uncle Blue's New Boat* (1942), and *Peter and Lotta's Christmas* (1947).

Elsa Beskow has herself said that the first book about the three aunts was largely an artistic experiment because she felt she was in need of a softer and milder color scheme. The milieu she created in these books was not a contemporary one but was from the middle of the nineteenth century, as is shown by the crinolines and pantalettes the aunts wear. The story of how the two poor children, Peter and Lotta, are given a nice, warm home with the three aunts, who spoil them thoroughly, has a charming flavor of the past as well as timelessness. The boy and girl, as children do, pack the daily life of the three aunts with events and bring color into their lives.

There are few other artists who can describe as well as Elsa Beskow the things children love and understand. A good example of this is the opening scene in *Peter and Lotta's Christmas*. Here is the old-fashioned kitchen with striped rag mats on a well-scrubbed floor and a kitchen range in one corner. Aunt Brown and the children are busy filling tray after tray with brown ginger-biscuits to be put into the oven. Aunt Green is polishing the copper until it glows. Aunt Lavender is hanging up the freshly laundered curtains. Peter is busy rolling out the dough while Lotta, although also busy baking, is keeping a loving eye on little Spot, the dog, who is playing with his ball, and Esmeralda, the cat, seems to be watching with a slightly malicious eye.

The whole picture breathes the atmosphere of Christmas expectation; there is gaiety and fun. . . . This sequel of picture books dealing with Peter and Lotta and the three aunts is among the happiest examples of Elsa Beskow's work.

Little Lasse in the Garden (1920) is another picture book in which the garden flowers and berries come to life. *Peter's Voyage* (1921) is, as are many of Elsa Beskow's other books, in verse. It tells about a little boy's first adventure away from his home, in the safe company of his teddy bear. Alice Tegnér wrote the accompanying music.

From an artistic viewpoint, a conscious change in Elsa Beskow's style can be noticed at about this time. The details that children love and understand are fewer. Elsa Beskow had in this way succumbed to the demand of her time. This was regrettable, since so much of the vitality of her art work depended on an interaction between loving detail and a color scheme with mild nuances.

A Journey to the Land of Long-Ago (1923) is a story about two small children who, using a fallen tree trunk as a means of transport, visit a long-ago land, where among other things they liberate a beautiful princess from the cruel Gnome King. When one looks at the picture, drawn in deep blue tones, which shows the two children rescuing a knight from the deep dark hollow, one spontaneously thinks of the story her son Gunnar Beskow once told at a gathering: "It was amusing to play a knight in shining armour, but not so amusing to be a fairy or a princess." This story obviously shows that Elsa Beskow used her sons as models and their features are clearly portrayed in several of her picture books. *The Tale of the Little Deer* (1924) has a sad but charming tone, and the pictures are light and graceful.

The Year's Tale (1927) is yet another book beloved by Swedish children. Like a sort of calendar, it tells in pictures and verses about the twelve months of the year, during weekdays and holidays. As a matter of course, the wonders of nature are central themes, the various seasons unfold before us, as do the feasts and holidays. Even in this book, the Swedish winter has a limited space. Thus, the grey month of November, which in Sweden is the darkest and also the dreariest, is portrayed by a cheerful room with mother and children reading stories in front of the flaming Dutch-tiled stove. Through the window only, we envisage what is outside, a grey mist and a wind-bent tree. Accentuated are the spring, summer, and autumn, and that which germinates and grows. The drawings illustrating spring are soft and pale, while those of summer and autumn form a riot of glowing colors, both rich and splendid.

The Hat House, a picture book in verse, was published in 1930. It is a tale in which the children themselves fill in the rhymes. This story is didactic in other ways, too, as it deals with the danger of playing with matches, which obviously elves also like to do. The colors are beautiful and bright, and the pictures composed with a gay, airy lightness.

The Sun-Egg is about the animals of the wood and the little fairy whose home was in a hollow tree in the deep forest. The color scheme is rather dark and gives for once the feeling of autumn. *The Tale of the Curious Perch* (1933) shows that Elsa Beskow also could depict water-life and *Ocke, Nutta and Pillerill* (1939) tells in rhyme the story of how a squirrel family, always busy gathering nuts to store for the winter, gets a lodger who becomes one of them. This book has all the special aroma

of the Swedish woods. *Clever Annika* (1941) is about the Swedish summer landscape, seen through the eyes of a happy little girl. In *The A B C Journey* (1945) flowers, fruits, and friendly, happy animals are drawn climbing the various letters of the alphabet. The last two picture books by Elsa Beskow are *Mr. Peter* (1949), about an idealist who tries to help everybody, and *The Red Bus and the Green Car*, in which she has tried to express something of the new era in which she lived.

Elsa Beskow also illustrated *The Book of Flowers* (1905) with verses by Jeanna Oterdahl, a book which has joined the treasure of classic Swedish children's poetry. She also drew the pictures for Alice Tegnér's many song books, for example, *Mother's Little Olle and Other Songs* (1903) and *Burgomaster Munte* (1922). Thus, these collections of songs were transformed into beautiful picture books.

Besides her picture books for which she always wrote the text herself, she has also published eight collections of fairy tales with her own illustrations. She modelled her fairy tales on the old folk tale, and she was also greatly influenced by H. C. Andersen and Zacharias Topelius. The first book in the fairy tale series was called *Fairy Tale Book* (1915), and this is also the one Elsa Beskow loved best. . . . The collection contains six fairy stories. Her sons helped with the illustrations of one of them, the tale of *Mr. Dumpty of Dumptyland.* (pp. 246-49)

Merry-eyes was published in 1919 and contains "**When the Big Blueberry Mountain Comes to Town,**" one of her most delightful tales. This mountain is completely covered with ripe blueberries, and one day it takes itself off to town so that the poor townspeople can enjoy some of its delicious fare. However, the townspeople do not behave quite as they should and so the mountain stamps back home again.

Bubbelemuck and Other Tales came in 1921 and in 1922 *Grandma's Patchwork Quilt*, a collection of tales told in a gentle old-fashioned way. *The Chest in the Manor House Loft* was published in 1926, and in 1930 the collection called *Grandma and Lightfoot.* In this latter book, the authoress shows that she could tell fairy stories even with a modern setting. *Once upon a Time* (1944) is a collection of fairy tales, illustrated in black and white. And finally came *The Little Weaver*, which was published posthumously in 1954, one year after her death. . . .

Elsa Beskow also wrote plays for children. For example, she dramatized *Aunt Green, Aunt Brown and Aunt Lavender,* in a play called *Little Spot's Adventures.* (p. 249)

Elsa Beskow writes about the fundamental things that children love and understand and that her childhood-land remains, despite the great changes Swedish society has undergone.

Brightness, lightness, and a great ability for happiness were Elsa Beskow's secret. Beneath everything she created ran the current of life. She knew, as few others do, how to write a text which was comprehensible to children; she knew the language of childhood. She made children feel both liked and happy; she knew their taste for the close and recognizable, and in her books they find security, warmth, and soft humor. She loved the ordinary things of everyday life, but also play and fantasy. Her knowledge of children was deep and she realized, as few others do, a child's feeling of insignificance in the large world of grownups. She diminished the Swedish woods so that the children could peep round the corner, she peopled it with animals and friendly fairy tale figures who talked a language children could understand. Elsa Beskow was often didactic, but her understanding of children was modern in the best sense. In her books she always met the children halfway. (p. 250)

Mary Ørvig, "Elsa Beskow Maartman: 1874-1953," in Top of the News, *Vol. XXII, No. 3, April, 1966, pp. 240-52.*

BETTINA HÜRLIMANN

[Elsa Beskow's] best-loved work about the little boy in the bilberry wood, *Putte i blåbärsskogen,* brings us back once more to the subject of the tiny human creature who is thereby enabled so much better to get under nature's skin. This is a theme to which we are well enough accustomed through *Alice in Wonderland, Nils Holgersson,* and countless fairy stories, but it is here varied in a way particularly enjoyable to young children. This writer's other books betray an even stronger relationship to [Ernst] Kreidolf and are less well known outside Sweden, although they possess great charm in their somewhat modified 'art nouveau' style. (pp. 207-08)

Bettina Hürlimann, "Picture-Books in the Twentieth Century," in her Three Centuries of Children's Books in Europe, *edited and translated by Brian W. Alderson, second edition, Oxford University Press, London, 1967, pp. 201-45.*

MARY ØRVIG AND NINA WEIBULL

[It] was not until 1882 that children's book illustrations of Swedish origin appeared. It was then that *Barnkammarens bok* appeared with twenty color plates by the artist Jenny Nyström, based on a collection of nursery rhymes. The book was a great success, and in 1886-1887 another important collection of nursery rhymes was published under the title *Svenska barnboken* with numerous black-and-white illustrations by Jenny Nyström and several hundred rhymes based on the collection of the folklorist Johan Nordlander.

These two titles introduced a period of picture book production in Sweden which culminated at about the turn of the century, when two women wrote and illustrated a series of books which have been nursery classics ever since. They were Ottilia Adelborg and Elsa Beskow. (p. 38)

Elsa Beskow began her literary career with the picture book *Sagan om den lilla, lilla gumman* (1897), based on an old nursery rhyme. In *Tomtebobarnen* Elsa Beskow describes the passing seasons in the Swedish forest with a detailed naturalism which replaced the stylization so characteristic of the turn-of-the-century art. The book shows the members of the Elf family occupied with various activities, and their diligent handiwork calls attention to the industrious domestic activities of the farming community. The figures are outlined in charcoal against the light water color background.

In the series of five picture books beginning with *Tant Grön, tant Brun och tant Gredelin* the scene changes to an idyllic small town in mid-nineteenth century Sweden where elderly people are portrayed with affection and humor. *Pelles nya kläder* describes country crafts and the barter economy of bygone agrarian Sweden, but above all it is a eulogy of human community feeling and kindness, presented moreover in a manner which has held the interest of Swedish children for over half a century.

Her last picture book, *Röda bussen och gröna bilen,* appeared in 1952, the year before she died. She wrote and illustrated more than thirty picture books and song books, as well as several collections of fairy tales and plays. She contributed to the field of school readers with a series called *Vill du läsa?*

which eventually superseded the readers by Anna Maria Roos. . . . Realism, psychological insight, affection, and a genuine feeling for nature—these are the characteristics of Elsa Beskow's picture books, with their portraits of children absorbed by everyday games. (pp. 38-9)

Mary Ørvig and Nina Weibull, "Children's Book Illustrations in Sweden: An Outline of Developments," in Culture for Swedish Children *by Mary Ørvig, Nina Weibull, and others, The Swedish Institute for Children's Books, 1981, pp. 38-52.*

PUTTES ÄVENTYR I BLÅBÄRSSKOGEN [BUDDY'S ADVENTURES IN THE BLUEBERRY PATCH] **(U.S. edition as** *Peter's Adventures in Blueberry Land;* **British edition as** *Peter in Blueberryland)* **(1901)**

[*Peter's Adventures in Blueberry Land was published in 1975. Peter in Blueberryland was published in 1982.*]

Elsa Beskow wrote for an earlier generation of Swedish children and we are told that she is still popular there. If invented here and now, the story of Peter, reduced in size by an elvish little forest fellow who enlists seven "blueberry boys" and five red lingonberry girls to help fill his berry baskets for his mother's birthday, could only be considered senseless and cloying. But Beskow's naive verse and gentle watercolors in art nouveau borders do have an innocent sweetness that couldn't be simulated today.

A review of "Peter's Adventures in Blueberry Land," in Kirkus Reviews, *Vol. XLIII, No. 10, May 15, 1975, p. 561.*

This unbelievably boring picture-book text has luckily been redeemed by images that excite the imagination. The story itself is composed of perfectly childlike, simple elements. On his mother's birthday, Peter searches for lingonberries and blueberries, but he fails to find a single one until Father Blueberry takes him to his enchanted kingdom. In that Thumbelina paradise, Peter sails in a boat made of bark, gallops wildly on a mouse, swings in a spider's web; and when he finally returns home, he totes two baskets of berries. Possibly something has been lost in the translation and adaptation of this much-praised Swedish picture book, for the writing is weak and precious, the sentences limp, and the language totally uninventive. But Elsa Beskow, a superb colorist and evocator of the natural world, fashioned illustrations that combine fantastic situations and precise, believable detail. Because of this, and because of the beauty of her delicate watercolors, the best of her work in this book deserves to be placed beside that of Beatrix Potter.

Anita Silvey, in a review of "Peter's Adventures in Blueberry Land," in The Horn Book Magazine, *Vol. LI, No. 4, August, 1975, p. 367.*

Elsa Beskow's books rest on folktale tradition to which she gives her own characteristic domestic flavour. . . . The illustrations [in *Peter in Blueberry Land*], on matt paper in serene, muted colours, are contained in neat frames decked with quaint figures, emphasising the play of imagination on a quiet country scene.

Margery Fisher, in a review of "Peter in Blueberry Land," in Growing Point, *Vol. 21, No. 5, January, 1983, p. 4012.*

OLLES SKIDFÄRD [OLLE'S SKI TRIP] (British edition as *Ollie's Ski Trip*) (1907)

The outdoor life of the North is shown in all its glory in this charming picturebook. The text, telling of winter days and the final rout of King Winter by Old Woman Thaw, accompanies pictures that are delightful both in conception and execution.

> *A review of "Olle's Ski Trip," in* The Booklist, *Vol. 25, No. 5, February, 1929, p. 215.*

TOMTEBOBARNEN [ELF CHILDREN OF THE WOODS] (1910; also published as *Children of the Forest*)

> [The U.S. edition of Children of the Forest *was published in 1970 with a verse adaptation by William Jay Smith; the British edition was published in 1982 with English text by Alison Sage.*]

A family of tiny forest people enjoys the changing seasons in this . . . rhymed adaptation of a European children's classic. . . . The four children, all in dotted red caps, encounter fairies and an ogre, gather mushrooms and berries, attend a kindergarten conducted by Mistress Owl, play in snow and summer streams, and watch their father slay a serpent in his suit of pine-cone armor. The simple, unhurried story and the clear, glowing watercolors, brimming with life, activity and charming detail, have a distinctly old-fashioned flavor but are saved from coyness by their creator's still fresh observation and affection for her human and animal creatures. (pp. 107-08)

> *Sada Fretz, in a review of "Children of the Forest," in* School Library Journal, *an appendix to* Library Journal, *Vol. 16, No. 8, April, 1970, pp. 107-08.*

No need for concept geography books when you have folktales to hand. . . . Elsa Beskow's *Children of the Forest* opens up a landscape subtly different from English woodland, in which a bearded father and his bonneted wife watch over their children as they play with squirrels or frogs, run from a troll while blackberrying, weave rugs from woven grass and gather nuts, mushrooms and crab-apples for the winter. Small children should find it easy enough to imagine themselves riding on a toboggan drawn by a hare or behaving demurely at Mrs. Owl's school: the quiet humour and delectable details of Elsa Beskow's gentle colours and shapes make it easy to accept the community of fairy children and animals, while the humane approach to wild life makes its unconscious appeal.

> *Margery Fisher, in a review of "Children of the Forest," in* Growing Point, *Vol. 21, No. 2, July, 1982, p. 3921.*

Elsa Beskow is the most consistently popular author-artist in her native country. . . . *Children of the Forest* is perhaps Beskow's best-loved picture book. The text in the original is in verse, neat and precise, and with immaculate rhythm and rhyme—much of the book's appeal to children lies in anticipating the last word of each couplet. In the English version, the verses have—probably wisely—been replaced by prose and without the rhythm to hold it together, the text, which describes a typical year with a family of little people, has taken on a rather distant voice. One of the features which accounts for the book's huge, long-standing success is presumably the fascination of seeing tiny people surrounded by and putting into use vastly enlarged, familiar objects. A Swedish child has an instant emotional response to a pine forest and its contents here so lovingly reproduced: adders, pismires in an anthill, wild fungi (chanterelles, boletus, fly agaric), linnaea growing on

mossy ground, a tiny forest tarn reflecting the white sky of a Nordic summer night. But to an English child, all this may seem more exotic and therefore less absorbing. Nevertheless much of the book's delicate charm has survived.

> *Kicki Moxon Browne, "Romantic and Real," in* The Times Literary Supplement, *No. 4138, July 23, 1982, p. 793.*

PELLES NYA KLÄDER [PELLE'S NEW SUIT] (1912)

Although books with far-flung settings may come early in the experience of a young child, the ethnic impact of such books is small compared to the impression these books may make on children of greater maturity. For example Elsa Beskow's *Pelle's New Suit,* the story of a Swedish farm boy, may just as well take place in a preschooler's neighborhood, while later on in the same story may serve to broaden a child's understanding of communities outside his own. (p. 88)

> *Constantine Georgiou, "Picture Books and Picture Storybooks," in his* Children and Their Literature, *Prentice-Hall, Inc., 1969, pp. 61-106.*

Pelle's New Suit, Elsa Beskow's one realistic picture book to be published in America, was acceptable to the advocates of the here-and-now school. It has been loved through the years, however, for the very unfamiliarity of its charm in telling how Pelle's new suit grew from his pet sheep's wool to its first wearing by Pelle on a bright Sunday morning. (pp. 650-51)

> *Ruth Hill Viguers, "The Artist as Storyteller," in* A Critical History of Children's Literature *by Cornelia Meigs and others, edited by Cornelia Meigs, revised edition, Macmillan Publishing Company, 1969, pp. 633-53.*

Although a few picture books attempt to portray the problems of the elderly, others stress the competence and wisdom that age brings. Elsa Beskow's *Pelle's New Suit* is a realistic picture book that portrays the skills of the elderly and stresses cooperation between the old and the young. Pelle is a Swedish boy who needs a new coat. He shears his lamb and gives the wool to his grandmother to card for him. In return, she asks that he pull the weeds in her garden. Then Pelle asks his other grandmother to spin the wool into yarn, and she agrees if he will tend her cows. The book pictures various other adults whose skills Pelle uses, and he provides them with labor in return. In the end, Pelle is outfitted in a fine new suit, one made by old and young working together. (p. 80)

> *Myra Pollack Sadker and David Miller Sadker, in a review of "Pelle's New Suit," in their* Now Upon a Time: A Contemporary View of Children's Literature, *Harper & Row Publishers, 1977, p. 80.*

TANT GRÖN, TANT BRUN OCH TANT GREDELIN [AUNT GREEN, AUNT BROWN, AND AUNT LAVENDER] (1918)

> There was once a little town, and in that town there was a little street, and in that street there was a little yellow house, and in the little yellow house there lived the sisters—Aunt Green, Aunt Brown and Aunt Lavender.

So begins the delightful story of the aunts and little Pet. One puts it down with a sigh and the wish that there were more picture books as eminently satisfactory as this: as simple in

From Aunt Green, Aunt Brown, and Aunt Lavender, *written and illustrated by Elsa Beskow. Harper and Brothers, 1928. Reprinted by permission of Harper & Row, Publishers, Inc.*

text, as dramatic in picturization, as good in color, and with that atmosphere of a natural, happy home life so almost universally found in the best children's picture books that come to us from the Continent.

It must have been ten years ago that one holiday season we discovered in a Scandinavian book-shop this little book in paper covers with Swedish text only. It was bought solely for the pictures, for it was evident at a glance that these were story-telling pictures. A great deal of the story we had to guess at. And now, a decade later, an American publisher brings the book out in boards and in an excellent translation by Siri Andrews, and we may know all about it at last—why little Pet, the black poodle, wore a black rosette on his tail in the first picture and a colored one on each ear and his tail in the last one; why the children were crying when Aunt Brown met them on the high road, and why the policeman walks at the tail of the procession when they all come home again.

There is one attribute possessed to perfection by Elsa Beskow and very evident in this book, one which not all illustrators possess. It is that of absolute consistency and of perfect fidelity to the story. When she draws a kitchen with copper pots on the shelves and strips of rag carpet on the floor you may be sure that when later in the story this room is used as a setting you will find the same number of shelves, the right shaped

pots, and rugs with the same stripes. Little children notice these things and take a huge delight in their accuracy. How often have we counted almost unconsciously the blackbirds in Caldecott's Sing a Song for Sixpence! Had there been twenty-three or twenty-five birds the great artist would have gone down pegs and pegs in our estimation.

One can give only the merest notion of the simplicity and charm of the story. There is, for instance, a naive and altogether childish pleasure in good things to eat. . . .

And when little Pet is lost and the mourning aunts must decide which road each is to follow in search of him, how simply it is all decided! They draw lots as they sit under the oak tree at the fork of the roads—with ginger cookies.

> The one who got a heart was to go to the left, the one who got a star was to go to the right, and the one who got a plain round cooky was to follow the highway straight forward.

This is the sort of conceit that brings chuckles of appreciation from childish readers of whatever age.

Even more than in her other charming picture books Elsa Beskow in Aunt Green, Aunt Brown and Aunt Lavender shows that her work belongs in the line of the best tradition in picture books for children, that which shows unmistakably in every line the delight that its creator has taken in doing it.

Marcia Dalphin, "Three Nice Aunts," in New York Herald Tribune Books, March 3, 1929, p. 8.

PETTER OCH LOTTA PÅ ÄVENTYR: BILDERBOK [THE ADVENTURES OF PETER AND LOTTA] (1931)

This is the third and best of the three books which Elsa Beskow has written about Aunt Green, Aunt Brown and Aunt Lavender, Uncle Blue and the two children who lived with them. *The Adventures of Peter and Lotta* has more to say about the children and less about the grown-ups and so makes a stronger appeal to boys and girls who find Peter's and Lotta's mild escapades and disasters entertaining and well within their range of interest. The incidents of the tale, Peter and Lotta finding a home for the kittens, losing their way in the woods, bathing in the brook, riding the bear in the circus in their borrowed clothes, while not such experiences as children are likely to have themselves, seem to young readers natural and logical and, above all, highly amusing. The illustrations have the usual charm of Elsa Beskow's pictures. They present everyday things and scenes with a touch of poetry and suggest the atmosphere of a Spring day.

Anne T. Eaton, in a review of "The Adventures of Peter and Lotta: A Story Told and Illustrated," in The New York Times Book Review, November 1, 1931, p. 24.

SOLÄGGET [THE SUN-EGG] (1932)

Fairies look as fairies should in Elsa Beskow's *The Sun Egg* the first publication here of one of the most attractive picture-books by this Scandinavian artist. . . . The elves and gnomes in a wood find an orange, dropped by a little boy. A sun-egg, can it be? They learn the delicious truth from a bird which knows what Andersen called "the warm countries". In the big woodland paintings, with life-size detail, fairies are fairylike

(as I have said): old gnome is more Merlin than Disney; the animals' restaurant has a notice: GUESTS ARE FORBIDDEN TO EAT EACH OTHER. A real child's book, seen at child-level.

Naomi Lewis, "Marriages of True Minds," in The Times Educational Supplement, No. 3361, November 21, 1980, p. 29.

PETTERS OCH LOTTAS JUL [PETER AND LOTTA'S CHRISTMAS] (1947)

The customs of a century ago are reflected in a simple chronicle of seasonal festivities in forest and homestead, with the Christmas Goat as an alternative to Father Christmas. The gentle air of mystification occasioned by Aunt Lavender's tale of an enchanted prince gives an extra dimension to the children's activities. Domestic affection is evoked in the illustrations, their matt colour and quiet interpretation of mood and setting characteristic of the artist and her period.

Margery Fisher, in a review of "Peter and Lotta's Christmas," in Growing Point, Vol. 19, No. 6, March, 1981, p. 3852.

RÖDA BUSSEN OCH GRÖNA BILEN [THE RED BUS AND THE GREEN CAR] (1952)

The authoress dedicates this book to her grandson and it contains two amusing stories in verse about his favourite toys, the bus and the car. It is very suitable for children of 3-6. It is not one of Elsa Beskow's best books, but a new book by this artist and writer of nearly 80 is always welcome. During her long life she has drawn and told stories to many generations of children, and it would be hard to overestimate what her beautiful and delightful books have meant to them.

A review of "Röda Busen och Gröna Bilen," in The Junior Bookshelf, Vol. 17, No. 4, October, 1953, p. 160.

Jamake (Mamake) Highwater

1942(?)-

(Tribal name Piitai Sahkomaapii) Native American author of fiction and nonfiction and poet.

Highwater is regarded as an expert storyteller who dramatically recounts the struggles of American Indians faced with the obliteration of their heritage by Western society. Considered an authority on Indian culture, he is also the author of well-received informational books for young adults and adults on such subjects as Indian art, music, and philosophy. Of Blackfeet and Cherokee heritage, Highwater uses the imagery and cadence of Native American oral folklore to craft works rich with metaphor which impress young readers with the importance of nurturing and respecting other cultures. He is perhaps best known as the creator of *Anpao: An American Indian Odyssey* (1977), a folktale which synthesizes stories from several North American tribes. Blending realism and mysticism, this story of a young man's quest through space and time to achieve self-understanding has been compared to Homer's *Odyssey* for its successful use of the oral tradition. *The Sun He Dies: A Novel about the End of the Aztec World* (1980) is acknowledged as the first historical novel on Cortes's conquest to take the Aztec point of view. With the "Ghost Horse Cycle"—*Legend Days* (1984), *The Ceremony of Innocence* (1985), and *I Wear the Morning Star* (1986)—Highwater traces the saga of three generations of Northern Plains Indians from the devastation of a nineteenth century smallpox epidemic to the pain of alienation in modern times. This trilogy represents several of the predominant topics found in Highwater's works: the fierce determination of some Native Americans to maintain a unique cultural identity, the insistence of others on conforming with white Western society, the role of artists in perpetuating the vision of their people, and relationships among both family members and individuals of differing backgrounds. Highwater has also written a historical novel based on the life of Dr. Charles Alexander Eastman, a general reference survey of Amerindian civilization as represented in works of art and in artifacts, and a picture book which lyrically proclaims the wonders of nature in a tone poem.

Critics laud Highwater's ability to render the tragic and enduring effects of the brutal treatment of Indians during the colonization of America as well as the dignity and creativity which helped them survive. Reviewers also praise him for offering young readers a rare view of a culture that differs greatly from the predominant Western one, for expressing an extraordinary depth of feeling through his protagonists, for his understanding of both adolescents and the elderly, and for his meticulous scholarship. Although the authenticity of his Native American heritage has been questioned and a few detractors fault his characterizations, writing style, and emphasis on the abstract, most critics decidedly approve of Highwater's facility in demonstrating the fortitude and aesthetic contributions of his people in works which are considered universally appealing.

Anpao was selected as a Newbery Honor Book and was a *Boston Globe-Horn Book* honor book in 1978. *Many Smokes, Many Moons* won the Jane Addams Children's Book Award in 1979. As a tribute to Highwater's work on behalf of Native Amer-

Courtesy of The Native Land Foundation

icans, the tribal name Piitai Sahkomaapii ("Eagle Son") was conferred on him by Ed Calf Robe, Elder of the Blood Reserve of Blackfeet Indians, in 1979.

(See also *Contemporary Literary Criticism*, Vol. 12; *Something about the Author*, Vols. 30, 32; *Contemporary Authors New Revision Series*, Vol. 10; *Contemporary Authors*, Vols. 65-68; *Dictionary of Literary Biography*, Vol. 52: *American Writers for Children since 1960: Fiction;* and *Dictonary of Literary Biography Yearbook: 1985.*)

AUTHOR'S COMMENTARY

[The following excerpt is taken from an interview with Jane B. Katz on June 26, 1978.]

In a very real sense, I am the brother of the fox. My whole life revolves around my kinship with four-legged things. I am rooted in the natural world. I'm two people joined into one body. The contradiction doesn't bother me. But people always assume the one they're talking to is the only one there is. That bothers me. There is a little of the legendary Anpao in me, but also a little of Mick Jagger. I stand in both those worlds, not between them. I'm very much a twentieth-century man, and yet I'm a traditional Northern Plains Indian.

I speak eleven languages and can joke in eleven languages. That facility enables me to reach out to people of many different cultures. I'm at home in New York and Europe. My house in Turkey overlooking the Aegean Sea is surrounded by a field of red poppies and golden hay. And yet I need to go home to my origins, to Indian land. There is some place in me where the animal tracks are still fresh.

I'm cautious about my success, and about my visibility. As a tribal person, I've had the rewarding experience of having Native Americans from all tribal backgrounds say, ''What you're doing is good.'' I'm touched by that, because from one side of me, I'm really just standing up and saying my say at a council meeting. And if the elders and the people nod their heads, that's as much achievement as I can expect. But I also live in that other world that gives its recognition in red and yellow lights on buildings. I'm happy if there's a full-page ad for one of my books in the *New York Times*. For if I'm going to make my personal view of the Indian world more visible, then I must do it for Indians and have them nod their heads quietly and say yes, and I must also do it for the kind of billboard mentality that the dominant world lives in, although I do have my priorities and limits.

I've always had an enormous regard for the intellect. Still, I like to go home to my people, who are in touch with the beginning of things. At home, people are carpenters; some are poets, painters, and teachers; some work on construction jobs. They are people who perceive the importance of small things that are easily missed by those of us who move much too quickly. I admire and respect that. People will say, ''Shall we take a walk?'' We'll walk along quietly. And they'll say, ''What is Jimmy Carter thinking?'' I'll say, ''It's hard for me to say.'' They'll say, ''Did you see the way the moon looked last night?'' And we'll talk about that.

In New York City, when I look above the crowds and the carnival atmosphere and comment on the sky and the crowds, people think it's quaint, part of my professional Indian stance.

I was born in the early forties and was raised in northern Montana and southern Alberta, Canada. I'm not enrolled in the Blackfeet tribe, but I spent my first thirteen years among Blackfeet and Cree people. We were very poor, but like most poor people, I didn't know it, didn't know why we always had the same thing for dinner.... Our house was warm in the winter, cool in the summer. We sang, and we were content.

My mother and father are gone now. My father was a founding member of the American Indian Rodeo Association. He was a very good rider. He was also an alcoholic who often fell off his horse. He got a reputation for being very funny, so he became a rodeo clown. My father was a handsome, brave, and wise man, without any education in the traditional Western sense, who worked by hard hoping to build a life for my mother, my brother, and me. But in some strange way he was poisoned with a deep sense of rage about his situation and blamed most of his failures on the fact that he wasn't given chances. I think that probably ninety percent of the time he was right, but ten percent of the time he was fooling himself and, like so many Indians, he didn't take chances. There are those in the dominant culture, too, who forget that although they have been beaten down, they can do something about it. My father, unfortunately, could not.

Filmmakers came to Montana and the Dakotas and hired Native Americans because that was an inexpensive way of getting ''extras'' for the cowboy-and-Indian crowd scenes. They heard that my dad was a very funny fellow—fell off horses, got on backwards, made people laugh—and so my father became a stunt man in the movies.... He traveled with the film companies, taking his family along, and I became a carney kid. I have vague recollections of Betty Hutton screaming on a Hollywood set, of seeing fog pumped onto the set of a Charlie Chan movie, a body floating in an indoor ocean. But I didn't know they were movies; I thought it was some sort of adult game with non-Indians playing Indians and non-Orientals playing Orientals (even then I knew we never played ourselves). (pp. 171-74)

My father was killed in a head-on collision. He certainly didn't feel it, for he was very drunk. My older brother was killed in Korea his second day of combat. My mother, who was an extraordinary person, lived on long enough to see that I had made it in this crazy life of mine. She was a very traditional Indian woman who had no grasp of why I would want to go to a university, study anthropology, and become a writer.

I came to terms with the solemn aspects of life very early. I was always among Indians, for we traveled the powwow circuit. I was always listening to some older person telling stories. They are nameless to me now, and countless, because there were so many. I was introduced to the Indian world as children in my tribe were in the 1870s when we were a nomadic people. I was rootless, yet connected to a vital tradition. The elders talked to me and gave me a sense of the meaning of my existence.

I talk and think as a poet, but I don't want to perpetuate the romantic notion of the Indian as watching chipmunks his entire life, waiting to see which side of the tree the moss grows on. For the Indian, art is not reserved for a leisure class, as it is in Anglo society. It is part of our fundamental way of thinking. We are an aesthetic people. Most primal people are. We represent a constant chord that's been resounding ever since man began. While those Cro-Magnon people in the caves of southern France (at least according to Western mentality) should have been out worrying about the great likelihood that they wouldn't survive, they were building scaffolds fifty or sixty feet high and with tiny oil lamps were painting the ceilings of their caves with marvelous magical images. These images were an implicit and important part of their lives. For us, this aesthetic reality is a continuous process. The kiva murals of the Hopi and the Mimbres pottery rival the finest accomplishments of Western art. This idea of life as art is part of being Indian. It's not quaint or curious or charming. It's fundamental, like plowing a field. There's great beauty in plowing a field.

The twentieth century is rediscovering what it is to be a primal person, to be human. It has finally become apparent that Indians have something to contribute, that were one of the last reservoirs on earth for this aesthetic mentality—not through our isolation, but through our tenaciousness. We have something urgent to say and something vital to be. But on the other hand, that doesn't mean that we are incapable of being brutes or sexist, being insensitive and drinking too much. We are who we are; we're people, with many facets to our nature. We know how to live in the twentieth century. Because if we didn't, we'd be like the dinosaur or the dodo bird—we'd be gone.

I think Indians have become a metaphor for a larger idea. We are building bridges toward cultures. Some people in white society are also building bridges toward us, and they sometimes join together. That means that it's possible for everyone to find the Indian in himself. It's a kind of sensibility that I'm talking about.

Indians have always had the greatest facility of all: the power of transformation. It's the thing white society is most stubborn about. They won't let people change, except perhaps nuns, priests, and peoples who take on a mystical relation to the deity. Women are permitted to change their names and loyalties, but only because they're not considered much to begin with. It's sad. We are committed like prisoners to our identities in the Western world. We cannot become who we believe ourselves to be. Indians, on the other hand, transform themselves into different beings in ceremonies. We go through initiation, wear special garments and become kachinas, masked figures who impersonate deities. Indian and non-Indian dancers don't just do a dance; they become the dance. All dancers are "Indians." Artists are all Indians, too. This capacity to believe in transformation is what makes art urgent. Because art is essentially a form of transformation.

What were my doorways into Western culture? How did I get a Ph.D., and why did I want one? How is it that I was reading Proust when I was nine, and listening to Edgard Varèse's music? Well, it's all because of a woman named Alta Black, my teacher and great friend from the time I was seven or eight. A white woman, she came West in a covered wagon. So outrageous for her time, she learned the Blackfeet language so she could teach Indian children. When I was eight, she gave me an old typewriter and a book and said I was to learn to type because I would be a writer.

I ran around with a bunch of hostile Indians boys. I was a big kid, violent, a sort of gang leader. We beat up white kids who we felt insulted us. But Alta Black believed in me. She continued as my teacher through the sixth grade and tutored me when I entered the university at thirteen. I grew a mustache at thirteen and ran around in a trench coat. As my spiritual guide, she introduced me to the whole of Western culture. At the end, when she was dying of cancer, she wrote me her death song. She's gone now, but I'm not sure that Alta Black is dead.

All I've done is carry out my instructions. All I really am is what I was made to be. The talent is in me—I don't know where it came from. When I write, I go away for hours at a time. I don't know where I've been or who does the writing. I have to give myself up to it entirely. I'm a technician. I use a typewriter. But I can't take credit for my work. In some way I feel I'm just a conduit. You have to be a very good conduit, like a good Amati violin, but I think someone else plays me.

As Indians, we are extensions of a people. I am not a person, I am a people, a Blackfeet. I am one aspect of a rainbow, part of a whole spectrum. I don't make any sense by myself. I only make sense in terms of the continuity of the whole. I think this is true of all people, but some of us have lost touch with it.

I care what happens to Indian people. I feel that we are a spiritual body. We are dreamers; we believe in dreams. We are brought together by the beautiful. But the word beauty has been distorted. For the Native American there can be great beauty in a cypress tree that's been lashed and twisted by the wind. There is beauty in being ourselves.

I'm concerned about what happens to young Indian boys and girls who are the way I was. I'm involved anonymously with Indian political and social service organizations—that's part of my tribal heritage. If what has happened to me means anything, it means that we can be transformed. We are like clay. With help and guidance, we can shape ourselves into absolutely anything. We can become what we believe in. It takes courage.

After all, we are all going to die. How much better to give back a plump, ripe fruit to the earth that it can grow on, than something that's hardly developed.

That's the important thing, to give something back to the earth. (pp. 174-77)

> *Jamake Highwater, in an excerpt in* This Song Remembers: Self-Portraits of Native Americans in the Arts, *edited by Jane B. Katz, Houghton Mifflin Company, 1980, pp. 171-77.*

GENERAL COMMENTARY

BERNICE E. CULLINAN with MARY K. KARRER and ARLENE M. PILLAR

Highwater is special in his ability to share his ancestors' culture, linking Native American and contemporary American experience. . . .

The stories that Jamake Highwater weaves continue the river of memory of his people and courageously influence current thinking. His novels and nonfiction are only a part of his contribution to building a heritage for tomorrow, for he also comments on music, dance, and art.

> *Bernice E. Cullinan with Mary K. Karrer and Arlene M. Pillar, in an excerpt in their* Literature and the Child, *Harcourt Brace Jovanovich, 1981, p. 352.*

JACK ANDERSON

> [*In the following excerpt, Anderson reports that Highwater has lied about his biographical and educational background and that he may not be an Indian.*]

One of the country's most celebrated Indians has fabricated much of the background that made him famous. In fact, some Indian leaders doubt that he is an Indian.

The name he goes by is Jamake Highwater. He has written several books and academic articles on Indian culture, detailing the pain of his life as an Indian. With his dark hair, sculpted profile and majestic presence, he appears to be the very model of an Indian. And his credentials as an Indian have been accepted without question by TV personality Bill Moyers, *Who's Who, The New York Times, The Christian Science Monitor* and other leading newspapers.

Highwater has produced recordings and television programs. Thirty years ago he founded a dance troupe in San Francisco. The Corp. for Public Broadcasting has put up $250,000 for a TV show now being produced by his nonprofit corporation.

CPB and the Public Broadcasting System have offered him $600,000 more if he can find matching funds for another TV production that would cost more than $2 millon.

Yet under persistent questioning by my associate Les Whitten, Highwater finally admitted that he has lied repeatedly about many details of his life. Asked why someone of such genuine and extraordinary talent felt he had to concoct a spurious background, Highwater said he felt that doors would not have opened for him if he had relied on his talent alone.

"Society puts certain pressures on people," he explained. At one point, he said, "Maybe I should have been more forthright."

Although he still insists he is an Indian, Highwater has dropped any claim to Indianhood from his approved press release. "I'm not going to say I'm an Indian any more," he told Whitten.

"But (expletive deleted), I'm an Indian. . . . I've taken a lot of (expletive deleted) being an Indian." He has also made a pile of money as an Indian.

Here are some highlights, culled from various sources:

• Highwater gave *Who's Who* his birthdate as Feb. 14, 1942. But when confronted with an old newspaper clipping that named him as founder of a professional dance company in San Francisco in 1954—when he would have been 12—he said he had guessed at his birthdate, and could be as much as 10 years off.

• His place of birth has been listed variously as Los Angeles, Canada, South Dakota, Montana and Normandy, France, though he said he was misquoted on the last site. Told that the place he gave *Who's Who*—Glacier Country, Mont.—has no record of his birth, Highwater said he picked it "right off the top of my head."

• He has claimed bachelor's and master's degrees from the University of California at Berkeley, and a Ph.D. from the University of Chicago. In fact, he admitted, he never got any such degrees.

• Highwater says his mother was a Blackfeet and his father a Cherokee. But beyond an affidavit in 1974 from his adoptive mother and another from his foster sister, attesting their belief that he is an Indian, he has no proof. He is not on the official Blackfeet tribal rolls, and such respected Indian leaders as Vine DeLoria Jr. and Hank Adams say flatly that Highwater is not an Indian.

• Highwater's father was either an "illustrious motion picture director," an "alcoholic stunt man" or a rodeo clown, and died when the boy was 7 (or 9 or 10 or 13). His mother, according to Highwater's promotional materials and published interviews, either married a rich man or was destitute—or wasn't a Blackfeet at all, but a Cherokee who ran away at 15 to marry a Greek-born circus aerialist.

> *Jack Anderson, "Lots of Smoke Rises around This 'Indian',"* in The Washington Post District Weekly, *February 16, 1984, p. D.C.II.*

SCHOOL LIBRARY JOURNAL

[The following excerpt is taken from an interview with Highwater in which he refutes published allegations that he is not an Indian, has lied about various biographical and educational information, and has written unauthentic works.]

"Lots of Smoke Rises around This 'Indian'" headlines Jack Anderson's column published in the February 16th [1984] edition of the *Washington Post* [see excerpt above]. "Tempest in a Tepee" by John Ashton appeared on the front page of the November 23, 1983, issue of *Westword*, Denver's News and Arts Weekly. The subject of these articles is Jamake Highwater, who is a well-known and highly regarded author of books for children and adults, a contributor to newspapers and magazines, a lecturer at New York University, and an assistant professor at the Graduate School of Architecture at Columbia University. He speaks on behalf of Indians and writes as an authority on Indian culture.

Anderson, who called Highwater "one of the country's most celebrated Indians," says that he "fabricated much of the background that made him famous." . . . Anderson then itemized "highlights" in Highwater's life and statements detailing his career, many of which, he claims, are conflicting and cast doubt on Highwater's credentials as an Indian.

Ashton's lengthy article, subtitled "Just who does Jamake Highwater think he is anyway?", also points out conflicting statements, either from an interview with Highwater, with Indian activists or critics, or taken from other publications. Much of the report concerns Highwater's date and place of birth, his claim to Indian parentage, his educational background, the authenticity of his writings, and the information he has offered about himself over the years. Says Ashton, "Highwater is a friendly, erudite fellow, and it's difficult to imagine him lying. . . . What he is, for his sake, had better be an Indian, because Hank Adams (one of his critics) is trying to get several U.S. senators and representatives to pass a law making it a federal offense to pretend to be an Indian. In writing to these lawmakers, Adams uses Highwater as an example of how bad things can be."

When these articles arrived at [*School Library Journal's*] news desk, a call to Highwater produced a statement from his attorney, Jonathan W. Lubell. This was followed by several phone interviews with Highwater, who resides in New York City. Highwater, who said that he chose to respond to the articles because of his tremendous respect for the integrity of librarians who read *SLJ* and his books, replied that he was "crushed, confused, and bewildered by this situation." He was particularly distressed because those making the accusations did not know his work—"a human being should be judged by his or her work." He maintained that many statements credited to him were taken out of context. When *SLJ* asked why this controversy about his credentials surfaced, he replied that gossip about his background has been repeated over the last three years "by persons who shall remain unnamed."

Highwater, in his interview and in Lubell's 7-page statement of clarification, confirmed that he did not know all the details of his life—his adoptive family chose not to disclose parts of his early childhood, his adoption, and his Indian heritage. He still refuses to reveal the identity of his adoptive family. Most biographical sources give his birth date as February 14, 1942 (the right year—the date is an estimate, says Highwater); the place of birth as Glacier Country, Montana. An affidavit from his foster mother confirms that his parents were Indian (Highwater says his mother was a mixture of French Canadian and Blackfeet (Blood) ancestry; his father, Cherokee). Writing in the *American Indian Journal* (July, 1980), Highwater states, "The grand climax of my professional and personal life took place on March 28th, 1979, at the Lethbridge University in Alberta, Canada, when Ed Calf Robe, Elder of the Blood Reserve of Blackfeet Indians . . . conferred a new name upon me to honor my achievements on behalf of my people. . . . My new name is Piitai Sahomaapii, meaning 'Eagle Son.' This name-ceremony was the vindication of my mother's constant efforts to keep my heritage alive within me." He went on to say that the Blackfeet would not have bestowed such an honor if there were any doubt of his Indian ancestry.

In the early 60's, Highwater, under the name J Marks (one source said this was his adoptive name), participated in a San Francisco dance troupe, which later evolved into the San Francisco Contemporary Theater, and wrote under this pseudonym, but dropped it in 1969 when he regained interest in his Indian heritage and resumed the use of his father's name. He states in his article, "Second Class Indians," published in *American Indian Journal*: "My work has given me abundant access to many different regions and many kinds of Native peoples whose desire to be proud of their Indian blood has stirred and heartened me. I have heard all of the cruel jokes and I have endured all the half truths and stupid innuendos. And having found my way into acceptance, I feel that I must not hide behind my achievements, but speak for all second-class Indians.''

Categorizing Ashton's charges of plagiarism as ''false, without the semblance of even a piece of proof to support them,'' Highwater's attorney Lubell concludes, ''The attempt to damage Highwater as a person is unfortunate, petty, and unjustified. However, the 'genuine and extraordinary talent' of Jamake Highwater, to use an American phrase, remains intact; and the integrity and historical and cultural significance of his work is unimpeachable.''

> *"Indian Heritage Queried: Highwater Refutes Charges," in* School Library Journal, *Vol. 30, No. 8, April, 1984, p. 7.*

EVIE WILSON

No author for young people has made the ''smell of pain'' suffered by the American Indian more real than Jamake Highwater. No author has so well represented the blood ties, the enduring dignity, and the persevering cultural creativity which has enabled the American Indian to survive the brutality, condescension, and attempted cultural annihilation in white man's America. ***Legend Days, The Ceremony of Innocence***, and *I Wear the Morning Star* stand in equal and impressive literary excellence.

> *Evie Wilson, in a review of ''I Wear the Morning Star,'' in* Voice of Youth Advocates, *Vol. 9, Nos. 3 & 4, August & October, 1986, p. 144.*

ANPAO: AN AMERICAN INDIAN ODYSSEY (1977)

AUTHOR'S COMMENTARY

These stories, like ancient Indian designs, have been passed from one generation to the next and sometimes have been borrowed by one tribe from another. None of the tales is my own invention; they were all born long before I came into the world. The words, like the threads of a weaving, are new, and these are mine, but the stories belong to everyone. (p. 239)

The character called Anpao is a fabrication. There is no such central Indian hero. . . . I created Anpao out of many stories of the boyhood of early Indians, and from my own experience as well, in order to make an Indian ''Ulysses'' who could become the central dramatic character in the saga of Indian life in North America. (p. 240)

North American Indians did not evolve a written language, at least not the kind of language familiar to the peoples of Europe. This book is my personal effort to use the vast facilities of the tradition of written literature to convey the energy, uniqueness, and imagery of Indian oral tradition. I have approached it, however, not as a stenographer or as an ethnologist, who would tend to value verbatim transcriptions. I have written these stories as a writer. But I have been careful to preserve the qualities unique to non-written folk history.

It is possible that readers will wonder what I have contributed to the stories of *Anpao* other than collecting them from countless tellers. I suspect I have done the same thing that many prior generations of tellers of history have done, only the creative process in my effort is much more like the methods used by contemporary Indian painters than the techniques of ancient storytellers. Like modern Indian painters I have made use of new potentials of technique and imagination which I have learned through the education available in the twentieth century. I be-

lieve, as do contemporary Indian painters, in the existence of some sort of transcendent Indian sensibility, and I believe that its power and its truth can be expressed in modes typical of our day as well as in the venerated, old style of the traditionalists. Just as young Indian painters with a command of modern methods have reinterpreted Indian iconography and history in a new style, so I have recounted the stories I have heard all my life in a prose which tries to merge the old and the new.

I believe that there are images and ideas which are uniquely Indian and remain uniquely Indian no matter what mannerisms are employed to present them. These Indian ideas are central to the stories in *Anpao*. My aim has been to illuminate them as self-contained realities, without drawing parallels to non-Indian rationale or attempting to ''apologize'' for them or to ''explain'' them. I have presented these old tales neither as curiosities nor as naive fiction, but as an alternative vision of the world and as an alternative process of history. (pp. 241-42)

> *Jamake Highwater, ''The Storyteller's Farewell,'' in his* Anpao: An American Indian Odyssey, *J. B. Lippincott Company, 1977, pp. 239-46.*

Highwater has created an exceptional book of rare beauty and insight. To say that Highwater did for American Indian culture what Homer did for the people of Ancient Greece may seem astonishing or perhaps overstated, but it is true. Using traditional tales from many North American Indian tribes, Highwater has skillfully woven them until they form the odyssey of Anpao who because of his love for the beautiful Ko-ko-mik-e-is must undertake the dangerous quest of finding the house of the sun so that he can ask the sun to remove the scar from his face as proof that these two young people may marry. Two of the stories, **''The Farting Boy''** and **''Deer Woman''** have elements that may be objectionable to some readers; however, they are presented with such good taste that they are likely to offend no one except those who can't wait to be offended. The moral tone of the stories is by nature Indian and will provide an interesting comparison and contrast to those of the Judeo-Christian tradition. Space does not permit pointing out the many fascinating aspects of this book except to say that without question this is a superior book which highly deserves the attention of all readers grades 7 and up.

> *James Norsworthy, in a review of ''ANPAO: An American Indian Odyssey,'' in* Catholic Library World, *Vol. 49, No. 5, December, 1977, p. 235.*

Jamake Highwater, of Blackfeet/Cherokee heritage, calls himself the Indian Homer who has written in *Anpao* an American Indian Odyssey. He almost pulls it off. . . .

The novel is well written, smooth, pleasing to the eye and ear. But as a novel it is no more than the linking of old tales. The character of Anpao is never developed. His more interesting brother Oapna dies in the first section. Ko-ko-mik-e-is is simply a beautiful and faithful woman, a little like Penelope perhaps, but with none of Penelope's inventive dedication. Folk characters in any culture tend to be types, prototypes who serve the theme of the tale. Highwater has written an extended folktale, not a novel, for his characters never breathe.

Jamake Highwater has already set up his defenses. At the end of the book, in an afterword to the story, he writes: ''When I had completed *Anpao* and it was read by several elder Indian friends, they asked me if I thought that many white men would be able to grasp what I had written.'' I may borrow that and substitute for a few of the nouns, for what author or artist when faced with a less than rave review ever thinks the critic has been able to grasp what was written?

I applaud Highwater's effort. His retelling of the tales is fluid and in many instances compelling. The book cries to be read aloud. But it is not a novel. And it is nowhere near as great a narrative as the *Odyssey*.

> Jane Yolen, in a review of "Anpao: An American Indian Odyssey," in The New York Times Book Review, February 5, 1978, p. 26.

Occasionally, not often enough, in the world of young people's books—or anyone's—there appears a timeless work which defies delimiting of audience. Such a book is **Anpao**, a synthesis of native American folklore. . . .

[Jamake Highwater] has woven across the main threads of his legendary hero's quest a significant weft of American Indian mythology. . . .

[In] his meticulous bibliography of sources he cites at least one book in which each tale can be read in its oral form. . . .

Some of [Anpao's] adventures are recounted as complete stories in themselves, like the Cheyenne tale of **"Snake Boy"** who eats the large greenish eggs of some unseen creature and turns into a serpentine water-dweller. A creation story, **"The Dawn of the World,"** also comes from the Cheyenne. Here Highwater's poetic narration begs to be read aloud: "At the place where all things began, there was first the black world. And Old Man, the all-spirit, lived in this void, silently and without motion. For he was he. . . . Because he was everything, Old Man was not lonely. But as he radiated through the endless time of nothingness, it seemed to him that something might be more interesting than nothing.". . .

Passages like [this] show that not only the uniqueness and significance of the content make this an enduring book, but also the author's gift for using the poetic, dignified language required of tellers of great epics.

> Virginia Haviland, "Tales of the Tribes," in Book World—The Washington Post, February 12, 1978, p. G4.

[Bringing] expectations to a work may result in a serious misreading of a work. (p. 93)

I myself have recently been guilty of [a serious misreading based on false expectations]. In this paper, I should like to examine the expectations which led to what I now believe to be an erroneous interpretation of Jamake Highwater's **Anpao** and to show how a reevaluation of these expectations have led me to reconsider the novel and to create what is, I believe, a far more valid reading.

When I first read **Anpao** just over two years ago, I was overjoyed. Here was the book I had long been waiting for: an inside narrative, a novel written by a Native American dealing with legend and history from within the culture. I started my reading with two expectations; by the end of the first chapter I had added a third; when I read the afterword, entitled "The Storyteller's Farewell," there was a fourth. Shortly after I Highwater's **The Primal Mind** [an adult work], which reinforced my initial expectations, which in turn had been reinforced by my reading of the afterword. I now had the framework necessary to create a detailed reading, one which, when I had completed it, confirmed my initial expectations.

Because I thought that Highwater was one of the new group of Native writers and painters who were proudly rediscovering and reinterpreting the old traditions, I expected to find traditional material and positive attitude. Like Leslie Silko, he would, I expected, show new hope for a long depressed people. The expectations were reinforced by the subtitle with its word "Odyssey" and the connotations of a successful homecoming after a long, painful, and often unhappy journey. When I discovered a very close resemblance to the Scarface legend collected by John Bird Grinnell, I was sure that my expectations were on the right track, for both dealt with an arduous journey and joyous homecoming. All I needed was the afterword, in which Highwater, contrasting Native and Western approaches to existence, spoke positively of the Native viewpoint, which he felt was superior to the prevailing Western attitudes and which he had embodied in the novel. **The Primal Mind** merely examined in much greater detail the ideas of the afterword.

The reading I created by allowing my expectations to influence my study of the text stated that Anpao was a great hero, one who had engaged in a long quest for self-knowledge and had used that knowledge to help a chosen few of his people prepare for the inevitable Native renaissance.

At the beginning of the narrative, Anpao is destitute, living from hand to mouth in a village which is not his own. He has no knowledge of his past. However, within him are the seeds of greatness; when he is laughed at, he tells his tormentors: "We are alone. But we are noble—for everything in the world is noble—and we are proud. . . . We are not yet wise, but we are seeking wisdom." When Ko-ko-mik-e-is, who has rejected all other suitors, agrees to marry him, Anpao accepts her condition: he must journey to the Sun, and if the Sun removes the scar from his face, he may return to her.

Anpao overcomes the greatest danger of the early part of his journey when he rescues his twin brother, Oapna, from the Lodge of the Moon. He realizes that he must accept the help of the old Swan Lady and that, even though he is filled with fear, he cannot leave his brother to die while he continues his own quest. After the rescue, Anpao also learns about his past, and, when he is united with his brother to become a complete being, he proclaims: "[My Grandmother Spider] would be pleased that I have found a vision from the dark side of the Moon. Now I can see light through the imperfections of the darkness. And I have become a person with a memory of the past and with a vision of the future."

In the long central section of the book entitled "The Lessons of Heaven and Earth," Anpao continues his journey and achieves the wisdom necessary for him to reach his destination. Although he cannot save a boy who has eaten sacred eggs or two boys who have treated a giant turtle with disrespect, he avoids their fate because he understands the necessity for reverence to all aspects of the world. By turning away from Deer Woman, he rejects the temptations of lust, and, by refusing to give in in the face of despair or to take the easy way and marry one of the girls in the villages he visits, he gains great inner strength.

At last he reaches the Sun where he proves his trustworthiness by not taking weapons found by the side of a trail and his courage by rescuing the Sun's son, his half-brother Morning Star, from giant thunderbirds. Even the Moon, who had tried to obstruct his progress throughout the travels, is reconciled to him. The Sun rejoices at having found his long lost son, rewards him with a horse, removes the scar from his face, and gives him the secrets of the Medicine Lodge. However, more troubles confront Anpao on his return trip. The world has changed since he left home: the white men have arrived, the landscape is desolate, many tribes have become degenerate, and smallpox devastates the people. But Anpao is equal to the difficulties he encounters. Controlling his fear, he tricks Smallpox and races to his village, where the people refuse to listen to his warnings. Having learned from previous experience the futility of convincing those who will not listen, he takes his loyal followers and his bride, Ko-ko-mik-e-is, to a village beneath the waves of a lake. There, he realizes, they will be safe from the death sweeping the land. He is their savior, having acquired the knowledge, courage, and self-confidence to choose the right path for those who will listen. The book ends with a hopeful note as the people beneath the water sing: "We shall live again." Anpao has prepared his people for a glorious future.

Such was the reading of *Anpao* which provided the basis for lectures in my Children's Literature classes for the past two years and which was to have been the framework for this article. However, a few months ago, I received two articles which caused me to question seriously both the reading and the expectations which had led to that reading. Jack Anderson, writing in *The Washington Post* on February 16, 1984 [see excerpt above in General Commentary], and Hank Adams, an Assiniboine Sioux, writing in the Native periodical, *Awkwesasne Notes*, late summer 1984, charged that Highwater was not, as he claimed, of Blackfoot/Cherokee heritage, but was, in fact, the son of Greek immigrants and was born George Markopolis, in Toledo, Ohio [see excerpt dated April, 1984, in General Commentary Highwater's denial of these allegations]. I had heard similar rumours before, but had discounted them, although they had made me uneasy.

What discovery of these articles did was to make me ask whether or not my initial literary expectations, based on my belief that Highwater was a Native writer, had caused me to read the book in a way which did not stick closely to the text. Was I, on the basis of this first assumption, ready to find anything that would make *Anpao* a novelistic equivalent to the Blackfoot legend of Scarface and Homer's *Odyssey?* And had I perhaps allowed the afterword and *The Primal Mind* to reconfirm what I had in reality only thought I had found? Clearly, my doubts were now strong enough to warrant a careful rereading of the novel.

I began by reading the last four pages, in which Anpao, after unsuccessfully warning the tribe, takes the believing few beneath the waters. This event was a marked departure from the conclusion of the Scarface legend, in which the hero had, after having been joyously reunited with his bride, lived a long and happy life. (It was also different from the *Odyssey,* in which Odysseus had returned home and reasserted peace with his powerful arms and personality.) There was another marked difference from the Scarface legend. The ultimate purpose of the traditional hero's journey had been to bring back to the people the secrets of building the Medicine Lodge. In fact, the subtitle of Grinnell's version (which Highwater cites as a source in his bibliography) was "The Origins of the Medicine Lodge." In *Anpao,* although the Sun gives the secret to Anpao, he, in turn, does not give it to the people. Instead, he begins his jeremiad. When we remember that the Medicine Lodge was, and still is, an integral part of the Sundance Ceremonies of the Plains people and was used as a means of restoring health and well-being, Anpao's failure to bestow the knowledge is very serious. Surely, with Smallpox stalking the land and threatening the people, they had great need of the Medicine Lodge. Instead, as he goes beneath the waves, he offers them an apoc-

alyptic vision of future hope: "Do not be afraid. The buffaloes and all the dead will return. They will come with a great explosion and in a cloud of smoke. The fireboat-walks-on-mountains will bring the people back again, whooping joyously as they come to us, waving their arms and shouting victoriously."

Anpao's vision is essentially that of the late 19th Century prophet, Wodziwob and was part of the Ghost Dance ceremonies, which in his afterword, Highwater referred to as something the Indians "grasped desperately at." In *The Primal Mind*, Highwater noted that the hopes inspired by the Ghost Dance movement had been destroyed by 1890 with the Massacre at Wounded Knee. . . . (pp. 94-7)

Clearly, in the light of the above observations, the conclusion of *Anpao* is inconsistent with the rest of the novel. The hero's actions are not what one would expect of a person who, as a result of his long travels, had gained great spiritual wisdom. However, the conclusion is inconsistent only when the book is read in the light of the interpretation I offered above. When one refuses to read the novel in the face of the initial expectations outlines early in this paper, but as a structural unit in which earlier and later parts interact ironically, a new reading emerges, one in which Anpao is not seen as a great Pan-Indian hero, but as an ironic hero, a failed leader who has never achieved the great insight he believes he possesses.

The opening section of *Anpao,* "In the Days of the Plentiful," sees the hero receive his injunction from his beloved, begin his journey, and rescue his brother from the Lodge of the Moon. The title of this section may itself be ironic, for Anpao and his twin brother Oapna live in poverty, their journey is long and arduous, and they often experience despair and fear.

Anpao's journey is clouded with ignorance. He does not know who he is, he is unaware of the location of the Sun's lodge, his destination, and he does not realize that he is in fact going to visit his own father. The key incident occurs when his twin, Oapna, who speaks in contraries, unintentionally insults the Moon and is taken away by her. When we later learn that Oapna is, in fact, a part of Anpao, his actions take on retrospective meaning: his foolishness is in fact part of his brother's personality.

When Oapna begins making his insulting statements, Anpao reacts in a manner that will be seen again and again throughout the novel. He warns his brother to stop, but to no avail; his message is unheeded. In the adventures with the boy who eats the snake eggs and the boys who insult the turtle, and in his final actions with his people, he does not avert catastrophe. He is ineffectual.

In order to save his brother, Anpao must accept the help of the Swan Lady. We are told that "At first Anpao did not trust her, but her voice was agreeable and there was no malice in her laugh." This trust will turn out to be ironically misplaced, for his helper is the Moon in disguise. Although Anpao is told by the Swan Lady about the Moon's vindictive anger, he makes several foolish statements. "I do not care at all about the problems of the Moon" and "I have seen the Moon and I do not fear her!" His opinions will prove to be wrong. The problems of the Moon will be of great concern to him and he will indeed come to fear the Moon. However, at this point Anpao is revealing a character trait that will be repeated again and again during his adventures: the making of brash statements which shortly after are revealed to be unfounded. For example, he tells the Swan Lady that "I cannot run away and hide." Yet, retreat from danger becomes Anpao's major way of dealing with difficulty, particularly in the conclusion of the novel. We are beginning to see that Anpao's character may have developed very little in the course of the novel.

In the second section of the novel, "The Dawn of the World," Anpao is told the story of his origins and the origins of the world. Now, he supposedly has the knowledge necessary to enable him to proceed more successfully on his quest. What is important to notice is that the story is told to him by the Moon in the disguise of the Swan Lady and that the story contains many messages, teachings which, if Anpao had observed them, would have stood him in good stead.

The major lesson to be learned from the stories is that death is inevitable. When Anpao's mother tosses a stone into the water and it sinks, Napi, the Old Man announces: "Now there must be an end to all the people of Earth. . . . Nothing is permanent and nothing can remain unchanged and something must become nothing as it was in the beginning." This message of death is reinforced when Anpao's mother falls from the rope dangling from heaven and is killed.

Throughout this section, death is linked to water. Napi's life shows that, although life emerges from water—he himself had floated on the waves and the coot had dived into and returned from the depths with earth to create the land—death involves a return to water. He himself is covered by water in his last moments. Later in his travels, Anpao sees the giant turtle take the disrespectful boys to their deaths in the putrid lake. But he does not recall the message of these stories when he makes his trip into the lake at the end of the novel. As he is still beneath the waters when Wasicong tells the story, it seems more likely that his is a one way trip like Old Man's rather than a return journey like that of the coot.

The story of Anpao's mother also provides many useful lessons. After she has foolishly cast the rock into the water and so created death, she regrets her decision but is told that it cannot be undone. However, she fails to realize this, remarking as she prepares to leave the Sun: "I have won over death both by entering the World-Above-the-World without dying and by reclaiming my child from the Sun. I am too clever to be caught." Her son, too, will make statements which will prove to be incorrect, and like her, he will also disobey injunctions which have been made in his best interests.

Grandmother Spider teaches the boy how to survive in the world, giving him advice which, if he follows it, will be to his advantage. His failure to obey her warning not to throw his hoop into the air leads to his being divided in two and his having to leave her home. She is correct when she assesses the symbolic significance of his actions: "You have become your own friend." Anpao's character is marked by a self-absorption not unlike his mother's. In instructing him, Grandmother Spider emphasizes that he must take a second look at everything he sees and that he must not be deceived by the evil ones: "They will tell you that they are good and that they wish you well. They will promise you many things that you know are impossible. Slowly, as you listen to them, you will come to hope for what cannot be. The Evil Ones will tell you that you must be something which you cannot be." Anpao's later actions will prove that he has not heeded this advice.

In fact, the very situation in which he finds himself indicates that he has not remembered the words Grandmother Spider had told him long ago. The Swan Lady, who as we have seen is in fact his great enemy the Moon, has deceived him into believing that she is his friend. She tells him everything that he must know because she realizes that he did not heed the words when he heard them the first time and that he will not heed them in the future. She recognizes him as a fool and so can speak without fear for herself. In fact, she tells him the story while he is in a dream-like trance, unable to fully comprehend. Twice she explains the significance of what she is relating: that he is mortal, that he will die. "You will not be born again," she announces early in her narration; and "You are dying," she hisses near the conclusion. Although she removes her swan-disguise, Anpao does not seem to recall the moment after he awakens and is reunited with his brother Oapna. Ironically, the last chapter of this section is entitled "All That Happened Must Happen Again." Presumably this is an implicit reference to Anpao in relation to his mother's experiences. He will repeat her foolish mistakes and will attempt to escape death.

After we have read the third section, "The Lessons of Heaven and Earth," we are in doubt as to whether Anpao has learned much. He leaves the camp of the Moon blithely and optimistically calling to his father: "I am not afraid of the Moon. . . . My Grandmother Spider tried to teach me but I was too young to understand. She would be pleased that I have found a vision from the dark side of the Moon. Now I can see light through the imperfections of the darkness. And I have become a person with a memory of the past and with a vision of the future." Ensuing events will reveal that he still has reason to fear the Moon and that the memory of the past has not taught him a great deal. The author casts doubt on these words a few lines later when he makes references to "the colorless camp where the Moon had tricked him." There is no evidence to indicate that Anpao realizes that he has been tricked, or, that if he does, he understands the full extent of the trick.

A survey of the episodes that make up the third section reveals several recurrent elements which reinforce our ironic reading. First, Anpao does not play a very active role in the events. Falling into the ravine where he breaks his leg, he must depend on the evil old man to save his life and later on the Thunders to rescue him from the old man. When a mysterious sickness affects his leg, it is Amana who brings rescue by courageously visiting the old healer. Moreover, as we have seen, he is powerless to save one boy from turning into a snake and two others from drowning on the back of the turtle. And when Deer Woman menaces the group of dancers, he does not act until the next morning, by which time she has killed her victim.

Generally, the positive actions he takes are motivated by self-interest. When he delays at various villages, it seems that he enjoys the adulation of the audiences to whom he tells his stories. While we do not hear the stories themselves, the audience reaction implies that they are recounted in such a manner as to place Anpao in a better light than, in fact, his behavior warrants. He is not above temptation, as his desires for Deer Woman reveal; and when he does continue his journey it is because of his dreams of Ko-ko-mik-e-is. He proceeds for himself. His most positive action in this section is the bringing of the buffalo to the world, but he does so not for the good of the people, but to gain for himself the spirit powers that eating buffalo meat will bestow. (Moreover, when he returns to the world after his visit to the Sun, the buffalo are gone.) Even then, his liberation of the buffalo does not bring total good to the people. Along with the buffalo, he releases sorcerers who control good and evil in the world. They cause him to undergo a deathlike dream state which results in the coming of corn. But because he had treated them haughtily, they disguise themselves so that people are no longer able to spot them. Because of Anpao's character and actions, life will be more, rather than less, difficult for human beings.

In spite of the warnings from Grandmother Spider and the repetition of these warnings in Swan Lady-Moon's story, Anpao continues to be deceived during this section. Significantly, he does not realize that Moon is still playing a role in his journey, impeding it at every possible step. When Anpao drinks the poisoned water innocently brought to him by Amana, "the Moon came out from behind a cloud," the implication being that she has induced the poison. Later, when Anpao leaves Amana, a girl whom, it is suggested, might well be the best helpmeet for him, "The Moon came from behind a cloud and smiled a dreadful, pallid smile. Silently she combed her long black hair and sang a little song to pleasure herself." When the Sun tries to save his son from death at the hands of the sorcerers, she will not let him take action. And, in the final lines of this section, as the boys are drowned on the back of the turtle and darkness falls, we are told: "There was nothing left now. Only darkness. Then the black clouds slithered back across the pallid sky, and the Moon slowly turned her head toward Anpao and smiled." Although she watches Anpao near the goal of his quest, she realizes that he has not illustrated qualities of character which will make his return to earth successful.

Finally, we should notice that death, rather than life, pervades the section. Anpao is twice near death and experiences a death-like dream; three of his companions die. The "Lessons of Heaven and Earth" are that death is the greatest reality. The end of the section is dark and gloomy. No wonder the vengeful moon is smiling.

We should now be prepared to view the title of the final chapter ironically. Whereas earlier, coming from water had signalled birth, "Invasion From the Sea" signals death. The white people in their fire boats do not come from out of the sea, they come across it and it does not touch them. Although the first part of this section seems to indicate the triumphal conclusion of Anpao's journey, it is in reality a false hope, one which merely creates a contrast to the elegiac mood which dominates the concluding thirty pages of the book.

As had been the case before in his adventures, Anpao proceeds in an ironically confident mood: "He started carefully down the trail, knowing that at any moment something unexpected might happen . . . knowing that nothing was exactly what it seemed to be." When he meets the Moon, she is not what he expected: she appears to be kind and helpful, and, although he recognizes that she is jealous, Anpao believes in her kindness. But he does not recognize her hypocrisy, even when she tells him a blatant lie, one he should have seen as such: "That woman and her bastard child died together and are gone forever." Knowing full-well that Anpao, like his mother, had not been able to obey prohibitions, she asks him not to take her son, Morning Star, hunting near the lake of the great Thunderbirds. She also tells him that he will be safe, for "they only kill the children of the Sun." Unaccountably, Anpao forgets that he too is a child of the Sun. Certainly the Moon seems to be attempting to lure him to his death. When he survives, she hypocritically appears to welcome him as a son, and she gives him the gift of raven feathers so that this bride can build a Medicine Lodge. Knowing him as she does, she knows that the gift will never be put to its intended use.

Anpao, when he arrives at the sun, announces that he will never be afraid again. Soon, however, he falls into despair,

thinking that he will never win the love of Ko-ko-mik-e-is. And when he encounters Smallpox on his journey home, he experiences fear several times. When he learns of the devastation created by the arrival of the white people, he moans: "No miracle is great enough to help me now." However, Morning Star's announcement that the horse will provide the appropriate miracle gives him new confidence. Ironically, when he first meets Smallpox, that person is also riding a horse.

On his return home, he exhibits the pattern of behavior he had often shown before. Rather than confront his enemies, he tries to escape them, hurriedly leaving the degenerate village and after tricking Smallpox, riding away in panic. It is no wonder that, when he returns to Ko-ko-mik-e-is' village, he forgets to bestow the boon of the Medicine Lodge, but instead, gives weak warnings and then prepares to escape, operating, for the final time in the novel on assumptions based, not on wisdom, but on false hope. He has abandoned his people, thinking only of himself and the fulfillment of his desires for life with Ko-ko-mik-e-is. His character in the conclusion, which does not present true vision, but self-deception and retreat, is thus consistent with his character as it has been developed through the novel. The individual who has attempted to ignore the inevitability of death has led his people not to rebirth, but to death.

Two other aspects of the novel reinforce this ironic reading. First is the fact that the story is narrated by a holy man whose name is Wasicong. The word is derived from the Dakota word meaning one who is imbued with spiritual powers. However, it has, for the past century at least, also had a derogatory meaning: it is a scornful term for white people, who, the Natives first believed, did have spiritual powers; now it is painfully evident that they do not. Perhaps, when we apply this ironic meaning to the narrator's name, we will realize that we are not intended to take his words at face value. What he tells is not a story about great spiritual power, but about a person who is misguided, who does not have wisdom but false visions. This is reinforced by the fact that Wasicong assumes the shape of an owl, a bird, as Highwater well knew, symbolizing death. Finally, we should note that Wasicong wears a cloak of raven feathers. Remembering that Raven was a trickster, we should be alerted to the fact that everything Waiscong says might well be a trick as well. The story of a holy vision about a hero with spirit powers capable of overcoming death is really an ironic story, told by a death figure, who, beneath his guise of giver of wisdom, is really telling us about the foolishness of one who tried to avoid death.

Further reinforcement for this view comes from the fact that the epigraph for the book comes from *Black Elk Speaks*. The autobiography of the Sioux holy man is not hopeful; it is, in fact, depressingly elegiac. Black Elk admits this himself, when, early in his narration he remarks: "Now that I can see it all as from a lonely hilltop, I know that it was the story of a mighty vision given to a man too weak to use it. . . ." Black Elk seems to say that his life story is a testament of failure. By attaching a quotation from this book to his novel, Highwater seems to be implying that his story, too, will be a testament of failure.

External reinforcement for this ironic reading of *Anpao* comes from three sources: two works by Highwater and the works of a literary critic well-known to him. In *The Sun He Dies*, a novel written in 1980 and describing the downfall of the Aztec world as a result not only of the invasion of the Spaniards but also of the weaknesses within Montezuma's empire. Highwater's first person narrator opens his account in a manner which resembles the gloomy opening of Melville's *Moby-Dick* and the darker sections of "The Book of Job": "Call me Nanautzin. For I am the one who threw himself into the fire so the Sun would rise. And I am the last of my race which has fallen into a reckless night. Call me *tlamatini*, for I am one of the wise men, a broken mirror in which the world makes its fragile shadows. I alone have escaped to tell what has come down upon my people." The novel clearly parallels the events of *Anpao;* the chief difference in it is that the tone is explicitly rather than implicitly elegiac. Highwater's recurrent theme seems to be the fall of the Native world.

In *The Primal Mind,* published in 1981, there are many statements which, read in relation to the actions of Anpao, cast the hero's actions in a decidedly unfavorable light. For example, speaking of the value of story, Highwater states: "The teller's or writer's story is a means of raising one's self to a higher level of achieved power." However, as we have seen, Anpao's frequent recountings of his adventures are usually followed by his failure to perform great deeds and, indeed, are generally told only as a means of gaining the approval of his hosts. Highwater also states: "In tribal religions there is no salvation apart from the continuance of the tribe itself, because the existence of the individual presupposes the existence of the community." He also notes, "It is taboo among primal people like Indians for someone to depart from communal mentality. Traditional Indians reject this kind of behavior as antisocial and treasonous." Anpao's final actions are certainly a departure from tribal mentality and community interrelationships.

Finally, Anpao's actions from the time he leaves the lodge of his father, the Sun, are consistent with the pattern of the failed hero described by Joseph Campbell in his book *The Hero With a Thousand Faces.* For the hero, Campbell writes, the most important phase of the journey he undertakes is the return to his people. "When the hero-quest has been accomplished . . . the adventurer must still return with his life-transmitting trophy. The full round, the norm of the monomyth, requires that the hero shall now begin the labor of bringing [the boon] back into the kingdom of humanity, where the boon may redound to the renewing of the community, the nation, the planet, or the ten thousand worlds. But the responsibility has been frequently refused. . . . Numerous indeed are the heroes fabled to have taken up residence forever in the blessed isle of the un-aging Goddess of Immortal Being." However, Campbell notes, the return is not easy; in fact, the people the hero has to save may represent the greatest obstacles to the completion of his quest. "He has yet to reenter with his boon the long forgotten atmosphere where men who are fractions imagine themselves to be complete. He has yet to confront society with his ego-shattering, life-redeeming elixir, and to take the return blow of reasonable queries, hard resentment, and good people at a loss to comprehend." As we have seen, Anpao does not give the boon of the knowledge of the restoring Medicine Lodge to his people; he is unable to survive the questioning and resentment of the limited villagers; instead, he opts out, he abandons his people. It could be said that, like Natty Bumpo of James Fenimore Cooper's Leatherstocking books, or Huckleberry Finn, he lights out the territory. In this respect, he is less a great Pan-Indian hero than a figure from within the main stream of white American literature, one who chooses individual salvation over social responsibility. Given Highwater's recent statements that he is working on a pilot television series based on the concepts of Joseph Campbell, it seems highly likely that the Campbell ideas expressed above were in his mind when he wrote the conclusion of *Anpao.*

This reading of *Anpao* is not intended to be offered as evidence in the continuing debate about the true nature of Highwater's heritage. Rather it is an attempt to offer a reading which looks clearly at the work, and uses literary experience and training to discover what the text says instead of what we expect it to say. (pp. 97-105)

> *Jon C. Stott, "Narrative Expectations and Textual Misreadings: Jamake Highwater's 'Anpao' Analyzed and Reanalyzed," in* Studies in the Literary Imagination, *Vol. XVIII, No. 2, Fall, 1985, pp. 93-105.*

***MANY SMOKES, MANY MOONS: A CHRONOLOGY OF AMERICAN INDIAN HISTORY THROUGH INDIAN ART* (1978)**

AUTHOR'S COMMENTARY

I grew up in two Americas—the ancient one that existed for my ancestors for tens of thousands of years, and the new one that is written about in history books. . . . . [The] tales of these two Americas are rarely compatible. It is for this reason that the arts of American Indians are precious—they provide a glimpse into their own history, into the world of the *other* America.

For a long time the viewpoint of primal peoples, such as Indians, was considered naïve and primitive, especially if the peoples kept their history alive through oral and pictorial traditions rather than by writing history books. Today we are learning that people are not the same, and that we cannot evaluate all experience the same way. We are also learning that everybody doesn't have to be the same in order to be equal. It is no longer realistic for dominant cultures to send out missionaries to convert everyone to their ideas of the "truth." Today we are beginning to look into the ideas of groups outside the dominant culture, and we are finding different kinds of "truth" that make the world we live in far bigger than we ever dreamed it could be—for the greatest distance between people is not geographical space, but culture. This book is an effort to make bridges across the vast spaces between Indians and non-Indians and to explore the America of native Americans as it is made visible through Indian art. (p. 14)

> *Jamake Highwater, "Preface: One Land, Two Worlds," in his* Many Smokes, Many Moons: A Chronology of American Indian History through Indian Art, *J. B. Lippincott Company, 1978, pp. 9-14.*

Many Smokes, Many Moons is, like Shirley Glubok's book [*The Art of the Southeastern Indians*], a general survey, but it is larger and treats the Americas as a whole. Mr. Highwater writes in his preface: "This book is an effort to make bridges across the vast spaces between Indians and non-Indians and to explore the America of native Americans as it is made visible through Indian art" [see Author's Commentary for this title]. Actually, the book is not nearly so ambitious as that sentence suggests. The "bridges" are simply brief chronological entries in a calendar of events that mark the experience of American Indians from prehistoric to contemporary times. The book, then, is a kind of clock, the bare outline of an enormous record yet to be set down in writing. As such it is more nearly a reference book than anything else.

Yet the principle of selection seems highly arbitrary; indeed, it seems at times curiously rhetorical, even contentious. Under 1528-36, for example, the single entry refers to the incredible odyssey of Cabeza de Vaca and his three companions, who walked across the American Southwest and were the first white-men to encounter the Indians of that region. Theirs is surely one of the great stories of survival in human history; they must have suffered unimaginable hardships. But Mr. Highwater ends the entry with this sentence: "Though Spanish history books make these men out to be heroes, Indians have accused the party of exploitation and aggression, and Esteban, in particular, is looked upon by Pueblo Indians as a thief and a rapist." This may be true, so far as it goes, but it certainly isn't the whole truth, nor is it the point that ought to be made here.

> *N. Scott Momaday, "Indian Facts and Artifacts,"*
> *in* The New York Times Book Review, *April 30,*
> *1978, p. 42.*

The subtitle is misleading. Handsomely designed, this really consists of archaeological, then historical snippets (most only a few lines to a paragraph long), some of them fitted out with black and white pictures . . . which illustrate the notes with varying pertinence. . . . After 1492 the coming of Europeans and the subsequent great changes and disasters are seen (some-times) from the Indians' viewpoint—but not as eloquently or informatively as in Nabakov's *Native American Testimony.* As for American Indian art as a subject for comment, Highwater makes passing mention of several developments but with no apparent system or sense of proportion; political observations are similarly sketchy and unconnected. The pictures as a group do not make this a notable art book; neither is it a coherent history or a particularly pointed reminder of the human diver-sity Highwater emphasizes in his introduction. Perhaps it will find a place somewhere between the coffee table and the quick-reference shelf.

> *A review of "Many Smokes, Many Moons: A Chro-*
> *nology of American Indian History through Indian*
> *Art," in* Kirkus Reviews, *Vol. XLVI, No. 15, August*
> *1, 1978, p. 813.*

Highwater uses artifacts, pottery, paintings, and drawings to reinforce the idea that all people are not the same in his selective chronological history. By understanding the cultural distance between Indian and non-Indian worlds, we become better pre-pared to bridge that distance. . . . Although about half of the book concerns post-seventeenth century, a time chart hidden in back of the index stops at the seventeenth century. As the book is arranged, it is difficult to gauge the passage of time between events and the relative importance of each occurrence.

In the prefacing essay, Highwater exhibits the conformity that he deplores. To see America as Indian and non-Indian is short-sighted, even from the Indian perspective, and contrary to the spirit of the author's own words. More than "two worlds" exist in our "one land." The American Indian's world is not ". . . the *other* America," but *another* America. Nevertheless, read the book for its insight, language, and the tasteful Indian art reproductions.

> *Ruth M. Stein, in a review of "Many Smokes, Many*
> *Moons: A Chronology of American Indian History*
> *through Indian Art," in* Language Arts, *Vol. 56, No.*
> *2, February, 1979, p. 188.*

THE SUN HE DIES: A NOVEL ABOUT THE END OF THE AZTEC WORLD (1980)

Nanautzin, the Ugly One, an Aztec Indian, is caught chopping firewood in a nobleman's forest. Decrying ruler Montezuma's harsh treatment of the people, he does not know it is Monte-

zuma to whom he speaks. Rewarded for his honesty, Nanautzin is transformed into Montezuma's chief orator. Through his eyes, we see the approach of Cortes and the destruction of the Aztec empire. How the Aztecs received the Spanish as gods and were barbarously betrayed by them for the sake of gold is a story familiar to school-children; what Highwater brings to the telling is the richness of Aztec cosmology and daily life, and a pictorial sensibility that helps us to see the battle scenes, especially. But Nanautzin, purposefully, is underdeveloped in traditional fictional terms, and Highwater's attempt at an epic seems more like a curious procession of narrated paintings than a novel.

> *A review of "The Sun, He Dies," in* Publishers
> Weekly, *Vol. 217, No. 11, March 21, 1980, p. 54.*

This work is a historical novel dealing with the conquest of Mexico. Highwater wants to tell the story from a native point of view, and he has made good use of the surviving Nahuatl sources. The authenticity of his materials is attested by the concluding apparatus, comprising an afterword, maps, glos-sary, and bibliography. The author's intentions as expressed in the afterword are fascinating: he wishes to convey a tradi-tional world view, through a narrative employing "the energy, uniqueness, and imagery of Indian oral tradition." The char-acters are presented as archetypes—as stylized characters from folk tales. The conclusion of the novel is meant to move beyond the traditional world view and the characterization typical of its art; the narrator, Nanautzin, evolves into an individual of the "post-Columbian" sort to which the readers of modern fiction are accustomed. This experiment in point of view is not entirely convincing, and the novel is weakened by diction that suggests costume novels more than an oral tradition. These problems aside, the book is ambitious and readable.

> *A review of "The Sun, He Dies," in* Choice, *Vol.*
> *18, No. 2, October, 1980, p. 248.*

The destruction of the powerful Aztec culture in the 16th Cen-tury by a handful of Spanish adventurers has been chronicled before, but never has it been told with the eloquent, progres-sively angry Indian voice Highwater has created. . . . Nanaut-zin's progress to the highest ranks of Aztec society provides varied insights into the culture as Highwater weaves history, cosmology and religious ritual seamlessly into the story. The immediate perception and measured cadence of an Indian nar-rator works well, as it did for the author in *Anpao: an American Indian Odyssey.* Though the story of Montezuma, the invasion of Tenochtitlan and the relation of the Spanish to the Aztec belief in the return of the exiled white god Quetzalcoatl has always been complex, Nanautzin's gradual understanding of the nuances of religion and politics is a good vehicle for YAs to learn more about the subject. This "cultural autobiography," as Highwater calls it, contrasts biased historical accounts of White-Indian encounters, and his rigorous scholarship (de-scribed in an Afterword) is apparent in the powerful story.

> *John Adams, in a review of "The Sun, He Dies,"*
> *in* School Library Journal, *Vol. 27, No. 2, October,*
> *1980, p. 167.*

MOONSONG LULLABY (1981)

The Newbery Honor author's lovely lines were inspired by stories told by his people of the Blackfeet and Cherokee tribes. Mothers cuddle their children and sing the lullaby: "Listen carefully, the Moon moves into the evening sky, her soft light streaming through the treetops. She is singing, singing to the People of the campfire.'' In the lyrical story, the mothers recall the trials and joys of the past and chant the praises of the natural world that gives the People life. [Marcia] Keegan's grand color photos of Native Americans and the landscapes of an unspoiled (so far) Western country illustrate Highwater's outstanding creation.

> *A review of ''Moonsong Lullaby,'' in* Publishers Weekly, *Vol. 220, No. 13, September 25, 1981, p. 88.*

A tone poem, quiet and reverent, has a warmth that is nicely contrasted with the cool night skies of the handsome color photographs. . . . The moment for this book may have to be chosen, but at the right moment this celebration of the affinity between the Native American and the natural world should reach and touch children.

> *Zena Sutherland, in a review of ''Moonsong Lullaby,'' in* Bulletin of the Center for Children's Books, *Vol. 35, No. 2, October, 1981, p. 31.*

[**Moonsong Lullaby** begins with] a somewhat anachronistic evocation of the ''People of the campfire'' . . . followed, for the greater part of the book, by some lyricizing about the Moon and the night and the morn. Little of this, however, is within a child's scope of thinking or expression . . . and, indeed, the more one ponders the words, the more strained they seem. . . . But the chief difficulty is that everything rests on words . . . that have no particular resonance and little concrete meaning. (pp. 2-3)

> *A review of ''Moonsong Lullaby,'' in* Kirkus Reviews, *Vol. L, No. 1, January 1, 1982, pp. 2-3.*

LEGEND DAYS (1984)

During Amana's tenth winter ''a strong man crept inside of her and refused to go away.'' It was the winter that smallpox decimated her tribe; forced to flee, Amana was rescued by a fox, who gave her refuge from the sickness and from a terrifying owl that stalked her. In the fox's cave she slept and dreamed and was filled with the power of the fox. A song within her told of her gifts: '' 'You must take this vision we give to you and draw it into your heart, where it must remain like the storm that fills the cloud with lightning.' '' She emerged from the cave ''more handsome and strong than the greatest of young warriors.'' Reunited with the remnants of her tribe, Amana carefully guarded her secret. She married the husband of her invalid sister and reluctantly settled into a life of caring for the three of them. But through the years of hardships— famine, decreasing buffalo herds, and the humiliation of reservation life—Amana yearned to help her people survive, although she feared she would never again hear the song of the fox. Much to the consternation of her indulgent husband, she was a stubborn, spirited woman, constantly defying convention; and the sometimes humorous confrontations between the two revealed their love and respect for each other. The book is written in powerful, rhythmic prose. Layered with symbolism and the supernatural, the story reveals the spiritual richness of the Indian people even as their culture hovered on the brink of annihilation. And on a different level the book provides a detailed portrayal of everyday life among the people of the Northern Plains, their social customs and their methods of hunting, of preparing and preserving food, and of moving camp. But holding the novel's different layers together is the strong

characterization of Amana—an inspiring heroine, full of courage, strength, and life. (pp. 336-37)

> *Kate M. Flanagan, in a review of ''Legend Days: Part One of the Ghost Horse Cycle,'' in* The Horn Book Magazine, *Vol. LX, No. 3, June, 1984, pp. 336-37.*

Highwater's theme is the end of legend days—Indian culture— at the hands of the encroaching white race's civilization; however, there is a spiritual progression to the story, as well as an historical one. . . . Highwater's writing is poetic; his use of mythic symbolism does not interfere with the telling of the story. While there are episodes of violence and gore, they stem from the survival aspects of the tale and are crucial to the story. The Indian culture lives in this book, and begins to die— although the fox's vision of Amana provides the hope that the old ways will at least be remembered. A haunting story which is accessible but which requires some afterthought.

> *Dorcas Hand, in a review of ''Legend Days,'' in* School Library Journal, *Vol. 30, No. 10, August, 1984, p. 84.*

The work of Jamake Highwater has always been something of a problem for me. With the exception of **Anpao,** which I liked very much but have not reread, none of his books ''feels'' very Indian to me. For me, they lack some balance, a certain pattern of thought—*something*—that keeps them, unlike the writing of Leslie Silko, Simon J. Ortiz, Wendy Rose and many, many others, from delivering that instantaneous whap! that comes with the recognition of *kin*.

So it is with **Legend Days.** The ''supernatural'' parts seem poorly integrated into the ''realistic'' whole of the narrative, and it bothers me a lot that Highwater has seen fit to drag out that Hollywood B movie cliché, the abandonment of the old during times of trouble. Although this procedure seems to be accepted as commonplace, I have never personally heard anyone tell of an instance where such abandonment was done at anything but the insistence of the Elder him/herself. You don't deliberately go off and leave your wisdom, your religion, your history—and your love—if you don't absolutely have to.

It will be interesting to see the other two books in this cycle. (pp. 18-19)

> *Doris Seale, in a review of ''Legend Days,'' in* Interracial Books for Children Bulletin, *Vol. 16, No. 8, 1985, pp. 18-19.*

THE CEREMONY OF INNOCENCE (1985)

In a powerful sequel to **Legend Days,** Highwater continues his Ghost Horse Cycle, based on the grim fate of the northern Plains Indians as the whites take over their land. It is three years since Amana's husband has died and her decimated Blood people have driven her out for acting as a warrior-hunter. Alone among strangers, she survives by begging from camp to trading post. She finds brief happiness with a French Canadian—but he abandons her, and her child Jemina is born on the desolate reservation. Saved by her one friend, the French-Cree Amalia, Amana finds work washing dishes in a town restaurant and rears her child in Amalia's brothel. As the settlers swarm west, their railroads transforming the land, Amana sees her daughter grow up without tradition or identity, aping the whites. From Jemina's doomed marriage to Jamie Ghost Horse, a once-proud Indian stunt-rider beaten down through the Depression years to alcoholism and brutality, two children are born. For a time Amana cares for them in the ancient Blackfeet homelands; and though the first child is beguiled by images of being a happy American, the younger boy, Sitko, hears his grandmother's stories and feels the gladness and dread of the sacred ceremonies. More realistic and more accessible than *Legend Days,* this has the same lucid and lyrical prose and vital characterizations (except for Jemina and her husband, who are not well developed). There are scenes of intense anguish: as when the broken and hungry tribal elders, prisoners in their own land, are forced to lead their people to the wasteland of the reservation; or when Amana, howling like an animal, feeds her own vomit to her starving baby. Amana's alienation is piercingly dramatized, and so is her endurance: she is sustained by friendship, by the fragile traces of her dreams, and by her hope that her grandson will not allow the ways of their people to die. (pp. 1325-26)

> *Hazel Rochman, in a review of "The Ceremony of Innocence," in* Booklist, *Vol. 81, No. 18, May 15, 1985, pp. 1325-26.*

The *Ceremony of Innocence* is the second book of the Ghost Horse Cycle, tracing the lives of three generations of a Northern Plains Indian family. . . .

Highwater continues to display a rare combination of gifts. Among them an unusual understanding of the contributions of the elderly revealed in his splendid tribute to a grandmother long remembered. The author shares a powerful reflection on the Indian experience and the plight of women in the early 20th century, similar to Alice Walker's achievement for blacks and women in *The Color Purple.* There is also in this book, an understanding of the sometimes willfulness and self-interest of adolescents. Jemina, though for different reasons, is not unlike her own mother who struggled with the male warrior tradition in her longing to be recognized as a warrior within the tribe. Throughout, there is a clear warning that much is lost in progress, and not only for Indians. . . .

A beautiful, moving rendering of the ties that bind us in our age to generations past and future.

> *Evie Wilson, in a review of "The Ceremony of Innocence," in* Voice of Youth Advocates, *Vol. 8, No. 3, August, 1985, p. 184.*

[The] lives of Highwater's characters become metaphor for all that happened to Native Americans between two world wars.

One problem with using fictional figures to make a statement in this fashion is that they must experience many more events than seem realistic for one group of people. Another is that it becomes difficult to allow them to be *believable* people, and that is a major flaw in *Ceremony of Innocence.* One might also be tempted to cite the author for his helpless and ineffectual women, were it not for the fact that none of his characters seem competent to cope with life on any level. The reader unfamiliar with Native history will be at a loss to understand from this book how the People managed to survive at all. Highwater's apparent attempt to convey the horror of one of the worst periods of Native American history does his subject no justice; rather, it seems likely to inspire only confusion and disbelief. The overwrought style of writing certainly does not help:

> She cried out in rage and she shook her fists, and she thrust back her head and shouted, "Sa!. . . No . . .

Sa!" again and again. "I swear to you, child," she howled. "I swear it! You will not die!"

The quintessential "middle" book, *Ceremony of Innocence* does not stand on its own, nor does it leave the reader with any particular interest in what is to come.

> *Doris Seale, in a review of "The Ceremony of Innocence," in* Interracial Books for Children Bulletin, *Vol. 17, No. 1, 1986, p. 6.*

EYES OF DARKNESS (1985)

Magical, engrossing and filled with echoes of a lost people, Highwater's novel of a young Indian's passage into manhood is the kind of full-bodied literature that promotes a sorely needed understanding of the native Americans' tragic defeat. Set in the late 19th-century, the story portrays the gradual and poignant decline of the Western tribes, culminating with the Wounded Knee massacre in 1890.

The story of Yesa and his life among his people is rich in historical detail and poetic imagery, conveying a sense of daily life and ritual. Raised under the wise tutelage of his paternal grandmother Uncheeda and his uncle Many Lightnings, Yesa becomes both a warrior and a deeply spiritual youth. The unexpected return of his father, long presumed dead, brings a new predicament. Yesa becomes an unwilling prisoner to this stranger, who no longer lives the life of an Indian warrior, who has been converted to Christianity by white settlers. Faced with the inevitable terror of a new world far different from anything he has known before, Yesa must summon all his courage to survive and keep intact the sacred teachings of his heritage.

Readers will gain much insight from this remarkable book— a tale of desperation and hope, capturing the spirit of these tribes that perished without mercy.

> *A review of "Eyes of Darkness," in* Kirkus Reviews, *Vol. LIII, No. 18, September 15, 1985, p. 990.*

Disappointingly dry fare from the author of such powerful, even poetic novels about the American Indian as *Anpao* and *Legend Days.* Written in the straightforward style of a junior biography, *Eyes of Darkness* is instead a fictionalized account of Dr. Charles Alexander Eastman, a Sioux Indian who was taken from his people at age 17 to live among the white men. . . . Yesa, renamed Alexander East by his white teacher, identifies his special mission in life as "to use the white man's wisdom to keep his Indian heritage alive.". . . Highwater fails in this novel, however, to bring Yesa's Sioux heritage to life in the scenes of the Dance, the warpath or the buffalo hunt. Here is none of the evocative imagery of the previous novels. The parallel opening and closing chapters are flawed and confusing. Young readers without background knowledge of the Ghost Dance or the Battle of Wounded Knee are likely to miss the connection and the full impact of these events. Both Alexander's and the historical Dr. Eastman's struggles and accomplishments are slighted by this treatment.

> *Deborah M. Locke, in a review of "The Eyes of Darkness," in* School Library Journal, *Vol. 32, No. 3, November, 1985, p. 96.*

The central, major part of the story is stately in pace and vividly detailed, a tribute to the good life of the People of the Plains, a sympathetic picture of an Indian boy's growth and acculturation that is often touching. The frame of reality of the (then) present is harsh, the contrast between the two a reflection of one man's sadness because he must forget the past and live with the cruel change that has come. The boy Hadakah who became the young man Yesa who became Dr. East is a memorable character, and Highwater gives depth and immediacy by writing from the sad hero's point of view. (pp. 68-9)

A review of "Eyes of Darkness," in Bulletin of the Center for Children's Books, *Vol. 39, No. 4, December, 1985, pp. 68-9.*

I WEAR THE MORNING STAR   (1986)

The last of the three novels in the Ghost Horse Cycle is a bleakly realistic first-person narrative about a contemporary Indian boy's struggle for survival. Abandoned by his mother in an orphanage where he is regarded as a freak outsider, Sitko resists the brutal attempts to break him, clinging fiercely to his Indian identity and the myths he heard from his beloved grandmother, Amana. When he is adopted by his mother's rich Greek lover, the pressures to assimilate increase, especially from Sitko's charming older brother, Reno, who claims he is white. The story ends in tragedy for Reno as well as for the boys' broken Indian father and their aimless mother. But Sitko is supported by Amana (who even sends him on a vision quest) and by a white friend; and he finds himself as a talented artist who expresses the vision of his people. Highwater's style sometimes becomes strained and repetitive, with heavy comment about "desperation and confusion" and "a wondrous thing that is called art." But at its best the language is simple and intense: "I live here, and I am lost." The story powerfully dramatizes the modern Indian conflict about identity and acceptance. It also shows Sitko's bond with others who are different. He feels the pain of the displaced and alienated, such as the poor white farmers and those immigrants and Jews who have denied their heritage. In "this longest night" of suffering he finds hope through love and the creative imagination that connect the generations.

Hazel Rochman, in a review of "I Wear the Morning Star," in Booklist, *Vol. 82, No. 13, March 1, 1986, p. 973.*

A fascinating blending of realism with mystical elements, told in poetic prose. . . . *I Wear the Morning Star* is as original and powerful as the first two in the series. All have the same unique melding of Amer-Indian mysticism with realism and incorporate themes dealing with interpersonal relationships among family members as well as people with differing racial and cultural backgrounds. Sitko and the other characters are well-limned protagonists whose believable exploits enable readers to better understand another culture and its people.

David A. Lindsey, in a review of "I Wear the Morning Star: Part Three of the Ghost Horse Cycle," in School Library Journal, *Vol. 32, No. 8, April, 1986, p. 97.*

This lacks the strong pacing of the previous books; the first third, set at the orphanage, has a static, mopey tone, while events pile up too quickly toward the end, teetering toward melodrama. The strongest scenes here are between Sitko (although the characterization lacks depth) and Reno: loving each other deeply, they helplessly move apart as Sitko gains strength through his painting and heritage, while Reno, desperate to be accepted as white, descends into alcoholism and corruption.

Roger Sutton, in a review of "I Wear the Morning Star," in Bulletin of the Center for Children's Books, *Vol. 40, No. 1, September, 1986, p. 9.*

(James) Langston Hughes

1902-1967

Black American poet and author of nonfiction.

Described as "the leading African-American poet of this century" by critic Richard K. Barksdale, Hughes was a prolific author of literature in a wide variety of formats who is lauded as a spokesperson for his people. Acknowledged as the poet laureate of the Harlem Renaissance, he addresses racial injustice, social struggle, and interracial relations in poems which have their roots in jazz and the blues and are written in a simple, colloquial style. Hughes used the musical rhythms and vernacular of urban blacks—a controversial decision for its time—to present powerful messages of protest and hope in his poetry, which mixes blank verse, lyric verse, and dialect. Although he expresses anger and sadness at the oppression of the American black, Hughes underscores his poetry with characteristic humor, optimism, and belief in humanity. Even though Hughes did not direct his poetry to children, his poems have been eagerly received by the young; many of his verses have been anthologized and are popular in the classroom. *The Dream Keeper and Other Poems* (1932), a volume of his poetry which Hughes compiled especially for young people, is considered one of his best works. Largely based on the adult collections *The Weary Blues* (1926) and *Fine Clothes to the Jew* (1927), *The Dream Keeper* is noted for conveying themes of ethnic pride, joy, bitterness, and love of adventure through Hughes's vivid imagery, dramatic conviction, and acute sense of sound and beauty. Hughes's prose works for children and adolescents also reflect his background, philosophy, and interests. Beginning with *Popo and Fifina: Children of Haiti* (1932)—a travel book on which he collaborated with black writer Arna Bontemps—and concluding with nonfiction series on black music, history, and biography, these works reveal competent research, insight, and lucid, lyrical narratives. With children's author Milton Meltzer, Hughes also wrote *A Pictorial History of the Negro in America* (1956) and *Black Magic: A Pictorial History of the Negro in American Entertainment* (1967), richly illustrated gift books which are popular with young adults. *Black Misery* (1969), a captioned picture book which represents the trials of black childhood, and *Don't You Turn Back* (1969), a collection of Hughes's poems selected by educator Lee Bennett Hopkins, were published posthumously.

As a writer for children, Hughes is praised for the immediacy and universality of his poetry as well as for the depth and clarity of his nonfiction; several of his informational books are acclaimed as superior examples of their genre. Although critics point to occasional factual errors in his nonfiction, Hughes is recognized as the creator of stimulating, moving works which demonstrate his skill both as a poet and as a teacher of the young.

Hughes received numerous awards and honors for his adult works.

(See also *Contemporary Literary Criticism*, Vols. 1, 5, 10, 15, 35, 44; *Something about the Author*, Vols. 4, 33; *Contemporary Authors New Revision Series*, Vols. 1, 25-28 [obituary]; *Contemporary Authors*, Vol. 1, rev. ed.; and *Dictionary of Literary Biography*, Vol. 4: *American Poets since World War II, Part 1:*

A-K; Dictionary of Literary Biography, Vol. 7: *Twentieth-Century American Dramatists, Part 1: A-J; Dictionary of Literary Biography*, Vol. 48: *American Poets, 1880-1945 second series; Dictionary of Literary Biography*, Vol. 51: *Afro American Writers from the Harlem Renaissance to 1940.*)

GENERAL COMMENTARY

BENJAMIN BRAWLEY

The significance of Langston Hughes grows out of the fact that, whatever may be his shortcomings, he has been singularly honest in adhering to his point of view and in emphasizing the racial idea. Far more than most men he has rebelled against conventional patterns and lived his life as to himself seemed best. The freedom he has sought for himself he has also insisted upon for others. (pp. 246-47)

Popo and Fifina, Children of Haiti is a book for young people written in collaboration with Arna Bontemps and illustrated by E. Simms Campbell. *The Dream Keeper and Other Poems,* also a collection for children, is in every way one of the best thing Mr. Hughes has done. There are rollicking songs and some typical "blues," but also stanzas in serious vein and lyrics of mystery and beauty. To some extent the book is indebted to the author's previous collections, but it shows far more faith in humanity than either of the earlier works. (p. 250)

Benjamin Brawley, "The New Realists," in his The Negro Genius: A New Appraisal of the Achievement of the American Negro in Literature and the Fine Arts, *Dodd, Mead & Company, 1937, pp. 231-68.*

LELAND JACOBS

Langston Hughes's poem **"City,"** with splendid economy of impression and word, praises two urban moods:

> In the morning the city
> Spreads its wings
> Making a song
> In stone that sings.
>
> In the evening the city
> Goes to bed
> Hanging lights
> About its head.

Notice the comparison of the city morning with the wing motions of a bird—graceful, vibrant movements. Like a bird, the city quivers and stretches, poised for action. The comparison seems apt. "A song in stone that sings" suggests the many sounds of the city orchestrated for the beginning of its multitudinous daily activity. In the second stanza, in parallel form, the feeling for the burst of illumination that becomes the hallmark of the city at night is graphically presented. Children could be encouraged to go on capturing in their own words other moods: the city at noon, at twilight; the city in fog, in wind; the city in summer rain, in winter snow.

"Cycle" may not be a word that young children have in their working vocabulary. But as Langston Hughes develops his poem of that title, they will know its essence:

> So many little flowers
> Drop their tiny heads
> But newer buds come to bloom
> In their place instead.
>
> I miss the little flowers
> That have gone away.
> But the newly blossoming buds
> Are equally gay.

The matter-of-fact way the poet speaks of blossoms going and coming is sensitive but not sentimental. It is an optimistic viewpoint: Though we lose something lovely, other lovely things follow in turn. Notice that this idea is presented twice. In the first stanza he states the fact of nature objectively—as nature's way. In the second stanza he personalizes this observation of the natural phenomenon. Therefore, one reads these stanzas differently—the first as observer of the fact, the second as reactor to the observed fact. Notice, too, the easy vernacular of everyday speech used poetically. Without artifice, the language is as natural as the phenomenon described. The fact that "heads" and "instead" do not rhyme exactly will not bother the young. To a child such rhyming is the type he himself might do, as is also the broken metrical pattern of the second stanza. In these brief lines, children can surely feel the meaning of the beginnings and endings and the great continuity in the cycle of life.

Again Langston Hughes comments on meanings from nature in **"Snail."**

> Little snail,
> Dreaming you go.
> Weather and rose
> Is all you know.

> Weather and rose
> Is all you see,
> Drinking
> The dewdrop's
> Mystery.

The child surely recognizes that what he learns largely comes from what is in his immediate environment, what he experiences firsthand. This idea Langston Hughes captures precisely, by using the weather and growing things as the symbols of the snail's environment in the first stanza. In the second stanza, he repeats that learning comes through seeing the observable but he adds a second dimension to knowing—the intuitive, that which is felt ("the dewdrop's mystery") but not known logically or factually. While this is a somewhat subtle poem, one way to help children comprehend its fuller meaning might be to have the children choose other creatures, such as a bee, a grasshopper, a fly, a frog. Then ask: What would this creature know? What, to it, would be the great mystery?

In quite different mood is **"African Dance."**

> The low beating of the tom-toms,
> The slow beating of the tom-toms,
> Low . . . . slow
> Slow . . . . . . low—
> Stirs your blood,
>   Dance!
> A night-veiled girl
>   Whirls softly into a
>   Circle of light.
> Whirls softly . . . . slowly,
> Like a wisp of smoke around the fire—
>   And the tom-toms beat,
>   And the tom-toms beat,
> And the low beating of the tom-toms
>   Stirs your blood.

In the first stanza, the effect of the tom-tom's hypnotic drumming sound is caught. The second stanza describes the response, through dancing, to the rhythm of the tom-toms—not, to be sure, a mechanical dance, but one that syncopates the preciseness of the drumming. The grace and appeal of the girl as she moves, as she interprets the appealing beat in her own dance patterns, is carried in several ways: in the poet's pointed descriptions ("night-veiled girl," "Circle of light," "Like a wisp of smoke"); and the varied tonal qualities of the words used in the changing intensity of the lines; and the quickly shifting metrical arrangements. This stanza ends with the reminder that basic to the girl's artistic accomplishment are the tom-tom's tones. And, in the last stanza, the poet notes that (while the visualization of the dancing has been pure delight) the haunting sound of the African drums is what prevails, holds, enthralls, truly excites the listener.

"April Rain Song" is an unrhymed cataloging of the delights of spring rain:

> Let the rain kiss you.
> Let the rain beat upon your head with silver liquid drops.
> Let the rain sing you a lullaby.
>
> The rain makes still pools on the sidewalk.
> The rain makes running pools in the gutter.
> The rain plays a little sleep-song on our roof at night—
>
> And I love the rain.

In the first stanza, note the behaviors associated with genuine affection used by the poet to suggest the gentleness of the rain. The word "beat" in the second line does not suggest violence; the beat of "silver liquid drops" could only be pleasantly positive. From what the rain does to the person, the poet moves on to catch in the next three lines some precise, clear observations of the rain—its movement, its effects, its sound. And the reader is amply prepared for the poet's personal observation in the closing line. How else could one feel about this natural phenomenon, as Hughes has so delightfully described it?

Other poems by Langston Hughes that children can comprehend and interpret well are:

"In Time of Silver Rain," in which the wonder of life, in the newness of springtime, is given praise.

"Mexican Market Woman," a brief poetic portrait of a poor old woman ''selling her scanty wares.''

"Proposition," Langston Hughes's translation of a Cuban poem about the moon, a sensitive word picture.

Langston Hughes's poems offer children pointed imagery, delightful verbal designs, and appealing sound patterns. More than this, he helps readers, young and old, sense the vibrancy and immediacy of the world as it affects humankind, as it aesthetically touches the human spirit. (pp. 28, 116-17)

> *Leland Jacobs, ''Langston Hughes,'' in* Instructor, *Vol. LXXIII, No. 7, March, 1964, pp. 28, 116-17.*

JAMES A. EMANUEL

Hughes's work of the 1950's revealed a widening interest in Negro history. He had written historical articles before.... But in this decade he published seven books historical or predominantly historical in treatment, augmented by two collaborative works—*The Sweet Flypaper of Life* and *A Pictorial History of the Negro in America*—and by his Folkways phonodisc ''The Glory of Negro History.''.... [*A Pictorial History of the Negro in America*] earned distinct approval in the press. Its approximately one thousand high-quality illustrations presented the first authoritative panorama of the Negroes' total participation in American life, from the bringing of the first slaves to Virginia in 1619 to the Montgomery bus boycott. The careful research and concise writing of Hughes and Milton Meltzer made this volume a useful reference. It was a timely survey for people unprepared for the Supreme Court decision of May 17, 1954.

Three of the seven historical and biographical books represent most of Hughes's contribution to the First Book Series of Franklin Watts, Incorporated, whose so-called ''horizon-pushers'' for young people quickly drew praise from child guidance experts, teachers, and librarians. All three received good reviews. His *First Book of Negroes* anticipated the larger task accomplished by his pictorial history. Using attractive illustrations and the travels of a New York boy to unfold a rather patriotic narrative of famous Negroes and pertinent events, it optimistically answers many questions normal to children in multiracial, color-conscious America. *The First Book of Jazz,* undertaking a harder job, clearly defines technical terms; gives musical-form samples of such specialities as breaks, riffs, and twelve-bar blues; and discusses subjects like ''Ten Basic Elements of Jazz.'' Employing the life of Louis Armstrong as a frame for the evolution of work songs, spirituals, field hollers, minstrel songs, blues, and ragtime (but treating elsewhere other famous jazz musicians), the book encourages a constructive attitude toward jazz. Folkways cut a long-play record, narrated by Hughes, of twenty-seven musical selections to accompany the reading of the book.

The First Book of the West Indies, which has a few minor geographical errors, charmingly compares and contrasts the Antilles: their similar birds and trees, and their differing remnants of Spanish, English, and African customs. Hughes records Caribbean rhythms, gives much economic, cultural, and historical information, and ends his book with a list of eminent people of West Indian birth, including Alexandre Dumas, Toussaint L'Ouverture, and Alexander Hamilton.

The other four books of this decade are more strictly historical except for a collaborative volume on folklore. *Famous American Negroes* sketches seventeen lives from a dozen or more vocational and professional areas. Hughes acquaints his young readers with persons new to most of them: Dr. Daniel Hale Williams, first surgeon to perform a successful open-heart operation; Ira Aldridge, one of the greatest Shakespearean actors of the nineteenth century; and insurance magnate Charles C. Spaulding, builder of the largest all-Negro business firm in the world.

Famous Negro Music Makers, ranging from banjoes, bones, and popular music to operas and symphonies, destroys some misconceptions about ''Negro music.'' Young readers learn that James A. Bland, the world's greatest minstrel singer, wrote *Carry Me Back to Old Virginny* and *In the Evening by the Moonlight;* that Dean Dixon organized an interracial chamber orchestra and conducted the New York Philharmonic; and that Mahalia Jackson and Bessie Smith both were titled ''queens'' over rather different realms. (pp. 44-5)

Hughes's *Famous Negro Heroes of America,* a 202-page continuation of an extensive subject, tells the memorable and often dangerous roads to fame taken by sixteen Negroes. Readers already initiated can hurry through the pages on Crispus Attucks, who was the first American to die for the nation's liberty, Frederick Douglass, and Harriet Tubman. But they can learn about Gabriel Prosser, the martyred Virginia slave insurrectionist; Robert Smalls, the bold young slave who stole a Confederate ship past Fort Sumter guns into the control of the blockading Union fleet; and Matthew Henson, who planted the American flag at the North Pole forty-five minutes before Admiral Peary arrived. (p. 46)

Not only did Hughes do some of his best translation in the 1950's, but he also explained, edited, and otherwise commented on poetry.... He added to his juveniles one that must have given him pleasure to write: *The First Book of Rhythms.* This deceptively profound little book no doubt had its origins in his talks to youngsters in the Laboratory School at the University of Chicago, and in similar sessions in the children's rooms of various libraries. [The] book explains the growth of human rhythm from man's primitive realization of his heartbeat, through his drumming, chanting, clapping, and stamping in work and play, to his adaptations of rhythmic principles in the instruments, buildings, and machines of an electronic age. (p. 48)

> *James A. Emanuel, in his* Langston Hughes, *Twayne Publishers, 1967, 192 p.*

MILTON MELTZER

[*A noted author of informational books for middle grade, junior high, and high school students, Meltzer collaborated with Hughes on* A Pictorial History of the Negro in America *(1956) and on* Black Magic: A Pictorial History of the Negro in American Entertainment *(1967). The following excerpt is from* Langston Hughes: A Biography, *which was a National Book Award finalist in 1969.*]

Good writing, Langston Hughes believed, comes out of your own life. You start at home, with what you know best—your own family, your neighborhood, your city. One of the first things he remembered from childhood was a voice on Independence Avenue in Kansas City. It was singing the blues.

He tried early to capture on paper the sound of the blues. It was a hard thing to do, working with words alone. But he learned how. . . . (p. ix)

To start with what he was: an American, and black. Except for the Indians, every American is a hyphenate, beginning with the Anglo-Americans who landed at Jamestown and Plymouth Rock. But for the Afro-American, who came here just as early, life in the land where "white is right" has always been different.

It is that difference which Langston Hughes' poetry illuminates. He voiced the condition of the black American. He listened closely, and heard; he saw, and understood; he touched, and felt; he knew, and remembered. Within a few years of his first book, he was the poet laureate of his people. Their life was his life, and he wrote about it as it was. He was a poet first, but he used every form—the short story, novel, play, song, musical comedy, opera, history, humor, autobiography. At the end, the shelf of his published work ran over forty volumes and with it should be included his many recordings, radio and television scripts, and hundreds of columns and articles for newspapers and magazines. It was a staggering production for a man who never seemed to be in a hurry. (pp. ix-x)

[Langston] was simply himself, the kind of man who must have been there always for all of us who need someone like him. He would last, if anything in life would. It was a quiet durability he had, like some element deep in the earth that powerful pressures had not fractured or scarred, but had made into a glowing diamond. (p. xiii)

The conventional poet's beauty and lyricism were not for him. . . .

For him, as for most other black poets, the basic subject was freedom. No matter what forms Negro poetry has taken, the words are about freedom. Race, color, and the emotions related to them in a land that treats its black citizens like pariahs—how many Negro writers have been able to forget about them? (p. 253)

To Langston's early poems can be traced the word that has lately come to mean so much to black Americans. "Soul." Look back at the refrain of "The Negro Speaks of Rivers"—

> My soul has grown deep like the rivers.

It was the first time, Arna Bontemps has pointed out, that the word was used with the meaning it has for young Negroes today. (p. 254)

Langston Hughes' poetry has long been neglected by the dominant school of American literary criticism. Not all of his poetry, of course, deserves equal attention. Even at its best it was distant from the formal traditions the academic critics respect, and they chose to overlook it. Its seeming simplicity deceived them. They thought of him—when they noticed him at all—as only "an inspired reporter of the surface of things." (p. 255)

But Langston Hughes went on being a writer, a black writer, he would say, not "just a writer," and never afraid to use the material and the language of his people. He knew that the local and the regional can—and do—become universal. As with Burns or O'Casey. To young Negro writers he said, "Do not be afraid of yourselves. *You* are the world." (p. 257)

"I document the feelings of our time in relation to myself and my own people, and, of course, the problems of our democracy," he told an interviewer in 1963.

"Feeling"—that is the heart of it. His work, no matter what form it took, rang with true feeling. The man was his work, the work, the man. (pp. 259-60)

Other Negro writers, such as Richard Wright, have paid tribute to Langston Hughes for opening the way to realism and honesty in Negro literature. He portrayed Negro life and interpreted it for countless people at home and abroad. Around the world he was heard as the voice of the American Negro, a designation that probably embarrassed him, for he knew that every writer speaks first for himself and himself alone. If he is aware and has the talent, he explores a range of values that reveal the humanity he shares with others.

It was his poems that first made him known, and it is still his poems that are the root of his reputation. But he ventured into many other forms of writing. (pp. 260-61)

He made many contributions to the popularizing of Negro history, with books designed for adults and for young people. Standard volumes in their fields are *A Pictorial History of the Negro in America* and *Black Magic: A Pictorial History of the Negro in American Entertainment* (both done in collaboration with Milton Meltzer). (p. 261)

In 1952 he began writing for young readers, and in the next eight years produced many books on Negro heroes, on Negro

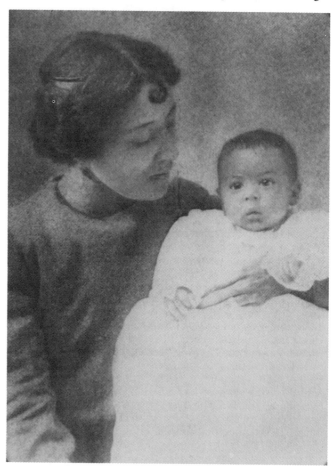

Hughes with his mother Carrie in 1902.

musicians, on jazz, on rhythms, on the West Indies, on Africa. He was surprised to discover how successful these were. When the first title went rapidly into a second printing he voiced his delight to an editor at Knopf. Perhaps I should have turned to this long ago, he wrote. (pp. 261-62)

> *Milton Meltzer, in his* Langston Hughes: A Biography, *Thomas Y. Crowell Company, 1968, 281 p.*

RICHARD K. BARKSDALE

In general, Hughes's publications during the final fifteen years of his life (1952-67) reflected two major emphases. First, in several books—*Famous Negro Music-Makers, First Book of Jazz, Famous Negro Heroes of America*—he wrote with spirit and fervor about black Americans, giving to a world of many colors and races a full view of America's largest and most troubled minority, even as Martin Luther King's program of nonviolent social change was beginning to affect and change basic patterns of racial relations in America. A second emphasis was on books stressing the growing cultural unity of black societies in Africa, the Caribbean, and Latin America. Examples of this emphasis are *The First Book of the West Indies, First Book of Africa*, and such anthologies as *An African Treasury* and *Poems from Black Africa, Ethiopia, and Other Countries*. (p. 103)

> *Richard K. Barksdale, in his* Langston Hughes: The Poet and His Critics, *American Library Association, 1977, 155 p.*

CHARLOTTE S. HUCK

Beginning in the 1920s Langston Hughes was the first to write poems of black protest and pride. It was his voice that asked: **"What Happens to a Dream Deferred?"**, and reminded the world that: **"I, too, sing America."** Some of his poems are bitter, proud, and militant; others are as soft and sensitive as his lovely tribute **"My People."** The voices of Gwendolyn Brooks, Le Roi Jones, Mari Evans, Nikki Giovanni, and others have joined with Hughes to produce a fine body of black poetry. (p. 341)

The harsh realities and futility of war have been the subject of many poems of protest. (p. 342)

Lee Bennett Hopkins has compiled an anthology of the poems of Langston Hughes that speak directly to young people of today. The title of this book, *Don't You Turn Back*, is from a line of Hughes' most poignant poem, **"Mother to Son"**:

> So, boy, don't you turn back.
> Don't you set down on the steps
> 'Cause you find it kinder hard.
> Don't you fall now—
> For I'se still goin', honey,
> I'se still climbin'
> And life for me ain't been no crystal stair.
>   Langston Hughes

This collection contains such well-known poems as **"The Negro Speaks of Rivers," "April Rain Song," "Dreams,"** and **"I, Too, Sing America."** Some of Ann Grifalconi's finest woodcuts illustrate this outstanding book. (p. 347)

> *Charlotte S. Huck, "Poetry: Selecting Poetry for Children," in her* Children's Literature in the Elementary School, *third edition, updated, Holt, Rinehart and Winston, 1979, pp. 324-52.*

ZENA SUTHERLAND AND MAY HILL ARBUTHNOT

Although many of his poems speak for and about black people, Hughes also wrote poetry that speaks for all humankind.... [There] is an ironic humor in much of Hughes' writing, both poetry and prose. Although he wrote several books for children (on jazz, on Africa, on black heroes), his poetry was not created for them. They have, however, overruled him and claimed his poetry for their own. Children enjoy its candor, its humor, and the melodic style that is often reminiscent of ballads and the blues. (p. 312)

> *Zena Sutherland and May Hill Arbuthnot, "Poetry: The Range of Poets for Children," in their* Children and Books, *seventh edition, Scott, Foresman and Company, 1986, pp. 297-320.*

DONNA E. NORTON

Although Hughes is not considered primarily a children's poet, his poetry explores human feelings, asks difficult questions, and expresses hopes and desires that are meaningful to readers of any age. Some of his poems—such as **"Merry-Go-Round"**—can be used to help children understand and identify with the feelings and experiences of black people in earlier eras of American history. In another poem, Hughes provides vivid descriptions of what life would be like without dreams:

> *Dreams*
>
> Hold fast to dreams
> For if dreams die
> Life is a broken-winged bird
> That cannot fly.
> Hold fast to dreams
> For when dreams go
> Life is a barren field
> Frozen with snow.
>
>   Langston Hughes
>   *The Dream Keeper*, 1932, 1960.

The photograph that accompanies **"Dreams"** in the anthology *Reflections on a Gift of Watermelon Pickle . . . and Other Modern Verse*, edited by Dunning, Lueders, and Smith, shows a solitary dried weed surrounded by a barren field covered with ice crystals. When this poem was shared with a group of fifth graders, one of the students reminded the class that dreams did not need to die, but, like the weed, could be reborn in the spring. (pp. 349-50)

> *Donna E. Norton, "Poetry," in her* Through the Eyes of a Child: An Introduction to Children's Literature, *second edition, Merrill Publishing Company, 1987, pp. 326-75.*

THE DREAM KEEPER AND OTHER POEMS (1932)

> [*Effie L. Power, Director of Work with Children at the Cleveland Public Library, was one of the first to encourage Hughes in his writing of poetry.*]

Love of beauty, zest for adventure, a sense of humor, pride in his own race, and faith in humanity in general are some of the characteristics which make Langston Hughes a poet whom young people enjoy. (p. vii)

Today we hail him as a poet of the present generation who interprets first of all life itself and following that, the everyday happenings, the idealism, the high aspiration of the new American Negro.

This selection of poems has been made by the author expressly for young people. The collection includes short lyrics of great beauty, stanzas in serious vein, rollicking songs, and several typical Negro blues. *Negro Dancers, Po' Boy Blues, The Dream Keeper, Aunt Sue's Stories, Sun Song, Youth, I Too, Sing America,* have already become favorites among the older boys and girls who read for pleasure in the Cleveland Public Library and together we bid this gay new volume a friendly welcome. (pp. vii-viii)

> *Effie L. Power, in an introduction to* The Dream Keeper and Other Poems *by Langston Hughes, Alfred A. Knopf, 1932, pp. vii-viii.*

In this volume the poet has made for young people a selection from the verse included in *The Weary Blues* and *Fine Clothes to the Jew,* and has added some new poems. . . . It is not hard to understand the appeal of Langston Hughes to young people sensitive to poetry. Boys and girls will respond to the personal mood of such lovely lyrics as "**The Dream Keeper,**" "**Quiet Girl**" and "**I Love My Friend,**" and will feel the lilt and cadence of the poems in the group called "**Sea Charm,**" and of the poems written in the manner of the Negro folksongs known as the "**Blues.**" The group of poems called "**Walkers With the Dawn**" gives to the reader an imaginative understanding of the poet's feeling toward his own people. Helen Sewell's illustrations have beauty and an unaffected simplicity that suggest the poetic realism of the poems. A book that will be a welcome addition to the shelves of school and public libraries and to the personal libraries of older boys and girls.

> *Anne T. Eaton, in a review of "The Dream Keeper and Other Poems," in* The New York Times Book Review, *July 17, 1932, p. 13.*

It is not till the third section of the book, "Dressed Up" (with a note on the Blues), that one encounters the best work of [Langston Hughes], though several wistful fragments may delay us on the way. The last sentence of the poet's "Note" is a pregnant one: "The mood of the Blues is almost always despondency, but when they are sung people laugh." In this section Hughes's well-known "**The Weary Blues**" is included, one of his best things. "**Song,**" "**When Sue Wears Red,**" and "**Song for a Banjo Dance,**" are meritorious. In the next section, "**Feet o' Jesus**" and "**Judgment Day**" contain the essence of the spirituals. Following this section, "**Walkers with the Dawn**" contains the tribute to Booker Washington, "**Alabama Earth**"; the fine, simple "**My People**"; "**Dream Variations**"; the praised "**The Negro Speaks of Rivers**"; and "**I, Too,**" and "**Youth,**" which are of Hughes's best. Langston Hughes is not a first-rate poet, even among those of his own race, but he is distinctly an appealing one, a melodist who touches with sensitiveness the stops of his black flute.

> *William Rose Benét, "Chiefly on Langston Hughes," in* The Saturday Review of Literature, *Vol. IX, No. 17, November 12, 1932, p. 241.*

[Rhythm], sound, and figurative language contribute to compactness, and compactness to emotional intensity. Langston Hughes's poem "**Dream Deferred**" has emotional intensity, intensity created particularly by his skillful use of unusual figurative comparisons and sensory appeals:

> What happens to a dream deferred?
> Does it dry up
>   like a raisin in the sun?

Or fester like a sore—
And then run?
Does it stink like rotten meat?
Or crust and sugar over—
like a syrupy sweet?

Maybe it just sags
like a heavy load.

Or does it explode?

From the poem we have an intense emotional experience of frustration. A festering sore, stinking meat—these are ugly images that cause us to experience the emotions that accompany frustration. The images connote neglect, usefulness turned to decay. What was a simple sore is now painfully infected; what was edible meat is now stinking uselessness. (p. 200)

> *Rebecca J. Lukens, in a review of "The Dream Keeper and Other Poems," in her* A Critical Handbook of Children's Literature, *second edition, Scott, Foresman and Company, 1982, p. 200.*

POPO AND FIFINA, CHILDREN OF HAITI   (with Arna Bontemps, 1932)

Here is a travel book that is a model of its kind. Facts, indeed, the reader acquires, but unconsciously, for what he feels is the atmosphere of the island of Haiti, dusty little roads that wind along the hills, sun-drenched silences only broken by the droning of insects and the cry of tropical birds, silver sails on clear green water, sheets of warm white rain.

Little black Popo and Fifina and their father and mother are slightly drawn, since the book is small in size; but the family creates in the reader's mind the feeling of reality. One follows their adventures, the simple everyday happenings, with interest. The book has some of the simple homelike atmosphere that has made *The Dutch Twins* such a favorite. Older readers will recognize that the beauty of the style has much to do in holding the reader's attention, and younger readers will unconsciously be held by the same quality. *Popo and Fifina* tempts us to wish that all our travel books for children might be written by poets. (pp. 13, 16)

> *Anne T. Eaton, in a review of "Popo and Fifina: Children of Haiti," in* The New York Times Book Review, *October 23, 1932, pp. 13, 16.*

Popo and Fifina, Papa Jean, Mamma Anna, and the baby, who lived in Haiti, traveled from the hills to live on the seacoast so that Papa Jean might be a fisherman. What they saw and what they did will interest children of fourth and fifth grades. The story is told with sincerity and appreciation of the simple, colorful life of the native black people of Haiti.

> *A review of "Popo and Fifina, Children of Haiti," in* The Booklist, *Vol. 29, No. 4, December, 1932, p. 118.*

THE FIRST BOOK OF NEGROES   (1952)

A poet, dramatist, short story writer makes signal contribution to a series designed to provide introductory material on a wide range of subjects. Here he tells the story of his people in lyric prose, with warm understanding and mellow judgment. Through the tenuous thread of story linking the scattered segments together, he shows Terry of Harlem, whose father is connected with U.N., learning the story of his race. The roots of Negro history and racial traits in other lands; the steps by which they were thrust into slavery and won their present position here; the contributions made by outstanding Negroes in all fields, education, history, politics, religion, music, literature, science and athletics; he even lets Terry learn the blight of discrimination which still mars the story. Through specific Negro figures, from the Queen of Sheba, the explorer Estevanico, the patriot, Jean Christophe—he goes on to as varied a roster as Harriet Tubman, Booker T. Washington, Louis Armstrong, Jackie Robinson, Marian Anderson, Ralph Bunche. A superb job of concentration, which should find a vital place with children everywhere.

> *A review of "The First Book of Negroes," in* Virginia Kirkus' Bookshop Service, *Vol. XX, No. 19, October 1, 1952, p. 659.*

The story of the Negro is always a rich field for the story teller. A writer would have to be extremely mediocre not to achieve some success in holding the attention of his readers with the colorful pageant of Negro life teeming with pathos, struggle, adventure, aspiration and achievements. Even a novice could demand some attention with the interesting glimpses of the part the Negro has played and is playing in helping to enrich the American scene. But what Langston Hughes has done in the *First Book of Negroes* is a stroke of rare genius.

In this interesting and beautifully written story, a combination of the story teller's art, the poet's insight and the researcher's accuracy, one sees the Negro on the vast stage of America, revealing himself not only as an important actor, but in many instances playing a stellar role in the ever unfolding drama of American History. (p. 94)

> *Gertrude Parthenia McBrown, in a review of "The First Book of Negroes," in* The Negro History Bulletin, *Vol. 16, No. 4, January, 1953, pp. 94-5.*

[*The First Book of Negroes*] begins with the exciting and readable story of the Negro explorer, Estevan, who came to this country with the Spaniards in search of the Seven Cities of Cibola and who discovered a part of what is now Arizona and New Mexico.

Following the story of Estevan a chapter, "Songs of Freedom: the Spirituals," discusses the bringing of the Negro slaves to this country and presents a few facts about how the slaves fared here and their final emancipation; however, only a brief half-page is devoted to the spirituals themselves. Not until the third chapter does the author introduce Terry Lane, the little Negro boy in New York City, who supposedly hearing these stories from his parents and grandmother, furnishes the frame upon which the stories are hung. From this point on, the arrangement of the book is haphazard, jumping from humorous folk tales (which seem more appropriate to the great-grandmother than to a grandmother of today) to the Bible stories of brown kings and queens in ancient lands, back to Negroes in the Caribbean, then to conditions in the South, and finally to the achievements of individual Negroes.

Terry's trip to the South, which serves to introduce him (and the reader) to the present day segregation and discrimination patterns of the region, may bring some objection from parents who have convictions about the proper time to develop in young children an awareness of this problem. (pp. 343-44)

A lack of organization is one of the more serious weaknesses of this little book. It would have been less confusing to younger readers had the author arranged the stories and pictures so that

historical periods and personalities, contemporary individuals and events, and folklore and legendary materials would have fallen into more appropriate groupings. Despite this fault, many of the stories are told in an inspiring and dramatic manner, particularly those dealing with Estevan, Toussaint, Christophe and Harriet Tubman. (p. 344)

> *Hallie Beachem Brooks, in a review of "The First Book of Negroes," in* PHYLON: The Atlanta University Review of Race and Culture, *Vol. XIV, No. 3, third quarter (September, 1953), pp. 343-44.*

FAMOUS AMERICAN NEGROES (1954)

There is always a need for this kind of collected biography in connection with school assignments and as stimulation to further reading of full-length biography. In this volume, perhaps some of the more familiar personalities, such as Booker T. Washington, could have been left out and equally illustrious but less well-known figures included. However, since some similar books are out of print, this is recommended for all children's and young people's collections.

> *Ann Nelson, in a review of "Famous American Negroes," in* Library Journal, *Vol. 79, No. 5, March 1, 1954, p. 461.*

"American democracy has produced the largest group of outstanding Negroes in the world," says Langston Hughes who is himself an outstanding American Negro writer. "They have worked in almost all fields of human endeavor from the sciences to politics, the arts to sports, religion to business." The seventeen men and women whose achievements he briefly records here include representatives from all these fields, from the Colonial poet, Phillis Wheatley, to Jackie Robinson.

Here, inevitably and properly, are Frederick Douglass, Booker T. Washington, George Washington Carver, Ralph Bunche and Marian Anderson. There are also figures less familiar to the average reader, such as Ira Aldrich, the actor who charmed nineteenth century Europe; Charles C. Spaulding, business and civic leader; Robert S. Abbott, newspaper publisher and editor. The sketches of these lesser-known men make this collection a particularly interesting addition to the biography shelf.

> *Ellen Lewis Buell, "Seventeen Leaders," in* The New York Times Book Review, *May 2, 1954, p. 26.*

A collection of short biographies of famous Negroes is coming to require considerably more careful selection of names than used to be the case. A few years ago, it was likely that any such work would include Frederick Douglass, Booker T. Washington, George Washington Carver, Sojourner Truth, Harriet Tubman, Mary McLeod Bethune, Walter White, and W.E.B. DuBois. Half of these names are omitted from the present volume, but how many more have been added! Richard Allen, Daniel Hale Williams, and Charles C. Spaulding are likely to be new to many readers who are as ignorant of Negro history as is the average American; and the inclusion of such varied living persons as W. C. Handy, A. Philip Randolph, Ralph J. Bunche, Marian Anderson, and Jackie Robinson emphasizes that not all greatness is in the past.

It is, of course, inevitable that many of the same people will be included in this work that have been written about many times before. However, the seventeen chosen—some limits had to be drawn, obviously—are taken from such wide areas as religion, poetry, medicine, art, the theater, music, statesmanship, sports, journalism, academic life, and science. The young people for whom this book is intended, many of whom will be reading about Negroes for the first time, cannot fail to be impressed by the way in which they all overcame economic and social obstacles to achieve greatness.

A good many grownups will profit by using *Famous American Negroes* to refresh their minds and add some fascinating details to their earlier knowledge. Langston Hughes has written a very readable, human group of biographies which make warm flesh-and-blood people out of what might easily have remained shadowy figures in history books.

> *Mabel M. Smythe, in a review of "Famous American Negroes," in* The Crisis, *Vol. 62, No. 1, January, 1955, p. 58.*

THE FIRST BOOK OF RHYTHMS (1954)

[Personal] and unusual is Mr. Hughes' book, which might well be read aloud with any first poetry book, but also belongs to older boys and girls up to fourteen. He begins "Let's make a rhythm" with a pencil on paper, goes on to the rhythms of music, painting, sculpture, of nature, of building, of folksongs, poetry, dancing, athletics, machines. All his ideas are briefly put and introductory. We rather longed for that old musicians' trick of being able to count different rhythms with hands, feet, head, and for an explanation of syncopated time. The charming finale is called "This Wonderful World," its place, our place, in the rhythm of the universe.

A true poet here talks to children with dignity, and with zest that will stimulate them to think about the world in a creative way. . . . It is interesting to hear that the book resulted from a talk given often to children of various ages by this famous writer.

> *A review of "The First Book of Rhythms," in* New York Herald Tribune Book Review, *May 16, 1954, p. 17.*

For the blasé, the bored, the tired, the restless and most certainly the uninformed (parents as well as children), Langston Hughes has fashioned a rewarding look into our everyday world. Few will leave *The First Book of Rhythms* without a sharper eye and a keener sense of sound and smell.

Mr. Hughes, poet, playwright and author of juvenile books, starts the exploration with a simple, wavy line, but before he has had his full lyrical say, the reader has been painlessly exposed to a world crowded with exciting rhythms: falling rain, an Egyptian pyramid, sea shells, verse, Stan Musial batting a ball and a scientist charting the force of the atom. Mr. Hughes deftly ties it all together into one big, beautiful package. It's an adventure for children that may require some parental assistance; it's certainly ideal for classroom use.

> *Pat Clark, "Everyday Wonders," in* The New York Times Book Review, *August 15, 1954, p. 20.*

An unusual book, beautifully written, to introduce to children the rhythms that are around them, showing how rhythms are to be found in every aspect of life, in all movement, in sounds, and even in the feel and smell of things. The way in which all things are tied to all other things through rhythms is simply but clearly expressed. The book will be excellent to introduce young readers to an awareness of the harmonies of life around them, and also to stimulate them to try to create more rhythms

Arna Bontemps and Hughes. Yale Collection of American Literature, Beinecke Rare Book and Manuscript Library, Yale University.

of their own in drawings, music, poetry, and other aspects of living. Teachers at the elementary level will find the book helpful for their own use to give them ideas of ways in which the idea of rhythms can be presented to young children. Readers at the upper elementary and junior high school level will be able to use the book by themselves.

> *A review of "The First Book of Rhythms," in* Bulletin of the Children's Book Center, *Vol. VIII, No. 4, December, 1954, p. 32.*

THE FIRST BOOK OF JAZZ (1955)

Hughes' appraisal and short history of jazz is a poet's and an appreciator's and thus makes a warm, relishing account of the music we can really call our own. To set the scene, there's an opening description of the New Orleans of Louis Armstrong's youth—the day of the spasm bands and their playing that marked the basic quality of jazz—playing for fun. Tracing the influences then, fascinating material emerges in the comments on early West African rhythms and the first Negro-White contacts; the characteristics of improvisation and movement rather than pre-composing and listening; the first southern brass and the sidewheeler bands; Negro songs—spiritual, minstrel and blues, and in 1800 the first "ragtime" bands that got their name from literally "tearing a tune to tatters". Completing his cycle, Hughes picks up Armstrong's story again and in portraying his life as the life of modern jazz, explains many of its parts—syncopation, counter melodies, the different beats and so forth. A good grasp of the subject for any age.

> *A review of "The First Book of Jazz," in* Virginia Kirkus' Bookshop Service, *Vol. XXII, No. 20, October 15, 1954, p. 711.*

Jazz, Langston Hughes says firmly, is fun. Unlike many of its devotees, he doesn't regard it as a peculiarly esoteric art; instead he writes with a refreshing lack of pomposity and with a clarity which will delight those who might be, reasonably enough, confused at the differences between cool and hot, swing and bebop. His analysis of the components and various styles of jazz is adroitly threaded into a colorful historical outline. He shows how certain elements from the spirituals, the blues and the weary field hollers of the slaves were mingled with merrier elements of the jubilees, street songs, minstrel songs and eventually evolved into distinctively American art. Homage is paid to the influences and achievements of the great figures of jazz—especially to Louis Armstrong, whose career, says Mr. Hughes, "is almost the whole story of orchestral jazz in America." There are two lists of records—one illustrating the historical stages of jazz and one containing 100 of the author's own favorites.

> *Ellen Lewis Buell, "Take a Blue Note . . . ," in* The New York Times Book Review, *January 30, 1955, p. 24.*

For many a substantial American home the term "jazz" has long maintained its existence outside the pale of respectability mainly because its experiences have been not so much with jazz *per se* as with a corruption of it. Traditionally, the term has carried a connotation that is sometimes unhealthful, sometimes hectic, and sometimes coarse to the n'th degree. *The First Book of Jazz* proceeds to expose this so-called negative influence as simply a normal social phenomenon that was begun and nurtured in our own back yards. The treatise is based on the sound assumption that the factual approach to a social phenomenon may disclose many an imaginary skeleton in the closet, and likewise that relaxed human beings engaging in an activity merely for the fun of it are not necessarily bad ones as some have been wont to think.

Brief in compass, running to exactly sixty-five pages and refreshingly lucid in style, *The First Book of Jazz* invites favorable comparison with Paul Whiteman's *Jazz* (1926), Iain Lang's *Jazz in Perspective* (1952), and Rex Harris' *Jazz* (1952); and like two of these volumes embraces the entire sweep of jazz in America from the appearance of Louis Armstrong's improvised jazz orchestra on the street corners of his New Orleans hometown to the "hot jazz" one finds at the Birdland, one of New York City's swankiest night clubs. And even though in quite a remote way jazz is reputed to be an outgrowth "of the beating of African drums," it has developed as an American creation. . . . (p. 318)

As to the evolution of jazz in America, Mr. Hughes points out that

> the roll of the African drums, the dancing guadrilles of old New Orleans, the marching tunes of that city's brass bands, the work songs of the levees, the field hollers of the cotton plantations, the spirituals, the jubilees, the blues, the off-beats of ragtime, each in a sense complementing or elaborating the other, have all gone into the making of jazz as we know it today in America and around the world.

In this brilliantly-written exposé, our poet-historian presents a clear account of how all this came about, points up its impact upon the totality of American music, and lists a sort of Who's Who among jazzmen (Louis "Satchmo" Armstrong being among the foremost of the crop) to whom the rise and the development of American jazz are eternally indebted. And among Hughes' one hundred favorite recordings of jazz, blues, folk songs, and jazz-influenced performers, one discovers such popular titles as "The St. Louis Blues," "Pine Top's Boogie," "Round

about Midnight," and "Tea for Two." "Jazz," Mr. Hughes insists, "is a *way of playing* music more than it is composed music. Almost any music can become jazz if it is played with jazz treatment." It began and has usually persisted without the benefit of written music; the tunes are remembered or made up as the players proceed and the whole thing is or was originally done "just for fun."

The First Book of Jazz is timely too. Written against the backwash of a turbulent era, the volume attests not only to Mr. Hughes' expanding interest in the American youth problem, but likewise in many present-day adults already afflicted by the nervous tensions of the atomic age. They move in a culture in which some get on while others sicken and die. Their lives lack calm and direction and rhythm and activity "just for fun" which historically jazz has set about to provide.

Langston Hughes' new volume has the distinction of being the first history of jazz to be written by a Negro author. It is a tribute to his genius as a story teller and as a prose stylist. (pp. 318-19)

> *John W. Parker, in a review of "The First Book of Jazz," in* PHYLON: The Atlanta University Review of Race and Culture, *Vol. XVI, No. 3, third quarter (September, 1955), pp. 318-19.*

[*The First Book of Jazz was revised in 1976.*]

Now in an updated version, *The First Book of Jazz* is once again the foremost children's book on the subject. The text flows easily and is devoid of the nostalgic sentimentality that mars Studs Terkel's comparable *Giants of Jazz.* Hughes considers jazz to be a developing art form rather than a specific musical style, and he emphatically demonstrates that "the whole history of jazz is alive and playing well." The essential chapter in the update, "New Forms of Jazz," provides an excellent overview of jazz's development since the early 50's, making this a worthy replacement for the 1955 edition. (pp. 107-08)

> *Diane Haas, in a review of "Jazz," in* School Library Journal, *Vol. 23, No. 2, October, 1976, pp. 107-08.*

FAMOUS NEGRO MUSIC MAKERS (1955)

Some of Langston Hughes' liveliness and depth of feeling as a poet come into these twenty or so sketches of Negro musicians who have enriched our culture. Starting with the Fisk Jubilee Singers, seven of whom were born in slavery, Hughes tells how all suffered post-Civil War hardships while they furthered a significant branch of Negro music. Continuing with a wealth of other names—James A. Bland the minstrel composer, Leadbelly who caught the essence of folk music, Roland Hayes and Marian Anderson—two concert artists, Duke Ellington and more, the accounts indicate both qualities and meanings of the wide varieties of Negro music. A good market for this lies in the interest in jazz and Negro music.

> *A review of "Famous Negro Music Makers," in* Virginia Kirkus' Service, *Vol. XXIII, No. 14, July 15, 1955, p. 499.*

This is a collection of short biographical sketches of American Negroes . . . who have achieved fame or made a large contribution to music in this country. As such it is informative and interesting and it includes people like James Bland and Mahalia Jackson, who should be better known. It is also, however, as one reads of the difficulties endured by most of these artists, the story of the gradual breaking down of the color line in the United States and a reminder of the fight still to be fought against prejudice. (pp. 76-7)

> *Lillian Morrison, in a review of "Famous Negro Music Makers," in* The Saturday Review, *New York, Vol. XXXVIII, No. 46, November 12, 1955, pp. 76-7.*

THE FIRST BOOK OF THE WEST INDIES (1956; British edition as *The First Book of the Caribbean*)

A look at the Caribbean Islands includes a substantial amount of information on customs, trade, geographical characteristics, history, etc., but lacks the swinging and imaginative quality of Langston's other *First Books* on *Jazz* and *Rhythms*. Two general introductory sections deal with the area's colorful background, the Indians which were there originally, discovery and the periods of piracy which followed. Moving then to the islands and groups of islands, there are notes on Cuba, Puerto Rico, Haiti, the Dominican Republic, the Virgin Islands, and the Antilles. Though extensive enough, these read more like a geography text than the personalized narrative which has often been successful in *First Books* about other countries.

> *A review of "The First Book of the West Indies," in* Virginia Kirkus' Service, *Vol. XXIV, No. 12, June 15, 1956, p. 406.*

A well-written, effectively illustrated book [the pictures are by Robert Bruce] affords an introductory view of the history, geography, products, life, and customs of the islands of the West Indies. Although uneven as to amount and kind of information about each island the book does convey the unique characteristics of each. Appended are listings of plants of the West Indies and of famous men and women of West Indian birth and a statistical table giving capital, population, area, and products of each island. (pp. 125-26)

> *A review of "The First Book of the West Indies," in* The Booklist and Subscription Books Bulletin, *Vol. 53, No. 5, November 1, 1956, pp. 125-26.*

An experienced traveler, Langston Hughes guides young readers through the island chain that "curves out from the Gulf of Mexico in a long tropical arch all the way down to the northern coast of South America." He invests this present-day jaunt with a sense of history—of the great age of discovery, the days of pirates and of early battles for freedom—and at the same time gives exciting reality to contemporary island peoples and scenes.

Facts, statistics, geographical data, pronouncing guides, a brief who's who of famous islanders will send interested readers on to deeper research.

> *Helen Lorraine Hultz, "Island Chain," in* The New York Times Book Review, *December 30, 1956, p. 12.*

A PICTORIAL HISTORY OF THE NEGRO IN AMERICA (with Milton Meltzer, 1956)

History is many things: it is legend and myth, fable and fact, and sometimes—rarely—truth. But mostly it is men, and men come grandly alive in the pages of this illustrated history. They are mostly Negro men; but of course no history of the Negro in America can be told without telling as well nearly the whole story of America. This is a fact too often overlooked by the academic historians, even the good ones, who research and write as if the coming of Negroes to these shores was an incident of no consequence, when in truth it was of the greatest possible consequence to our political development, our institutions and ourselves.

Mr. Hughes and Mr. Meltzer have not made the academicians' mistake. They have kept the true historic proportions, and given a kind of majestic sweep to a story which, when told at all, is usually made niggling and constrained. Some may hold its sweep against it as history, for its very force knocks aside the kind of detail that is the meat of scholars. And after all, what is the swift lightning of an Armisted Revolt compared to the thunderous storm of John Brown? And how can the Congressional debates of 1850-1860 match the rush of men and events roaring toward tragic fulfillment in the Civil War? If the sweep of the story is against it as history, it is certainly for it as drama.

Since relatively few people read and learn from history as written by scholars, the fast-paced narrative style of Hughes' text may be all to the good. The pictures—photographs, prints, cartoons—compound the value. They set forth the whole story from 1619 down to the Supreme Court decision of 1954, and they make clear who the American Negro is and how he has affected and in turn been affected by American life and thought. This is a kind of knowledge that is needed as background upon which to project the news of American race relations that lately fills the national and international press. But apart from telling us a great deal about the past and the present of the American Negro, the authors take a considered look at the future, and what they see should give encouragement to all those, white and Negro, who believe that the ancient idealism of the American creed still lives in the hearts of the American people.

> *Saunders Redding, "The American Negro's Role in History," in* New York Herald Tribune Book Review, *November 18, 1956, p. 7.*

[*A Pictorial History of the Negro in America*] succeeds in giving the best one volume picture of the Negro's niche in America—not in any depth but interestingly and pleasurably. The authors have managed to collect some excellent and apt photographs and drawings to illustrate their subject. This is popular history at its most popular with emphasis on little-known facts. The articles are briefly and lucidly written by the famous Negro poet. Recommended for even the tiniest public library and young adult collection and browsing collections.

> *Milton S. Byam, in a review of "A Pictorial History of the Negro in America," in* Library Journal, *Vol. 81, No. 21, December 1, 1956, p. 2849.*

I think the most dramatic feature in the record of our nation, is the history of the American Negro people. Its exciting quality makes the idea of Langston Hughes and Milton Meltzer—to portray that history visually, with a minimum of text—particularly apt. On the whole, they have realized their vision well and produced an excellent gift-volume of permanent value.

The scope of the book encompasses the Africa of pre-Columbus days to those immediately following the Supreme Court's desegregation decision of 1954. Many of the hundreds of illustrations are exceedingly scarce; all are of great interest and the quality of reproduction throughout is very high.

The general attitude of the volume is sharply anti-racist; its political orientation is New Dealish. As one might expect from a volume of illustrations, the work is descriptive, not analytical, and its overall approach strives for simplicity, and once in a while falls into simplification.

Factual errors are sprinkled through the text—thus, slaves from Georgia and South Carolina did fight as soldiers in the Revolution, the Negroes brought to Virginia in 1619 were not sold as slaves, etc.—but their number is not extraordinary, and generally they are not very serious. The absence of any real concern with cause produces somewhat more serious errors of omission and commission. For example, in discussing the era of the Populist movement, one reads: ''Whites of all parties decided to keep the franchise lily-white and to fight their political battles among themselves,'' ignoring imperialism, ignoring class-divisions among the whites, which made their reactions much more complex than this sentence would suggest, etc.

No doubt the form of the work dictates this kind of superficiality, but its presence must be pointed out, nevertheless. Yet the volume does convey an overall sense of achievement in the face of extraordinary odds, some feeling of the constant struggle by the Negro people, and a general impression of noteworthy contributions in all areas by Negro men and women. In regard to the latter, there is, too, less of an atmosphere that the book is a record of ''distinguished'' Negroes, and more that it is one of a mass accomplishment than is generally true with works of this kind; that, of course, is all to the good.

Two-thirds of the volume is devoted to the period up to and including Reconstruction. This reviewer would have preferred a contrary arrangement, with most of the space devoted to the last seventy or eighty years, but then historical writing as a whole still suffers from this unbalance, and one must not blame Messrs. Hughes and Meltzer for a failing that marks the historical guild as a whole, up to the present.

Related to this disproportion is the volume's underplaying of the Left, and particularly the impact of socialist and communist thinking and organizations upon the history of the Negro people. The fact is that since the founding of the NAACP (in which Socialists played an outstanding part), through the struggles of the New Deal era, and to World War II, the Marxist ingredient was a major feature in American Negro life and thought and organizational activity. To ignore this, as the present book does, is to misrepresent history. Connected with this is a picture of Negro life today that is prettified. For example: ''As citizens of the U.S., Negroes are Americans and their way of life is much the same as that of other Americans.'' At the same time, the impact upon other Americans of the policy of second-class citizenship is obscured.

But we repeat, the work is distinctly anti-racist and its message is directed towards the elimination of Jim Crow. This, plus of course, the frequently fascinating pictures makes the volume enjoyable. (pp. 62-3)

> *Herbert Aptheker, ''Negro Panorama,'' in* Mainstream, *Vol. 10, No. 2, February, 1957, pp. 62-3.*

FAMOUS NEGRO HEROES OF AMERICA (1958)

The author states that '' 'a hero,' says the dictionary, 'is a doer of great or brave deeds; a man of distinguished valor or intrepidity; a prominent or central personage in any remarkable action or event'.'' This surely qualifies such people as Esteban, Crispus Attucks, Harriet Tubman, and Dorrie Miller for inclusion among the 16 Negroes selected as famous heroes and heroines. Style of writing is lively and the biographical material

interesting and inspiring. Companion volume to *Famous American Negroes.* Recommended for ages 12-16.

> *Augusta Baker, in a review of ''Famous Negro Heroes of America,'' in* Junior Libraries, *Vol. 4, No. 9, May, 1958, p. 49.*

Langston Hughes is a distinguished writer, but *Famous Negro Heroes of America* is not a distinguished book, even though it is informative in its brief accounts of sixteen lives. Some of its figures are standard to all collections of American Negro lives, such as Harriet Tubman, Frederick Douglass, and Crispus Attucks. Others are less familiar, such as Esteban, early explorer of Arizona; Du Sable, first settler on the site of Chicago; and Gabriel Prosser, leader of one of the plans for a slave mutiny.

A few of the modern figures included here may not yet rate the canonization of this collection. One of the best chapters is that dealing with Matthew A. Henson, who accompanied Peary to the North Pole. The general weakness of the book is its stock, inspirational tone.

> *Edmund Fuller, ''Sixteen Lives,'' in* The New York Times Book Review, *July 27, 1958, p. 14.*

With the exception of Crispus Attucks, Frederick Douglass and Harriet Tubman, the subjects of these sixteen brief accounts are generally not well known. They all should be, however, for these pioneers, explorers, seamen, journalists, abolitionists, war heroes, and the rest, played important parts in the history and development of the United States, and it is good to have them presented here in these dramatic biographies.

> *Ruth Hill Viguers, in a review of ''Famous Negro Heroes of America,'' in* The Horn Book Magazine, *Vol. XXXIV, No. 4, August, 1958, p. 281.*

THE FIRST BOOK OF AFRICA (1960)

[This] is a comprehensive study, clarifying one of the most complex areas in the world today. The geography of Africa is described, the various racial and cultural strains of which it is comprised are stated, a picture of colonial life and its accompanying problems are dispassionately reviewed. Illustrated with photographs and replete with a chart of statistics pertaining to each country, this is a superb introduction to a troubled and vastly rich frontier land.

> *A review of ''The First Book of Africa,'' in* Virginia Kirkus' Service, *Vol. XXVIII, No. 12, June 15, 1960, p. 455.*

Poet Langston Hughes has long been a student of African affairs and so brings to the subject a knowledge of and a sensitivity for the people and their problems. The material in this book is necessarily brief, but it is well selected and organized and, added to the photographs, makes up an attractive, small volume with a great deal of accurate and pertinent information for elementary school children. Highly recommended.

> *Augusta Baker, in a review of ''The First Book of Africa,'' in* Junior Libraries, *Vol. 7, No. 1, September, 1960, p. 64.*

The First Book of Africa claims such a vast field for its subject that we did not hope for much enlightenment for young readers, but we were quite wrong. It is an excellent introductory book, head and shoulders above the others in the ''first book'' series,

Hughes with a group of students. Schomburg Center for Research in Black Culture, The New York Public Library, Astor, Lenox and Tilden Foundations.

or in those of the "Getting to Know" or "Let's Visit." The author is not content with bland summaries but poses the burning question of today fairly and dispassionately, even offering a brief final chapter on "U.S.A., the UN and Africa" (written before July 1, 1960, of course). About a third of the book is historical, with interesting bits about the medieval Negro kingdoms and the Moslem influence as well as the familiar story of European colonization; another third is about the peoples and their governments and the last third touches on the most difficult problems of Kenya, Belgian Congo, Guinea, Liberia and Ghana.

"Ancient Lands, Africa Now," in New York Herald Tribune Book Review, *November 13, 1960, p. 32.*

BLACK MAGIC: A PICTORIAL HISTORY OF THE NEGRO IN AMERICAN ENTERTAINMENT (with Milton Meltzer, 1967)

This is another rare instance of a published work fulfilling its promise. Not only is the book a tribute to the Negro performing artist, it is an eloquent statement about the human spirit's victory over suppression. . . . That Langston Hughes was coauthor should override any possible criticism of pictorial examples of bigotry in the book. . . . This splendid volume, together

with Loften Mitchell's *Black Drama,* will assure representative coverage in the field.

Edward Mapp, in a review of "Black Magic: A Pictorial History of the Negro in American Entertainment," in Library Journal, *Vol. 93, No. 4, February 15, 1968, p. 770.*

Twelve years ago Langston Hughes and Milton Meltzer published *A Pictorial History of the Negro in America,* a book which deserved many more readers than it probably acquired. *Black Magic,* as its subtitle indicates, surveys only one phase of that history, but it does so comprehensively, simply, and interestingly. The title has nothing to do with the historical meaning of the term *black magic;* it refers generically to the genius which Negroes have evidenced in the arts of music, dramatics, and dancing through the various media of expression, including motion pictures, radio, and television. The thirty chapters and their accompanying, well-chosen illustrations are arranged in approximately chronological order, beginning with an account of "the syncopated beat which the captive Africans brought with them" to the New World and ending with notations of present-day Negro performers at home and abroad. The texts of the several chapters consist of running comments in which many names of persons—famous and near-famous, incidental facts, and some interpretative and critical views are mentioned.

First among the Negro performers in the arts to be acclaimed, as Hughes and Meltzer observed, were the musicians. Especially notable among those of this group who flourished during the middle of the nineteenth century and afterwards were Elizabeth Taylor Greenfield (''the Black Swan''), the Luca Family, and Thomas Green Bethune (''Blind Tom''). . . . [Hughes and Meltzer] also brought back to memory some nineteenth-century songwriters, like James A. Bland, who was already well-known, and some who have never been well-known, like Gussie L. Davis of Cincinnati and Richard Milburn of Philadelphia, the composers respectively of *In the Baggage Coach Ahead* and *Listen to the Mockingbird*.

Most of **Black Magic** is appropriately devoted to the history of Negroes in the theater as actors, writers of musical comedies, and playwrights. Still most famous among the actors is Ira Frederick Aldridge (1807-1867). Since so much misinformation about Aldridge has so long been prevalent, it would have been good if Hughes and Meltzer had written more extensively than they did about him, as they could have done authoritatively on the basis of Herbert Marshall and Mildred Stock's thoroughly researched *Ira Aldridge: The Negro Tragedian*. They did mention this biography, however, in passing.

As Hughes and Meltzer indicated, Negroes made their way on the American stage at the turn of the nineteenth and twentieth centuries in musical comedies of their own creation. This they did principally in New York, which has been the theatrical capital of the United States at least since the beginning of the republic. In many instances the composers of the words and the music of the songs in which the musical comedies abounded were persons who had already achieved or were soon to achieve distinction as poets or musicians. Among the poets were Paul Laurence Dunbar and James Weldon Johnson, and among the musicians were Will Marion Cook and J. Rosamond Johnson. Throughout most of his career as a poet, Hughes himself wrote lyrics for shows. Some of these lyrics were set to music by Negro musicians and some by white musicians. From the beginning the performers in these shows have been Negroes. One of them who later became a show in himself was Bert Williams. Influenced by the tradition of the musical comedies, in which singing and dancing were featured, Negro musicians of one generation after another have been inspired to write the popular songs which Americans have sung from time to time generally without knowing who composed them. Likewise performers in these shows have brought into vogue one dance after another—like the cakewalk, now forgotten, the Charleston, and the Lindy hop—only to replace each in turn with a new one.

As Hughes and Meltzer might have noted for the sake of historical completeness but did not, William Wells Brown pioneered among Negroes in the writing of dramas and published in 1858 his *The Escape; Or, A Leap for Freedom*, an antislavery melodrama in five acts. This is still generally considered the first play published, although certainly not the first one written, by an American Negro. This play seems never to have been professionally produced, nor was any other play by a Negro author thus presented during the next sixty-odd years. Not until the 1910's, as Hughes and Meltzer discovered, were Negro actors cast in important roles in plays produced by white theatrical companies, and not until the 1920's were plays by Negro dramatists presented on Broadway. The reasons for both of these delays were, of course, racial rather than artistic. It should also be remembered that more often than otherwise Negro actors and playwrights arrived on Broadway by way of the Apollo and the Lafayette Theatres in Harlem.

It has indeed been a long way from the plantation buffoonery with which slaves were often compelled to entertain slaveholders even while their own hearts were breaking, to the Uncle Tom shows, to the minstrel shows, to the unfulfilled plan for Sissieretta Jones (''the Black Patti'') to sing roles in *Aïda* and *L'Africaine* in the Metropolitan Opera House in 1892, to the musical comedies, to the birth of jazz and the blues, to celebrated dance troupes, the gospel singing—one of the songs being Thomas A. Dorsey's *Precious Lord, Take My Hand*, to the success of those whom Hughes and Meltzer listed as ''The Golden Dozens'' of actors, musicians of various kinds, dancers, ''jazz personalities,'' and ''very versatile artists who can hardly be classed correctly in a single category.'' It has been almost as long a way from Brown's writing *The Escape* to the Broadway productions of Garland Anderson's *Appearances* in 1925, Hughes's *Mulatto* in 1935, Louis Peterson's *Take a Giant Step* in 1953, Hughes's *Simply Heavenly* in 1957, and Lorraine Hansberry's *A Raisin in the Sun* in 1959. In **Black Magic** Hughes and Meltzer have retraced and illuminated these ways very well. (pp. 367-69)

> *W. Edward Farrison, in a review of ''Black Magic: A Pictorial History of the Negro in American Entertainment,'' in CLA Journal, Vol. XI, No. 4, June, 1968, pp. 367-69.*

Black Magic, Langston Hughes's final book . . . , is a truly impressive account of Negro entertainers in this country. Its 600 illustrations, which complement the text, are equally excellent for their variety and liveliness. Together they cover virtually every Negro performer of consequence from Sam Lucas, a 19th-century minstrel, to Duke Ellington, the modern jazz master. The book, though, is not just a compendium or a volume of praise, but a sensitive and poetic evocation of the creativity and performances of Negroes in all phases of entertainment. It is a fitting testament to Mr. Hughes's devotion to Negro life and letters.

> *Alden Whitman, ''End Papers,'' in The New York Times, June 1, 1968, p. 25.*

BLACK MISERY (1969)

Few books have moved us, at a glimpse, to laughter and sadness as this one has. The reaction's personal, but without a doubt the late, truly-lovable Langston Hughes strikes a deep and universal note in the simple text-and-caption book he left behind, here first published with the perfectly harmonizing line-and-wash drawings of Arouni. Hughes reaches down beneath the skin of us all with his poignant yet laugh-provoking one-liners that cut through the sad folly of the concept of ''race.'' We wish we could quote endlessly, but we can't. Black misery . . . ''is when somebody meaning no harm called your little black dog 'nigger' and he just wagged his tail and wiggled . . .'' and it's when ''your white teacher tells the class all Negroes can sing and you can't even carry a tune.''

> *A review of ''Black Misery,'' in Publishers Weekly, Vol. 195, No. 10, March 10, 1969, p. 67.*

In a conversation . . . , Hughes told this reviewer that he always had on hand a large store of verse from which to choose selections for his volumes of poems.

Apparently Hughes was long in the habit not only of writing down many of his ideas and reflections in verse but also of

Hughes and Milton Meltzer during a lecture trip in 1956. Courtesy of the Worcester Telegram and Gazette.

recording an appreciable number of them in prose. ***Black Misery,*** a black and white booklet of sixty-three unnumbered pages, consists of the latter kind of reflections. According to the "Publishers' Note," "Just before Langston Hughes died, he finished the captions [the reflective statements] which appear in this book." There are twenty-seven of them, each of which begins with the formula "Misery is when—" and each of which is accompanied by an illustration by Arouni that illuminates it and in turn is illuminated by it. In the illustrations the bearers of the misery are Negro children of grammar-school or high-school ages. Together the twenty-seven statements and the illustrations define compositely and satirically the misery of being black—that is, the disadvantages of being a Negro—in America.

The subjects of the statements range widely over ghetto existence, myths concerning Negro characteristics, the sensitiveness of some Negroes, racial proscription, name-calling, integration, etc. In "Misery is when your white teacher tells the class that all Negroes can sing and you can't even carry a tune," the myth that Negroes are born singers is gently but effectively exploded. In "Misery is when you learn that you are not supposed to like watermelon but you do," and "when your own mother won't let you play your new banjo in front of the *other* race," there is implied ridicule of Negroes who

are oversensitive lest they give proof to some of the myths concerning Negro characteristics.

As in everyday life, the misery in some of the instances in ***Black Misery,*** like that in the three just cited, is somewhat lightened by humor. But also as in everyday life, the misery in some of the instances in the booklet is totally devoid of humor. In "Misery is when you find out your bosom [white] buddy can go in the swimming pool but you can't," for example, there is only a cruel lesson in racial proscription for the teen-age black boy concerned. The part that name-calling has been made to play in racism is revealed to the Negro child who suddenly becomes aware that "Misery is when you start to play a game and someone begins to count out 'Eenie, meenie, minie, mo . . .'" The last statement in the booklet refers to the misery experienced by Negro children who had to have the help of the national guard—Federal troops in Little Rock, Arkansas—to get into an integrated school.

All of the statements in ***Black Misery*** are so compact, informal, and simple that they are apparently naive. To discerning readers, nevertheless, they suggest much more than they explicitly say. Herein lies the value of the booklet. It is a new and challenging reminder to those who have faith in the democratic ideals of America, as Hughes himself had, to speak, vote, and strive in all other severally available reasonable ways for the realization of those ideals. (pp. 87-8)

*W. Edward Farrison, in a review of "Black Misery,"
in* CLA Journal, *Vol. XIII, No. 1, September, 1969,
pp. 87-8.*

This is a book for whitey—Negroes are well acquainted with black misery. The format is similar to such books as Schulz's *Happiness is a Warm Puppy*, with a simple picture opposite a short statement like: "Misery is when you learn that you are not supposed to like watermelon but you do."; or "Misery is when your own mother won't let you play your new banjo in front of the *other* race." The captions were completed just before Mr. Hughes died and they are every bit as moving as his other work. Short, but heavy on impact; YAs should dig. (pp. 2687-88)

Regina Minudri, in a review of "Black Misery," in
School Library Journal, *Vol. 16, No. 1, September,
1969, p. 176.*

DON'T YOU TURN BACK   (1969)

An excellent presentation for children of 45 poems by the late, renowned Negro poet, selected by an educator [Lee Bennett Hopkins], whose readings have evoked enthusiastic response to Hughes's poetry from school children across the country. The collection is divided into four sections: "My People,"

"Prayers and Dreams," "Out to Sea," and "I Am a Negro." None of the poems is more than a page long and many contain only a few short lines, but each is awarded a separate page. The result is an attractive volume that invites browsing and illustrates the power of space-filled pages to involve hesitant readers. Ann Grifalconi's woodcuts, black and brownish-red against the white backgrounds, have a dignity and strength that match the poet's concise images of hardship and hope.

*Sada Fretz, in a review of "Don't You Turn Back:
Poems," in* School Library Journal, *Vol. 17, No. 1,
September, 1970, p. 161.*

Langston Hughes . . . speaks with immediacy and freshness to children, and his poetry has been selected for them in the collection *Don't You Turn Back.* His work expresses black pride, anger, and courage in the musical rhythms of black speech and the blues. With all their ironic humor, bluntness, and gravity, his poems are still universal in their treatment of elemental human emotions, offering Blake-like nature lyrics, murmuring lullabies, and poignant confessions such as **"Mother to Son"**. . . .

*Sheila A. Egoff, in a review of "Don't You Turn
Back," in her* Thursday's Child: Trends and Patterns
in Contemporary Children's Literature, *American Library Association, 1981, p. 239.*

Phyllis Reynolds Naylor

1933-

American author of fiction, nonfiction, and picture books, and journalist.

Naylor is regarded as a prolific and versatile author for middle and upper grade readers whose works display an especially extensive range. Throughout her career, she has been commended for consistently portraying likable protagonists from caring families who grow toward maturity by finding the strength to prevail despite adversity. As a writer of fiction, Naylor is perhaps best known for creating two trilogies which exemplify her passionate determination to treat sensitive issues and distinctively couple elements from gothic fiction with situations from contemporary family life. In *Witch's Sister* (1975), *Witch Water* (1977), and *The Witch Herself* (1978), young Lynn Morley becomes involved in the battle between good and evil when she tries to convince her parents that her sister and a neighbor are witches; concurrently, Lynn attempts to help a friend adjust to her parents' divorce while fretting about the stability of the marriage of her own parents. In the York trilogy—*Shadows on the Wall* (1980), *Faces in the Water* (1981), and *Footprints at the Window* (1981)—adolescent Dan Roberts learns to live with the threat of inheriting Huntington's chorea by traveling through time to ancient Britain to help a gypsy family. In her other stories for young adults, Naylor addresses such serious topics as crib death, mental illness, and war while utilizing contemporary settings and exciting, often mysterious plots. Several of her books are instructional in nature, teaching young people about such subjects as writing as a profession and techniques for effective interaction with parents and teachers. Naylor has also written several regional novels, works with historical settings, and lighthearted books for primary graders on such whimsical subjects as facing the annoyances of being the oldest child in the family and outwitting a demanding babysitter.

Critics are quick to praise Naylor's ability to create complex characters who have a special appeal to the young. Although some reviewers maintain that her largely episodic plots tend to lose momentum, especially in her gothic fiction, most observers admire the suspense and unearthly atmosphere of these books. They find that Naylor successfully invests all her works with optimism and clear-headed advice, qualities that reflect her sympathetic understanding of the myriad trials of childhood and adolescence.

How I Came to Be a Writer won the Golden Kite Award for nonfiction in 1978. In 1984, *Night Cry* received the Edgar Allan Poe Award for best juvenile novel.

(See also *Something about the Author*, Vol. 12; *Contemporary Authors*, Vols. 21-24, rev. ed.; and *Contemporary Authors New Revision Series*, Vol. 8.)

Photograph by Rex Naylor. Courtesy of Phyllis Naylor.

AUTHOR'S COMMENTARY

[If] few people really understand the writing process, it is excusable because we writers often do not understand it either. I don't even know why it is that writing is what I like to do best. Why we become what we are is a result of luck, circumstance, motivation, and all kinds of things the guidance counselors never tell us. The philosophies of our parents and grandparents affect us more than we know. I am sure that three major attitudes of my own relatives probably helped determine the course of my life:

The first all-pervading attitude of both maternal and paternal grandparents was that we are put on this earth for a purpose, and it's up to us to find out what that purpose is. Somehow, my mother always said, in some way, the world should be a better place because of us. She never said we had to be famous—merely constructive. Or, as an old German grandmother used to say, "Everyone can serve, if only as a horrible example." Perhaps writing, for me, is a way to serve.

The second attitude was that time is our most valuable possession. I am geared, I'm afraid, to see a twelve-hour day in allotments of fifteen minutes each, and from the moment I get up, I have a fair idea of what each fifteen minute segment will hold. Neurotic? You bet. But think how much writing I get done this way. What else could I be doing when I'm waiting in line at the supermart or riding the bus or sitting under the hairdryer?

The third attitude is that the less one has to start with, the more noble the accomplishment. The musician, with nothing more than a flute, makes beautiful music. Ah! The artist, who takes simple clay and some paint and creates a gorgeous ceramic bowl. Even better! The writer, who with nothing more than a stub of a pencil and a scrap of paper, invents a story. The ultimate! "Writing," said a relative of dubious charm, "is starting with nothing and making something of it."

Writing is very definitely an addiction. Once the thrill of putting words on paper had a hold on me, the magic of it never left. Though this is certainly not true for all writers, ideas now come faster than I can handle them. By the time I am halfway through one book, a new plot is already forming in my mind, distracting me and making me miserable until I can end the first manuscript and start the second. I already know what my next five books will be, and this is probably the way it will be for the rest of my life. On my deathbed, I am sure, I will gasp, "But I still have five more books to write!" I feel as though I am eternally pregnant, and at the birth of each new book, another is already on the way. Every author leaves a little of himself in whatever he writes, and if he writes enough books or stories, eventually his whole personality and life history will be laid out before him, all mixed up, of course, with fantasy and imaginings.

I am happy and miserable and excited and devastated and encouraged and depressed all at the same time. But accepted or rejected, I will go on writing, because an idea in the head is like a rock in my shoe; I just can't wait to get it out. (pp. 130-33)

> *Phyllis Reynolds Naylor, in her* How I Came to Be a Writer, *Atheneum, 1978, 133 p.*

THE GALLOPING GOAT AND OTHER STORIES   (1965)

These nine short stories about children in other lands have appeared previously in magazines. The stories are uniformly trite and predictable, and the characterization is bland except for the last story **"The Donkey and the Kettle."** This tale of Spanish gypsies has humor and life. The collection as a whole, however, cannot be recommended.

> *Dorothy English, in a review of "The Galloping Goat and Other Stories," in* School Library Journal, *Vol. 12, No. 3, November, 1965, p. 64.*

TO SHAKE A SHADOW   (1967)

The "shadow" that crosses 14-year-old Brad Willson's life is the discovery that his father, the town's respected bank vice president, has cheated on his income tax and faces a prison term. The middle-class values that up to then had sustained him suddenly take on another, less benign aspect and set him on a path of self-discovery through bitterness, a rash flirtation with petty crime, estrangement from members of his family and, finally, to acceptance of himself in a less-than-perfect world.

Mrs. Naylor's third book offers a good story, despite her reluctance to set the characters free from the strictures of textbook psychology. Writing in a crisp, businesslike style, she has the storyteller's ability of keeping the reader interested and turning the page to find out what happens next.

> *George Gent, in a review of "To Shake a Shadow," in* The New York Times Book Review, *September 17, 1967, p. 34.*

A 14-year-old's slow groping towards maturity and his acceptance of human nature, especially his father's, are convincingly handled in a plot paced by enough family bouts and junior gang intrigue to hold adolescent interest. Major characters, sometimes acting and reacting within a tight psychological framework, could do with more spontaneity, but this is only a minor annoyance in an otherwise solid story.

> *Susan A. Roth, in a review of "To Shake a Shadow," in* School Library Journal, *Vol. 14, No. 2, October, 1967, p. 79.*

WHAT THE GULLS WERE SINGING   (1967)

Mrs. Naylor has another small tractarian story this season (*To Shake a Shadow*) and this changes the labels to put across roughly the same ideas about family amity and community accord. The Buckleys are by the seashore for the summer and Marilyn, the second oldest of four, ten, resents Peter, eleven, who gets the best marks, the new bike, and to room with Nico the Greek boy they have just taken in. Appearances are not what they are (even though Niko is called "greaseball" and "spic") and differences are equally deceptive—Cassandra who lives alone in the village and is suspect; the baby Ricky who is mentally retarded. By the end of this, a non-story (though there are incidents) in a nondescript style, Marilyn understands about "love." A lesson learned while fingers stick to the page.

> *A review of "What the Gulls Were Singing," in* Kirkus Service, *Vol. XXXV, No. 18, September 15, 1967, p. 1135.*

The welter of subplots concerning the boarders and their love affairs, mysterious events, rowdy surfers, and a retarded baby brother will smother the reader's interest in either Marilyn or the book as a whole. The writing is mediocre, while the point about love, expounded without subtlety by the beach girl Cassandra, is presented in terms difficult for children to grasp whatever their emotional experience might be. (pp. 73, 75)

> *Elena Fiant, in a review of "What the Gulls Were Singing," in* School Library Journal, *Vol. 14, No. 4, December, 1967, pp. 73, 75.*

JENNIFER JEAN, THE CROSS-EYED QUEEN   (1967)

"The Cross-Eyed Queen" was one of the things other children said to tease Jennifer Jean; she didn't mind too much—she could see pretty well, and in a way it was nice to be different. But when Jennifer was four, she was taken to a doctor; first she wore an eye-patch, then eyeglasses; then she did exercises, and after a while her eyes really were straight again. A realistic treatment of the problem: Jennifer Jean is teased, but not unmercifully; she has trouble with some activities, but not all; she would like to have straight eyes, but is used to being cross-eyed. The parental attitude is commendably relaxed, and the story—although not well written, and both sedate and purposive—should encourage children who suffer from being cross-eyed and educate other children.

> *Zena Sutherland, in a review of "Jennifer Jean, the Cross-Eyed Queen," in* Bulletin of the Center for Children's Books, *Vol. 21, No. 5, January, 1968, p. 81.*

A sensitively told story of how children are affected by physical differences. . . . This well-written story also mentions a couple of other minor afflictions, such as big feet and ears that stick out, and, so, might be used to give a class a sense of empathy or sympathy with any members who have disabilities.

Joan Lear Sher, in a review of "Jennifer Jean, the Cross-Eyed Queen," in School Library Journal, *Vol. 14, No. 6, February, 1968, p. 70.*

MEET MURDOCK (1969)

To appreciate the full blown fun, this must be read aloud. It's a zany tale of a retired sailor named Murdock who is "hardly fond of children," has a parrot named Sir Walter, and lives in the basement of an apartment house where he is custodian. Three children, ages 7, 6, and 4, live with their families in the house, and are determined to play in the basement. Murdock's "Closed" and "Keep Out" signs are no more successful than his dire warnings of trolls, goblins, and dragons. It is when they make a raft in the cellar "in case there's a flood," and then set out to make it rain (just enough for a tiny flood) that they really begin to get to Murdock. All their efforts, as funny as they are unscientific, fail. No rain. Just snow. But luckily, a pipe bursts! The cellar is flooded for real. And guess who is on board the raft, captain's hat atop his head, and leading a rousing sea chantey. The illustrations [by Gioia Fiammenghi] are as fresh and comically successful as the story.

Jeraline Nerney, in a review of "Meet Murdock," in Library Journal, *Vol. 94, No. 13, July, 1969, p. 2673.*

TO MAKE A WEE MOON (1969)

Skill in developing a picture of rural Wisconsin life and a remarkably acute recalling of childhood feelings give notable reality to the family story. From the opening, when Jean and young Brian take a long train ride from West Virginia coal country to Grandmother's farm, to the conclusion, when father and mother at last find land on which to make their own way, the story has the ring of truth. Each person is clearly individualized: Grandmother (from Skye) who "had the look of a troll about her" (she does believe in the wee folk); Donald Harvie, the hired man, who elopes with Aunt Gwen to become "Uncle" to Jean; creative Aunt Gwen, who helps Jean make a most ingenious doll's house; Preacher Bean in his revival tent gaining crowds as he talks against the sins of Mr. Murray's carnival; and abandoned Tommy Pepper, whose effect on all—including schoolmates—is a remarkable, salutary one. Their problems, presented more openly than in some such stories, become part of Jean's growing up. She realizes that it is "possible to like a person partly and partly not like him at all." A rewarding book.

Virginia Haviland, in a review of "To Make a Wee Moon," in The Horn Book Magazine, *Vol. XLVI, No. 1, February, 1970, p. 42.*

A slow-moving, mediocre story about two children who are sent to their grandmother's Wisconsin farm until their parents can gather their resources to join them, and who find themselves in a thoroughly miserable situation. An ungentle grandmother whose life is ruled by the fairies she imported from Scotland, a mannish aunt who finally elopes with the unambitious hired man, and a small assortment of preachers, teachers, and carnival barkers present an unattractive but no doubt realistic picture of rural life an unspecified number of years ago. "To make a wee moon," Aunt Gwen keeps saying, "all we need is a little patience and a lot of hard work." Patience and hard work abound, but little real interest, and most girls

will wonder if the resulting "wee moon" was worth quite so much moralizing.

Katherine Heylman, in a review of "To Make a Wee Moon," in School Library Journal, *Vol. 16, No. 7, March, 1970, p. 139.*

NO EASY CIRCLE (1972)

An average contemporary story about a 15-year-old girl concerned with her physical immaturity, her divorced parents and her friend Pogo's escape to a crash pad and subsequent pregnancy. Shelley moves through various eye-opening episodes: from early dating to the youth culture at Washington's Dupont Circle. When she arrives home unexpectedly from a slumber party and discovers that her mother has been keeping late company with a male friend, Shelley decides to split for "The Circle" in search of her girlfriend. But after spending one night on a mattress next to an inebriated 14-year-old, Shelley finds the crash scene (dirt, drugs and casual sex) repulsive and eventually returns home. Most of Shelley's adventures are fairly conceivable, but the author unfortunately attempts to get in as many contemporary problems as possible. The relationship between Shelley and a psychiatric social worker is well-handled, but Shelley's bland character lacks force and credibility even though she does mature somewhat by the end of the story.

Ronna Dishnica, in a review of "No Easy Circle," in School Library Journal, *Vol. 19, No. 1, September, 1972, p. 95.*

Naylor presents the problems of divorce but then only dallies around its periphery. In fact the subject is nearly lost in this with-it, kitchen-sink conglomeration of teen-age writing. The departure point is the split nucleus of two divorced and unfeeling parents and one salvageable, 15-year-old girl. From there we are taken on a dreary tour of the Washington, D.C. hippie scene, homosexual marriages, drugs and drunken 14-year-olds, a teen-age pregnancy, a near-suicide—and a mother found out with yet another man. It's a tediously long journey around the circumference of this circle before we find psychological—if not literary—salvation.

Lael Scott, "Divorce Juvenile-Style," in The New York Times Book Review, *September 3, 1972, p. 8.*

TO WALK THE SKY PATH (1973)

Billie Tommie goes to the white man's school, the only member of his three-generation family who has had the chance at an education. The Tommies are Seminoles, living on the outskirts of civilization in the Everglades. Billie is faced with the inevitable conflicts of trying to learn new ways and also adhere to the standards set for him by his beloved grandfather, Abraham. The author writes with sympathy and respect for the Seminoles. She paints a compelling picture of a proud people, their privacy invaded by crass tourists. But the somber scene is leavened by humor and a note of hope as Billie grows in strength and maturity.

A review of "To Walk the Sky Path," in Publishers Weekly, *Vol. 203, No. 19, May 7, 1973, p. 66.*

To Walk the Sky Path is about the conflict in the life of a ten-year-old Seminole boy between the traditional ways of his forbears and more modern, American ways. Since the problem is set up this way in the book, the author has good opportunity to indicate attitudes about both poles of the dilemma, and this she does, showing the advantages and disadvantages of both. She has sympathy for the ways of the Indians, and she shows scorn and disdain for some aspects of modern American life (mostly the ill manners of tourists and prejudiced whites). She indicates a good and convincing knowledge of her subject. Everyone, however, would not agree that, all things considered, the young boy is better off choosing modern America. The grandfather's dying at the end represents a value judgment which is at best questionable. The danger of this book is clearly seen if its implications are imagined as being translated into public policy. The argument of the book is that it is in the best interest of Indians to be integrated into American life. I do not think all Indians would agree.

> *Donald B. Gibson, in a review of "To Walk the Sky Path," in* Children's Literature: Annual of the Modern Language Association Seminar on Children's Literature and The Children's Literature Association, *Vol. 3, 1974, p. 232.*

A number of overused Indian characteristics are included in **To Walk the Sky Path.** For example, Tommie's grandfather extols the virtues of stoicism, and Tommie's uncle remains polite and smiling while being abused by tourists, but then drinks "himself into a stupor." In spite of such stereotypic characteristics, **To Walk the Sky Path** does focus on the conflict between Indian civilization and white schooling, between the old and the new Indian. (p. 173)

> *Myra Pollack Sadker and David Miller Sadker, "Native Americans in Children's Books," in* Now Upon a Time: A Contemporary View of Children's Literature, *Harper & Row, Publishers, 1977, pp. 163-90.*

AN AMISH FAMILY   (1974)

An authentic and sympathetic text gives much information about a particularly exclusive American minority. . . . The account focuses on the Stolzfus family, part of the Amish Community in Pennsylvania and explains the *Ordnung,* rules which govern Amish life. Ms. Naylor tells how the Plain People are often bedevilled by insensitive tourists who invade their privacy and (worst trial of all) try to snap their pictures. The Amish are forbidden to allow any image of themselves to be created. The practice of shunning is discussed—a method of punishing members of the community for offenses—as are other demands of the *Ordnung.* This is an interesting book but rather limited in that it concentrates on positive aspects of Amish life and skims lightly over the grimmer side.

> *A review of "An Amish Family," in* Publishers Weekly, *Vol. 207, No. 22, June 22, 1975, p. 54.*

Naylor gives a really excellent survey of Amish life, using descriptions of the members of a three-generation family to illustrate living patterns, attitudes, roles, and relationships. Beyond this, she provides full historical background, assesses the problems of an isolate group in a disparate society and those within the Mennonite religion and the Amish sects that sprang from it. The tone is sympathetic, respectful of the tenets of the Amish but objective about dissident elements within their community. As useful as it is interesting, the book can serve as a minor reference source. A bibliography and an extensive relative index are appended.

> *Zena Sutherland, in a review of "An Amish Family," in* Bulletin of the Center for Children's Books, *Vol. 29, No. 3, November, 1975, p. 51.*

Through incidents in the lives of Benjamin and Rebecca Stoltzfus and their children, readers get an extremely thorough and vivid picture of the Amish life (e.g., manners, customs, holidays, education, courtship, weddings, funerals, baptisms, barnraisings, and language). The text is flawed by occasional wandering from specific events to detailed descriptions of the Amish background, but the presentation is objective and informative in relating the conflicts the children face as Plain People in a modern world. . . . A necessary addition for libraries wanting up-to-date information on the Amish (history of the Amish religion from 1517 until the present is also included).

> *Sara Rupnik, in a review of "An Amish Family," in* School Library Journal, *Vol. 22, No. 7, March, 1976, p. 116.*

WITCH'S SISTER   (1975)

Lynn Morley suspects her older sister Judith of being a witch. Lynn's fertile imagination works on such readily explainable incidents as Judith not getting poison ivy when both her siblings did until she is convinced that her sister plans to harm their younger brother. The climax is exciting and would even be frightening if readers could really believe that Judith is a witch; unfortunately, the evidence never seems to warrant such a farfetched conclusion—a weak spot in an otherwise lively and well-written book.

> *Susan Davie, in a review of "Witch's Sister," in* School Library Journal, *Vol. 21, No. 8, April, 1975, p. 56.*

The author carefully builds up the equivocal evidence that feeds the flames of Lynn's imagination and fear; but the reader is never quite persuaded, and the story—though meticulously plotted and well-written—is a pleasant diversion but scarcely a thriller.

> *Ethel L. Heins, in a review of "Witch's Sister," in* The Horn Book Magazine, *Vol. LI, No. 4, August, 1975, p. 383.*

There's some suspense, certainly some insight into the imaginative convictions of the pre-teenager, good parent-child relationships, and a capable writing style, but the book is weakened by a plethora of small coincidences: Lynn learns that a witch keeps a box of ashes, and Judith has one that is never explained; witches bathe the children they are about to destroy, and the neighbor dips the brother's hand in milk (explained but too pat) and witches "hex" those who pursue them, so Lynn knows why her pots of daisies die, why her friend becomes ill, et cetera. (pp. 68-9)

> *Zena Sutherland, in a review of "Witch's Sister," in* Bulletin of the Center for Children's Books, *Vol. 29, No. 4, December, 1975, pp. 68-9.*

WALKING THROUGH THE DARK   (1976)

Poverty transcended is interesting, even uplifting. Poverty endured is dull. The Wheelers endure. Ruth is just about to enter high school in Chicago in 1932 when the Depression hits, knocking her father out of work, the mortgage payments on their house off-schedule, and her dreams of an assured college future into a cocked hat. Ruth's encounters with first love, living conditions of others worse off, hunger, and adult financial desperation are relentlessly centered on money and the lack of it. Ruth's emotional growth from selfishness to compassion, is a slow, monotonous trip punctuated with dollar signs. And, her story isn't ended. Does she go to college and become a teacher? Does she marry Ed Galvin? Who knows? The book ends in her junior year in high school with an historical note on economic recovery and the beginning of W.W.II. Ruth would be in spitting distance of Social Security now if she hacked it through from a story that only starts. No competition here for that warm, wet *Waltons* TV series.

> *Lillian N. Gerhardt, in a review of "Walking through the Dark," in* School Library Journal, *Vol. 22, No. 8, April, 1976, p. 92.*

[When her family was reduced to poverty] Ruth responded to events first with impatience and a lack of understanding, then with bitterness and self-pity, and finally with stoical acceptance. Ruth mourned the loss of her happy girlhood, but her much-admired teacher made her understand that experience of any sort is always valuable. The relationship between the parents is well-presented; they lost all sense of humor and their affection for each other became submerged in worry. The problems and adjustments that were forced on people during the Depression and the normal and often humorous vicissitudes of adolescent life add depth to a study of a sad but interesting era in American life.

> *Ann A. Flowers, in a review of "Walking through the Dark," in* The Horn Book Magazine, *Vol. LII, No. 3, June, 1976, p. 295.*

Ruth's diary records the notable events from 1931 to 1933, the entries taking us to the day of her sixteenth birthday. Attention to detail recreates Chicago in the early thirties—Hoovervilles alongside the World's Fair. The author's lavish care makes a depressing time in history come alive. Her people do not. Ruth and her family seem to be a product of the seventies, not the thirties. The litany of disasters that befalls the Wheelers resembles a welfare worker's report. If you are looking for a way to end the "good old days" syndrome, this book should qualify.

> *Ruth M. Stein, in a review of "Walking through the Dark," in* Language Arts, *Vol. 53, No. 6, September, 1976, p. 701.*

GETTING ALONG IN YOUR FAMILY (1976)

A readable description of some typical family tensions emphasizes acceptance of the family as a diverse group of individuals bound together by ties of love, experience, and practical considerations that make it important for everybody to show as much tolerant understanding as possible. The predominant slant here is toward children adjusting—the reader should try going that extra mile—and the author assumes reasonable, caring parents and strong, articulate children. There are no therapeutic solutions outside the theme that love goes a long way, but the book itself could go a long way in airing grievances and opening up discussion if shared by parent and child; there are several situations presented with a concluding question "Fair or not?" and several problems presented first from one point of view and then from the other. Altogether, this offers

commonsense perspective on the minor irritations of basically healthy relationships.

> *Betsy Hearne, in a review of "Getting Along in Your Family," in* Booklist, *Vol. 73, No. 6, November 15, 1976, p. 476.*

Recommending many of the same therapeutic techniques as Ginott's *Between Parent and Child* (1965), an adult title cited in the bibliography, this is a well-intentioned but plodding attempt to help children understand and express anger appropriately and relate to brothers, sisters, and parents in a considerate and loving way. Naylor makes it clear that all families have problems, and most of the common ones—e.g., sibling rivalry, intergenerational conflict, alcoholism and divorce—are discussed here. Although Naylor's counseling will provide some reassurance and comfort, none of the topics is explored in any depth [and] the tone is often preachy. . . .

> *Joan Scherer Brewer, in a review of "Getting Along in Your Family," in* School Library Journal, *Vol. 23, No. 4, December, 1976, p. 56.*

This readable and realistic little book is admirably suited to the difficult task of opening channels of communication between a child and other family members. Moreover, it could serve as a springboard for problem-oriented discussions in educational or therapeutic settings. . . . Problems and controversies are presented from the point of view of both child and parent. This format encourages the child to see situations from the point of view of the parent and to see the parent as a person who has needs and feelings too. . . . Specific examples and vignettes are well written and provide excellent focus.

> *S. Joyce Brotsky, in a review of "Getting Along in Your Family," in* Science Books & Films, *Vol. XIII, No. 2, September, 1977, p. 93.*

WITCH WATER 1977

A popular theme in Gothic fiction for adolescents is the way the heroine—usually an intelligent, gifted, and oftentimes alienated pre-teen—works out a problematic relationship with her family and friends. The dramatic build-up involves the use of literary trappings, as they are known, drawn from late eighteenth- and early nineteenth-century British and German Gothic traditions, like haunting voices, animal and human vessels, and harbingers of evil spirits—typically cats, crows, and old ladies who live alone. (The eccentric old ladies here have a particularly American flavor inasmuch as they resemble Puritan spinsters or town scolds.)

But when the central focus of the novel shifts away from a nineteenth-century reliance on outer trappings, like enchanted forests and conventional corridors peopled by ghosts, to a psychological presentation of the pre-teen heroine's troubled emotional life—her suspicions, fears and terrors—in the form of her obsessive need for secrets and/or her using time by herself for indulging escapist fantasies in order to resolve her problems, then the Gothic genre can transcend its historical confines and become more seemingly realistic and accessible to a contemporary audience.

Of the three new Gothic novels for adolescents [*Witch Water, The Haunting of Julie Unger* by Valerie Lutters, and *Time Tangle* by Frances Eagar] . . . , only the first presents with total believability the delicate, potentially volatile balance which exists in the sensitive heroine's mind between her world of escapist fantasy and her actual situation in ordinary reality. (p. 111)

In *Witch Water* . . . the thin line between fantasy and reality is drawn with skill and finesse, as when the heroine, Lynn Morley, can at once speak with maturity and awareness to her mother about the big-sisterly concern she feels for her best friend, Marjorie Beasley, whose parents just got divorced, and at the same time repress childishly the terror which Marjorie's depression also makes her feel. . . . (p. 113)

There are in *Witch Water* the typical Gothic extremes in plot—natural calamities and reversals—such as when crows ambush Lynn and Marjorie on a night they sleep alone together in an otherwise empty house, and the grand finale when Lynn initiates a confrontation with Mrs. Tuggles' cat in the town lake, and the reader learns that Lynn's paranoia has developed to such an extent that she wants to murder the cat by drowning it. When, in the closing scene which takes place the morning after the confrontation, Mrs. Tuggles' cat appears to Lynn, Mrs. Morley, and Mrs. Tuggles who are assembled in the cabin, it becomes clear that Lynn imagined the drowning, that her developed expression of the ghoulish fantasy was that "dark night of the soul" experience she needed to undergo to exorcise herself from holding a jealous and false vision of Mrs. Tuggles as the witch of her projections. . . .

Of [the three previously mentioned] new Gothic novels for adolescents, only *Witch Water* presents an engaging, dynamic account of the way a frightened pre-teen resolves a serious emotional crisis. (p. 115)

> *Sharon Leder, "Contemporary Adolescent Gothic," in* The Lion and the Unicorn, *Vol. 1, No. 2, Fall, 1977, pp. 111-15.*

In this sequel to *Witch's Sister,* Lynn Morley and her friend Mouse fear that old Mrs. Tuggle is a witch determined to bring the girls into her power. No one else regards lonely, eccentric Mrs. Tuggle as a threat, but the friends are convinced that Mrs. Tuggle has summoned nine crows to follow Mouse. Characters are nicely drawn, and the plot is well crafted with a genuine aura of evil contributing to the carefully built tension.

> *Susan Davie, in a review of "Witch Water," in* School Library Journal, *Vol. 24, No. 1, September 1, 1977, p. 134.*

The American origin of this book presents no problems. I question the wisdom of stimulating interest in the occult for the over-eights, however engrossing the story may be—and this one certainly is. Fairy tale witches on broomsticks are part of our cultural heritage: modern tales of modern witches in a modern environment have the power to instil false or disquieting ideas—and even in *Witch Water* doubts about Mrs. Tuggle remain unresolved. (pp. 328-29)

> *G. Bott, in a review of "Witch Water," in* The Junior Bookshelf, *Vol. 43, No. 6, December, 1979, pp. 328-29.*

HOW I CAME TO BE A WRITER (1978)

Would-be writers should be spared this shallow autobiographical account, which comes with family-album photos of the author from angelic tyke to coiffured success. The author of less than memorable juvenile novels (*Witch's Sister, Walking Through the Dark*), Naylor includes here samples of her earliest (elementary school) efforts plus, in toto, her first published story ("Sure Mike," the famous athlete assures the injured boy, "Anyone can succeed if he tries hard enough and long enough")—solicited by a former teacher for a church school paper when Phyllis was 16. There are more stories, exchanges with editors, reviews of her books—but the closest Naylor comes to considering the art of writing is an early "glimpse [of] the possibilities in writing the unexpected. What if a mother was *not* soft-spoken? . . . Why should children always be the ones at fault?" Naylor ends with a housewifey chat on how she fits her writing in with the sock-sorting and such, and some banal advice for those who would do likewise: "Read good books as well as junk. How [else] can you tell the difference?"; "Live a full life with many types of experiences." But there is no evidence here that she's been touched by either good books or experience (despite the hairy ones recalled in her adult, autobiographical *Crazy Love*). Book publication by a respectable house seems the ultimate goal; reading this, one wonders how she ever got that far. (pp. 309-10)

> *A review of "How I Came to Be a Writer," in* Kirkus Reviews, *Vol. XLVI, No. 6, March 15, 1978, pp. 309-10.*

The book contains autobiographical fragments interspersed with detailed accounts of publishing procedures. The author has included many samples of her own writing—stories, poems, and pieces of novels at various stages of completion—as well as illustrations and jackets from published work. She has also included examples of rejection slips, notes of advice from her editors, and mixed reviews from the critics. Thus the reader is shown the development of a work from its inception to its final publication. Though the integration of all these parts is not as fluid as it might have been and the number of sample pieces seems a bit too profuse, the book presents an interesting personal account of what it is like to be a professional writer. Discussions of the psychological and emotional demands are lightened by humorous anecdotes which show that although the author takes her work very seriously, she has learned not to take herself so: "I refuse to go on vacation until my last book is done, and then I leave it on my desk with all sorts of little notes attached so that if I should drown at the ocean, my grieving relatives will know how I intended to revise it." (p. 411)

> *Karen M. Klockner, in a review of "How I Came to Be a Writer," in* The Horn Book Magazine, *Vol. LIV, No. 4, August, 1978, pp. 410-11.*

[Naylor] uses a workaday voice, dividing her approach between autobiographical anecdotes and minilectures on the craft (e.g., to expect rejection slips and not postpone work by holding out for one special pen). The beginning personal chapters and photographs have a liveliness that the facile career advice lacks. Passages from the author's novels illustrate editorial changes, but the book includes several poorly chosen selections that serve no purpose (e.g., an example of a galley proof that doesn't differ in format or typography from the rest of the printed text; amateurish stories; a series of four photos labelled "Editor," "Designer," "Copyeditor," and "Manuscript reader" whose functions are visually indistinguishable). Naylor talks clearly about revisions and plots, but she doesn't differentiate between formulaic writing and creative spark. (p. 145)

> *Sharon Elswit, in a review of "How I Came to Be a Writer," in* School Library Journal, *Vol. 25, No. 1, September 1, 1978, pp. 144-45.*

THE WITCH HERSELF (1978)

Although Lynn Morley and her chum "Mouse" Beasley were convinced that the aged Mrs. Tuggle was a witch, none of the adults in whom they confided accepted their opinion. Most of the ominous events could somehow be rationalized by their less observant elders as evidence of eccentricity rather than of demonic intent. Of particular concern to Lynn was the sinister change in her mother's personality—a change which became more noticeable, even to other members of the family, after Mrs. Morley moved her writing studio into the old woman's home. Realizing that Mrs. Tuggle saw them as adversaries, Lynn and Mouse began delving into her past and found in an ancient journal that there had once been a woman who, like themselves, suspected Mrs. Tuggle's power but who disappeared in a flood before her theory became public knowledge. To add to their terror, Mouse's experiments with hypnotism indicated that Mrs. Tuggle could someday control them by communicating with the dark side of their natures unless they fought against such manipulation. Exactly how the battle between good and evil would be resolved is the central question of the concluding volume of a trilogy which combines elements of the contemporary family story with motifs from Gothic romances. The sense of terror is heightened by the contrast between the prescience of the girls and the rational perceptions of the adults. (pp. 519-20)

> *Mary M. Burns, in a review of "The Witch Herself,"
> in* The Horn Book Magazine, *Vol. LV, No. 5, Oc-
> tober, 1978, pp. 519-20.*

Is Mrs. Tuggle's witchcraft all in Lynn's head, as Mother had suggested in **The Witch's Sister,** or is the old woman really on the way to capturing Mother for her coven? Naylor almost seems to be having it both ways in this last of three adventures, each of which has Lynn worried about Mrs. Tuggle's influence on a close friend or family member, each of which climaxes in a scary midnight confrontation.... Formula shivers—but followers of the series won't be disappointed.

> *A review of "The Witch Herself," in* Kirkus Re-
> views, *Vol. XLVI, No. 20, October 15, 1978, p.
> 1139.*

Lynn and Mouse discover they can not blame all that goes wrong on witchcraft; there is a good and bad side to everyone. Characters are well developed, and the plot is carefully executed to give readers a chill up the spine.

> *Hilarie D. Morrow Kane, in a review of "The Witch
> Herself," in* School Library Journal, *Vol. 25, No. 6,
> February, 1979, p. 58.*

HOW LAZY CAN YOU GET? (1979)

Really a broad comedy sketch, this short story details the week that humorless Miss Brasscoat spends with the three Meggle-thorp children while their parents are away on business. She cooks them unappetizingly nutritious meals and sets them to dusting and cleaning more than they've ever dreamed possible. They suffer duly, but not without some comic responses, including a dinner fiasco that finally accomplishes the impossible—a smile from Miss Brasscoat. Light, but not to be dismissed in an age range where humor is scarce.

> *Denise M. Wilms, in a review of "How Lazy Can
> You Get?" in* Booklist, *Vol. 76, No. 2, September
> 15, 1979, p. 126.*

Breezy humor, rooted in family situations, resembles that in Helen Cresswell's *Bagthorpe* chronicles, of which this book seems to be a spoofing counterpart. The baby-sitter Hildegarde Brasscoat arrives to stay for a week and lays down the law to the young Megglethorps; among her rules is an edict that "lay-about children" are up to no good. When she spontaneously complains, "How lazy can you get,'" they take her literally and cause more havoc than ever. The line-and-wash pictures [by Alan Daniel] . . . indicate the hyperbolic quality of the text.

> *Virginia Haviland, in a review of "How Lazy Can
> You Get?" in* The Horn Book Magazine, *Vol. LV,
> No. 6, December, 1979, p. 664.*

This brief tale will do nothing to displace Travers' *Mary Poppins* in "Nanny" literature. But it is well written and amusing, although slight; the characters are vivid if not drawn with any depth; and innocent children against stuffy adult antagonists is always an appealing theme.

> *Anne Hanst Parker, in a review of "How Lazy Can
> You Get?" in* School Library Journal, *Vol. 26, No.
> 4, December, 1979, p. 88.*

GETTING ALONG WITH YOUR FRIENDS (1980)

A popular psychology title in the vein of *I'm O.K., You're O.K.* for the middle grades. It deals with knowing yourself and your friends and accepting both the good points and the warts. The advice and examples are practical and in good taste, if sometimes erring on the side of optimism. Generally the book teaches but does not preach. Might be useful for counseling a child having problems with relationships.

> *Barbara Baker, in a review of "Getting Along with
> Your Friends," in* Children's Book Review Service,
> *Vol. 8, No. 9, April, 1980, p. 89.*

This examination of making and keeping friends lays some sound groundwork in simple terms for readers interested in their ability to relate to others. Friendly discussions push at self-awareness, self-acceptance, and recognizing the needs of others; and there are plenty of examples to pinpoint the lessons. Naylor begins by suggesting that readers make an analytic list of their friends, which might reveal patterns in why the friendships came to be. That exercise is, in essence, a vantage point for closer looks on the issues it might bring up—insecurity, low self-esteem, bossiness, manipulative tendencies, and a host of other significant behavior patterns. There is also consideration of fighting and the process of people's changing, two potentially painful aspects of friendship. It's interesting to see, in a discussion of bullies, examples showing both violent and nonviolent solutions to the problem: "What you do will depend partly on what you have been taught by your parents." Useful both for self-help and classroom discussion.

> *Denise M. Wilms, in a review of "Getting Along
> with Your Friends," in* Booklist, *Vol. 76, No. 16,
> April 15, 1980, p. 1206.*

For a younger audience than Neimark's *Getting Along: How To Be Happy with Yourself and Others* (1979), this self-help book also has a more extroverted focus. . . . Unfortunately, the fictive examples are numerous and the analytic passages, brief.

Gale Eaton, in a review of "Getting Along with Your Friends," in School Library Journal, *Vol. 27, No. 1, September, 1980, p. 76.*

EDDIE, INCORPORATED   (1980)

Eddie, Incorporated presents a light look into the world of careers and economics. Eddie, upset with his status as the only non-working member of his family, takes it upon himself to begin a business venture. Despite many failures, Eddie keeps trying, and the reader will feel compelled to find out if Eddie does finally succeed. This humorous, realistic novel will entertain independent readers, and it will be equally appealing when read aloud. The book presents a unified, caring, loving family, and an untroubled hero. It is a pleasant departure from much of today's realistic fiction.

Fellis L. Jordan, in a review of "Eddie, Incorporated," in Children's Book Review Service, *Vol. 8, No. 12, Spring, 1980, p. 119.*

A healthy celebration of a sixth grader's first commercial triumph. . . . The story is honestly child-oriented, and therefore involving; its vocabulary is carefully controlled yet varied and interesting. Echoing the hopes of many youngsters, it captures a child's frustration at being ambitious within an economic system designed for adults.

Liza Bliss, in a review of "Eddie, Incorporated," in School Library Journal, *Vol. 26, No. 9, May, 1980, p. 71.*

The process by which [Eddie learns] that no business is trouble-free and that fulfilling an obligation brings its own satisfaction is unfolded humorously and sympathetically in a fast-paced, vivacious episodic story. The characters are broadly outlined rather than developed, but plot is the dominant element in the story, and Eddie's tribulations are believable in their absurdity.

Mary M. Burns, in a review of "Eddie, Incorporated," in The Horn Book Magazine, *Vol. LVI, No. 3, June, 1980, p. 302.*

SHADOWS ON THE WALL   (1980)

On a trip to York, England, 15-year-old Dan Roberts is distressed by his parents' unusual secrecy and a strange sense of dread he feels near some ancient Roman ruins. By accident, he discovers that his mother is researching his father's generational lines to trace a hereditary disease that could seriously affect both Dan and his father. Furthermore, several ghostly encounters with Roman legionnaires from out of the past seem mysteriously linked to Joe Stanton, an eccentric cab driver who befriends Dan, as well as to the Faws, an old gypsy family who live by ancient traditions. In the first of what is to be the York Trilogy, the seeds of many situations, relationships, and plot complexities are sown, and Naylor uses suspense and atmosphere well. Whether or not the harvest matches the planting, however, will have to await judgement. Though Dan departs for home more or less at peace with what has happened, the final vignette leaves readers intrigued with a foreshadowing of more to come.

Barbara Elleman, in a review of "Shadows on the Wall," in Booklist, *Vol. 77, No. 2, September 15, 1980, p. 118.*

The characterization of likable, introspective Dan and of the gypsies is good, and the author is skillful at establishing a gray brooding mood, but the connection she makes between Huntington's Chorea and enhanced psychic receptivity is very dubious and detracts from the story's credibility. Also, the plot is just starting to liven up when the book (the first in a three-part series) ends with all questions still unresolved. William Mayne's *Earthfasts* (1966) is a more exciting and rewarding story. (pp. 71-2)

Chuck Schacht, in a review of "Shadows on the Wall," in School Library Journal, *Vol. 27, No. 5, January, 1981, pp. 71-2.*

There's a strong evocation of atmosphere and setting, although perhaps a plethora of historical details is introduced as part of the dialogue; the characters are interesting, albeit drawn with little depth. It is the plot that's weak, with no clean story line emerging from the various incidents and encounters, and with no definition in the ending.

Zena Sutherland, in a review of "Shadows on the Wall: The York Trilogy, Book One," in Bulletin of the Center for Children's Books, *Vol. 34, No. 6, February, 1981, p. 115.*

GETTING ALONG WITH YOUR TEACHERS   (1981)

Teachers have good days and bad days; give them an ounce of understanding, suggests Naylor, and getting along might not be so hard. Also, turn in assignments on time, and follow basic classroom rules. Besides these obvious down-to-earth directives, Naylor counsels against prejudging teachers on the basis of hearsay, lest bad rumors become self-fulfilling prophecy. And where there is really trouble—an honest personality clash, for example—she suggests talking things out with the teacher privately or in the presence of an authoritative third party. If no good comes of it, a transfer may be in order. Just about all commentary presumes reasonable attitudes on the part of both teacher and student, which can't be faulted but may be insufficient where the situation has become strained.

Denise M. Wilms, in a review of "Getting Along with Your Teachers," in Booklist, *Vol. 77, No. 16, April 15, 1981, p. 1156.*

Unfortunately, since the book has no index and since the chapter headings are not indicative of specific content ("Getting Yourself Together," "Going by the Rules," "Real Trouble") there is little to guide the reader to identifiable problems in teacher-student relations. The text is well organized, and is only moderately well written; there are several fictional episodes that are designed as examples but that do not expand on what is already in the text. It may be realistic to assume that it is usually the student who is required to adapt, adjust, tolerate, etc. rather than the teacher, but it can't be very encouraging to the reader. The text may, however, help some readers to understand that all relationships are susceptible to change if either party takes the initiative and tries to improve them.

Zena Sutherland, in a review of "Getting Along with Your Teachers," in Bulletin of the Center for Children's Books, *Vol. 34, No. 9, May, 1981, p. 177.*

Naylor at approximately eight years old. Courtesy of Phyllis Naylor.

FACES IN THE WATER (1981)

In a sequel to **Shadows on the Wall,** Naylor continues her story of Dan Roberts and his confrontations with the past as he attempts to sort out the future, which contains the possibility of incapacitation from a hereditary disease. During a summer visit to his grandmother's Pennsylvania farm, Dan again finds himself involved with the gypsy family of Ambrose Faw—and the daughter Orlenda, in particular—as well as with his grandmother's strange hired hand, who is somehow mysteriously connected to the ancient Faws. Though Naylor writes with vitality and assurance and her story is compelling, the final direction of the trilogy is uncertain, and judgment of the novel's success will need to wait completion of the final volume.

> *Barbara Elleman, in a review of "Faces in the Water: The York Trilogy, Book Two," in* Booklist, *Vol. 77, No. 17, May 1, 1981, p. 1198.*

No doubt the stories will come together in the final volume. Meanwhile we have some smooth and fairly complex interweaving of the characters' various manifestations; some spooky effects that are effective until, once more, they pile up ludicrously; some fairly shallow musings on time and time-travel; and a general gloss of grade-B melodramatic writing.

> *A review of "Faces in the Water," in* Kirkus Reviews, *Vol. XLIX, No. 10, May 15, 1981, p. 636.*

The second volume of the projected trilogy demands a knowledge of the first. . . . By her own admission the author is anxious to show that young people have always been faced with such agonizing problems as war and disease, and in another story combining realism and fantasy, she writes with skill and a degree of passion. Whether she can reconcile the disparate elements of her plot and bring the trilogy to a unified conclusion still remains to be seen.

> *Ethel L. Heins, in a review of "Faces in the Water: The York Trilogy, Book Two," in* The Horn Book Magazine, *Vol. LVII, No. 4, August, 1981, p. 435.*

ALL BECAUSE I'M OLDER (1981)

Eight-year-old John is convinced that his troubles are caused by the machinations of his five-year-old brother. Peter *always* starts something bad, John finishes it, and John is the one who gets in trouble. A truly classic trip to the grocery store with father and baby sister has everything going wrong in a very funny way. It ends happily with both boys doing things *right* on the drive home. . . . Timely situations, two believable little boys, and some funny scenes will make this a winner in the middle grades.

> *Barbara Baker, in a review of "All Because I'm Older," in* Children's Book Review Service, *Vol. 9, No. 14, August, 1981, p. 124.*

This isn't a story but a series of anecdotes that demonstrate (according to John's viewpoint) the pathetic plight of the innocent older child. Nicely told, not very substantial, often funny, and realistic enough to evoke a recognition reflex on the part of any current or former young siblings.

> *Zena Sutherland, in a review of "All Because I'm Older," in* Bulletin of the Center for Children's Books, *Vol. 35, No. 2, October, 1981, p. 34.*

The story line paints a pretty true picture of family dynamics—only John's constant lamentation over his unfair position as the oldest child may be overdrawn (in fact, it makes him sound on the plaintive, whiny side). To Naylor's credit, she plants sympathy with the focal character without causing John's siblings to seem mean, stupid, or in any way unlikable. This book is a possibility for inexperienced readers because of its episodic structure; vignettes vary in length, but average on the short side of one page.

> *Liza Bliss, in a review of "All Because I'm Older," in* School Library Journal, *Vol. 28, No. 4, December, 1981, p. 67.*

FOOTPRINTS AT THE WINDOW (1981)

In the two earlier volumes of Naylor's York Trilogy, American teenager Dan Roberts becomes involved with a gypsy family he meets while visiting in York, England, and later with different incarnations of that same family as tribespeople in Roman England and, back home, as migrant gypsies near his Grandmother's farm on the Susquehanna. Some of the same figures turn up among his grandmother's ancestors and, in this volume, Dan is reunited with another version of the family back in York during the bubonic plague. Dan's felt need to rescue the daughter of the family persists through all these encounters, as does a Roman coin that keeps changing hands with varying implications. Here, in his time-trip to York, Dan finally accomplishes his mission by obtaining a horse that will take the girl to a plague-free area. Once he does, the ghosts from other times stop bothering him and he is able to take a more philosophical approach to the other worry that has plagued him through all three volumes: the possibility that his father, and thus he too, might have the genes for Huntington's disease. But the connection between this worry and all the other business remains remote and arbitrary; the rescue that should climax the time-trips' action is flat and minor, and certainly insufficient reason for all the ghostly disturbances of the usual order of things; the first part of the book consists entirely of reminders of previous visions and encounters, confusing to new readers and dramatic to none; and the end leaves you feeling that you've been jerked through a lot of mumbo-jumbo and shifting veils to no particular purpose.

> *A review of "Footprints at the Window," in* Kirkus Reviews, *Vol. XLIX, No. 19, October 1, 1981, p. 1241.*

This is an imaginative tale for young readers who are becoming slightly too old for comic books and are still a bit too young for Tolstoy. The plot is a simple one; the style quite easy to follow. The touches of mystery and suspense immediately call to mind the adventures of Nancy Drew and the Hardy Boys.

One point on which Naylor is to be especially commended is her presentation of the mature judgments and sound values of the characters. When Dan realizes that Orlenda is in danger from the plague, his thoughts are turned away from himself and towards another's safety. Bill, Dan's friend and editor of the school newspaper, is concerned about the potential for nuclear conflict and doesn't spend his time eating ice cream in front of the TV.

Overall, this book is a fine one for young people. It will instruct as well as entertain.

> *Joseph P. Manfredi, in a review of "Footprints at the Window," in* Best Sellers, *Vol. 41, No. 8, November, 1981, p. 319.*

The final volume of the series is so tightly bound to its companions that it is difficult to consider separately.... The suspense that propelled the previous volumes is tempered somewhat as Dan considers the metaphysical questions behind his adventures; and younger readers intrigued by the element of fantasy may be impatient with his contemplation of life and death, war and chance. Still, for the thoughtful reader the author provides an accessible grip on such questions within the framework of a believable fantasy.

> *Dudley B. Carlson, in a review of "Footprints at the Window: The York Trilogy, Book Three," in* The Horn Book Magazine, *Vol. LVIII, No. 1, February, 1982, p. 54.*

A STRING OF CHANCES (1982)

Evie Hutchins, daughter of a small-town fundamentalist preacher, has never seriously questioned her faith until her sixteenth summer, which she spends with her cousin Donna Jean and husband Tom Rawley to help out when their baby is born. Various people and experiences awaken a questioning in Evie, but the shattering impact of the tragic crib death of the Rawleys' beloved baby pushes her first into a denial of faith and then into a search for a God in whom she can believe. Though the story centers on Evie's emotions and experiences, making her

a fully realized character, it also gives other characters enough depth and emotional play to make them both viable and essential to the plot. Specific scenes and themes—contemplation of religious beliefs; the baby's birth, which is handled with tasteful realism; the stark grief felt by the parents and by Evie when the baby dies and their eventual coming to grips with his death; intergenerational and peer interactions and relationships; small-town and family life—all smoothly converge and interlock to give vivid dimension to the story and to delineate the individuals within it. The effect is totally involving and moving.

> *Sally Estes, in a review of "A String of Chances," in* Booklist, *Vol. 78, No. 22, August, 1982, p. 1518.*

The style is sensible and warm, but not florid. Naylor's handling of a large cast of characters is skillful, and her depiction of contemporary small-town life is exact and evocative, without sentimentality.

> *Roger Sutton, in a review of "A String of Chances," in* School Library Journal, *Vol. 29, No. 1, September, 1982, p. 142.*

[Evie's story] has a deft fusion of major plot threads (the relationships with Matt and another boy, Evie's love for the baby and grief at his death, and her despair and anger as she begins to examine her doubts about the tenets of her faith) and minor ones. Characterization and dialogue are handled with smoothness and depth, as Evie moves toward tolerance of others and understanding of herself.

> *Zena Sutherland, in a review of "A String of Chances," in* Bulletin of the Center for Children's Books, *Vol. 36, No. 2, October, 1982, p. 33.*

THE BOY WITH THE HELIUM HEAD (1982)

The boy with the helium head is a disturbing, silly fantasy.... Major flaws in the text are: unresolved sibling rivalry, Jonathan's inexplicably large feet and, most of all, playing out a child's bleak fear of doctors. All ends well, but the content is far too advanced for the picture-book format.

> *Leslie Chamberlin, in a review of "The Boy with the Helium Head," in* School Library Journal, *Vol. 29, No. 2, October, 1982, p. 144.*

Jonathan just knew it was going to be one of those days. If there's anything worse than an upcoming flu shot, it's the certainty that Duke Duncan is going to clobber him for sitting on Duke's sandwich. But Duke's plan is spoiled when the harried doctor who has been giving helium balloons to those receiving flu shots puts medicine in the balloon and helium in Jonathan's arm. Just as Duke is about to pounce—whish!—Jonathan floats up in the air away from his tormentor. After Jonathan's many adventures land him in the news media, Duke finds himself solidly in Jonathan's cheering section. Way too long, this nevertheless has some happy moments.... The leap into fantasy from what is at first a realistic story seems forced, but Jonathan's unexpected flight taps into a dream of many kids.

> *Ilene Cooper, in a review of "The Boy with the Helium Head," in* Booklist, *Vol. 79, No. 3, October 1, 1982, p. 248.*

Like many fantasies, this is based on one improbable premise; here the switch from realism . . . isn't quite believable; first, a doctor isn't likely to make such a mistake, second, helium shot into the arm wouldn't necessarily go into the head. . . . Mildly funny, but contrived.

> *Zena Sutherland, in a review of "The Boy with the Helium Head," in* Bulletin of the Center for Children's Books, *Vol. 36, No. 4, December, 1982, p. 74.*

NEVER BORN A HERO (1982)

Never Born A Hero is a collection of 15 "true to life" stories for and about "young teens." The attractive cover photograph and the full page photographs sprinkled throughout the book are an accurate clue to its text. Young people are shown alone, with adults, with friends, thinking, playing, and working. They are quite normal and natural looking in their sweatshirts, sweaters or polo shirts with jeans or corduroys. Maybe somewhat unusual, though, is that they are all well groomed, and while some may be pensive, they all are content.

These fast-paced stories are all about young people who are victorious. Although most of the narrations are third person, all of the stories are told from the young characters' points of view. The reader lives through various realistic difficulties with them and watches them overcome such personal flaws as self-ishness, narrow-mindedness, and self-consciousness. The difficulties, like parents' divorces, diabetes, gossip, or strict parents, don't always go away, but the characters' inability to cope with them does.

> *Holly Ein Kane, in a review of "Never Born a Hero," in* Voice of Youth Advocates, *Vol. 6, No. 1, April, 1983, p. 40.*

THE SOLOMON SYSTEM (1983)

Thanks to the artless, sometimes naturally humorous and moving voice of the 13-year-old narrator, Naylor's new novel is one of relatively few honest and effective stories for young readers about broken families. At summer camp, Ted Solomon trusts the comradeship of his brother Nory, 16, to help him ease the worry of their parents' impending divorce. But this year, Nory's fancies run to girls; Ted sees the collapse of the "Solomon System" that has been the boys' armor in earlier crises. Even Grandma Rose, the brothers' champion, can't offer much now but love. Naylor's uncontrived handling of the plot, with the two boys working out their sad problem, leads to a satisfying close. The characters are all appealing, even the squabbling parents, and the author merits extra points for giving us Grandma Rose, a person, not a stereotypical Jewish mother.

> *A review of "The Solomon System," in* Publishers Weekly, *Vol. 224, No. 13, September 23, 1983, p. 72.*

A very realistic look at the heartache and loneliness that divorce causes children to bear. The selfishness and immaturity of the parents is well balanced against the finely drawn personalities of the two brothers. Each boy suffers changes in his personality and outlook before the conclusion and the "Solomon system" changes as well. Readers of *It's Not the End of the World* (1972) by Judy Blume, *Guy Lenny* (1977) by Harry Mazer or Angell's *What's Best for You* (1981) will also like this one.

> *Gayle Berge, in a review of "The Solomon System," in* School Library Journal, *Vol. 30, No. 2, October, 1983, p. 161.*

OLD SADIE AND THE CHRISTMAS BEAR (1984)

Naylor weaves a spell, persuading us that her tender story could be true on so magic a time as Christmas Eve. Amos the bear awakens and tells his wife Esmerelda he's going out to investigate a strangeness in the air. Shuffling into town, Amos beholds ornately trimmed fir trees; he watches and listens as singers stroll from house to house. At the cottage of old Miss Sadie, who is almost blind, Amos receives a warm welcome and the invitation to supper. He accepts and they sit and visit like dear friends, sharing their treats with Miss Sadie's cat and even with the mice who venture out of hiding. Amos has lots to tell Esmerelda when he gets back to the cave. (pp. 436-37)

> *A review of "Old Sadie and the Christmas Bear," in* Publishers Weekly, *Vol. 226, No. 9, August 31, 1984, pp. 436-37.*

Soft pictures [by Patricia Montgomery Newton], touched with red tints, beautifully tactile but—especially in interior scenes—often crowded, illustrate a sentimentalized and not very convincing fantasy about a bear who comes out of hibernation, sensing something (Christmas, it develops) in the air. He drops in to share a meal with an elderly woman who is so near-sighted that she never realizes that her guest is a bear. (They have a conversation, of course.) When the bear goes, Old Sadie (as stereotypical as she can be) moves into his warm chair to continue her nap. That's the "gift" of the Christmas Bear. This is insubstantial as cotton candy, and almost as sugary.

> *Zena Sutherland, in a review of "Old Sadie and the Christmas Bear," in* Bulletin of the Center for Children's Books, *Vol. 38, No. 2, October, 1984, p. 33.*

NIGHT CRY (1984)

Naylor stretches a bit to pull the plot elements into a cohesive whole, but for most readers the facts that the heroine is intrepid (believably) and that suspense builds nicely in a dramatic story will compensate for what contrivance is used. Thirteen, motherless, living on a Mississippi farm, Ellen's disturbed when her father takes a salesman's job and leaves her for several days at a time. She's competent, but she's frightened by the horse that's thrown and killed her only brother, by the dire warnings of an eccentric old neighbor, and by the strange man who's been doing farm work in return for food for himself and the sick wife Ellen's never seen. The man proves to be a kidnapper (his wife, not at all ill, is his associate) and it is Ellen who faces all her fears to rescue the four-year-old son of a wealthy man, receiving kudos and financial gain. Just this side of credible, the book is adequately written structurally and has some good (and some overdrawn) characterization; readers will enjoy the tension and the action.

> *Zena Sutherland, in a review of "Night Cry," in* Bulletin of the Center for Children's Books, *Vol. 37, No. 7, March, 1984, p. 132.*

A series of events plausibly lead to an exciting climax and satisfying resolution. Naylor skillfully creates a tangible setting effectively using all the senses. Readers can smell the lush southern growth, hear the thunder rumbling in the distance, feel summer's humidity. The characterizations are consistent and well developed; each one comes to life as the fast-paced, credible and suspenseful plot unfolds. Ellen's growth is evident as she gradually allows fearful beliefs based on Granny Bo's superstitious portentions to be replaced by growing acceptance and understanding of her broadening world.

> *Maria Salvadore, in a review of "Night Cry," in* School Library Journal, *Vol. 30, No. 8, April, 1984, p. 126.*

The dialogue is enriched by the backwoods dialect of a large cast of characters; and the sense of place integral to the author's fiction provides the backdrop for Ellen's suspenseful struggle to cope logically with unreasonable fears.

> *Charlotte W. Draper, in a review of "Night Cry," in* The Horn Book Magazine, *Vol. LX, No. 3, June, 1984, p. 331.*

Thirteen-year-old Ellen Stump is in two ways the heroine of this novel, set in the backwoods hill country of Mississippi. First, she is the main character, on stage all the time, and what we know as readers we experience through her senses and thoughts. Second, she is heroic in overcoming her greatest fear and saving another's life through deeds of daring. . . . So skillful is Naylor's portrayal of Ellen that aspects of the background and plot that might sound melodramatic are convincing, seen through the girl's eyes.

> *Carolyn Phelan, in a review of "Night Cry," in* Booklist, *Vol. 80, No. 21, July, 1984, p. 1550.*

THE DARK OF THE TUNNEL (1985)

Naylor combines political commentary with personal tragedy in her latest novel about a high school senior grappling with questions about death and responsibility as he leaves his youth behind. Generally one to keep things to himself, 17-year-old Craig Sheldon begins to doubt that strategy when he is suddenly confronted with the loss of his mother to incurable cancer. His tendency toward passivity and self-involvement is challenged further as he watches his uncle prepare for a totally ludicrous and costly civil defense drill, which ultimately becomes the vehicle of tragedy for a reclusive, disturbed Vietnam veteran. Naylor's story is heavy-handed and uneven—its separate parts and characters never quite gel—but she manages some genuine flashes of insight and emotion, especially as she portrays Craig's relationship with his 11-year-old brother, and her denunciation of governmental nuclear policies is not only an unusual focus for a teenage novel, but also an invitation for young adults to become involved. (pp. 1051-52)

> *Stephanie Zvirin, in a review of "The Dark of the Tunnel," in* Booklist, *Vol. 81, No. 14, March 15, 1985, pp. 1051-52.*

The need for communication and the effects of the lack of it are demonstrated throughout this story. . . . There are many characters, each with his own story which is an integral part of the whole. Naylor has made each of them a unique, three-dimensional person. Readers are plummeted into the depression that Craig experiences when he is deluged with problems and feels that he has no one with whom to discuss them. Gradually the understanding that more can be accomplished by being truthful with others than by trying to protect either them or yourself from reality emerges.

> *Nancy P. Reeder, in a review of "The Dark of the Tunnel," in* School Library Journal, *Vol. 31, No. 9, May, 1985, p. 103.*

The tunnel in this novel is a focal point for the author and for the reader. However, the tunnel's importance is more symbolic than realistic. . . . As the story progresses, Mrs. Sheldon's illness and the family's reactions to it occur against the backdrop of threatened nuclear war with Russia and their small community's plans for civilian defense, hence the real tunnel of the book's title. . . .

While the backdrop is well-handled with a wealth of interesting secondary characters, the focus of most of the book is really Mrs. Sheldon's *dying*, not only her death, and this is truly the strength of the novel. Naylor's handling of the dying of the boys' mother is exceptional. Here is the tunnel as it represents the problems of the main characters—and their attempts to work out their problems. Without going into great details, I would have to say that this is one of the best adolescent novels dealing with death that I have read, mainly since it concerns itself with the dying process and the recognition of the two young people and their mother. A book about dying can be both maudlin and melodramatic. A good book about dying— a confusing phrase in itself—can be a learning experience for every reader. This is one!

> *John R. Lord, in a review of "The Dark of the Tunnel," in* Voice of Youth Advocates, *Vol. 8, No. 3, August, 1985, p. 188.*

THE AGONY OF ALICE (1985)

Motherless Alice goes through sixth grade in an agony of humiliation, longing for a female role model to show her how to behave. Her father tries his best, but he can't help her with things like buying her first bra, and the Sears catalog only confuses her. She's grateful when the girlfriend of her older brother Lester talks to her about pantyhose and about how to take care of your cuticles—"I didn't even know I *had* cuticles." she longs to be in the class of glamorous Miss Cole, and hates her teacher, pear-shaped Mrs. Plotkin. But Mrs. Plotkin proves kind; she knows Alice at her worst and likes her. Alice begins to accept herself: a cousin helps her buy a bra; her period comes and it's no big deal; she reaches out to comfort her brother in trouble, and they have "an entire conversation without being rude to each other once." Although the resolution is a little too easy, Naylor's characters are drawn with subtlety and affection, and there is no heavy moralizing. Alice has just a glimpse of Miss Cole's shallow behavior. Mrs. Plotkin delivers few homilies besides telling Alice that her "agonies" happen to everyone. A wonderfully funny and touching story that will make readers smile with wry recognition. (pp. 264-65)

> *Hazel Rochman, in a review of "The Agony of Alice," in* Booklist, *Vol. 82, No. 3, October 1, 1985, pp. 264-65.*

Through a series of incidents both hilarious and poignant, Alice searches for a female to help her cope with her adolescent anxieties. . . . The lively style exhibits a deft touch at capturing the essence of an endearing heroine growing up without a mother. Alice's forthcoming fans will agonize with her and await her further adventures.

Caroline Ward Romans, in a review of "The Agony of Alice," in School Library Journal, *Vol. 32, No. 5, January, 1986, p. 70.*

THE KEEPER (1986)

As Nick's father's paranoid behavior becomes increasingly bizarre, both he and his mother begin to accept the fact that Mr. Karpinski is mentally ill. Refusing to acknowledge his illness, Mr. Karpinski isn't about to have himself committed or even seek help, and Nick and his mother are nearly powerless to force him. Until he becomes a danger to himself or others, the family does the only thing they know how to—barely cope over a period of several painful months until Mr. Karpinski deteriorates to the point where committing him is clearly the only alternative. As Naylor charts this man's descent into madness, she also attunes readers to the feelings of Nick and his mother and the dynamics these emotions create: Mrs. Karpinski initially refuses to acknowledge her husband's symptoms and, when they are all too clear, postpones getting help. Nick, who readily grasps the seriousness of his father's problem, feels a terrible paralysis when it comes to taking—or provoking—action that will result in his father's unwilling commitment. Yet despite all this anguish, life goes on. Nick develops a circle of friends and, in the midst of the painful chaos at home, manages to go out on a successful first date. Loosely based on Naylor's adult book, *Crazy Love: An Autobiographical Account of Marriage and Madness,* this is a sensitively wrought novel with no happy ending but certainly with an affirmation of individual strength and emotional survival in the face of adversity.

Denise M. Wilms, in a review of "The Keeper," in Booklist, *Vol. 82, No. 15, April 1, 1986, p. 1144.*

The focus on the problem is unrelenting, but the story is grippingly detailed, with characters emerging full-dimensioned rather than being cast into roles of typical reaction (the exception to this is a girl who breaks her date with Nick after his father's hospitalization). Nick's stages of realization, anger, and pain are subtly developed, as is his mother's realistic mixture of strength and limitation and two school friends' genuine affection for Nick. (p. 176)

A review of "The Keeper," in Bulletin of the Center for Children's Books, *Vol. 39, No. 9, May, 1986, pp. 175-76.*

Mental illness of a parent is not a subject commonly dealt with in books for young people, yet it must happen more frequently than we are aware of. The author gives us a meticulous description, almost a case history, of the terrifying transformation of Jacob Karpinski from a quiet, but loving and conscientious, husband and father into a paranoid, dangerous madman. . . . Although Wanda [Nick's mother] is a weak character and certainly ill-advised in hiding their problems and Nick seems at times to be a mere sounding board, the author is extremely adept at showing us the destruction of comfort and happiness and the horror and misery of having someone we know and love turn into a frightening, suspicious stranger. A book of considerable power on a subject that affects many people. (pp. 598-99)

Ann A. Flowers, in a review of "The Keeper," in The Horn Book Magazine, *Vol. LXII, No. 5, September-October, 1986, pp. 598-99.*

THE BODIES IN THE BESSLEDORF HOTEL (1986)

Naylor dishes up a frothy, light-hearted farce for young mystery readers. The story centers around the strange happenings at the Bessledorf Hotel in Middleburg, Indiana, which Bernie Magruder's father manages. The trouble starts when two guests die in their hotel rooms—but the bodies disappear. The situation obviously threatens Mr. Magruder's job, and the family valiantly attempts to keep the hotel's business afloat. However, after a body from the funeral parlor next door appears in one of the rooms, the hotel owner dismisses the Magruders in no uncertain terms. In the meantime, Bernie's mother has received a rose and a mysterious love letter, and Bernie worries that she will leave the family. As it turns out, Mrs. Magruder's suitor from the past is the key to the mystery, and all ends well for the Magruders and the Bessledorf Hotel. One jarring note is the dialogue of the cleaning woman, whose poor grammar may be a weak attempt to show that she is black. Aside from that, both avid and reluctant readers should enjoy this zany diversionary tale.

Cynthia Percak Infantino, in a review of "The Bodies in the Bessledorf Hotel," in School Library Journal, *Vol. 33, No. 4, December, 1986, p. 107.*

The subject of bodies, which I feared might be a bit touchy, is treated comically. On the book's opening page, Officer Feeney of the local police walks around the park with Bernie "talking bodies," as the author puts it. Since the Bessledorf Hotel is right next door to a funeral parlor, Bernie has seen one corpse. Officer Feeney, however, admits to having seen a total of six. "What do they look like, really?" Bernie, as any child might, asks. "Same as when they were alive," Feeney tells him, "but a bit more relaxed." Throughout the book, Naylor gives us one-liners like these.

And her talent for caricature is just as great.

When the hotel regulars gather in the hall, screaming and gesturing and in one case even writing obituaries in rhyme, it's hard not to laugh out loud. Even the pets, a Great Dane named Mixed Blessing and two cats called Lewis and Clark, are funny. But best rendered is Bernie's wacky family. His parents are gems, but his older sister Delores, who works in a parachute factory, isn't far behind. And Bernie's younger brother, Lester, gets center stage for a page or two as he churns up a gloppy drink that will test, if not exercise, every reader's gag reflex.

As I neared the close of this volume, I just couldn't believe that Naylor was going to be able to tie up the seemingly disparate threads of plot. I'm happy to report that she does so in a way that will surprise and please.

Carolyn Banks, "Murder Most Hilarious," in Book World—The Washington Post, *December 14, 1986, p. 8.*

The ending is more than slightly concocted (the Magruders are vindicated) when the culprit is caught due to the efforts of Bernie and his friends, but the light tone, the comic moments, the action, and the element of mystery should make the story appealing.

Zena Sutherland, in a review of "The Bodies in the Bessledorf Hotel," in Bulletin of the Center for Children's Books, *Vol. 40, No. 5, January, 1987, p. 94.*

THE YEAR OF THE GOPHER (1987)

Despite (or, more likely, because of) his father's insistence upon an Ivy League education, George doesn't want to go to college—not until he knows better what he wants to do. "I mean, if you don't know where you're going, you won't know if you're halfway to the place you're supposed to be, if you get what I mean." So, after intentionally botching up his applications, George stays home to work as a "go-fer," first at a garden nursery, then as a bicycling messenger. While George's narration—of the changes in his family relations, escapades with friends, his first sexual experience—is appealingly ingenuous, it gets bogged down with superficial insights tacked on to each event, insights readers could easily spot for themselves. George and his buddies are well-drawn in effective (if not complex) characterizations; his "achievement-oriented" parents seem two-dimensional, evolving only in service to the overstated theme.

> *R. S., in a review of "The Year of the Gopher," in* Bulletin of the Center for Children's Books, *Vol. 40, No. 9, May, 1987, p. 175.*

Pressured college-bound YAs will identify with George's confusion and applaud his rebellion against parents who seem more interested in how the world views the family than in what's right for each family member. Naylor's realistic portrayal of a teenage boy rings very true to anyone who has ever lived with one!

A delightful and insightful story, lighter than some of Naylor's other books; with a plucky, likable hero.

> *Carole A. Barham, in a review of "The Year of the Gopher," in* Voice of Youth Advocates, *Vol. 10, No. 2, June, 1987, p. 81.*

The first-person contemporary novel provides a thought-provoking look at an achievement-oriented family; by probing effectively into their relationships, the author has created an interesting and intricate web of emotions. George makes a believable, articulate narrator whose peaks and valleys will surely be familiar geography to young adult readers. (p. 473)

> *Karen Jameyson, in a review of "The Year of the Gopher," in* The Horn Book Magazine, *Vol. LXIII, No. 4, July-August, 1987, pp. 472-73.*

THE BABY, THE BED, AND THE ROSE (1987)

This picture book makes ordinary moments of family life interesting, appealing, and comforting. Molly is fussing, and neither a diaper change nor food settle her down. Mom, Molly's two loving brothers, and Grandpa comfort the restless baby. Crayon and pencil drawings [by Mary Szilagyi] focus on the baby, but the entire household will get readers' attention. Children will feel the love in this family through the smooth text and softly-colored illustrations, and they'll appreciate the gently surprising ending.

> *Anna Biagioni Hart, in a review of "The Baby, the Bed, and the Rose," in* School Library Journal, *Vol. 33, No. 10, June-July, 1987, p. 87.*

This warm story, although self-consciously told, basks in an aura of familial love and sharing. Its extreme emphasis on positive interplay only, however, lends it a somewhat unnatural cast.

> *P. H., in a review of "The Baby, the Bed, and the Rose," in* Children's Book Review Service, *Vol. 15, No. 14, August, 1987, p. 150.*

BEETLES, LIGHTLY TOASTED (1987)

Out to win the annual essay prize (subject: conservation), Andy devises three protein-rich recipes with unusual ingredients.

Designed to elicit the sort of ingenuity the prize-donor likes to remember in his late fifth-grade son (lost in a tumble from a local Iowa silo), this year's topic at first provokes yawns. But when rival Cousin Jack enters, Andy is galvanized into action. Writing to an expert for ideas, he soon produces brownies flecked with crunchy beetles, crisp fried worms, and grub-laced egg salad, each of which is tried on unsuspecting friends and relatives, though Andy himself (the ultimate picky eater) abstains. Jack and Andy tie as winners, and Andy courageously faces the consequences: he consumes his inventions for the benefit of the local paper's photographer—and to the satisfaction of the previous unwitting samplers.

Reminiscent of Rockwell's ever-popular *How to Eat Fried Worms*, this almost-as-funny story is a bit less frivolous. With its realistically-drawn extended farm family and classroom rivalries and friendships, it is more than humorous. Andy's aversion to prickly Aunt Wanda's cooking (featuring Okra Surprise) and his friendship with Sam, whose family has opened a soul-food restaurant that serves delicious food, suggest thoughtful consideration of what people find edible and why. And the final scene where the three boys share Andy's concoctions is not only hilarious but also one of those moments of truth where old antagonists see each other with new appreciation. This should be popular.

> *A review of "Beetles, Lightly Toasted," in* Kirkus Reviews, *Vol. LV, No. 12, July 1, 1987, p. 997.*

This fast-paced novel, with its likable protagonist and strongly evoked rural Iowa farm setting, will remind readers of Thomas Rockwell's *How to Eat Fried Worms*. But the family of black characters, described as having "skin the color of gravy," emerges as tired stereotypes. They run a soul-food restaurant and eat fried chicken, catfish and hush puppies; the kids slap each other's hands and say, "Hey, man, gimme five!" and "All right!" and they tend to drop verbs, as in "How you doing?" Though the interracial friendship between Andy and Sam is well-intentioned and serves as a positive element in the story, Sam the character is merely one-dimensional, a collage of hackneyed clichés. And such disappointment is hard to ignore, coming from the notable author.

> *A review of "Beetles, Lightly Toasted," in* Publishers Weekly, *Vol. 232, No. 9, August 28, 1987, p. 80.*

The premise of the insect eating is thinly stretched—in fact, the book is half over before the first antenna is downed. Meanwhile, readers must digest a medley of vignettes and characters—the family that owns the local soul food restaurant, a rivalry between Andy and a spoiled cousin, and a crusty aunt with a near-poisonous okra recipe. Intended to depict life in this close rural community, these subplots bounce off one another randomly, only to fall predictably into place at the book's close. The plot is further elongated by the sometimes blow-by-blow nature of its telling, which further slows an already languorous pace. Andy's motives seem more spiteful than funny, leaving readers' sympathies with his victims. Doubtless the enticing nature of the title and the familiarity of the author's name will tempt readers to pick up the book, but they will find it meager fare with too long a wait between courses.

> *Joanne Aswell, in a review of "Beetles, Lightly Toasted," in* School Library Journal, *Vol. 34, No. 2, October, 1987, p. 128.*

MAUDIE IN THE MIDDLE (with Lura Schield Reynolds, 1988)

Naylor bases this novel on the remembrances of her mother, who is credited as coauthor. Set in the early 1900s, its heroine is eight-year-old Maudie Mae Simms, stuck in the middle of seven children. Although Maudie loves her family, she resents the lack of special attention—her dream is to be her beloved Auntie Sylvie's godchild, so she can be number one with someone. Maudie feels if she were truly a good person she might make that dream come true. She does make the effort, but goodness ebbs and flows. For every moment of pure goodness, such as turning the other cheek when her brother spills her new perfume, there's a time when Maudie listens in on the partyline or, worse, plays on the roof. The authors present a warm, realistic look at life at the turn of the century, reminiscent of the early volumes in Maude Hart Lovelace's Betsy-Tacy series. And as in those books, religion plays an integral part in life, supporting characters are well realized, and readers have a heroine with whom they can identify despite the span of time.

> *Ilene Cooper, in a review of "Maudie in the Middle," in* Booklist, *Vol. 84, No. 15, April 1, 1988, p. 1352.*

All of the characters are marvelously believable. Each chapter covers a separate episode in Maudie's life, making the book good for reading aloud. Children who are searching for something after the "Little House" books or *Caddie Woodlawn* should enjoy Maudie.

> *Margaret C. Howell, in a review of "Maudie in the Middle," in* School Library Journal, *Vol. 35, No. 8, May, 1988, p. 100.*

Mordecai Richler

1931-

Canadian author of fiction and scriptwriter.

As a writer for children, Richler is recognized as the creator of *Jacob Two-Two Meets the Hooded Fang* (1976), a popular humorous fantasy for primary graders. As a writer for adults, he is renowned for creating realistic fiction and essays in which he reflects characteristic sarcasm and acerbic wit to satirize Canadian and Jewish culture by depicting a barbaric world filled with insecure, alienated inhabitants. Richler's fourth novel, *The Apprenticeship of Duddy Kravitz* (1956), which many critics still consider his best work, has long been a favorite with Canadian adolescents and has been used as a textbook in Canadian high schools. *Duddy Kravitz* is also noted for Richler's searingly accurate picture of life on St. Urbain Street in Montreal's Jewish ghetto—the area in which Richler grew up—during the 1940s. The protagonist, a motherless boy who lives in a world dominated by dishonest businessmen and petty criminals, sets out to acquire property by any possible means after misinterpreting his grandfather's advice that "a man without land is nobody." While tracking Duddy's progression from a conniving fifteen-year-old to a ruthless entrepreneur, Richler takes great pains to give his readers a sense of Duddy's predicament. Raised by a father who teaches him to idolize small-time racketeer Jerry "Boy Wonder" Dingleman and rejected by his family in favor of his scholarly older brother, Duddy searches for a hint that someone does—or could—love him. At the end of the novel, Duddy is a nineteen-year-old landowner who is rejected by his friends as well as by his grandfather, the one person he has genuinely tried to impress. Duddy is, however, embraced by his father, who sees in him the promise of another Boy Wonder. Observers note that Richler's ambivalence toward his protagonist, who is portrayed as both a grasping, self-centered opportunist and an underprivileged, confused teenager, forces readers to constantly reassess the character. In Richler's adult novel *St. Urbain's Horseman* (1971), Duddy reappears in a minor role; now middleaged, he is an unscrupulous, unloved millionaire.

In *Duddy Kravitz*, Richler analyzes the effect of society on the individual and strives to elicit sympathy for his main character, an attitude with which he also invests *Jacob Two-Two Meets the Hooded Fang*. The youngest of five children, Jacob has acquired his nickname from having to repeat everything twice before anyone will listen to him. Teased by his siblings, whose names are those of Richler's own children, and living in a world planned for—and by—grownups, Jacob dreams that he is spirited away to the horrible Slimers' Isle and put on trial by a group of adults simply for being a child. He is imprisoned in a dungeon presided over by the dreaded Hooded Fang, an ex-wrestler. Undaunted, Jacob uncovers the weaknesses of his jailer and saves the other children with whom he has been incarcerated. Originally begun as a bedtime tale to amuse Richler's youngest child, *Jacob Two-Two* is now considered a classic of Canadian juvenile literature. In its sequel *Jacob Two-Two and the Dinosaur* (1987), eight-year-old Jacob receives a small reptile, which grows into an enormous diplodocus, as a gift. The book follows Jacob and Dippy as they

successfully elude the malicious public officials intent on destroying the dinosaur.

While reviewers debate over the character of Duddy in *The Apprenticeship of Duddy Kravitz*, arguing whether he is a villain or a victim, they are nearly unanimous in viewing the novel as an impressive attempt to chronicle the inevitable corrupting influence of the postwar world on a young adult. Although the *Jacob Two-Two* books have met with a mixed reception, most observers applaud Richler's portrayal of a downtrodden but not defenseless child, and applaud the author's wit and true-to-life family situations. *Duddy Kravitz* and the *Jacob Two-Two* books generally are embraced with enthusiasm by the young, who appreciate Richler's sensitivity to their plight, the colloquial liveliness of his style, and the humor and fast pace of his narratives.

In 1976 *Jacob Two-Two Meets the Hooded Fang* received the Canadian Library Association Book of the Year for Children award and the first Ruth Schwartz Children's Book Award.

(See also *Contemporary Literary Criticism*, Vols. 3, 5, 9, 13, 18, 46; *Something about the Author*, Vols. 27, 44; *Contemporary Authors*, Vols. 65-68; *Dictionary of Literary Biography: Canadian Writers Since 1960*, Vol. 53; and *Authors in the News*, Vol. 1.)

AUTHOR'S COMMENTARY

Why do you write?

Doctors are seldom asked why they practice, shoemakers how come they cobble, or baseball players why they don't drive a coal truck instead, but again and again writers, like house-breakers, are asked why they do it.

Orwell, as might be expected, supplies the most honest answer in his essay "Why I Write":

"1. Sheer egoism. Desire to seem clever, to be talked about, to be remembered after death, to get your own back on grown-ups who snubbed you in childhood, etc. etc." To this I would add, egoism informed by imagination, style, and a desire to be known, yes, *but only on your own conditions.*

Nobody is more embittered than the neglected writer and, obviously, allowed a certain recognition, I am a happier and more generous man than I would otherwise be. But nothing I have done to win this recognition appals me, has gone against my nature. I fervently believe that all a writer should send into the marketplace to be judged is his own work; the rest should remain private: I deplore the writer as personality, however large and undoubted the talent, as is the case with Norman Mailer. I also do not believe in special license for so-called artistic temperament. After all, my problems, as I grudgingly come within spitting distance of middle age, are the same as anybody else's. Easier maybe. I can bend my anxieties to subversive uses. Making stories of them. When I'm not writing, I'm a husband and a father of five. Worried about pollution. The population explosion. My sons' report cards.

"2. Aesthetic enthusiasm. Perception of beauty in the external world, or, on the other hand, in words and their right arrangement." The agonies involved in creating a novel, the unsatisfying draft, the scenes you never get right, are redeemed by those rare and memorable days when, seemingly without reason, everything falls right. Bonus days. Blessed days when, drawing on resources unsuspected, you pluck ideas and prose out of your skull that you never dreamt yourself capable of.

Such, such are the real joys.

Unfortunately, I don't feel that I've ever been able to sustain such flights for a novel's length. So the passages that flow are balanced with those which were forced in the hothouse. Of all the novels I've written, it is *The Apprenticeship of Duddy Kravitz* and *Cocksure* which come closest to my intentions and, therefore, give me the most pleasure. I should add that I'm still lumbered with the characters and ideas, the social concerns I first attempted in *The Acrobats.* Every serious writer has, I think, one theme, many variations to play on it.

Like any serious writer, I want to write one novel that will last, something that will make me remembered after death, and so I'm compelled to keep trying.

"3. Historical impulse. Desire to see things as they are. . . ." No matter how long I continue to live abroad, I do feel forever rooted in Montreal's St. Urbain Street. That was my time, my place, and I have elected myself to get it right.

"4. Political purpose—using the word 'political' in the widest possible sense. Desire to push the world in a certain direction, to alter other people's idea of the kind of society that they should strive after."

Not an overlarge consideration in my work, though I would say that any serious writer is a moralist and only incidentally an entertainer. (pp. 44-6)

> *Mordecai Richler, "Why I Write," in his* Notes on an Endangered Species and Others, *Alfred A. Knopf, 1974, pp. 36-48.*

THE APPRENTICESHIP OF DUDDY KRAVITZ   (1959)

What made Duddy Kravitz run was an old adage his grandfather used to repeat to him: "A man without land is nothing." This is the story of a Jewish Studs Lonigan growing up in Montreal and trying to live up to his grandfather's injunction. At the end, he has his land; but he also has lost the respect and friendship of those who cared for him. Although the dialogue and the writing are generally quite good, the story stretches the imagination in many places. It is moreover a coarse, earthy novel whose central character, aggressive and given to vulgar language, arouses little sympathy. The sly tirades against Judaism and Christianity may be regular fare in the gutters of Montreal but do not come off so well in a more restrained environment. Recommended to drugstore clientele but not to public libraries.

> *Norbert Bernstein, in a review of "The Apprenticeship of Duddy Kravitz," in* Library Journal, *Vol. 84, No. 17, October 1, 1959, p. 3058.*

Mordecai Richler's *The Apprenticeship of Duddy Kravitz* is a tough, raucously funny, boldly unsentimental novel about still another Jewish immigrant world—that of Montreal, rather than the more literally familiar one of Chicago, Brooklyn or the Bronx. (The speech and the frantic tug of war between generations, as well as the potato latkes, appear to turn out pretty much the same on either side of the border.) If this doesn't seem to be saying anything very special about Richler's book except that it is extremely skillful and has a rambunctious vitality not often encountered in novels about any world these days, one has only to read it side by side with *The Time of the Peaches,* Arthur Granit's account of his childhood in Brooklyn's Brownsville. It is a sharp reminder that writing by and about the sons and daughters of Russian immigrant Jews, in the last 10 years or so, has taken on a kind of slick-magazine haze of sentimental "niceness," and has relied too much on a neat and tidy pastiche of "colorful" detail and lovable old picturesque types talking a tiresomely cute Yiddish-English. Though many of these writers are blessed with very acute ears and definite memories, they have settled for creating a phony "sweet" folklore for its own sake—as though the fact that a writer had grown up in this immigrant world could make up for the fact that at bottom he had absolutely nothing to say about it.

But Richler, like Saul Bellow before him, is more concerned with being a novelist than a Nice Jewish Boy, and he has a great deal to feel and say and evoke about his at once appalling and appealing roughneck Duddy Kravitz, who certainly is Jewish but, just as certainly, isn't nice and doesn't give a damn who knows it. Fifteen years old when we first encounter him, a skinny, narrow-chested punk bullying his teachers into early straitjackets at Fletcher's Field High School, Duddy is not quite 20 when the author lets him go, but the brevity of the time span doesn't matter; what does is the unsparing, searching, powerfully insistent look one is given at Duddy Kravitz and his family, a novel in which nothing is simplified, everything is ventured, and a memorable fictional complexity is gained.

By the end of Duddy's apprenticeship, one knows his frenzied, demoniacally ambitious, pathetic, generous, awkward, brash, vulgarly overweening, devoted and at the same time traitorous soul as no sequel could possibly improve upon.

In some ways, Duddy is a blood brother to Budd Schulberg's Sammy Glick—but with some important differences. What made Sammy run—at least, Schulberg was content to leave it at that—was a meanhearted, ruthless, brutal greed for power, for the fleshpots that go with power, and the women who go with the fleshpots. Duddy, like Sammy, is certainly one possessed, and his hunger to succeed is nothing if not rampageous, but Duddy has a vision that goes beyond himself. When he was seven, his stern and inflexibly proud grandfather Simcha, who persisted in worrying the earth in the yard back of his shoemaker's shop though the vegetables always came up scrawny and stunted, had said to his grandson, ''A man without land is nobody. Remember that, Duddel.'' Land was the spur that drove Duddy after that—to own land was the measure of "being somebody," and over and again Duddy keeps saying to himself, ''I'm going to be somebody.'' (p. 18)

[Like] a bush-league Columbus, Duddy stumbles on the land he wants, on an idyllic lake in the Laurentians. He hurls himself, sparing neither himself nor any scruples that might be lurking inside him, into a dozen money-making schemes at once.

From this point, only one thing really matters—somehow, anyhow, getting the money to buy up that dream. (Some of this franticness also makes for some of Richler's more wildly inspired and hilarious comic writing—notably his account of Duddy's venture into private movie-making—of bar-mitzvahs and weddings—with an alcoholic English documentary-film man who turns out *the* arty-cinema experiment in claptrap surrealism to finish off that genre once and for all.) But the recklessness of Duddy's furious thrust to buy up his land before someone else can get it also leads to the permanent crippling of an innocent and pathetic friend, and to the loss of his girl Yvette, and to his committing the final unforgivable swindling sin against the one person who trusts him most and has least reason to trust him at all. When his grandfather finds out about this, Duddy loses him, too.

Yet if Richler had been aiming for just another portrait of a monumentally self-seeking scoundrel, *The Apprenticeship of Duddy Kravitz* would be a lesser book than it is, and only another variation on the theme of Sammy Glick. Where this novel leaps way out beyond Schulberg's class is in the unflinching comprehension Richler brings to his portrayal—at once sardonic, tender, harsh and sad—of a family, and of all the enigmatic and inexorable cross-strains of duty and love and hatred and resentment that course through members of a family in their feelings and acts toward one another. Perhaps because his mother died when he was a kid, Duddy never can escape what his father and Uncle Benjy and his beloved grandfather keep telling him—

> You've got to love them, Duddel. You've got to take them to your heart no matter what. They're the family, remember. . . .

No matter how cold-bloodedly Duddy cheats and hurts and double-crosses whomever he can, Duddy is the one who has to take time out from his frenzied conniving, and get his medical-student brother Lennie out of really serious trouble. When his rich Uncle Benjy, who always treated him like dirt and lavished his favors on Lennie, is dying, Duddy is the one who

has to bring his giddy and foolish aunt back to her husband's deathbed. But to assume that Richler is thus trying to show what a sweet boy Duddy really is would be to miss his point— he is interested in a reality about people more difficult to confront and to write about than easy answers can ever cope with.

What Duddy does for his family is part of what he helplessly, entirely is, almost despite himself, and not because a sudden "niceness" has bloomed in a formerly black heart. The delight and futility and bitterness and love that members of a family can inflict on each other give an almost intolerable dramatic force to the end of the novel. If it was his grandfather who instilled in Duddy his fierce vision of how to ''be somebody,'' it is his grandfather, finally, who turns his grandson's crass victory into a rejecion that robs it of all triumph. With the instinct blood endows, the one human being Duddy really cared to impress is the one who hurts him the most—perhaps because only this person can know where to aim and how to hit most woundingly. Refusing to believe in cant, but knowing why people like Duddy and his father have to rely on it, Richler can understand both the wonder and cruelty of family feeling without underestimating either. It is an enormously impressive achievement. (p. 19)

> *Pearl Kazin, ''Chicken Soup and the Jewish Novel,''* in The New Leader, *Vol. XLIII, No. 12, March 21, 1960, pp. 18-19.*

[Mordecai Richler's] first three novels are studies of ruined lives: André, the guilt-haunted Canadian artist, who is eventually murdered by the Nazi, Kraus, whose sister Theresa then commits suicide; the guilt-ridden homosexual, Derek, his equally guilty sister, Jessie, and her equally guilty husband, the alcoholic, Barney; the Wellington College professor, Theo Hall and his wife, Miriam; Norman, the American Fifth Amendment expatriate, whose brother is murdered by Ernst, the German youth whom Sally, the Toronto girl, ruins her life trying to save. All of these persons reach out, cry out, for any masks other than the ones they have.

And they testify to Richler's affinity with that side of modern life where the misbegotten wander through ruined Spains of self-pity, poisoned to the point of near and at times actual madness by self-loathing. However, Richler does not seek out these persons in order to demonstrate several times over that we are wrapped up like so many sweating sardines in world misery, world guilt, world sorrow. Like André, Norman and Noah, the protagonists of these novels, he is inside the misery looking for a way out. What looks out is a courageous intelligence struggling to realize that the tormented sleep of self loathing which he explores is just that—a sleep, a dream, a nightmare: but not the reality.

In his fourth novel, *The Apprenticeship of Duddy Kravitz,* the sleeper begins to come awake. The nightmare is still there, but it is not the same nightmare. In *The Acrobats* and *A Choice of Enemies,* Richler chooses areas of world guilt as the basis for dream terror. The Spanish war, the second world war, the victims of these wars and of their ideologies make up the manifest content, the general human failure which images and invites the latent personal failures represented. People whose lives have gone smash drift into areas where life has gone smash and consort with the ghosts who have survived. In *Duddy Kravitz* the scope contracts. Both the ghosts who make up the nightmare and the ideologies through which they wander have faded from mind. Duddy's father, his brother Lenny, his uncle and aunt, his teacher MacPherson, his friend Virgil, his enemy

Dingleman, and his shiksa Yvette all live tangled lives in a world where they do not know themselves. But they are caught up by personal disorders rather than world disorder, family strife rather than international strife, individual conflict rather than ideological conflict. And within the localized dream we meet an entirely different dreamer. We meet the direct intelligence and colloquial exuberance that is Duddy's style—and Richler's.

T. S. Eliot has said that poetry in our time is a mug's game. So is fiction, and Richler is one of the mugs. Duddy has ceased to care for appearances and this insouciance releases him from the nightmare. All of the other people in the novel cannot possess themselves because their vital energies are devoted full-time to maintaining the false appearances in terms of which they identify themselves. These appearances—the cultural, ethical, communal pretensions to which they cling—mask over but scarcely conceal the distinctly uncultured, unethical, isolated actuality in which they participate. Hence the importance in their lives of Dingleman, the Boy Wonder, who is a projection of their actual longings to be at ease in Zion in a Cadillac at the same time as he is a projection of the limitation of these longings, being hopelessly crippled. But Duddy, who has ceased to care for appearances, sees people for what they are, himself included. And what he sees, he accepts—himself included. In an acquisitive world he is exuberantly acquisitive. When he is tricked, he weeps. When threatened, he becomes dangerous. When attacked, he bites back. When befriended, he is generous. When hard-pressed he becomes frantic. When denied, he is filled with wrath. From the weave of this erratic shuttling, a self struggles into presence, a naive yet shrewd latter-day Huck Finn, floating on a battered money raft down a sleazy neon river through a drift of lives, wanting to light out for somewhere, wanting somewhere to light out for.

Plato tells us that when a new music is heard the walls of the city tremble. The music in Duddy Kravitz is where in novels it always is, in the style. The groove in which the style runs is that of an exuberance, shifting into exaggeration, shifting into those distortions by which Richler achieves his comic vision of Montreal. The finest parts of the novel are those in which Richler most freely indulges the distortions: the sequence in which the documentary film director Friar produces a wedding ceremony masterpiece which views like the stream of consciousness of a lunatic, a fantasia of the contemporary mind; the entire portrait of Virgil who wants to organize the epileptics of the world and be "their Sister Kenny", as well as the more sombre portraits of Dingleman and Duddy's aunt Ida. Because Duddy has ceased to care for appearances, he moves past all of the genteel surfaces of the city and encounters an actuality in which all that is characteristically human has retreated to small corners of consciousness and life becomes a grotesque game played by bewildered grotesques. The persons who make up this gallery not only fail to invoke self but can scarcely recognize what it is to be a human being. They are like uncertain creatures in a fabulous but confusing zoo, not sure why they are there, not even sure what human forest they once inhabited.

They testify in the language of the sometimes comic, sometimes grim, distortions Richler has created to the oppressive weight of doubt, guilt, remorse, shame and regret that history has imposed upon modern man, particularly upon man in the city, where the effects of history, most closely organized, are most acutely felt. The greater the system of threats to self, the more extensive the system of appearances needed to ward off those threats, the more marked the distortions of characteristic human need and desire. And the more marked the distortions, the more difficult the artist's task. For sensibility, that active sum of the artist's self, never does exist in relation to itself alone. It exists in relation to what is—actual persons, an actual city, actual lives. When the impact of accomplished history imposes distortions upon that actuality, sensibility must adjust itself to the distortions. The story of these adjustments is, I think, the most significant feature of North American fiction in our time. Long ago and far away, before World War One o'clock, Theodore Dreiser could look at the world with direct eyes. Characteristic human impulses of love, sorrow, hope, fear, existed in the actual world as love, sorrow, hope, fear; and Dreiser could direct his powerful sensibility into representation which was, as they say, "like life". But after World War One, in The Great Gatsby, possibly the most significant of the between-wars novels, there is open recognition of a distorted actuality necessitating a re-ordering of sensibility, one which both Gatsby and Fitzgerald fail to achieve.

Since World War Two the need for adjustment has become even more marked, simply because the distortions have become more pronounced. In Duddy Kravitz, Richler follows closely in the groove of Duddy's exuberance and on out into the exaggerations and distortions which make up his adjustment to actual Montreal. By doing so he is able to achieve an authentic relationship to life in that city—Duddy's dream of Caliban along the drear streets of Zoo. In this Richler is at one with the considerable group of contemporary writers—call them mugs, call them angry, call them beat—who all are seeking in their art those re-adjustments which will permit them to relate their sensibilities to what actually is. History has had and continues to have her say. These writers are trying to answer back. If the vision which Richler achieves in answer to history jars upon our sensibilities, that is because we have all heard of Prospero's cloud capped towers and gorgeous palaces. Yet, if the style which conveys the vision twangles from glib to brash, from colloquial to obscene, that is because the true North American tone, at long past World War Two o'clock, is much closer to that of Caliban than ever it has been to that of Prospero whose magic was a European magic, long sunk from sight, and whose daughter and her beau and their world are out of fashion like old tunes or like the lovers on Keats' urn, maybe forever but address unknown. The brave new world toward which Duddy's self quickens is the lake property he covets throughout the novel and finally possesses. When he dives in, seeking a rebirth, he scrapes bottom. But he doesn't care, he doesn't care, he doesn't care. Which is why the mug can make with the music.

D. H. Lawrence contended that in the visions of art a relatively finer vision is substituted for the relatively cruder visions extant. But in North America . . . , finer is relatively crude, because frequently untrue, and crude can be relatively fine. All too often, in fiction as in life, those pretensions which we seek out because they make us fine provide false furnishings for the actual house in which we live. This fine is crude. Duddy, who would not know a pretension if he met one, wanders for this reason by accident and mostly unaware into the actual house. His crude is relatively fine. True, there are no gods hovering over Duddy's lake, no grandiose hotel, no summer camp for children. There is only old mother North America with her snow hair, her mountain forehead, her prairie eyes, and her wolf teeth, her wind songs and her vague head of old Indian memories. And what has she to do with Duddy Kravitz? A lot, I think. For when the house is repossessed the gods come back—snow gods, dust gods, wind gods, wolf gods—but life gods too. And life is the value. When history conspires against life, ruining the house, life will fight back in the only way it can, by not caring. Heavy, heavy doesn't hang over Duddy's head. And that is his value. (pp. 44-8)

> Warren Tallman, "Wolf in the Snow, Part Two: The House Repossessed," in Canadian Literature, No. 6, Autumn, 1960, pp. 41-8.

[The following excerpt originally appeared in the Summer, 1966 issue of Canadian Literature.*]*

The publication of Mordecai Richler's ***The Apprenticeship of Duddy Kravitz*** and Hugh MacLennan's *The Watch that Ends the Night* makes 1959 one of the important years for recent Canadian fiction. The two works seem at first to be strangely paired. One is a pungently ironic comedy, the other a serious metaphysical study that verges at times on the sentimental. Richler relies on a sprawling picaresque method, and MacLennan on a muted allegory. Even their flaws are different. The tendency to verboseness that afflicts the end of MacLennan's book is nowhere found in Richler's, but Richler will sacrifice the overall balance of his novel for the sake of big comic set scenes. Fortunately his novel survives because his wit is successful, just as MacLennan's work succeeds because the reader becomes sympathetically involved in the reality which the author has created. Yet for all their differences, the two works have the same basic situation. The discovery and habitation of a new land becomes a metaphor for an attitude of mind, and that attitude is at the forefront of present literary thought.

Richler's novel is concerned with the apprenticeship, the voyage, as it were, that ultimately takes Duddy to a new world and gives him the power to create there a recognizable individuality. His childhood position is analogous to that of Jerome Martell in *The Watch that Ends the Night*. While Jerome has known no father, Duddy at the age of fifteen has been unable to find in his father the qualities he wants to admire, and he invents an extra brother Bradley to satisfy this need. While Jerome has not experienced the ordinary expressions of love from his mother, Duddy has not known his mother and is therefore unsure of ever having experienced that love himself. He "couldn't bring himself to risk" asking about this, a key phrase, considering what he will risk, for his incomprehension either of love or of relationship awaits his discovery of an acceptable self. Like Jerome he has a journey to go through part of life, not only inevitable but necessary.

Exactly where the journey should aim and should end is Duddy's problem. When he was only seven he had been told by his grandfather: "A man without land is nobody. Remember that, Duddel." To find and own land becomes in time, therefore, equated in Duddy's mind with the identity for which he also seeks. But to be a somebody is more than this; to be a somebody is to be adult, not only in the self, but also recognized as being adult by a world to which the self bears some relationship. Maturity does not occur with the discovery of a new world, for this tends not to be a satisfactory end in itself. The dimensions of the new world are greater than the old identity can fill out, and there must be a realistic matching between an individual's potentialities and the place he can occupy. Duddy notes that "South America . . . could no longer be discovered. It had been found." But in re-enacting not only the Canadian but also the twentieth-century conflict, he can find a smaller niche elsewhere.

The humour that pervades the book is not gentle and it serves a quite different purpose from that in, for example, Mitchell's *Who Has Seen the Wind;* there is no necessity here to prevent sentimentality from repelling the reader. Duddy moves through a complicated but essentially extra-human sequence of events which, because incongruous, excites laughter. The laughter is directed at an outsider to the ordinary human predicament whose conflict is yet typical of it, and because he can surmount his difficulties in unorthodox and cumulatively extravagant ways, he wins, like Donleavy's Ginger Man, a sort of admiration without respect, a sufferance without approval, an attraction without sympathy, and an attachment without involved concern. At once more than the conventional society and an inherent element in it, Duddy follows a course of life in order to locate an appropriate pattern for it. Though this is pursued in iconoclastic—but innocent, and therefore laughable—terms, it illustrates a growth to maturity which is fundamentally parallel to the serious situations involving MacLennan's George Stewart. The changes that take place in Duddy prepare him for the discovery of Lac St. Pierre, and the discovery is an essential step in his growing up.

Duddy is a comer; he pushes his way to success not by having any idea of a reasonable means to do this, but rather by not having any idea and so using every means as though it were a reasonable one. The losses he incurs in a crooked roulette game stem from his naïveté, and they recall his earlier loss of a much smaller capital invested in a stock of obscene comic books. His earlier reaction had been to burn the stock for fear of being caught with it; the reaction at Ste. Agathe is to run away; yet both are childish in a way that Duddy cannot be if he is to emerge from his apprenticeship in his own terms. The novel has its limited success because the reader will let Duddy have those terms; they reverse standard values, but they become values in themselves.

Because he is a comic figure, a sort of latter-day *picaron* seeking ruthlessly and ultimately successfully for social promotion, Richler must not cultivate for him the reader's pity. If there were a total identification between the reader and the central character, the comic effect would be destroyed, for it is the sense of apartness, of differentiation between the character perceived and the concept the reader has of himself, that is part of the ironic comedy. Duddy, that is, must remain innocent even in success, even though he moves through his failures to a triumph that he does not fully comprehend. The identity that he finally achieves, successful in spite of its disregard for social convention, is both typical of the society he has been scorning and yet beyond it. The 'maturity' he reaches by the end of his apprenticeship is a recognition of a place in relation to society that will probably through time generate social acceptance as well; at that time, perhaps, reader and character could move closer together, but not until. His solution is distinct, then, from that found within a social code by George Stewart, though it is related to the individual one formulated by Jerome Martell.

Duddy's childishness concerning the comics and the roulette must be avoided not because it is socially irresponsible but because it does not contribute to the self for which he aims. Because he has been reared in the St. Urbain Street world of Montreal, a sort of Jewish enclave of low average income, he has been brought up to expect defensive protection as necessary. Several choices are open to him as routes to success: immersion in the Gentile world with concomitant loss of identity, continuation of the St. Urbain Street world of his childhood, participation in the establishment of the new Jewish state of Israel, or the achievement of an independence that will let him be himself in any situation. An attempt to achieve independence, however, makes Duddy uneasy and suspicious because he is insecure. The very defences that protect against any envelopment by the 'alien' culture preserve the St. Urbain Street childhood identity as well. Duddy's brother Lennie removes those defences in his contact with the Westmount Gentiles, but that society only consumes him. He thinks he finds there a freedom that his own deliberate childhood existence did not supply: "They're just themselves and glad of it. Nothing scares them. . . . *They're young.*" But Duddy voices the truth later when he says: "It's hard to be a gentleman—a Jew, I mean—it's hard to be. Period."

To achieve independence in the Gentile world, Duddy assumes he needs money. When he was a child, the identity he had wanted was bound up with his appraisal of Jerry Dingleman, the Boy Wonder, the Mr. Big of a narcotics underworld.

> Duddy wanted to be a somebody. Another Boy Wonder maybe. Not a loser, certainly.

But the Boy Wonder is exactly that, a *boy* wonder, because in spite of his power in a localized area and in spite of his wealth, he does not achieve recognition by the Westmount world. Before Duddy recognizes that the Wonder is "only famous on St. Urbain Street," he is used, unaware, to smuggle heroin. Dingleman says of him: "The boy is innocent. He's perfect." The innocence that Dingleman sees in Duddy is a naïveté perfect for being exploited. Because the boy seeks to masquerade in an imagined sophistication, he will avoid questioning what he does not understand when questioning would be the very act that would bring him real knowledge. To come out of apprenticeship, Duddy needs not only to discover truth in the world in which he wants to live but also to know what to do with truth. Dingleman can be defeated not by confronting him with fact (which he has known and disregarded all along) but only by an independence that can afford to disregard him. Duddy's various schemes for achieving the wealth to purchase Lac St. Pierre give him a measure of the experience he needs to be independent of Dingleman; what he needs also, in the way of position, achieved through a recognition by self and by others, he has yet to find out.

Duddy must both extend trust and be extended trust before he can achieve recognizable adult status. For this to be part of any development in him in Richler's comic terms as well, it must be his extension of trust that brings him knowledge of the nature of this relationship but the extension of trust to him that in fact brings with it the success that is maturity and mastery. Duddy's grandfather, Simcha, is an adult of the old order; he merits trust in his neighbourhood and is given it, and it is a measure of his position. But for Duddy the estimation of that world is insufficient, and though one of his plans in securing Lac St. Pierre is to please his grandfather, this must ultimately give way to the more basic need to fulfill himself. He cannot live in Simcha's world; no more can Simcha live in his. The final recognition of their separate identities is prefigured when early in the novel Abramovitch says to his father: "this is modern times."

When Duddy trusts others, his comic naïveté takes him into situations that more experienced persons would avoid, but it is simply because he is naïve that he can emerge unscathed, though more knowing, developing cunning in the process. He lets Dingleman use him for smuggling heroin, for example; he unknowingly lets Peter John Friar make *avant garde* films of

a *bar mitzvah* ceremony for him; he purchases Lac St. Pierre in Yvette's name, saying, "A friend is a friend. You've got to trust somebody. . . ." But it is in his central and significant relationship with his brother that the difference betweeen intelligent trust and foolhardiness crystallizes for him, that he learns he must make a choice of enemies. Lennie had tried to become part of Westmount society and in so doing was gulled into foolhardy action; he is a promising medical student, and yet he jeopardizes his career by performing—and botching—an illegal abortion, and then running away childishly, to hide from the act. Duddy, however, can not only diagnose the cause but also prescribe the cure: "Don't you know better than to go bareback?" If mature life is a healthy self-possession, then the life lived prior to maturity must be based on self-protection. When Duddy then takes Lennie's problem from him and solves it, earning Lennie's trust, he has achieved part of the relationship that will ultimately give him his final position. Lennie finds his own identity by breaking with Westmount and participating in the building of Israel, by taking his doctor's capacity for healing to a new world that he can inhabit; but Duddy's place remains in the Gentile world. He is therefore different from Cohen, who says: "We're two of a kind, you know. . . . A plague on all the *goyim*, that's my motto." He is different because, for Duddy, this is not a satisfactory guide; he cannot choose to align himself on religious terms. When his film of Bernie Cohen's *bar mitzvah* shows "the pregnant moment, the meeting of time past and time present, when the priest and his initiate reach the *ho'mat*," and shows it, in a hilariously funny scene, by techniques of symbolism and montage, the orthodox apprenticeship to position within the religion is contrasted with Duddy's unorthodox but vigorous apprenticeship to an identity all his own.

Though the story is related in terms of a Jewish boy's rise to adult status, its implications go beyond the strictly racial-religious extension. Duddy's Uncle Benjy is wrong when his estimation of the boy begins and ends here: "Because you're a *pusherke*. A little Jew-boy on the make." What Duddy comes to and in fact must come to if his apprenticeship to life is to be successful is *a* self rather than *the* self. He cannot accept an order that is established for him by race or religion or duty or family, and when Benjy leaves him a letter—which Duddy must be ready to read, somewhat like Nick Adams or Ike McCaslin having to be ready to fish or hunt—the warning it contains to the boy must even yet undergo seachange within him before he can become a man:

> You've got to love [the family], Duddel . . . A boy can be two, three, four potential people, but a man is only one. He murders the others.

The relationship of family love is only valid for him up to a point. Inheritance of family ties—in individual or even in political terms, for the 'ghetto', for Montreal, and for the Canadian society of the story—must not interfere with the establishment of individual identity. Lennie and Riva find their "God's Little Acre" in Israel, but though this satisfies them, it cannot become *ergo* a necessary reason for Duddy's embracing the same solution. His own little acre lies at Lac St. Pierre, neither in Israel nor in St. Urbain Street, and love that enmeshes him elsewhere than in that self deprives him of his full potentialities and ends by being no love.

He has to become a Somebody, and for this to occur, the demanding love that had attempted to form the child's identity must be exchanged for a trust in the identity that the adult forms for himself. Lennie has to trust Duddy in the matter of the abortion; Max has to trust him with a thousand dollar loan; Benjy has to show his trust by willing Duddy his house. Duddy's particular personality causes a change when the comic reversal of intent takes place; not only does he avoid all other selves in his master of one, but he also turns to his own development the trusts that are placed in him by others. The abortion affair leads to his business ventures with Hugh Calder of Westmount, for example; the house that Benjy leaves him, tied up as it is by legal limitations so that Duddy can only own the legacy and not profit in his own cash terms by it, he empties of its furniture in order to raise money anyway and invest it in the acquisition of his own land. What Yvette will not willingly give him is the opportunity ultimately to be adult; she wants a cessation of imaginative investment and practical energy which is objectified in her care for the paralytic Virgil. Whereas Duddy finds himself by expending, Virgil remains fearful and in need of protection by trying to save intact a bequest that has been left to him. When Duddy sacrifices that tradition to his own effort, he brings the traditional world—albeit weak and by now impotent: Simcha, Dingleman, Virgil—into opposition against him. But when he is recognized as the Owner of the new world, his apprenticeship of discovery is over. He is given a trust that makes him at last the Somebody he wants to be ("That's all right, sir. We'll mark it.") adult, individual, and master in his own terms in his own land.

Success is therefore possible in Richler's fictional world, though his ironic eye builds it only out of breaking traditions. This seems at first to be so partial as to deny adequate scope to the novel, and in Richler's other works this is essentially true. The acrimony of *The Incomparable Atuk,* for example, makes that work merely repellent instead of provocative. *A Choice of Enemies* and *Son of a Smaller Hero* offer only fragmentary views of society, and hence the reader never quite believes in their reality. But the world of Duddy Kravitz is whole, and Duddy himself, while not particularly likeable, is very much alive. He wins readers to his side, moreover, because his reaction to traditions is a positive one. His iconoclasm is of value not for itself, but because it is a route toward inhabiting a new world and fulfilling a social individuality. As he is a comic figure, his apparently destructive tendencies can paradoxically be a means for constructing life, but the fictional tone and technique are necessarily different for depicting this than they are for showing a comparable process of discovery in *The Watch that Ends the Night.* MacLennan's study is of the crossing of political and metaphysical frontiers and it ends in peace, whereas Richler's novel, of a different kind, ends in a comic triumph. That both might be empty victories was a view that hindsight would support; in 1959, they seemed the culmination of a tense but strangely expectant decade. (pp. 108-16)

W. H. New, *"The Apprenticeship of Discovery: Richler and MacLennan,"* in his Articulating West: Essays on Purpose and Form in Modern Canadian Literature, *New Press, 1972, pp. 108-27.*

[*The following excerpt is from an essay originally published as the introduction to the 1969 edition of* The Apprenticeship of Duddy Kravitz.]

At first glance, Mordecai Richler's novel seems to fit into the tradition of Joyce's *Portrait of the Artist* and Lawrence's *Sons and Lovers,* each of which deals with the growing up of a young man to the point where he is on his own, alone and lonely, ready to strike out in life freed from the ties of his youth. Stephen Dedalus deliberately separates himself from Ireland and all it stands for in order to become a writer: "To forge in the smithy of my soul the uncreated conscience of my race." His solitary condition is the result of long thought and much self-examination; he has made a choice and has consciously accepted the responsibility for his own life. The reader shares with him some of his elation, some of his excitement, the novel ending as an affirmation of man's creative spirit. Lawrence's hero, Paul Morel, turns at the end of the novel back towards the lights of the city, walking quickly away from the darkness that had embraced his dead mother: "He would not take that direction, to the darkness, to follow her. He walked towards the faintly humming, glowing town, quickly." Again we are made to feel as the novel ends that the young man has made a choice, has re-entered the world of life and vitality. In both of these earlier novels the protagonist has made a choice of direction, aware of the chain of events that had made such a choice possible and necessary. Each has made a decision, based on thought and self-awareness, and each has chosen a way of life that is an affirmation of man's greatness or potential greatness.

Richler's novel, however, in spite of its superficial affinity with the two novels mentioned above, ends with no such affirmation. His protagonist, who has never weighed the consequences of his actions in any but material terms, is less alone in the physical sense than the earlier young men, but he is also much less of a man. His decisions have been made on the wrong terms, have been based on nothing at all. He has destroyed himself and others for a piece of land that means nothing to those who have loved him. He has devoted his energy to acquiring property; he has done nothing to develop himself. Whereas the other two, Stephen Dedalus and Paul Morel, have matured, and have decided the course of their lives for themselves, poor Duddy has simply gone along without realizing where he was headed. He is a modern "anti-hero" (something like the protagonist in Anthony Burgess's *A Clockwork Orange)* who lives in a largely deterministic world, a world where decisions are not decisions and where choice is not really choice.

In another sense Duddy reminds us (at least he reminds me) of Tom Jones the foundling. Duddy has no mother and not much of a father; he asks all his relatives about his mother but never actually finds out if she had ever loved him. He is almost as much an orphan as Tom Jones, and like Tom he sets out to find his place in the world. Moreover, Duddy's search for himself has strongly picaresque overtones; like Tom he ranges through a very broad spectrum of his society, exposing to the reader the vices and follies of the world in which he is forced to make his way. He is less fortunate than Tom, for whom everything works out beautifully, since Duddy discovers at the end of the novel that he belongs to the world of Max and Eddy and Jerry Dingleman. He learns that there is no place for him in the gentle, loving and kindly world of his grandfather, or even in the world of Yvette and Virgil. His frantic headlong search ends with his discovery that he fits all too well into a vulgar and raucous world devoid of understanding and love. If we take Duddy seriously as a character, and I think we should, the novel ends on a very sad note.

Duddy Kravitz, obsessed with the land he eventually is successful in acquiring, is destroyed by following an assortment of false gods he picks up at random from all sorts of people in his life. Like a parrot, he hears and then adopts phrases and ideas that no doubt have had some special significance to the people who first used them, but to Duddy they have become not much more than verbal bromides. He uncritically swallows and later throws out as his own such undigested gems as Lennie's "Anatomy is the big killer," and Cohen's "There's not a businessman in town who hasn't at least one bankruptcy in his pocket," and most important of all his grandfather's "A man without land is nobody." It is this last speech that directs Duddy's actions throughout the novel. Ironically, it is the comment of Simcha Kravitz, the chief representative in the novel of the old lost world of solid virtues and sound values, that turns his grandson into a person possessed of a materialistic demon. Duddy becomes a ruthless entrepreneur with an impressive list of sins of omission and commission to his discredit, and all to follow the dream implanted in him by the kindly old Simcha.

Duddy gets his land; but, because he believes that any means can be justified by the beauty of his vision of the future, he emerges at the end of the novel as a failure in all the relationships that should have mattered to him. He is rejected by his grandfather, and by Yvette and Virgil, and is left with the loud unthinking admiration of his father, Max the Hack. (We agree with Uncle Benjy that "Max is not very bright.") The people Duddy admires have come to see him for what he is, whereas those who have learned to admire him see only what he has accomplished. Max knows nothing about the conniving tricks; the others do. When Duddy tells himself that "I'm going to get that land no matter what, see?" he expresses to himself much the same idea as the earlier accusation of his brother Lennie, "What's in it for me, that's your philosophy."

It is difficult to feel very much sympathy for Duddy until perhaps the end of the novel; he is just too aware of the enormity of his own actions to pass for an innocent, and he causes the destruction of too many people to be seen only as a victim of his unfortunate environment. From one point of view we are presented to Duddy as a poor little neglected underprivileged boy from the slums and therefore one who cannot be blamed for trying to improve his lot even by slippery tactics. But the Duddy that we usually see is the one described as "a cretinous little money-grubber," as "a little Jew-boy on the make," as "a busy, conniving little Yid," and as a "scheming little bastard." It is true that his Uncle Benjy, who is one of the "lousy intelligent people!" (to use Duddy's description of him), realizes just before his own death that there might be something else about his nephew:

> You're two people . . . The scheming little bastard I saw so easily and the fine intelligent boy underneath that your grandfather, bless him, saw.

He goes on to tell Duddy that "a boy can be two, three, four potential people, but a man is only one. He murders the others." Richler obviously presents Uncle Benjy as one of the spokesmen for the minority view, a sort of chorus figure commenting on the central character and indirectly on society at large. We're prepared by the author to accept Uncle Benjy's reading of Duddy's character and we see Duddy as we saw him, and at the end of the novel we see that all the other potential people present in the boy have been murdered by the scheming little bastard. He has become another Boy Wonder!

The original Boy Wonder, Jerry Dingleman, is an important character in the novel. As Max describes the exploits of the Boy Wonder in words and tone suited to an epic hero, Dingleman the racketeer becomes to Duddy the living symbol of success. He has money, power and girls, and he made it all himself . . . When we actually meet the Boy Wonder as presented directly by Richler and not through the gullible eyes of Max, we immediately recognize him as an unscrupulous, predatory, and successful crook. His physical appearance, changed

greatly for the worse by his "personal troubles" (polio), is to the reader clearly indicative of his moral corruption, another personal trouble that has had at least as much effect upon the impression he makes upon others. It takes poor Duddy a long, long time to recognize his hero for what he really is, a "two-bit, dope-smuggling cripple." Max, it is interesting to note, continues in his admiration of Dingleman, and his highest praise of Duddy is to see his son in the same way. In the last paragraph of the novel, after Duddy has been rejected by Simcha, Yvette and Virgil, he returns to the admiration of Max, apparently accepting it as the real, the genuine, the true evaluation of his achievement: "And suddenly Duddy did smile. He laughed. He grabbed Max, hugged him, and spun him around. 'You see,' he said, his voice filed with marvel. 'You see.' " His triumph is on the scale of values set up by the Boy Wonder, whose greatest advocate is the not-very-bright Max the Hack.

The novel ends then as a devastating attack on the world of Duddy Kravitz, which is the world of Jewish Montreal. It is interesting to note that Duddy's Montreal is a bi-cultural city, Jewish and non-Jewish. All non-Jews, French and English, are seen as pretty much the same; the two-culture theme of *Two Solitudes* takes on a new look in Richler's novel. He is obviously very aware of the flaws in his own society, and on one plane the novel is a bitter revelation of the vulgarity and raw materialism of middle-class Canadian life, for Richler well exemplified by the world he still probably knows best. There are a few admirable Jews presented very briefly and used to reveal even more clearly by contrast the glittering false standards of the many; but for the most part Richler emphasizes all too strongly the aspects of Jewish society that the anti-Semites do. The few warm and unselfish characters we meet remain largely undeveloped and lifeless: Simcha, the representative of the old world; Hersh, the only student at school who openly criticizes Duddy's destruction of MacPherson, the alcoholic teacher whose invalid wife dies answering one of Duddy's anonymous and scurrilous phone calls; Bernie Altman, the one fellow-waiter not dedicated to ridiculing the outsider; perhaps Yvette, Duddy's Girl Friday; and Virgil, the epileptic ruthlessly used by Duddy. But it is not only the sympathetic characters who fail to come to life; we also get to know very little about any character other than Duddy himself. Other characters are seen only in terms of their relationship with Duddy, whose apprenticeship is the subject of the novel. There are brilliant sketches of many minor characters, such as Auntie Ida, Cuckoo Kaplan, Rabbi Goldstone and many others, but they remain as extras.

Duddy and his development as a full-fledged member of his world occupy the centre of the stage at all times. And we do have a chance to know him. At least we see him in action, and we are allowed to enter his mind and to see what his motives are and what he wants to do with his life. Unfortunately for Duddy he doesn't always know himself very well, not well enough to see that he is consistently following the wrong set of values, even though these are the accepted values of the world in which he lives. Max, proudly reminiscing about his highly successful son, gives praise for the wrong acts:

> You could see from the day of his birth that he was slated for fame and fortune. A comer. Why I remember when he was still at F.F.H.S. they had a teacher there, an anti-Semite of the anti-Semites, a lushhead, and my boy was the one who led the fight against him and drove him out of the school.

Of course, Duddy does know himself better than Max knows him, and he does have some uneasy thoughts about his share in the ruin of the kindly MacPherson and even wonders if he did somehow kill Mrs. MacPherson by accident by phoning when old Mac was not at home. It is in Duddy's occasional moments of self-examination that the reader develops some sympathy for the kid "born on the wrong side of the tracks with a rusty spoon in his mouth, so to speak, and the spark of rebellion in him."

Canadian novelists seem to me to be a very conventional lot, at least as far as experiments with form go (*The Double Hook* stands out for me as the shining exception to the rule), and certainly in this novel Richler is a traditionalist. We do have a short break in the generally straightforward chronology when, after meeting Duddy as a particularly nasty, fifteen-year old schoolboy, we go back to learn something about his earlier exploits, and especially about his relationship with his grandfather, a relationship that gave the old man's friends cause to worry: "The round-shouldered old men looked at Duddy and decided he was mean, a crafty boy, and they hoped he would not hurt Simcha too hard." Then we move back to Duddy at seventeen and carry on from there. There is no playing with any experimental form here either. We see everything as Duddy sees it, but not through any stream-of-consciousness; Duddy is always fully conscious, and with only minor excursions into his dream world we follow all the action as Duddy scurries from job to job, from deal to deal, from scrape to scrape. In the narrative and descriptive sections of the novel Richler writes good, sound, correct English, perhaps a bit too much like a good term essay. It seems to me that Richler handles dialogue exceptionally well, giving us conversations of great range and convincing authenticity: Duddy and his schoolmates with their smutty and suggestive comments on life and love; the loud, vulgar, and raucous remarks on the film HAPPY BARMITZVAH, BERNIE!; the talk of Max and his mates; the maudlin psychological jargon of Auntie Ida; and many others. The book comes to life through its dialogue, and the vitality of dialogue is usually a reliable test of the success of a novel.

There is always a temptation to evaluate Canadian writers by comparison with other Canadians. Written by a Canadian and about Canadians in Canada's largest city, this novel with its satiric-tragic-comic attitude to man in the modern world is much more than a "mere" Canadian work. Richler's novel, it seems to me, can stand on its own by any standard. (pp. 84-91)

> A. R. Bevan, "The Apprenticeship of Duddy Krav-
> itz," in Mordecai Richler, *edited by G. David Sheps,
> Ryerson Press, 1971, pp. 84-91.*

My reason for writing about *The Apprenticeship of Duddy Kravitz* is simple. I think it is a good novel, arguably the best of Mordecai Richler's seven novels. . . . I think it is true to say that *The Apprenticeship of Duddy Kravitz* has divided its critics. If we read, for example, Warren Tallman's and A. R. Bevan's accounts of the novel, we might find it hard to believe that we have read critical assessments of the same book. Tallman provides us with a total vindication of Duddy [see excerpt dated Autumn, 1960] and Bevan with a complete denunciation of him [see excerpt dated 1969]. Certainly, Duddy Kravitz is an ambiguous character, but he is not totally ambiguous. In fact, not sufficiently ambiguous to have provoked such widely divergent estimations of his character and conduct.

Although I am more sympathetic to Bevan's assessment of Duddy than I am to Tallman's, I think that both critics have, in obviously different ways, misread the novel. And while the critical disagreements they have raised are capable of solution

by a careful re-reading of the text of the novel itself, since we have recently received such helpful external evidence as a fictional reappearance of Duddy [in *St. Urbain's Horseman* (1971)] and an interview with his author who discusses his character at some length it would be silly to pass such assistance by in any attempt to come to a fuller understanding of Duddy Kravitz and of Mordecai Richler's intentions and achievement in his fourth and, perhaps, best novel. (p. 77)

The Apprenticeship of Duddy Kravitz depends for its total effect upon an oscillating pattern of sympathetic and judicial response to its central character. This pattern seems to be consciously created but whether this is so or not is finally unimportant. Such a pattern is after all a fairly regular device in tragic drama. What seems to have happened in the criticism of *Duddy Kravitz* though is that Warren Tallman, for example, has been attentive only to the novel's pattern of sympathy, while A. R. Bevan has responded almost solely to its pattern of judgement. To gain a fuller appreciation of what this novel is about we need to attend to both patterns and their skillful interaction. This ultimately involves a double response (not necessarily an ambiguous one) to the novel's conclusion. Tallman feels happy about the ending of the novel because Duddy is successful, whereas Bevan feels that the novel ends on a sad note because Duddy has destroyed his moral nature. A fuller sense of the ending allows us to applaud Duddy's dismissal of Jerry Dingleman from his land, yet realize the delusions that Duddy labours under and the way in which he has become like Dingleman. At the close of the novel Duddy Kravitz is both a victor and a victim. And this seems to be what Richler wants to put before us. In the acquisitive stakes of North American life Duddy is a winner. He has his land. But humanly and morally he is a loser. Richler considers one of the novelist's chief roles to be "the loser's advocate" and this is precisely what he is in *The Apprenticeship of Duddy Kravitz*. In Duddy's attack on Uncle Benjy, Richler puts Duddy's case compellingly before us, yet Duddy is ultimately a loser because he loses humanly. At the end of the novel, without Yvette's love or his *zeyda's* respect, he is alone. And the point is that the kind of double response which we have at the close of the novel has been the dominant pattern of dramatization throughout the book. One of the best things about this novel, in fact, is the way it moves, perhaps a little too stridently and cinematically at times, but it sustains our interest in ways that Richler's first two novels especially do not. (p. 78)

Incident and suspense are well handled [in *The Apprenticeship of Duddy Kravitz*] and support the shifting response to the hero that I have mentioned.

The first physical description we are given of Duddy Kravitz introduces the complex response we are to have towards him throughout. We receive from it simultaneously a sense of Duddy's deprived background and his adolescent lust for manhood:

> Duddy Kravitz was a small, narrow-chested boy of
> fifteen with a thin face. His black eyes were ringed
> with dark circles and his pale, bony cheeks were
> criss-crossed with scratches as he shaved twice daily
> in his attempt to encourage a beard. Duddy was pres-
> ident of room forty-one.

Our sympathy extends to the boy brought up without a mother's love but is qualified by his treatment of MacPherson and his wife which is both cruel and cowardly despite the fact that there are some extenuating reasons for Duddy's behaviour. We measure Duddy's vindictiveness against Hersh's sympathy for the beleaguered teacher. However, the inadequate familial attitudes of Max, Uncle Benjy and Lennie tend to increase our sympathy for Duddy and make the invention of his fantasy brother Bradley understandable. . . . Duddy is regarded as a puzzle by his family and friends, his grandfather Simcha is respected by his fellow immigrants but, apart from by each other, both are unloved. It is this lack of love and the belief that he is essentially unlovable which lies at the root of Duddy Kravitz's problem. . . . His aggressiveness proceeds directly from a sense of deprivation and while we may judge its manifestations adversely we sympathise with Duddy because we see that its causes are real enough.

Duddy's treatment by Uncle Benjy during his first job and his treatment by Irwin Shubert at Ste. Agathe considerably increase our sympathy for him. The roulette game in particular finds us on Duddy's side and opposed to Linda and Irwin. It is in the beginnings of his relationship with Yvette that we begin again to misdoubt him. A crucial passage occurs on page 92 of the novel:

> She [Yvette] led him towards the railroad tracks as the stars started to fade and light began to spread across the sky. Duddy saw for the first time the part of Ste. Agathe where the poorer French-Canadians lived and the summer residents and tourists never came. The unpainted houses had been washed grey by the wind and the rain. Roosters crowded in yards littered with junk and small hopeless vegetable patches and Duddy was reminded of his grandfather and St. Dominique Street, and he promised himself to send the old man a postcard tomorrow. There were faded Robin Hood Flour signs on some walls and there a barn roof or window had been healed with a tin Sweet Caporal sign.

It is one of the best descriptive passages in the book, the details of poverty are authentic and strike home, and in this passage we also discover the limits of Duddy Kravitz's human sympathy. The place reminds him of his grandfather but he cannot establish a wider human sympathy than this. Duddy is able to love and help his family but his love cannot extend beyond this point. . . . This is Duddy's problem and it is where we find him wanting. He is unable to love Yvette and Virgil, the two *goys* who offer him love and friendship. So when Yvette shows Duddy the lake he is more excited by the possibilities of ownership than by Yvette's human love. He makes love to her hastily and in a very real and perverse sense his sexual energies are here re-routed into the acquisition of land. . . . Duddy has found the lodestone for his ambitions and henceforward is governed by his lust for land.

> His heart began to pound again and he laughed more happily than he had ever laughed before . . . He would never surrender control of course.

A subtle irony comes into play here which both qualifies our response to Duddy's enthusiasm and helps us to discover the degree of his enslavement to his dream. Cuckoo Kaplan, the unsuccessful comedian, who Duddy befriends but later humiliates closes the first part of the novel with a comment which focuses the reader's response to Duddy.

> 'I'm worried, though. He seemed so sick like last night. I don't mean the fever. I mean sick in the head. He went on and on about some lake . . . I was just going to get the show on the road,' Cuckoo said.

For Duddy, who is now running the show is, indeed, on the road. A second-hand American dream of ownership has trapped him and Cuckoo's antics provide an appropriate ironic measurement for what Duddy has now been captured by.

To indicate further the working of the oscillating pattern under consideration it is interesting to notice on Duddy's return to Montreal that when he hastens to embrace his father, his father retreats from him. Our sympathy for Duddy is reinvoked as it is in the naivety of his transactions with Peter John Friar and his disappointment in the arranged meeting with his father's idol, Jerry Dingleman, the Boy Wonder.

The *bar-mitzvah* film provides the novel's comic centre. In a novel about apprenticeship a ritual of initiation for a young man would naturally seem to gain this kind of strategic relevance. The film is Duddy's *bar-mitzvah* for the business world. And it seems to me both funnier and more fully functional than the equivalent expatriate baseball game sequence in *St. Urbain's Horseman*. We respond to Duddy's chagrin and elation and this emotional mixing provides a kind of diminuendo to the poles of judgement and sympathy between which we respond to Duddy throughout. At this point in his career we are also made fully aware of the kind of toll which the pursuit of success is taking on his nature:

> At ten the next morning Duddy came charging out of a bottomless sleep, unsure of his surroundings but prepared for instant struggle, the alibi for a crime unremembered already half-born, panting, scratching, and ready to bolt if necessary.

Yet he is still prepared here to trust Yvette with the deeds to his land which he eventually is unable to do after his final heinous act against Virgil. If he cannot contemplate marriage to his *shiksa*, his "Girl Friday," he still possesses a belief in friendship at this point. As he tells Friar, " 'A friend is a friend. You've got to trust somebody.' " (pp. 78-9)

If we misdoubt Duddy's means of pursuing his goal we respect the way he saves his brother Lennie's career. Duddy is always generous when it comes to assisting his family. We see this again when Uncle Benjy is dying and Duddy undertakes to bring Auntie Ida back from New York. But here Richler sharpens the ironic focus through which we view his hero since Virgil's accident follows hard upon the discovery of Uncle Benjy's terminal cancer. Although Duddy had always hated Uncle Benjy and liked Virgil he responds to the former's illness with concern and the latter's accident with revulsion. Clearly, responsibility is what is at issue here. Duddy is not responsible for Uncle Benjy's illness but he is responsible for Virgil's accident and to be fully sympathetic to Virgil would involve a full acknowledgement of his responsibility. This Duddy is unprepared for. Besides, Uncle Benjy is "family", Virgil is just a *goy* and we gain from this a clear sense of Duddy's confused values and inner division. He is, indeed, two people, the behemoth and the gentleman that Uncle Benjy mentions. Richler in *Duddy Kravitz* provides us with yet another treatment of the theme of division which has been such a perennial concern in Canadian literature. Duddy Kravitz is a divided man. And this is probably why the critical response to him has been so divergent. But the truth of the matter is that Duddy Kravitz is neither a hero nor a villain. In a sense he is both and neither. He is in many ways a North American everyman and through creating him and following his progress Mordecai Richler has been able to test the way we live on this continent. Duddy Kravitz expresses our materialism and our lack of love. We both sympathize with and judge him but we can neither account for him nor dismiss him easily. He mirrors too accurately, too painfully what goes on here, what passes for life on this continent. (pp. 79-80)

At the close of *The Apprenticeship* Simcha is the thorn in Duddy's side when he goes to show his land to his family. Simcha represents the conscience of the race and he shows the way in which acquisitiveness constitutes a betrayal of the true spirit of Hebraism. . . .

> I can see what you have planned for me, Duddel. You'll be good to me. You'd give me everything I wanted. And that would settle your conscience when you went out to swindle others.

Duddy drives Dingleman off his land but ironically accepts and quotes Dingleman's assessment of Simcha's moral integrity.

> You don't want a farm. You never have. You're scared stiff of the country and you want to die in that stinky old shoe repair shop.

Duddy no longer respects his grandfather's poverty as he had earlier with Yvette at Ste. Agathe. Of course, he is injured by his grandfather's moral judgment and he wants to hurt him back. Duddy can't accept that the end does not justify the means. Simcha would have been proud to possess his grandson's farm if it had been honestly acquired. It was after all Simcha who originally told his grandson that a man without land is nobody. What is at issue is *how* the land is acquired and in acquiring his land Duddy has become like another Jerry Dingleman. Thus, we leave Duddy at the end of the novel caught in the illusion of success's tinsel dream:

> 'That's all right, sir. We'll mark it.'

> And suddenly Duddy did smile. He laughed. He grabbed Max, hugged him, and spun him around. 'You see,' he said, his voice filled with marvel. 'You see.'

We are reminded of the blind man who said he could see when he couldn't see at all. The novel's pattern is complete. We both pass the necessary judgement here and feel the kind of sympathy that is felt for someone irrevocably locked in a state of illusion. The winner of land becomes a moral and human loser. Richler is beyond his hot defence of Duddy in the face of his patronising, intellectual critics like Uncle Benjy and the rest of us, he shows us, whether consciously or not does not matter, the void, the hollowness of merely material success. (p. 80)

John Ferns, "Sympathy and Judgement in Mordecai Richler's 'The Apprenticeship of Duddy Kravitz'," in Journal of Canadian Fiction, Vol. III, No. 1, Winter, 1974, pp. 77-82.

JACOB TWO-TWO MEETS THE HOODED FANG (1975)

AUTHOR'S COMMENTARY

I have five children who, when they were very young, were told again and again it was too early for them to read *Cocksure*. Or even *The Apprenticeship of Duddy Kravitz*. Well then, one of them asked, not unreasonably, isn't there anything of yours we are not too young to read? The short answer was no, but I also promised that one day I would write something that would be just for them; and that's how I came to write *Jacob Two-Two Meets The Hooded Fang*. The book was meant to be family fun, with certain built-in family jokes. It began, innocently enough, as a bedtime tale told to amuse our youngest child, Jacob, and as it made him (and even the others) giggle I started to write it down.

To backtrack briefly.

As a child, I never read children's books myself, but cut my intellectual teeth on *Superman, Captain Marvel,* and *The Batman,* moving on from there to Ellery Queen and Perry Mason, and finally, at the age of twelve or thereabouts, to the first novel that I ever read, *All Quiet On The Western Front.* So my experience of children's books, such as it is, came to me from reading aloud to our children, an office that is usually filled by my wife. In reading aloud to them I was somewhat shocked to discover that a few classics old and modern, and the incomparable Dr. Seuss, aside, most children's books were awfully boring or insufferably didactic or sometimes both. These dreary, ill-written books were conceived for profit or to teach the kids racial tolerance, hygiene, or other knee-jerk liberal responses. In Canada, tiresome Eskimo or Indian legends seemed to be the rule. In contemporary children's stories parents were never hungover or short-tempered and the kids were generally adorable. I decided if I ever got round to writing a book for my kids its intention would be to amuse. Pure fun, not instruction, is what I had in mind.

But I resisted sitting down to *Jacob Two-Two* for more than a year, because I also have a prejudice against children's books, too many of which are written by third-rate writers for children already old enough to enjoy at least some adult books. Say, Mark Twain, some Dickens, certainly *The Scarlet Pimpernel,* and our own Farley Mowat on the north. Put simply, I think bright children beyond the age of twelve are ready for the real stuff, properly selected. Presented with it, they will respond or are already beyond the pale, destined to be *Reader's Digest* subscribers no matter what you do.

So *Jacob* was to be for the younger child, our Jacob actually, who was not yet ready for adult books. Writing it, really, was not very different than writing an adult novel, which is to say it was largely hard work, and, as is usually the case with me, went through many drafts. I did not worry overmuch about vocabulary, my feeling being that if a child didn't understand a word he could look it up in a dictionary. On the other hand, I did feel a rape scene might be inappropriate. I wrote it, first of all, for my own pleasure (and in fulfilment of a rash promise). Of course, I hoped, as I always do, that it would appeal to a large audience, but that is never a consideration in the actual writing.

Something else.

I have no special attitude towards children as a breed. They are, after all, merely little people, some of them obnoxious, many more stupid, and a few, a cherished few, absolutely enchanting.

The success of *Jacob Two-Two* has surprised, even embarrassed me. It was immediately accepted for publication in England and Canada and, after something like seven rejections in the U.S.A., was finally taken on there by my adult book publisher, Knopf. It has come out in a Bantam edition and will soon be a Puffin. It has been translated into several languages. Christopher Plummer has done a delightful recording of the story and there has also been a film version, which may be released one of these days. The Children's Theatre in Toronto is to present a musical adaptation this autumn. Most delightful of all, hardly a week goes by when I don't get a batch of letters from children in Canada or the United States. They want to know if it's a true story or just something I made up out of my own head. My favourite letter, one I keep pinned to a board on my office wall, is from a boy who begins by saying, "I really liked your book Jacob Two-Two Meets The Hooded Fag.''

Ironically, I suppose, *Jacob Two-Two,* in hard cover, has already outsold even my most successful adult novel, *St. Urbain's Horseman.* Maybe I missed my true vocation. (pp. 6-8)

Mordecai Richler, "Writing Jacob Two-Two," in Canadian Literature, *No. 78, Autumn, 1978, pp. 6-8.*

As black satirist, fearless lambaster of Jew and WASP, dirty comic writer, Mordecai Richler has consistently displayed a resolute sneer. But in his first children's book, *Jacob Two-Two Meets The Hooded Fang,* Richler stands revealed. Beneath the hardened accretions of cynicism, there's an incorrigible softy. Richler knows and loves children. Astonishingly, he accepts them for what they are.

The book has a relaxed air about it that makes it more often delightful than relentlessly involving. It falls in a safe zone somewhere between banal, librarian-approved, no-scare classics (which children loathe and aunties love) and the fiery apocalyptic comics in which costumed heroes smash their amazing fists into the lime jello faces of space monsters. While Richler, understandably, has leaned toward the scary tastes of children, he has not created merely an expensive replay of a comic book. Though Jacob Two-Two wrangles with monsters of sorts —and even eventually earns a dazzling outfit of golden cape, Child Power T-shirt, and Day-Glo blue jeans—he is for the most part a real-live six-year-old with some excruciatingly real six-year-old problems. Jacob, in fact, is all too human. Unavoidably young and clumsy, he is an embarrassment to older brothers and sisters and still too small in his parents' eyes to accomplish much that's useful.

Sent out to buy "two pounds of firm, red tomatoes" at the green grocer, Jacob Two-Two is ridiculed for having to say everything twice. Humiliated once more (it has been a rough day), he flees the store to a nearby park where he collapses in weariness and frustration. The next thing he knows, he's being hauled before the kangaroo court of Mr. Justice Rough on a charge of impertinence, defended only by Louis the Loser, a lawyer who has never won a case. Mr. Justice Rough leads the entire adult court in a chorus of anti-child bile. "Big People Are Never, Never Wrong," they shout on cue. Of course, Jacob Two-Two is automatically guilty and is sent off to a miserable dungeon on the fog-shrouded Slimers' Isle "from which no brats return." His gruesome guards, Master Fish and Mistress Fowl, inform him that "the only birds that ever flew over the island were buzzards, and the land could support no animal life other than gray wolverines with yellow snaggle-teeth and millions of deathwatch beetles. There were no flowers . . . but nettles thrived everywhere, hiding the quicksand." Bungler in the outside world, Jacob Two-Two doesn't do too badly conspiring against the Slimers. He's discerning, intelligent, clever. He not only sees through the studied paedophobia of the chief Slimer, The Hooded Fang (an ex-wrestler), he eventually manages to release all the child prisoners from the island.

In the Austrian-English artist Fritz Wegner, Richler has a strong collaborator. Wegner's ink and wash representations of the miserable creeps who prey on children effectively compensate for the paucity of textual descriptions. In violation of the spirit of the text, though, his children have the disappointing look of those characterless blanks one finds in How-to-Draw-Chil-

dren-in-Five-Easy-Steps manuals. Nevertheless, *Jacob Two-Two Meets The Hooded Fang* has the look of a book which belongs more to children than to adults—a subversive but happy accomplishment. (pp. 65-6)

John Ayre, "Mordecai Richler's Subversive Accomplishment," in Saturday Night, *Vol. 90, No. 3, July-August, 1975, pp. 65-6.*

Seeing that Mordecai Richler has intended his latest (no. 11 in the canon) book for a juvenile audience, the ideal person to provide a proper assessment would appear to be one of the New (Brand New) Critics. So here then is Louise, age 10 (academic qualifications: grade 5, clear standing; writing credits: numerous classroom stories and essays, and penmanship exercises):

> *Jacob Two-Two Meets The Hooded Fang* is one of the best books I've read. It is mysterious and it holds a lot of suspense. You don't need to hear what I think about it. Just listen to the title. It almost draws you to reading it.

Thus, it would seem that Richler has thoroughly succeeded in his first attempt at writing for the youngsters; so any further comment is probably redundant. Nevertheless, here is what one of the Old Critics has to say.

When first learning some months ago that Mordecai Richler was bringing out a children's book one was naturally interested—and apprehensive. Could a man who has spent the past two decades perfecting his Black Humour craftsmanship suddenly abandon his customary cynicism and enter a child's world of magic and delight? What could he bring to the children's literature genre that wouldn't be grossly unsuitable? Well, the kiddies do like *Mad* Magazine, don't they? Perhaps then something like that.

As it turns out, though, here is what *Jacob Two-Two Meets The Hooded Fang* is really like. Jacob, who is six years of age (or, as he puts it, "two plus two plus two years old"), lives with his family—two older brothers, two older sisters, and mother and father—"in a rambling old house on Kingston Hill in England." The "Two-Two" nickname comes from the fact that Jacob feels obliged to say everything twice, so that the bigger people around him will have to pay some attention.

However, this word-repeating habit of his gets him into difficulty, eventually bringing about his meeting with the dreaded Hooded Fang. Believing that Jacob is mocking him, the greengrocer, Mr. Cooper, teases the lad in return, going to the extent of calling in a policeman and charging Jacob with "insulting behavior to a big person." In alarm, the boy dashes out of the shop and into Richmond Park, where he sinks to the grass, exhausted—and dreams.

We soon find Jacob in court, where he is inadequately defended by the barrister Louis Loser. The result is that the judge, Mr. Justice Rough, to punish Jacob for his offensive conduct toward the greengrocer, sentences him to "two years, two months, two weeks, two days, two hours and two minutes in the darkest dungeons of the children's prison"—which is located on "Slimers' Isle", "A marshy island in the foggiest part of England, a place where the sun never shone." The island is surrounded by crocodiles and inhabited by "gray wolverines with yellow snaggle-teeth and millions of deathwatch beetles." And the warden, we discover, turns out to be the frightful-looking Hooded Fang. A onetime wrestler, The Hooded Fang had to leave his former profession because one day a child laughed at him; the news quickly spread and soon all the wrestling fans were treating The Hooded Fang with derision, thereby making it impossible for him to continue his career as the terrifying figure in the ring.

What follows next are The Hooded Fang's attempts to break Jacob's spirit (Jacob also finds the ex-wrestler amusing) and make him cringe in fear as do all the other youthful prisoners. Eventually, though, The Hooded Fang acknowledges defeat; however, Jacob must pay a terrible price for failing to be suitably impressed. The Hooded Fang announces: "Tuesday afternoon at two o'clock, *I'm going to feed you to not one,* but two hungry sharks. Ho, ho!"

What then? Will Jacob be able to escape this dire fate? (Actually The Hooded Fang is a kind-hearted fellow, who sneaks candies into Jacob's cell, but he seems determined to carry out this threat. After all, he does have his image around the prison to maintain.) Will Jacob be rescued in time by the leaders of Child Power, the Infamous Two—also known as the intrepid Shapiro and the fearless O'Toole (in everyday life, Jacob's sister Emma and his brother Noah)?

Such is the story of *Jacob Two-Two Meets The Hooded Fang*— a story that is "mysterious" with "a lot of suspense", as is rightly claimed by the youthful collaborator in this review. However, there are other elements in here as well. In essence, the book concerns the lot of the child in our society—the relatively helpless position he or she is in because of psychological and physical dependence upon the adults. Hence Jacob's exploits represent wish-fulfilment (the secret, of course, of the adult best-seller), and hence Richler's tale is of natural appeal to the juvenile reader—who also undoubtedly would be quite appreciative of this author's customary satiric detail. For example, here is what Jacob has to put up with in the courtroom scene: "'. . . BIG PEOPLE ARE NEVER, NEVER WRONG. . . . If they punish you . . . it's . . . FOR YOUR OWN GOOD. . . . And it hurts them. . . . MORE THAN IT HURTS YOU. . . .'" And in the same episode: "'Everything you have—' continued Mr. Justice Rough. '—YOU OWE TO US,' chimed in the big people."

So what we have here is a satiric view of the adult world through child-like eyes. (Usually, in his adult fiction Richler seems jaded; on this occasion, though, he appears totally fresh—in two senses, it might be added.) An adult world which can create such injustices as: "No-flow ketchup, guaranteed to stick in the bottle"; "Jigsaw puzzles too complicated to solve"; and "major news stories concocted to break only when they could replace favorite television programs."

Other sinister adult practices originate with the toy saboteur Mr. Fox, who transfers vital parts around in model kits, exchanges wires in electric train and racing cars sets, replaces English-language model kit instructions with those written in Japanese, and switches the labels on chemistry set tubes ("That ought to make for an explosion or two," he cackled).

No doubt *Jacob Two-Two Meets The Hooded Fang* has some significance or other in relation to Richler's grown-up books. . . . For instance, one notices in his most "mature" novel (the novel, that is, containing the fullest expression to date of his fictional powers), *St. Urbain's Horseman,* that in the midst of all the social shambles one value remains steadfast for the protagonist Jacob Hersh. (Incidentally, could there be some symbolic connection between this middle-aged Jacob and the present six-year-old Jacob?) And this value is love for and love from one's family. Society at large may be emotionally adrift

because of vainglorious striving, forlorn ego quests; nevertheless, family security is always there to fall back on. Jacob appears condemned to just go on being a commercial hack film director—no Ingmar Bergman-like artistic self-fulfilment for him; yet he has gained one achievement in life: the love of wife Nancy and the little Hershes.

So it would seem that after twenty years of nihilistic satire Mordecai Richler has turned sentimentalist. (Of course, it could be maintained that Richler never really has been all-out Black Humorist, but rather an indignant reactionary moralist—as is clearly conveyed by *Cocksure*.) And *Jacob Two-Two Meets The Hooded Fang* appears to be following in this sentimental comedy vein. Obviously intended as light entertainment for the juvenile set, this book presents nothing reprehensible about Jacob's family (as might be the case with Jacob Hersh's family, the possibly objectionable member being Daddy himself). The young Jacob's only difficulty with them is that because of his diminutive stature he does not command much attention.

No indications of any overt, or even covert, cruelty appear in the story, just love and affection. Discovered eventually in Richmond Park, where he had been sleeping, Jacob obtains this response: "His father shook him awake. 'Jacob Two-Two,' he said beaming, 'thank God, you're safe.'" And even the greengrocer, Mr. Cooper, from whom Jacob had fled in fear, welcomes the boy back joyfully. . . . (pp. 96-8)

Thus, *Jacob Two-Two Meets The Hooded Fang* could be regarded as an extension of the values displayed in *St. Urbain's Horseman.* However, could it be that this latest book represents something more—a new direction in Richler's development as an artist? The story closes with the boy's mother saying: "'Jacob Two-Two, you are too much. You're a dreamer.'" And the author adds: "A dreamer? Maybe." Then

> that night, after Jacob Two-Two had gone to bed, he was paid a visit by the fearless O'Toole, accompanied by the intrepid Shapiro. They brought him a child power uniform that was different from all the others. It contained a pair of Day-Glo blue jeans and a golden cape, but the *Child Power* emblem was emblazoned on the T-Shirt two times.

Perhaps then this book is actually "A Portrait of the artist as a Young Child" type of story, with Jacob, as the Artist in question, achieving power, or at least worthwhile human significance, through the strength of his imagination. It might also be noted that he does have one advantage here over his namesake, Jacob, the film director. Young Jacob merely has to transform an essentially kindly, well-ordered world and make himself master of it, whereas Jacob Hersh has to contend with an Absurdist milieu. The boy inhabits a pastoral England, but middle-aged Jacob is part of a fallen world, a society based on tawdry dreams.

One could speculate further on the part that England has played in Richler's writing over the years. Evidently semi-autobiographical, his fiction up to now has displayed a rejection of the author's Montreal St. Urbain Street background in favor of a new identity in English media land, and the subsequent failure of his various protagonists, or alter egos, to find anything spiritually refreshing there. In contrast, though, to Richler's "serious" books, this children's story expresses the golden essence of the Albion escapist vision—a Garden of Eden-like existence on Kingston Hill, the fictional home of Jacob and his family and the onetime real-life home of the Mordecai Richler family. (And a further autobiographical connection is that the names of the novelist's five children—according to the book's dedication note—are the same as those of Jacob and his brothers and sisters.)

Anyway, a fully developed discussion of how *Jacob Two-Two Meets The Hooded Fang* relates to the rest of Richler's work belongs in some other study. What is of principal interest here is how this book is related to other Canadian children's literature.

A noted commentator in this field, Sheila A. Egoff, in her article "The Writing and Publishing of Canadian Children's Books in English" (in *Royal Commission on Book Publishing Background Papers,* 1972), states:

> The didactic tradition was broken in England in the 1850's and after, when outstanding writers turned their talents to pleasing children rather than informing them . . . Canadian writers stood aloof from this change and particularly from the great stream of fantasy. . . . While imaginative writing failed to find adherents in Canada, sentimentality did become a favorite theme. . . . through the writings of Margaret Marshall Saunders (1891-1947), Nellie McClung (1873-1951), and L. M. Montgomery (1873-1942).

And to jump ahead a number of years:

> With the advent of the 1960's, children's books, particularly those written in the United States, began to take on a psychological and sociological cast. . . . While other English-speaking children, as seen through their books, are coping with ineffectual parents, no parents, one parent, being unhappy, tuning in, dropping out, brushing up against drugs, alcoholism, homosexuality, and racism—Canadian children are still visiting a lighthouse, crossing the barrens, discovering a cache of Indian relics, escaping a murderer, catching a bank robber, or getting a pony for Christmas.

So then, how does Richler's children's book fit in with these traditions of sentimentality and adventure-story writing? Well, for one thing he evidently has revived the Saunders-McClung-Montgomery sentimental tale. However, *Jacob Two-Two Meets The Hooded Fang* is not strictly speaking an adventure story, but rather a fantasy. Or at least a fantasy with a realistic context. Thus, Richler's achievement would appear to be to have finally brought some "imaginative writing" into Canadian children's literature, also to have caught up with recent U. S. developments, children's material with a "psychological . . . cast." (And more on Richler's true-to-life qualities shortly.)

Another way, though, of approaching Mordecai Richler's contribution to CanLit Junior is to relate it to the offerings of other contemporary authors who write primarily for the adults but who do occasionally bring out something for the youngsters. For example, the comic essayist Robert Thomas Allen, who in 1963 published *The Mystery of the Missing Emerald;* and a novelist of urban despair, Richard B. Wright, who actually started off as a children's writer with *Andrew Tolliver* in 1965. However, neither author appears to be extending his customary artistic preoccupations into juvenile literature with these catching-a-robber boys' adventure stories. (pp. 99-100)

So it is evidently to Richler's credit then that he has remained true to his artistic vision, turning in a genuinely creative performance, rather than hackishly reproducing some standard item for the young set. Still, this is not an entirely unique achievement, since we do have before us the example of the afore-mentioned *Luke Baldwin's Vow* by Morley Callaghan (first published in 1948 and reissued in 1974), another children's book that illustrated adult themes. (p. 100)

Now that *Jacob Two-Two Meets The Hooded Fang* has been categorized in various ways, what exactly are its literary merits? As already stated, two readers (one juvenile, one adult) have enjoyed the book. But it must be admitted that the adult reader at least does have certain reservations. To put it bluntly, where does justifiable literary influence end and plagiarism begin? Louis Loser, the barrister defending Jacob Two-Two in court, seems curiously reminiscent of Morgenhall, the ineffectual barrister in John Mortimer's play *The Dock Brief.* Furthermore, when Jacob first meets Louis and sees how incompetent the courtroom defense will be, he responds with: " 'I have faith in you, Mr. Loser,' he said, his voice wobbly." The lawyer then replies:

> In that event . . . we can't lose. Because if you have faith in me, I'm going to plead insanity on your behalf. You're nuts, my boy. Positively crackers.

So we would appear then to have strayed into Joseph Heller's *Catch-22* territory.

Anyway, the kiddies probably wouldn't be aware of Richler's having studied up on his Mortimer and Heller, and no doubt would appreciate the literary enrichment, no matter how it got in there. However, there are other aspects of Richler's first children's book that might disconcert them. For instance, when Jacob is brought into court, the judge Mr. Justice Rough, says:

> This is serious. Extremely serious. If you got away with it, it could only lead to more monstrous crimes, like hiding comics under your pillow or peeing without lifting the seat.

"Peeing"? A proper term or even concept for a children's story? Mordecai Richler is not going to get himself the Good Housekeeping Seal of Approval with language like that. Still, while we're on the subject, what exactly is the appropriate word? Tinkling? . . . Urinating? . . . Unfortunately, L. M. Montgomery and the other giants in the children's lit field have set no precedents to lead us out of this impasse.

Of course, it could be argued that this use of a vulgarism is quite in keeping with the current trend toward realism in children's books, as noted by Sheila A. Egoff. Or possibly Richler is making use of a shock device, characteristic of his adult fiction. If so, can one then conclude that he is trying to estabish himself as an *adult terrible* for a youth audience?

In any case, there's no point in going on and on about a mere one word in this book. A much more significant problem is the story itself. Certainly an agreeable enough fantasy; however, why did Mordecai Richler feel obliged to present it as a dream sequence? Do children really require a prosaic explanation to account for Jacob's extraordinary experiences with The Hooded Fang and the Slimers? (Perhaps, though, the author is basing his narrative strategy here upon that employed in the movie version of *The Wizard of Oz;* whereas he would have been better off to stick to what Frank L. Baum originally had in mind—an actual visit to fantasy land for his Dorothy, rather than some kind of hallucination.)

Nevertheless, despite all the foregoing objections—the use of an impolite six-letter word, possible copyright infringement, and the realistic undercutting of his fantasy material—one would like to think that Mordecai Richler has created a Canadian children's literature classic. For this is a compellingly presented tale, replete with comic detail and story-line inventiveness.

Hopefully, *Jacob Two-Two Meets The Hooded Fang* does not represent some mere literary exercise for its author, a way of keeping himself in creative trim (and in money) while he gets ready to attempt another major adult novel. One would like to look forward to further children's stories from Mordecai Richler—stories which, if he pays close heed to the above critical observations, will have to be entirely masterful. (pp. 101-02)

John Parr, "Richler Rejuvenated," in Canadian Children's Literature: A Journal of Criticism and Review, *Vol. 1, No. 3, Autumn, 1975, pp. 96-102.*

What is one to make of a children's book in which a six-year-old boy is sent to prison on a false charge of insulting a grown-up; in which his jailor tells him that he is to be fed to the sharks, adding: "I will personally bring you your last meal"; in which, on his first night in solitary confinement, he is forced to listen to the Happy Nightmare Hour: "One of our snakes is missing and is rumoured to be slithering through the cell-blocks right now in search of some tasty toes"? There are many other similar details in *Jacob Two-Two meets the Hooded Fang* . . . , a book which left me feeling slightly sick. However, remembering how strange it is that many adults have hangups about books like *Where the Wild Things Are* and most children certainly don't, I did not feel I could trust my judgment until I had shown the book to several other adults. Their unanimous opinion was that while older children might find it amusing—though it is not often that a ten-year-old wants to read a book in which the central character is six—for the six-year-old it could well be the basis of several nightmares. Catherine Storr rightly said that it is perfectly proper to expose children to fear and evil in literature, otherwise they will not be able to cope with such things in real life; but, she added, one should try to avoid exposing them to the kind of sick fear that leaves them depressed and unable to cope. After reading *Jacob Two-Two meets the Hooded Fang* many a nervous or fearful child may have any sense of loss or separation he has experienced reinforced.

What has gone wrong? It would seem likely that the book originated from the author telling stories to his family . . . perhaps as bedtime stories that were designed to help overcome Jacob's problems. But what may have been perfectly acceptable by the fireside or in the bedroom has here, on the printed page, become chilling. Of course, from an author of the quality of Mordecai Richler, there is much excellent writing and considerable wit, and the story is indeed properly resolved; but this is not sufficient recompense for the horrors encountered en route. I am well aware that children are subjected to such things as the gory horrors of the battle of Stalingrad on television, but these will not produce nightmares; the events depicted are too remote from them. However, when a young child reads this book, he will be Jacob: that is the problem.

David Rees, "Over-Exposed," in The Times Literary Supplement, *No. 3864, April 2, 1976, p. 376.*

"Once there was a boy named Jacob Two-Two." At first glance, that "once" in the opening sentence of *Jacob Two-Two Meets the Hooded Fang* seems like a miscalculation. The story happens in a time and a place quite unlike the "once" of fairy tales, that mysterious world in which impossible things are a matter of fact. *Jacob Two-Two* is certainly no fairy tale.

It is not even much of a fantasy. The novel contains no unusual beasts, no magical objects or mystical rituals. Its settings include department stores and prisons, its artifacts television and electronic bleepers—things not usually found in worlds of fantasy. And while there is a slightly unusual device that makes fog in *Jacob Two-Two,* there are none of the wildly impossible machines we demand from science fiction. Furthermore, and what is most surprising, the novel offers none of those impossible leaps from time to time or place to place that we expect of dream-worlds.

Nevertheless, once Jacob begins his dream (for, as Richler insists, a dream it clearly is), things happen that do not accord with our usual sense of reality—not so much things that are impossible as things that stretch possibility.

In fact, the distinguishing quality of Jacob's dream-world is that it exaggerates reality. While cruel judges and intolerant juries do exist, they rarely act with the intense malevolence of Jacob's judge and jury—nor seem so funny in their malevolence. And while children like to believe that grownups have it in for them, not all grownups do, at least not to the degree they do in Jacob's dream. *Jacob Two-Two* is more like what we call satire than what we normally expect of fantasy; it depicts evil in an exaggerated way, so that things that are merely bad tendencies in reality are magnified into unqualified traits, and become laughable in the process.

But if *Jacob Two-Two* were only satire, it could not allow its hero the tremendous victory he achieves. In a satire, Jacob would inevitably rot in prison for eternity, in order to confirm the prejudice, accepted by Jacob and expressed by the judge, that ". . . in this court, as in life, little people are considered guilty, unless they can prove themselves innocent, which is just short of impossible." The satiric intensity of statements like that one—and the book contains many—depends on everything forever remaining just as horrible as it is; since the point is to show how corrupt things are, corrupt they must always remain. But things do get better for Jacob Two-Two. Much better.

In fact, Jacob seems to get everything he wants from the experiences the novel describes. His cynical interpretation of reality may be confirmed by the horrid judges and dark prisons he encounters; he is treated badly simply because he is young. But eventually, his genius is recognized, and not in spite of his youth, but because of it.

It seems, then, that the world described in *Jacob Two-Two* is neither like our own nor very consistent in the ways in which it is unlike our own. To some extent it is a satiric nightmare, a comical depiction of a world that is ugly, corrupt, and designed to hurt children. But it is also a wish-fulfillment, a depiction of how things ought to be. It is both satire and utopia, both worse than the real world and better than it.

The apparent inconsistencies of this world may be explained by the circumstances of its creation. In the first two chapters of the novel, Jacob confronts real situations in his normal life; but after Jacob "rubbed his eyes" at the end of the second chapter, he has fallen asleep. At the end of the book, Jacob's mother says to him, "You're a dreamer," and while the author adds a "maybe," there is little doubt that he has been dreaming. John Parr suggests this is "a significant problem with the novel . . . why did Richler feel obliged to present it as a dream sequence?" [see excerpt dated 1975].

He had a good reason for doing so; in insisting that Jacob is dreaming, Richler demands that we see the relationship between the dream and the reality. (pp. 31-2)

In fact, the oddities of the world Jacob dreams are directly related to the particulars of his life in the real world. In the real world, he is told by his older brother that at school ". . .

they had punishment cells . . . dark and gloomy, with double-locked doors, and that naughty boys ultimately had to appear before a judge.'' In his dream, he is placed in such a cell and appears before such a judge. In the real world, the grocer says, ''I demand justice. This exasperating little boy . . . must be charged with insulting behaviour to a big person.'' In his dream he is charged with just that.

Of course, as Richler is careful to point out, the grocer is ''only teasing.'' But significantly, Jacob is not amused. The dream Jacob bases on his experience with the grocer tells us how Jacob himself understood the experience—it is Jacob's version of reality, and given the way it ends, it appears to perform a positive function for him; it certainly makes him a hero. Apparently *Jacob Two-Two* is one of those fantasies in which, as Eleanor Cameron suggests, ''waking dreams of children are realized.''

But since the world he dreams is so ugly, we might wonder how such ugliness could possibly satisfy anybody's perception of reality. A closer look at its characteristics should reveal what the dream offers, both for Jacob and for young readers of the novel.

Within Jacob's dream, grownups are unreasonably cruel to children, and take it for granted that they have a right to be so. The very existence of a judge who deals strictly with ''girls who grow out of their shoes too soon'' and of a prison for the punishment of such crimes, confirms that unreasonable cruelty. There is no logic in being punished for what you cannot help, or in being punished so extravagantly. And since that is true, there is no need to feel guilty. The nastier the judge and the crueller the punishment, the freer Jacob can feel of responsibility for his inadequacies. Ironically, the dream world gets more satisfying as it gets uglier.

Furthermore, grownups act this way in Jacob's dream world for no good reason. They simply assume their right to do so. It is the way of the world to be nasty to children. The jury members spout their typically grownup aphorisms with an ease that comes with great familiarity, and the only purpose of the goods made on Slimers' Isle is to make children miserable: ''Jigsaw puzzles too complicated to solve. . . . Ping-Pong tables with a net bound to collapse the first time it was struck by a ball'' and so on; ''in a word, anything to torment little people.'' But the nastier these grownups are, the more ridiculous they become. They are, in fact, not terrible but ''funny,'' as the child points out when he sees through the deception of The Hooded Fang. The sneaky trick Jacob's dream plays on grownups is to exaggerate the bad tendencies of adults until they become too ridiculous to be respected, or even to be hated. They become figures of fun; that is why *Jacob Two-Two* is such a funny novel, and why some grownups, who may recognize their own behaviour in the exaggerated madness of the grownups in the novel, fail to see the humour.

But despite their laughability, Jacob's imaginary grownups do have a motive for their cruelty, and it makes them even more satisfying for Jacob and for children who read the novel. They secretly know, and do not dare admit, that children are, in fact, superior to grownups. That is why they spend all their time and effort keeping children in their place. If the world were not so beautifully designed to keep children in their place, then grownups would have to bow to the superiority of children and give up the power they enjoy but do not deserve.

The superiority of children, as defined in Jacob's dream, lies in their wisdom. It is not surprising that The Hooded Fang hates all children because a child once realized that he was funny instead of terrible. The child was wise enough not to be taken in by the Fang's fake terror. So is Jacob when he realizes that the Fang is secretly ''a nice man.'' In fact, it is this wise realization that leads to the Fang's eventual downfall.

But if that is true, the wisdom of children lies in their lack of knowledge of what the grownup world conceives to be the truth. Neither the child who laughed nor Jacob has understood the conventional response the grownup world expects them to have to The Hooded Fang; they are too innocent to see things the way they are supposed to see them, so they see them the way they actually are.

Ironically, the main tool grownups use to keep children in their place is this same innocence. Except grownups call it ignorance. In the real world, Jacob is told again and again that he is ignorant of what he ought to know—how to slice bread, how to count sheets, and so on. Even his brothers and sisters, who are ''taller and much more capable than he,'' will not let him play with them because ''our game's too complicated for you.'' In the exaggerated world of his dream, Master Fish and Mistress Fowl tell him that ''. . . little people are always doing the wrong thing,'' and finally call him an ''ignorant little troublemaker.''

''Ignorance'' is the secret weapon. The hold grownups have over children is their ability to persuade children that they are too stupid to understand anything or to do anything that really matters; that they are, in fact, inferior. And Jacob *is* finally ''convinced by his tormentors that there simply had to be a prison for little people as obnoxious as he was.'' But since Jacob's ''ignorance'' leads to the unmasking of The Hooded Fang and the destruction of Slimers' Isle, there is clearly some question about its value; in Jacob's dream, what is ''obnoxious'' to grownups is actually what is best about childhood.

It seems that the world of Jacob's dream has three important characteristics. The first is that grownups have all the power within it, keep it by persuading children of their ignorance, and are more funny than terrible. The second is that children are superior to grownups because their theoretical ignorance is simply an inability to understand things that are in fact incomprehensible, or wrong, or just plain silly; that their ignorance is really a wise innocence. And the third, of course, is Richler's insistence that this *is* a dream, that Jacob has imagined this distorted vision of reality for his own satisfaction.

If we take these three things together, we discover that they amount to something very *like* a paranoid delusion. Psychologically speaking, paranoia is the ascription of personal difficulties to the supposed hostility of others; ''the paranoid individual . . . cannot accept disappointment in himself, and reacts by developing fictions of superiority and by blaming his shortcomings on the machinations of others.''

In the real world, Jacob is disappointed by his inability to ''cut a slice of bread that wasn't a foot thick on one end and thin as a sheet of paper on the other,'' and about the fact that ''. . . he was not allowed to sit in a big chair at the kitchen table, but what good was it when he could hardly see over the dinner plate . . .? He cannot help these inadequacies—they exist because he is a child, not yet physically big enough to cope with grownup artifacts like kitchen chairs or physically skilled enough to handle grownup artifacts like knives.

Jacob realizes that these difficulties are merely conditions of being a child, not personal inadequacies. He knows that ''. . .

life was becoming more tolerable,'' that his capabilities are growing and will keep growing. Nevertheless, his inability to cope inevitably disturbs him personally. In fact, and paradoxically, Jacob is annoyed by his difficulties because he is mature enough to recognize them. He is young enough to fail, but old enough to realize that he is failing and be annoyed by it.

Jacob's solution to that is his paranoia-like delusion, a kind of wish-fulfilment. In his dream, his failures are not his own fault. Grownup artifacts were specifically designed by grownups to torment children, and represent grownup hostility, not childish inadequacy. The list of objects made on Slimers' Isle includes ''Shoes made especially for children to outgrow within three months'' and ''Rain for picnics.'' It takes a certain amount of protective self-delusion to imagine that the problem is the shoes and not the feet, and that even the weather has been designed by THEM to get YOU. It also takes a lot of egocentric arrogance; but what makes the persecution bearable is the belief that one is important enough to be the object of such intense persecution.

In fact, the world of Jacob's dream is much *like* Freud's description of paranoid delusions: an attempt, and a successful one, ''to re-create the world, to build up in its stead another world in which its most unbearable features are eliminated and replaced by others that are in conformity with one's own wishes.'' According to Freud, ''each one of us behaves in some respect like a paranoiac, corrects some aspect of the world which is unbearable to him by the construction of a wish and introduces this delusion into reality.'' The delusion Jacob introduces into reality, at least into the reality of his dream, allows him to put up with his own failings.

But we should not forget Richler's careful insistence that Jacob is in fact dreaming. It shows us that Jacob realizes his dream is not the truth—only a temporary replacement for it. Jon C. Stott says that Jacob ''misunderstands the attitudes of older people toward little kids.'' But he does not really misunderstand. His parents do feel he is incompetent (and to some extent, he *is* incompetent); and the older children really do not want to play with him. Stott says Jacob has a ''persecution complex,'' but Jacob really *is* persecuted.

Furthermore, he understands the true nature of the persecution. When Jacob flees the grocery store, he does so, not because he is terrified by the grocer's threatened punishment, but because he knows the grocer is merely teasing. If we assume that Jacob's response to the exaggerated cruelty of the grownups he imagines in his dream represent his attitude toward the pretend cruelty of the grocer, then what bothers Jacob is that the grocer is belittling him. Either Jacob is dumb enough to believe the grocer, or weak enough to have to put up with cruel teasing. Either way, the grocer is a fool—and in his dream, Jacob makes grownups into fools. He does not misunderstand the grownup world (and his own place in it) so much as he dislikes it; that is why he transforms it into something easy to dislike, and himself into something so easy to admire.

In any case, the dream itself contains an acknowledgement of its own exaggeration. We are told that the various inventions of Slimers' Isle are designed to get children ''in trouble with big people who did, in fact, love them.'' So Jacob acknowledges that such people do exist, even if none appear within the dream. The dream is not something Jacob confuses with the truth, but something he uses to make the truth more bearable. Jacob is not a paranoid with a persecution complex, in

need of clinical treatment; he is a sane and successful user of paranoid delusion.

In fact, the best thing about Jacob's dream is that it is, in fact, just a dream. Knowing that grownups are not really unthinking, ridiculous monsters with nothing on their minds but the repression of children, children who read the novel can instead pretend for awhile that grownups *are* such monsters, and purge their feelings of repression with laughter.

In this sense, *Jacob Two-Two* is a subversive book—a comical attack on grownup supremacy that undermines the control grownups have over children. Within Jacob's dream, he possesses the power he lacks in reality, and it is no wonder that the phrase ''Child Power'' operates so significantly in the novel. Paranoid fantasy is a means of power for those who are otherwise powerless, and in *Jacob Two-Two* Richler associates with other members of powerless groups who feel repressed by the society they live in. The control over their own existences such people lack is available to them only in fantasy, and we are all familiar with books by Blacks about magnificent Blacks and hilariously weakminded Whites, or books by women about magnificent women and unnecessarily arrogant men. In such literature the powerful are made figures of fun, and the weak become blameless heroes. *Jacob Two-Two* offers children similar consolations if they feel similarly powerless; for not only does Jacob have power within the dream, but perhaps more significantly, the power to dream is itself a significant replacement for the power he lacks in reality. It does not change the world, or even himself; but he can continue to operate in the real world because of his indulgence in the dream one. He can bear persecution if he has power over his persecutors—especially since it is only in his imagination.

It is a large part of Richler's genius as a novelist for children that he recognizes, and allows his youthful protagonist to enjoy, the pleasures of paranoia. Jacob manages to be what Richler says he himself and too many other contemporary writers too often are: ''triumphant in our vengeful imaginations as we never were in actuality.'' It may well be a flaw in theoretically mature novelists that they re-invent the circumstances of their lives in order to make themselves feel better about them. But for Jacob, who is too powerless to have other means of feeling better about himself, a vengeful imagination turns out to be a boon and not a failing. (pp. 32-7)

> *Perry Nodelman, ''Jacob Two-Two and the Satisfactions of Paranoia,'' in* Canadian Children's Literature: A Journal of Criticism and Review, *Nos. 15 & 16, 1980, pp. 31-7.*

Clumsy adults get their comeuppance in scores of humorous children's books. The success of *Jacob Two-Two Meets the Hooded Fang*, Mordecai Richler's bestseller, is testament to the allure of this theme. The book has real liabilities—an overload of belabored jokes, cliché, and sagging plotlines. Worse, it has moments of embarrassing sentimentality and falseness. The villains of Slimers' Island, we are told, shroud the place in fog because they can't stand sunshine. Why? Because ''any big person who cannot stand little ones also fears the sun'' (also pets, flowers, and laughter). The ending is a bit of a cheat, too. After all the hoopla and the uproariously gothic plot, Jacob awakens on a park bench, and we are left to decide whether the entire story wasn't just a dream.

Still, in addition to occasional flights of inspired verbal tomfoolery, the book has another basic strength, and that is the accurate perception of how it feels to be the youngest in the family, the one who always gets teased, tricked, put-upon, left out, and drowned out by ebullient older siblings. If Jacob Two-Two cannot ride a bike or cut a straight slice of bread, he can nevertheless enjoy a comic triumph by seeing clearly through the hypocrisies of adults, judge and jailer alike.

Michele Landsberg, in a review of "Jacob Two-Two Meets the Hooded Fang," in her Reading for the Love of It: Best Books for Young Readers, *Prentice Hall Press, 1987, p. 82.*

JACOB TWO-TWO AND THE DINOSAUR (1987)

One of the happy publishing events of 1975 was the appearance of *Jacob Two-Two and the Hooded Fang.* . . . Richler's new story, *Jacob Two-Two and the Dinosaur,* demonstrates some of the virtues of the original and a few more shortcomings.

Now eight years old and more independent of spirit, Jacob still suffers the teasing of his older brothers and sisters. While their parents are away on a trip to Africa, a well-meaning aunt, Aunt Good-For-You, takes the children to the museum, where Jacob learns all about dinosaurs. Soon the parents return, and their gift for their youngest son is a small green lizard. Before long, Dippy is as big as a house—no ordinary lizard but a real, live dinosaur. Because people are afraid of live dinosaurs, Jacob and Dippy (who suddenly reveals a gift for speaking English) must head for the hills—in fact, the Rocky Mountains, where, it is said, dinosaurs once roamed free.

The fugitives are pursued by a collection of refugees from Richler's adult satirical mind: Prime Minister Perry Pleaser, his adviser Professor Wacko Kilowatt, and Bulldog Burke, chief of army intelligence. The most enjoyable moment in the chase for the reader will be Dippy's discovery of pizza with the works, an addiction resulting in fogs of garlic wind blowing through the valleys of British Columbia.

Like Dippy's pizza, the new *Jacob Two-Two* contains a number of undigested elements. It's loose in structure, with a clutter of topics sprinkled through the story: information about dinosaurs, a taste of political satire, the too brief walk-on of Aunt Good-For-You. The story will entertain kids, but it may not have the shelf-life of the original.

Peter Carver, in a review of "Jacob Two-Two and the Dinosaur," in Books for Young People, *Vol. 1, No. 2, April, 1987, p. 9.*

Jacob Two-Two, Mordecai Richler's pint-sized protagonist, is back after 12 years. The Montreal novelist's first book for children, *Jacob Two-Two Meets the Hooded Fang,* introduced Jacob as a plucky six-year-old beset by four older siblings. In Richler's long-awaited sequel, *Jacob Two-Two and the Dinosaur,* his hero has moved from Britain to Montreal (like Richler himself), and he has grown marginally older and tangibly wiser. Now 8, Jacob can dial a phone number, do "joined-up writing of a sort," and, to the reader's relief, no longer has to say everything twice to be heard. Once again he is in trouble with mean-spirited grown-ups. But the adventures of Two-Two II are far more imaginative and amusing than those of Two-Two I. Indeed, the ogre-and-dungeon fantasy of *The Hooded Fang* seems positively lugubrious next to the Swiftian satire of *Dinosaur,* a fable cunningly designed to delight children and parents alike. . . .

There is a reckless momentum to Richler's narrative, a rhythm of slapdash invention that mimics the frantic pace of childhood

fantasy. Yet Richler's tale is well-ventilated with adult wit. Professor Kilowatt brags about the tolerance of his country club, which accepts "a few members who are black or Jewish or Greek, so long as they are also filthy rich." Later, Prime Minister Pleaser's coterie of "yes-men and yes-women" applaud wildly when he ties his shoelaces "without help from anybody."

Unfortunately, Richler has so far produced only two *Two-Two* books. The first was charming and clever but catered perversely to juvenile obsessions with ugly monsters and prisons. *Jacob Two-Two and the Dinosaur* is a split-level fantasy that taps an ageless sense of insolence. And Dippy the talking dinosaur makes an ideal mascot for children—or adults—out of sync with the grown-up world.

Brian D. Johnson, "Jacob Two-Two in Love," in Maclean's Magazine, *Vol. 100, No. 22, June 1, 1987, p. 52.*

The first *Jacob Two-Two* was well-written, carefully plotted, nicely illustrated, morally satisfying, and, above all, funny to young and old alike. The sequel, alas, has none of those qualities.

Jacob Two-Two is now two years older, and his penchant for saying everything two times has almost entirely disappeared. Since that habit was the source of much of the first book's humour, Richler has sacrificed a great deal in allowing Jacob to age. To portray Jacob's difference from the other kids, Richler resorts to stale jokes. Asked by his teacher, Miss Pickle, to define the word "denote," Jacob repeats what his brother has told him: "Denote is what you write with de pencil and de paper." This response earns Jacob the admiration of the rest of the class and the displeasure of his teacher, the first in a long line of adults who threaten his happiness.

The conflict between adults and children was also at the heart of *The Hooded Fang,* but in that book the satire is light-hearted and directed against the conventional attitudes of adults towards children. (p. 43)

In the new book, however, adults are divided into two distinct groups: Jacob's parents (who are Good) and all other authority figures (who are Bad). Teachers are mean, relatives are oppressive, scientists are foolish cowards, politicians are egotistical maniacs, rich people are snobs, and the government works hand-in-hand with the army to destroy Jacob's pet. (pp. 43-4)

The size of Dippy . . . causes problems for Jacob's family: one day he trots through the grounds of the Certified Snobs' Golf and Country Club, where Jacob has been taking swimming lessons. This episode prompts an attempt at satire at the expense of the Certified Snob's Club. . . . The president of the club, Professor Wacko Kilowatt, summons Jacob's father and delivers an ultimatum:

> "Look here", Wacko said, "we are now, in spite of what hopelessly inferior people say, a very tolerant club. We have come to accept a few members who are black or Italian or Jewish or Greek, so long as they are also filthy rich. We even accept children for swimming classes whose parents . . . were not intelligent enough to inherit money and actually work for a living. But we must draw the line somewhere. We will simply not accept any green monsters in our club."

It is difficult to imagine what audience Richler could have in mind for this sort of bald sarcasm. Children wouldn't see the irony, and most adults would find it too obvious to be funny. Only readers who assume that all rich people are ignorant, bigoted, and snobbish would be likely to smile at this.

Wacko Kilowatt is the scientific advisor to Prime Minister Perry Pleaser, who bears a suspicious resemblance to our current PM (the illustrator has given him a pronounced chin). Perry Pleaser is prime target for Richler's satire:

> On awakening each morning, Perry Pleaser, even before he brushed his teeth, would hug himself and kiss his reflection in the mirror. He wanted all the people to love him at least as much as he loved himself, which was proving very, very difficult.

A little of this kind of humour goes a long way, but Richler evidently felt that he had struck the motherlode with the self-obsessed PM, and he mines it for all it is worth, which is not much. Pleaser has surrounded himself with a chorus of yes men (and yes women) and hardly a chapter goes by without a ringing chorus of ''yes'' from these sycophants. Unlike the Jacob Two-Two of *The Hooded Fang,* whose repetition of every speech becomes a significant element in the plot, and evokes sympathetic laughter, the yes men are ultimately boring.

Predictably, Perry Pleaser and Wacko Kilowatt decide that Dippy must be eliminated. The dinosaur, who up to this point has been mute, suddenly begins to speak. This enables him to have witty conversations with Jacob, using lines borrowed from old Mel Brooks routines. When Jacob says, ''Aw, who needs girls,'' Dippy replies: ''It's okay for you to talk—you're only eight. But I'll bet when you get to be sixty-five million-plus

years you'll be interested in girls too.'' When apprised that he is being hunted down, Dippy protests: ''But I'm a law-abiding citizen. In more than sixty-five million years I've never even had a ticket for jaywalking.'' Dippy has forgotten that for all but a few months of that time he was apparently only a few inches long and living underground in Kenya. But what does consistency matter if the humour is clever and appealing to readers of all ages? Unfortunately, it isn't.

Reviewers who enjoyed *Jacob Two-Two meets the Hooded Fang* praised it as much for its warmth and compassion as for its humour. It's difficult to imagine anyone praising *Jacob Two-Two and the dinosaur* for those reasons. This is a mean-spirited book, which promotes an Us vs. Them philosophy, and suggests that Canadian scientists, politicians, and military men are corrupt, self-serving, and vicious. The same attitude pervades Richler's last novel, *Joshua then and now,* a disappointing imitation of *St. Urbain's Horseman. Horseman* was characterized by compassion and a clear sense of a moral norm, whereas, *Joshua* seems to be motivated by feelings of revenge and My Family Right or Wrong. Morality in the novel crumbles when it runs up against the brick wall of family ties. *Jacob Two-Two and the Dinosaur* is the product of a similar approach to the world, in which Jacob and his family are right, and everyone else is wrong—and not only wrong, but evil, stupid, and incompetent. One hopes and expects that children will not care for this book. (pp. 44-5)

Michael Darling, ''An Unappealing Sequel,'' in Canadian Children's Literature: A Journal of Criticism and Review, *No. 49, 1988, pp. 43-5.*

Ouida Sebestyen

1924-

American author of fiction.

Sebestyen's realistic stories for young adults convey the resilience of youth, the importance of families, and her overriding belief in the power of good. Noted for her portrayal of plucky adolescent protagonists who triumph over adversity, Sebestyen sets her themes of survival, the search for identity, and the universal need to belong against a formidable background of poverty, injustice, desertion, and death. Her vivid narrative style, interspersed with convincing dialogue and seasoned with humor, serves to offset the seriousness of her topics and to assist the flow of her multi-level stories. Sebestyen is best known for her first book, the controversial *Words by Heart* (1979). Set in 1910, the story is told by twelve-year-old Lena, a black minister's daughter, who moves with her family to a small, all-white Texas town. During the course of the novel, Lena wins a Bible memorization contest over the favored white contestant and then must learn to live out the scriptural injunction to "turn the other cheek," her father's method of coping with the prejudice and violence which their family encounters. The book's title reflects Lena's journey from merely memorizing biblical verses to living by them, which is to know them "by heart." Although *Words by Heart* was acclaimed by many in the literary establishment, Sebestyen faced accusations of racism in perpetuating stereotypical images of passive blacks and bigoted whites. Her second novel, *Far from Home* (1980), focuses on thirteen-year-old Salty's struggle to care for his great-grandmother after the death of his mother, and authentically recreates the atmosphere of Texas in 1929. A contemporary story loosely based on Sebestyen's relationship with her son, *IOU's* (1982) depicts the close bond between young Stowe and his divorced mother Annie as the boy strives to make up both for the husband who left his mother and the father who disinherited her. *On Fire* (1985) takes up the tangled story of sixteen-year-old Tater, the killer of Lena's father in *Words by Heart*. The novel is told by Tater's younger brother Sammy, who follows his confused sibling to the coal mines of Colorado to save him from himself. In all of her books, Sebestyen emphasizes the worth of the individual and the interrelationships that bind people together.

Critics praise Sebestyen for her strong characterizations, substantial themes, polished craftsmanship, and perennial optimism. Although opponents decry her regressive message in *Words by Heart* and attack the credibility of the novel's ending, reviewers generally applaud her stories of young people overcoming obstacles and recommend reading her books for discussion of their thought-provoking concerns. Sebestyen is generally considered an insightful, eloquent writer whose tough yet tender works emphasize the dignity and resolution of the young.

Words by Heart won the International Reading Association Children's Book Award in 1980 and was a finalist in the hardcover fiction category of the American Book Award in the same year; in 1982 the paperback version won the American Book Award. *Far from Home* was nominated for the American Book Award in 1981 and received the Zilveren Griffel (Silver

Pencil) Award from the Netherlands as the best translated children's book of 1984.

(See also *Contemporary Literary Criticism*, Vol. 30; *Something about the Author*, Vol. 39; and *Contemporary Authors*, Vol. 107.)

AUTHOR'S COMMENTARY

Probably I became a writer, with a berm of scratch paper and dictionaries buffering me from the world, because I don't think too fast, or well, on my feet. When someone in a recent audience asked me why I had made a parent-child relationship the focus of each of my books, I was speechless. That is to say, I didn't have the answer in my speech, and had to settle for looking mysterious and going home to think about it sitting down.

With my feet propped and the butterflies of extemporaneous speaking weighted by a peanut butter sandwich, I could readily see that I had indeed built my three books around children and parents—around families—and especially around a full range of mothers, from expectant ones to a great-grandmother. It seemed clear to me, pondering at my leisure, that I'd done it because I like examining and commenting on what it's like to be a part of the human family, with all its problems, responsibilities, joys and—to a writer—dramatic possibilities.

I just happened to love families, kids, homes, kinships, pets, interrelationships, the whole bit. You'd think I could have explained something that simple standing up.

I could see three or four other reasons, perhaps more personal, when I stopped to look. I write fiction because it gives me permission to do something I enjoy: creating my own little worlds. Certainly every family is a world, teeming with life, symbiotic, ancient and futuristic, sending little spaceships out, first to visit grandma, then off to college, and finally out to people other colonies. On the other hand, I like trying to reduce things to basics, and it's hard to get more basic than a baby. Or to construct a stronger, more economical shape than the triangle of man, woman and child.

Also, I'm only comfortable writing about what I know, or think I know, and I've spent my life being either a daughter or a mother, and nearly twenty years being both at once, hands-on. Maybe, as an only child with an only child, I've been more aware of the parent-child ties and stresses than more thickly-branched, sibling-rich families are. While I was struggling with the technical aspects of plot, character, dialogue and all the rest, in those first books, I may instinctively have chosen families as the subject matter I could feel—well, *familiar* with.

But my reasons weren't all personal. I was writing for young readers, and I truly believed that young lives are shaped mainly by the family they are part of. This shaping would have to include the flip side, too: managing without a family, or finding or rebuilding it, or losing or leaving it. Family is both heredity and environment in one. Everything branches from it like the twigs of a genealogical chart.

Still, by family I don't mean, necessarily, the traditional father and mother and two and a half children. Even my most traditional family, the one in [*Words by Heart*], had a step-mother and half brothers and sisters. In *IOU's,* a single parent and an only child create their unique and workable version. And in *Far From Home* a family has to evolve from the flawed and disparate characters gathered in a boardinghouse. But *family* originally meant all the people living in the same house. Maybe I stretch this a tiny bit, to include all the people living on the same planet.

Physically, having a book is a lot like having a baby. It looks easy until you try it. There's the same early mixture of apprehension and high hopes, the feeling of being burdened and blessed and happily scared. Later comes the struggle to share this tender new creation trustfully with the world. Sending a manuscript off to a publisher leaves the same aching end-of-an-era empty space as sending a child off to school. Editors and educators and the realities of life are waiting out there, sure and persuasive, to start the second shaping.

I was a writer, unpublished but undauntedly A Writer, a long time before I was a parent. Through all the years that my friends were getting married and having babies, I was having books and getting rejection slips. Both motherhood and success in my work came late. The efforts fell roughly into eighteen-year segments. I tentatively started a novel for adults when I was nineteen. It was never accepted by a publisher, nor were the three that followed it. The baby came more or less in the nick of time when I was thirty-seven. The first book was published when I was fifty-five. It was slightly overdue, for an overnight success, but overwhelming just the same.

Motherhood was the turning point of both my life and my career. I couldn't have written my three books before my son was born. Out poured all those powerful instincts to nourish and protect, to comfort and praise, to advise and guide. The kid was inundated. Suddenly I had hooked into the generations. I had rediscovered loving and giving. I longed to explain all the sad, bad things so they wouldn't hurt so much. I wanted to pass on to him all the funny, hard, delightful things I'd learned, or done, or read or imagined. We shared childhoods. I watched his unfold, feeling a second-time-around enthusiasm. He listened to mine with a patience that failed only once when, at the age of three, he said, "Why don't you hush and let me tell about when *I* was a little dirl?"

Happily, the instincts were still flowing when he reached the saturation point. My short stories for adults began to contain young people, then to be written directly for teenagers. It was wonderful to be, without apology, as upbeat and idealistic and silly and uncertain about life as my readers. My high-heeled attempts at sophistication had never felt right. It was lovely to stop teetering and tripping, and to feel solid ground under my bare feet. And one of the three stories I actually sold during that last eighteen-year period became the inspiration for, and with minor changes the first section of, the novel *Heart*.

With that first book, I began what I later realized was a goodby to my father. We had shared thirty-eight close and loving years, but last things are never fully said. I kept saying them, in all three books. As my characters worked through their losses I worked through mine. I was grateful that he lived to see his grandson. It was during those strange few months when their lives overlapped that I began to feel the grand designs in families.

Years later I was able to say in *Heart:* Something always comes to fill the empty spaces.

It was true then, and later. My mother and my son and I filled each other's spaces when my divorce and her widowhood turned us into a three-generation family, without a home or livelihood but undoubtedly rich in everything except money. It was in the two-mother household which all of us had created together that I began to write desperately in a last try for success before I gave up the crazy dream and got a real job. Supported on either side by two generations whose faith in me divided all the hardships into thirds, how could I help but write about the wonders of being family?

My mother lived to hold the first published book in her hands, nearly as proud of having it dedicated to her as she had been of an earlier gift from me—that one and only grandchild. Six months later she died, the day after I finished the last page of *Far From Home*. If my father's spirit shines out of *Heart,* my mother's brave last days are echoed in the indomitable Mam of that second book.

The third book, *IOU's,* moved on into the present generation. It's not my son's story, or mine, but I confess to using some of the antics of his thirteenth summer that were better than I could make up. We were certainly there, on the sidelines, nodding in recognition, as the mother and son of that story stretched their us-against-the-world ideas of family larger than they thought they could.

Having children and writing books for them are both acts of faith and giving. Parents and writers make the first leap when they choose to love what doesn't yet exist but is coming and will someday be. It takes faith to bring something to life and see it to its maturity—faith in communication and communion and themselves. They must believe they will have, or find, the strengths and capabilities they will need.

I keep Longfellow's lines over my desk: *Give what you have. To someone it may be better than you dare to think.* Those words help my words creep out onto the blank sheets of typing paper. They keep me making motherly soup from whatever I find in the kitchen.

Writers and parents put a lot of energy and time into earning trust, being fair, and keeping a tolerant dialogue going between the generations. Consciously or not they pass on the gifts of their own parents, and their teachers and friends and heroes, struggling to put the bits and pieces into forms that are wise or beautiful or affecting enough to deserve being handed down. A book written for young readers has to come out of the child in the writer as well as the adult, from the same memory-place where parents find empathy. Both parents and writers need to do more than hold the mirror up to life for those they're speaking to. They need to tilt the mirror so it catches light, and suggests not only how life is, but how it ought to be.

At the end of *Far From Home* I leave the main characters accepting each other's love on faith. I tried to fill the book with joyful things: babies, jokers, parades, fireworks, to counter the poignancy of a boy's search for a place to call home and someone to belong to. One of the main characters never appears in the book, but is the catalyst, just the same, of the whole story. It's the boy's mother, naturally. Who else would I pick? She leaves him a note just before she dies. It's a gentle command of ten words, and nearly everyone who reviewed the book quoted them. They promise the boy he'll be taken in. And one of the ten words is love. I hope one out of every ten words in the book, and the other books, too, conjures up love, because in my mind love, and the miracles of acceptance and connection it generates, are the ultimate things to write about.

My son graduated from high school on the day my first book was published. I remember hoping that I was sending *both* my children out into the world, to be a worthy addition and edition, respectively. So far they've brought me nothing but a joy. I'm grateful for all the ways they've forced me to grow. Now one is off to Europe for awhile, and his life opens up in all directions. It's been a fascinating experience, evolving from mother to friend. I hear my other offspring is being made into a drama for Public Television. I'll have no control over what happens to it—my baby's an adult now, on its own. But to have it appear in another form, recognizable but uniquely itself, may be close to what it's like to have a grandchild. Just the thought of it starts the old instincts flowing . . .

Belonging is a human need. Miraculously, the instinct for accepting our own is strong in all of us. What is lacking is a reminder of how far the concept of Our Own should be stretched. We all live in the same house. We may not all be writers, or parents, but we've all been children, with our common roots in love and hope. That makes us family, and family matters. It tells us where we come from and how we're connected. It reminds us, in books and in life, how varied and generous our kinship can be, if we only let it. (pp. 1-3)

> *Ouida Sebestyen, "Family Matters," in* The ALAN Review, *Vol. 11, No. 3, Spring, 1984, pp. 1-3.*

GENERAL COMMENTARY

BEVERLY HALEY

Everything has its price. To gain something, you must lose something. And the dearer the prize, the greater the cost. [In *Words by Heart*] Lena wins the Bible recitation contest, but she pays with her personal pride. And later, to gain her father's respect, she must force herself to bring those memorized words to life. "A price must be paid" recurs as a major theme in Ouida Sebestyen's novels—*Words By Heart, Far From Home,* and *IOU's.* Coming to her own success later in life than many authors . . . , Sebestyen's years of apprenticeship are now yielding awards-winning works. She tries, she says, to create a "sense of miraculous heroes, a sense of individual worth and potential." She wants her stories to show how things have been, how they ought to be, how they can be.

Sebestyen's characters provide the vehicle for dramatizing the themes. Family plays a central role in all three novels, but not family in the traditional sense. *Words By Heart* centers around a black family in an early 1900's all white Western town. Lena, the protagonist, idolizes her father Ben and loves her young stepmother, Claudie, half-brother Roy, half-sister Armilla, and the baby. Ben Sills, who once studied to be a minister, forms the strength and the center of the family; and he demands of his family that each one be at once strong and gentle.

Far From Home features a family menagerie. Again set earlier in this century, the story opens with the death of Salty Yeager's deaf-mute mother. Though he has never heard his mother's voice, he has known the strength of her penetrating love and the need to live up to that love. Now Salty must find a way to care for Mam, as he calls his great grandmother, and himself. But no one will hire Salty. Evicted from the small shack on a farm several miles from town, Salty must also get living quarters for himself, Mam, and Tollybosky, the pet gander he refuses to abandon. The last hope is The Buckley Arms Hotel, where his mother had worked hard and faithfully for as long as Salty knew. Tom and Babe Buckley—who own, run, and live in the shabby old hotel that looks "like a dignified bum who still thought it was somebody" reluctantly take the three in. Hardy McCaslin—who can't grow up, can't get or hold a job, just wants to have a good time—and his wife Rose Ann live there, too, as part of the hotel family. Briefly, the Buckleys also provide shelter for Jo Miller, who has run away from her irresponsible husband just when it is time for their first child's birth. Salty, who has never known who his father is, feels compelled, with his mother dead, to find the father he doesn't know.

The family in *IOU's,* a story set in the present in the Rocky Mountain foothills, consists only of mother and son, Annie and Stowe Garrett. Annie's father disowned her when she ran away to marry a man he disapproved of; her husband abandoned her when Stowe was very small to pursue a life of personal pleasure (Sebestyen's men tend to have weakness of character, though Ben Sills in *Words* makes up for all the rest.) The conflict comes for Stowe when he learns that the grandfather he has never seen is dying and wants to see Stowe, but not Annie, before that moment. Stowe is torn between wanting to be loyal to his mother, hating both his grandfather and father for what they have done to Annie and him, and longing to see them, to know them, to let them into his life, to find other pieces to the puzzle of his identity. (The search for identity runs strong through both *Far From Home* and *IOU's.*)

Reminiscent of Steinbeck's worlds, Sebestyen's protagonists suffer the effects of poverty, of being misfits, and of doing battle against the world in general and themselves in particular. Despite their lack of material wealth, Sebestyen's heroes gleam with a sense of nobility and purpose that the glimpses of those characters wealthy in possessions fail generally to reveal.

Their situations demand of each protagonist—Lena, Salty, Stowe—that they grow up prematurely. All experience a death in the family that forces additional maturity on them. This early maturing imposes pain, but it also endows them with a largeness of purpose and of character that most teenagers do not acquire in such breadth and depth. But they lack experience to help them fulfill the demands on them, so they sometimes falter in their attempts. Lena steals books from Mrs. Chism, justifying that act to herself and her father by saying,

> "I just wanted to read them . . . Books are to read. They'll just ruin up there (the attic). She don't care if the rats eat them—she's wasteful. She's ignorant and selfish."

Salty resents the burden that Mam is. . . . Stowe, in *IOU's,* resents having to think about things instead of just doing them as his friend Brownie is free to do. . . . (pp. 3-4)

Each of the protagonists discovers, too, the power to hurt others. Lena knows she has hurt her father by being dishonest. . . . Salty recognizes this power to hurt others in this passage:

> He could hurt people. He had never had that kind of power before. He had lives in his hand. It scared him, in a way nothing else ever had.

Stowe deliberately uses his power to hurt his mother Annie. . . . (p. 4)

Just as Sebestyen dramatizes the irony that the materially rich may be poor in common sense and decency while the materially poor possess riches of other kinds, so too do the teenagers rise to become the adults when that role is demanded. Tom Buckley in *Far From Home* can love only one person. . . . Salty, the teenager, must grow taller than Tom, the adult who can't love his own son. Salty is left alone, Sebestyen explains, "to find his place in a complex world, a safe, loving center."

In *Words,* Lena must be a bigger person than Mrs. Chism in that rich woman's irrational demands; bigger than Mr. Starnes, who forbids his son Winslow to associate with the black girl (later in the novel, Winslow becomes the adult when he calmly stands up for his friend Lena); and bigger than the Haneys, the poor white trash competing for Mrs. Chism's favors. When Lena's father dies, the preacher admits his inability to be the adult comforter of the child. . . . (pp. 4, 6)

Throughout *IOU's,* Stowe attempts to protect his mother, to be a strength to her. . . .

Sebestyen's protagonists are spirited, independent teenagers bent on being better than they are now and better than others. They are honest, loyal, proud, and loving. Yet they could not be accused of being goody-goody. They flame orange-red in their passion to possess the best in life; they push; they lie; they use their power to hurt; they have their moments of despair. They are human beings trembling on the edge of adulthood who grow up through the events in their lives. They grow stronger as a result of adversity and the fact that they are misfits in society because of age, social class, race, or sex. And for those minor characters who are in most ways flabby and weak of will, there come small deeds or words to surprise the protagonist and the reader with redeeming traits.

Violence erupts—the knife driven through the loaf of bread on the Sillses' kitchen table, the mysterious death of the pet dog, the violation of human dignity because of racial prejudice in *Words;* jeers from neighbors, rejection by his own father, the loneliness of Jo in her birth-giving, the quarreling between Hardy and Rose Ann in *Home;* and in *IOU's* the humiliations of having to return part of the groceries at the checkout stand because Annie doesn't have enough money, the embarrassment of Brownie and Stowe making fools of themselves in their anger over Karla's growing up before they do and leaving them behind and out of her life, getting lost in the cave on the mountain campout. These and other violences are set in relief against the tenderness between people who love deeply and who fight for that love.

Sebestyen lightens the opposing tones of violence and of tenderness with a third tone—that of playfulness and an enduring sense of hope. The protagonists are, after all, children. One not merely hopes but believes they will never lose the child within that makes them laugh and be bold and believe in a happy ending somewhere, that takes delight in the joy of now. (p. 6)

The author's diction captures the flavor of a time, a place, and particular people. Its poetic, musical simplicity elevates the people who are poor materially to match their richness of character. Wealthy Mrs. Chism, on the other hand, reveals her baseness of character through her "back-of-the-barn" language. Thus diction and style add texture to the writer's use of force/counterforce in characters, themes, and events.

Sebestyen's aim beyond telling a story is, she says, to nourish and enlarge young minds. Those of any age who read her words risk catching the fire of life as Salty does at the close of *Far From Home:*

> He took his punk stick from between his knees and touched it to a Sphinx. A flame rose, as green as love, and burst into sparks, snow, goose down, tears— he wasn't sure which. But it was for everything that was his, out there.

> Quickly he groped in the box and put his punk to a sparkle stick. The gray-coated wire flickered and faded, unable to catch. Then sparkles burst from the grayness, flying, hot against his skin. He stood up, so Idalee could see from her window, and conducted a band of chimneys. He made a great charmed circle over the Buckley Arms, and wrote his name in light. (p. 13)

> *Beverly Haley, "Words by Ouida Sebestyen," in* The ALAN Review, *Vol. 10, No. 3, Spring, 1983, pp. 3-4, 6, 13.*

LYN LITTLEFIELD HOOPES

To read Ouida Sebestyen is to feel deeply the power of good. Her prose holds us at the edge of our senses, where awareness is acute and meaning bursts forth from the most ordinary. In each of her four novels for young adults we see the chain of evil—of hatred, resentment, fear—being broken, and in the face of much hardship, rendered powerless by good.

In *Words By Heart,* Sebestyen's award-winning first novel, a black family strikes out for freedom and comes face to face with prejudice in an all-white town early in this century. Ben Sills, a deeply Christian man, has raised his daughter, Lena, with the imperative of good: "Be not overcome by evil, but overcome evil with good." But words must be lived. Just as the Sills family begins to get a foothold in the community, Lena's father is killed, and Lena is left to struggle alone with a mandate of goodness. Out of this deeper sense of life's purpose comes the courage to forgive, which Lena demonstrates when she saves the life of Tater Haney, the boy who has killed her father.

On Fire carries on the story from Tater Haney's perspective. Tormented by the murder he has committed, Tater faces the problem of what to do now that his life has been spared: "Sometimes I wish the law would just take me . . . but I guess that's too easy . . . you don't get to just die. . . . Like they give me back this life . . . And what am I doing with it . . ."

What am I doing with it? is the heart of Sebestyen's story. At first Tater plunges headlong into further wrong. But his younger brother Sammy and friend Yankee persevere, refusing to write him off, and in the last hour Tater makes a dramatic leap for freedom.

In *Far From Home,* young Salty Yaeger searches for the father he has never known. His mother has died, leaving him with the command to "Go to Tom Buckley . . . Love him." Salty finds Tom, and soon discovers him to be his father. A terrific struggle of wills ensues, of blame, of resentment for past wrongs, and of the question of responsibility. But through the strife they come to an acceptance of each other that fulfills Salty's mother's imperative to love.

In *IOU's,* the main character, Annie, has raised her son, Stowe, on her own, cut off from her father after his renunciation of her. After years of bitterness, Annie and Stowe's willingness to trust in good brings forgiveness and a move toward reconciliation. Ironically, Annie's father dies before they reach him, but Sebestyen shows us that the change in thought itself raises Annie and Stowe above the limitations of the past, and again evil is overcome.

> *Lyn Littlefield Hoopes, "Novels of Ouida Sebestyen Share Thread of Good," in* The Christian Science Monitor, *May 3, 1985, p. B6.*

WORDS BY HEART (1979)

AUTHOR'S COMMENTARY

Sometimes writing fiction is a struggle, sometimes a joy. Most of the time it's like a chronic backache or a ringing in the ears that won't go away. I get the feeling, looking back, that I began to write not long after I began to read, trying in some half-understood way to pass on some of the pleasure that reading had given me. It seemed like reasonable work for a shy, delicate type, a loner lost in a sturdy clan of farmers and teachers. I wrote little half-baked stories, and plays in blank verse. No one clamored for them. I wrote my first novel when I was twenty, Off it went, with my heart and soul in it. Back it came. Off again. Back again. Over and over. It happened that Little, Brown and Company was the first publisher I ever sent a manuscript to. They told me, "Sorry—but keep trying us." Thirty-five years later they published me. I guess they figured I'd finally got the hang of it.

For years I wrote hopefully. Success was coming. I told myself that, every five years, when I sold a story. Naturally I had days—what am I saying, I had *years*—when I thought of giving up. But there was nothing else in the world that I wanted so badly to do. Writing incorporated all my other enthusiasms. And that was a big order because I was an artsy-craftsy amateur at everything. I knew I was a one-thing-at-a-time person. I could never be all the things I wanted to be if I lived to be a hundred, but the people in my fiction could. I knew writing was a career I could carry anywhere in the world and tuck into the spaces around two other activities that were beginning to appeal to me very much—being a homemaker and a mother. I liked working alone, maybe not speaking to a soul all day.

Doing exactly what seemed right for me. I wanted the freedom of being my own boss. I wasn't about to give up just because I couldn't write!

If all this sounds impractical, if not downright arrogant, it was. It made for years of frustration and teetering along the poverty line. In those years I began to tack quotations on the bulletin board behind my desk to keep my spirits up. One—the only line I remember from Will Durant's *The Story of Civilization*—I took as my aim: "To seek, beneath the universal strife, the hidden harmony of things." And because writing was a lonely, self-revealing business, I needed another quotation from Longfellow to help the words come: "Give what you have. To some one it may be better than you dare to think." And a little one by Emerson: "Do the thing, and ye shall have the power."

I did my thing. I wrote and wrote. And I didn't have the power. (p. 440)

I did sell three short stories, but I sold them over a period of ten years. (p. 441)

One of those three stories I'd sold had been an enlargement of a little incident my aunt had told me—how as a child she had won a contest and got a prize that obviously had been meant for the boy everyone had expected to win. During an especially low period in my writing, I remembered the story I'd made of it, and since I'd tried and failed at everything *but* children's stories, and since the main character was young, I sent it to the children's editor at Atlantic Monthly Press. I think I started with the A's, planning to go right through every publisher in the alphabet. I asked if it had any possibilities as a book. I didn't know. I thought maybe they could add lots of pictures or something. The editor said if I'd like to try to enlarge the story and make a novel about that spunky little girl and her family, she would like to see the results. It wasn't a promise of anything. It would all be on speculation. But that letter of encouragement after all the years of rejection slips absolutely electrified me. If she had asked me to write a sequel to *War and Peace,* I would have tried. I looked at my bulletin board. It said: Do the thing, and ye shall have the power. And I did. Three months later I sent her *Words by Heart*.

Then I waited. Weeks went by. I read in the paper that our post office had been robbed. I could picture my manuscript lying discarded in a ditch. Finally the phone rang. A soft voice said, "Did you know you've written a beautiful book?" At that moment I didn't know *anything*. The voice said, "I sobbed when I read it. The assistant editor sobbed. That doesn't happen very often in this business. And we want your book."

I don't know whether I had finally learned how to put a story together, very simply and, I hope, truly, or whether speaking to children released something natural and idealistic and naive that I had been trying to camouflage as I wrote for adults. Or whether I was taken over, in the strange process that writers sometimes feel. Or whether it was a massive stroke of luck. But something went right. *Words by Heart* was published. The generous reviews took my breath away. It was honored and translated and paperbacked and condensed and dramatized. Everyone was so kind. And, of course, all the friends and relatives who gave up on me years ago told me they knew all along I could do it.

So here I am—Cinderella. The oldest promising young writer ever to become an overnight success. I'm so thankful. (pp. 441-42)

Ouida Sebestyen, "On Being Published," in Innocence & Experience: Essays & Conversations on
Children's Literature, *edited by Barbara Harrison
and Gregory Maguire, Lothrop, Lee & Shepard Books,
1987, pp. 440-42.*

The eloquent story, though circumscribed in time and setting,
dramatizes the Black people's long struggle for equal opportunity and freedom. The year is 1910; Ben Sills, ambitious for
his children, has bravely moved his family from the compar-
ative security of an all-Black Southern town to take up life as
American citizens in a white community further west. Ben is
hard-working and dependable and soon incurs the enmity of
the Haneys, a family of shiftless, ignorant sharecroppers.
Moreover, Ben's oldest child, twelve-year-old Lena, hungry
for book-reading and learning and almost always at the head
of the class, is making the townspeople uneasy; the old Southern fear and animosity are ignited anew. When Ben is hired
by wealthy old Mrs. Chism to do Mr. Haney's neglected work,
he is doomed by the tenant farmer's vengeance. The writing
is vivid, well-seasoned with figures of speech, and sometimes
even humorous; there is poignancy without sentimentality,
tragedy without melodrama. Ben and Lena dominate the book,
and the bond between them is unusually strong. A loving,
Bible-quoting man who once wanted to be a preacher, Ben is
a complex character, a person of unshakable faith and rational
conviction; he dies without hating his enemy but says to his
daughter, "'I want you to know your place. You have a right
to an education . . . and the chance to use your gifts. I pray to
God you won't ever have to live your life by somebody else's
rules.'" (pp. 303-04)

> *Ethel L. Heins, in a review of "Words by Heart,"
> in* The Horn Book Magazine, *Vol. LV, No. 3, June,
> 1979, pp. 303-04.*

This novel, like life itself for Afro-Americans in the post-Bakke
1970s, is an anguish-provoking experience in backward time
travel. Its sincerity is unquestionable, its eloquence seductive—
but its message is even more regressive than the many setbacks
from the gains of the '60s that blacks have suffered in this
Second Reconstruction.

Appropriately, **Words by Heart** is set during the closing years
of the First Reconstruction. . . .

The most puzzling and distressing aspect of Lena's character
development is that she begins as a proud fighter and ends as
a model of meek Christian forbearance, exactly, as Claudie
observes with resignation, like her saintly father. The Bible
contains, along with everything else, counsel for both modes
of behavior, making Lena's transformation from sword-wielder
to cross-bearer especially difficult for this reader to accept.
She has learned her verses under Papa Ben's tutelage, of course,
but early in the book, to his reminder that "The Lord commanded, Thou shalt not kill,'" she responds quickly, "But
Papa, in the very next chapter Moses says anybody that smited
a man and killed him shall surely die."

How Lena comes to learn Papa's favorite verses and not her
own "by heart," in view of all the evils that beset her family,
is unaccountable. One threat to their safety is the capricious
nature of their employer, Mrs. Chism, a wealthy old dragon
of a landowner who suffers unpredictable attacks of decency.
She is perhaps the most complex and intriguing character in
the book, but if she and people like her were consistently cruel,

Lena, her family and the rest of us would be better off. Mrs.
Chism is, for instance, too soft-hearted to get rid of her shiftless, dishonest poor white tenant farmers, the Haneys who are
incapable of anything but harm, until too late.

That Lena is able to feel sympathy for the Haneys at points in
the novel, in spite of the threat they pose to her family; that,
at the grim ending of the final and most suspenseful chapter,
she decides to follow her father's dictum to "Love thy enemies
and do good to them that hate you" is both appalling and
incredible. One of the author's best phrases is: "Something
always comes to fill the empty places . . . Something comes
to take the place of what you lose." But if Sebestyen's brand
of meek, turn-the-other cheek Christianity is supposed to fill
the voids left by Malcolm and, yes, Martin, then we blacks
and our youngsters will be in even deeper trouble.

> *Kristin Hunter, "Blurred View of Black Childhood,"
> in* Book World—The Washington Post, *June 10, 1979,
> p. E3.*

"Those words that you memorized," Ben Sills tells his daughter, Lena, "are not cotton to see how much you can stuff in
your sack and get rewarded for. They're rules to live by. They're
to aspire to. It means to reach up to something high, with all
your heart."

Though early signposts point to a classic black tragedy, a female *Sounder*, this deceptively simple but strong first novel is
mostly about words—from the Bible, Walt Whitman and Ben
Sills.

Twelve-year-old Lena is determined to win a contest to see
who can recite the most verses from the Bible. Tonight her
father will be proud, she vows, and her white schoolmates will
notice her "Magic Mind," not her black skin. . . .

Throughout the novel, the voice is Lena's. She listens to Ben
and Claudie argue over her head; she hopes; she becomes angry;
she learns to be afraid. Sometimes her voice rankles like that
of an angry adolescent. Sometimes it strains, stretching credibility: "Events are blinks of time in endless time." Some of
her metaphors are strained.

But sometimes, as in the beautiful contrapuntal passage during
the Bible-recitation contest, in which verse and history and
Lena's thoughts and memories are skillfully interwoven, Lena
leaps to life, full of promise and confusion, as real as the words
that astound or confound or dazzle her.

No small feat. The author—who grew up in the South and
moved to West Texas and is not black—has "aspired" bravely,
reaching high with all her heart. Despite the transparent plot,
and characters who state the novel's themes too bluntly, Ouida
Sebestyen has written a many-layered book. She has wrapped
a story with poetry, wrapped me with it, too, caught and held
me, made me feel with Lena and Claudie and Ben. And then—
in the last chapter, a kind of welcome coda—she shows her
optimism, changing her characters from timid to heroic, vengeful to generous, pointing toward love, not cynicism, without
painting black history white.

> *Cynthia King, in a review of "Words by Heart," in*
> The New York Times Book Review, *August 26, 1979,
> p. 34.*

Words by Heart brings back childhood memories of family
reunions in my parents' native state of Texas. It was during
the post-Depression years, at those gatherings of white cousins,
aunts and uncles, that my earliest impressions of the nature of

Sebestyen with son Corbin and dog Neptune above Boulder, Colorado. Photograph by Corbin Sebestyen. Courtesy of Ouida Sebestyen.

Black/white relationships were formed. The world I encountered in that small Texas town was completely white on the surface. Although Black people were about one-third of the population, for my family they were in the background, seldom mentioned, rarely heard and little seen. My memories of them are dim. Yet all the attitudes and actions of my relatives were influenced by the nature of their relationships to Black people. If any one trait characterized that relationship, it was silence. It was not until I was an adult—and then only through my mother—that I learned of my uncle's Klan activities, that one of our grandparents had been a slave owner, that the tree I had climbed in the town square was "the hanging tree." Those things—and many more—were simply not discussed. They did not exist.

Silence is good soil for the raising of myths. Was my uncle really one of the night riders who strung "rowdy niggers" from the hanging tree? Not even my mother was ever certain of her brother's involvement in those Saturday night rituals. Surely the aunts and uncles and grandparents whom I loved were good people. Where was the evidence to deny it? In that world of unspoken exploitation and violence, my relatives were nurtured on myths about good whites, contented Blacks, and an orderly way of life that suggested that things were as they should be.

I think my relatives, as I knew them in the late 1930s, would have liked **Words by Heart** because it nourishes their myths.

Here is the story of Black people who, above all else, want to protect white folks. The white community can absorb reminders that Black people are intelligent—as long as the basic hierarchical nature of the social system is undisturbed, as it is in Sebestyen's fantasy of Black/white relationships.

Not only has she made Blacks nurturing of white, she has also projected onto them the *desire* to be, with a few rumblings of discontent held in control by the gentle Black man whose wisdom is unquestioned. After his death, his wife tries to assert herself, not with the threat of rebellion, but with the implication that her children will make changes in the future. This kind of talk is not very disturbing. After all, deep inside ourselves, we whites know that Blacks harbor desires of rebellion. But dear Lord, please not now. White folks profess the need for change, but pray that it will be postponed until some indeterminate time in the future. Sebestyen's message is reassuring.

Mythology is further promoted by the portrayal of white people who seem to behave oppressively only because of prejudice on the part of certain individuals. Nowhere is there a hint of the deeply entrenched racism in the society at large that makes oppression inevitable. The author has invented a way of life that hides the ugly truth, and created characters who bear little resemblance to real people. The reader could easily conclude that exploitation of Black people in the U.S. results from individual prejudice which can be overcome if only Black people will continue to be loyal, passive and forgiving.

The final insult to reality comes in the scene of the Black-hating, self-hating white man picking cotton for the Black family whose husband/father has been murdered. Perhaps that is the ultimate fantasy in the mythological land of white goodness and Black helplessness—and the need to say that things are really not so bad, after all.

That *Words by Heart* has been highly praised by many white critics is a disheartening sign of the continued need for mythology. As white people, we cling to the myths because we want so much to convince ourselves that we are good people. What clearer indication could there be of the destructiveness of racism to white people than the unrelenting need to be reassured of our basic worth as human beings.

Racism nurtures a spirit of violence through its suppression of people, ideas, behavior, speech. White people are just as surely victimized by the violence of racism as Black people, for we have paid a high price for maintaining a racist society. We have been censored and repressed so that we would not disturb the system, our thought and behavior molded by numerous influences, our education distorted. In all of this, mythology has played a pivotal role, for it keeps us from understanding that unconsciously and unwittingly we are acting against the very principles we value most highly—freedom, independence, equal opportunity, justice.

Only when we as white people recognize that we too are damaged by racism will we be prepared to see the muzzling effect of books like *Words by Heart*. However well-intentioned the author, she does us no favor to perpetuate mythology, for it is like an addiction. The more we behave in ways that support racism, the more we hang onto mythology in order to ease the pain and guilt and to avoid taking action. And the mythology in turn perpetuates the racism. Writers who help us are those who break our needles instead of supplying us with more narcotics.

Kathy Baxter, " 'Words by Heart': A White Perspective," in Interracial Books for Children Bulletin, *Vol. 11, No. 7, 1980, p. 18.*

Words by Heart is the latest book honored by the literary establishment even though it perpetuates negative images and stereotypes. . . . It joins such books as *The Cay, Sounder* and *The Slave Dancer* in purportedly presenting a sympathetic picture of Blacks even as it misinforms readers and reinforces racist attitudes. Like the other prize winners, it has been honored for the excellence of the author's craft, but it is flawed because it presents an outsider's perspective on Black lives and fails to recognize the political, racial and social realities that shape the Black Experience in this country. And like *The Cay*, it features the death of a "noble" Black man, that very expendable literary creation.

Based on a short story published in 1968, *Words by Heart* shares with other late sixties children's fiction about Blacks the implied purpose of raising the consciousness of white readers to racial injustice. *The Horn Book* suggests that "it dramatizes the Black people's long struggle for equal opportunity and freedom" [see excerpt above dated June, 1979], but the dramatization fails because the statements the book makes about the human condition are fallacious. Unlike books written from a Black perspective—Mildred Taylor's *Roll of Thunder, Hear My Cry*, for example—*Words by Heart*, for all its literary artistry, fails to do more than evoke pity and compassion through heart-rending sentimentality. (p. 12)

On the surface this is a well-written, poignant story, offering such time-honored themes as "Love thy neighbor" and "Overcome evil with good." . . . The Sills family is portrayed as warm, close and strong. The father is, in many ways, admirable—wanting a better life for his family and placing a high value on education. However, the portrait of this Black family, supposedly seen from its center (Lena's point of view), is out of focus. The viewpoint remains that of an ethnocentric outsider. In its totality, the book perpetuates some negative images, some tired stereotypes and some implicit themes that are, from a Black perspective, questionable at the very least. There are both major and minor problems.

One problem, indicative of the book's perspective, is the tendency to associate things black with things negative. . . . Lena sees in her reflection "spiky plaits and a rascal face." At the contest, "Then everybody looked at Lena, smiling behind their eyes because she was different and comical looking oozing like dark dough over the edges of last year's Sunday dress." No matter that *everybody* in this case includes her family, who would hardly view her that way. The rest of the audience is "an orchard of pink-cheeked peaches," and the standard of beauty that is invoked reflects their ethnocentric perspective.

The main problem with Scattercreek, too, seems to have been that it was all Black. While the move west represented potential freedom from the oppression prevalent in the South of that era, the book suggests that Scattercreek also provided refuge, but was inferior because it was an all-Black town. Sills explains that because they could not live in some Southern towns, Black people made "their own communities like Scattercreek, with their own schools and churches and stores. It eases some of the trouble." And "She [Claudie] felt safe when we moved to Scattercreek." But then he says, ". . . it was easier there, but I wasn't proud of myself." Earlier he had said, "I wanted *more* for us than Scattercreek" (emphasis added). What is not clear is what Bethel Springs offers that is more, and why he was not proud to live in an all-Black town. He does cite his right as a U.S. citizen to live where he chooses, but the implication is that he chose an all-white town because there was something shameful about living in an all-Black one. This attitude contrasts to positive descriptions, like those given by Zora Neale Hurston of the richness of life in Eatonville, Florida, the "pure Negro" town in which she was born.

It is through Sills' talks with Lena that the most insidious messages about the nature of racism occur. Sills stubbornly refuses to acknowledge racism as the motivation for the hatred the Haneys—and others—express. There are threats and name-calling, the mysterious death of the Sills' dog, a knife thrust through a fresh loaf of bread the night Lena wins the contest. Yet Sills insists: "This is a good town we've come to . . . they took us in." He attributes whites' behavior to their fear of change or to their hopelessness and frustrations with being poor share-croppers, rather than to racism. He proposes that the white people's actions be met with understanding: "It's not your place to judge people," he tells Lena. "That's for God." When Sills' wife Claudie urges him to tell Lena about racism and about the family's earlier experiences in the South, Sills softens the telling with the suggestion that the isolation Claudie experiences in a white town exaggerates her fears that those "bad old times" could happen again. Although Ben does recognize that, even in Bethel Springs, some cannot accept them, for the most part Claudie's fears are made to seem almost unreasonable in this "good town." (Moreover, the "bad old times" were hardly past since this story takes place during the period historians call "The Nadir" because it was a time of intensified violence and brutality against Blacks; there is no sense of this reality in the book, however.)

When discussing the family's history and the Black Experience in general, Sills refuses to place the blame where it belongs: "They reconstructed us—one little loss at a time. . . . Somehow we got put in our place again." The anonymous, unspecified forces at work are never labeled, never named. The violence that Black people experienced the post-Civil War period is only touched on in one brief paragraph and, in fact, some of the historical information given is not correct. (Black people did not, for example, only *begin* to read and write after the Civil War; freed people aside, many slaves learned to read and write, even when it was illegal. And to say about the Civil War, "all those people fighting for our rights," as Sills does, is to minimize the role that Black people played in fighting for their own freedom.) The entire section is clearly a contrived bit of writing designed to bring in some historical information.

The most overtly racist behavior comes from unsympathetic characters whose behavior can be "explained away" in large part by their situation or personality traits. The Haneys are stereotypes of poor-white Southerners—lazy, hard-drinking, irresponsible, gun-toting males, dirty children and women kept barefoot, pregnant and silent. Another prejudiced person in the story is Mrs. Chism, the woman for whom both Sills and Haney work and from whom Ben Sills rents his home. She is an eccentric elderly woman—lonely, unhappy, seemingly oblivious to the effects of placing Sills and Haney in competition with each other and indifferent to the effects of her sharp-tongued barbs on other people. Neither her own children nor her neighbors like her, and only one person attends what was meant to be her large and elaborate dinner party. The pompous school teacher at one point asserts the inferiority of Blacks and is disputed by Lena and a white boy whose father then forbids him to associate further with Lena. Predictably in a book of this type, at the end of the story the boy openly and publicly defies his father to befriend Lena's family, an act which lacks credibility. In any case, the portrayal of the "bad guys" as mostly atypical or unlikeable people projects a picture of a utopian town where racism is an aberration.

Moreover, the cumulative picture of Ben Sills is the prototype of the "good Negro"—hard-working, Bible-quoting, understanding, passive, loving and forgiving towards whites, and willing to "wait on the Lord" until whites are ready to accept his family. (Sills' favorite Bible verse is "They that wait upon the Lord shall renew their strength. . . .") Sills lives to serve others—and those others (outside of his family) are white. When Lena asks why her family must always work for others, Sills replies: "What's wrong with working for people? That's what we are here for, to serve each other. . . ." That is a questionable generalization, since no whites "serve" any Blacks in the story. This stereotypic portrait of passivity does not advance the art of writing about the Black Experience, and in the late 1970's it need not have been perpetuated.

The characterization of Sills will be justified by the fact that he had wanted to be a minister, but it is false to equate godliness with passivity. Furthermore, Black ministers have been in the forefront of the struggle for freedom. Dr. Martin Luther King, Jr. was non-violent, but not passive. His counsel was not to "wait on the Lord," but to recognize "why we can't wait."

Many works, both fictional and historical, provide alternative portraits. Nate Shaw's story, told in *All God's Dangers*, and even the popular *Roots*, suggest that Ben Sills is unreal. Even James Weldon Johnson, a staunch integrationist, wrote in 1934 in *Negro Americans, What Now?*,

> There come times when the most persistent integrationist becomes an isolationist, when he curses the white world and consigns it to Hell. This tendency toward isolation is strong because it springs from a deep-seated, natural desire—a desire for respite from the unremitting, grueling struggle; for a place in which refuge might be taken.

It is the recognition of this truth that is glossed over in the portrait of Ben Sills.

The most disturbing aspect of this book is its ending. Given the characterization of Ben Sills, it is entirely consistent for him to crawl, though fatally wounded, a considerable distance to help Tater, his attacker. (Sills doesn't even try to leave to get help for himself; that option "never occurred to him.") Given the described relationship between Lena and her father, it is also consistent for her to help Tater—for her father's sake and for the sake of her own humanity. But only if one can equate justice with vengeance can the message implicit in Lena's decision to lie about her knowledge of her father's murder be seen as consistent behavior—or acceptable. The message is that if a white boy, as part of his rite of passage into male adulthood, even goes so far as to kill a Black person, the proper Christian response is to "let God handle it." (Can you imagine literary prizes bestowed on a book in which a rotten Black boy murders an angelic white man and is forgiven by the white man's daughter?) That message remains untempered despite the intimation that Tater may eventually be healed both physically and morally, and despite the closing scene in which Tater's father silently picks the cotton of the family his son has made fatherless. He knows that the cotton crop represents money the Sills family will need to survive, but the question of whether his helping is motivated by remorse, guilt or a desire to buy Lena's continued silence is left unanswered. Given the characterization of Haney as hate-filled and lacking in hope, Lena's hope that he has acquired a new sense of morality is totally unfounded.

The message is certainly untempered by Claudie's speech to Mrs. Chism and other white town leaders. Says Claudie:

> We know how to earn our keep and we know how to knuckle to you. Only we mean to work and knuckle the way we choose to, and where we choose to. I have two boys coming up to be the same threat to you all that Ben was. You better be ready for them because I'm going to have them ready for you.

The idea that hard work and submission and gradualism will overcome is untenable. Hard work is no threat to people on whom one depends for one's livelihood. Hard work was never a defense against oppression; it is not today. This is an irresponsible message to give to any young readers. In addition, Claudie's dramatic speech misses the point, touched on earlier in the book, that it is Lena's facile mind and her thirst for knowledge that are the real potential threat.

"Love thy neighbor" and "overcome evil with good" are worthwhile themes. In an ideal world, where racial differences don't count, it wouldn't matter which characters exemplify those themes. However, in a book set in the real world, where racial differences *do* count, when the responsibility for loving, forgiving and overcoming evil with good lies solely with the book's Black characters, the action takes on racist overtones. The implication is that white people should be understood and forgiven, even for violent racist acts. In all likelihood, many aware young Black readers will reject this message, and the book with it. They understand that passivity will not cure racism. Others may not be so aware. If they, along with young white readers, come away with the message that passivity is acceptable and that whites are to be forgiven rather than held accountable for racist actions, the damage will be doubly done.

In these troubled times, when the KKK still operates on the assumption that they can threaten and kill with relative impunity, it is important to recognize that *Words by Heart* invokes a third Judeo-Christian tenet—''Thou shalt not kill.'' A prize-winning book that plays ''overcome evil with good'' against ''thou shalt not kill'' has a responsibility to see that the latter receives equal time. (pp. 12-15, 17)

> *Rudine Sims, '' 'Words by Heart': A Black Perspective,'' in* Interracial Books for Children Bulletin, *Vol. 11, No. 7, 1980, pp. 12-15, 17.*

FAR FROM HOME (1980)

Salty was thirteen. He had no idea who his father was; his mother (a mute woman) was dead, as were his grandparents; he lived alone with his great-grandmother and they were facing eviction. He took the note his mother had left, telling him to go into town to the home of Tom and Babe Buckley, where she had worked for many years. ''GO TO TOM BUCKLEY HE TAKE YOU IN LOVE HIM,'' it said. The boy and the old woman are taken in on sufferance, Salty determined to earn his keep; the house is an almost-bankrupt boarding house; there are six adults and Salty. It will probably be clear to the reader before it is understood by Salty that Tom is his father and that the fact must be kept from Babe, who has had many miscarriages and who is loved and protected by her husband. This is not a childlike story, but should have some of the same kind of appeal that *To Kill a Mockingbird* has had to many adolescent and pre-adolescent readers: a vividly created microcosm of society, an abundance of sentiment without sentimentality, and a protagonist who is drawn with compassionate percipience. All of the characters are drawn in depth, in a moving story in which several of them change believably in response to the others. For some it develops that the boarding house can never be a home; for Salty, once he accepts the limitations that Tom puts on their relationship, it becomes a home. While Salty is the only child in the story, he is the focal point; in him are the passion for justice, the need for love and security, and the need to identify and belong that all children feel. A fine novel.

> *Zena Sutherland, in a review of ''Far from Home,'' in* Bulletin of the Center for Children's Books, *Vol. 34, No. 1, September, 1980, p. 21.*

It is risky for an author to tackle stock characters and stock situations in a novel. Take *Far From Home.* Down-and-out orphan of deaf-and-dumb mother begs mother's former employer (and maybe lover) for room at failing boarding house only to meet aging prankster, pregnant bootlegger's wife and nosey neighborhood kid. Not only could this have ended up a stock story, it could have ended up a melodrama.

It didn't, largely because of an honest character named Salty. With all the gangly, fumbling energy of a 13-year-old who feels life has not been fair, Salty not only pushes for a home for himself, his grandmother ''Mam'' and his pet gander Tollybosky, he pushes to the very edge of discovering who his real father is. Landlord Tom Buckley warns, ''You're edging

along something you're not old enough or smart enough to handle,'' but Salty is stubborn.

At times the activity around Buckley Arms, a kind of 1920's Noah's ark, flips by like a penny movie. The prankster Hardy is forever clowning, Jo has her baby in Salty's room, Mam runs away, and a Fourth of July parade almost steals the ending. But while Salty goes along with it all, he is never taken over by it. Author Sebestyen sees to that with moments like Salty's first lonely night at the Arms, when he gets lost in the yard stumbling over tin cans and ''grabbing at moon shadows.''

Amid the parades and fireworks Ouida Sebestyen lets her character touch the others honestly ''with a little bluster of hope'' and produces an aching irony, for it is July 1929, the end of an era. One only wonders if she needed the nonstop action and a cast that size when she had a year like '29, a character like Salty and a notably sensitive style.

> *Patricia Lee Gauch, in a review of ''Far from Home,'' in* The New York Times Book Review, *January 18, 1981, p. 31.*

Sebestyen's style includes humor to offset the serious tone of the book and sensitivity to help us understand the many dimensions of the characters. Salty learns about different kinds of love through the novel: love of a mother for a newborn baby; love of older people; love of friends who share life experiences. In spite of the poverty surrounding them, everyone finds some way to extend a helping hand to those who need it, but to Salty especially. A quiet story told with gentleness and honesty.

> *Ruth Cline, in a review of ''Far from Home,'' in* The ALAN Review, *Vol. 11, No. 1, Fall, 1983, p. 17.*

IOU'S (1982)

Like *Words by Heart* and *Far from Home,* Sebestyen's new novel is an unforgettable story that adults and young readers both will lose themselves in. With insight, unforced humor and tenderness, the author relates events arising from changes in the lives of 13-year-old Stowe and his divorced mother, Annie. They have been inseparable always; Stowe has never known his father. Annie supports them precariously by tending little children, work that allows her to share her son's growing years. But now the pangs of adolescence and poverty cause Stowe to challenge Annie's independence. He confronts her with such questions as why she doesn't get a better job or ''marry somebody.'' Mother and son together decide a vital question when kin in a distant city offer a home and security, a resolution that is delivered in the book's only slightly weak part. Here, the otherwise excellent narrative becomes rather talky—an unimportant flaw, however, in a story about characters who compel our attention and concern.

> *A review of ''IOU's,'' in* Publishers Weekly, *Vol. 221, No. 7, February 12, 1982, p. 98.*

Written from the adolescent's perspective, the story explores with sensitivity and insight the relationship between two remarkable individuals—Stowe and his unconventional mother Annie.... The resolution is neither glib nor simple but rather reflective of reality where large losses are sometimes followed by small advances. What is most important is that Stowe and his mother emerge from adversity not necessarily unscathed but undaunted. With feeling, but not without humor the novel works on many levels. The characters, developed in action and dialogue, are remarkably well rounded, and the theme, as in *Words by Heart,* is a substantial one.

> *Mary M. Burns, in a review of "IOU's," in* The Horn Book Magazine, *Vol. LVIII, No. 4, August, 1982, p. 418.*

Stowe's ambivalence is wonderfully captured. He has moments of sudden recklessness, exhilarated at having risked pursuing his way even if his mother might be right. But he also nurses a secret prayer: "Let me be better to her than they were. . . . I want to make it up to my mother."

The crisis of his grandfather's dying helps release Stowe's dammed-up feelings. He lets go of his hatred and exposes himself to the terror of loss. With Annie's love he feels able to travel "the scariness of new country" and to begin the search for his own father, breaking the pattern of what happened with hers.

Although Ouida Sebestyen allows her characters to talk too explicitly about these themes, making connections for the reader that would be better left tentative, this is a powerful story. As in Miss Sebestyen's award-winning *Words by Heart,* the young protagonist, strengthened by the love and integrity of a parent, takes on moral responsibility in a harsh world.

> *Hazel Rochman, in a review of "IOU's," in* The New York Times Book Review, *September 19, 1982, p. 41.*

ON FIRE (1985)

1911. The Haneys, dirt poor and without hope, are on the road in a stolen wagon and team. Humiliation fuels the rage of Tater Haney, 16, who has shot Ben Sills, the black man who had taken the job Tater's father proved too shiftless to do *(Words by Heart)*. Sammy, 12, idolizes his older brother, excuses his rages and is ignorant of Tater's crime. When Pap is jailed for drunkenness, leaving the family totally without any resources, Tater—as the eldest—decides to take a job he has seen advertised. Through a chance meeting with Yankee Belew, as poor and desperate as the Haneys and caretaker of her dead sister's baby, Sammy finds out that Tater's job—strikebreaker in the mines—is extremely dangerous. With Yankee as his protector, Sammy follows Tater to save him. It is Yankee, with her compassion and intelligence, who finally makes Sammy see the truth about his brother and enables him to defuse the anger that threatens to consume Tater. It is also Yankee who finally brings the Haneys back together after Pap's suicide in jail and enables them to face the future secure in the strength of their regard for each other. If Sammy is the hero who saves his brother, it is Yankee, with her "soft froggy voice," her determination to survive, her bright belief in the future and her affectionate nature who is the heroine of this eloquent story that takes place in a time when there were no economic safety nets, when children worked side by side with adults, when

labor was locked in combat with management. Without reading *Words by Heart,* it may be hard to understand why Tater was not prosecuted and why his vocal, virulent hatred of blacks is so much a part of his life. The book is so subtle that many readers may miss the fact that Tater's prejudice is a product of his own self hatred. The racism issue is not explored, and although Sammy is uncomfortable with Tater's attitude, he never verbalizes his discomfort. This is not as accessible as *Words by Heart.* A more mature sense of implication, imagery and nuance is needed to mine the riches of the writing and uncover the levels of love, pride and survival so beautifully portrayed. Booktalking the scene between Tater and his father in the prison may be powerful enough to tempt readers to pick this one up. They won't soon forget it.

> *Marjorie Lewis, in a review of "On Fire," in* School Library Journal, *Vol. 31, No. 8, April, 1985, p. 100.*

The 1911 Colorado setting provides the social and economic conditions that make this a story of physical as well as psychological survival. The characterizations are vivid, and Sebestyen's style, as always, is faultless. But what stands out here are the moral dilemmas, the compromising solutions, the tough choices. This book has real beauty, but it is about ugly things: poverty, hatred, callousness, prejudice. From its audience it will require more maturity than advanced reading skill.

> *Janet Hickman, in a review of "On Fire," in* Language Arts, *Vol. 63, No. 2, February, 1986, p. 191.*

The book is a tough and realistic exploration of the possible motivations behind the racist behaviors of a poor white young man early in this century. Tater suffers no legal consequences for his acts, but they are neithr excused nor condoned by the characters in the book. Tater's characterization remains consistent, and his eventual change of heart and expression of remorse is believable.

The book is actually more Sammy's story than Tater's, and it is a "growing up" story for Sammy, too; he must learn to see his brother for what he is and make his own decisions about right and wrong. He is aided by Yankee Belew, who sometimes seems too wise for her fifteen years. The character of Mrs. Haney is still hard to take. She remains silent, always referred to by her sons as "she" or "her"; she needs, in their eyes, "somebody to tell her what to do and think now that Pap couldn't." It is not until the end that she if forced to make a decision that may be the first one she's made since her marriage, if not the first ever.

The book ends on a hopeful note, but certainly not with a fairy-tale ending. It is a provocative book, worth reading, worth thinking about, worth discussing with young people. (p. 34)

> *Rudine Sims, in a review of "On Fire," in* Interracial Books for Children Bulletin, *Vol. 17, Nos. 3 & 4, 1986, pp. 34-5.*

Maurice (Bernard) Sendak

1928-

American author and illustrator of picture books, fiction, and nonfiction.

Called "the Picasso of picture books" by a reviewer for *Time Magazine*, Sendak is perhaps the most well known and well respected illustrator of his generation. A prolific author and artist who is often lauded as a genius, he is considered responsible for liberating the picture book genre by creating highly individualistic works which highlight the emotional complexity of childhood. Sendak is credited with successfully using the medium of the illustrated book to address personal issues while developing an artistic style based on both popular culture and the works of classic illustrators. He is often noted as the first artist to deal openly with the feelings of children, a subject he is praised for addressing with significant depth and sensitivity. Drawing on the recollected emotions of his childhood, Sendak explores primary longings, fears, needs, and beliefs—anger, sexuality, sibling rivalry, jealousy, loss, grief, the desire for love and approval, and other issues—in a forthright and often profound manner. The creator of a mythology based on both personal and cultural archetypes, he provides his audience with an unsentimental assessment of the universal childhood unconscious while attempting to come to terms with the essential points of his life; on this subject, Sendak has said, "I live inside the picture book. . . . It's where I fight all my battles and where, hopefully, I win my wars." Sendak is perhaps best known for writing and illustrating three books which he calls his trilogy: *Where the Wild Things Are* (1963), *In the Night Kitchen* (1970), and *Outside Over There* (1981). In each volume, the young protagonist is separated from his or her parents, confronts a traumatic situation, solves it through assertiveness in a cathartic dream or fantasy, and returns to the security of home. These works are acknowledged as landmarks in the field of children's literature for their frank depiction of the child mind and innovative approach in text and illustration. As a writer, Sendak is recognized for his economy and expressiveness; as an illustrator, he is applauded for his versatility, the excellence of his draftsmanship, and his use of contrast and page design. His style varies from book to book, ranging from humorous line drawings to impressionistic watercolors, bright poster-style pictures, and detailed black-and-white pieces which exhibit his characteristic crosshatching technique.

Beginning his career as the illustrator of works by such noted authors as Marcel Aymé, Ruth Sawyer, Beatrice Schenk de Regniers, and Meindert DeJong, Sendak first came to prominence as the illustrator of *A Hole Is to Dig* (1952), a book of children's definitions by Ruth Krauss. By depicting a world of natural youngsters playing spontaneously, Sendak went against the conventions of the time; his active, dumpy figures are often considered the first realistic children in picture books. Sendak has continued to illustrate works for other authors throughout his career, providing well-received pictures for such writers as Else Holmelund Minarik, Janice May Udry, Leo Tolstoy, Hans Christian Andersen, Jacob and Wilhelm Grimm, George MacDonald, Isaac Bashevis Singer, and Randall Jarrell; Sendak has also illustrated two books by his brother,

© Nancy Crampton

Jack, and one by his father, Philip. Sendak's first original books, *Kenny's Window* (1956) and *Very Far Away* (1957), introduce his characteristic theme of the child's relationship with fantasy and reality. *The Sign on Rosie's Door* (1960) is unusual among Sendak's works in portraying the activities of a group of children rather than those of an individual child; the character of Rosie, a lively and imaginative young girl who lures the children on her block into sharing her fantasies, is considered Sendak's first completely realized character. *The Nutshell Library* (1962), a boxed set of four miniature volumes which includes an alphabet book, a book about the seasons, a counting rhyme, and a cautionary tale, is esteemed as an especially successful merging of text, illustration, and design. With *Where the Wild Things Are*, Sendak created a work often recognized as the first modern picture book. The story describes how Max, a young boy dressed in a wolf costume who is sent to bed without supper after misbehaving, imagines that he travels to the island of the Wild Things and becomes their king; later, Max emerges from his reverie to find that his mother has left him a hot supper in his room. *Wild Things* established Sendak as a major talent while making him the center of a controversy that continues to this day: some librarians, educators, and parents have objected consistently to the story's potentially horrifying monsters as well as to the depiction of Max's uncouth behavior. However, *Wild Things* was embraced immediately by children, who identified with Max and were amused by the characters he meets on his journey.

After writing and illustrating *Hector Protector and As I Went Over the Water* (1965), a tribute to English illustrator Randolph Caldecott, and *Higglety Pigglety Pop! Or There Must Be More to Life* (1967), a poetic fantasy about the artist's beloved Sealyham terrier, Sendak created *In the Night Kitchen*. This work, which Sendak says comes "from the direct middle of me," is a joyous celebration of a child's self-discovery. Influenced by American cartoonist Winsor McCay's "Little Nemo in Slumberland" as well as by the movies of the 1930s and the works of American animator Walt Disney, *Night Kitchen* uses a comic strip format to describe how little Mickey wakes to a noise in the night, falls out of his clothes into the Night Kitchen, and is placed in the batter which three bakers—all images of comedian Oliver Hardy—are making into a cake; after Mickey escapes and supplies the bakers with milk for their batter, he crows his triumph and slides down the milk bottle into bed. Like *Wild Things*, *Night Kitchen* was received with both delight and disapproval. Mickey's frontal nudity offended some librarians, a few of whom drew shorts on him, but other observers welcomed *Night Kitchen* as Sendak's most interesting and most artistic book. During the rest of the 1970s, he created *Maurice Sendak's Really Rosie: Starring the Nutshell Kids* (1975), an adaptation of *The Sign on Rosie's Door* and *The Nutshell Library* which was based on an animated musical television program; *Some Swell Pup; or Are You Sure You Want a Dog?* (1976), an instructional book coauthored by Matthew Margolis which attracted controversy for its graphic representation of a puppy's natural functions; and *Seven Little Monsters* (1977), a counting book based on Sendak's drawings for an animated sequence which had aired on "Sesame Street."

With *Outside Over There*, Sendak created the picture book which he says will be his last; he calls it "the release of something that has long pressured my internal self. . . . If for only once in my life, I have touched the place where I wanted to go." The first work to be published simultaneously as both an adult and children's book, *Outside Over There* tells the story of Ida, a young girl who bravely rescues her baby sister after she has been kidnapped by goblins. *Outside Over There* is acknowledged as a new departure for Sendak: drawing from influences as diverse as the Brothers Grimm, Mozart, the Dionne quintuplets, German Romantic painting, and the kidnapping of the Lindbergh baby, the book is a textured, mysterious, and lyrical work crowded with images and symbols. Sendak illustrates the book with lush, rich paintings which underscore the surrealistic quality of Ida's quest. After *Outside Over There* was completed, Sendak pursued several theatrical projects; the illustrated versions of E. T. A. Hoffman's *Nutcracker* (1984) and Frank Corsaro's *The Love for Three Oranges* (1984) grew out of productions on which Sendak worked as a designer.

Sendak is saluted as an ambitious and highly influential creator of works which have set new standards for juvenile literature; critic John Rowe Townsend has called him "the greatest creator of picture books in the hundred years' history of the form." Some reviewers complain that Sendak's books have become too obscure and inaccessible and that his recent works show a lessening in quality; other critics berate his art for being too reminiscent of its influences and attack him for producing books about children rather than for them. However, most commentators extol Sendak as a brilliant author and illustrator whose understanding of the young is reflected in their consistently enthusiastic response to his works.

Sendak received the Caldecott Medal in 1964 for *Where the Wild Things Are*, which also received the Lewis Carroll Shelf Award the same year and was placed on the International Board of Books for Young People (IBBY) Honour List in 1966. *In the Night Kitchen* was chosen as a Caldecott Honor Book in 1971 as was *Outside Over There* in 1982; the latter also received a *Boston Globe-Horn Book Award* in 1981 and an American Book Award in 1982. Several works illustrated by Sendak were also named Caldecott Honor Books: *A Very Special House*, written by Ruth Krauss, in 1954; *What Do You Say, Dear? A Book of Manners for All Occasions*, written by Sesyle Joslin, in 1959; *The Moon Jumpers*, written by Janice May Udry, in 1960; *Little Bear's Visit*, written by Else Holmelund Minarik, in 1962; and *Mr. Rabbit and the Lovely Present*, written by Charlotte Zolotow, in 1963. In 1970, Sendak became the first American to win the Hans Christian Andersen Illustrator Medal, an award he received for his body of work. In 1981, he was presented with the University of Southern Mississippi Medallion for his contribution to the field of children's literature; in 1983, he won the Laura Ingalls Wilder Award for his body of work. Sendak was made an Honorary Doctor of Humane Letters by Boston University in 1977.

(See also *CLR*. Vol. 1; *Something about the Author*, Vols. 1, 27; *Contemporary Authors New Revision Series*, Vol. 11; *Contemporary Authors*, Vol. 5-8, rev. ed.; and *Dictionary of Literary Biography*, Vol. 61: *Poets, Illustrators, and Nonfiction Authors*.)

AUTHOR'S COMMENTARY

All my life I have been fortunate enough to do work that comes naturally and spontaneously to me: illustrating and writing books for children. Happily, an essential part of myself—my dreaming life—still lives in the potent, urgent light of childhood, in my case an American childhood composed of strangely concocted elements. I had a conglomerate fantasy life as a child, typical of many first-generation children in America, particularly those in a land called Brooklyn, a regulated, tree-lined ghetto-land separated only by a river from the most magical of all lands, New York City—that fantastic place rarely visited but much dreamed of.

Mine was a childhood colored with memories of village life in Poland, never actually experienced but passed on to me as persuasive reality by my immigrant parents. On the one hand, I lived snugly in their old-country world, a world far from urban society where the laws and customs of a small Jewish village were scrupulously and lovingly obeyed. And on the other hand, I was bombarded with the intoxicating gush of America in that convulsed decade, the thirties. Two emblems represent that era for me: a photograph of my severe, bearded grandfather (I never actually saw him) that haunts me to this day and which, as a child, I believed to be the exact image of God; and Mickey Mouse. These two lived side by side in a bizarre togetherness that I accepted as natural. For me, childhood was *shtetl* life transplanted. Brooklyn colored by old-world reverberations and Walt Disney and the occasional trip to the incredibly windowed "uptown" that was New York-America. All in all, what with loving parents and sister and brother, it was a satisfying childhood. Was it American? Everybody's America is different.

And then there were the books I loved—those wonderful, cheap, pulp-papered, bad-smelling, gorgeously if vulgarly colored comic books and story books, full of mystifying magic men and women dressed in gleaming aluminum clothes and whizzing over some great American metropolis and into the vast unknown. Best of all, perhaps, were the movies of my childhood. With their exotic, glossy fantasticalness, they permanently dyed my imagination a silvery Hollywood color. Aspects of the movies that might be rejected by an adult mind were perfectly suited to a child devoted to making up stories and, from an early age, putting them down on paper. The pleasurably dreaded King Kong, the graphically vivid, absurdly endearing figures of Mickey Mouse and Charlie Chaplin were the most direct influences on me as a young artist.

As a child I felt that books were holy objects, to be caressed, rapturously sniffed, and devoutly provided for. I gave my life to them—I still do. I continue to do what I did as a child: dream of books, make books, and collect books. As I grew older and could cross that river with ease into a New York that remained magical, my taste and interest in books became more sophisticated. On my own I discovered artists from all over the world who seemed to speak directly to me; and as a young man, trying to discover my creative self, I leaned heavily on these sympathetic friends. They were a very cultivated bunch. From the first, my great and abiding love was William Blake, my teacher in all things. And from two other Englishmen, Thomas Rowlandson and George Cruikshank, I borrowed techniques and tried to forge them into a personal language. The Frenchman Boutet de Monvel refined my eye and quickened my heart and ambition. The Germans Wilhelm Busch and Heinrich Hoffmann provided me with the basis of a style and hinted at a kind of content that developed much later in my own work. When I was sixteen I first saw the edition of *Pinocchio* illustrated by Attilio Mussino and I know that was a turning point. My eyes were opened by the offhand virtuosity of the man, the ease with which he commanded a variety of styles, controlling them all, blending them, and still managing to keep them subservient to the tale. He taught me at once and the same time respect for finish and style as well as a certain disregard for these qualities. Style counts, I now saw, only insofar as it conveys the inner meaning of the text being illustrated.

There were other artists who taught me, who coaxed me into becoming myself—too many to bring up here. But I cannot leave unmentioned the great Swiss illustrators—Rodolphe Topffer, Ernst Kreidolf and Hans Fischer, all of whom influenced me significantly during my apprentice years.

My passion for making books has lately led me to a distinct vision of what I want my books to be, a vision difficult to verbalize. I no longer want simply to illustrate—or, for that matter, simply to write. I am now in search of a form more purely and essentially my own. In a way I'd rather have been a composer of operas and songs, and I must turn to music to describe something of what I am after. The concentrated face of Verdi's *Falstaff*, or a Hugo Wolf song, where music and words mix and blend and incredibly excite, defines my ideal. Here words and music form a magic compound, a "something else"—more than music, more than words. My wish is to combine—in words and pictures, faithfully and fantastically—my weird, old-country, new-country childhood; my obsession of *shtetel* life, its spirit; and the illuminating visions especially loved artists have shown me. All this mixed and beaten and smoothed into a picture-book form that has something resembling the lush, immediate beauty of music and all its deep, unanalyzable mystery. Most of all the mystery—that is the cherished goal.

Hans Christian Andersen described his life as a fairy tale, a pronouncement that, taken literally, might provoke a shudder or bring to mind a particular coyness that has often been detrimental to the serious work of writing and illustrating for children. But in the metaphoric sense Andersen intended, I can say the same thing and mean it. What could be more fairy-tale-ish than a childhood dream coming true? As a small boy I pasted and clipped my bits of books together and hoped only for a life that would permit me to earn my bread by pasting and clipping more bits of books. And here I am, all grown up—at least physically—and *still* at home making books. (pp. 366-69)

> *Maurice Sendak, " 'The Coming Together of All My Various Worlds'," in* Top of the News, *Vol. 26, No. 4, June, 1970, pp. 366-69.*

GENERAL COMMENTARY

LEO WOLFE

"Mr. Sendak is a 'children's illustrator,' for people who want to pigeonhole things. He is, in fact, (to repigeonhole) a fantasist in the great tradition of Sir John Tenniel and Edward Lear." So wrote Brian O'Doherty, art critic of the New York *Times,* in his review of Sendak's first one-man show, a retrospective that encompassed drawings from *A Hole Is to Dig* and some sketches done a few weeks before the show opened last March.

Most people who concern themselves with children's books today would eagerly agree that Sendak's name can be pronounced in the same breath as Tenniel's or Lear's, and that mentioning both of them justly symbolizes the breadth of Sendak's work. For, like Tenniel, he has responded to distinguished manuscripts with pictures of distinction; and, like Lear, he has created both words and pictures for children's books born of a unique personal vision. (p. 254)

> *Leo Wolfe, "Maurice Sendak," in* Newbery and Caldecott Medal Books: 1956-1965, *edited by Lee Kingman, The Horn Book, Incorporated, 1965, pp. 254-57.*

J. H. DOHM

[Maurice Sendak] has proved a consistently interesting illustrator, intelligent and versatile, able to add something to any book he works on, but is occasionally disappointing and irritating. (p. 104)

Unfortunately, some of us find his Medal winning book the most disappointing and irritating of all—obviously he was due to receive the medal before long, probably more than once, but it seemed a pity it should go first to a book of such surpassing silliness. He and his most ardent admirers seem to feel the only fault others can find with it is the "scariness" of the Wild Things encountered by young Max when he takes a magical journey to their island after being sent to bed without his supper. Actually there is little fearful about these beasts except the idiocy of their expressions, for there is always something terrifying about the drunken or idiotic; these creatures do not seem so much wild as *non compos mentis.* Max is a bit scary himself for he has a calculating eye and a mean mouth; it is impossible to believe he may grow up to become one of Sendak's nice heavy-set father-figures. He is clad in a "wolf suit" which has few wolfish attributes and joins the Things in a mild sort of orgy—surely the most inadequate piece of wildness presented since the Bolshoi Ballet's Walpurgisnacht—swinging from trees, yelling, simpering and sniggering like mad. Everything is carefully planned, the picture size gradually expanding until whole double page spreads are filled at orgy-time, but the whole thing seems very flat and inane. It was surprising to learn from Mr. Sendak's medal-acceptance speech that Max represents his perpetual hero-figure, the child searching for respite from the pressures of the adult world; it is to be hoped most children can imagine something better by way of respite. Of course there are good things in the book as well; there are always good things in a Sendak book, even if he can't draw a three-dimensional bed this time and always has trouble with hands. The idea of the walls giving way to the woods and a sea with a little boat coming along to take Max to the island is entirely successful, the colour is charming and the whole book looks expert enough at first glance, but it seems less satisfactory at the second and the closer scrutiny turned on it as a Medal winner make its weaknesses loom larger than they should.

Much of the disappointment comes because Mr. Sendak can do so much better work, especially when he is supporting a stronger text. He has probably done his best work so far for the books of Meindert DeJong, who is also a highly individual and sensitive artist with a wildly fluctuating series of successes and near-misses to his credit. Sendak can match him perfectly, whatever the background of the story or nature of its characters may be, and it was gratifying to see that DeJong recognised this when he dedicated *The Singing Hill:* "To Maurice Sendak who illuminates my things, because we are a pair."

Sendak first captivated the public when he illustrated Ruth Krauss' picture book of "first definitions," *A Hole is to Dig,* in 1952, and the little children he drew there were the first of many to jump about, usually with tight-shut eyes, through the pages of dozens of picture books of the past decade, not all of them illustrated by Sendak. He does seem to have been one of the originators of the type, perhaps *the* originator; his little jumpers are the best of the lot and either he was the first to point them out to us or has somehow influenced the children through his drawings for America is now full of children who look exactly like those in his picture books; they had not been noticed before his books appeared, surely an indication of his creative powers! He says he draws to carefully selected music and likes to make a sort of progressive dance throughout these books and in many the children do indeed create a continuing pattern, conferring, arguing, solitary or acting as a mass, often almost hysterical in their activity. The authors of the books, Mrs. Krauss, Beatrice Schenck de Regniers and Janice Udry in particular, have more or less turned themselves into tape-recorders of children's prattle; they are hyper-conscious of the small child's world and in attempting to enter it have sometimes lost perspective altogether. Each generation has its own stories in this genre, however—those of the 19th century being told in a baby-talk which now appals us—and although Sendak's work sometimes joins in the silly moments all too whole-heartedly, it also captures the moments of truth very well indeed. His own texts have been less successful, showing a fragmentary dreamworld, painfully self-conscious and precious. His tiny **"Nutshell Library"** of four miniature booklets limiting the text to little more than the alphabet and numbers nonsensically set forth, contains his best and most ingenious texts so far.

Perhaps his most influential work has been done for Mrs. Minarik's series of **"Little Bear"** books for early readers. There are many good picture books to promote a pre-school interest in art work, but almost nothing else to make children illustration-conscious while they learn to read, and these quaint, af-

fectionate pictures come to them at a crucial stage. His most ambitious work seems to be that done for some 19th century tales by Brentano, Hauff and Frank Stockton; this is also his most derivative work, with echoes of Richter, von Schwind, Rowlandson and others. The German-style pictures appear to have been blown up from smaller drawings but this may be the result of attempting to reproduce wood engravings with pen and ink; it is harder to forgive his tampering with the text of a Stockton tale. If the author specified a griffon minus hind-legs why wilfully add them; we know from Tenniel how they look so why introduce them contrary to the text? More forgivable is the copy-work, for it must be tempting to employ such styles; children no longer have access to the originals and should be given a taste of their work and there is always enough of Sendak present to keep it from being theft—it is more of a tribute and a graceful one at that. His sources in other books are not always easy to trace—a touch of Ben Shahn here, Chagall there, of Oscar Pletsch and the engravings in 19th century magazines and schoolbooks in another place. There is less borrowing noticeable from the work of artists Sendak especially admires—Caldecott, Boutet de Monvel, Busch, Hans Fischer and André Francois, a surprisingly extrovert, message-less group considering the introvert sound of Sendak himself. From the articles and the film, "The lively art of picture books," comes an impression of a man still young, working alone in a dark studio filled with gramophone music, surrounded by fetishes, full of theories about the psychological needs of children. As he says, it's foolish to pretend that children trail nothing but clouds of glory, to ignore their fears and resentments. His own pictures sometimes show carefree children and perhaps even over-emphasise their irresponsible moments at times, for although most children need to be naturally silly, some books can promote artificial silliness of a sterile kind. But he does appear to view them through a distorting glass, possibly that of the Brooklyn window through which he drew them when in his 'teens. And his ideas can hardly have been dispelled by the lady authors who listen-in to the nursery world, scavenging for book ideas, or by the lady editors at Harpers who were so frightened by the first sight of the Wild Things. On the other hand, the picture conjured up by the articles may be pretty distorted itself and it would be both unjust and ungenerous to sneer at the editors of Harpers who were amongst the first to recognise and foster the talent of the young Sendak.

Since Sendak seems peculiarly well equipped to capture the narcissistic atmosphere of childhood popular in picture books just now it would be stupid to suggest that he should rush out and see the world as full of adult stir and bustle as that of Caldecott, as "lustige" as that of Wilhelm Busch—heaven forbid!—or full of the grave dignity and lovely pattern Boutet de Monvel displayed in his books. Sendak has something of his own to offer, but although he has illustrated over fifty books, most of them very ably, he has yet to attain his full stature and has still a long way to go before equalling the masters whose work he rightly venerates. He has given much pleasure, his work is witty, skilful, individual, but as a picture book artist he seems to fall short of his full promise. It may be that the Medal was a good idea, after all, for he says himself that his style is only now beginning to "jell" and perhaps he needed this sign of approval before taking the next step. He has the qualifications to eventually astonish us with a picture book which can be simply enjoyed without analysis or reservations—may it come soon!

• • • • •

Since this article was written three new books have appeared with Sendak illustrations. I have not seen Jarrell's posthumous story but can report that *Hector Protector* uses a Caldecottian method of pictorial writing between the lines to give a most Sendakian twist to the plots of two nursery rhymes, while *Lullabies and Night Songs* provides a series of charming nocturnes with a sprinkling of jolly strip-type drawings with an 18th century flavour in a beautifully planned book. The children should enjoy both full-heartedly and there is much for adults to enjoy whatever their reservations, but the reservations are there and it is difficult to define the cause. Mr. Sendak's latest *verbal* publication, a spirited defence of Beatrix Potter in the Wilson Library Bulletin of December, 1965, written as a staircase reply to a gentleman who questioned her merits at a meeting—and as Sendak says how *can* you reply directly except with "Well, if you can't see!" or a punch on the nose!—set me to comparing his approach with that of the artist he had defended. And Joan Bodger's *How the Heather Looks*, with its opening chapters on Caldecott country, brought Caldecott's approach into consideration as well. Admittedly such comparisons are fairly full of flaws themselves and perhaps the only valid conclusion is that Mr. Sendak lives in a different time, place and atmosphere. But it does seem that neither Caldecott nor Beatrix Potter gave much thought to children or childhood as such, and although they remembered and retained much from their own particular time as children they seldom referred to pictures they had enjoyed as children. Caldecott drew the life he saw and took part in as a man, Beatrix Potter's insight into animals and humans was born in her and not so much developed as refined with age; both drew what they saw as adults, a world peopled mainly with adults. But Mr. Sendak draws mainly children and tries to see them as a child would and he draws *upon* his memories of his own childhood, particularly the pictures he enjoyed as a child, and on his theories of what children are like. This makes his work different in kind, and while there's no reason why it might not be as good in quality eventually, right now it seems impossible to say that Mr. Sendak inhabits the world he depicts as Caldecott and Beatrix Potter inhabited theirs. (pp. 105-09)

> J. H. Dohm, "20th Century Illustrators: Maurice Sendak," in The Junior Bookshelf, *Vol. 30, No. 2, April, 1966, pp. 103-11.*

SAUL BRAUN

[Maurice Sendak] is probably the best known and almost certainly the most beloved illustrator of the day. (p. 34)

Sendak shouts a resounding "No!" to the idea that there is something inherently good about a tidy, obedient child. His world is peculiarly relevant in these times of stress and conflict. In some sense, his heroes all face the problem that confronts today's child: how to maintain identity and integrity in an uncomprehending adult world that appears to want to deprive him of his noblest (that is, most natural) feelings. This has always been the case. What is interesting is that Sendak's heroes, like young people today, do not seem willing to make some of those significant compromises which appear to them to be of dubious value, and which we call "growing up." (p. 37)

> Saul Braun, "Sendak Raises the Shade on Childhood," in The New York Times Magazine, *June 7, 1970, pp. 34-54.*

MURIEL HARRIS

Sendak's children have always threatened parents, the Establishment and have tamed the wildest, most ferocious of beasts with the greatest of ease. Sendak's children have stuck their tongues out at queens, leave home and go very far away, stand on their heads on chairs, threaten to eat tigers, rats, even robbers, squeeze cobras by the neck, or scream "No" and "I don't care," and put their heads in lions' mouths. They even threaten a herd of ugly, clawing, growling, bulbous-eyed creatures that they'll be sent to bed without supper. What immense bravery! What courage! What necessary fantasy!

Where the Wild Things Are won the coveted Caldecott Medal in 1964. A new era in children's literature had emerged. Up until now children behaved dutifully in literature, minded their p's and q's, bowed and curtsied, smiled and said "Thank you," to their elders. . . . But along came the roaring and crescendo of *Wild Things* and the literary world literally somersaulted. (p. 828)

Why do children like his books? A child spins concentric circles around himself. The nucleus never fails to be the "I." The "I" for identity and the "I" for "me." The ego is one big circus balloon swelling, soaring, ready to burst within the child. And when he opens a Sendak book he's peering into a mirror seeking, feeling, hearing, touching his own thoughts, his own actions. He sees Himself. (p. 829)

While Sendak represents Renaissance Man he also represents the hippie culture of today in that he's rebelling against the saccharine content of most of American children's literature, eager to get down to the nitty gritty. Every one of his children rebels against the Establishment. Each one seeks his real identity through fantasy only to discover what the flower children profess, love is all . . . as he fights to grow through the elemental need of fantasy.

Freud once said in a letter to Wilheim Fliess, ". . . a man like me cannot live without a hobbyhorse, a consuming passion—in Schiller's word a tyrant. I have found my tyrant, and in his service I know no limits. My tyrant is psychology."

And so it is with Maurice Sendak. His consuming passion, his tyrant is his art, his books. (p. 832)

> Muriel Harris, "Impressions of Sendak," in Elementary English, *Vol. XLVIII, No. 7, November, 1971, pp. 825-32.*

JENNIFER R. WALLER

In an interview, Sendak describes [William Blake] as "from the first, my great and abiding love . . . my teacher in all things." While the influence of George MacDonald, Randolph Caldecott, Attilio Massiono, and the tradition of the American comic book are all much more immediately definable in Sendak's work, the strength of his emotional response to William Blake is undeniable. In the same interview, he asserts Blake to be his favorite artist and goes on to explain that "of course, the *Songs of Innocence* and the *Songs of Experience* tell you all about this: what it is to be a child—not childish, but a child inside your adult self—and how much better a person you are for being such."

In this paper I want to suggest the usefulness of comparing Sendak's insights into childhood with Blake's and, as well, to compare their responses to the challenge of combining artistic vision and entertainment in a composite medium. For Blake, the state of childhood, with its innocent ignorance of destructive reason and of the processes of the adult's self-conscious rationalization and self-justification, represented a time when the human imagination was most potent. (p. 130)

Like Blake, Sendak draws unusual strength from the vision of imagination. Like Blake too, he uses the image of childhood to represent the liberation of his creativity: "An essential part of myself—my dreaming life—still lives in the potent urgent light of childhood." Commenting directly on his own work, he defines the relationship he has with "the kid I was"—an interesting phrase—who did not grow "up into me" but "still exists somewhere in the most graphic, plastic, physical way." The presence of this child is indispensable to his work, for as he asserts, "one of my worst fears is losing contact with him." To lose contact with this vision of childhood would be to destroy the substance of Sendak's creative talent—his extraordinary powers of evocative imagination and his sensitivity to the experience of childhood.

Both artists, as illustrators *and* authors, seek to use their composite form to express their vision through structural tension. Often their words may rationalize experience which may be either elaborated, or sometimes, contradicted by the illustrations, which bring out more fully the dreamlike, wordless level of the unconscious. Since Blake was obsessed with the intention of destroying the dualistic world of mind and body, time and space, he saw in the composite medium the possibilities of dramatizing "the interaction of the apparent dualities in experiences." Sendak on the other hand, because he was writing and illustrating children's books, was forced to the realization that a child's book is not simply read or rationally understood: "There's so much more to a book than just the reading; there is a sensuousness. I've seen children touch books, fondle books, smell books." Sendak is similarly conscious of certain contraries in human experience, which he attempts to assimilate in his composite form. He describes his desire to combine the disparate elements in his own experience of his "weird old-country, new country childhood." He speaks of his "obsession of *shtetel* life," and "the illuminating visions especially loved artists" have shown him in "words and pictures."

Any artist working in a composite medium clearly faces special problems. Sendak has developed a style of illustration which can initially be explained by reference to the **"Little Bear"** books. Here the text and Sendak's illustration are both enclosed within a formal decorative border. Like Blake, Sendak is not merely aiming for some kind of aesthetically satisfying unit. Neither does he want to make the pictures express only the fabric of the text. This would in Sendak's estimation be a "serious pitfall." He hopes to allow "the story to speak for itself; with my picture as a kind of background music—music in the right style and always in tune with the words." Background music such as that which accompanies film, it should be noted, is an essential element of the dramatic structure, making the listener only partially aware of feelings which he may be unwilling or unable to verbalize. Sendak's concern in this way to assimilate divergent art forms into a harmonious unity seems to be becoming more insistent recently as he establishes his reputation in the no-man's land where he is both author and artist. With Sendak's own works, *Where the Wild Things Are* and *In the Night Kitchen,* we can go a step further and put him in an explicitly Blakean context. He seems to be responding to the challenge presented by such a poem as Blake's "Infant Joy":

> I have no name
> I am but two days old.—
> What shall I call thee?
> I happy am
> Joy is my name,—
> Sweet joy befall thee!

> Pretty joy!
> Sweet joy but two days old.
> Sweet joy I call thee:
> Thou dost smile.
> I sing the while
> Sweet joy befall thee.

Encircling the words of the poem and the ostensibly simple domestic scene of mother and child it describes, is a twining vine bearing flamboyant flowers, suggesting passion and sexuality. The lower leaves of the plant are angular and strained and suggest a hint of impending experience—experience which may transform the simplicity of domestic love through the expressions of frank sexuality and are, of course, the origins of the scene. The eventual complexity of human love is suggested in this encircling illustration. It thus provides a portent, as well as the orchestration for pain and sorrow evoked in the equivalent poem in the *Songs of Experience:*

> My mother groaned! My father wept.
> Into the dangerous world I leapt:
> Helpless, naked, piping loud;
> Like a friend hid in a cloud.
> Struggling in my father's hands:
> Striving against my swadling bands:
> Bound and weary I thought best
> To sulk upon my mother's breast.

Some of the same intention is apparent in *Where the Wild Things Are.* Max's rebellion and frustration at his punishment spread over four pages and are described in the text:

> That very night in Max's room a forest grew / and grew— / and grew until his ceiling hung with vines and the walls became the world all around / and an ocean tumbled by with a private boat for Max and he sailed off through night and day.

As the bedroom is transformed into the land "where the wild things are," the phrases become longer and more unwieldy until the reader must gasp for breath. Each stage in the transition is marked by the physical act of turning a page, and by the time the rumpus commences the visual images have taken over entirely from the words. The illustrations, which initially remained neatly contained within a white border on one side of the centerfold, have now swamped the page. The tensions between the competing mediums of prose and picture illustrate the transformation from Max's initial reasoned reaction, described in words, to his wild frenzy and cathartic rage, which can only be illustrated in wordless pictures. Inside the space of one children's picture book, the illustrations, comparable in function to the border of Blake's "Infant Joy," have conquered the page leaving the child in the midst of Experience like Blake's child in "The Garden of Love":

> So I turn'd to the Garden of Love
> That so many sweet Flowers bore,
> And I saw it was filled with graves,
> And tombstones where flowers should be:
> And priests in black gowns, were walking their rounds,
> And binding with briars my joys and desires.

Where the Wild Things Are, surely one of the best children's books of our time, presents a responsiveness to childhood strikingly akin to Blake's in which childhood is not a world of idyllic escapism but of combined vulnerability and creativity. . . . [The thrust of Blake's work] was to express, for the first time in English literature, such spontaneous experiences of childhood and such assertions of the independence and integrity of childhood experience as the children's reply in ''Nurse's Song'':

> No no let us play, for it is yet day
> And we cannot go to sleep
> Besides in the sky, the little birds fly
> And the hills are all covered with sheep
> Well well go & play till the light fades way
> And then go home to bed
> The little ones leaped & shouted & laugh'd
> And all the hills echoed

The *Songs of Innocence,* in particular, asserts that childhood is a time of freedom from the constricting demands that lie behind the adult's acceptance of established theology and philosophy.... It was not a totally idyllic world, for the world of innocence is full of the portents of experience. The predominant tone of the poems is still one of vulnerability, weeping, and lamentation—even if this sorrow is ultimately controlled.... This awareness of the ambivalence of childhood experience separates Blake's responses to the child from later Romantic exploitations of the symbol of childhood. Blake's child, like Wordsworth's, possesses an intuitive power of responding and knowing. But Blake does not contemplate the state of childhood nostalgically. Wordsworth looks at childhood through the eyes of an adult awakening to his lost innocence and attempting to recapture it simply because he is adult and aware of his lost security. Blake, rather, leaps into a state of childhood and re-creates the moment when pain and vulnerability mingle with joy, perception, and lack of cynicism. Blake's child is not observed coming from heaven ''trailing clouds of glory''; rather he *is* that glory for a brief and vulnerable moment. We see feelingly through his liberated responsiveness.

Generations of post-Romantic children's writers have wallowed in their own sense of nostalgia for their younger selves, so that childhood is usually portrayed as a time of innocence and only fleeting pain. But for Blake, and I would argue, Sendak, the approach is different. Sendak's evocation of childhood separates him from most contemporary children's writers in much the same way as Blake's creation of childhood separated him from Wordsworth's contemplation of the state. This is not to deny that Sendak is in the Romantic tradition. He is extremely conscious that elements of subjective biographical experience and responsiveness are the substance of his art. His description of the genesis of his books—''if something strikes me and I get excited, then I want it to be a book''—sounds like a vaguely expressed Wordsworthian ''overflow of powerful feelings.'' But in describing the impact of childhood experience on his work, he makes an important distinction between the act of remembering childhood or ''pretending that I'm a child'' and the action of a ''creative artist who also gets freer and freer with each book and opens up more and more.'' In another instance he insists on the continued existence of the ''kid I was'' continuing ''somewhere, in the most graphic, plastic, physical way.'' Perhaps most significantly, he destroys the connection between himself as adult and the child when he speculates that ''the kid I was never grew up into me.'' Thus, like Blake, he does not use the child to comment upon himself as the adult. The connection implicit in Wordsworth's phrase, ''The child is father of the man,'' does not exist for Sendak in the context of his imaginative creation. Like Blake, he seems to be asserting that ''Imagination has nothing to do with Memory,'' rather it is ''Divine Vision.'' Thus he attempts to shear off the partisan preoccupations which invade our own memories of childhood now that we are adult—our nostalgia, our obsessions with the lost opportunities and pastimes of childhood.

His assault on our more conventional responses to childhood is revealing. Some reviewers agonized over the disturbing evocations of *Where the Wild Things Are* or the unveiling of a small boy's penis in *The Night Kitchen.* Psychologists and librarians have reacted with their own understanding of childhood—or rather their own need to believe that some part of human existence can be, and therefore should be, protected from pain, fear, and the menace of chaos. For such readers, Max in *Where the Wild Things Are* may be a disturbing creation; his imagination makes him as vulnerable as the playful children in the pastures of Innocence. His world of mischievous make-believe is so fragile that his mother's anger can shatter it and thurst him into the expanding world of his own rage and fear, the world of Experience. In this state he creates from within himself demons which are really reflections of his own agression. Eventually these menaces will be overcome and controlled and the child will return to bed and thus to what may be read as analogous to Blake's state of further or mature innocence, where the lamb and the tiger are reconciled. The book's ending is not merely a happy conclusion. There is a real sense of ''look we have come through''—as Sendak has explained, he risked his own imagination in writing the tale: ''When I write and draw I'm experiencing what the child in the book is going through. I was as relieved to get back from Max's journey as he was. Or rather, I like to think I got back.''

Like Blake, Sendak has taken seriously the horror and the largely helpless frustration of childhood that have to be sublimated into fantasies. Wordsworth's child meditates and broods on the beauty and challenge of nature. Self-consciously he appears to be preparing himself for the time when he will be a man. Blake's children are laughing, playing, weeping, and above all asking questions or arguing with others.... One of the most striking characteristics about Sendak's recurring prototypal figure of Max in each of his forms—human or canine— is his assertiveness and his astonishing curiosity. Kenny in *Kenny's Window* dares loneliness and despair on his mission to find answers for his questions: ''What is an only goat?''; ''Can you fix a broken promise?''; ''What is a Very Narrow Escape?''. Maybe he would even dare to ask: ''Tyger, did he who made the Lamb make thee?'' Moreover, like the questioner in *Innocence and Experience,* Kenny sometimes receives only half-answers or answers which are truer to feeling than they are to logic.

Generations of critics have argued about the nature of Blake's states of Innocence and Experience. Certainly in the *Songs of Experience,* cynicism and self-consciousness creep into the imagined world making previous situations suddenly seem unendurable and tragic. The change is not one from happiness to sadness, for sadness has already been present in *Innocence.* Rather, the world of Urizen—of definition and order—has destroyed freedom and sensitivity. When children are observed at play, jealous nostalgia invades the ''Nurse's Song'':

> When the voices of children, are heard on the green
> And whisprings are in the dale:
> The days of my youth rise fresh in my mind,
> My face turns green and pale.
>
> Then come home my children, the sun is gone down
> And the dews of the night arise
> Your spring & your day, are wasted in play
> And your winter and night in disguise.

Sexuality becomes corrupt as man's intellect reasons that:

> The Sexes sprung from Shame & Pride
> Blow'd in the morn: in evening died. . . .

It is in this context that Mickey's penis is clothed and the fears of Jenny's search for "experience" in *Higglety Pigglety Pop!* become unendurable. It is also in this context that criticism of Sendak's frank approach to the ambivalence of childhood grows. Defending himself against the charge that he frightens our little ones, Sendak describes what he sees as the experience of childhood in terms which significantly parallel Blake's creation of joy and love, of curiosity and knowledge, intermingled with vulnerability and pain. Children are not, he claims, "drab, but they're not innocent of experience either. Too many parents and too many writers of children's books don't respect the fact that kids know a great deal of pleasure, but often they look defenceless too. Being defenceless is a primary element of childhood."

Sendak's approach to childhood is as unsentimental as Blake's. Like Blake, he regards the material of his childhood experience as the substance of his imaginative powers. His childhood world is invaded by fears which may be unendurable if perceived wholly by an adult but which may eventually be controlled by the courage of a child's imagination. (pp. 131-38)

Like Blake's children, Sendak's Mickey [of *In the Night Kitchen*] lives in a separate world of ingenuity, sensitivity, and sometimes delight. He is often vulnerable, subjected to fear and pain, but his courage and his persistent imagination finally defeat the self-obsessed adult world. For all the terrors Mickey encounters, the book remains amusing and ingenious; just as the world of Innocence, for all its portents of sorrow, is one of peace and love. Sendak's trust in the ability of the childhood imagination to ultimately accommodate the terrors of experience is obvious.

Sendak's books, unlike many contemporary works for children, are not therapeutic in intent. They do not explain to the child how to imagine, what to imagine, how to reinterpret the adult world. They simply attempt to reflect and evoke the child's imaginative experience. Perhaps for this reason, children quickly identify with the protagonists and can easily act out plays about *Where the Wild Things Are* or what it is like to be Max or Mickey or Hector. Like Blake, Sendak has preferred to leap into the middle of the experience of childhood rather than to contemplate it from a nostalgic viewpoint. To place Sendak alongside Blake in the manner I have sketched in this paper is necessarily to ignore many of the evident influences upon his work. But it does, I believe, illuminate a central part of his genius. When we compare their visions of childhood in particular, we understand something of how Sendak's Max is a totally believable and fascinating child in his own right, in a way in which probably no other book child is. It demonstrates how, despite the brevity of the text in most of his books, so many complicated human experiences and emotions are evoked. It shows also that it is not simply technical superiority and slick promotion that make Sendak the most popular children's writer-illustrator of the 1960s and 1970s. Rather, it is the singular depth of perception of the nature of childhood experience which he possesses. In a very real sense he has emancipated the children's picture book. He has demonstrated that it may actually be about children, not just about loveable steam shovels or cute dogs or shapes—or even about the children we as adults want to remember or imagine. He presents the child as the Human Force Divine, in a very real Blakean sense. (pp. 139-40)

Jennifer R. Waller, "Maurice Sendak and the Blakean Vision of Childhood," in Children's Literature: Annual of the Modern Language Association Seminar on Children's Literature and The Children's Literature Association, *Vol. 6, 1977, pp. 130-40.*

JILL P. MAY

In his own country, American Maurice Sendak is today's most controversial creator of children's books, and while he is not as well known a part of popular culture as Walt Disney or the Sesame Street gang, he is an arresting artistic leader. His creations are enjoyed by many U.S. children and are familiar to most (if not all) children's librarians and educators. Sendak's productions have often aroused strong adult criticism. . . . *Where the Wild Things Are* has been criticized for its frightening monsters. Yet, these monsters could easily have posed for the later production of Sesame Street monsters. And, although Sendak's works seem disgusting to some U.S. educators, librarians, and parents, his books are found in most public libraries and elementary school libraries. Children will not recognize his name, but they will usually be introduced to at least one of his books in a public classroom, a library story hour, or through a school paperback book club. Over 70 books contain his illustrations.

Sendak is interesting to the field of popular culture not because he is a prolific author / illustrator. It is his use of twentieth century popular culture combined with his bold style that make his artistry fascinating. Librarians may sniff and scoff at Walt Disney, but Sendak does not. He credits popular culture as the inspiration for much in his original fantasies. His characters may at times seem ethnic, but they are truly American children, surrounded by familiar U.S. vignettes. (p. 30)

Maurice Sendak's childhood, his fascination with music and animation, and his vision of the preschool ego have helped him produce some of the finest preschool experiences available for the modern child. He has established a picture book prototype of the American preschooler: a robust child, self-centered and assertive, who appeals to both girls and boys.

Recently, when one two-year-old picked up *In the Night Kitchen* she exlaimed, "There's Pierre!" In fact, although Sendak does not call his character by one name, but gives him many—Max, Pierre, Hector Protector, Kenny or Mickey—his hero is always identifiable to any child. It really does not matter to the child what this impish boy's name is. His adventure is worth emulating to the preschooler because it is fantasy based on an early childhood experience. Sendak's hero is a modern uninhibited youngster, capable of maintaining his self-love in spite of adult reprimand. (pp. 30-1)

[Sendak] remains the most controversial American children's artist of this era.

Adult critics have never quite understood and appreciated Sendak's picture books as much as young people have. Already acclaimed a fine author and a substantial children's artist by 1972 when his **"Nutshell Library"** arrived, Sendak's reviewers began acknowledging that he did have unusual talents, but some did not see these stories as particularly unusual or noteworthy. Their charm comes from the subtle use of art and text to create a rare twentieth century fantasy. Each of these small books appeals to children for very different reasons. *One Was Johnny* contains a concise plot told in 195 words. The action is quick and to the point. More important, it is an animated book; when the child flips the pages from back to front Johnny actually comes alive. *Alligators All Around* is simply a nonsensical alphabet story, but Sendak's use of alliteration has the same

From Where the Wild Things Are, *written and illustrated by Maurice Sendak. Harper & Row, Publishers,* 1963. Copyright © 1963 by Maurice Sendak. All rights reserved. Reprinted by permission of Harper & Row, Publishers, Inc.

auditory appeal found in Mother Goose. ***Chicken Soup With Rice*** introduces the months of the year with such a buoyant rhyme that children repeated it sing-song fashion long before it was put to music in Sendak's film ***Really Rosie***. Finally, ***Pierre: A Cautionary Tale*** combines some of Sendak's best storytelling techniques: doting parents, a rude preschooler, a wild beast and the security of a happy family circle. Sendak's use of a miniature format immediately thrills the young child. A youngster is able to carry all four books inside their own complimentary small box, or to take them out and randomly page through the books with their animated cartoon-like illustrations. The stories are simple enough for him to tell after a few readings. Any preschooler can tuck this fantastic world of make-believe into its box and put it under his arm even if he is only a toddler.

In 1964 Sendak received the Caldecott award for his book ***Where the Wild Things Are.*** When it was first announced the winner, many teachers, parents and librarians feared that children would not be able to differentiate between the real and imagined adventure. They felt that the monsters would frighten children, and that the mother's punishment would make them feel insecure.

Children have not reacted in terror because the book's hero is typical of those heroes they like best. Max is a doing hero. He is a self-confident little boy. He shows neither remorse nor fear when he is sent to his room. His life goes on; he is capable of having a good time. Over a decade has passed and children continue to enjoy Max's adventures. If the book is discussed after sharing it, someone will usually point out that monsters are pretend. But the fact that the child in the book was able to cope with frustration and to continue to be exuberant fascinates children. They see no need for Max to act sad, and are satisfied that Max's mother has anguished over her decision to punish him when they hear that supper is waiting for him.

Although these early works are substantial and are still as modern in theme and plot as they were when first published,

they are not as complex in artistic style as two more recent Sendak creations. The book ***In The Night Kitchen*** and the film ***Really Rosie*** best achieve Sendak's desire to create a visual representation of his American childhood. Both are accurate interpretations of the child's understanding of his freedom as a small U.S. citizen and of his use of adult pop culture. Each is an unique experience for the modern child. They are similar in artistic style, but they have different strengths and weaknesses. Yet, they are both landmarks in children's media.

Maurice Sendak, like most substantial artists, seems always to know where he got his artistic inspiration. Concerning ***In The Night Kitchen*** he wrote:

> "Night Kitchen" . . . reflect[s] a popular American art both crass and oddly surrealistic, an art that encompasses the Empire State Building, syncopated Disney cartoons, and aluminum-clad, comic book heroes, an Art Moderne whose richness of detail was most sensuously catalogued in the movies.

Adult critics at once applauded and chastised Sendak's use of American pop culture. They were upset with his use of a comic strip format (including ballooning people's words), with his nudity, with his use of familiar adult movie stars and vulgarities. Some feared that it was a much more frightening experience than his previous Caldecott winner. To librarians who disliked the first story, this could only be met with contempt. (pp. 31-2)

Some libraries put shorts on Mickey to cover up his obvious penis, some kept it behind the desk; many simply did not order it. Adult censors were well meaning—they knew the implications of Mickey's saying ''cock-a-doodle-doo''—but they were also destructive. They failed to come to grips with a timeless technique used in children's literature: writing and illustrating one plot for two audiences.

Sendak's stylistic plan was not new; Randolph Caldecott's nursery stories are illustrated to appeal to adult humor and to reflect the adult social life of the time. Lewis Carroll's characters were created around sophisticated adult humor, and reflected the absurd conditions of the English court in that era. Probably Sendak never assumed he was doing anything revolutionary in this picture book fantasy. And while, in the large sense, Sendak did not change children's literature, he did begin a minor twentieth century revolution for picture book authors and artists.

He created a free American preschool child who is unaffected by adult social hypocrisy. His child is uninhibited by the adult moral code since it has no real meaning to him. He is pleased with himself, not because he is so sexually attuned to his situation, but because by mentally and physically being creative he is capable of solving problems that are insurmountable to the adults. Thus, Sendak indirectly states the adult theme that dominated children in the seventies: you can be anything you want to be and nothing can keep you down. This book most clearly shows the child as the creator of order from chaos, and directly states that "thanks to Mickey, we [adults included] have cake every morning." Mickey is the forerunner in picture book presentations of the liberated American child. He is self assured and happy, and because of this he never doubts his abilities. He was the first most nude (and therefore rude according to adult critics) child, but he certainly was not the last. Other less boisterous nude children have since appeared. By freeing his main character from adult sexual implications, Sendak created a realistic preschooler.

Children's comments on *In The Night Kitchen* demonstrate that they look at the book in terms of their everyday life and their fantasy world. It is important to remember that U.S. children are expected to watch television, believe in God, the U.S. government, Santa Claus and the tooth fairy without having psychological traumas. It would be unrealistic not to expect them to enjoy fantasy literature based on their culture. Not one preschooler I have shared this book with has objected to Mickey's being nude. In fact, one child was most unhappy when he got his dough suit and said, "he shouldn't have those clothes." The bakers are neither too frightening nor too realistic for children. Most do not notice their resemblance to Hardy since he is not seen in current media. Children do recognize that the bakers are merry fellows who work earnestly at their profession, and they will be alert to find the bakers in U.S. pop art. To my surprise, a four year old was looking at a box of Sunshine cookies one day and pointed at the small picture of a robust baker exclaiming, "There's the baker who baked the cakes!" The baker does look strangely like Sendak's version, but he is so small that the adult would not notice. Further, when Mickey cries "cock-a-doodle-doo!" children say, "The sun is coming up!"

Probably Sendak did not realize the impact his book would have on small children. Certainly adult critics cannot judge the appeal that this combination of everyday objects with fantasy has for a small child. We have long known that the young child's imaginary play is very real and very important to him. Sendak captured the essence of play and drew common kitchen paraphernalia in a scene that any American child would have been able to identify. It was at once real and unreal. It was unique, because it showed ordinary objects caught as a backdrop for a preschool creative drama. (pp. 32-4)

The film version of *The Sign on Rosie's Door* and "**The Nutshell Library**" is a gutsy children's musical that combines Sendak's ability to bring alive the child's pretend world with modern compositions written and sung by Carole King. The visuals reflect Sendak's earlier techniques: independent children capable of believing in the reality of play who aptly integrate well known products and items with pure nonsense. Ms. King's uninhibited voice gives her compositions that hardy sound that is characteristic of children's pretenses. The movie reaffirms Sendak's belief that U.S. children live in a world of pretend closely linked to their everyday life and to their natural meter and rhyme.

Rosie is a brassy little girl whose sharp answers and quick wit make her the natural leader in neighborhood play. She dresses up in mother's cast off clothes and plays movie star. She directs the other characters' participation and casually puts them down. She is slightly obnoxious (even to the other children in the film), but she is great fun to know. Most children were not familiar with her before the film. Many older children were anxious to read *The Sign on Rosie's Door* and to see her other adventures. "**The Nutshell Library**"'s words are gay and catchy. They are well captured in the songs, and are more enjoyable to some as songs than they were as stories. The children in these stories come alive and are funny to small children because of their quick movements and strong personalities. But Rosie and Chicken Soup are the dominant characters, and they best reflect Sendak's interpretation of modern American children. They are casual, clever and audacious; they are also in need of an audience and of companionship in their own familiar surroundings.

Sendak graphically captured the American duplicity of adult criteria for child behavior and artistic endeavors in children's literature in both *Really Rosie* and *In the Night Kitchen*. He has always presented a picture that was bawdy to those who could not sense its underlying currents. . . . Children immediately see the modern realism of these fantasies. Adults dismiss them as irresolute in theme.

When accepting the Hans Christian Andersen award [see excerpt above in Author's Commentary], Sendak said:

> I no longer want simply to illustrate—or, for that matter, simply to write. I am now in search of a form more purely and essentially my own.

That form was initiated in *Night Kitchen* and resolved in *Really Rosie*. The only fear must be that Maurice Sendak will grow up and forfeit his perception of American society's effects on the preschool child. (pp. 34-5)

Jill P. May, "Sendak's American Hero," in Journal of Popular Culture, *Vol. XII, No. 1, Summer, 1978, pp. 30-5.*

HILTON KRAMER

The great appeal of Mr. Sendak's work lies precisely in his success in transforming [a] psychoanalytical vision of experience into fictional fantasies that have something of the quality and mystery of traditional folk tales and fairy stories. His audacity in opening up the traditional children's story to the terrors, including the sexual terrors, that are disclosed to us in psychotherapy, is the very mark of his originality. (p. 69)

Hilton Kramer, "Audacious Fantasist," in The New York Times Book Review, *November 9, 1980, pp. 47, 69.*

SELMA G. LANES

[*The following excerpt is from* The Art of Maurice Sendak, *the first extended monograph on a twentieth-century American creator of picture books.*]

There is no better-known illustrator of children's books in our time than Maurice Sendak. . . . Sendak is credited by many critics, educators, and knowledgeable readers of children's books with being the first artist to deal openly with the feelings of young children. His receipt in 1970 of the international Hans Christian Andersen Medal, the closest approximation to a Nobel Prize in the world of children's books, for the body of his illustration gave official confirmation to what his admirers already knew: that his pictures had made and were continuing to make a major contribution to the literature of childhood. The artist has said of his work, "If I have an unusual gift, it's not that I draw particularly better or write particularly better than other people—I've never fooled myself about that. Rather, it's that I remember things other people don't recall: the sounds and feelings and images—the emotional quality—of particular moments in childhood.". . .

[Sendak is] the most important children's book illustrator of our time. (p. 7)

Anyone familiar with Sendak's work knows that certain images and themes recur from book to book, year after year. The subject of food and eating—or being eaten up, for one, has been a central concern since the artist was a child. (p. 237)

Food—or the lack of it—is a crucial element in **Where the Wild Things Are.** For talking back to his mother (angrily threatening to eat her up), Max is sent to bed "without eating anything," and this is more than half the reason for his rage. Once he has made himself king of all wild things and has presided over a triumphal wild rumpus, however, Max willingly gives up his throne when "all around from far away across the world he smelled good things to eat." And the book's perfect ending is achieved as Max, back in his very own room, finds "his supper waiting for him, and it was still hot." The small listener instinctively knows that where there is hot food, there is also forgiveness and maternal love restored.

In Sendak's next picture book, **Hector Protector and As I Went over the Water,** both nursery-rhyme improvisations revolve around food and eating. Hector, the ill-tempered messenger, deliberately sets off without his edible dispatch—the cake his mother is sending to the Queen. The entire pictorial interpretation is a comic consideration of unloving behavior (the withholding of food by the hero) and its punishment (food being withheld from the hero). The companion rhyme, **As I Went over the Water,** begins with an act of oral aggression: a disconcertingly cheerful, underwater monster swallows a ship whole. With the behemoth's regurgitation of the ship, all feelings of aggression are presumably assuaged, and the entire cast—small sea captain, sea predator, and two toothless blackbirds—are last viewed as a comradely foursome.

In Sendak's **Higglety Pigglety Pop!,** eating is the dog-heroine Jennie's consuming passion. Voraciously, she devours all the sandwiches a pig has to offer, wolfs down a milk-wagon-full of dairy products, and then gets an unsuspecting parlor-maid to whip her up a batch of buttermilk pancakes because she is, presumably, faint from hunger. An unfulfilled artist, Jennie cannot find food enough (or love enough?) in this world to satisfy her. Perhaps this is the meaning of her existential lament, "There must be more to life than having everything." Only when she wins the leading lady's role in the World Mother Goose Theatre is she able to satisfy her insatiable appetite. (Jennie's part requires her to consume a mop made out of salami during every performance.) An artist's ultimate satisfaction is in the practice of her—or his—art; it is food for the spirit and the means of achieving immortality.

In the Night Kitchen is, from beginning to end, a paean to the sights, sounds, and smells of that most familiar and comforting childhood haven, the kitchen. If warmth and love dominate its food-filled province, there is also an element of danger. Mickey, the hero, is almost consumed—baked in a cake for others to eat. Ultimately, however, Mickey the pilot helps to feed us all, by providing "cake every morning," thus fulfilling the artist's childhood longing to be able to watch, and perhaps to join, the Sunshine Bakers at their nighttime labors. As it did in *Wild Things,* food provides the perfect grace note on which to end a joyous dream about the sensual pleasures of being a young child.

When the question of food is raised, Sendak says, "The business of eating is such an immensely important part of life for a child. The Grimms' tales are full of things being eaten and then disgorged. It's an image that constantly appeals to me, and to most children, too. The scene where the monster eats the boat and regurgitates it in *As I Went over the Water* struck me as hilarious when I drew it. I have the mind of a child." (pp. 238-39)

If anything looms larger than food in Sendak's work, particularly in his later work, it is babies. From the comically irresistible cartoon in *The Bee-Man of Orn* of the Bee-Man transformed back into babyhood, to the first use of family photographs to depict infants in *Zlateh the Goat,* the artist has exhibited a marked affinity for babies as subjects. In *Higglety Pigglety Pop!,* Sendak, for the first time, used a photograph of himself to fashion the character of Baby. In 1968, the artist drew an arresting frontal view of a nude baby girl floating in air—MacDonald's Light Princess as an infant. For *The Juniper Tree* in 1973, Sendak provided the commanding frontispiece baby for "The Goblins." In Randall Jarrell's *Fly by Night,* the artist again made use of himself as a baby, this time enfolded in his mother's arms. During the seventies, too, Sendak did two drawings of babies for the Op-Ed page of the *New York Times,* one of a somewhat dubious-looking infant proffering a toast to the new year, another of an infant in thrall before a television set. And in *Outside Over There,* not only did Sendak use posed photographs of an infant in order to develop one of his two leading characters, he turned to a German photographic album to characterize the five goblin babies, the villains of the tale.

On an obvious level, the artist's interest in babies can be attributed to his fascination with his own childhood and babyhood. In each of the works of his picture-book trilogy, there is a progressively younger hero or heroine. Max of *Wild Things* is older than Mickey of *Night Kitchen,* who, in turn, is older than the baby in *Outside Over There.* (pp. 239-47)

From the time Sendak first read Dorothy Baruch's case study of a disturbed child, *One Little Boy,* and was moved by her documentation that "the thoughts of childhood are deep and dark," he has been looking back at his own childhood and trying to unravel "this loose mystery of myself, the psychic reality of my own childhood." At the time he was working on *Outside Over There,* Sendak was fascinated by a study of preverbal language, the signals babies give to make their needs and wants known. And as an artist, he has long been intrigued by "the physicalness of babies, the endless variety of baby movements and otherworldly expressions." For him, drawing them is akin to a sensual pleasure.

Among other recurring images in Sendak's work are flying and falling figures, staples since his earliest illustrations appeared. In Ruth Krauss's *A Very Special House,* the small hero, while not actually in flight, is dancingly airborne for much of the book. In one dreamlike sequence in Krauss's *Charlotte and the White Horse,* done while the artist was still influenced by the paintings of Chagall, the heroine actually flies. Both the hero of Krauss's *I Want to Paint My Bathroom Blue* and the heroine of Doris Orgel's *Sarah's Room* are airborne for a good part of their stories, and Mickey of *In the Night Kitchen* free-falls from his bed down two floors into the Night Kitchen, a variation of flying. The hero of Jarrell's *Fly by Night* is in flight for most of his story, as is Ida, the heroine of *Outside Over There.* Whatever else it may signify, a flying figure is one that has escaped the bounds of everyday reality and clearly announces to the child viewer that the realm of fantasy has been entered. In psychoanalytic terms, a flying figure is a symbol of power and potency. Certainly dreams of flying are common in childhood.

Windows, an integral part of Sendak's imaginative life since he was a small boy, also play an important role—often a magical one—in many of his books and fantasy drawings. In Ruth Krauss's *I Want to Paint My Bathroom Blue,* they float in space with the hero. Time and again, a Sendak character will pass through a window only to be transformed into something or someone else. In *Kenny's Window,* the aperture serves as the border between the familiar reality of the boy's bedroom and both the real world beyond and the fantasy world within himself. ("A window" is the answer to one of Kenny's seven vital questions: "What looks inside and what looks outside?") A window, too, is a protection from the unknown world outside. One of Kenny's tin soldiers comments wistfully on looking through the window, "That's the world and it is miles long. We'll get lost." In *Outside Over There,* the heroine Ida's exit via a window signifies her passage from the safety and comfort of home into that unexplored dream / nightmare realm where the goblins live.

In Sendak's fantasy pages done to pieces of music, the same themes and motifs can be found—flying and falling figures, characters eating and being eaten, windows serving as passageways to other realms, and babies wailing, nursing, devouring their mothers, or being carried off. These drawings, some perfunctory in execution, others of high polish and charm, form the psychic raw material of Sendak's imaginative world. (pp. 247-48)

When asked specifically what his single obsession is, Sendak has become less articulate as the years pass. "I know in my gut what it is, but it's not easy to verbalize anymore. I can't really say my theme is what children are as related to their parents, though it is certainly partly that. But it's something more as well. Whenever I get really close to it, I think 'no, it's from some deeper part of myself than my head.'"

If one were to try to verbalize Sendak's major theme on the basis of a close examination of all his books and writings, it would certainly have something to do with his unending exploration of the normal child's burden of rage, confusion, fear of and frustration with the various uncontrollable factors in his own life: adults who don't understand, limitations that restrict and inhibit, situations beyond coping with.

In his continuing attempt "to make contact with the real, underlying child," Sendak has forthrightly confronted such sensitive subject matter as childhood anger, sexuality, or the occasionally murderous impulses of raw sibling rivalry. Whenever adult critics find his work baffling or downright frightening, he is quick to point out that children are their own best censors

and will neither listen to nor read on their own things that make them uncomfortable. As an author / artist of the post-Freudian world, one who has spent more time and conscious effort keeping in touch with his child-self than any previous practitioner of the art of illustration, he doubtless knows whereof he speaks. (pp. 248-49)

Selma G. Lanes, in her The Art of Maurice Sendak, *Harry N. Abrams, Inc., 1980, 278 p.*

ERIC A. KIMMEL

While I am sure that many children will certainly have a look at *Outside Over There,* I suspect that most will pass it by in favor of *Mike Mulligan and his Steamshovel, Blueberries for Sal,* and *Where The Wild Things Are.* Like *The Juniper Tree,* it will enrapture the critics and leave children cold. Now why should that be? Is it because children have no taste? Hardly. It was the delighted response of children to *Where The Wild Things Are* that made Sendak a superstar in the first place. Back in '63, many grown-ups did not know what to make of such vivid monsters in a children's book. Fortunately, kids did. However, since that time, the bulk of Sendak's work has exhibited a darker, more idiosyncratic vision; astonishing conceptions, but not nearly as popular with children as they are with adults. Sendak's critical reputation is enormous. Abram's publication of *The Art of Maurice Sendak* [by Selma G. Lanes; see excerpt above], complete with pop-ups, is an unheard-of tribute to a living artist, let alone a kid's book illustrator. Yet the cold fact is that with the exception of *Where The Wild Things Are,* "The Nutshell Library," and a few early titles, Sendak's overall popularity with children is much less than that of Ezra Jack Keats, Leo Lionni, or Tomie de Paola. (pp. 38-9)

Eric A. Kimmel, "Children's Literature without Children," in Children's literature in education, *Vol. 13, No. 1, Spring, 1982, pp. 38-43.*

JOHN CECH

From the 1960s on, it has become increasingly clear that one person stands out from the crowd as a primary innovator and extender of the form and subject matter of the picture book: Maurice Sendak. Since Max and the Wild Things' astonishing rumpus into our lives in 1963, Sendak's work has challenged conventions, drawn controversy, set new standards, and, quite simply, delighted and dazzled us. But we may tend to forget that, even before the Wild Things broke through, Sendak had given us a number of books that would have secured him a respected, memorable place in the history of children's book illustration: *A Hole Is to Dig; Charlotte and the White Horse;* the "Little Bear Books" and "The Nutshell Library." No other illustrator since Caldecott has had such all-pervasive, if sometimes unacknowledged, impact.

As we know from studying Sendak's art and reading his remarks about those figures who have influenced him, he has built his work on sources from the deep and recent past. Like Autolycus, his "borrowings" are famous and often invisible. Dürer, William Blake, Henry Fuseli, Samuel Palmer, George Cruikshank, Winslow Homer, Marc Chagall, Caldecott, Winsor McCay, and Walt Disney, to name just a few, have inspired his work. . . . Yet Sendak's genius has lain in his unique creative alchemy, in his ability to transmute the influence of the masters into a substance that is always and profoundly himself. (p. 178)

Through Sendak's capacity to remain true to his own childhood, and through what John Keats called negative capability, Sendak labors to give shape and meaning to its fragmented and frightening fantasies. This creative effort has allowed him to chart and thus guide us through the visions that occupy not only his own, personal childhood but all childhoods. Taken as a whole, his work has provided us with a weave of archetypal expressions that constitute a true, living mythology, a body of stories, both verbal and visual, that touch our deepest longings, misgivings, fears, and beliefs. He shapes anew for the modern child and adult (since there is not a generation of adults that has grown up on his works) that primal stuff that we may try to turn away from but that is inescapably there, in the "rag and bone shop of the heart"—ignored, unspoken, repressed, unconscious, but nonetheless there, present. We do not usually speak of Sendak in these terms, preferring to stay on the surface of his art, but it is time we did: he is our childhood's mythologist. (p. 179)

> *John Cech, "Sendak's Mythic Childhood," in* Children's Literature: Annual of the Modern Language Association Seminar on Children's Literature and The Children's Literature Association, *Vol. 10, 1982, pp. 178-82.*

GERALDINE DeLUCA

There are some books that seem to touch us all, children and adults, in a primary way. *Charlotte's Web* comes most immediately to mind. But Sendak, in his quest for both audiences, may actually be leaving the child behind. *Higglety, Pigglety, Pop* and the selections of Grimm tales for *The Juniper Tree* suggest his interest in taking the forms and genres of children's literature into the adult world. Neither work really seems appropriate for children. And his most recent work, *Outside Over There,* despite its handling of sibling rivalry and oedipal feelings, seemingly so close to a child's experience, may also be a heavier burden than some children can be expected to bear.

The difficulties, the obscurities of *Outside Over There* seem to spring from what is essentially an allegorical sensibility, a sensibility that needs to charge its works with layer upon layer of meaning, one that is obsessive, that thrives on detail, that must cover every inch of literal and metaphorical ground. This is not, of course, a negative quality in itself. Some of the greatest artists of our culture seem to have worked from the same impulses. It does account, however, for the extravagant, secretive quality of Sendak's work and may explain why he sometimes passes the child by.

Even in art for adults, allegory has not, at least since the nineteenth century, been a particularly popular form. It has traditionally been regarded with suspicion and impatience as being too doctrinal and mechanical, in contrast to "symbolic" literature, wherein the symbol is felt to inhere in the work, to be more intrinsically related, rather than being tediously strung along throughout.... More recently, structuralist and poststructuralist critics, concerned with the uncertainties of the critical, interpretive activity itself, have begun to find the allegorical mode particularly attractive. (pp. 4-5)

[The] sense that reality is impossible to represent, and that the desire to try to represent it grows out of a sense of loss, sheds much light on the quality of Sendak's work. It may account for its fussiness—its cantankerousness, I might almost say—for its themes of childhood anger and struggle, and for Sendak's increasing tendency to depict the child's triumphs as fragile, partial, and sorely bought.

That Sendak sees himself as working in a tradition that seeks to reveal difficult, perhaps ultimately ineffable truths is evident from his own commentary on his work. Regarding his illustrations for the Grimm fairy tales, for example, he says, "The tales work on two levels: first, as stories; second, as the unraveling of deep psychological dramas"; further, "I wanted my pictures to tell any reader who thinks the stories are simple to go back to the beginning and read them again. I searched for what was really underneath. It was hard. There was not one story that gave its secret right away." Allegory, of course, is not the only mode that speaks to us on more than one level. We can read any realistic piece of fiction and take from it not only the story but some more essential statement about life. But allegory compels us into that interpretive frame of mind. The story qua story is strange, enigmatic, distorted; it demands a reading. This may seem inappropriate for children's stories, stories whose success we would assume to lie in their simplicity. At times, as I am arguing here, Sendak does go too far. But at times the allegorical mode does work. Fairy tales, despite their spare surface, are not simple, and by and large children love them. They haunt us with their threats and promises, their taboos, their intimations of life that lie below their surface. And this is what Sendak strives for in his works.

Moreover, while we might, on first consideration, expect a children's book writer to move toward simplicity, from another point of view it makes sense that children's literature would yield multiple meanings. At the very least any children's book writer has to sustain two visions: the adult's and the child's. In some way he has to become connected to his own childhood, to his perceptions of the world of his past, from its physical scale in relation to himself, to his confusions and fears and naive interpretations of things he could not possibly understand fully. So there is always a certain amount of irony in children's books, from the adult's point of view, due to simplifications of information and necessary deletions of certain kinds of experience.

These distinctions between big and small, innocence and experience, provide an important source of layering in Sendak's work. His childhood remembrances seem more vivid and acute than those of most adults—perhaps the effect of writing for children, but possibly his reason for doing so. He depends in a very conscious way on his unconscious—his repository of childhood experiences—to supply him with material, expressing a clear perference for the kind of material the unconscious can offer him.... (pp. 6-7)

The obsessive devotion to the treasures of the unconscious ... is manifested in much of Sendak's work, as in his quest narratives that represent the conscious self in some relation to the unconscious. As he says, his three major picture books, the self-styled trilogy of *Where the Wild Things Are, In the Night Kitchen,* and *Outside Over There,* all deal with "how children master various feelings—anger, boredom, fear, frustration, jealousy—and manage to come to grips with the realities of their lives." All three dreamlike fantasy journeys, and as the "fascination of what's difficult" has grown in Sendak, each has become deliberately more laden with "meaning." (p. 7)

[*Outside Over There*] is a book that is at times disturbingly implausible on a literal level, surrendering some of its harmony for hidden meanings, some universal but some highly idiosyncratic, that lie heavily on us.

Sendak's comments on his work show quite clearly his inclinations toward allegory. To be sure, most of his works are not fully developed examples, but even the simplest of them displays aspects of allegorical art, and looking at them with a definition of allegory in mind makes it clear where a work like *Outside Over There* comes from. Angus Fletcher's definition of allegory is particularly helpful because it analyzes allegorical art in terms of its component parts—agency, imagery, themes, action, causation, and values—and this analysis helps us to see where the non-allegorical works, or rather those that are not full allegories, share characteristics of the mode.

Briefly, in Fletcher's scheme, allegorical characters (he calls them "daemonic agents") act as if possessed by daemons who "compartmentalize function" so that they seem pathologically single-minded. Such characters are remarkably rigid and restricted in behavior, always tending toward becoming icons in an allegorical cosmos. Daemonic agents perceive the characters around them as aspects of the conflicts within themselves. And "by analyzing the projections, we determine what is going on in the mind of the highly imaginative projector." With his restricted view of the universe, the daemonic agent reminds us that we see only what our preoccupied minds allow us to see. On the simplest, most childish level—and children are often remarkably like this—we have Pierre, "who only would say 'I don't care,'" and Chicken Soup, who is what he eats: chicken soup with rice twelve months a year. In *Chicken Soup with Rice* Sendak is reflecting a small child's pleasure in routine and repetition. In *Pierre* he reflects the child's negativism. Neither work reveals allegorical dimensions, although one could spend a little time talking about Pierre's getting swallowed by the lion. But all of these motifs—the repetitions, the obsessiveness, the self-containment, the child-eating lion—are used again allegorically in *Higglety, Pigglety, Pop*, a work that does demand interpretation. It is a more difficult, more serious work in which Sendak comes to terms with the death of his dog Jennie by giving her eternal life as the leading lady in the World Mother Goose Theatre where every day she gets to eat a mop made of salami.

The world of *Higglety, Pigglety, Pop* is world of enchantment, a world constructed to test Jennie's mettle. As the Red Cross Knight's universe is centered upon holiness and its enemies, Jennie's is centered upon food. Gluttony, we might say, is her abiding sin, and thus all her adventures involve eating. . . . What she lacks is "experience," a commodity, Sendak tenderly implies, that she could never get under his hothouse care. So she goes out into the world, genuinely on a quest, though like most untried heroes not quite sure what she is looking for. But the other characters, all members of the World Mother Goose Theatre, do know what she needs, and beguiling her with food, they lead her to the house of Baby, who won't eat, and whose name nobody knows, except for her parents at Castle Yonder. Castle Yonder is clearly heaven, and Lanes points out that at the time of the writing, Sendak was also anticipating his mother's death. It is not surprising then that Baby looks like Sendak's own baby pictures. Jennie, who is determined to feed Baby, winds up eating the breakfast herself and thus failing at her "experience." But she is prepared to sacrifice herself to save his life. Putting her head into the lion's mouth, she is saved at the final moment unwittingly by saying Baby's name, Mother Goose. Baby and the lion then immediately disappear to Castle Yonder and Jennie, who had everything, now finds herself in a wood with nothing. But she has gained experience. She has learned to sacrifice for someone else, to stop eating, to let herself in fact be food for a lion. She has endured—and died—and is ready to be led to the Mother Goose Theatre, at Castle Yonder, by Mother Goose herself, who was Baby / Sendak, now transformed into an orchestrator of tales.

Jennie's "final reward" is to live forever in the nursery rhyme of the title.

It is clear that Jennie is a daemonic agent rather than a fully rounded, mimetic character. One might well answer that she is a dog, after all; how complex can she be? But if we compare her, say, to William Steig's Dominic, we can see the difference. Dominic's doglike nature is not ignored. But he travels through a universe that is fuller and more varied, that has an existence apart from him. The world of Sendak's story, by contrast, reads like a projection of Jennie's mind. The pig wears a sandwich board that contains free sandwiches; the milkman's truck is filled with milk that Jennie drinks. Like the world of dreams, it all pertains to her; she has to figure out what it means and without her it does not exist.

The imagery in such a world is what Fletcher terms "cosmic," which is to say that every item appearing before us has its place in the cosmic hierarchy and is to be regarded as a sign. The macrocosm is reflected as well in the microcosm; nothing is too large or too small to be ignored. The protagonist traveling through such a landscape is generally in a state of anxiety because he cannot read the signs (see Sendak's statement about his unconscious) or because he is trying to ignore the import. And while the gap between the sign and the thing signified may never be fully bridged, so that one will never be completely assured that what he perceives is reality, part of the reader's pleasure, nonetheless, is in trying to decode the signs and understand the meaning of the protagonist's response to them. Names, dress, and place are all a part of this universe of signs, reflecting to an extraordinary degree the state of one's mind or soul and one's position in the cosmos. (pp. 8-10)

The basic movement in allegory is the quest—the journey away from the familiar to hidden external and internal truths. It includes alternating states of progress and battle, interspersed with periods of rest and understanding. For the allegorical hero, however, there is almost never total peace or harmony, at least not while he is on this earth. Ambivalence haunts him, the degree to which it is resolved depending on how idealistic the work is. But even the most hopeful of allegories are by their very nature filled with conflict, with characters pulled by polar desires, since it is the function of allegory to set up an intellectual and emotional dialectic that the hero must work through.

Sendak's simplest representation of the child's quest "to come to grips with the realities of his life" is, as he says, *Where the Wild Things Are.* In an early version of the story Max's mother turns into a wolf, embodying the agent-to-image change that sometimes occurs in allegory. And an early draft of the text has a passage of commands and conflictingly alluring visual messages reminiscent of passages in Spenser: "He entered a magic garden though the sign said do not enter and looked round the tree though the sign said do not look. He thought this might be the place where the wild horses are." But Sendak finally pared away the florid excesses and what remains is a beautifully clean visual and verbal story of Max's rebellion—his working through his hostility to his mother, being the wild thing that his wolf suit says he is, charging through the tiny space of the first pages into the vast double-page spreads where the wild things are. Eating, a favorite subject of Sendak's, and a common source of sensual pleasure in children's books, is here the vehicle through which Max reveals his aggressions. "I'll eat you up," he tells his mother and is sent to bed without his supper. One is reminded of Sendak's sequence of sketches of the baby who begins by sucking at its mother's breast and ends by contentedly swallowing her. Max, in his wolfish state of mind, might be inclined to do the same. But then what would he do for his next meal?

The quest, then, for all that it is liberating and wish-fulfilling, with Max ordering everyone around, is also, as it is for Jennie, civilizing. Max may rule the wild things but they are not giving him anything to eat. They can only offer to "eat him up [they] love him so," which is in the right spirit, but the wrong solution. Max needs someone unlike himself to "love him best of all" and cook his supper, regardless of the compromise to his freedom. The story is a remarkably subtle and affectionate rendition of a child's desire for independence and dominance in conflict with his need for security and love, and we finish reading it with a sense of comic, cathartic relief.

Visually as well as textually *Where the Wild Things Are* is a wonderful work, the gray confining space of the house opening up, as the borders disappear, into the expansive, rosy fantasy world and pages of "wild rumpus," a sublime conception that is also, by virtue of its preciousness and safety, picturesque. One could call such a work simple—once it is all laid out it seems so clear—but such simplicity is deceptive. The book is inspired and rendered with remarkable balance and restraint. Surface and underlying meaning are close; that it is not a "difficult," enigmatic book is part of its charm. It is truly an allegory for a small child, one that can be apprehended in its totality, without explanation.

In the Night Kitchen is a more complicated, idiosyncratic work, presenting us with a more self-consciously allegorical Sendak, someone more fully exploiting the potential of the mode. Mickey's night sky / city / pantry is a surreal world conjured up by innocence with perfect logic, given the fragmentary state of a child's understanding of terms like the Milky Way. Everything in this night kitchen is comfortingly labeled, as food boxes are. Everything has a name, a place, a significance that can be read. To be sure, Sendak embeds his own private associations in the pictures: June 10, 1928, a date on a box, is, as we might have guessed, his own birthday, and other names are those of people important in his life. But what makes the work so appealing is that the images are not merely clever; Sendak can turn the giant milk bottle into a womb and have it make perfect sense psychologically. Drinking from the bottle as he floats in the milk, Mickey says, "I'm in the milk and the milk's in me. God bless milk and God bless me." It's an intriguing image that expresses a preoccupation of Sendak's—being inside and outside at the same time, being in the womb, contained, and at the same time incorporating, containing; being supremely sheltered and yet conquering. Conflicting, ambivalent desires are momentarily resolved in this image of infantile sensual pleasure. And the overriding statement of the work, focusing of Mickey's driving need to learn what goes on in the night kitchen and save the day by finding milk, is true to a child's experience.

Mickey's fantasy is more social than Max's, involving an awareness of what one could call community that Max doesn't yet have. Mickey is both showing off and doing something useful. "And that's why, thanks to Mickey, we have milk every morning." For both children, however, the struggle is purely self-centered. And for the time being, in each case, that is enough. It is not the case, however, for Ida in *Outside Over There*. The eldest and most complex of the three protagonists, her story is quite different.

Structurally the third book follows the same form as the first two, moving from the inside, Ida's room—though it's not her private bedroom but a day room that she shares with her sister—to a place of fantasy and risk, to "outside over there." The phrase represents the abstract concept of externality, otherness, a child might state it. For while all three books bring the child from one relatively safe place to another where one tests one's prowess, this third book not only involves getting beyond one's room but also past the night places of one's own fantasy world to a place that encompasses the needs and will of other people, outside the mind itself. Of course this is still Ida's struggle with herself—conquering the goblins in herself that would do away with her sister. But Ida's quest is also social. She is older than Max and Mickey, who are hardly more than babies themselves, and she is female. One is grateful to Sendak for recognizing how early in life girls learn to feel the conflict between their desire to achieve for themselves and the demands placed on them to take care of others. Another writer might have indicated that Ida's achievement *was* in taking care of the baby, and, of course, in part it is, but while he allows approval to Ida for finally being a good sister, Sendak keeps the two roles separate.

Another sign that this quest is more complex is that Ida needs help in completing it. Max and Mickey had only to dream, becoming in their dreams figures appropriately dressed—or undressed—to express their psychic state, both conjuring up and conquering their adversaries. Ida, as Sendak says, starts out badly and only recovers by listening to her father's song—her father being the traditional guardian figure of the fairy tale, the wise part of the psyche, which helps to "turn her around" and allow her to find her strength. Another indication of the complexity of her problem is that there is no food in this work. Ida takes her pleasure and solace in her wonder horn, her music being both what distracts her from her sister and what she uses to bring the sister back. This is a world not of sensuality but of work and art.

As Fletcher and others have noted, allegory is "the art of subterfuge par excellence," an art "proper to those moments when nothing but subterfuge will work." The situation in *Outside Over There* is clearly such a moment for a child. Placing Ida in charge of her baby sister while her father is away at sea and her mother sits immobile in the arbor, Sendak creates a tableau of oedipal feelings, and from beginning to end there is not an easy moment. These are the great taboos of childhood—the longings from which the dreamwork of allegory springs. The feelings to which Sendak gives shape are terrible and frightening, and the excessively careful narrative just barely veils what is going on.

We can understand the rationale of the situation as simple story: papas go to sea, children help with younger siblings. That's the grown-up and moral way. Yet we still feel the unfairness of it, from Ida's point of view. There is something suspect about the parents, the profoundly passive mother so wrapped in missing papa she can hardly move, the father so unattainable and beyond reproach, and Ida stuck with the baby, big, heavy, and helpless, requiring Ida's undivided attention. Turn away for a second and the goblins come. And papa from afar—his picture hanging watchfully on the wall—knows just what's happening.

We feel for Ida not only as we feel for a child but as we feel for ourselves. She is anyone feeling abandoned and burdened, needing love, recognition, and time to herself, anyone feeling guilt at not being all she is expected to be. That Sendak manages to embody so much in her is impressive. He expresses the depth and complexity of a universal situation. But his handling of other aspects of the story is disturbing. On a simple narrative level, for example, the kidnapping of the baby by the goblins is horrifying: the terrified baby is hustled out the window while Ida "never knowing" plays her horn; on the next page we see Ida embracing the changeling "ice thing" and saying "how I love you." These are nightmare images and one keeps turning back to them, wondering how a child would understand them. By now such complaints must be an old song for Sendak. But perhaps all one can do is worry anew over each new frightening image and try to make distinctions among them. In this story, as opposed to **Wild Things,** there is no humor to lighten the burden. We are not seeing a child brazenly seeking out an adorably depicted danger; rather, a totally innocent and helpless baby is being threatened because of the neglect of her sister.

And why are the goblins babies? It seems a bit arch and coy at first, tied up as it is with Sendak's private associations about the Dionne quintuplets and the Lindbergh kidnapping. But symbolically it does make sense. It is characteristic of allegorical imagery that false creatures mimic their true counterparts. Consider Una and false Una in Book I of *The Faerie Queene* or Florimell and false Florimell, who, like the ice baby, is an effigy in snow. Ida's unconscious might well depict the goblins as babies since that is the form that troubles her. She is angry at babies. In some way the baby is to blame. Furthermore it makes the rescue more complex. Ida cannot simply pluck her sister away. Everyone looks the same. How can she tell the false from the true? It is an essential question in allegory. And since appearances are always deceiving, there is no direct way to find out. With her father's help, she must discover her own resources—her music—and let its power work for her. For the goblins the music is Dionysian; it makes them sick. But it leaves her sister safely reborn to Ida in the eggshell. This is the way with allegory. The truth can only be known through signs and rituals: the baby that doesn't dance itself into a frenzy is the human child.

Ida seems bewildered through most of the story, but on a symbolic level it all makes sense. She begins her journey to rescue her sister by putting on her mother's yellow cloak and floating backwards out the window. Why is she floating and why backwards? She is still too passive and still looking inward rather than to "outside over there," where the world and her responsibility lie. And her mother's cloak can only hinder her because she has failed in taking her mother's place. Only her father can help her now (who else, we think smugly), by revealing her own strength to her. So even though she seems in a state of shock through most of the experience, Ida is learning, simply by virtue of enduring.

When her ordeal is over, Ida passes through a wood, a picturesque setting where Mozart sits in a little house playing the harpsichord. Sendak told Selma Lanes that he played nothing but Mozart throughout the composition of this book—the horn and the kidnapping are allusions to *The Magic Flute.* So a Mozartean spirit is meant to infuse the work. Mozart is its reigning deity. And Ida, like many allegorical heroes having endured a struggle and accomplished the quest, has her moment of peace in his presence. Fletcher calls such places as this house in the wood "temples in the labyrinth." Northrop Frye earlier labeled them "houses of recognition." They are a common feature of allegorical literature. But Ida doesn't go near the house; she seems, in fact, unaware of it—which is another problem in the work. Ida's perpetual isolation is oppressive. Nonetheless she is in an enchanted place. Earlier she loomed

large, awkward, engulfed in the luminous lightning-colored cape, in a world full of distortions. Now order and proportion are restored. The shepherd tends his sheep; there are butterflies. Lest we forget, however, that we are never really out of danger, there are also, as John Gardner points out, sinister, skull-shaped leaves in the foreground [see excerpt dated April 30, 1981 for *Outside Over There*], and the limbs of the tree next to Ida are threatening hands. But things are somewhat better when Ida returns home. Though he is still away, her father has sent a letter, her mother has perked up a bit, and she still has her horn.

The artwork for this book is a striking departure from that of the two previous picture books, though its delicate loveliness is present elsewhere in Sendak. *Outside Over There* has a sumptuous painterly quality totally different from the cartoon drawings of the other two works. The change is, of course, appropriate to this more serious, complex work, and Ida has a dignity in her troubled state that Max and Mickey don't really need. But the characteristic allegorical distortions are there. The painting is mannered and the imagery borders on the surreal in a subtler way than it does in **Night Kitchen,** where the giant milk bottle is a playful and clearly understood surrealistic sign. Mannerism and surrealism are characteristic of allegorical art, each suggesting, in its degree of distortion, the importance of certain features and objects symbolically. Fletcher describes surrealism as implying "obsessional and dream imagery, unexpected, even shocking collocations of heterogeneous objects, psychological emblems (usually Freudian), hyperdefinite draftsmanship, distortions of perspective—with all these working together to produce enigmatic combinations of materials." Naturally in a children's book such qualities will be minimized, but they do characterize Sendak's art, with its compression of landscapes and exaggeration of features. Ears and eyes are larger than they should be; Ida's ankles and sturdy feet are peculiarly prominent. And even though one recognizes the proportions in live children, they here remain dis-integrated, isolated, "hyperdefinite," as Fletcher says. It is a style Sendak may have developed in reaction to the doll-like drawings of earlier illustrators, but his own drawings, particularly in this work, have their own sentimental effect, the square, solid little bodies and bewildered faces of children suggesting an awful, almost unbearable vulnerability.

And objects, too, are scaled or selected to produce slightly surreal effects. Consider the enormous sunflowers—sinister, sublime foliage—pushing their way through Ida's window. Throughout the work the figures are compressed into an extravagantly detailed, slightly miniature landscape, a landscape that seems made for slightly smaller people than those who inhabit it, but which nonetheless encompasses sea, sky, and land. It is a segmented, claustrophobic world, wherein the father's boat, the mother's arbor, the enormous dog, the goblins, the proper hats (that seem, after a while, curiously important emblems of order)—all must find their place. Sendak also produces a subtle sense of disorientation by combining different styles on a page. The enormous German shepherd, for example, is drawn in a far more realistic style than the characters, so that when the baby extends her slightly cartoonish hand toward the animal, it is as if she is reaching out toward a creature of a different medium.

The language of the book is disorienting and one suspects that the lack of comedy afflicts it as well. Sendak's picture book prose style is generally characterized by shifting rhythms, movements in and out of rhyme, and much assonance and

From In the Night Kitchen, *written and illustrated by Maurice Sendak. Harper & Row, Publishers, 1970. Copyright © 1970 by Maurice Sendak. All rights reserved. Reprinted by permission of Harper & Row, Publishers, Inc.*

alliteration, the last being features of allegorical writing, words that sound the same not only providing pleasant aural effects but also suggesting connections between objects signified. The style is apparent in *Wild Things*. . . . The style is coy and petulant—like Max, and its preciousness is bearable for that reason.

In *Night Kitchen* the techniques are refined and further exploited, producing a text that is a kind of playful poem. . . . The narrative moves in and out of small sections of verse, with frequent shifts of rhythm, and while at times the shifts seem capricious, the overall effect is appealing. Again, it is fitting to Mickey.

The playfulness, however, is missing from *Outside Over There,* leaving the work with an old, labored syntax that calls attention to itself continually. . . . This borders on verse in a way similar to the text of the other two books, but it is awkward because of its humorlessness and the need for each word in this very abbreviated narrative to function the way the language of poetry does—when much of it simply isn't poetic. The narrative details are presented in a way that suggests an archetypal situation but that also echoes the pretend intimacy of baby talk: ''Mama and Papa,'' ''pulled baby out,'' ''the goblins came.'' And there are lines that are not poetic or musical or significant in any way, lines that simply convey information but by virtue of the strange syntax and fussiness of detail seem to be trying to do more: ''Now Ida in a hurry / snatched her Mama's yellow rain cloak.''

Recognizing Sendak's allegorical leanings helps one to understand the quality of this writing, with its portentous subtext hinted at, its Freudian themes waiting to be apprehended by the intuitive reader. But one feels uneasiness here that goes beyond the state of mind of a heroine who is just beginning to struggle with the complex relationships of her life. One feels pressure in this work to transcend, to create a picture book more psychologically astute, more complex, more visually dazzling than anything Sendak had done yet, a picture book that adults would embrace as a fine work of art. In some ways Sendak succeeds. The book has its achingly beautiful moments. It is often richer and more risk-taking than anything else around. But it is also overworked, self-conscious, its surface meaning sometimes disturbing and absurd. One needs Sendak's own descriptions of what he has done as a running gloss. The book is also curiously static and bleak, Ida's face often frozen into a bewildered half-smile. The seriousness of her plight seems contrived, so that even while one is moved by this delicately terrifying story and the beauty of its characters, a kind of better judgment frowns on it, distancing one from the work as too melodramatic and manipulative. And there is no release. One looks, in the moment after Ida's struggle, for something to suggest relaxation. But there is nothing there, and when the book ends, its last line ''And that is just what Ida did'' suggesting resolution, we nevertheless still feel oppressed. Is this the way it is psychologically? Perhaps. But sometimes we all need a break—not happiness ever after, but something to hold onto. It is as great a human need as the need to tell the truth about emotions, and we—particularly children—are left at the end of this work with too much pain.

If it is true, as contemporary critics contend, that allegory grows out of longing, that it exprsses the impossibility of ever fully recovering that which we have lost or of fully articulating that loss, then perhaps the sadness of this most recent book of Sendak's is inevitable. Certainly the strain one senses in the work has to do with his need to get ever nearer to some final and immensely complex statement through indirection. But one still hopes that now that the trilogy has been completed and the statement of that trilogy has come as close to being made as it perhaps will be, something more spontaneous will next emerge. For whatever reservations we may have about individual works, Sendak is certainly one of the great children's artists of our time and, given the astonishing fertility and inventiveness of his work to date, I look forward to whatever he has in store. (pp. 12-22)

> *Geraldine DeLuca, "Exploring the Levels of Childhood: The Allegorical Sensibility of Maurice Sendak," in* Children's Literature: Annual of the Modern Language Association Seminar on Children's Literature and The Children's Literature Association, *Vol. 12, 1984, pp. 3-24.*

DONNARAE MacCANN AND OLGA RICHARD

Unless art can be split into two discrete kinds of experience—one kind for the young and one for the adult—Selma Lanes' title [*The Art of Maurice Sendak*] is a misnomer [see excerpt above dated 1970].... In a majority of cases, the Sendak illustrations that Selma Lanes designates as "art" should be called "popular art." They don't survive scrutiny from a fine arts perspective. (p. 135)

As a distinct branch of graphic art, illustration can make explicit reference to material that a text refers to, or it can express the spirit of that text. In both cases the drawings can make their illustrative points. But in either instance illustrations must qualify as good art before they can qualify as good illustration. As noted by Bob Gill and John Lewis, "Today there should be no difference in the aesthetic standards of painting and illustration."

Artists with this frame of reference value individual expression, the exploration of new art forms, new ways of seeing and communicating, and the discovery of new dimensions in life's experiences. None of these features place their works outside the range of children.

Sendak has occasionally been a creative artist of this latter sort. More often his art is an escape from, rather than a means to, originality. He clings to modes from the past—usually 19th century Romanticism or 1920's Art Deco. Quoting Sendak, Lanes refers to his determination in 1961 to "have a new, thoroughly contemporary look" in Clemens Brentano's *The Tale of Gockel, Hinkel and Gackeliah.* He wanted a "modern look" because "everything was ultra-sophisticated in illustration at that time." We can't tell what his vision of modern is or how he relates his own sense of form to that "look." He seems to be thinking of contemporary works as simply offering another standard model to emulate. He then returned to copying chiefly 19th century artists, and by the time he reached his assignment on *The Juniper Tree and Other Tales from Grimm* he was borrowing freely from Durer's "Pontius Pilate," from the Swiss-English artist Henry Fuseli, and from Ludwig Grimm's frontispiece engraving for the second edition of the tales.

In the popular arts such restatements of the old and accepted constitute the heart of the work's appeal. Conventional techniques and images are selected by the popular artist, and by giving them a certain emphasis, the artist can sometimes produce a kind of creative surprise. But Sendak relies upon a heavy Romantic style to the point where his work in *The Light Princess, Fly by Night,* and *Outside Over There* is drearily nostalgic and sentimental. Unlike Edward Gorey, who borrows from the Romantic style to create a unique blend of ironic contrasts, Sendak lets the seeming security of tradition get in the way of his own creative talent. And this weakness—this subordination of sensibilities to the mode of another time, another artist—is the very element eulogized by Selma Lanes. It would have been more helpful to Sendak had Lanes followed the example of the art dealer, Julian Levy, in 1931. When the painter, Arshile Gorky, told him "I was *with* Cezanne for a long time, and now naturally I am *with* Picasso," Levy replied that he would give him an exhibition "someday, when you are *with* Gorky."

Popular culture is a collective product in the sense that the kind of borrowing which results in a popular object represents something important to a sizeable cultural group. For this reason, psychological concepts can be applied to works of popular art. Lanes describes Sendak's works principally in terms of story (what the people in the picture are doing), or in terms of psychological meaning (how a picture ties in with Sendak's memories or subconscious). She doesn't elaborate upon how his problems relate to those of other middle class Brooklynites of his generation. But the material is there for any student of American civilization.

Sendak describes forces which helped shape many individuals and families. He was the "child" of the Great Depression, the redundant cartoons by Disney, the charms and banalities of movie musicals, the incongruities of scrubby Brooklyn and glamorous Manhattan, the ferocity of a World War, the facile reductionism of Freud, the arduous strivings of immigrant parents, the mysteries of an ancient, dynamic religion, and the peculiarly American ambivalence about fine art. The insecurities Sendak describes to Selma Lanes could well be rooted in such prevailing social tensions. Ironically, while these insecurities seem to hamper Sendak's necessary self-expression and risk-taking in art, they are the very lines of contact with collective 20th century experience which elicit a loyal following.

Both the trauma and exaltation of group experience rapidly find their way into children's books. Consequently this branch of literature provides an illuminating instance of popular culture. The special artistic hazard lies in the fact that the makers are always "above" the receivers in terms of age. This induces condescension. If you then add the celebratory feature—the love of certain insights authors want to pass "down"—this combination of the didactic and panegyric generates either sentimentality or banality. Sendak speaks frequently about the "bit of truth" he wants to pass along, but he succeeds only when he overcomes in some degree the self-conscious "them" and "me" gap. His comment about the vacuous *Outside Over There* reveals a disrespect for "them"—the child audience—which doesn't correspond with his typical advocacy of childhood. He says, "I had waited a long time to be taken out of kiddy-book land...." He is failing to identify correctly the thing he really needs to escape from: stagy, derivative visual effects.

Like some of his predecessors (children's book authors Louisa May Alcott, Horatio Alger, Kate Greenaway, and so on) Sendak provides enlightening source material for the study of an age. But it is a great mistake to give children objects of popular culture and call them original art. It means that works which are truly superlative (spatially creative, individualistic, lively, complex, enduring, profound) may be left out of a child's life altogether. (pp. 136-37)

Hilaire Belloc once made this remark: "There is no one that cannot tell some sort of story to a child. . . . As to writing really good rhymes and really good stories . . . a very few people can do it. All the remaining millions cannot do it." Sendak should be definitely singled out from the millions who "cannot do it." Yet his immersion in popular culture and its spurious elegance has limited his creativity. (p. 139)

> *Donnarae MacCann and Olga Richard, in a review of "The Art of Maurice Sendak," in* The First Steps: Best of the Early "ChLA Quarterly," *edited by Patricia Dooley, ChLA Publications, 1984, pp. 135-39.*

ELAINE MOSS

Unquestionably the artist who has most profoundly changed the scope of contemporary picture-book art, Sendak has many imitators—mostly unworthy. He is an artist and writer who can peel back the years and remember acutely his feelings as a sickly child in the tough back streets of Brooklyn. His pleasures (other children's make-believe, comics, early Hollywood anarchic movies) and his fears (night-time defencelessness, loss of love) come strongly to the surface in his picture books. A child of the Freudian age, an admirer of William Blake as well as of Walt Disney, Maurice Sendak is the creator of books that delight the eye, educate the ear, challenge the observation of the reader of any age. (p. 20)

> *Elaine Moss, "Maurice Sendak," in her* Picture Books for Young People 9-13, *second edition, The Thimble Press, 1985, pp. 20-3.*

JANE DOONAN

Jonathan Swift said, 'Vision is the art of seeing things invisible', which encapsulates for me Sendak's greatest gift. He gives precise delineation to the fantasies of childhood. He is able to take the moment of anger, or irritation, or hunger, or sheer cockadoodledoo-dom and develop it through observed detail and homely facts—a door handle set too high for a child to reach, a hot supper, a toy plane mobile, a little girl twisting the end of her hair as an important letter is read out to her. The extraordinary territory to which Sendak takes his reader-viewers is but an extension of the ordinary; the frontier between the two is fluid, shifting; the unwelcome weight of a sturdy baby, an uncomfortable burden to carry, is the point of departure, and the horror of the faceless goblin is a logical extension.

The boldness of the subject matter and the themes of his picture-book trilogy are further evidence of Sendak's originality, in the sense of 'a return to our origins'. He has not lost touch with the child within himself whose feelings he explores. In their expression he does not sentimentalize or trivialize their potency as a concession to young readers. Nor does he—unlike some picture-book artists—make any concessions for adults who may be sharing the material with a child. There is in his work a merciful absence of cynicism and conscious irony.

Where the Wild Things Are is, quite simply, a perfect picture book: spare in its verbal text, undecorated in its visual style, yet when the two narratives are received as one, the composite text—the one that exists in the reader-viewer's head—is as bold as Max himself and as satisfying as his supper. *In the Night Kitchen* is an intriguing flourish—complex, sensual and

humorous in tone, a visual assault course for its spectators yet looking as if set down effortlessly by its creator. It is true that *Outside Over There* lacks the seamless unity enjoyed by the other two books in the trilogy. Nevertheless, this 'portrait' of Mozart and exemplar of the Northern Romantic tradition is one of the works that extends the range of how far it is possible to travel—historically, culturally and psychologically—inside the covers of a picture book. (pp. 185-86)

> *Jane Doonan, "'Outside Over There': A Journey in Style, Part Two," in* Signal, *No. 51, September, 1986, pp. 172-87.*

THE SIGN ON ROSIE'S DOOR (1960)

Rosie, a perfectly ordinary little girl, like all perfectly ordinary children, is filled with strange and wonderful fancies. When it gets too monotonous being just plain Rosie, she transforms herself into a variety of alluring creatures all of whom hear the mark of the original Rosie in their whimsy and intensity. Maurice Sendak, both through text and illustrations, fuses the appealingly familiar with the magical in an *I Can Read* book of outstanding charm.

> *A review of "The Sign on Rosie's Door," in* Virginia Kirkus' Service, *Vol. XXVIII, No. 19, October 1, 1960, p. 867.*

Through a wide range of styles from *A Hole Is to Dig* to *The Moon Jumpers* to *Kenny's Window*, Maurice Sendak's illustrations evoke the very real world of make-believe, in which children are unabashedly themselves. In this . . . imaginative children will readily identify with Rosie who is never more herself than when she is somebody (or something) else—Alinda the lovely lady singer, the lost girl, or even a big red firecracker.

Mr. Sendak's text has humor and insight and a cozy feeling of children accepted as they are, but it is often over-long and wandering, a slice of life *about* children rather than *for* them. The final chapter, however, which demonstrates that being a firecracker is as good as having one, is, by itself, a highly successful read-aloud story—if the audience will refrain from participating long enough to listen. Second- and third-grade readers find the format tempting, though for many the content is young; parents, in particular, will welcome the book as a reminder that children who appear aimlessly occupied are often doing something very important.

> *Alice Low, "Pretending," in* The New York Times Book Review, *October 16, 1960, p. 40.*

Those anxious adults who expected [Maurice Sendak's] delightful *Where the Wild Things Are* to fill their children with fear and nightmares will be much reassured by his domestic ditty *The Sign on Rosie's Door,* just published in this country. It is a pure fun book showing Rosie and her friends in that delightful playworld of childhood. They dress up, fight, have pangs of hunger and put on a show with that complete absorption which only children and animals, the young and the uninhibited still retain.

Sendak's eye for the attitudes of children is as clear as ever—Max's determined stomp is replaced by Rosie's bossy command of every situation in spite of annoying interruptions like firemen, and revolution of the would-be entertainers. The world of make believe is brought vividly alive for the 4-8 year olds in this enchanting house-next-door extravaganza. (pp. 205-06)

A review of "The Sign on Rosie's Door," in The Junior Bookshelf, *Vol. 34, No. 4, August, 1970, pp. 205-06.*

WHERE THE WILD THINGS ARE   (1963)

[*The following excerpt is from a classic essay by Dr. Bruno Bettelheim, who at the time of its publication in 1969 was Rowley Professor of Education at the University of Chicago's Sonia Shankman Orthogenic School. In this essay, Dr. Bettelheim evaluates* Where the Wild Things Are *in a conversation with three mothers. In the subsequent excerpt, Mary Agnes Taylor counters Dr. Bettelheim's arguments against the book.*]

First Mother: A few nights ago, in the middle of the night, my four-year-old son called me into his room and told me he'd seen a bad man outside his window. I looked outside and said, "Well, there isn't anybody out there now. But if you ever see anybody out there, call your daddy right away and he'll take care of it." But then my husband said I shouldn't have admitted there were bad men, because the next day that's all my son talked about. He wouldn't even go to the bathroom by himself. My husband reassured him that while there are bad men in the world, there aren't any bad men around here. So now he's going through a monster kick, talking about monsters, and I still think it all started with that one incident. . . .

I was afraid the monsters came from a book I got him recently called **Where the Wild Things Are**. It has beautiful monsters in it.

Dr. B.: But why do we give children books with monsters in them?

Second Mother: My child has this book, too, and I think one reason the children enjoy it so much is that the child in the book controls the monsters. The child is king of the monsters and tells them what to do. And they are beautiful, but still frightening. They have horns and hair and teeth and claws, but the child controls them. This is its particular appeal.

Third Mother: The story begins where the child wears a wolf costume, and behaves badly, and his mother tells him he's behaving like a wild thing and has to be punished. It's at that point that he conjures up the monsters and controls them. I think it got the award for the best pictures in a children's book for the year. So everybody seems to be buying it.

Dr. B.: I don't know the book, but I'm skeptical. You haven't convinced me that the child *really* believes that the monsters are his invention and that he therefore controls them. It's entirely possible that some children believe this; on the other hand (like the sorcerer's apprentice), when you've got a monster by the tail you can't know for sure that it won't turn against you.

First Mother: The thing I didn't like about the book was that while my son had talked about monsters before, he didn't really have a conception of what monsters looked like. I think the pictures are worse than what he had in his own mind.

Dr. B.: This raises the problem of so many well-intentioned efforts to help children with their emotional problems. In many cases it comes out of the psychology of the writer, or, later on, the parents or nursery-school teacher; it doesn't come out of the psychology of the child. The old-fashioned fairy tale, which was gruesome enough, had one redeeming feature. It came out of the fantasy of an adult, not out of what the adult thought was the fantasy of the child, and in this way it was

more or less authentic. Storybooks like the one you have mentioned and, as I say, I don't know the book; it may be very unfair on my part; but I've seen others—come out of the fantasy of adults who believe they really know the fantasy of children. But the child's fantasies are quite different from the adult's.

Let's look at what the author might have had in mind. The author had in mind a very sound therapeutic procedure. That is, in psychoanalytic child therapy we must eventually put the child in control of his own monster fantasies. We have to show him that these persecuting figures are really the creation of his own mind. Now, if that could be done simply by the reading of a book, people like me would be out of business. It takes me a year or more of very hard work, of doing a wide variety of things, to get a disturbed child to the point where he's in control of the persecuting figures he creates in his imagination. And this only happens when the child begins to realize why he produced them in the first place. Sure, you can tell him "these are your fantasies and you can therefore manipulate them in any way you want." But this is much too rational a way to deal with the irrational. Let's look at the beginning of this book. How does it begin?

Second Mother: At night the child wore his wolf suit and made mischief of one kind and another. And his mother called him "wild thing." So the boy said, "I'll eat you up," and he was sent to bed without his supper.

Dr. B.: Stop there and let's look at this situation. What does this little story tell us about life, if we take it at face value?

First Mother: Only the good things are accepted. If you're bad or if you represent a bad thing, you're punished.

Dr. B.: Right, and what is the punishment?

Third Mother: You don't get any food.

Dr. B.: Yes, or, looked at differently: If you're trying to assert your power—as he said, "I'm going to eat you up"—what happens?

Third Mother: Powerlessness.

Dr. B.: Exactly. Somebody much more powerful than you beats you down. And you really think the appeal here is that it gives children the conviction that they're in control?

Third Mother: But why do children *love* this book?

Dr. B.: I don't doubt that children enjoy it. But, after all, children also enjoyed the fairy tales where everybody's cut to pieces and eaten up. Those, too, they asked to have read to them over and over again. We decided that wasn't very good fare for children. Maybe it was a wrong decision, I don't know. But it's interesting that when it comes to our aversion to gruesome things (fairy stories) nobody says, "but the children love them and want them read over and over again" as justification for keeping them. Enlightened parents decided that these gruesome fairy tales were bad. So I don't think this argument is a very good one—that the child enjoys the story and wants it read over and over again.

I'm a firm believer that in most things the end is in the beginning, because the beginning sets the stage. And the beginning, here, goes as follows: You have aggressive tendencies, want to eat up your mother, and for having such tendencies, mother takes her revenge. Then the best you can do is to take your revenge on mother. You get these monsters under your control.

Third Mother: Do you think books with scary parts should be eliminated?

Dr. B.: No, I don't think so at all. All I'm saying is we shouldn't fool ourselves that these books do for children what they don't. You see, fairy stories were very gruesome, but most of them held a very clear message: the evil-doer gets punished and the good are rewarded and live happily ever after. So, as gruesome as they were, the message that the good are rewarded and the bad are punished is very clear. It leaves the child with the convicion that, while life isn't easy, all I have to do is be good, and I'm safe. Now, I'm not pleading here for some of these gruesome fairy stories. All I say is that what the three-, four- or five-year-old needs is a clear, definite message. And however much the fairy stories differed, the message was always essentially the same.

Now let's look at what this new story really says. It says: If, in reality, you give way to your unsocialized tendencies, though you only try to eat up your mother in fantasy, then mother starves you in reality. Now, there's hardly ever a mother who withdraws food for good. But the small child doesn't know that.

Second Mother: At the end of the book, on the last page, he gets his supper. That's how the book ends.

Dr. B.: But what kind of a mother is it who first sends him to bed without supper? If it's security we're after, a book could be much more reassuring if it tells children they needn't be afraid of not getting their food, that it's perfectly all right to say what's on their mind, and that they won't be punished for saying it, only for doing it. Don't forget that in the fairy stories nobody ever gets punished for what he *says*, but only for what he *does*. So actually this story goes the cruel fairy tale one better. In the fairy stories only those got punished who did bad things. This modern psychologist who wrote the story seems to say it's all right to say what you think—except that if you do, you get punished. If we start out by evoking the image of starvation anxiety, in reality, and then put the child in control of monsters in fantasy, I think the child still ends up with a deficit.

Fourth Mother: But the book isn't necessarily harmful to a secure child.

Dr. B.: Nothing is necessarily harmful. Falling out of a first-floor window isn't always harmful either, but I wouldn't suggest it. . . .

Third Mother: It's interesting that we look at the story and let it go, even though none of us would consider sending our kids to bed without supper.

Dr. B.: There's another thing that was true of the old fairy tale. It was told by one adult to a child where the adult knew the child or the children, and there was flexible adjustment in the telling. The story was embroidered or toned down or exaggerated as the teller went along, and the child interrupted for questions. That has all gone out of fashion. Even in some of our nursery schools where teachers still tell stories, or read them, I've heard the teacher tell the children, "Now be quiet and listen." And this happens in a day and age when we say we must activate children.

Bruno Bettelheim, "The Care and Feeding of Monsters," in Ladies' Home Journal, Vol. LXXXVI, No. 3, March, 1969, p. 48.

It is difficult for the Sendak worshiper to believe that there still exists a reading public which views askance the delightfully impudent antics of Max and the wild things. However, unfavorable attitudes toward Maurice Sendak's *Where the Wild Things Are* do exist, and in the relatively recent past unfavorable statements have been voiced by individuals as well known as Dr. Bruno Bettelheim. . . .

These unfavorable statements appeared in a regular feature article, "Dialogue with Mothers," in *The Ladies Home Journal* under the title of "The Care and Feeding of Monsters" [see excerpt above]. Understandably, such statements arouse concern on the part of conscientious parents and teachers charged with the responsibility of selecting children's literature. But there is certainly room for dissent, and Dr. Bettelheim's statements should be studied with care. A long, inquiring look at them readily reveals at least three major weaknesses in his argument.

First, and most disturbing, is Dr. Bettelheim's admission that he has not read *Where the Wild Things Are*. In literary criticism, the admission that one has not read a given work usually eliminates him as an effectual critic. But not in this case. Confused readers seemed unimpressed by the fact that early in the dialogue Dr. Bettelheim says, "I don't know the book, but I'm skeptical." One logically asks then why should anyone take seriously the subsequent comments attending such an admission. The answer is probably that our current society is highly oriented toward psychological interpretation; hence, if a child's book is pronounced psychologically unsound, the public is receptive to the criticism. When the criticism is made by an individual who is as well known and respected in the field of psychology as Dr. Bettelheim, all the more credence is given to it. That the critic's statements may be perceptive in one context but irrelevant in another is easily overlooked.

A second weakness is that he treats a modern picture-book fantasy as if it were a traditional fairy tale. Dr. Bettelheim fails to recognize the fundamental difference in the structural techniques of the picture book and the fairy tale. The fairy tale was developed primarily as a verbal and aural experience for adults; the modern picture book is basically a visual experience deliberately designed to transcend the verbal limitations of the very young. Although an aural experience usually accompanies the picture book, the fact remains that the young child must depend more on what he sees than on what he reads or hears if he is to comprehend the full meaning of a picture story.

Dr. Bettelheim contends that "in the fairy stories nobody ever gets punished for what he *says*, but only for what he *does*." He adds that only those were punished who "did bad things." Clearly, in Sendak's first two pages, Max pictorially "did bad things." He deliberately hammered a rope of knotted fabric on opposite walls to support his blanket tent; he gleefully chased his terrier down the stairs with the pronged end of a fork. His mother, in the first speech of the book, called him "'WILD THING!'" In keeping with her suggested tone, Max responded, "'I'LL EAT YOU UP!'" and thus "he was sent to bed without eating anything." To which Bettelheim says, "This modern psychologist who wrote the story seems to say it's all right to say what you think—except that if you do, you get punished." If one looks carefully at the book, one sees that here as in the fairy tale, the hero is punished primarily for what he does rather than for what he says.

Furthermore, Bettelheim speaks in favor of the fairy tale as against the picture book by emphasizing, "that what the three-, four- or five-year-old needs is a clear, definite message." And he explains that the message in the fairy tale was always the same: good versus evil with the good ever triumphant. But at this point a warning from May Hill Arbuthnot is in place. In her *Children and Books* she cautions that one of the common misuses of the traditional fairy tale is too early an introduction. She and other authorities in the field of children's literature agree that with the exception of a few nursery tales, the ideal age range for the traditional fairy tale is seven to nine. Prior to that age, the child is unable to cope with the adult content and the generally abstract theme of the old fairy tale. Thus the modern picture book is advantageous for the preschool child, overcoming pictorially both the thematic abstractions of fairy tales and the limitations of infant vocabulary by visually giving the child the "clear, definite message" Bettelheim demands. Obviously, any criticism of the modern picture book must include a criticism of illustrations as well as of text, for in this particular genre, the two function inseparably.

And thirdly, just as one cannot condemn the modern picture book because it does not fill the role of the traditional fairy tale, neither can one rightly call psychologically unfit a piece intended for the average child because it is not suited to the needs of the disturbed child. The slant of the general content in "The Care and Feeding of Monsters" is bent entirely toward the needs of the disturbed child. Furthermore, Dr. Bettelheim seemingly presumes Sendak's purpose to be clinical, for he says, "The author had in mind a very sound therapeutic procedure. That is, in psychoanalytic child therapy we must eventually put the child in control of his own monster fantasies." He adds that if this could be done by reading a book, people such as he would be out of business. Although Sendak's book may serve incidentally and temporarily as a mild psychological balm, it is highly doubtful that he ever intended to evoke anything more from his child reader than mere delight and joyful empathy.

Where the Wild Things Are is juvenile escape literature on an exceptionally high artistic level. This fact was at last partially understood by the "Fourth Mother" of the dialogue: "But the book isn't necessarily harmful to a secure child." To which Dr. Bettelheim replied, "Nothing is necessarily harmful. Falling out of a first-floor window isn't always harmful either, but I wouldn't suggest it."

Negative reactions by adults to children's reading matter are not without tradition. . . . Bettelheim echoes a clean-it-up philosophy that was in vogue during the second quarter of the twentieth century. Of children's casual acceptance of the gory fairy tale he says, "We decided it wasn't very good fare for children."

Writers of children's fantasy have usually been aware of such adult censure. Fortunately, most have ignored it. C. S. Lewis, in *The Lion, the Witch, and the Wardrobe: A Story for Children,* even confided to his young readers that he could tell them a great deal more about the creatures that participated in Aslan's death, but that if he did, grown-ups would not let them read his book.

Although Lewis's remarks pass as a private joke between him and the child reader, one must remember that they reflect existing adult thought. Thought that children—especially the wild ones—would never understand. The tumultuous parade of five-year-olds who have rocked kindergartens from coast to coast with their improvised dances of the "'wild rumpus'" could scarcely be bothered about an adult fear that the inspiration of

their creative activity was psychologically unsound. Nor would all the naughty, but loved, little boys who, in their swiftly flowing stream-of-consciousnes, have run away from home and promptly returned to a warm supper, care whether their sojourns are considered traditional fairy tales or modern fantasies. Decisive response is not their problem. Their problem—and it is one that can be relieved for them only by knowledgeable, mature providers—is that they be allowed free choice in their selections of literature and that their choices not be limited by opinionated adults.

Children bring to books a selectivity that is unique to childhood and immune to adult opinion. They can ferret out the fairy-tale quality of *Pilgrim's Progress*—probably that element which John Bunyan himself credits to his early exposure to the chapbooks—and ignore the sermonizing. . . . They can make *Charlotte's Web* a classic, although adults did not agree to its selection for the Newbery Award. There is so much to their credit in this matter of unerring selection of literature that one is forced to admit their collective possession of uncanny wisdom. Furthermore, if the adult were completely honest with himself, he might also admit to a wish that he were sufficiently uncalcified to go whisking away with Max and his young readers to "where the wild things are." (pp. 642-46)

Mary Agnes Taylor, "*In Defense of the Wild Things*," in The Horn Book Magazine, *Vol. XLVI, No. 6, December, 1970, pp. 642-46.*

[The] text and drawings of *Wild Things* contribute to a subtle crescendo of mastery as the boy controls the wild things, and then a decrescendo as he returns to his room. As the size of the drawings increases and then shrinks, all sorts of other developments, such as the metaphors of time and place, the topics of the illustrations, the compounding style of both text and drawing, also expand and contract, drawing us into this ordered, controlled experience. The entire enterprise—text, drawings, printing, story—becomes one metaphor for Max's going and coming. For he does not control his anger with a weapon (the hammers and forks he uses in the opening panels are left behind); rather he exerts his will and manages the wild things in that place, in himself, so that in the last drawing he can remove the hood of his wolf suit and sleepily scratch his head, child-like for the first time. Just as Max's parents controlled him by their authority, so he controls his anger through his own will. So Sendak controls us subtly, structurally, covertly.

This contrast of control by management or intimidation lies at the heart of the distinction I am proposing between the interplay of content and style in [*Where the Wild Things Are* and Mercer Mayer's *There's a Nightmare in My Closet*]. A comparison of the two reveals that *Where the Wild Things Are* is an excellent book because every aspect of it—drawing, layout, and story—contributes to the central theme of control. Each facet of the book's style reinforces another, so that the experience of the book for the reader emulates Max's experience. Thus, the artist gives no explicit moral, and the reader, no matter of what age, is left without a lesson. Like the wild things, which become Max's playmates, we are drawn into the experience unconscious of the artist's manipulation. We are conscious only of pleasure because patterns such as coordination, expansion and contraction, and repetition manage our responses as Max manages both the wild things and his own anger. (pp. 126-27)

Paul G. Arakelian, "*Text and Illustration: A Stylistic Analysis of Books by Sendak and Mayer*," in Children's Literature Association Quarterly, *Vol. 10, No. 3, Fall, 1985, pp. 122-27.*

Maurice Sendak's Caldecott winner *Where the Wild Things Are* upended many notions about children's sensibilities. Controversy surrounded the two questions of whether Sendak should have portrayed monsters . . . and whether he should have depicted Max's behavior as so uncivilized. . . . But decades later, the controversy persists: some primary-grade teachers still do not want the book in their classroom.

Sendak's portrayal of an unreal world of wild jungle fantasy has been said to have changed the way the real world of childhood is viewed by adults. *Wild Things* stands unique in its time for appealing to more sophisticated sensibilities in children, whom Sendak felt to have a higher level of appreciation for complexity in plot and in art than was then explored in picture books. Before this the status quo in children's literature had stressed prettiness, wholesome attitudes, gently decorous humor, and a strong reliance on adult authority. . . . Sendak had begun to break with this prevalent view in earlier illustrations for titles by Ruth Krauss: *A Hole to Dig* and *I'll Be You and You Be Me,* which presented children having day-to-day problems. In *Wild Things,* he said, many of his ideas finally came together as one.

For the most part, children themselves have accepted Sendak's deviation from the picture-book norm with glee. Many adults in 1963, and indeed a few today, simply could not and cannot share the children's positive reaction toward Max's problems. Another reviewer's tongue-in-cheek note perhaps sums up the ongoing differences of opinion about *Wild Things:* "Boys and girls may have to shield their parents from this book. Parents are very easily scared."

Worldwide recognition has most certainly come to Sendak. . . . This illustrator of some seventy titles is often thought of in a category by himself as a mad genius or eccentric visionary. Whatever Sendak himself thinks of such quaint praise, the children surely consider it rubbish, for most of them have welcomed this eccentric as one of their own. After all, he gives them his best and they think—as he does—that they deserve it.

If there are truths about childhood in *Wild Things,* then what might those truths be, and how has Sendak presented them in his artistic vision for young children? The truths are quite simple ones: primary-age youngsters are intellectually intrigued by creatures from the wild, are fascinated by dinosaur and monster books, and often develop an early interest in exotic environments unlike their own. Socially they set a great deal of store in surprises, birthday wishes, and daydreams that hold heartfelt hope for their own lives. They enjoy games, like to win, and to be boss. They can be sassy and become resentful over imagined injustice when punished. They need love and security but often don't show it. Most play "pretend"—not always wild or scary pretending, but if someone else's pretending isn't as interesting as their own would be, they can get bored. In case this paints too sweet a picture of childhood, it is also important to point out that these same children can ruthlessly break all the rules to win, boss siblings and pets to the breaking point, throw red-faced tantrums when punished, scare each other so badly that nightmares develop, act most unlovably in a crowded supermarket, and if *too* bored, have been known to amuse themselves with peeling off wallpaper. In short, children are not little adults, but like homemade wine, most improve with age.

Little wonder, then, that so many of these normal children have loved *Wild Things* in much the same way that they love Hal-loween night. Sendak's book relates directly to the good and the bad, the comfortable and the scary, the known and the unknown, the realities and the fantasies they have experienced in their own lives. Since the book appeared, children's picture books and Saturday morning TV cartoons have become more flamboyant, even surrealistic, so that today's children are not nearly as impressed by the illustrator's monsters and Max's behavior as were children in the 1960s. In fact many youngsters today do not think of the Wild Things as really fearsome at all but instead rather homely, absurd in a couple of instances, and downright pathetic when unloved and left behind.

However, *Wild Things* is one of the few titles still remembered by young adults who were elementary-school children when the book first appeared. They remember because the Wild Things were indeed scary in 1963 and were unheared of in their other books. Sendak gave form to the nightmarish unknown these young people recall being frightened of: there were "The Monsters" and if "They" were pictured in a book, then just maybe other people thought about "Them" too, and perhaps "They" need not be so feared. After all, as naughty as Max was, he did have the bravery to stand up to "Their" bluff and win as "boss of Them All." People in their twenties may articulate for us what children have been trying to tell us all along but have lacked the vocabulary to express: *Wild Things* in a very real way assuages childhood's fears and pains by labeling as universal the inner monster we all have known, a monster that must be controlled if we are to survive emotionally. (pp. 107-09)

A comparison of illustrations in *Wild Things* with the paintings of Henri Rousseau, a forerunner of the surrealists in the twentieth century, would be of interest to children. Rousseau's fantasy worlds of exotic images set in mysterious, tropical landscapes remind us hauntingly of the combination of reality and dreaming that Sendak has given in his Award winner. The controversy that surrounded Rousseau when his work first appeared was similar to the dispute over *Wild Things*. Luckily Sendak continued to picture for children his own version of truthfulness to life, however unsettling that may be. "It seems to be the gift I have . . . catching hold of those moments that are the experiences of all human animals when they're small children. I don't stifle the child in me. I hear it loud and clear." Children will be listening to the child's voice that comes from Maurice Sendak for years to come. (pp. 110-11)

Lyn Ellen Lacy, "Light and Dark: 'The Little House', 'Where the Wild Things Are', and 'Jumanji'," in her Art and Design in Children's Picture Books: An Analysis of Caldecott Award-Winning Illustrations, American Library Association, 1986, pp. 104-43.

The quest myth represented in Max's imaginary journey is indeed central to *Where the Wild Things Are,* but equally important to this now classic picture book is how Sendak expands Max's quest both spatially and temporally.

Traditionally, the plot of *Where the Wild Things Are* would have been seen as time-oriented and the illustrations as space-oriented, but the theories of Joseph Frank, Rudolf Arnheim, and E. H. Gombrich about the integral and complex relationships between space and time, and the application of these theories by literary critics such as Sharon Spencer, Eric S. Rabkin, W.J.T. Mitchell, and others, now allow us to view both text and illustration more fluidly, for the interdependence of word and picture is paralleled by the interdependence of time and space. . . . Sendak himself has emphasized the importance of both space and time in his work, asserting that "You must leave a space in the text so the picture can do the work. Then you must come back with the word and the word does its best, and now the picture beats time." In contrast to standard expectations, then, Sendak associates the traditionally spatial form of the picture with *time* and the traditionally temporal, or narrative, text with *space*. The resultant use of spatial and temporal forms in *Where the Wild Things Are* is indeed complex, existing on at least four levels: textual, physical, psychological, and mythic.

Perhaps the most obvious textual characteristic of *Where the Wild Things Are* is Sendak's use of white space, decreasing in the first half of the book and increasing in the second half. (pp. 86-7)

[The] text itself—the way in which white space, print, and illustration appear on the page—is a basic spatial construct of the work, with the relationship between white space and illustration serving as the key to physical reality on the one hand and imaginative, or psychic and mythic, realities, on the other. The white space itself comes to represent the real world, perhaps suggesting its vacuity when compared with the depths of psyche and myth, for the white space is most overpowering at the beginning and the end of the book when Max is most absorbed in the sensual realities of playing and eating. Moreover, the white space itself completely disappears in the three double-spread pages that appear at the climax of Max's imaginary journey. These spatial aspects of the literal text are paralleled by the temporal, for as [W.J.T.] Mitchell has observed, "We cannot experience a spatial form except in time." That is, though the spatial form exists of itself, it is perceived by the observer only in time. And indeed, the child or adult who "reads" *Where the Wild Things Are* will spend as much or more time decoding the textual space of the illustrations as that of the print.

The physical space in *Where the Wild Things Are* is that of Max's house, primarily that of his bedroom. According to Gaston Bachelard, the house image "shelters daydreaming, the house protects the dreamer, the house allows one to dream in peace"; and indeed, even before the reassurance of his hot supper, Max must feel sheltered and secure in the space of his room to be able to imagine such a delightfully scary adventure. Like the normal four- or five-year-old child categorized by Piaget as being in the preconceptual stage, Max egocentrically derives the representational schema of his daydream from "his own immediate world," attributing "life and feeling, in the first place, to all objects, though later only to those that move," and believing that natural objects "can be influenced by his wishes or by actions at a distance." Thus, in his imaginative daydream, Max seeks escape from his mother and the confined space and time of his physical room, willing the walls to become "the world all around."

In the opening scene of the book, Max is outside his own physical space—his bedroom—in a room that he is trying to make his own through imaginative play with a tent and a wolf suit, both images foreshadowing those of his daydream. Juxtaposed with this scene is an illustration of Max chasing a Sealyham terrier in front of a picture of a monster. As shown by both text—"The night Max wore his wolf suit and made mischief of one kind / and another"—and illustration, the connection between these scenes is more spatial than temporal, for, though the second scene is more intense than the first, there is no causal relationship between the two. The third scene in which Max is banished to his room for threatening to eat

his mother up corresponds to traditional narrative expectations, to character motivation, and to temporal sequence. In the fourth scene, however, a forest begins to grow in Max's room, a sign that he has shifted into a fantasy world, into the space and time of psyche and myth. In the following scenes, as [Paul G.] Arakelian has observed, "violations of place and time are used to separate Max from the 'real' world and isolate him in dream or fantasy" [see excerpt above dated Fall, 1985], but in the final scene he returns to the physical space and time of his room. The reader has no way of knowing how much time has passed between the third and final scenes—enough for Max's mother to have forgiven him and brought him his supper, but not so much that his food has gotten cold—but it is apparent that we are dealing with different levels of space and time, with not only the closed spatiotemporality of Max's room but also with the open spatiotemporality of the daydream. One explanation of this apparent warp in space and time is Havelock Ellis's description of a dream, or we may substitute daydream, as "a kind of cinematographic drama which has been condensed and run together . . . so that although the whole story seems to be shown in constant movement, in reality the action of hours is condensed into moments."

As Geraldine DeLuca has observed, the physical directional movement in *Where the Wild Things Are,* as well as in the other two volumes of Sendak's trilogy, is from inside to outside "to a place of fantasy and risk, to 'outside over there.'" But just as time and space are difficult to separate conceptually, so are the dynamics of inside and outside, for when Max is inside his room, he is in the physical world but outside of his own imagination; in contrast, when he moves imaginatively outside his room to "where the wild things are," he is more truly inside not only his own mind but also inside the universal mind of myth, as shown by the archetypal images of boat, water, monster, and moon. (pp. 87-9)

In Max's imaginary journey . . . he crosses over the line of realistic space and time into the dream world of fantasy. Moreover, the symbolic events of this journey vivify Jung's theories that the dream, or daydream, is a doorway to both the personal and the collective unconscious, to the individual psyche and to archetypal myth. Max's psychological development is reflected spatially through the illustrations, for just as the pictures expand so does he grow and develop psychologically. The changing moon, which has baffled critics, indicates that Max's development occurs outside of clock time.

I would argue, however, that though the changing moon in *Where the Wild Things Are* may indeed be inexplicable according to chronological time, it is perfectly logical according to "moon time," for moon time is cyclical and cosmic, representing not hours and minutes but stages in Max's psychological growth. Initially, shining in the sky outside Max's window, the moon is crescent shaped with a shadowed fullness symbolizing Max's potential growth. After Max's voyage in his private boat across a vast ocean, suggestive in Jungian psychology of the collective unconscious that connects the personal psyche to universal archetype, the moon reappears as an unshadowed crescent. At the climax of the book when Max is spontaneously and joyfully cavorting and prancing with the monsters of his imagination—*his* monsters—the moon is suddenly full. Moreover, when Max returns to his room, the moon outside his window remains full, a reminder that the psychological growth that he has expereinced in his journey will remain with him in his physical world.

From Outside Over There, *written and illustrated by Maurice Sendak. Harper & Row, Publishers, 1981.*

The journey motif itself links Max's personal psychological development with the universal archetype of the quest myth as identified and analyzed by Joseph Campbell. Max is almost absurdly young to be a "hero" in the sense of Jason or Perseus or Odysseus, and yet how can we as adults say that Perseus' Medusa or Jason's Medea or any of Odysseus' monsters were more frightening to them than Max's "monsters" of anger, guilt, and fear are to him? Perhaps the use of the hero archetype with such a miniscule hero is what makes *Where the Wild Things Are* lighter in tone and yet, I think, at least as deeply reverberating as the latter two volumes of the trilogy.

As appropriate to the quest of a child hero, Max's quest is comparatively simple, though the major stages of separation, initiation, and return identified by Campbell are clearly present. Before Max's imaginary journey, he perceives his world to have "a symbolical deficiency" (Campbell, *The Hero with a Thousand Faces*), for he feels unloved and rejected by his mother. As a result, he issues and accepts his own "call to adventure" (ibid.), separating himself from his real world and moving across the threshold of his forest room to a boat on an imaginary ocean. Campbell's description of the typical place of initiation as "a dream landscape of curiously fluid, ambiguous forms, where he [the hero] must survive a succession of trials" (ibid.) is a remarkably apt description of the dreamscape

of "where the wild things are." Moreover, the ambiguity of the monsters is crucial. Max's monsters are at once the foes to be conquered and the supernatural helpers of myth and fairy tales, for they are his own feelings—his love as well as his anger, his forgiveness as well as his guilt. Then after Max releases his emotions in the cathartic dance, he, like a true hero, is ready to return to his world carrying with him the "ultimate boon" (Campbell) of his understanding and growth as symbolized, of course, by the full moon. (pp. 87-91)

Various images of space and time in *Where the Wild Things Are* also connect the psychological and mythical levels of the book. Piaget believes that in a child of four years old, the "conception of the world is similar to that of men in many primitive societies." Interestingly, a comparison of some of Marshall McLuhan's observations about tribal, or primitive, man and modern, or literate, man to the images and incidents in Max's journey reveals that this child hero's quest delves not only into his own mind but also back in time to the elemental truths of tribal life. First of all, McLuhan believes that the square housing of modern man fragments and separates whereas the round housing of tribal people unifies. Significantly, Max feels separated from his mother in his *square* room with its closed door, but after his ritualistic dance with the wild things he sits in an open cosmos in front of a *round* tent. In addition,

McLuhan believes that print itself detribalizes man whereas the absence of print integrates. Significantly, it is where print occurs in the text, especially at the beginning of *Where the Wild Things Are,* that Max feels most alienated from his mother, whereas during the dance in the middle of the book, where *no* print occurs, he apparently feels the greatest freedom as well as the greatest acceptance of and unity with the "wild things" inside and outside himself. Moreover, the double-page dance spreads at the center of the book are the most naturally rhythmic—a characteristic inevitably associated with the tribal rituals of primitive man.

The dance sequence itself is indeed crucial to Sendak's use of space and time in *Where the Wild Things Are.* Since the scenes shift from night to day and back to night, the sequence has the appearance, on the one hand, of a vast stretch of time. On the other hand, however, because each page is an *image* presenting, as Ezra Pound has perceived, "an intellectual and emotional complex in an instant of time," the effect is actually one of the suspension of time. . . . We are reminded of Sendak's statement about creating "a space in the text," for that is exactly what these full-page spreads do: they create silent spaces in the text in which the reader must, as if watching a silent movie, interpret and create meaning. . . . What the illustrative text demands in the dance sequence is, I believe, music, for the rhythms of music, like those of myth, not only connect modern man to his ancient roots but also reveal the integral relationships between space and time—relationships suggested by the very etymology of the word *rhythm,* which was once associated with the act of drawing or inscribing. Sendak's personal infatuation with music is well known, of course. For instance, in his acceptance speech for the Caldecott Award, he stated that the "musical accompaniment" provided the "very quality he has sought" in his own books. [See excerpt above in Author's Commentary for *Where the Wild Things Are*]. . . . Sendak called Caldecott's *The Three Jovial Huntsmen* a "contrapuntal play between words and pictures, a comic fugue." The term *fugue,* implying as it does the complex simultaneity of space and time relationships, is also an excellent description of *Where the Wild Things Are.*

No doubt, my reading of *Where the Wild Things Are* is unusually elaborate for a picture book—after all, it's just a simple nursery tale, isn't it? But, of course, it is simple in the same way that the fairy tales and myths are simple: superficially simple, direct, and dramatic but reverberating throughout with various layers of meaning and structure occurring on textual, physical, psychological, and mythical levels. Like *In the Night Kitchen,* the conflicts and images of *Where the Wild Things Are* come not only from the "direct middle" [as Sendak says in Selma G. Lanes's *The Art of Maurice Sendak*] of Sendak but also from the direct middle of all of us. (pp. 91-2)

> *Ann Moseley, "The Journey through the 'Space in the Text' to 'Where the Wild Things Are'," in Children's literature in education, Vol. 19, No. 2, Summer, 1988, pp. 86-93.*

IN THE NIGHT KITCHEN (1970)

If you haven't read Mr. Sendak's latest contribution to literature for the very young, borrow a copy and do so. Don't bother to buy it, unless you want to use it as a device to relieve the monotony of dull cocktail parties, because you most probably will not want to use it with the audience for whom it is intended. (One can only speculate that the intended audience is the pre

and primary school child for, contrary to Harper's usual practice, the book's jacket does not suggest an age-level.) (p. 262)

It just may be that America's children have been waiting with bated breath for this opportunity to vicariously wallow nude in cake dough and skinny-dip in milk—not to mention the thrill of kneading, punching, pounding, and pulling. Somehow, I doubt it.

Perhaps, at the sub-conscious level, our childen need liberation from the Puritan convention that, while children should be seen and not heard, only selected parts of the anatomy should be seen in public. If that is the case, then Mr. Sendak has struck a literary blow for the Kid Lib movement. It can never again be said that the penis has not been displayed in children's books—Mickey's dangles conspicuously throughout most of his adventures. (Sendak has already given his readers a ground-level view of the vagina in his illustrations for George MacDonald's *The Light Princess.*) As to Freudian sex symbols, there are so many that it is a romp to identify and discuss them.

As Little Orphan Annie was wont to say, "Gloryosky, Sandy!"

It seems that Mr. Sendak has used one of the most weary of all literary devices—that of the dream—to get into his story which proves in its execution, in both text and illustration, to be heavy, self-conscious, pointless, and—worst of all—dull.

The judges who selected the New York Times' list of best illustrated children's books of 1970 "were unanimously enthusiastic in their selection of *In the Night Kitchen.*" They hailed it for "breaking new ground in the children's field as well as marking a significant event in his [Mr. Sendak's] own career."

So be it!

Now that Mr. Sendak has had his own signficant event, let us hope that he turns once again to creating significant events for children. (p. 263)

> *Shelton L. Root, Jr., in a review of "In the Night Kitchen," in Elementary English, Vol. XLVIII, No. 2, February, 1971, pp. 262-63.*

Children's imaginations work in a surrealist way, jumping from one thing to another in a perfectly logical if zany sequence. Sendak knows this and his dream stories are always plausible to the childlike mind. Sometimes they impinge on the nightmarish but if they do it does not last and everything ends happily. Mickey falls out of bed into the night kitchen where three cooks, all looking rather like the fat half of the Laurel and Hardy partnership, are baking a cake. The frightening part comes when the boy is baked inside it, but calmly and resourcefully he gets out and after more adventures ends snugly tucked up in bed again. The pictures have a complete unity with the text, which in any case consists rather of captions than a continuous story. The colours are mostly secondary as befits a night adventure, but they are anything but gloomy with their pinks and blues and buffs. Sometimes there is a double spread, sometimes the illustrations are two or three or four to a page. Only Sendak could have produced this book, which is another way of saying that the draughtsmanship is unfaltering and that the style has something from Pop art, something from that of seventy years ago, but wherever it comes from the result is unique. This is quite one of the most satisfactory works we have had from this author-artist, perhaps second only to *The Wild Things.* However, reactions to Sendak vary enormously and everyone will want to form his own opinion, but the children will like it. (pp. 165-66)

C. Martin, in a review of "In the Night Kitchen," in The Junior Bookshelf, Vol. 35, No. 3, June, 1971, pp. 165-66.

In reading *In the Night Kitchen* this reader . . . has been concerned that so few reviewers have suggested that Sendak's surface and implied concoction is just that—a concoction (*n. to cook together crude materials*) with questionable nourishment for the very young members of our society.

Using a trademark of a popular radio/television series which has slipped to vernacular use, "The facts, just give us the facts, please," we may approach the analysis of *In the Night Kitchen.*

Cover of the book. The single detailed graphic reflects certain surface and implied messages. As is customary the cover cites the title, the author-illustrator and a graphic representation of the contents. A young lad is flying a fanciful open cockpit airplane into a star and moon studded sky. In the background is a fanciful city setting symbolizing both real and transformed objects. A salt shaker, screws, jars, elevator trains, paper cream containers and large urban buildings are obvious. It is through this transforming graphic technique that Sendak encourages the reader to anticipate implied meaning from the sixty or so further pages of the book. The first generative interpretation this viewer received from the cover graphic was the teasing hint of Freudian interpretation of graphics of the green beans and vines. Having taught literature for the young over several decades, it has been exciting to watch the invasion of one discipline by another. Sigmund Freud stimulated a review of the mythical and folk characters for implied messages. Universals that are to be found all through the world's cultures maintain the significant position that storytellers and writers of the past reflect much the same picture of human life as that to be found in the work of exact and insightful writers of today. Freud's impression-repression premise of the natural forces in the self which conjures up ids or scapegoats for pressure release is surely as valid today as when he devised it. Those thinkers-reviewers following Freud's method of inquiry were quick to read possible implied meaning into the folk character of Jack and the magic episode of beans growing to non-rational proportions in the night.

Unfortunately, some reviewers over-read the folk characters and stories without the necessary in-depth historical research. Sendak's age suggests that his generation was the one which became enamoured with this Freudian technique of inquiry. Other books by this author-illustrator, most notably *Higglety Pigglety Pop! Or There Must Be More to Life* communicate this in an allusionary-allegorical form.

Progressing beyond the book's cover, the first major surface and implied interpretation is given by Sendak on page 3. Mickey, in falling through the dark, mysteriously loses his pajamas, leaving him naked (a point at which Mickey's adventure will surely be a puzzle to the myriads of adults with subtle mid-Victorian inheritance). The sequences which follow directly after this appearance of nudity feature patterned curtains which dominate the night sky outside the window. As Mickey passes his parents bedroom door an idea and word code message informs the reader that help from his parents was not wanted even though the child's chronological age judged from size and body stage places him in the much "below ten years" group.

This age-body interpretation is a clue to the inappropriateness of the illustrator in using the descendant or blood brother of Pierre in the *Nutshell Library* or Max in *Where the Wild Things Are* for this story. It is as if Sendak is mocking his own previously successful creations by not expanding his skill and facility.

When Mickey lands in the *Night Kitchen*'s dough-filled utensil the second major implied graphic message appears. The three bakers are mirrored images of Oliver Hardy.

The use of Oliver Hardy is deplorable to this reader. A well-known and unique performer who has entertained millions of viewers still lives after death in the hearts of people the world over. The Laurel and Hardy personalities have contributed substantially to Man's universal quest for the humor in life. In making three Oliver cooks, it is as if Sendak envisions three film-created wise men awaiting the very young in dream symphonies, mixing laughter with mystery, confusing reality with fancy.

It may be questioned whether Sendak controlled himself in attempting to relate a fanciful world with reality. Had he created some other bakers his message might have had the strength to battle the taboo it appears he intended to break in literature for the young.

In the ditty-like exclamation of Mickey's "I'm not the milk and milk's not me! I'm Mickey!" there is another surface indication that the boy has mental control of the events rather than dream involvement. At this point the model of Carroll's *Alice's Adventures in Wonderland* has taken root only to be confused by the author-illustrator encasing Mickey in bread dough all ready to rise in the night kitchen.

In the word code signal given in the trade name of the cook stove, *Mickey Oven*, once again Sendak slapstickingly slips into the cultural domain of Walt Disney and the current saying "This is a lot of Mickey Mousing."

In the split screen graphics where Mickey falls into the bread dough a large bottle of liquid blueing appears. It bears alphabetic writing on its label which is not repeated exactly when this same symbolic bottle reappears as the apartment house called CHASE-O. Why this change in labeling on page 13 and page 23?

In detailed reading of the graphics and text following Mickey's swim in the 1930 milk bottle we encounter words and graphics which might be interpreted as integrating realistic male body functions and night's fanciful adventure.

The cry of Mickey in the *Night Kitchen* before he slides down the side of the milk bottle uses a rural, small town boy's language habits more than those of an urban child where trains travel on Jennie's Street and high rise buildings share the natural elements of stars, sky and moonlight.

The number of questions raised by *In the Night Kitchen*'s detailed graphic message can be answered only by Sendak himself. Why those particular patterns in the curtains? What are the meanings (surface and implied) of *Fandango, Cole's Orange Flower Water,* sugar in salt containers, *Safe Yeast,* with the trademark of a sun, yet presenting the phrase "up with the moon," and cream in graters? Should nonsense be the thrust and intent of the author, it most surely could have been explored with more nonsensical use of word-sound play than the obvious use of male names found on the kitchen items. Such names as *Woody, Louis, Philip, Taylor,* and *Eugene* detract from the nonsensical word play of *TA-KA-KAKE* in one spot. To this reviewer the mixture of three types of names and messages used on the city buildings is a sign of weakness rather than the gift of the polished writer-illustrator who produced *Where the Wild Things Are.*

Reading and re-reading *In the Night Kitchen* does not convince one that it is a child's delightful imaginative adventure. The overwhelming impact of this story, even though inexperienced young readers will not be able to express it to others, may well be the generation of more puzzlement where enough is generated in even the most permissive real life home environments.

The surface-implied message and the author's-reader's casual recognition of personal-social-cultural thoughts places this piece of literature in the contemporary sexual liberation movement in this writer's opinion. One of the bakers can flippantly strum a wooden spoon and shout "—AND NOTHING'S THE MATTER" but his action only points out the shallowness of playing unauthentically with moral and social mores within the young child's mind.

Would this reviewer have been disturbed with the messages he has received from *In the Night Kitchen,* he asks himself, *if* Sendak had directed his impulse or compulsion toward the literature for children of "ten and above" and created for it a boy character who was at least an *older Pierre or Max,* or better yet, a *new* character and a trio of bakers who were individuals in their own right?

Probably not, he answers himself. (pp. 860-63)

> *David C. Davis, "Wrong Recipe Used 'In the Night Kitchen'," in* Elementary English, *Vol. XLVIII, No. 7, November, 1971, pp. 856-64.*

When in 1970 *In the Night Kitchen* appeared, as much awaited as any picturebook has been, it was, as touted, unlike anything Sendak had done before; but more like *Hector Protector* than anything he had done since. No mists or quavers, just a *thump, dump, clump* and Mickey waking up and shouting "QUIET DOWN THERE!"

And he "fell through the dark (OH), out of his clothes (AAH) past the moon (OOH) & his mama and papa sleeping tight (MAMA! PAPA!) into the light of the night kitchen? (p. 518)

Until Mickey is aloft, it's not to be stopped; until the words stop, that is, and we are once again, as with the wild things, all eyes. But the text prints effectively in paragraph form, you'll notice, as that for *Where the Wild Things Are* wouldn't; and yet it is composed, piece by piece, of captions in panels and talk enclosed in speech balloons.

In making his comic book Sendak has combined the two modes of comic-strip 'narration,' the caption and the balloon, exposition and dialogue, where one or the other was usually chosen; and in combining them he has integrated them into a continuous text that we could reproduce by enclosing the spoken words in quotation marks—a continuous rhythmic text, moreover, borne along by internal rhyme and near rhyme: a text designed to be read aloud, as a comic-strip text isn't.

Captions and balloons are one because both are bounded by the same heavy even line and the balloons, far from floating, are squared off, while the captions, rather than being appendages, are part of the total picture too. So, indeed, is the handsome lettering, like in weight, variable in size. It is a matter, now, of visual design, of treating the page as a unit in the manner of an illuminated manuscript; and Sendak, further,

plays with his pictures as the illuminators did, letting them burst out of frames that in comic strips are usually sacrosanct. His model, notoriously, was Winsor McKay's "Little Nemo"; but the divergences are hardly less interesting than the resemblances. (pp. 518-20)

It will not have escaped anyone's attention that the dramatic structure of *In the Night Kitchen*—out of bed, adventure and back—is that of "Little Nemo in Slumberland" as much as the pictorial structure; and that the central episode, Mickey as a dough-boy, is prefigured by the Sixth Trick of *Max and Moritz*. But so does *A Very Speical House* anticipate the bounces and spills, and *I'll Be You and You Be Me* the magic transformations. The example of "Little Nemo," the specific motif of Busch, are catalysts: in the first and more important instance structuring—simplifying and fortifying—what had appeared as a spontaneous flow of invention.

As he made a picturebook text of comic-strip narration, so Sendak makes a volume that is a picturebook, not a comic book, in design; that translates McKay's structural flexibility into picturebook terms. Thus we have great full-page, page-filling pictures of the Oliver Hardy cooks; and overleaf a double-spread of the batter borne ceremoniously to the oven, with the grocery-built city looming behind. We have Mickey skipping one, two, three out of the oven, the separate panels breaking his fall even as they mark his descent; but though McKay continues his setting from one frame to the next, Sendak, doing him one better—and undoing the very idea of comic-strip sequence—backs his batter up from the last frame to the first.

On the right-hand page comes (1) the kneading and (2) the punching and (3) the pounding and (4) the pulling; and the looking and the wondering and the guessing . . . "till [overleaf] it looked okay." Wordlessly, below, Mickey spins the propeller; and when he's finally up and away, the book disappears, as it were, and what took on the aspect of a frieze in *Where the Wild Things Are* becomes a full-screen trick scene from a Thirties movie spectacle.

McKay, a prophet not without honor hitherto, has been referred to as a 'poet of the urban world.' His cityscapes, drawn when cities had just come to look as he drew them, have, even in their meticulous rendering, a visionary quality, and he drew visionary cities as well. Sendak's fantasy makes of McKay's city, and Hollywood's, the kitchen-cabinet assemblage that we see, where egg beaters top one building and a shaker is the dome of another. A grown-up child's magic make-believe city, with lights shining from a breadloaf el train.

There, "over the top of the Milky Way," Mickey is about to dive into the giant bottle (not part of the city proper but impossible without it); and, leaving his plane, losing his bread-batter suit, to swim about, bare as he was without his pajamas, singing: "I'm in the milk and the milk's in me, God Bless Milk and God Bless Me!" The cake finally baked, Mickey, with a "COCK-A-DOODLE DOO!" slides down the side of the bottle "straight into bed cakefree and dried."

Mickey unclothed offended sensibilities, and a naked Mickey lolling in the milk and, after, crowing 'Cock-a-doodle doo,' was suggestive, period. There is much sensual pleasure, real and potential, in the Night Kitchen; or one could say that *In the Night Kitchen* is where sensual pleasure takes precedence, and stop there. But Mickey in clothes would be a mess in the batter and a drowning fly in the milk: we need him unclothed to avoid incongruity, we need him out of his everyday self— just as painters needed their nude Athenas and Psyches—so that he can be a figurative figure. Martin, you'll recall, put on a cowboy suit and a mustache 'for a disguise' and Max, of course, had his wolf suit. Dressed in a T-shirt, Max would be a tourist in Disneyland.

More even than the *Wild Things,* however, *In the Night Kitchen* has to be *seen*. Max's story can be summarized, sensibly, in a sentence; to put the *Night Kitchen* into a sentence or two—a little boy falls out of bed into the 'night kitchen' where three bakers mix him in a cake, etc—is to render it meaningless, not to say ridiculous. Similarly, the *Wild Things,* recorded, makes good listening with or without the book (noises do nicely for the beasts) while the *Night Kitchen,* heard and not seen, is literally unimaginable. Smooth-flowing as the text is, a narrative poem in effect, the pictures are the essential counterpoint; and, as in a piece of music, the two develop together.

We could expand on this, we could look further into the book: of all of Sendak's picturebooks, it is what one would call the most interesting. And to my mind, he has never drawn better. . . . It is vital, forcible drawing, broad and clear and bold and yet quick with life. The marvelous dusky shades, meanwhile, take us back and away; this is stage coloring, an aura, almost an aroma of color. As a creation, the book could hardly be more successful.

It falters, I think, as a story. In Slumberland, Little Nemo has adventures, exciting, frightening adventures; Max, within and without, has an adventure too: in his own way he goes forth, to borrow Dorothy White's definition, "from security to insecurity and back to port." Mickey's pleasant dream—enough said?—is an escapade. He is popped into the oven, true, but not as a consequence of anything he's done (Max and Moritz) or a wish to do anything to him (Hansel and Gretel). It's a case of mistaken identity—"I'm not the milk and the milk's not me! I'm Mickey!"—and as innocent, as harmless as the kind of Marx Brothers routine that is back of it. Otherwise Mickey's wishes are fulfilled with no more struggle than the effort to shape the plane; and even to speak of tension is to speak another language.

On the last page is a picture of Mickey, his arm around a bottle of milk, in a sunbeam aureole, and around it the legend: "And that's why, thanks to Mickey, we have cake every morning." Intimations of a trademark, that's obvious (of the Fisk Rubber baby with candle and tire, perhaps); and Sendak's little joke, but otherwise?

He has spoken often about his work and what it means to him; usually what it means to him is what it says to us, in the yield is the intent. But as a chlid he had, it seems, not only the common yearning to be part of the nighttime world, he had a specific beef against the Sunshine Bakers, "We Bake While You Sleep." . . . (pp. 522-24)

Well, I had forgotten the Sunshine Bakers though I remember well the Fisk baby (whose significance to me was not what the ad intended either), which is not to say that the book depends on a recollection which, in any case, children can't have, but that the particular form that Mickey's—and Sendak's—wanting to stay up at night takes does not communicate the intensity of the experience. The meaning of the book to others falls short of its meaning to him.

But from it he made a coloring book: from this very personal, painstakingly wrought and expensively produced volume he made a sow's ear. It isn't only that kids could color it any which way, they could, if they wanted, try to color it his way;

and either way—anyway—we've heard for years that coloring books are bad for children, that they stifle the imagination, impede creativity. Paper-doll books might pass muster, but coloring books, never. To children, though, coloring is more like lacing—or the cutting out of paper dolls—than it is like drawing or painting; an objective accomplishment, that is, over a subjective expression. Operative also perhaps is the impulse to fill a vacuum: old books will almost invariably be found with the outline drawings colored in. But theory apart, coloring books were generally dismissed—since those early efforts of Françoise's that we saw—as intrinsically unworthy, déclassé, dime-store rubbish.

If it was characteristic for Sendak to produce a coloring book because kids enjoy them and he makes books the way, indeed, bakers bake—now a macaroon, now a napoleon, now a tart—it was no less characteristic of him to make something plebeian. Beyond the manifold influence of his work, it has served to bring together the 'popular' and the 'artistic' strains that [diverged] upon the appearance of the aesthetic book. And in reconciling he creates anew: whatever its antecedents, *In the Night Kitchen* is not Tolstoy sweating alongside the peasants nor is it Pop art. (p. 524)

> *Barbara Bader, "Maurice Sendak," in her Ameri-*
> *can Picturebooks from Noah's Ark to the Beast Within,*
> *Macmillan Publishing Co., Inc., 1976, pp. 495-524.*

MAURICE SENDAK'S REALLY ROSIE: STARRING THE NUTSHELL KIDS   (1975)

The complete, action-packed half-hour script for the television special adapted from Sendak's **"Nutshell Library"** and *The Sign on Rosie's Door*. Brilliant inked celluloids from the animation largely replace Sendak's original muted pastels. It is **unfortunate that space limitations allow only a handful of il**lustrations from each of the Nutshell stories, but even so, each page offers plenty to see. Carole King's lilting music is included with the Sendak lyrics. This is a first-rate picture-book play, superior to television's usual animated offerings, way above the stilted little plays for little players fobbed off on kids, and a godsend to everyone's neighborhood Rosie.

> *Helen Gregory, in a review of "Really Rosie Starring*
> *the Nutshell Kids," in* School Library Journal, *Vol.*
> *22, No. 4, December, 1975, p. 48.*

A charming, animated television special, **"Maurice Sendak's Really Rosie,"** has spawned a hodgepodge of a book, combining Sendak's script and lyrics with color pictures reproduced from the show, some of Sendak's preliminary drawings, and Carole King's music. One purpose clearly served is to make available the sheet music for Carole King's seven songs, but the point of putting all this together in one package escapes me.

Sendak's spunky, expressive kids are a natural for animation techniques. But in this book they are at two removes. Most of the pictures were drawn for the cartoon special by the artists of D & R Productions based on Sendak's sketches. They're good, but they don't have the gutsiness of Sendak's own scratchy, pencil sketches which are scattered through the book. In the large color pictures, the stylistic difference between Rosie and the kids in outline and pure solid colors, against more muted, blurrier, more naturalistic backgrounds of brick buildings and a cellar, seems extremely peculiar. And all these backgrounds which had a luminous quality on TV are muddy and disturbingly overcast here.

I wonder, too, what is the point of reproducing the script? It's not a play suitable for children to put on. Even a professional group of performers would be hard put to find a way to use it well. The script for **Really Rosie** follows the bossy Rosie as she auditions the kids on her block for parts in the classy movie of her life. Evening comes, the kids are tired and hungry, and the fantasy peters out till tomorrow. It's essentially an undramatic structure, though it worked adequately to link the production numbers based on the four books of the "**Nutshell Library**" and the other songs, and succeeded in placing diverse characters in a context where you could imagine them all together. Unfortunately, there are no production numbers in this book. The texts of the "**Nutshell**" books are included and set off with borders along with a meager assortment of illustrations. But the page-by-page visual excitement and wit of the tiny books is missing.

So the special qualities of the TV special have disappeared and we are left with an organized clutter.

> *Burt Supree, in a review of "Maurice Sendak's Really Rosie," in* the New York Times Book Review, *February 29, 1976, p. 26.*

If the reaction to the first showing of the TV special "**Really Rosie**" is any gauge, Rosie will be around for quite a while. Perhaps many children and adults will be interested in seeing the scenario and many will try to act it out. . . . A delight for TV fans of all ages, but will be a "special book" for older children interested in drama, music or animation.

> *Donald J. Bissett, in a review of "Maurice Sendak's Really Rosie: Starring the Nutshell Kids," in* Language Arts, *Vol. 53, No. 5, May, 1976, pp. 502-03.*

SOME SWELL PUP; OR, ARE YOU SURE YOU WANT A DOG? (with Matthew Margolis, 1976)

Obedience training, not for pets but for their young masters who are exhorted in sequential cartoon panels to cut the rough stuff and pile on the Tender Loving Care. (Sound enough, but that's about all the counsel there is, except for a suggested three-month grace period before paper training, which seems too long by half.) Presiding over this cautionary comic strip, the caftan'd canine who functions as patron saint to Pup and guiding light to two benighted kids is just the kind of odd touch Sendak fans have come to expect; the sequence with the most oomph—asleep, the kids each envision their own dream doggy—also has the artist's unmistakable stamp. Sendak is up front about dog droppings, liberally sprinkling in piles and puddles and deliberately risking a flap similar to the one over frontal nudity in . . . **Night Kitchen;** unaccountably, though, the running joke over Pup's gender never leads to an anatomy lesson. Although sure to be the most lovingly and expensively produced comic book around, the winsome mutt's misbehavior and the whacked-out antics of hammy first-time owners are the only bones tossed to readers in what still rates as second-level Sendak.

> *Pamela D. Pollack, in a review of "Some Swell Pup or Are You Sure You Want a Dog?" in* School Library Journal, *Vol. 22, No. 9, May, 1976, p. 54.*

Aidan Chambers gave utterance to an evaluation of Maurice Sendak that almost everyone has come to acknowledge: "Ar-

tistically, he stands head and shoulders above everyone else . . . a true genius." But whatever else it may be, the artist's latest book does not seem to be the product of that genius. . . . Even though the text contains some humor and some information, the artwork is so banal that one would simply yawn, were it not for the name of the illustrator. Sendak has dipped into the well of the comic strip before; but if **In the Night Kitchen** evolved from some of the fabulous and eerie scenes of "Little Nemo," this book depends more on the lifeless artwork seen in "Nancy"—flat, nonexistent backgrounds, caricaturish faces, dull colors. One of the few picture-book artists who has really demanded versatility of himself, Sendak has always refused to produce a book like his last one, has always attempted to change and to grow, and this book is no exception to that admirable pattern. But it is clearly lesser Sendak, and it will probably, like many bad paintings by great artists, still get more attention than it deserves.

> *Anita Silvey, in a review of "Some Swell Pup or Are You Sure You Want a Dog?" in* The Horn Book Magazine, *Vol. LII, No. 5, October, 1976, p. 495.*

A willingness to learn from expert opinion, and to change personal attitudes and modify cherished beliefs in light of new information, would appear to be useful characteristics for the scientific mind. If this is true, then young childen have available to them some excellent examples in Maurice Sendak's picture book **Some Swell Pup**. Written and illustrated in comic book style, to avoid appearing pedantic, the book lightly imparts some important concepts.

On the opening pages we see "Sendak's kids" wishing they had a puppy, and we also see an adult figure who has a homeless puppy. Until the inherent nature of their "baby" animal manifests itself in the form of "messing", the kids are delighted with their puppy. Then the kids scornfully reject their puppy precisely because of its biological nature and normal behavior. Training is tried, but a puppy is too young to be trained. What to do?

To begin with, the children completely fail to see that a puppy has certain natural limitations, so they engage in inappropriate and unwarranted criticism and blame. They call their puppy "bad", "dirty", and a "fiend", and become personally ashamed of what is perfectly natural behavior for a puppy. In brief, they show no understanding or tolerance for the inherent, biological limitations of a young animal.

At this point the adult expert authority enters the picture and explains to the children that their puppy is behaving normally and therefore must be regarded as innocent of blame. Puppy is just behaving according to his inherent nature and therefore blame and beatings are inappropriate and of no use. Needless to say, the kids accept the words of the expert and change their attitudes toward their puppy.

After a great deal of help, the children learn more useful and adaptive ways of interpreting the behavior of a young animal. They learn that a living thing has an inherent nature which causes it to behave in certain specific ways. They also come to believe that irrational attitudes and punishment must be replaced by love and understanding, or they will never be able to teach their puppy anything. Living creatures have biological givens which must be understood and accepted.

Heavy lessons in biology from a comic book, perhaps, but if young children learn all of these things about a puppy, as adults they might have similar attitudes toward all living things, including their own children. Maybe that's just exactly what the author had in mind. (pp. 7-8)

> *Georgia L. Bartlett and Clarence C. Truesdell, "Science and the Young Child," in* Appraisal: Science Books for Young People, *Vol. 17, No. 2, Spring-Summer, 1984, pp. 4-9.*

SEVEN LITTLE MONSTERS (1977)

Sendak's latest offering takes all of a minute. With just nine crayon-and-ink sketches illustrating a nine-line rhyme, his rough, tossed off sketches depicting his inimitable monsters have more life than many artists' finished drawings, but this is still a ripoff.

> *Helen Gregory, in a review of "Seven Little Monsters," in* School Library Journal, *Vol. 23, No. 8, April, 1977, p. 56.*

Seven Little Monsters, by Maurice Sendak, is a slim quasi-counting book.... One adult critic has described it as "an indifferent effort" and reproached Sendak for having "his attention elsewhere." The children found its slightness manageable and approachable, especially the younger ones. Small children don't ask for sophisticated story lines—*Seven Little Monsters* has almost none—but Christopher "liked the story because it seems like a nice story. It just seems like fun." He added a small piece of advice for the author: "If I wroat the story, I wood have gave them a name." Six-year-olds were pleased with the simple little book "I loved this book" wrote Nicole. "I liked it," seconded Leah.

> *Brigitte Weeks, "Picture Books: A Consumers' Report," in* Book World—The Washington Post, *May 1, 1977, p. E3.*

A counting book of monsters is guaranteed to please preschool devotees of the exotic—particularly if the monsters have the deliciously naughty characteristics of children. Certainly, the amiable gathering depicted here is an annoyance rather than a threat to the scurrying townsfolk, who try a variety of ineffectual methods to eliminate their visitors. Consequently, they are calculated to delight rather than to terrify young audiences. Indeed, many of the creatures should look familiar, for they bear close resemblance to the wild things tamed by Max more than a decade ago. Even their postures suggest a relationship to the artwork of the earlier book. But it is unfortunate that the sequence of their activities does not reflect their respective positions on the initial page. Small children just learning numerical order may be confused when, for example, the third figure in the row of seven monsters is subsequently identified as the first. Further, Monster Six, although performing in his correct spot, seems to have changed his costume—which adds to the confusion. Derived from a series of sketches made for an animated film for *Sesame Street,* the book is a charming conceit, but the illustrations lack the multi-dimensional quality of Sendak's earlier work.

> *Mary M. Burns, in a review of "Seven Little Monsters," in* The Horn Book Magazine, *Vol. LIII, No. 3, June, 1977, p. 303.*

OUTSIDE OVER THERE (1981)

[*Outside Over There*] may well become a children's classic. (p. 49)

Both the words and the pictures give endless cause for musings, and the musings are in this case profound, dealing with the darkness every child must conquer. It is a book for children that treats the child-reader as a serious, intelligent, troubled and vulnerable human being. Another writer might have softened the tale's effect by humor. Mr. Sendak does something better: By the lyricism and gentle irony of his words and pictures, he transmutes guilt and insecurity—the dual bane of every child's existence—the things one can muse on without undue fear and escape triumphant. More specifically, he examines, with great accuracy and tenderness, the archetypal older girl-child's longing-filled love for her father and her jealousy toward her mother and younger sibling, and he shows how the father's love and respect are won.

The tale is of olden times, and of Ida, whose job is to tend her baby sister while her father is away at sea and her mother sits staring in an arbor. Unfortunately, Ida plays her horn and fails to watch, so goblins come and steal the baby, leaving in its place a baby made of ice. When she finally realizes what has happened, Ida pursues and at last rescues her sister. Henceforth she watches her sister—and her mother—more carefully.

Everywhere Mr. Sendak's words and pictures hint at life's dark potential, the irrationality in the world and within us that makes loving vigilance necessary and not easy. With the first words of the story, "When Papa was away at sea," we get a harbor landscape thick with round and jagged rocks, a storm-wind stirring the trees and Mama's scarf, and in the lower left corner, in a moored boat, goblins looking out to sea as do Ida's mama and Ida; the baby gazes warily past the reader's left shoulder, more or less in the direction of the goblins down left.

Will Papa's ship strike rocks and sink? Why is it young Ida, not her mother, that has to hold the chunky baby (an interesting, more than lifelike baby that recalls those in Mr. Sendak's illustrations of the Grimm fairy tales in Lore Segal's translation). And the goblins—though they don't look very dangerous (hooded robes, so that we can't see their faces—robes whose color happens to fall midway between the color of Ida's dress and the color of Ida's mama's)—what are the goblins up to? The sky, when one looks closely, looks exactly like choppy water. Strange!

In the next picture, Ida's mama stares off at nothing from her arbor seat while Ida still holds the baby (who is crying now) and looks down at the baby's bonnet, which Ida can't pick up without setting down the baby. In the lower left corner, the goblins are going somewhere with a ladder, under the very nose of a large, beautiful Alsatian, a watchdog as lost in thought as Ida's mama or the serene sailboat in the distance. No wonder that, in such a world, where the responsible powers are off at sea or lost in a sweetly domestic daze, "Ida played her wonder horn to rock the baby still—but never watched." In the accompanying illustration we see Ida playing a post-horn, facing a window filled with sunflowers and climbing roses, her back to the baby who leans toward her, interested in Ida's music, while at a window nearby two goblins, on a ladder, sneak in. From a portrait, up right, Ida's papa looks on.

In the next picture Ida is still playing, lost in a dream; the sunflowers and roses are burgeoning, pushing into the room, while the baby sister cries in vain from the arms of a departing goblin and the ice-baby stares at the reader with what looks like frozen shock and disbelief, or perhaps an exaggeration of the familiar dazed stare. Father stares from his portrait almost as before, concerned, not lost in thought, but unable to help.

Then come two pictures wonderfully striking, on facing pages because they need to be looked at together. The text for the first is, "Poor Ida, never knowing, hugged the changeling and she murmured: 'How I love you.'" The unbeautiful flowers have crowded farther into the room, and Ida dreamily hugs the staring ice-baby, failing to notice—as she *would* notice if she really loved her sister, not just her own image as loving sister/mother—that she's murmuring to a spooky thing of ice.

On the facing page, the ice has melted down, the ugly flowers have pushed in much farther, and Ida is standing up, angry and a trifle scared. Outside the window through which the goblins came we see a storm at sea, a stroke of lightning that echoes Ida's stance, and a sinking ship; we belatedly notice that on the earlier page, when Ida murmured "How I love you," what we saw through the window was a stately square-rigger headed homeward under a dark sky. At some level one cannot help feeling that Ida, our surrogate, is to blame for all this, the rough pushyness of nature, the suggested death of the father (her moods and his welfare are eerily connected), and the loss of baby sister, gone "to be a nasty goblin's bride," as Ida's jealous unconscious thinks fitting.

Ida furiously resolves to save her sister, snatches her magic horn and her mother's much too large rain cloak (another sad reminder of how unfair the world is to big sisters) and makes, we are told, "a serious mistake," climbing "backwards out her window into outside over there." What is the mistake, exactly? Climbing out backwards? If so, why is it bad? We're not told.

In pictures weirdly early-Renaissance—ominous, beautiful, with sly echoes of, among others, Goya, Brueghel and Salvador Dali—Ida floats over the landscape, gazing at the reader with a superbly rendered troubled look: insecure, guilty, lost in thought. "Foolish Ida never looking," the text sighs . . . but then, like help from some magical protector, her sailor papa's song guides her (turns her around) and Ida finds the goblin wedding where her baby sister is to be bride. The goblins are babies so much like her sister that Ida can't be sure which one her sister is, so she plays her "wonder horn," making them dance—plays mercilessly, though they cry out, sick and weary—plays "a frenzied jig, a hornpipe that makes sailors wild beneath the ocean moon." The goblins melt into a dancing stream, leaving Ida's sister "cozy in an eggshell."

Again, dark hints, more than I can mention. The baby sister one is supposed to love and care for is like a goblin, at least sometimes, and one's gone-away sailor papa is also a little goblinlike, dancing, like them, "wild beneath the ocean moon." (Another drowning hint, besides: "beneath the ocean," we read, then instantly correct to "ocean moon." There is more here, Freud would say, but I pass by with downcast eyes.) Ida's sternness as she plays the horn—again the facial expression is superbly rendered—is everything her dreamily murmured "How I love you" (to the ice-baby) was not. She is now in fact behaving like a mother, deserving her father's love (finding the baby in an eggshell helps to displace the mother as rival).

Out of this darkness, this sterner, more responsible love, comes light and order. Ida, no longer in her mama's cloak, carries her sister home through a peaceful landscape without goblins (instead there are butterflies, who have the goblins' color, as does a white-wigged Mozart-like figure seen through his orderly, sharply rectangular cottage door playing what is probably a harpsichord). In the distance is a shepherd whom we earlier saw sleeping, now awake, tending his flock. The only hint of evil remaining is the foreground flora, which suggest skull-shapes. When Ida and her sister reach home, the dog is on his feet and Mama has a letter from Papa, which reads, "I'll be home one day, and my brave, bright little Ida must watch the baby and her Mama for her Papa, who loves her always." Which, the final page tells us, is just what Ida did.

Outside Over There is in the literal sense dreamlike, crowded with obscure symbols, rooted in the real troubles of the psyche, in the end both satisfying and not: Papa is still away, Mama still not helpful; but Ida has learned things, above all the dutiful devotion that merits love. (Not that duty is all. There really is something deep and strange in the father-daughter relationship, as Mr. Sendak suggests through the father's calling song and sailors' dancing, and Ida's calling, dance-demanding horn.)

The vision offered is honest, carefully worked out, unsentimental. What Mr. Sendak offers, in short, is not an ordinary children's book done extraordinarily well but something different in kind from the ordinary children's book: a profound work of art for children. (pp. 64-5)

> John Gardner, "Fun and Games and Dark Imaginings," in The New York Times Book Review, April 26, 1981, pp. 49, 64-5.

"England invented the children's book as we know it," Maurice Sendak once stated in a lecture at the Library of Congress, later explaining that he had specifically been referring to the picture books of Randolph Caldecott in which "words are left out and the picture says it, pictures are left out and the word says it. . . . It's like a balancing ball, it goes back and forth. And this, to me, is the invention of the picture book."

No one in our own time has as masterfully continued and extended the Victorian tradition of children's picture books as Sendak himself. "I live inside the picture book," he once said. "It's where I fight all my battles, and where, hopefully, I win my wars." And in his greatest works in this genre—***Where the Wild Things Are*** and ***In the Night Kitchen***—Sendak depicted two of his most memorable child heroes, who deal with their troubling emotions by taking two fantastic journeys. . . .

"It comes from the direct middle of me," Sendak once wrote to a friend about the creation of ***Night Kitchen***, "and it hurt like hell extracting it. Yes, indeed, very birth-delivery type pains, and it's about as regressed as I imagine I can go." But in his newest picture book ***Outside Over There***—which he considers the third of the trilogy that began with ***Wild Things***—Sendak has imaginatively gone even further into his past. (p. 1)

Unlike ***Wild Things*** and ***Night Kitchen***—which drew their inspiration from ***King Kong***, Laurel and Hardy movies, and the cartoons of Winsor McCay—***Outside Over There*** presents a series of extraordinarily intense, luminous, almost frozen-in-time illustrations that reveal the influence of such visionary 18th-century German painters as Caspar David Friedrich and, especially, Philipp Otto Runge. In ***Outside Over There***, the simultaneous presentation of different moods, characters, and actions—we see the goblins planning and performing their kidnapping while Ida is obliviously taking care of her baby sister—testifies to Sendak's compositional brilliance. The double-page illustration showing Ida, in search of her sister, flying backwards seemingly over and through inner and outer worlds, is one of Sendak's greatest achievements, while the muted but rich colors of grass, trees, sunflowers, moons and skies are the means by which Sendak conveys the story's emotional content.

As Ida returns home with her sister through a wood, we notice a little cottage in which we see in silhouette the seated figure of Mozart, whose presence betokens his role as the muse of the book. For **Outside Over There** is, above all, an homage to the composer who is probably Sendak's greatest artistic inspiration (''My book is my *imagining* of Mozart's life,'' Sendak says). One can, in fact, almost hear the Queen of the Night's impassioned first aria from *The Magic Flute* as we see the skies darken outside Ida's window while she watches the changeling baby dissolve into water. And it was for a production of that opera by the Houston Opera . . . that Sendak created costumes and sets (caves appear in both opera and book) while he was working on **Outside Over There**.

We should not overlook the fact that this book is also, of course, *echt*-Sendak. With her pluckiness and indomitability, Ida might well be an incarnation of Rosie in **Really Rosie;** Ida and her infant sister remind us of the dog Jennie and Baby in **Higglety Pigglety Pop!;** Ida flying resembles David flying in **Fly By Night;** and Ida's rescue mission parallels Max's and Mickey's night journeys. But while Max contacts his feelings of anger and loneliness as he travels to the land of the Wild Things, and while Mickey explores the feelings of his unrepressed body as he journeys in the world of the Night Kitchen, Ida and her sister experience feelings of loss—the loss of identity and of dissolution—only to recover both themselves and each other.

In **Outside Over There,** it is as if Sendak, in the character of Ida, had returned to the first moments of conception—Ida's

Sendak in his studio in Ridgefield, Connecticut. © Nancy Crampton.

ritual encounter with the goblin infants just out of their eggshells hints at this. And it is interesting that in this book, Sendak has given us the first female protagonist of his trilogy. . . . It is as if he had contacted the realm of his anima—in the Jungian sense of the female side of a man's nature. One can make such speculations because **Outside Over There**, like most great fairy tales, has the simplicity of an elemental story and at the same time the mysteriousness, the depth, and the multiplicity of meanings of a dream . . . as we, like Ida, enter the underworld of the goblins' cave, where what is outer becomes inner, and where what is lost is found.

Outside Over There is the first of Sendak's works to be published and distributed as both a children's and an adult book. This is as it should be, for Sendak has always had the uncanny ability to make us, as adults, reexperience the way a child experiences his or her earliest emotions, reawakening in us our own childhoods. As Runge once said: ''We must become children again if we wish to achieve the best.'' And in **Outside Over There**, Maurice Sendak has achieved the best. (p. 2)

> Jonathan Cott, ''When Ida Blew Her Magic Horn,'' in Book World—The Washington Post, *May 10, 1981, pp. 1-2.*

Because people have two hands, they can say, ''on the other hand,'' and sometimes think they're done with it; if they were octopuses, perhaps they would not be so inclined towards dualism—towards thinking things have readily distinguishable and merely ''two'' sides. (p. 88)

Those books that nudge us into that multi-faceted reality beyond dualism are rare in any genre—but for some reason, we're not surprised that when they do appear, they are likely as not to be called ''children's books.'' One of those transcendent talents is at work today—Maurice Sendak—a maker of children's literature who knows that although we have two hands, and that the sun casts one shadow, we must look warily at our ordinary turf and discover how to count to three—to move beyond dualism into the complexity of imagination.

Sendak's new book, **Outside Over There** develops themes from his earlier works and radically transplants the viewer/reader to a planet more familiar, more strange than the ordinary one in which people blithely and blandly say, ''on the other hand . . . ,'' ignore their shadows, or think that children and adults cannot share the same picture book (or aesthetic elegance and psychological eloquence).

With words cumbersome, yet poetically scored, Maurice Sendak tells the story of Ida, a girl who forgets to watch and so must journey foolishly and courageously to recover what is lost. His words explode those capsule expressions and visions that have elusive significance. The story is so rich, compact, and lush, it must be eaten like a berry—all at once.

The exquisitely evocative pictures are of life made to hold still, like the staged photographs from which Sendak sometimes works, setting up a fake scene which illuminates an image of something interior—hard to capture, hard to expose. Resonant with the centuries of religious art behind her, Ida whirls in the air with her toy horn and in her Mama's yellow rain cloak; she is a child made to act a mother, an image we know we've seen before, of a delicate, disrupted madonna. The pictures must be consumed—almost like a holy feast.

Sendak is hardly the first to suggest that all the world's a stage—or even that it's edible; he is, nevertheless, original, with an originality that is at once quirky and profound.

In spite of his extraordinary popularity, too many people have remarked recently, "Oh, I don't like Sendak," and then add with not a little self-righteousness, "he would *frighten* my children." Or, I hear, "I haven't bought that new book *yet;* I can't allow myself to be frightened right now." Are these whimsies of Sendak's really terrifying? They often make you laugh out loud, they are graphically splendid, and they are textually (the books he has authored as well as illustrated) surprising—often profound. They celebrate the presence, the humor, the depth of children. Is this perhaps what is so—as the detractors insist—frightening?

The flirtation with fright in Sendak is mingled with an affirmation of the human spirit. Perhaps the people who have painted diapers on his naked children, or those who have rejected *Some Swell Pup* because the cartoon puppy all too naturalistically urinates and defecates, or those who think that the Grimm characters of grotesque visages in *The Juniper Tree* crowd up too close for our readerly comfort, might dare to look again. The frightening or repellent is also beautiful or funny, clever or charming; and Sendak's work holds it all in tension and does not permit us to take sides. The shadow-realm in the artist's view is not in opposition to the light. It is not to be eradicated by the light, but it is a part of the totality of vision.

Shadows, as all children know, are made visible only by means of some part of ourselves thrust into and posed in the path of a light. Shadow, unfortunately by some other standards, looms, not as the dramatic extension of ourselves, but as something alien or demonic. Dualistic visions of reality demand that the shadow, the other, the dark side must be conquered, overcome, overthrown. Sendak, though he plays at conquering, subverts our dualistic assumptions about the shadow.

The dualistic world-view of our culture has spawned two-dimensional imaginations which project on to images female, sexual, intellectual, or aesthetic, an evil which is named. But in Sendak, to the dualist's dismay, goblins and babies are almost indistinguishable, lions are great gobblers as well as pleasant weekend guests, outrageous willfulness may cause one's dinner to be withheld or may tame monsters. It's a complex world in which monstrousness may be a dimension of love and also the means to make and un-make monsters—not a mere two-sided world of good and evil, or ordinary reality and fantasy. Fantasy and palpable reality are so unified in Sendak's art, we cannot help but discover there that *other* and *mother* are closer than a rhyme.

"Fantasy is the core of all writing for children, as I think it is for the writing of any book—perhaps even for the art of living," the author has said.

This complexity, a construction of many sides and more mirrors, is a world exemplified by an interplay of artist and writer; each aspect of Sendak's imagination and skill enhances and enlarges upon the other. The eloquence of that interpretive interplay, story enlarging image, the visual extending the verbal, is like human experience, the shadow interpreting the light, daytime revealing the night, the dark. As Sendak has expressed it,

> You must never illustrate exactly what is written. You must find a space in the text so that pictures can do the work. Then you must let the words take over where words do it best. It's a funny kind of juggling act, which takes a lot of technique and experience to keep the rhythm going.

As it is with story and image in the work of Maurice Sendak, so it is with the interweaving of light and shadow—each fills up the spaces left by the other.

The latest book, *Outside Over There,* is the most triumphant of Sendak's ever-enlarged talent. All of us have experienced the purgatory of being left with baby. We empathize with Ida, who means well, playing "her wonder horn to rock the baby still, but never watched." So goblins snatch the baby, leaving a changeling made of ice in her place. (pp. 89-90)

Clever Ida "made a serious mistake" and "climbed backwards out her window into outside over there." Those serious mistakes take us into a realm—variously called in Sendak's trilogy, *Where the Wild Things Are, The Night Kitchen,* and *Outside Over There,* the place where the big things happen, where the stories come from, and which may be geographically charted, as the artist has claimed, "from the direct middle of me."

When Ida finally turns herself around, she's "smack in the middle of a wedding." The goblin thieves, when unveiled, are babies, identical to her baby sister. But they are celebrating an uncanny wedding—an event that resembles a collection of squally babies. Sometimes it takes a special charm to distinguish between a goblin and a real baby. Ida plays her horn so fiercely the goblins are "churned into a dancing stream," enabling her to discover the real baby cooing in an eggshell. She packs her back home. A letter from her distant sailor father, and the look of her even more remote mother who sits by in the arbor, prompts Ida to resolve to watch the baby, "which is just what Ida did."

A traditional Grimm tale, "**The Goblins,**" stunningly illustrated by Sendak several years ago, seems to lurk beneath some of the imagery and humor of Ida's story. The folk story tells of a mother's dilemma, when she realizes that goblins have stolen her child and left her a changeling "with thick head and staring eyes who did nothing but eat and drink." A neighbor woman prescribes the remedy: set the changeling before the fire and begin to boil water in egg shells; when the changeling sees it, he will laugh and be returned. The changeling baby laughs, "and as he laughed there suddenly came a lot of little goblins who brought the right child and set it on the hearth and took their friend away with them." The illustration depicts an enormous baby carried by little goblins—but which is it? The real baby or the changeling? That is the business of Sendak.

Sendakian characters, in book after book, eat, act, and float. The first book he ever owned, he says, he tried to bite; characters swallow one another over and over, 'til the reader can only say, "I'm in the book and the book's in me." The creatures act up and act out until we realize that what's pretended is what's real. The figures levitate, not so much to represent the power of flying, as the faith of floating.

No sissy bunnies bump around in Sendak pages, but erotic, sauntering rabbits advising girls on the mystery of color. Old worn photographs of relatives lost to the Holocaust, or of the author's own childhood lost to the past, act as models for the characters of his fantasies. The bodies formed by Sendak are large, stocky, yet page after page they're moving through the air. His art is the inner feeling made manifest—why else would his characters and objects look so saturated with substantiality, were it not conferred on them by the imagination rather than by mere physicality?

Yes, I suppose Sendak is scary. His humor, his heavy grace, have the power to levitate our own shadows.

An earlier book (and still my favorite), *Higglety Pigglety Pop,* tells of Jennie, the dog who knew there must be more to life than having everything. She goes off to gain experience (out-thinking a large baby unwilling to eat and a larger lion very willing to do so) so that she can join the World Mother Goose Theatre and act every day in a salami-propped, atrocious nurs-ery-rhyme drama and live at Castle Yonder. Jennie derived her wit, her courage, and her appetite from a real dog, transformed by Sendak into fiction—she becomes something that becomes part of all of us.

There are few things which can fall wholly onto one side of experience—the horrible or the beautiful. Experience is min-gled, and the more beauty in a vision, the more likely terror is to be there too. Indeed, once one gains enough experience to join the World Mother Goose Theatre, or to transgress into the milk of the Night Kitchen, or fall and float into Outside Over There, I suspect the sides are too many to count. After all, Ida doesn't seem to notice (but baby does) that Mozart plays on the opposite shore. (pp. 90-1)

> *Lynda Sexson, "Too Many Sides to Count," in Par-abola, Vol. VI, No. 4, Fall, 1981, pp. 88-91.*

According to Selma Lanes, Sendak derived the "bare-bones plot" of *Outside Over There* from the brief Grimms' tale, **"The Goblins,"** which he had illustrated in 1973. The connection with a story about a baby stolen by goblins is clear enough, and the artist seems to allude to his earlier illustration by pro-viding the hooded goblins of *Outside Over There* with the same kind of staff. But so far as I know, no critic has identified what seems to be a more fundamental and complex source for Sendak's text, George MacDonald's *The Princess and the Gob-lin,* and to a lesser extent Arthur Hughes's illustrations for that book and for MacDonald's *At the Back of the North Wind.* Nor has Sendak mentioned these in published interviews as influ-ences on the third volume of his trilogy.

Sendak has, however, in most of those interviews mentioned MacDonald as a "model . . . someone I try to copy in many ways." He has spoken of "ripping off" MacDonald, whose "fairytales . . . are for me the source book of much of my work." In a 1970 interview Sendak refers specifically to *The Princess and the Goblin,* and to Princess "Irene's travels through the cave with the goblins" as being so strange that "they can only come out of the deepest dream stuff." The greatest interest of the latter statement is the fact that eleven years before the publication of *Outside over There* Sendak has already in his memory transformed MacDonald's novel into something more like his as yet unwritten book than it really is: for although there is a goblin plot to kidnap Irene "to be a nasty goblin's bride" (Sendak's words in *Outside Over There*), and she does travel through their caves, she never actually comes into direct contact with the goblins, as Sendak's Ida is to do.

In *Outside Over There* Sendak was further to transform a kid-napping plot into an actual kidnapping, and the victim from a young girl into a baby sister in such a girl's charge. But the initial circumstances and even setting are similar. Irene lives in a great house halfway up a hill, her parents absent—father traveling throughout his kingdom and mother elsewhere be-cause of a serious illness. Ida, who also lives on a hill, must take the place of an absent-minded, preoccupied mother in caring for her little sister, while her father is "away at sea." The hill in Sendak's first two-page spread is similar to Hughes's first cut for *The Princess and the Goblin,* which also depicts

a stone bridge like that over which Sendak's goblins carry the baby.

But perhaps the most revealing evidence of Sendak's debt to MacDonald is a remark in his 1976 interview with Jonathan Cott: "The only way to find something is to lose oneself: that's what George MacDonald teaches us in his stories." Although in the immediate context Sendak is referring to Mahler's "los-ing himself" in his *Waldhütte,* the MacDonald reference would seem to be to Irene's earliest adventure, when she must lose herself in order to find the protective (and strangely erotic) figure of her "great-great-grandmother" at the top of the man-sion. MacDonald remarks that "it doesn't follow that she *was* lost, because she had lost herself"; and Irene's failure in the next attempt to find this mysterious figure whose love she so greatly needs, when she *is* described as being "lost," seems to stem from her failure to lose herself, her self-consciousness, her waking rationality. This matter of losing oneself fits the pattern of all three works in Sendak's trilogy (as well as many of MacDonald's works, such as "The Golden Key" and the adult fantasy, *Lilith*): the journey into the dream and back of *Where the Wild Things Are* and *In the Night Kitchen,* where the dream is a losing of oneself that effects a new reconciliation to one's life; and what I see as the more ambiguous experience of Ida and her sister's being lost and restored.

The forms of the recurrence of fictional situations from MacDonald to Sendak suggest that Sendak is not merley im-itating, or "ripping off," but transforming source elements. And as I read and reread, I find that I internalize those elements, which come to form a level of intertextual meaning in Sendak's text. Thus, Sendak's double-page spread, "If Ida backwards in the rain . . . ," where Ida's floating on her back in the air trailing the yellow raincoat resembles Arthur Hughes's en-graving of the North Wind floating in the air as she prepares to take Little Diamond to his final rest, assumes for me a special resonance because the North Wind is "saving" Diamond as Ida is saving her sister. Hughes's surprisingly erotic drawing and MacDonald's text associate the beautiful North Wind, like Irene's great-great-grandmother, with physical maternal love, spiritual goodness, and a vaguely defined afterlife. Though there is no exact resemblance—apart from that of saving a small child—between the functions of the North Wind and of Sendak's Ida, identifying this apparent influence helped to clar-ify my feelings about aspects of Sendak's text: feelings of loneliness, loss, and anxiety in childhood about sexuality and death.

The connections between *Outside Over There* and the work of MacDonald and his illustrator Hughes seem too obvious to be doubted. From *The Princess and the Goblin* in particular come the neglect of a child; actual or intended kidnapping by goblins for the purpose of a wedding; and the necessity of losing one-self. Perhaps even more fundamental is the way in which, in both texts, danger comes from *outside,* and from the depths of the earth. One answer to [critic] Susan Hankla's question as to where "outside over there" really is would seem to be (for MacDonald as well as Sendak) anywhere primal dangers might lurk, outside one's own comfortable bedroom, home, and family. Yet "outside over there" is also "inside in here," the domestic world where all the child's guilty feelings of oedipal desire, aggression, and jealousy originate; and Sen-dak's tale would almost be taken as a paradigm of how the *heimlich* (domestic, private, secret, forbidden) becomes the *unheimlich* (alien, threatening, strange, but also eerily famil-iar). (pp. 142-45)

My own reading now starts from the premise that Sendak's creative process is autobiographical and eclectic. This allows me to integrate what I see as his main sources and what I have learned about his life into my total understanding. But this is a point arrived at only with difficulty, after an initially negative response to the apparent obscurity and didacticism and the new graphic style of *Outside Over There*. That response was provoked, and the possibility of empathy was blocked, first of all, by a feeling of betrayal in Sendak's change of style. The flat, comic-book style of *In the Night Kitchen,* which recalled the tokens of love given to me especially when I was ill as a child, and the cross-hatching of *Higglety-Pigglety-Pop,* so reminiscent of my favorite, Cruikshank, had been replaced by a mode which, especially in its modeling of figures, recalled the despised *Saturday Evening Post* commercial art of my childhood. . . . But worse than the shock at Sendak's new style was my feeling about the apparently didactic implications of the story: girls, if they want to be happy and content, must take care of their baby sisters *and* their mothers. What I sensed as an attempt to provide reassurance for the reader just didn't work.

Discovering what I thought to be Sendak's main source in MacDonald provided a framework within which I could reconsider my response. If a single aspect of *The Princess and the Goblin* is dominant for me it is the combination of Irene's virtually orphaned state with her strong and determined sense of self, a combination which allows her both to find her succoring great-great-grandmother *and* to make the "mistake" (Sendak's word about Ida) of staying outside too long with her maid, thus putting herself in danger from the goblins. Of course it is this mistake that leads to her meeting Curdie whom she later saves from the goblins in the mine, and who in turn saves her from a "goblin wedding" (again, Sendak's expression). Because my identification is strongest with the lonely but self-possessed child, and secondarily with the older male child, Curdie, I find especially appealing MacDonald's notion that being a princess depends on inner rather than contingent (hereditary) qualities. And the narrative structure recalls childhood fantasies about the foundling who attains love, power, and acceptance.

The goblins' threat to Irene has affective significance for me in three ways. There is a guilty identification with the goblins in their desire to treat sadistically and possess sexually the pure young girl. Insofar as I identify with the princess as child, however, I also feel a fear of physical violation. And for my adult consciousness, an ongoing pleasure is provided by the extraordinary way Macdonald presents a pre-Freudian model of the human psyche, corresponding roughly to the id (the savage goblins in their deep caverns), the developing ego (Irene), the integrated ego (the miners, and especially Curdie, who can work in the mines but also functions rationally above ground), and, in the great-great-grandmother, a female ego-ideal which is given clear preference over the machismo of the super-ego King-Papa (as Irene calls him). Thus *The Princess and the Goblin* provided some insight into Sendak's creative process and an external framework which seemed to make *Outside Over There* more coherent. (pp. 146-47)

Upon reflection, it occurs to me that many of the greatest children's books, seemingly based on bizarre personal fantasies, have their incoherences and their hints of what Leon Edel has called the "tristimania" of great art, the feeling, beginning in childhood, of a fundamental sadness in life. Given my experiences with students who, not having read *Alice's Adventures in Wonderland* as children, find it both disturbing and incoherent, I should not be surprised at my own resistance to recognizing the emotional coherence of *Outside Over There.*

Probably the most seriously unresponsive aspect of my early readings of Sendak's tale was that I saw not only the conclusion, but also the intial situation, as approved by the narrator: "When Papa was away at sea, / and Mama in the arbor . . ." I can now see that both the initial two-page spreads include disturbing elements, not only the ominously lurking hooded goblins, but the evident ignoring of Ida and her screaming baby sister by their mother, and the frustrated look on Ida's face. Her sister's bonnet has just fallen on the ground and Ida is looking down at it as if hoping her mother will turn around and pick it up for her. Given this opening, where things are emotionally wrong, "Ida played her wonder horn to rock the baby still—but never watched" has connotations of deliberate and hostile neglect, emphasized by the visual parallel with the previous illustration, where Ida's mother's back is turned just as Ida's is here.

Sendak told Selma Lanes that he identified as much with Ida as with the baby, although it was he who was cared for as a child by his older sister; and it is Ida, rather than the baby, who is given strong emotions (though the baby's face is more expressive), the fear and jealousy. Ida's unawareness of the kidnapping seems to be due to her almost hypnotic fascination with the horn, roses, and sunflowers (which combine male sexual force in their tumescence with phallic and vaginal shapes in their leaves), just as her failure to see the ice changeling is due to her own icy feelings toward her burdensome sister. To say, as Susan Hankla does, that Sendak's is a "strikingly paranoid vision" which implies that without constant vigilance "the world as you know it can be replaced by one in which repulsive goblins steal real babies," apart from taking a symbolic (or, as Geraldine DeLuca argues, allegorical) tale too literally, denies a particularity to Ida's experience and overlooks the possibility that Ida herself is in conflict. That is, the kidnapping and saving of the baby, as manifestations of Ida's fantasies, represent a conflict between hostility and love.

The idea of psychological projection is borne out by the fact that Sendak (at least as I understand his use of MacDonald) changes the object of the goblins' lust and cruelty in MacDonald from the "I" (Irene, Ida) to the baby. That Ida symbolically tries to take on her mother's role by donning her raincoat seems clear, but why is it a "serious mistake" to climb "backwards out the window into outside over there"? Backwards may have various implications, including regression, but in the context of the previously turned backs of Ida and her mother, it suggests to me a continuation of unconscious neglect (since Ida is, after all, trying to save her sister). It is the voice of the father (psychologically the introjected father or super-ego) that provides Ida with the right kind of magic: in effect, the command, "Turn around and look!" This seems to be stressed in the double-page spread in which she is hearing her father's voice, through the inclusion of a portrayal of the neglectful (and, it should be remembered, maritally neglected) mother in her seat in the arbor, with the baby's bonnet still not picked up, and separated by many caves from her baby, the mother looking quite unaware that anything is happening.

The revelation to Ida that the goblins are "just babies like her sister!" has at least a double edge. While it can be seen as a defense against the threats that seem to loom in puberty, it also implies that for Ida her sister is indeed something of a goblin—screaming and making ugly faces when Ida wants to talk to her mother or play her horn. Of additional interest is the ambiguous gender of the goblin babies; all are naked, but the only sex (in two of the goblins) revealed is female, which suggests again that Ida's sister is as much of a "goblin" threat as the onset of her own sexual maturity. There is also a telling phrase which connects the scene to what Sendak has called his "individualized" childhood: "We're dancing sick and must to bed." Does this mean that Maurice himself is one of those troublemaking goblins in his fantasies about his childhood? (Sendak told [Jonathan] Cott that everyone in the book is female, including the five goblins, though I see no way of telling about three of them; and further, two unquestionably male sailors and a male shepherd are depicted in the two-page spread, "If Ida backwards . . ."). Again, in the "dancing sick" scene, the reference to the hornpipe making "sailors wild" recalls Ida's father the sailor, and a girl's ambivalence about her father's sexuality. In this same connection the eggshell in which Ida finds her sister seems to be a symbol of both the protective shell of childhood mentioned by [critic Elaine] Moss and a child's belief that chickens come from eggs and babies from mothers without any role for the father—although here it could also be a fantasy-denial of the mother's role. Indeed, it is only after being (apparently) born from the egg that Ida's sister is "crooning and clapping as a baby should," quite different behavior from that at the book's opening, when the mother is present.

A problem for some readers, and one of the main obstacles to my taking *Outside Over There* seriously, is the apparent didacticism of the conclusion. Returning with her sister to their mother, Ida finds that a letter has come from her father which instructs her to "watch the baby and her Mama for her Papa, who loves her always." Sendak reports that a friend found this disturbing, in the way it "dumps everything on Ida," but he refuses to commit himself to a definite meaning for this conclusion. Elaine Moss, apparently feeling a need of closure, construes the ending as reassuring, and I think my own reaction and that of Sendak's friend indicated a similar wish for closure but an inability to find it. It now seems more satisfying to take a clue from Sendak's demurral and consider that ending as a step reached in a process of emotional development for Ida (and perhaps her mother as well). One may venture a nonreductive Freudian reading at this point. The symbolic meaning of the father's absence and his letter, for Ida, is that the female child must come to recognize that she cannot have her father for herself and need not regard her mother as a rival. But because of the double configuration of the oedipus complex experienced by girls, the conclusion can also signify that the *mother* is not exclusively one's own—especially in the context of a sibling rivalry. Ida is, surely, accepting some of the func-

tions of a mother in relation to her baby sister. Yet it is a *step*, not a completed process. And if my earlier resistance to his ending was obtuse, this was perhaps because I, like Elaine Moss and Sendak's friend, was expecting a certain kind of resolution, in part because of unexamined assumptions about what a children's book should accomplish, and at a deeper level because of anxieties stemming from childhood, about loss and the fear of growing up.

At this point in the account of my story of reading, it seems relevant to turn again to *The Princess and the Goblin,* in order to stress the intertextual component of my response (and one might note that Sendak's view of his work is also intertextual, though so far he has cited texts other than the one I find most important). Irene's losses are greater than Ida's, for not only is her father mostly absent, but it is clear toward the end of the novel that her mother is dead. Yet Irene too has moved at least one step in her development: by taking the initiative to enter the mine and rescue Curdie, she has made possible the eventual routing of the goblins, symbols of male sexuality as dirty, violent, and demeaning. She thus clears the way for a mature relationship with Curdie, who will eventually (in *The Princess and Curdie*) replace Ida's King-Papa as her main love-object, after he goes through his own process of testing.

The Princess and the Goblin, **Outside Over There,** and *The Magic Flute,* one of Sendak's avowed sources, are all fantasies of the testing and development of individuals. It is evident from Sendak's published statements that at the time of writing **Outside Over There** he was consciously creating a tribute to Mozart (and the Grimms) rather than to MacDonald; I can only guess that if one of his interviewers had raised the question of MacDonald's influence on **Outside over There** we might have a different set of statements. But this is relatively unimportant for what has been the telling of a story of reading. Both MacDonald and Sendak have shown me the danger of reading their fantasies either too literally or too much as strict allegories. My experience of **Outside Over There** has also shown me the need to let one's response and thus understanding flow from a contact with one's (inevitably reconstructed) child-self. Neither *The Princess and the Goblin* nor **Outside Over There** should be defined as "children's" or "adult's" books; rather, they are works which demonstrate just how fine the line is between being a child and being an adult. (pp. 148-51)

Michael Steig, "Reading 'Outside Over There'," in Children's Literature: Annual of the Modern Language Association Seminar on Children's Literature and The Children's Literature Association, *Vol. 13, 1985, pp. 139-53.*

Anna Sewell

1820-1878

English author of fiction.

The following entry presents criticism of Sewell's *Black Beauty: His Grooms and Companions. The Autobiography of a Horse* (1877; U.S. edition as *Black Beauty: His Grooms and Companions. The Uncle Tom's Cabin of the Horse*).

Sewell is celebrated as the author of *Black Beauty*, perhaps the most successful and beloved animal story ever written. Her only book, *Black Beauty* is regarded as an exceptionally moving work which is responsible for improving the treatment of horses, influencing the realism of its genre, and affecting the emotions of generations of readers, most frequently preteen girls. The story is told by Black Beauty, a well-bred stallion who, through human neglect and abuse, descends from life in a gentleman's stable to status as a lowly cab horse; the happy ending reunites Beauty with an old friend, the impoverished but loving groom Joe Green. *Black Beauty* is clearly didactic in purpose. When Sewell wrote the story, horses were considered a primary means of transportation and a major source of labor. Despite their usefulness, the animals were often mistreated by their owners. Sewell directed *Black Beauty* to the English working class, who had consistent contact with horses. The novel demonstrates Sewell's desire to relieve the suffering of horses as well as her intention to abolish the bearing rein (or checkrein), a device used to make the animals look elegant by holding their heads in an unnatural upward position. While the cruelty of the bearing rein had been debated before the publication of *Black Beauty*, the book's popularity prompted a sympathetic awareness which caused the extinction of the device. In addition to achieving her humanitarian aims, Sewell created an especially memorable character with Black Beauty, who is now recognized as a universal figure.

Sewell presents an authoritative knowledge of horses and their needs in *Black Beauty*, an unusual quality for a Victorian woman; her challenge of such accepted practices as war and fox hunting are also distinctive for a person of her time. Sewell's views also include a refined distaste for drinking, smoking, and graft, which perhaps reflects her genteel background. The story of Sewell's life is often referred to as explanation for the depth of her humanity and intimate insight into helpless dependence. Crippled in adolescence, by her mid-30s she could get around only by pony cart and was bedridden for the last ten years of her life. Raised a Quaker, she was very close to her mother, Mary Sewell, an author of popular ballads and verses who devoted herself both to charity and to her daughter. Sewell spent seven years painstakingly handwriting *Black Beauty*, which was transcribed by her mother, and died within a year after the book's publication. At the time of her death, several thousand copies of the novel had been sold, and it continued to sell steadily. George T. Angell, the founder of such organizations as the Massachusetts Society for the Prevention of Cruelty to Animals and the American Humane Education Society, was looking for a book that would do for horses what *Uncle Tom's Cabin* did for slaves. When he discovered *Black Beauty*, Angell had it distributed as propaganda to the drivers of horses. The book became an immediate best seller, and its triumph led the Royal Society for the Prevention of Cruelty

to Animals to add a recommendation to the 1894 edition. One of the world's most popular works, *Black Beauty* has not been out of print since its initial publication. Although it was not originally written for them, children consider *Black Beauty* a particular favorite and are captured by its appealing subject and exciting story.

Sewell is consistently praised for her sincerity, simple and succinct writing style, precise and eloquent narrative skill, and success with characterization. She is also appreciated for her accurate detailing of both animal care and nineteenth-century English life as well as for her expert imparting of information. Although *Black Beauty* is often criticized for its excessive sentimentality and for the obviousness of its moral objectives, Sewell is admired for creating a work which continues to arouse compassion and respect for horses through her passionate conviction, integrity, and excellence as a storyteller.

(See also *Something about the Author*, Vol. 24)

AUTHOR'S COMMENTARY

[The following excerpt is taken from a collection of papers discovered after Sewell's death. Although its genesis is unknown, it is thought to be part of a letter or a journal from approximately 1877.]

I have for six years been confined to the house and to my sofa, and have from time to time, as I was able, been writing what I think will turn out a little book, its special aim being to induce kindness, sympathy and an understanding treatment of horses. In thinking of Cab-horses, I have been led to think of Cabmen, and I am anxious, if I can, to present their true conditions, and their great difficulties, in a correct and telling manner.

Some weeks ago I had a conversation at my open window with an intelligent Cabman who was waiting at our door, which has deeply impressed me. He led the conversation to the Sunday question, after telling me that he never plied on the Sabbath. I found there was a sore, even a bitter feeling against the religious people, who, by their use of cabs on Sunday, practically deny the Sabbath to the drivers. 'Even ministers do it, Ma'm,' he said, 'and I say it's a shame upon religion.' Then he told me of one of the London drivers who had driven a lady to church—as she stepped from the cab, she handed the driver a tract on the observance of the Sabbath. This naturally thoroughly disgusted the man. 'Now, Ma'am,' said my friend, 'I call that hypocrisy—don't you?' I suppose most of us agree with him, and yet it might not have been done hypocritically—so few Christians apparently realise the responsibility of taking a cab on Sunday. (pp. 178-79)

> *Anna Sewell, in an excerpt from* The Woman Who Wrote 'Black Beauty': A Life of Anna Sewell *by Susan Chitty, Hodder and Stoughton, 1971, pp. 178-79.*

MRS. TOYNBEE

[The following excerpt is taken from a letter written to Sewell's mother by Mrs. Toynbee on behalf of Edward Fordham Flower. The author of a number of pamplets on the humane treatment of horses, Flower was also considered an expert on the harness.]

January 29, 1878

Captain Toynbee and I went yesterday afternoon to see our friends the Flowers, in Hyde Park Gardens, and found Mr. Flower in a complete state of enthusiasm over ***Black Beauty.*** 'It is written by a veterinary surgeon,' he exclaimed; 'by a coachman, by a groom; there is not a mistake in the whole of it; not one thing I wish altered, except that the cabman should have taken that half-crown. I shall show Mr. Bright the passage about horses in war. I must make the lady's acquaintance; she must come to London sometimes. . . . He particularly wished me to say that he would like to write himself, but writing is troublesome to him, from the weakness of his hand. Are we right in supposing that the book is written (translated, by-the-by) by your daughter? Is it being actively circulated? That was a point Mr. Flower was very anxious about . . . Will you forgive so many questions, but Mr. Flower could talk of nothing else. Now and then, when the conversation strayed to the war, or anything else, he would exclaim, 'How could a lady know so much about horses?'

> *Mrs. Toynbee, in a letter to Mary Sewell on January 29, 1878, in* The Woman Who Wrote 'Black Beauty': A Life of Anna Sewell *by Susan Chitty, Hodder and Stoughton, 1971, p. 186.*

THE CRITIC, NEW YORK

Miss Sewell may not have a mind as powerful as that of the author of *Gulliver's Travels,* but ***Black Beauty: His Grooms and Companions*** will do vastly more than that incomparable satire to convince mankind of the stupidity of treating the horse as an infinitely inferior animal. The happy thought has occurred to her, not of making a plea for the horse, but of letting the horse make a plea for himself. And a still happier thought is that of robbing the plea of tediousness by making it dramatic. The little book . . . is the autobiography of a horse; and such is the author's skill in the art of narration, that the story is as readable as a novel—much *more* readable than the average novel of to-day. No wonder it has had so large a sale across the ocean. We should rejoice if its popularity in this country should prove to be even greater.

Black Beauty is the grandson of the winner of a famous race.

> The first place that I can well remember was a large pleasant meadow, with a pond of clear water in it. Some shady trees leaned over it, and rushes and water-lilies grew at the deep end. Over the hedge on one side we looked into a plowed field, and on the other we looked over a gate at our master's house, which stood by the roadside. At the top of the meadow was a grove of fir trees, and at the bottom a running brook overhung by a steep bank.

We call this an auspicious beginning; and we leave it to any imaginative reader whether he does not feel, in reading it, that he has seen that pleasant meadow through a horse's eyes. Till he is four years old, our autobiographer nibbles the grass at Farmer Grey's. Before half that time has passed, he has seen a man's neck broken and a horse's legs (his own brother's, they proved to be) in jumping a brook at the hunt. Then the unpleasant experience of being broken in to harness and the saddle has to be gone through. To accustom him to the steam-cars, he is turned into a meadow skirted by a railway, where some sheep and cows are feeding. A week or two of this, and he minds the noise and smoke as little as do the cows and sheep. 'Thanks to my good master's care, I am as fearless at railway stations as in my own stable.' As a four-year-old, Black Beauty is sold to Squire Gordon, whose son was the hapless youth that met his death while riding Black Beauty's brother.

At Birtwick Hall, Beauty's *entourage* consists of the Squire and his wife, their daughters Flora and Jessie ('Miss Flora' and 'Miss Jessie,' the autobiographer never fails to call them), John Manly the coachman, James Howard the stable-boy, Ginger the mare, Merrylegs the pony, the old brown hunter Sir Oliver, and Justice the roan cob. These various characters—the occupants of the stable being quite as distinctly individualized as the dwellers in the hall—run through a good part of the book; and if the reader fails to take a keen interest in them from the fact that they are described from the point of view of a horse, he should have his mind mended and his heart set in the right place before it is too late. When Mrs. Gordon's health fails and the household at Birtwick is broken up, Black Beauty and Ginger are sold to the Earl of W—— and sent off to Earlshall. Here their lot is less happy than when John Manly had them in charge: the coachman is well meaning, but Lady W —— has notions of stylishness that render her hateful to the team that has the honor to draw her carriage. Ginger is spoilt by hard riding, and Beauty has his knee's skinned by a drunken groom. We cannot follow the hero through all his changes of place and occupation; suffice it to say that he runs the whole range, from being my lady's carriage horse in the country, to serving at a cabstand in London (once with a good master, once with a bad). In this long experience, he discovers that it is not always the handsomest stable that makes the happiest home. Sometimes in his own person, sometimes in that of the other characters in the book, he lays down, informally, a complete body of rules by which men should be governed in their relations with dumb beasts, particularly horses.

And not only does one discover the whole duty of man in this connection, but the whole duty of horses is as plainly set forth. The tone of the tale is not namby-pamby: it is proved to demonstration that wise and considerate treatment of a horse yields the handsomest possible return in efficient service.

The sub-title of the book is *The "Uncle Tom's Cabin" of the Horse*. This may prejudice against it those who are weary of the changes that have been rung on a title excellent in itself but little capable of adjustment to other uses. But *Black Beauty* is a capital name, and will soon be a household word in this country. (pp. 305-06)

> A review of "Black Beauty," in The Critic, New York, n.s. Vol. XIII, No. 338, June 21, 1890, pp. 305-06.

GEORGE T. ANGELL

For more than twenty years this thought has been upon my mind.

Somebody must write a book which shall be as widely read as *Uncle Tom's Cabin,* and shall have as widespread and powerful influence in abolishing cruelty to horses, as *Uncle Tom's Cabin* had on the abolition of human slavery.

Many times, by letter and word of mouth, I have called the attention of American writers to this matter and asked them to undertake it.

At last the book has come to me; not from America, but from England, where already over ninety thousand copies have been sold.

It was written by a woman, Anna Sewell.

It is the autobiography of an English horse, telling of kind masters and cruel, of happiness and of suffering. I am glad to say that happiness predominates and finally triumphs.

I have read each of its two hundred and thirty-eight beautifully printed pages from its cheerful beginning to its happy end, and then called in the printers. (pp. 5-6)

I want to print immediately a hundred thousand copies.

I want the power to give away thousands of these to drivers of horses, and in public schools, and elsewhere.

I want to send a copy postpaid to the editors of each of about thirteen thousand American newspapers and magazines. (p. 6)

I would be glad, if I had the means, to put a copy of it in every home in America, for I am sure there has never been a book printed in any language, the reading of which will be more likely to inspire love and kind care for these dumb servants and friends who toil and die in our service. I hope to live long enough to print and distribute a million copies. (pp. 6-7)

> George T. Angell, in an introduction to Black Beauty: His Grooms and Companions by A. Sewell, American Humane Education Society, 1890, pp. 5-7.

THE BOOKMAN, LONDON

Black Beauty is a classic, and one which should be in the home of every child—and of every man who has dealings with horses. Children of several generations have given it their approval, and have been the better for reading it; for this autobiography of a horse does not appeal to the emotions by mere sentimentality: it is full of good sense, and a first-hand knowledge of horses and horse-nature.

> A review of "Black Beauty," in The Bookman, London, Vol. XLIII, No. 255, December, 1912, p. 134.

THE BOOKMAN, LONDON

That *Black Beauty* has taught people to understand and care for horses more than any book ever published is of course beyond doubt. . . . A book like this makes a universal appeal, and it matters not whether the reader is a girl, or boy, or grown-up man or woman; the truth and sincerity of the tale grips and holds the imagination. Those who love horses must ever bless the name of Miss Sewell for the wonderful work she has done for them. (pp. 51-2)

> A review of "Black Beauty," in The Bookman, London, Vol. LXII, No. 367, Spring, 1922, pp. 51-2.

VINCENT STARRETT

Centenary celebrations are posterity's tributes to the favored children of fame; sometimes they are tardy acknowledgements to genius. Too often does genius sup late, and sometimes it does not sup at all. One wonders whether, on the thirtieth day of March, 1920, in all the world there was a single thought of Anna Sewell. Certainly no celebration marked the day. Despite the unique popularity of her single book, there seems never to have been much interest in Miss Sewell as a person. Yet it has been asserted that since the invention of printing, than *Black Beauty* only the Bible has found a wider distribution; and it is certain that more than any other single agency this humane classic has improved the lot of the captive horse. The book has lived; the author has been forgotten.

Anna Sewell died in pain within a year of the success of her first and only volume. The story of her life explains the deep humanity of *Black Beauty*. Few lives perhaps have been less eventful in their worldly aspects than that of the crippled Quaker girl; yet it was a life freighted with great emotional crises, spiritual distresses, and physical pain. (p. 205)

[The first mention of *Black Beauty* occurs in Anna Sewell's] journal under date of November 6, 1871: "I am writing the life of a horse, and getting dolls and boxes ready for Christmas." There is no further entry on the subject until December 6, 1876; then: "I am getting on with my little book, *Black Beauty*." The next is dated August 21, 1877, and reads: "My first proofs of *Black Beauty* are come—very nice type."

There is an appealing modesty about this record; and it is a poignant thought that this "beautiful equine drama" was almost entirely thought out of the sofa where so much suffering daily was endured. When she was capable of supporting the fatigue of writing, the work was done with a pencil, and Mrs. Sewell, sitting beside her, received the paper from the tired hand and made a fair copy of it. (p. 217)

What was the germ of *Black Beauty*? It appears to have been Horace Bushnell's *Essay on Animals*, quoted to Anna by a friend, Mrs. Bayly. This is Mrs. Bayly's account of the incident:

> It was in the summer of 1862 that I first met Mrs. Sewell, at the home of her old friend Mrs. Ellis, at Hoddesdon. In the following summer I had the great pleasure of paying her a short visit at Blue Lodge, Wick.
>
> (pp. 218-19)

> The parting came all too soon. In the afternoon it poured with rain. When the carriage that was to take me to the station came to the door, Anna was standing in the hall, enveloped in a large mackintosh. The future writer of *Black Beauty* was to be my driver. I

found that she and her mother were in the habit of driving out on most days, without attendance, the understanding between themselves and their horse being perfect. The persistent rain obliged us to keep up our umbrellas. Anna seemed simply to hold the reins in her hand, trusting to her voice to give all needed directions to her horse. She evidently believed in a horse having a moral nature, if we may judge by her mode of remonstrance. 'Now thee shouldn't walk up this hill—don't thee see how it rains?' 'Now thee must go a little faster—thee would be sorry for us to be late at the station.'

I think it was during this drive that I told Anna of something Horace Bushnell had written about animals. Soon after the publication of *Black Beauty* I had a little note from her, written from her sofa, in which she says:

'The thoughts you gave me from Horace Bushnell years ago have followed me entirely though the writing of my book, and have, more than anything else, helped me to feel it was worth a great effort to *try*, at least, to bring the thoughts of men in harmony with the purposes of God on this subject.'

During the year 1876, Anna was sometimes able to dictate passages of *Black Beauty,* and the story was completed late in 1877. . . . The book was published near the end of the year 1877, and Anna lived just long enough to hear of its remarkable success. Almost at once it rushed into a popularity undreamed-of by its author. The joy of the success of her book was almost too much for Anna's delicate frame, but the devoted mother rejoiced and collected the reviews of *Black Beauty* with a happiness greater than she had found in this phase of her own writing life. The work was virtually a gift to the world. (pp. 219-21)

In the history of humane literature the book holds a place unique; in the history of all literature it maintains its position as an authentic classic, not alone for children but for their parents. (pp. 221-22)

It is no small thing to have written *Black Beauty,* a book whose missionary achievements in its own field it is impossible to measure. It is unquestionably the most successful animal story ever written; and it would seem that its author should be something more than a name in the card-index of a library. (p. 222)

Vincent Starrett, " 'Black Beauty' and Its Author,"
in his Buried Caesars: Essays in Literary Appreciation, *Covici-McGee Co., 1923, pp. 205-23.*

ALMA B. CALDWELL

What a treat is before the reader who is taking up this volume, whether it be for the first time or for the oft-repeated reading! It will bring forth many an appreciative thought for creatures in the animal world as well as create more sympathy for fellow creatures. . . .

If an animal could be gifted with powers of speech such as those attributed to Black Beauty, he could hardly make a more convincing appeal for kindness at the hands of his human masters. (p. ix)

Black Beauty's introduction is skilfully handled through his own story of himself as a colt. . . . Note how the suggestion was made as to why he should not kick or bite—because he was well-bred. (p. x)

The most inspiring part of this story is found "between the lines," where we read of the effort of this horse to maintain

a high standard of service when even though because of various hard experiences he found himself "going downhill" as to his prowess.

When instead of the gallant showy service he enjoyed while young he found himself obliged to perform menial tasks, he tried to keep his courage intact. Much was demanded of him, and his story of how he met these demands is an inspiration to human beings. The reader will rejoice in the account of the good home with which Black Beauty closes his story.

The story will never grow old. No speed story of plane or motor can rival the appeal to the best in human nature which prompts kindness to all dependents and subordinates, whether man or beast. No machine can give the satisfactory intelligent response to kind treatment that Black Beauty returned to associates, whether human or animal. Nor can a lifeless mechanical device create the sympathy and companionship which nearly every human being feels for the horse and the dog.

Many children who live in cities have little or no knowledge of horses or other animals. This story provides them worthwhile information along these lines. (pp. xi-xii)

Alma B. Caldwell, in an introduction to Black Beauty:
The Autobiography of a Horse *by Anna Sewell, The John C. Winston Company, 1927, pp. ix-xii.*

JOHN BIRKS

Anna Sewell's classic story is almost as popular now as it was seventy years ago when it first appeared. To me it reads like a product earlier still. It is smug and sentimental, but it has those qualities that give permanence to books. It is deeply sincere and shows the author's complete absorption in a subject she knows intimately. It is written in a starkly simple style; it preaches a series of little sermons, including one on the evils of alcoholic intemperance. But it is only fair to remember when reading it that it was written before the coming of the motor-car, a time when horses were the common motive power in all forms of transport, and all the cruelty carelessness and thoughtlessness against which the story inveighs were only too common. *Black Beauty* is a crusading book, but Anna Sewell was a gentle soul and she uses her whip much more gently than did many of the people she chastises on their overworked and broken-spirited drudges.

I have read *Black Beauty* many times and it still holds my interest even while it irritates me by its many virtues. Children will continue to enjoy it so long as there are horses to be seen in use in the service of man. They will weep over it and will be none the worse for that. (p. 170)

John Birks, "Horses in Books," in The Junior Bookshelf, *Vol. 10, No. 4, December, 1946, pp. 166-72.*

COLEMAN O. PARSONS

Nearly two centuries of humanitarian arguments, narratives, pleas, laws and organised work created the atmosphere which sustained Anna Sewell in the writing and dictating of *Black Beauty* between 1871 and 1877. But the most distinct single influence on her work was, I believe, George MacDonald's *At the Back of the North Wind.* . . .

MacDonald's story of a boy and a horse was serialized in twenty issues of the juvenile magazine, *Good Words for the Young,* between 1 Nov. 1868 and 1 Oct. 1870, and was published as a book in 1871. The plot may be reduced to a simple form: Mr. Coleman of The Wilderness, Chiswick, London, had a coachman, Joseph, who named his son Diamond after a fa-

Anna and Mary Sewell.

vourite horse, old Diamond. "God's baby" slept in the stable hayloft, where the North Wind visited him in the figure of a lady and bore him far away to the back of the North Wind, where he found peace and calm insight. When Mr. Coleman failed because of dishonesty, he sold old Diamond and discharged Joseph. After being out of work for some time, Joseph bought old Diamond off cab-master John Stonecrop and began hacking in London. Driving for a fortnight when his father was sick, young Diamond reunited Mr. Evans and Miss Coleman and was a wingless baby angel to a drunken cabman. The juvenile cabby picked up good Mr. Raymond, who later helped the boy's crossing-sweeper friend, Nanny. After testing Joseph's integrity by leaving a horse, Ruby, in his charge, Mr. Raymond took Joseph and his wife Martha, their three children, and Nanny and her lame friend Jim to his Kentish home, The Mound. There the author met little Diamond, who died peacefully one night, and went to the back of the North Wind.

In the equine part of the story, we have the pattern of willing service, decline in status, pathetically hard work, and rehabilitation of a horse whose name, Diamond, was suggested by "a white lozenge on his forehead." Although MacDonald, as far as I remember, does not mention old Diamond's colour, the first illustrator, Arthur Hughes, makes him black in *Good Words for the Young*, 1 Aug. 1870. Black Beauty's self-portrait is: "My coat . . . was bright black. I had one white foot, and a pretty white star on my forehead." (p. 156)

The parallels between *At the Back of the North Wind* and *Black Beauty* are fairly abundant. The horses think and speak. Whereas MacDonald is not absolutely certain of Diamond's mental processes, "for it is very difficult to find out what any old horse

is thinking," Anna Sewell shows no such diffidence. Yet even the cautious George MacDonald has young Diamond, perhaps walking in his sleep, overhear a conversation between old Diamond and Ruby, "in a strange language, which yet, somehow or other, he could understand, and turn over in his mind in English."

The general plot-development is the same. Both old Diamond and Black Beauty were thrust from their particular paradises of good treatment and moderate work through no fault of their own, the latter through the invalidism of Mrs. Gordon. Coachman and cabman are the same person in MacDonald; John Manly and Jerry Barker are different persons in Sewell, who points out their resemblances in more than one comparison. Both Joseph and Jerry fell sick from overwork and exposure. A benevolent patron rescued Joseph and old Diamond from their London bondage and made little Diamond his page. The Barkers were employed at last by Mrs. Fowler, Polly Barker's former mistress and one of Jerry's London fares; their son Harry became the good lady's page boy. As for Black Beauty, his salvation from killing toil had to be deferred in order that Miss Sewell might round out her narrative sermon on the proper and improper management of horses. When he had repeatedly proved himself a good and faithful, though much abused, servant, Black Beauty was sold by a kindly farmer to three maiden ladies, none other than the Blomefields, former playmates of the Gordon sisters. Their groom was Joe Green, whom Squire Gordon had employed as a boy. Thus known friends saved both horses from the final degradation portrayed by other writers and suggested by the title of Miss Sewell's twenty-seventh chapter, "Ruined, and Going Down-Hill."

Both authors moralize on the harm done to grooms and cabmen by drink. MacDonald presents only one ill-treater of horses, "the drunken cabman," who "put a stinging lash on his whip" and let his uncomplaining nag dwindle to "skin and bone." Here the blame rests on beer and a weak will, rather than on natural viciousness. Joseph recommended cold water, tea and coffee against the "thirsty devil" who induced the drunken cabman to strike his wife and almost starve his baby. Fortunately, young Diamond started a reformation in the drunkard's character. In ***Black Beauty*** Seedy Sam, the Governor, and other cabmen are subjects of the "drink devil." Jerry Barker was freed from the craving ten years earlier by good food, coffee, peppermint, and regard for his wife Polly. Black Beauty's friend, the ex-cavalry horse, Captain, was shot after being run down by a drunken drayman who had lost control of his horses. And most disastrously of all, the Earl of W——'s drunken groom, Reuben Smith, galloped Black Beauty over a dark, stony road when the animal had a loose shoe. The inevitable fall cost Reuben his life; his wife Susan and their six children went to the Union House; and Black Beauty, blemished for life by cut knees, was sold to the owner of livery stables in Bath.

In discussing anti-saloon sentiment, I must digress to mention the authoress's literarily prolific mother, Mrs. Mary Sewell, whose 'Homely Ballads for the Working Man's Fireside' (1858) includes 'The Drunkard's Wife':

> Then came a shadow o'er my life—
>   My husband took to drink;
> And lower down, and lower still,
>   My heart began to sink.

(p. 157)

In poetry and prose, Mrs. Sewell tempered a mass of didacticism with a modicum of reality, concentrating on sociologically typical cases; her daughter, in contrast, subordinated her message or warning to the demands of realism. I see little reason to suppose that Mrs. Sewell had any marked literary influence on her far more gifted daughter. If the example of the older woman's long activity was effective, it is rather strange that Anna Sewell waited until she was 51 years old—until her mother had been writing some forty years—to respond to that stimulus.

But to return to MacDonald's influence on Anna Sewell. Old Diamond's cab labours, with the London adventures of his namesake, fill up half of the narrative, *At the Back of the North Wind,* and Black Beauty's career as a cab horse makes up nearly a third of the later book. (pp. 157-58)

MacDonald's protest against the 6d. a mile legally fixed fare to which Joseph was held and his humane understanding that both cabmen and horses were victims of an economic wrong reappear in Anna Sewell's pages. In the chapters of *Black Beauty* that do not deal with cabbing, the authoress finds men and boys either good or bad in their treatment of horses. The exception, good Joe Green, through boyish ignorance gave Black Beauty cold water to drink when overheated and did not put a blanket on his back. A more complex and mature interpretation of injustice and final responsibility appears in the London passages. Seedy Sam had to pay Nicholas Skinner 18s. a day rental for a cab and two horses. He himself worked fourteen to sixteen hours a day at a pinching 6d. a mile, hardly ever got a Sunday off, and died at the age of 45, leaving a wife and children penniless. As Seedy Sam remarked, "It is hard lines for man, and it is hard lines for beast, and who's to mend it I don't know." Both MacDonald and Anna Sewell used the horse as a touchstone of human worth; coincidentally, in 1877, the year *Black Beauty* was published, the Scotch author introduced the demonic black mare, Kelpie, in *The Marquis of Lossie* as a test of integrity or duplicity.

Parallels, however, should not make a reader lose sight of differences. MacDonald emphasised good treatment of horses and concentrated chiefly on his human characters and his fantasy; Anna Sewell stressed ill-treatment, while introducing much material on sensible handling as exemplary instruction to bad grooms and owners, and she ranged much more widely in her special humanitarian field. Beyond the fact that old Diamond's somewhat mystical companion, Ruby, is a chestnut in colour, he bears no resemblance to Black Beauty's friend, Ginger, who performs a very special function in the novel. Whereas Black Beauty shows the effects on disposition of a gentle breaking-in and kind management, Ginger illustrates the proposition that horses are not born bad but are tragically made so by man: "I never had any one, horse or man, that was kind to me, or that I cared to please." No wonder that Ginger developed the vices of biting and snapping! After tempestuous protest against the bearing-rein, Ginger was turned over to the Earl of W——'s son, Lord George, whose hard riding touched her wind and strained her back. Sold and resold, poor Ginger died a cab horse and was carted off—probably to the London knacker's yard, where some four to five hundred horses were being reduced to commercial hides, hoofs for glue, and dogs' meat every week.

Besides her attack on the bearing-rein (to be discussed later), Miss Sewell exceeded MacDonald's scope in her objections to damp bedding, a cause of thrush; to inadequate lighting of stables, a cause of blindness; to docking of tails; to the use of blinkers, painful bits, and tight harness; to the theft of oats by grooms, the flogging of cart-horses, and the clumsy driving of

job or hired horses; to ploughboys' throwing stones at colts and boys' playing recklessly with ponies; to hunters' spoiling horses by hard riding and dangerous jumping; to cabmen's speeding for extra fares and driving seven days a week; and to many other abuses. (p. 158)

• • • • •

At the end of her life, Anna Sewell, whose birth preceded that of the R.S.P.C.A. [Royal Society for the Prevention of Cruelty to Animals] by four years, gathered together in *Black Beauty,* more often unconsciously than consciously, the quintessential details of humane literature and sentiment. She was both heir and spokesman of the growth, spread, and increased articulateness of English humanitarian attitudes towards the horse. One example of her relations to past and present may be developed at some length.

Miss Sewell's most eloquent propagandic work has been considered that against the use of the bearing-rein, which ran from the harness pad to the bit (or to its own separate bit) and gave an artifically beautiful lift and arch to the horse's head and neck. . . . One of the early attacks on the rein was *Observations on the Effect of the Fixed Bridle or Bearing-Rein, and a Few Words for the English Post-Horse* (1841), printed for the R.S.P.C.A. The pamphleteer protests against any use whatsoever of the bearing rein, as it produces "roaring" in the horse, "souring his temper, making him jib, deadening his mouth, wasting his strength, hurting his wind, injuring his sight, lessening his speed, abridging his services, shortening his days, throwing him down, and breaking his knees." (p. 230)

Anna Sewell's opposition to the bearing-rein was similarly all-inclusive (see particularly Chapters 8, 11, 22-3, and 46). She characterizes Black Beauty's first two owners, Farmer Grey and Squire Gordon, as crusaders against its use for over twenty years. But the wife of Black Beauty's third owner, the "tall, proud-looking" Countess of W —— fully illustrates the evils of fashion when followed instead of common sense. She insisted on having "those horses' heads [put] higher, they are not fit to be seen." The rein and extra bit, resulting in a bleeding tongue, aching neck, and constricted windpipe, had earlier ruined Ginger's mouth and temper and forced both "vices" and punishment on her. The chestnut mare again rebelled and was dismissed from carriage work, and her team mate, Black Beauty, remained to undergo more torment. But the blame is not always with the lady. Mrs. Gordon did missionary work, as did an unnamed London lady who persuaded carter Jakes to take off Black Beauty's bearing-rein at the bottom of a hill: "Is it not better to lead a good fashion, than to follow a bad one?"

That the humanitarians did not have an easy time of it is indicated by the Rev. John George Wood's *Horse and Man: Their Mutual Dependence and Duties* (1885). Two of the chapters are devoted to proving that the bearing-rein accomplishes just the opposite of improving the appearance of the horse, saving him from stumbling or falling, and preventing him from running away. Of course, the debate has flourished for years, but the entry in Margaret Cabell Self's *The Horseman's Encyclopedia* (1946), under the American term, *checkreins,* seems to prove that Youatt's position is central: "Properly adjusted they do not worry the horse and do prevent vices such as kicking, boring, bolting, etc."

The thoroughness of Anna Sewell's narrative discourse on the bearing-rein should make a reader wonder whether *Black Beauty* was written out of experience and observation alone, or whether well digested learning also contributed. It has been assumed that the authoress depended on first-hand knowledge. Enough is known about Anna Sewell's life to yield the fact that, in the healthier stretches of her invalidism, she rode and drove a pony. The essentially first-hand passages in *Black Beauty* therefore, may be those about Jessie and Flora Gordon's "little fat grey pony," Merrylegs. Indeed it is in these passages that more ordinary, less technical, material appears. The book starts and ends on happier, more familiar detail, events connected with kindly owners, Farmer Grey and Squire Gordon. Farmer Thoroughgood and the Misses Blomefield. The central portion of the book, Black Beauty's unhappy adventures at Earlshall, in Bath as a job horse, and in London as a cab horse under good Jerry Barker and bad Nicholas Skinner and as a baker's cart horse, relies, I believe, on some observation, imagination, facts gained from conversations, inspiration drawn from George MacDonald, and the reading of works on the horse.

In the same oversimplified fashion, Miss Sewell's humanitarianism has been explained as the insight of a sensitive Quaker nature given leisure for reflection by invalidism. But the humanity of *Black Beauty* is too definitely in the main stream of English thought on justice to animals—too much a narrative embodiment of this thought—to be of accidental and independent growth. The story was, in fact, the answer to a need expressed in the eighteenth century by William Upton and re-emphasized in the nineteenth by Sir Arthur Helps. (pp. 230-31)

The neglect of Black Beauty's humanitarian progenitors has been made easy by the impressive flood of editions of "the 'Uncle Tom's Cabin' of the horse"—of translations, dramatic adaptations, sequels, and narratives influenced by its autobiographical form. In content, *Black Beauty* is a highly effective synthesis of materials already available, with ethical mysticism and speculations about equine immortality omitted. Anna Sewell's originality is certainly not that of new materials, but rather of compelling fictional unity created out of confusing abundance. Her success invited a popular supplanting of the tradition out of which her masterpiece grew by the masterpiece itself. The final narrative expression of a movement of thought and feeling was, when itself imitated, mistakenly considered a great original, springing full bodied out of a vacuum.

In form, *Black Beauty* harks back to brief verse and prose life sketches from the lips of horses. Or Miss Sewell may consciously have been following in the footsteps of Thomas Smith, who represents Wily ("alone of my tribe . . . endowed with the power of . . . using" the quill pen) and nine other foxes as exchanging life stories one night: *The Life of a Fox Written by Himself* (1843). . . . The first to write a *full length*, first person horse story, Anna Sewell was followed by several writers who were probably acquainted with more than the title of *Black Beauty: the Autobiography of a Horse.* (pp. 231-32)

Miss Sewell's influence on the form of horse stories lasted longer than her influence on their content. When cruelty to horses had been largely checked by the work of humane societies and the sentiment of individuals, propagandic narratives on the subject became less and less functional. The two-century-old battle, waged by satirists, poets, preachers, horse experts, moralists, legislators, organizers, novelists, and writers of children's books, was at last won. With the increased use of bicycles and, afterwards, of automobiles, the horse was dissociated from everyday transportation, but he gained in strangeness and glamour through his identification with racing, circus, and cowboy life. Thus the horse, emancipated from cruelty, was given a somewhat exotic individuality of his own,

but he was not yet emancipated from servitude to man. Such a prospect of equine freedom would have been beyond the comprehension of Anna Sewell, who lived in the compact, populous, tamed island kingdom of Queen Victoria. (p. 232)

Coleman O. Parsons, "The Progenitors of 'Black Beauty' in Humanitarian Literature," in Notes and Queries, Vol. 192, Nos. 8 and 11, April 19 and May 31, 1947, pp.156-58; 230-32.

H. J. B. WOODFIELD

There is always a steady stream of books about horses written from various angles, unfortunately most often from the jodhpur, gymkhana, pony club angle. You might be inclined to be contemptuous of the old favourite *Black Beauty* because of what appears to be sickly sentimentality. But it is still read and enjoyed, nearly a hundred years after its first publication, by many thousands of young girls. The secret of its long life is that its author felt intensely about her subject and knew it intimately. She meant every word she wrote.

H. J. B. Woodfield, in a review of "Black Beauty," in The School Librarian and School Library Review, Vol. 4, No. 4, March, 1949, p. 169.

BULLETIN OF THE CHILDREN'S BOOK CENTER

[*The following excerpt is a review of the 1956 edition of* Black Beauty, *which was edited and abridged by Barbara Nolan.*]

Cut, re-written version of a story that has long since outlived its usefulness as a children's book. This account does nothing to correct the weaknesses of the original story and, in view of the innumerably good horse stories available for children today, has even less reason for being.

A review of "Black Beauty," in Bulletin of the Children's Book Center, Vol. X, No. 7, March, 1957, p. 96.

M. J. P. LAURENCE

[The] documentary story about animals, if I may so describe it, . . . sets out to give an accurate account of an animal in its habitat, but wraps it up in slight fictitious form, either by making the animal hero of its own story or by putting the story, as it were, in the mouth of the animal. These tales are favourite reading for Junior children. The classic of this kind is Anna Sewell's *Black Beauty,* still the favourite book of many a youngster, girls particularly. Old-fashioned in the way of life which it describes, horses being the chief means of ordinary transport, its matter-of-factness, its real love and observation of the horse, its straightforward morality, its use of anecdote and direct speech, make it unfailingly popular. (pp. 290-91)

M. J. P. Laurence, "Animals and 'Dressed Animals'," in The Junior Bookshelf, Vol. 21, No. 6, December, 1957, pp. 289-94.

NOEL STREATFEILD

Horses play an important part in the lives of most people in Britain. There are horse shows all over the country which families for miles around attend. Also, in London on the Monday after Whit Sunday there is a special show for working horses—those who draw the milk carts, brewers' drays, and the costers' barrows—just the type of horse in fact that in Anna Sewell's day so often was cruelly treated. Such horses now have no need of defenders, for they are cherished friends of their owners, and loved by the public. Recently when a mare unexpectedly foaled in a London street, people came running from every house carrying coats and rugs to keep the mother and child warm, until a horse ambulance arrived.

Horse riding, at one time exclusively an amusement of the rich, is now within the reach of all, for there are inexpensive riding clubs on the outskirts of most cities, and at horse shows the competitors come from every walk of life.

In this wonderful change in less than a hundred years *Black Beauty* has played a large part. The book is widely known, for not only is it in all children's libraries, but is a school reader. In fact so popular is it with British children that in many homes *Black Beauty* does not seem a fictional character, but as much part of the family as their pet cat or dog. Wouldn't Anna Sewell be pleased? (p. v)

> *Noel Streatfeild, in an introduction to* Black Beauty *by Anna Sewell, Franklin Watts, Inc., 1959, pp. iii-v.*

WILLIAM H. MAGEE

[*The following excerpt originally appeared in the Summer, 1964 issue of* The Dalhousie Review.]

The widespread use of animals in modern literature dates from the last quarter of the nineteenth century. In 1877 Anna Sewell began the vogue with *Black Beauty*. . . . Through her philanthropy Miss Sewell had hit on a purpose for her story which distinguishes animal characters from man, instead of stressing similarities. The artistic appeal for human readers is genuinely indirect, a good will based perhaps on the misery and cruelty suffered by all living creatures and caused by bad men. For the first time in literary history it was no longer desirable or even artistically sensible to draw manlike animals. Any failure to make the domestic animals credible on the part of Anna Sewell or her followers is the result only of failures in technique. (p. 223)

> *William H. Magee, "The Animal Story: A Challenge in Technique," in* Only Connect: Readings on Children's Literature, *Sheila Egoff, G. T. Stubbs, L. F. Ashley, eds., second edition, Oxford University Press, Canadian Branch, 1980, pp. 221-32.*

MAY HILL ARBUTHNOT

[*Black Beauty*] enjoyed tremendous popularity for many years. Some children wept over Beauty's sufferings and were never thereafter able to ride or drive a horse without being haunted by its probable agonies of mind or body. Only parents with a sense of humor could laugh and talk them out of Black Beauty vapors.

Black Beauty was written as a protest against the tight checkrein and other more serious cruelties to horses. It relates, in the first person, a good story of the ups and downs of a carriage horse. . . .

This story sounds all right, yet *Black Beauty* is rarely listed in careful bibliographies in spite of new and beautiful editions of it. One reason is that Black Beauty, while presumably a real horse, thinks and talks out of horse character. He is humanly sensitive to the social and moral tone of the people with whom he lives. His social judgments are those of a genteel lady, not a horse. He is ultraconservative about such habits as smoking, of which he heartily disapproves. Bad language, dirty clothes, and the smell of liquor offend his refined sensibilities—not as a horse, which might associate these things with cruel treatment, but as a perfect Victorian lady. Black Beauty is so full of human proprieties that he ceases to be convincing as a horse. The story is also morbidly sad, but it is the sentimentality and the overhumanizing of the species that make *Black Beauty* unconvincing as a horse story. (p. 401)

> *May Hill Arbuthnot, "Animal Stories," in her* Children and Books, *third edition, Scott, Foresman and Company, 1964, pp. 398-425.*

DOROTHY M. BRODERICK

My favorite candidate for nostalgia personified is *Black Beauty*. By any standards, it is a poor book; yet on it goes, and will probably continue to do so for another generation. Not much beyond that, though, because the days when such an embarrassment of maudlin sentiment could stir hearts are numbered. It is a book I would leave in the collection but would never recommend to any reader either directly or by putting it on lists. For the horse story readers of today, Marguerite Henry is a better author; and if the horse fans can be brought to the stage where they can read Will James's *Smoky*, we need not fear for their future growth as readers. (pp. 142-43)

> *Dorothy M. Broderick, in a review of "Black Beauty," in her* An Introduction to Children's Work in Public Libraries, *The H. W. Wilson Company, 1965, pp. 142-43.*

FRANCES CLARKE SAYERS

Genuine emotion on the part of an author quickens the interest of children in their reading. They will sniff it out, like hounds following a scent, and they will gladly range through endless brambles and briars of sickly sentimentalism in search of it.

Reading *Black Beauty* as an adult, one can hardly stomach the tale, but for many children it remains to this day among the best of the horse stories, because the author, Anna Sewell, wrote out of genuine feeling for animals, and with a zeal to better their treatment at the hands of humans.

Recently, in a class of teachers engaged in the reappraisal of books for children, a young man who confessed to having loved *Black Beauty* as a boy denounced the book to the class in the light of his mature judgment. "Of all the sentimental Victorian tear-jerkers, this is the worst," he said, "and what we mean by giving children such drivel, I'll never know."

The class went wild, some of them welcoming this break with tradition, and others acting as though the young man were dangerously subversive. The argument was ended for all time when one member of the class rose and declared simply, "What he say as is true, but the fact remains that when you read *Black Beauty* you feel like a horse."

The intensity of feeling and the absolute sincerity of the author—to these elements *Black Beauty* owes its long life. Children know, in eerie ways of their own, the genuine attitude from the assumed, and they will endure the dated, the old-fashioned, and the wordy if the intent is clear and the emotion has its own integrity. (pp. 159-60)

> *Frances Clarke Sayers, "Books That Enchant: What Makes a Classic?" in her* Summoned by Books, *edited by Marjeanne Jensen Blinn, The Viking Press, 1965, pp.152-61.*

SUSAN CHITTY

Inevitably one seeks, in Anna Sewell's life, the originals of the characters, places and events in her book, and for Black Beauty himself one does not have to seek far. [Anna's sister-in-law] Margaret Sewell never doubted that he was simply [her husband] Philip's Bessie after a change of sex. Even the names

The White House, Old Catton, Norwich, where Sewell wrote Black Beauty.

of the two horses are similar, for Bessie's full name was probably Black Bess, like Dick Turpin's famous mare.

The Sewell family used to tell many tales of Bessie's wisdom and foresight and one feels the incident of the flooded bridge in *Black Beauty* must almost certainly have been based on an event in her life. (p. 197)

In one respect, however, Bessie did not resemble her fictional self. She was a restless horse and would never have suffered the long hours on the cab-stand that Black Beauty did. She had a strong sense of propriety and would not allow social calls to last beyond the prescribed fifteen minutes. When she brought Anna's nieces to see her they would put their heads out of the window and plead with her to wait an extra five minutes, but Philip found it hard to hold her and the carriage was usually moving away down the road before the last one had climbed in, laughing and protesting. In the book Bessie's restlessness was transferred to Ginger.

The original of Merrylegs is also not hard to find. I am assured by Miss Lee Warner that her mother learnt to ride on this pony, lent to her by Anna when she became too ill to drive, and that he was the fat grey pony that took such an objection to the Norwich cobbles. Certainly it would have been very like Merrylegs to know better than his driver what was good for her. It will be recalled that he always knew what was best for his rider and used to end riding lessons by gently tipping his rider off backwards. 'Boys,' he explained, 'must be broken in as we are broken in as colts.' (pp. 197-98)

The original of Ginger is not known and it seems unlikely that Anna would have owned such a vicious animal. A mare she was much more likely to have driven was Peggy, the short-paced cob at the livery stable in Bath. Although not well-bred, 'she was a strong, well-made animal, of a bright dun colour, beautifully dappled, and with a dark brown mane and tail'. . . . Peggy's story ended happily for she was sold to two ladies living in Bath who drove themselves and wanted a good safe horse. These two ladies can surely have been none other than Anna and Mary Sewell.

Anna herself crops up several times in the course of the book. She makes her first appearance, one feels sure, as Jerry Bar-

ker's eight-year-old daughter, Dolly. Indeed Dolly and her brother Harry bear a strong resemblance to Anna and Philip as they were at Palatine Cottage, when they helped their parents with the running of the little farm. (pp. 198-99)

As an adult, Anna first appears in a somewhat idealised guise as Lady Anne, the daughter of the Earl of W—who was so romantically run away with by the skittish mare Lizzie and was rescued by young Colonel Blantyre on Black Beauty. 'She was a perfect horsewoman, and as gay and gentle as she was beautiful.' It was true that she had 'followed the hounds a great many times', but she also had a heart that could be touched by suffering. One of the labourers who came to her aid after her horse fell said, 'I'd risk my neck for the Lady Anne; she was uncommon good to my wife in the winter.'

Anna was also almost certainly Miss Ellen, the youngest of the three Miss Blomefields, a good and fearless driver with dark eyes and a merry face. But she makes her longest appearance in the chapter entitled 'Jakes and the Lady'. Jakes, it will be recalled, was the cruel carter who overloaded Black Beauty and drove him in bearing-rein. (p. 199)

It must be admitted that this portrait, like that of the Lady Anne, shows Anna as she would have liked to be, rather than as she was. In reality, as Margaret Sewell pointed out, the sight of cruelty drove her to such a frenzy that she was incapable of restraint. Like her mother, however, she would have preferred to have the self-mastery to address wrong-doers gently. (p. 200)

Black Beauty tells us a great deal about Anna Sewell's attitude to life. From it we can discover what were the real thoughts of this silent woman, who at times, seemed little more than the shadow of her mother. As one reads about Anna Sewell one finds oneself constantly asking the question, did she share Mary's philosophy of life or was she secretly a rebel? A careful reading of ***Black Beauty*** proves that she was not a rebel. Indeed, the book is a final proof of Mary's domination over Anna, for in it the daughter's view of life is seen to be a faithful reflection of the mother's.

Anna's attitude to the social structure was feudal. She believed in the good old days when everyone knew his place; the rich man's being in his castle and the poor man's at his gate. Although she was sympathetic to the sufferings of working men, she would have no truck with Socialism and indeed she had little use for any political party, as she stated clearly enough in a conversation between Jerry Barker and his son in a chapter headed 'The Election'. (p. 206)

Squire Gordon's family at Birtwick Park represented her ideal society in miniature. At the head of it was the master, Squire Gordon himself. Below him were the servants, John Manly, James Howard and little Joe Green. And below them were the horses. Just as it was the duty of the horses to serve the men, so it was the duty of the men to serve their masters.

This similarity between the position of servants and horses becomes more obvious still when we compare *Patience Hart*, Mary Sewell's autobiography of a kitchen-maid, with Anna Sewell's autobiography of a horse. It is true that Patience herself never descended the ladder of service in the way that Black Beauty did. On the other hand, the life history of her fellow servant, Honour Green, closely resembled that of the horse. Like Black Beauty, Honour was raised in a simple but happy country home, lost a good place through no fault of her own and descended to the lowest kind of work as a general servant in a boarding house. Here her final collapse occurred, and even this resembled that of Black Beauty for, while he fell pulling a load up Ludgate Hill, she fell while carrying a tray up a flight of stairs. After a period in hospital she, like Black Beauty, was rescued by a kindly old person and ended in a good home.

There are other characters in *Patience Hart* who have equivalents in **Black Beauty**. Abigail, the flighty house-maid who picks up bad habits in youth and lives to rue them, is a forerunner of Ginger, while Mrs. Trubody, the cook who is so given to quoting from the Good Book, is obviously a close relative of John Manly. The advice given to young horses in **Black Beauty** echoes that given to young servants in *Patience Hart*. 'Lift up your feet when you trot and never kick or bite,' says Black Beauty's mother to him when they part. 'Be sure to do *well* whatever you do; and remember servants must not have tempers,' says Mrs. Trubody to Patience.

But if Anna and her mother considered that servants should obey their masters as horses do, they also considered that masters had responsibilities. It was their duty to care for those beneath them, even at inconvenience to themselves. Squire Gordon walked to church on Sunday so that his servants could also attend a place of worship, and he took on John Manly as 'a raw boy from the plough tail', to save him from the workhouse.

Grooms equally had responsibilities for their horses. Indeed, Anna regarded the prevention of suffering as the duty of every human being and had no patience with those who pass by on the other side. (pp. 206-07)

Not only did Anna Sewell believe in a strict social hierarchy in human society. She believed in a parallel one in horse society. Black Beauty himself was an aristocrat, as his mother, named, appropriately enough, Duchess, was quick to inform him.

> I wish you to pay attention to what I am going to say to you. The colts who live here are very good colts, but they are cart horse colts, and of course they have not learned manners. You have been well-bred and well-born; your father has a great name in these parts, and your grandfather won the cup two years running at the Newmarket races.

Many of Black Beauty's associates were also out of the top drawer. Captain, Jerry Barker's grey horse, was the equine equivalent of a retired army officer, 'a high-bred, fine-mannered, noble old horse every inch of him'. Peggy at the livery stables, on the other hand, was but a common creature. 'There was no high breeding about her, but she was very pretty and remarkably sweet tempered and willing.'

Black Beauty himself descended the social scale as his misfortunes increased. . . . Yet, even when to all intents and purposes he was a broken-down screw, he was still a gentleman at heart, as Farmer Thoroughgood quickly saw. 'He might have been anything when he was young; look at his nostrils and ears, the shape of his neck and shoulders; there's a deal of breeding about that horse.'

Anna was opposed to the Industrial Revolution and the new era of technology. This was natural in one so attached to the established social order and the ideal of paternalism. Like her mother she deplored the severing of the old ties of master to man which followed upon the herding of the working classes into the manufacturing towns. Towns in **Black Beauty** were always symbols of evil. All his good masters lived in the country with one exception, Jerry Barker, and even he had finally to be transported to the heaven of a country home, for

he was too good for the city. We are given one glimpse of him in his natural setting when he takes Dinah Brown to visit her sick mother in the country. 'Jerry seemed to be quite as happy as I was. He sat down by a bank under a shady tree, and listened to the birds, then he sang to himself, and read out of the little brown book he is so fond of.'

Ironically the two men in the Sewell family were actively engaged in bringing about the very revolution that the women so deplored and whose harmful effects they attempted to remedy. Isaac, as a banker, no doubt financed many of the schemes that changed the face of England, and Philip was a builder of railways. Railways indeed play a part in the story of Black Beauty, but it is a sinister one. To Black Beauty as a foal, the train that ran along the bottom of his field was a thing of ill omen and sure enough it was the 'black frightful thing' that carried away his kind master and mistress.

Besides towns and railways, there was a third product of the Industrial Revolution to which Anna, like the ladies of Cranford, took great exception, and that was the class of persons she described as Cockneys. Black Beauty came in contact with many of these people when he was working as a job horse in Bath. They were usually people from towns who had never had a horse of their own. (pp. 208-09)

Anna's dislike of Cockneys spread to people of all classes whose chief concern was show, be they earls or stable-boys. She did not disguise her disapproval of the Countess of W— who insisted on the bearing-rein, and the chapter of Mr. Barry's groom, Alfred Smirk, was appropriately entitled 'A Humbug'.

> If ever there was a humbug in the shape of a groom Alfred Smirk was the man. He was very civil to me, and never used me ill; in fact, he did a great deal of stroking and patting when his master was there to see it. He always brushed my mane and tail with water and hoofs with oil before he brought me to the door, to make me look smart; but as to cleaning my feet or looking to my shoes, or grooming me thoroughly, he thought no more of that than if I had been a cow.

For Anna, as for her mother, the ideal society was still the one portrayed by their favourite schoolroom author Maria Edgeworth in the story *Simple Susan*. For them, as for Miss Edgeworth, the good characters were Squire Somers up at the big house and Farmer Price, his humble and grateful tenant. The villain was the get-rich-quick lawyer, Case.

Of the social vices of her day alcoholism was the one that Anna, like Mary, most deplored. Strong liquor was the cause of Black Beauty's undoing. ''It was all that cursed drink; why will they sell that cursed drink?'' sobbed Reuben's widow when her husband's dead body was brought to her. (pp. 210-11)

Another social evil that Anna in particular felt very strongly about was the seven-day week. It is true that Mary also considered Sunday work wrong for both men and horses. . . . Nevertheless, she never made the point as emphatically as Anna. Jerry Barker would never ply on a Sunday and lost his best customer by refusing to drive her to church. Mrs. Briggs paid down 'fair and honourable, like a lady . . . no beating down or making three hours into two hours and a half as some folks do'. But, as Jerry explained to her husband, 'I had a seven-days' license once, and the work was too hard for me, and too hard for my horses. Year in and year out, not a day's rest, and never a Sunday with my wife and children; and never able to go out to a place of worship, which I had always been used to do before I took to the driving box.' (pp. 211-12)

Jerry felt so strongly on the matter that he actually suggested a strike. '''If you Sunday drivers would all strike for a day of rest,'' he said, ''the thing would be done.''' Such a shocking suggestion would never have come from the pen of Mary Sewell. She never considered that strikes were justified. On this point at least the daughter's views diverged from the mother's. (p. 213)

Like *Gulliver's Travels* and *Robinson Crusoe*, **Black Beauty** was not originally intended for children. It was aimed at precisely the section of the public that Mary Sewell wrote for, the simple working folk, for it was these who were in daily contact with horses. . . . The account of Black Beauty's breaking-in by Farmer Grey is particularly full and accurate. (p. 214)

The most technical section of the book is Part II which covers Black Beauty's period at Bath. In the chapters devoted to his experiences as a job horse Anna Sewell went into some detail about the different styles of driving and deplored equally those who drive with too tight a rein under the impression that it is their duty to hold the horse up, and those who drive with too loose a rein. Her castigation of 'loose rein drivers' suggests that Mrs. Bayly's picture of Anna herself driving with the reins resting on her horse's back was not entirely accurate. She considered that a horse 'likes to feel the rein a little in going downhill . . . and to know that his driver is not gone to sleep'. Nor did she approve of lazy habits in a horse. 'Squire Gordon always kept us to our best paces and our best manners. He said that spoiling a horse and letting him get into bad habits was just as cruel as spoiling a child and both had to suffer for it afterward.'

A hazard to which a loose-rein driver's horse was exposed was that of travelling several miles with an undetected stone wedged in his hoof. Victorian roads did not have the smooth surfaces we are familiar with today. When newly made up they were often covered with loose chippings of the sort that caused Black Beauty's fatal fall with Reuben Smith. There were regulations about the maximum size of these chippings but, as Anna's admirer Mr. Flower pointed out in his book, *Macadam versus Vestries,* these regulations were often ignored. (pp. 215-16)

In the chapters devoted to Black Beauty's life as the hack of Mr. Barry, we are given an equally accurate account of faulty stable-management and some remarkably detailed diet sheets are given for horses under different circumstances. A cure for thrush is also given which involves packing the affected hoof with medicated wadding. In a previous chapter are included cures for pneumonia and broken knees.

Some might suppose that this detailed knowledge of horses was normal in an age of horses, for an age of horses the mid-Victorian era undoubtedly was. It is true that by 1845 the stage-coaches had gone but the trains that took their place had to be met by horse-drawn vehicles and the travelling public had never been so large. A woman who lived in this horse-drawn age, however, was no more expected to know about what went on in the stable than a modern woman is expected to know about what goes on under the bonnet of her car. Sweat and manure were not considered suitable subjects for ladies to discuss and even if a lady interested herself in horses she was certainly not expected to associate with grooms. Stablemen were considered the lowest of the low. . . . In creating the virtuous trio at Birtwick, John Manly, James Howard and Joe Green, Anna was breaking with tradition. The 'nice' girls today who can take

positions as grooms without loss of reputation may well have Anna Sewell to thank for the new image she gave to the stable yard. (pp. 216-17)

It has always been said that **Black Beauty** led to the abolition of the bearing-rein and this is essentially true. A contemporary admirer wrote, 'The testimony of those who mingle most among London drivers . . . has been that no society . . . has induced such humane treatment, as the influence and teaching gained by **Black Beauty**.' However, like all emphatic historical statements, it requires qualifying. Anna Sewell was neither the first nor the last campaigner in the field, although her appeal reached the largest and most impressionable section of the public. (p. 229)

Cases of cruelty through real neglect . . . are rare on both sides of the Atlantic and the few ill-used animals dwindle to insignificance beside the number of healthy, well-cared for ones. One likes to suppose that these owe something of their well-being to a book that taught their owners to turn pale at the sight of a stall without water or a groom entering a stable with a lighted cigarette in his mouth. (p. 237)

Over the years Black Beauty had proved a horse remarkable not only for speed but for stamina. Few of the improving books written a century ago are still to be found on sale. Yet any bookshop on either side of the Atlantic will produce several copies of **Black Beauty;** probably two paperbacks, a cheap hardcover version and a couple of 'classics'. Woolworths is rarely without a copy. (p. 238)

The persistent popularity of **Black Beauty** becomes all the more remarkable when one considers the fate of its contemporaries. . . .

Indeed, of the hundreds of books written with a humanitarian motive in the last century probably only a handful are now read. The titles that spring to mind are Charles Kingsley's *The Water Babies*, a book intended to inculcate kindness to children of *all* classes, and *Uncle Tom's Cabin* by Harriet Beecher Stowe. And of these two one suspects that the former survived not because of its good intentions but because it belongs to that timeless category, the fairy tale. (p. 241)

Black Beauty started a new category of book, the animal story. Of course there had been animal stories before. Anna as a child was familiar with the talking animals of La Fontaine (and indeed **Black Beauty** is a kind of extended fable, for in it animals talk and a moral is drawn). In her own century James Greenwood wrote a series of books about talking South African animals, including *Bear King*, and in 1861 Ballantyne's *The Dog Crusoe* appeared. But these books only amounted to a handful.

There was, however, a book published six years before **Black Beauty** that one feels certain Anna must have read. It was George Macdonald's *At the Back of the North Wind*, the haunting story of little Diamond, the boy who was swept off by the North Wind and, between magical adventures with her, drove his father's cab through the streets of London. The cab-horse, like the boy, was called Diamond, and there is a scene where he is overheard in conversation with his stable-mate which is extraordinarily reminiscent of **Black Beauty**. There are other points of similarity between the two stories, like the scene where the horse Diamond, disfigured by hard work, is recognised by his old groom. The story of George Macdonald's cabman and his son closely resembles that of Anna Sewell's. They also had a favourite regular customer, preferred to risk bronchitis to taking shelter in their own cab, had a rush to catch a train (at King's Cross Station this time) and regarded tea and coffee as superior to hard liquor. At the end of the story they, like Jerry Barker and his family, are whirled off to a happy home in the country.

At the Back of the North Wind, however, was not primarily an animal story and of the predecessors of *Black Beauty* in this genre it is hard to find one that could be definitely said to have influenced it. Its imitators, however, are legion. (pp. 241-42)

We are left with the task of explaining why *Black Beauty* has lasted so well. For me its charm is summed up in its opening sentence. 'The first place that I can well remember was a large pleasant meadow with a pond of clear water in it. Some shady trees leaned over it and water lilies grew at the deep end.' To lovers of the book these lines are deeply evocative. They speak of the doomed English countryside that even in Anna Sewell's day was under threat of demolition. *Black Beauty* is a book that smells of fields after rain and this is one of the reasons why it has lasted.

Strangely enough there are few actual descriptions of landscape. One of them occurs, symbolically, after Reuben Smith's fall.

> It was a calm, sweet April night; there were no sounds but a few low notes of a nightingale, and nothing moved but the white clouds near the moon and a brown owl that flitted over the hedge. It made me think of the summer nights long ago, when I used to lie beside my mother in the green pleasant meadow at Farmer Grey's.

For vividness combined with brevity this could hardly be bettered. And this brings us to the second reason for *Black Beauty*'s excellence; its economy with words. Of its forty-nine chapters few are more than five pages long. The style, no doubt because of the circumstances under which the book was written, is pared to the bone, a great selling-point to juvenile readers. Children also enjoy the opportunity to identify. Anna Sewell spirits them inside the gleaming hide of her horse. They learn what it is to go on four legs, to have ears that prick and a tail to swish off flies. They feel the cold steel of the bit between their teeth, the stiff crupper under their tails and the weight of the carriage that follows them everywhere whether they like it or not.

Not only are they inside the horse but they're *on* his side, for *Black Beauty* is a strongly partisan book. The world is made up of good and bad people and we may know them by their treatment of animals. (p. 244)

Black Beauty is a cathartic book; it purifies through pity and fear. The first comment of almost everyone who reads the book is, 'It's so sad!' And most children like sad books. . . .

And the book is exciting as well as sad. Many times during the story the reader holds his breath in suspense. Will Black Beauty escape from the burning stable? Will Jerry outbid the loud-voiced brute who wants to buy him at the horse fair? Will he die on Ludgate Hill? The chase after Lady Anne on her runaway horse Lizzie is as vivid as any in children's literature. (p. 245)

To children the practical nature of the book is attractive. The tips on grooming, care of diseased hooves and correct procedure if a horse falls are eagerly stored away for future use. And they appreciate its lack of sentimentality. Anna Sewell makes no bones about how a horse should end its life. It should be shot. The kindly Jerry puts a 'sure bullet' through Captain's head after the accident rather than sell 'a good old servant into

The first edition of Black Beauty, *presented by Sewell to her mother's three sisters.*

hard work' and there is no talk of horse heavens or ethereal cab-horses. Perhaps the quality one admires most in Anna Sewell was her refusal to allow even one pale-haired little girl to die of tuberculosis. The temptation was too much for almost all her contemporaries, including Harriet Beecher Stowe, whose child heroine is inevitably borne away by the 'soft insidious killer'.

Sentiments like these have rendered the vast bulk of Victorian children's books unpalatable to the present generation. Perhaps a subsidiary reason for *Black Beauty*'s long life is that it is free of them. It remains to be seen whether the book will survive the next hundred years as well as it has survived the last. (p. 246)

> *Susan Chitty, in her* The Woman Who Wrote 'Black Beauty': A Life of Anna Sewell, *Hodder and Stoughton, 1971, 256 p.*

MARY F. THWAITE

The variety of the animal story is well in evidence in the second half of the nineteenth century, and it was this period which produced perhaps the best loved animal tale yet to be written— *Black Beauty.* This imaginary history of the life of a horse . . . also presents a vivid social picture of the days before the internal combustion engine. But its success was due to its sincerity and powerful feeling. . . . [Anna Sewell] put into her book practical advice as well as moving incidents. Black Beauty, like the animals in earlier, more purposeful tales, tells his own story, thus making it more poignant, although he must step out of horse character. In spite of sentimentality and the device of narration, this is a most convincing, well told story, with many features to endear it to children. Beauty's descent in the world, his work as a cab-horse, his eventual rescue, his recognition by an old friend, Joe, once a stable lad, and his final return to happiness and security, have something of the sequence of a fairy tale. Few books have won from young readers such lasting and heartfelt allegiance.

> *Mary F. Thwaite, in a review of "Black Beauty,"*
> *in her* From Primer to Pleasure in Reading, *revised*
> *edition, The Horn Book, Inc., 1972, p. 186.*

DEIRDRE DWEN PITTS

We began in the last century to understand the meaning, and in this century the consequences, of the hostility between man and animals, and our guilt provoked a surge of literature intended for children but actually serving the adult need for expiation. Prototypical of such guilt-ridden literature is Anna Sewell's **Black Beauty,** whose sentimentality need no longer be described. It is worthwhile to note, however, that the novel is still regarded as a classic by some critics in spite of its flaws, which are both conceptual and technical. As an attempt at realistic fiction, it is flawed technically by the fabulous device of the talking animal. Conceptually, Beauty is an extension of man, condescendingly raised to a level of sensitivity and reasoning, which allows him no existence independent of man's will. (p. 170)

> *Deirdre Dwen Pitts, "Discerning the Animal of a*
> *Thousand Faces," in* Children's Literature: Annual
> of the Modern Language Association Seminar on
> Children's Literature and The Children's Literature
> Association, *Vol. 3, 1974, pp. 169-72.*

MARGARET BLOUNT

[**Black Beauty**], the most famous and best-loved animal book of all time, stands out as a landmark. It is perhaps the last of the moral tales, the last great first person narrative in the Listen-to-my-life style. It is not quite as original a work as it appears to be; Arabella Argus had already told the story of Jemmy Donkey, and there are cab-horse incidents in George Macdonald's *At the Back of the North Wind,* 1871—in its way, a far more unusual work, but of less popular appeal. But Black Beauty's vicissitudes have the truth of something experienced and there is no fantasy relief—unless you count the oddity of a reasoning, communicating horse. The world-wide popularity of Anna Sewell's book must be attributed not to its campaigning fervour for kindness to horses, but to the narrative itself. It is such a good story, full of incident, character and suspense, rousing intense partisan feelings about the clear-cut issues of good and bad. It imparts information so effortlessly that even the reader who knows nothing about horses and is not even particularly interested in them is at once involved and ends with as much horse-lore as if he had been studying a rider's and driver's manual.

That the book was written as a moral tale or tract is certain; copies of it were given away to drivers of railway vans, and in America to drivers, grooms and stablemen, on a vast scale. Anna Sewell was very much influenced by her mother [Mary], a prolific and successful writer of tracts and moral poems about suffering children, brave parents and the evils of drink. . . . Anna, permanently lame and often ill, overshadowed by the active and indefatigable Mary, bore a troubled life with great courage and patience, which is what Black Beauty does. It is impossible to think of this horse without seeing the author

incarnated, and thinking of a human soul imprisoned and dumb. The animal autobiography gives the speechless a chance to speak to humans, and the convention is that the animal *can* communicate somehow. (pp. 249-50)

To communicate at all, the animal has to have a human psychology. . . . This elevates the horse to a far higher status than it normally has, or had, so that kindness done to it brings emotions of memory and gratitude and reciprocal goodness. Cruelty is worse because it is cruelty to a fellow human who is powerless and cannot answer back or take revenge. Every event is magnified and given echoes, and feelings are aroused almost unfairly; or are they? The book had enormous influence for good in the treatment of horses and helped to abolish the bearing rein. It continues to be a bestseller a hundred years after it was written.

The factor that moves is that horses were, and are, victims used for pulling and carrying; and one of them is allowed to tell what being a victim feels like—this is special pleading. But there are no extraordinary tear-jerking or sentimental qualities in the narrative. The horse hero has good, gentle qualities—and in keeping with the period, a finer strain also: 'Ginger and I were not of the regular, tall, carriage horse breed: we had more of the racing blood in us.' The handsome, agreeable, sensitive nature of Black Beauty makes him interesting in human terms, and his downfall from carriage horse—sold with Ginger for three hundred pounds—to broken down hack—sold for five pounds and at a horse fair—is only just made bearable by rescue and happy ending.

Black Beauty's life embraces practically every event that can happen to a horse, and he experiences every kind of rider and driver, good and bad, from the coachman John Manly and the kindly and thoughtful cabdriver Jerry Barker, to the drunken Reuben Smith who ruins him by breaking his knees, and the extortioner Skinner who works his horses to death. Cabs and carriages exist no longer, but it is impossible to read about the horses' sufferings without being affected—no less so because a human voice is talking, Anna Sewell's, both in the person of the hero when told by his mother to 'do your work with a good will, lift up your feet when you trot, and never bite or kick, even in play,' and in the person of the kind lady who stops the insensitive carter and asks him to remove the bearing rein with gentle, persuasive fervour.

The book does give adults and children—who read it now and have done so ever sine it was written—an insight, not exactly into how a horse feels, but into what it would be like, if one could be so transformed, to feel the bit, the blinkers, the bearing rein, the good and foolish treatment, and to realise with the whole of one's moral nature what was being done without being able to alter one's lot. That Anna Sewell believed horses really had moral natures is rather doubtful. Very little can be told of her life other than is revealed in a few letters. . . . What she certainly did believe was that horses were put into the world for the use and service of man, and that as man does, or should do, God's will, so the vocation or animals was to do the will of man. Any human reading **Black Beauty** will be kinder to horses.

But one cannot help thinking about how the magic is worked. Humans look before and after, and pine for what is not, and Black Beauty experiences moral doubts: 'They were carrying young Gordon to the churchyard to bury him. He would never ride again. What they did with Rob Roy I never knew; but 'twas all for one little hare'; the pains of speechlessness: 'I held my face close to him, as that was all I could do to say goodbye, and then he was gone, and I have never seen him since'; and helpless regret, as at the climactic end of his pride and maturity he is left with broken knees and a dead rider: 'It was a calm, sweet April night . . . it made me think of the summer nights long ago, when I used to lie beside my mother in the green, pleasant meadow at Farmer Grey's.'

Unfair! Unfair, and yet the end justifies the means. This was the only book I have ever read right through, straight away, twice; but fond as I was—aged ten—I have not read it since and other books have been greater favourites and changed life more deeply. It made me look, on my way to school, more intelligently at the coal carts that plodded all day between the station and the gasworks, at the plaque on the wall that said for many years 'Please slacken bearing rein going up hill,' and I watched the carters putting on the metal brake shoes and wondered—as a horse—what it was like going downhill with a heavy load behind. But beyond these feelings was the one that if the horse were I, or anyone, and the story really about me, or people, then school was the breaking-in stable and many people were led or driven through life with a series of owners and made to run, walk or trot without being able to argue about it. The horse characters in *Black Beauty* are too human to be lightly dismissed or forgotten, and found immediate identification; Peggy, Captain, Lizzie, but more surely Ginger and Merrylegs. Aunt Merrylegs was the sturdy, self-confident one that nobody could argue with. Aunt Ginger, pale, angular, auburn and clever, but ruined by unlucky treatment in youth and difficulties and setbacks since, had reared, refused and bitten her way through life until 'bearing it on and on until the end'. In a way this animal book made one child love people more and understand them a little better. (pp. 250-54)

> Margaret Blount, ''If Only We Were They: The Humanised 'Nature' Story,'' in her *Animal Land: The Creatures of Children's Fiction, William Morrow & Company, Inc.,* 1975, pp. 245-64.

ANDREW STIBBS

In *Children's Reading Interests* Frank Whitehead, A C Capey, and Wendy Maddren describe *Black Beauty* as 'the most widely read of all children's books'.

They explain its popularity, despite its 'stiffly Victorian language' and out-of-date detail, by its provision of a central figure to identify with, by a specific 'feeling-tone' arising from the horse's child-like lack of control over misfortunes it nonetheless understands, and its thereby justified moral complacency vis à vis adults, by its wish-fulfilment ending, and by its being a 'haunting' cumulative record of the progression from youth to age. They cite the last two factors, together with 'detailed observation of human behaviour' as justification for including *Black Beauty* in their 'quality' list.

I think the factors in its popularity which they cite do play their part, but I think they are part of a syndrome, a comfortableness, a reassuring and unreasoned reinforcement of all its readers' mothers have told them of both what life is like and what they should or should not do. These add up to an ethos so passive and shortsighted, a moral complacency so infectious but *un*justified, that the book does not deserve to be considered one of 'quality'. John Manly's recipe for bringing up horses ('patience and gentleness, firmness and petting. . . . with commonsense') could well be applied to children. But *developing* children need an active, perhaps even antagonistic, stance towards the precepts of their protectors and mentors. Without

that they become pets. The stance of the eponymous character in *Black Beauty,* the one the child inevitably identifies with, is one of almost unquestioning acceptance of his role and lot. That stance is a dangerously limiting one.

As Whitehead *et al* point out, Black Beauty's model of the types of human nature is based on his experience of people who have power over him. These are the stereotypes of the angels and devils who inhabit the universe of the helpless, inexperienced, and overgeneralizing child. They include the violent and incomprehensible—like your dad; sweet, kind angels—like your mum; constant reliable oldsters—like your grandparents; companions who inexplicably go away—like your siblings.

The human beings in the book accord with the respectable young child's stereotypes, and the didactics in the book accord with the advice, moral and practical, pressed on him or her by adults. This is specially true of middle-class girls, and even though *Black Beauty* readership is not confined to them, that is an important guide to the nature of the book's appeal. The virtues preached are those of docility, keeping yourself to yourself, the pursuit of comfort, and simple-minded religiosity. (Jerry Barker says that if religious people are not better than irreligious people then they are not religious!) Precepts are unbacked by reasons—though sometimes by Biblical reference. As the Old Ostler says, horses 'are like children; train 'em up in the way they should go as the good book says, and when they are old they will not depart from it.' Even the areas of practical concern are the same—one example is the importance of good meals.

The book is the stimulus which activates the nurtured reflex of enjoyment in the well-conditioned subject (in this case the well-brought-up reader). In this it contrasts perhaps with myth and fairy tale which retain their appeal by embodying a child's 'natural' morality and instinctual model of experience in the inhabited universe, a morality and model as simple as those embodied in *Black Beauty* but more forceful.

The values the book betrays are in the class 'tales my mother told me': they form a passive-feminine-genteel-rural syndrome. It seems specially apt to extract socio-ethical values from *Black Beauty,* the one book, from the end of her life, of a lady of a moralistic and class-conscious era, and therefore likely to embody, however unconsciously, her beliefs and attitudes. It is overtly didactic ('being kind to animals' is only one of the kinds of behaviour it endorses, even though it is the only one it self-confessedly endorses). And the book has an allegorical appearance: some chapters, like 'The Old Ostler' and 'John Manly's Talk' are almost sermons interleaving the alarms and gallops (in this case 'The Fire'); the overall pattern, as Whitehead *et al* point out, is a life-journey, and it is a circular one to the Elysium of primal innocence; furthermore, it is the journey of an unchanging hero, for Black Beauty does not develop and his instructive experiences in no way broaden or deepen his (*ab initio* quite considerable) store of prejudice and precept; many of the names are quasi-allegorical (Farmer Thoroughgood for a thoroughly good farmer; Skinner, Filcher, and Smirk for villains who are, respectively, extortionist, thief, and humbug; and, amongst the horses, Merrylegs who is merry, Ginger who is hot and spicey, and Captain who is military—though 'Black Beauty' as a name is a surprise: he is an Uncle Tom to his species).

The book is imbued with features of the female sex-stereotype and one has to keep reminding oneself that Black Beauty is male. There is a comfortableness associated with all things good specially attached to the women in the book. Recurrent words are 'gentle', 'kind', and 'sweet'. For instance, the lady who remonstrates with Jakes, the overloading carter, has a 'sweet, earnest voice' and a 'gentle hand'. In the first of the book's four parts these words occur at least ten, eighteen, and seven times respectively, and 'nice' and 'good' (the latter frequently in such forms as 'good-tempered', 'good-mannered', or as 'well-bred') are similarly frequent, as are 'bad', 'nasty', and 'awful'. It is the language, and the ethos, of the genteel nursery.

The human vices which, in *Black Beauty,* are the main causes of equine misfortune are ones traditionally associated with men. Violence—practised exclusively by men, in the stable, in the hunt and in war—is censured in the book. The demon drink is invariably associated with cruelty and misfortune and you could extract an improving temperance tract from the book. Samson, Ginger's persecutor, is a drinker; the men who try to force Jerry to drive too fast 'came out of a tavern'; a carter guilty of brutality 'had clearly been drinking'; the voters whom Jerry so despises are 'half-drunken'; a drunken cabman does for Captain, and booze breaks Black Beauty's knees. No wonder (for smoking causes a fatal fire) Black Beauty says he prefers his men to smell of the hayloft rather than beer and tobacco.

Although Squire Gordon's employees look after their horses well and a male farmer (in accord with an even stronger polarity in the book) intervenes to save Black Beauty when he is a townee's job-horse, kindness to overworked horses is almost invariably practised, in the book, by females. At their worst, their fashion-following and vanity (practised by aristocratic, not genteel, ladies) causes inconvenience and discomfort rather than death and injury. It is the ladies who interfere with the professionals and, with one sweet and gentle word of remonstrance to the ignorant men whose livelihood is horses, convert them from unwise and brutal to wise and gentle ways. His first mistress, for instance, when she 'met a heavily-laden horse . . . would . . . reason with the driver in her sweet, serious voice, and try to show him how foolish and cruel it was.'

Anna Sewell was no mere amateur do-gooder: she would know her horses. As Eleanor Graham's biographical note in the Puffin edition makes clear, she was partially lame, and therefore dependent on horses most of her life. The book's didactics extend to presumably sound advice on horse care: from it you could compile a dietary, or manuals on driving, on tack, or on horse doctoring. No opportunity is lost to slip in a tip, even as blatantly as 'I may as well mention here what I suffered at this time from another cause' (a badly lit stable).

Is not the constant proffering of homespun advice another feature (one specially obvious to a young reader) of a concerned mother? The consequences of horses' drinking too much cold water after exercise have their equivalents in the warnings you and I have received about sitting in draughts or on pile-producing wet grass; and how often have I been told to eat—as reward, restorative, duty, or act of gratitude to the starving inhabitants of the Third World—the human equivalents of Anna Sewell's obsessive 'good bran mash' by a mother who, like Dolly Barker the human soup-kitchen, made a barrage of hot-pies and puddings emblems of familial love and the well-ordered household.

The domesticity of genteel ladies necessarily limits their horizons, and the limits are enshrined in *Black Beauty* and, possibly, dangerously conveyed to its susceptible readers. The fates of Ginger and Lady Anne are warnings to all high-mettled and aspirant females, horse or human. Morality is limited to personal relationships. It is as if there is an 'event horizon' beyond which all the interpersonal kindness, gentleness, and justice characteristic of the endorsed characters of the book disappear into a black hole of indifference. Beyond that horizon are people whose names we do not know, or those who have put themselves beyond concern by their nonconformity or disloyalty or unfortunate expulsion from the social model. Thus, boys or men inconsiderate to horses are sacked (Chapter 1), left in a thorn hedge (Chapter 13), imprisoned (Chapter 20), or killed (Chapter 25), by Anna Sewell, and the family of Reuben Smith are, in one sentence and without further comment, 'obliged to leave . . . and go into that great gloomy union house'. One cannot help wondering if the uncharacteristic irony at the end of the description of the Charge of the Light Brigade in Chapter 34 ('that is more than a horse can understand, but the enemy must have been awfully wicked people, if it was right to go all that way over the sea on purpose to kill them') is powered by disgust at the suffering caused to horses, rather than at the death of men. The only comparable irony in the book is directed at fox-hunting. A preference for kindness to animals over kindness to people is overt in 'they (the Gordons) were good and kind to everybody . . . If any of the village children were known to treat any creature cruelly, they soon heard about it from the Hall.'

This 'out of sight; out of mind' attitude is expressed in the 'wise speech of good little Merrylegs' at the end of a discussion about cruelty to animals: '. . . we won't talk about it here . . . master, and John, and James are always good to us, and talking against men in such a place as this doesn't seem fair or grateful'. With such metaphorical blinkers on, politics are unconsidered or despised by the main characters in the book, though the stuff of politics—injustice, poverty, inequality—is there in plenty. Jerry Baker despises the activities of 'An Election', and does nothing to counteract the abuses to which he and his kind are subject. His rural counterparts, the grooms and coachmen on the estates, accept the feudal order. This attitude is typical of that of the respectable and unliberated woman whose political consciousness is confined to voting, if at all, for the status quo—dreadful things go on, but there is nothing we can do about them so they are none of our business. (Anna Sewell had not learned that attitude from her mother, as we shall see later.)

In Chapter 6, Black Beauty regrets his loss of liberty—but 'I am not complaining for I know it must be so'. Such passivity and moral self-complacency are more likely to be learned by the child, as by Black Beauty, from a mother, than from its own analysis of the events it experiences.

There is one exception to the stereotyping of passive angelic women. This is the Duchess of W, whose vanity causes suffering to horses. But she is a rule-reinforcing exception, for she, alone of the women in the book, is not ruled by her husband. (The Duke of W blames his employees for obeying her.) Unquestioning obedience is as much a part of the perfect horse and child as is obedient unquestioningness. Black Beauty accepts his breaking in in one of the key chapters and takes pride in doing man's will. The unpleasantness of some parts of his breaking in is admitted—he feels like kicking—'but of course I could not kick such a good master'. He boasts of knowing what's required of him before he's asked, and says 'The better I behaved, the better I should be treated.' The breaking in of a horse is like the mixture of blackmail, brain-wash and beating by which a child is broken into docility and respectability. Were reminded of the Old Ostler's analogy above.

On the attitudes that informed Anna Sewell's own upbringing we can only speculate. Eleanor Graham describes her mother as anxious to see Anna grow up fearless and independent, but a quotation from one of the mother's letters ('She needs to get the habit of a cheerful surrender of her own will') reminds us that Anna Sewell was brought up in a period when middle-class (and, at the highpoints of Methodism, working-class) attitudes to work, authority, and childhood were dominated by nonconformist beliefs in original sin and the necessity of break-ing the will, beliefs which provided the rationale of child la-bour. However, the Sewells were not Methodists and Anna's mother had been a Quaker like her husband until subsiding into Anglicanism. But by the 1830s the Quakers' dissent was little more than token though they had begun their traditional espousal of liberal causes. . . . (pp. 128-32)

In *Black Beauty* the passive virtues are linked to class and breeding. Black Beauty's mother lectures him on the equiva-lence of gentleness and good breeding, and urges him to eschew the course behaviour of low-born cart horses, and a turf-cutter is prepared to risk his life for the foolish Lady Anne.

With one exception the villains are low-born. In the phrase 'low cruel boy' there is an almost medieval equivalence of the moral and social implications of 'low'. Similarly, proper be-haviour is called behaving like a lady ('she pays down fair and honourable like a lady'). There is also a suggestion that intel-ligence is linked to class. Men who work with horses seem to have less common sense about them than the parasites who use them for pleasure. A carter has to be shown the mechanical advantages of a loose rein by a passing lady, and John Manly—albeit one of the two low-born heroes of the book and one who says ignorance is 'the worst thing in the world, next to wicked-ness'—has to be told by his master what route to try out Black Beauty on.

Obedience is a palliative of low birth. Another is old age. On the whole, parents are better than their children (Mrs Ryder is kind but her son Samson is cruel). The Old Ostler is wiser and better than his younger assistant who lounges, smokes, ignores advice, and burns the stable down.) Again we are reminded of the nursery: respect your elders.

Old is better than young, and old is better than new. So the country, in *Black Beauty,* is better than the industrial town. This arcadianism, celebrated and asserted in this still-popular book, lives on in a middle-class urging of children to go to picnics rather than the pictures, rambling rather than dancing, and to join a young naturalists' club rather than a pop fan club, and it lives on in the illustrations of learning-to-read books. In *Black Beauty* all things rural (except fox hunting, which is cruel to horses) are good. All things urban are bad: even steam engines are 'monsters'. Anna Sewell's mother hated the city where she was forced to bring up her children, and Anna spent holidays with godparents in Norfolk, where she learnt to ride. The London of 1877 was an unplanned, uncontrolled cancer which had overgrown a once coherent and civilized centre. In *Black Beauty* it is a vicious place, characterized by crowds, elections, greed and rush.

Women—like the one struggling to hospital—are victims of the city; Ginger is killed by the city; Black Beauty escapes from it only by luck. Cockneys are ridiculed (and insultingly

An illustration from the first edition of Black Beauty *por-traying the fall of the drunkard Reuben Smith.*

compared to steam engines), and a farmer has to save Black Beauty from being lamed by an ignorant townee.

To Anna Sewell's implied censure of all things urban Jerry Barker is an exception, but again he is one who reinforces the rule. For Jerry, with his abstemiousness (he is a reformed drinker), his uxoriousness, his sabbatarianism, his dependence on the constantly administered drug of his wife's soup and pies, his fair language, and his refusal of bonuses, is a traitor to the habits and practices of both his sex and class. Symp-tomatically, his perfect day—a Sunday—is a rural interlude listening to the birds and reading his prayer book whilst Black Beauty rolls in the grass. At the end of the book, Jerry is rescued from the city by Mrs Fowler, a *dea ex machina*, and, like Black Beauty, ruined by the town, he is put out to Elysian grass.

The Barkers are the only lights in the murky city (and it nearly puts them out). Whereas in the country even the peasants can be good, in the city even gentlemen can be villains, like the gamblers whose inconsiderate delay keeps Jerry out in the rain on New Year's Eve.

One does not blame an author for embodying the attitudes of her time and class. But where those attitudes are irrelevant and, as I believe is the case here, disablingly limp and short-sighted, they reduce the book from the status of a 'quality' novel for children to that of an interesting case for critics (as well as an interesting case for consumer researchers and a popular novel for children). To retain its worth a book must transcend its author's background, and embody enduring and recurring situations and values. I do not think that *Black Beauty* does so, and reading it is a self-indulgence which may reinforce attitudes of which most of us would disapprove. And I do not think there is sufficient force in the language or details of the book, nor in its plot or overall shape, to provide a compensating tension to the texture of soft attitudes.

To me the language seems not 'stiffly Victorian' but as limp as the attitudes. It rises to memorability only with the death of Ginger, and that is symptomatically drawn back from:

> The head hung out of the cart-tail, the lifeless tongue
> was slowly dripping blood, and the sunken eyes! but
> I can't speak of them, the sight was too dreadful.

I find the events indistinguishable and predictable, and, as far as I can judge, unmemorable. . . . The story is broken when Black Beauty's knees are broken: it becomes a series of forced episodes in a didactic tract enlivened—if that is the word— only by the fates of Ginger and Jerry.

If only Ginger had written it and made it *The Ragged Fetlocked Philanthropists* or *The Female Gelding!* (pp. 132-34)

Andrew Stibbs, "'Black Beauty': Tales My Mother Told Me," in Children's literature in education, *No. 22, Autumn, 1976, pp. 128-34.*

MARGERY FISHER

Black Beauty is a classic because it is popular with the young, not because it is "great work". It was written for a purpose and the constant apostrophising of the reader dominates and sometimes impedes the narrative. The prose style is graceful and pleasing but, like the water-colours executed by the young ladies of the last century, it lacks the unmistakable shock of true originality. Nor should we expect any subtlety in character-drawing. The horses, including Black Beauty as narrator, are not really humanised, though they have voices and express opinions. Like the cats and dogs and inanimate heroes of so many "autobiographies" of a century and more ago, they are mouthpieces, enabling the author through them to outline a social abuse, or rule of horsemanship. Black Beauty's willingness and good temper are inherited from his dam but they are also fostered by the experienced and humane coachman John Manly and the honest cab-driver Jerry Barker; goodwill has become a habit, so that even in the dismal purlieus of Skinner's yard the horse remains docile. Rebellion is shown to be the result of prolonged ill-treatment. It is equine virtues and vices, not human counterparts, which are illustrated, and the fate of the nervous mare Ginger is no moral lesson to the young to be obedient but a direct appeal to them to learn how to be truly responsible in dealing with horses.

The structure of *Black Beauty* is very simple, with the contrasted Beauty and Ginger talking to or about other horses for the sake of variety—the cheerful old pony Merrylegs shows the harm thoughtless children can do, while the charger Captain's recollections of the Crimean War introduces a different element into the peaceful English scene. Noble mansion and London tenement, farmyard and crowded street, sunny days and stormy night—each scene is developed for a particular end and the human characters are chosen as strictly for this end as the horses are. Looked at as characters they may seem stilted and exaggerated—John Manly with his even temper and his

probity, Reuben Smith the hackneyed figure of the drunkard, the arrogant Countess of W— forcing the unwilling groom to tighten the bearing-rein on the carriage horses; but they are types, not characters. If generations of girls have their first taste of human feeling through reading this book, as I believe they have, it is because Anna Sewell's patent sincerity and open manner have given scope for each and every reader to bring to the story her own tentative feelings. No, Black Beauty is not a great book, nor is it outstanding as literature; it endures as a minor classic for its congenial recital of stable-details, its appealing incidents and its particularly honest emotional content.

Margery Fisher, in a review of "Black Beauty," in Growing Point, *Vol. 15, No. 7, January, 1977, p. 3038.*

NICHOLAS TUCKER

[It is not its] campaigning against cruelty to animals that has made this novel a success; more fundamentally, it is yet another variation on the Cinderella theme, where nobility and virtue go unrecognised, to be rescued at the last moment from dishonourable oblivion. It is easy for readers to identify with the interests of the main, sympathetic characters in such an eternally appealing plot, especially since Black Beauty is in no true sense an animal. He and Ginger, for example, exchange very conventional human sentiments; one of their phrases, 'Good Heavens!' was later objected to by a critic since it referred to 'A place not dreamt of in Equine philosophy'. It is not certain whether Anna Sewell would have accepted this comment, since in most other ways, except in his taste for oats and hay, Black Beauty's behaviour is what one might expect from a refined, sensitive young man who has suddenly had a saddle placed on his back and a crupper tied round his nether regions. As he says himself, 'Those who have never had a bit in their mouths cannot think how bad it feels'; readers, addressed so directly and perhaps fingering their own mouths, have little choice but to agree. He also has other typically human worries of a more class-conscious nature; from the earliest days, his mother had told him that he was 'well-bred and well-born', and for that reason should avoid the company of the young cart-horses who 'have not learned manners'. Later, he suffers the agony of social disgrace when he becomes a cab-horse, where he meets 'a good many like myself, handsome and high-bred, but fallen into the middle-class through some accident or blemish.'

This particular underdog view of life can be one that has particularly strong, natural attractions for child readers of whatever social class, living as they all do in an adult-dominated world where other people usually have the last word over their conduct and destiny. Used to being patronised in their own lives, it must be a pleasant change for children to be able to feel more socially competent and therefore protective about some animal characters who are inevitably confused about many of the ways of man. (pp. 158-59)

Domestic animals in fiction are also constantly liable to be bossed around in an arbitrary way with no court of appeal, beyond their sometimes uncaring masters, to protect them except in the most extreme cases. Child readers, in their turn also very dependent upon the adult world, can easily be spurred on by such stories to wonder how they might manage if they were similarly quite on their own—a fantasy that has always been very meaningful for children, and one reason for their general fascination with stories about orphans. A book like *Black Beauty,* therefore, about an ill-used, inarticulate animal who is also an orphan, has several obvious points of appeal.

In addition to this, Black Beauty himself is a very sympathetic hero to children; his own enforced lack of sexuality makes him childlike in other ways, and many of his chief preoccupations are to do with his physical state—an easy dimension for children to understand, whether it concerns hunger, exhaustion, pain or illness. He is, also a loving, friendly animal, again quite like a child in his ready affections and general anxiety to be accepted and to please. There is something childish, too, in his vanity, where he is so artlessly proud of his good looks and high quality.

There are more subtle themes in this book as well, giving it an extra interest for readers [between the ages of eleven and fourteen]. Anna Sewell, for example, could have blamed all cruelty to animals simply upon human wickedness, but instead she tries to guide readers towards a more complex view. Seedy Sam, for example, is a cab-driver who fearfully misuses his horses, but when criticised, he shows how his large family would certainly starve unless he worked his animals so hard. It is the social system that is wrong here—quite a stimulating jump in understanding for children to make, if they can, used as they once were to personifying evil simply as the individual responsibility of a few, unpleasant people. (pp. 159-60)

> *Nicholas Tucker, "Literature for Older Children (Ages 11-14)," in his* The Child and the Book: A Psychological and Literary Exploration, *Cambridge University Press, 1981, pp. 144-89.*

JOHN ROWE TOWNSEND

[The] first animal story of major importance was Anna Sewell's *Black Beauty*. . . .

The author is constantly concerned to put over her message; and from one point of view—which was probably her own—the whole book is a treatise on the care of horses, illustrated with numerous examples. But clearly a book does not survive on account of its message—particularly in a case like this, where the message has been largely outdated since the motorcar succeeded the horse. I think *Black Beauty* survives partly through its successful appeal to compassion in children and partly because the story carries conviction, in spite of some absurdly un-equine remarks in the horse's narration. And Miss Sewell proved her independence of mind, as well as her sincerity and courage, by condemning war and fox-hunting—two institutions which right-minded people were supposed to accept without question. (p. 105)

> *John Rowe Townsend, "Articulate Animals," in his* Written for Children: An Outline of English-Language Children's Literature, *second revised edition, J. B. Lippincott, 1983, pp. 103-13.*

James Stevenson

1929-

American author and illustrator of picture books and fiction, dramatist, and scriptwriter.

A prolific creator of books for preschoolers and grade school readers, Stevenson is acclaimed for his gently humorous, fast-moving stories which treat universal childhood experiences with imagination, insight, and wit. Often using a comic strip format to convey plot through pencil, watercolor, and dialogue balloons, he is considered an especially talented illustrator whose works combine the appeal of comic books with a strong aesthetic sensibility. Stevenson's themes frequently center on family life, friendships, and the traumas of children. He has addressed such subjects as quarrels with siblings, feelings of inadequacy, nighttime fears, and boredom. Throughout his works, Stevenson presents a positive, supportive attitude towards his audience, and is credited for delivering the morals underlying his stories without preaching. His message is one of consolation; the lonely, frightened, or worried child finds comfort in a Stevenson book, with its laugh-evoking plot and optimistic—but realistic—ending. Much of the tone of Stevenson's works is conveyed through his illustrations, which reflect a characteristically unrestrained, unpretentious style. Influenced by both comic strips and films, Stevenson uses line to capture expression, personality, emotion, and action while adding carefully planned color washes to elicit atmosphere and setting.

An artist and writer for the *New Yorker* since 1956, Stevenson began contributing to children's literature when he collaborated with his eight-year-old son James Walker Stevenson on the brief fantasy *If I Owned a Candy Factory* (1968), the story of a boy who dreams of possessing a candy factory and of sharing his sweets with his friends. Stevenson firmly established his career as a children's writer with the publication of *"Could Be Worse!"* (1977), the first of ten stories about Grandpa, the elderly gentleman who is perhaps Stevenson's most popular character. In *"Could Be Worse!"*, Grandpa deflates his grandchildren Mary Ann and Louie's assumption that his life is dull by telling them of his recent hair-raising adventure. In subsequent books about the same characters, the children bring a variety of problems to Grandpa, which he alleviates by relating tall tales of his exploits as a child. The preposterousness of these tales—which Stevenson illustrates with robust portrayals of Grandpa and his younger brother Wainwright as children, complete with mustaches—give Mary Ann and Louie new perspectives on their own situations. Interspersed among the Grandpa books are stories about Emma, the small witch who outsmarts two older disagreeable witches with the help of her animal friends; The Worst, a cantankerous antihero who discovers an unexpected need for companionship; and Monty, a good-natured crocodile. Stevenson has written several books with anthropomorphic animal protagonists which address such concerns as the importance of friendship and the appreciation of others; he has also created such works as an alphabet book, a modern-day fairy tale, a pop-up book, and a spoof of credit cards. With the publication of the autobiographical *When I Was Nine* (1986) and its companion volume *Higher on the Door* (1987), Stevenson made a notable depar-

Photograph by Edwina Stevenson. Courtesy of James Stevenson.

ture from his usual illustrative style. These works, filled with reminiscences and anecdotes about growing up in the 1930s, are illustrated with what Stevenson calls "minimal art," water-color paintings without defining lines which are considered particularly apt for rendering hazy memories of times long past. He is also the illustrator of books by several noted writers for children, including Dr. Seuss, Jack Prelutsky, John Donovan, and Charlotte Zolotow.

Reviewers applaud Stevenson's works for their appealing characterizations, economic texts, dexterous illustrations, and portrayals of strong intergenerational relationships. Most critics praise Stevenson for his childlike quality, sense of humor, and acute understanding of matters that bring concern or delight to children.

Many of Stevenson's books have been chosen for "best book" and "best illustrated" lists. *We Can't Sleep* won the Christopher Award in 1987.

(See also *Something about the Author*, Vols. 34, 42; and *Contemporary Authors*, Vol. 115.)

AUTHOR'S COMMENTARY

[The following excerpt is from an interview by Kimberly Olson Fakih.]

The little voice that bespoke the plot of James Stevenson's first children's book, *If I Owned A Candy Factory,* was not his own—it was that of one of his sons: "He was about this high," Stevenson remembers, as he indicates a point just slightly above the arm of his wooden chair. He is speaking from his office at the *New Yorker.* There, amidst the numerous illustrations, cartoons and magazine covers that are "filed" from floor to ceiling in envelopes and folders, he talks about that early work and his most recent book from Greenwillow, *Higher on the Door.*

"'Tell me a story,'" Stevenson recalls saying to his son, "'and we'll make a book.' He stood at my desk and narrated a story; I wrote it down and then did the pictures. It was a collaboration, and it was published. We split the royalties." . . .

[Manhattan is where Stevenson] works a couple of days a week, commuting between the world of topical cartoons and city interiors to his Connecticut home where he has been creating children's books for more than a decade. They have been published at the rate of approximately four titles a year, which may sound as if Stevenson eats, sleeps and breathes comic ideas and children's books.

He doesn't. "I have no ideas until I sit here with the paper in front of me," Stevenson says. "I never think of cartoon ideas until I'm here. For children's books, it's a different desk. One of the problems of working is that you try to stay fresh. You can't do it unless you just stop and do something else."

"Staying fresh" by doing "something else" may be particular key phrases behind a career that was never actually launched, but seems to have simply evolved. Stevenson began selling cartoon ideas to the *New Yorker* while at Yale (Class of '51) and in the Marines.

[He] eventually began drawing his own cartoons and also contributed "Talk of the Town" columns and "Profiles." Recently, however, most of his writing time has been given over to children's books; he now estimates that 50% of his work time is spent on cartoons and the rest on picture books.

The binding factor, of course, is humor. The approach to each is quite different; according to Sevenson, "a cartoon is a formalization of a certain situation . . . something topical, reflecting the news. The challenge is in taking an issue and trying to reduce it to simplicity, to make the point—preferably with no words, but at least with as few words as possible.

"A children's book, on the other hand, is like making a movie. I often use the comic strip form because it's cinematic. You write the story and you produce it, and direct it and cast it and do the costumes and you do the cinematography," he says, adding a couple of distinguishing points. "You're not waiting for any set-up, or lights. You don't have to deal with weather changes, or personalities—you can just do it." Does that mean appropriating a godlike role? Stevenson shrugs that off with a laugh. "Never mind the theology, it's just that it's faster doing it yourself!"

There are areas of thematic overlap in cartooning and children's books. In one case, a character in a *New Yorker* cartoon became the star of what is now a burgeoning picture book series. Stevenson's longtime editor at Greenwillow, Susan Hirschman, made the suggestion after spotting a witch he'd drawn. The first book was about *Emma,* an apprentice witch, and her two cranky rivals, Dolores and Lavinia. The second book was *Yuck!;* last fall the witches appeared in a non-Halloween adventure, *Fried Feathers for Thanksgiving.* Stevenson recently completed

the fourth book of the series, about which he will only say that it has a Valentine's Day setting. "Witches have their own holidays," he blithely adds. Stevenson has published over 30 books with Greenwillow since 1977, when he debuted on their list with *"Could Be Worse!"* That book, too, launched a character that would become part of series for Stevenson—Grandpa, whom some consider a codgerly incarnation of Stevenson himself. Grandpa is around when Mary Ann and Louie have had a terrible first day of school *(That Dreadful Day),* find themselves in an intimidating new neighborhood *(No Friends)* or, among other problems, can't put their heads to pillows at night *(We Can't Sleep).* By detailing his outlandish exploits (or outrageous lies, depending on the reader's level of gullibility), Grandpa soothes away their concerns—and not without a belly laugh or two. (p. 148)

Although Stevenson's children's books have for the most part been well-received, he is a bit wary of reviews. "About the 10th time I read a review describing my 'effortless' watercolors I decided: to hell with this! . . . "

He softens, though, when he refers to *Higher on the Door* and the book's stylistic predecessor, *When I Was Nine.* These titles are departures from his black line illustrations with color washes. "I am interested in seeing if people got something from those books; they're kind of minimal art," Stevenson comments. He has long been curious about the power of visual suggestion. Reviewers have pointed out that the art—indefinite dabs of color representing familiar surroundings—forces readers to supply much of the details in their minds.

He recalls that he had been working with photographs when he began to experiment with "how little you could have of a subject and still get the emotional response and the recognition of what it was. The idea of reducing the visual information and yet seeing what would remain and cross over to the reader or the viewer. How specific do you have to be to get a response? Most things are so familiar visually that we don't need that whole story."

Stevenson adds that there is a risk involved in this minimalist approach. "You need to trigger it with something specific. If it's too universal it's nothing. If you're writing a play you don't want to have a character named John Smith because nobody gives a damn about John Smith. Someone with a real *name* is immediately a little more real for the audience." . . .

For those two books, Stevenson relied on his own memories about growing up in the suburban Hudson River area in the '30s for the stories. One of the major influences of his childhood was an elementary school that he describes as "extremely involved in social issues and political issues of the day. I remember writing letters to Roosevelt when I was seven, asking him to lift the arms embargo on Spain. I did political cartoons about Chamberlain later on. In one of the school plays I was a banker foreclosing mortgages on farmers in the dust bowl or something like that."

Stevenson recalls that the area in which he lived had "a history of the arts and communism and bohemianism." But one of the most significant factors in his development was certainly "this school that had a kind of policy of telling you that everybody could do everything. Everybody could sing, dance, act, play musical instruments, write stories, make pictures and change the world."

Stevenson's father was an architect and watercolorist, an ability Stevenson obviously inherited and has passed along to his own family. Of his nine children, one—Suçie—is writing and illustrating children's books. One is an art director in advertising, another is studying art. . . .

Stevenson says that he has spent much of his life reassuring his own children. "And now they're reassuring me," he adds. But he still does not connect his family with the number of books he has produced—and continues to produce. "I think that most people, maybe especially me, have a limited number of stories to tell. Sometimes you think you only have one story to tell, and you keep telling it in different ways."

Does he know what that story is? "No . . . reassurance is certainly a theme that comes through. A lot of dealing with children is telling them either it's not so bad or it's going to be all right. Yes. Reassurance." (p. 149)

> *Kimberly Olson Fakih, "James Stevenson," in Publishers Weekly, Vol. 231, No. 8, February 27, 1987, pp. 148-49.*

GENERAL COMMENTARY

JANE LANGTON

Some good picture books show the labor that went into every square inch. Others look as simple as breathing, even when they aren't. After running through one of James Stevenson's easygoing stories you feel he has merely picked up a pen and a box of watercolors and said, "Hey, look—I had the craziest day."

> *Jane Langton, in a review of "'Could be Worse!',"*
> *in The New York Times Book Review, August 7, 1977, p. 24.*

NAOMI LEWIS

Brilliant James Stevenson is certainly not unknown, yet evidence suggests that his picture books must be the most undiscovered major treat of their kind to be found today for under eights and adults who have the very young in their care. Or class. Each is not only a miniature topical fairy tale, funny, witty and moving at any level you like, but an experience—one which a young child can reflect on long after the book is closed. In . . . *The Night After Christmas*, snow falls on the rubbish bins, and on two abandoned toys, hopeful Teddy, benign though torn, and Annie, a glum rag doll. A kindly dog takes them on his back to a shelter of sorts ("It's not fancy but it's warm")—the basement of a block of flats, all pipes and brooms and junk. Later, sensing the need for finding them new children and new homes, he places them at the gates of a junior school just before the home-time rush.

The subject, and the expressive poignancy of the pictures should make the book a ready favourite; but it is not to my mind, the best of all Stevenson. You may prefer *Monty* . . . —a perfect book for very young children. A good natured crocodile gives several juniors a lift to school across the river twice a day; once there, once back. But do they thank him? Are they grateful? One day he announces that he is on holiday. Read on; you will want to. *Howard* too has its devotees. Here, a young wild duck loses his way when the rest of the group are heading south, and spends the winter with newfound bird and animal friends in various city hideouts; a ruined theatre is one. What good friends friends in need can be! Anyone whose heart does not leap at the unexpected end does not deserve this book.

Possibly most inspired of all is *Clams Can't Sing*. . . . The shore is full of noises with its grasshoppers, gulls and crabs and

things. Skeek! quack! chomp-chomp! glop! klonk! whoosh! zizza-zizza! Even the mussels clack. A concert is planned. Pity about Benny and Beatrice Clam—they can't do anything. But can't they? Secretly they devise their Symphony for Two Clams . . . "Take a bow!" cry the joyful audience. "We don't do bows," says Beatrice. Unlike Aesop or La Fontaine, Stevenson has no need to spell out the message in his stories. *Clams Can't Sing* affirms that everyone can do something. You can't have a better thought than that, or, at its own level, one more engagingly rendered.

> *Naomi Lewis, "Funny, Witty and Moving," in The Times Educational Supplement, No. 3477, February 18, 1983, p. 30.*

GERTRUDE HERMAN

A more engaging character than Grandpa has not emerged in recent picture books. Laconic storyteller and intrepid adventurer, Grandpa shares universal childhood experiences with his grandchildren, goggle-eyed Louie and Mary Ann. . . .

A swift and always surprising sequence of events; framed and free pictorial elements in varying page layouts; a range of graffiti to suggest sound effects and dialogue; plot, character, personality, fantasy, emotion, and humor created by unerring line; elegant discrimination in color use: These are some elements of Stevenson's inventive genius as a picture book artist.

> *Gertrude Herman, "A Picture is Worth Several Hundred Words," in The Horn Book Magazine, Vol. LXI, No. 5, September-October, 1985, p. 605.*

MARGARET CARTER

Imagine this: you're looking out of the window on a pretty stormy night: you're doing no harm—just looking out of the window in company with your young brother, who's a bit of a drag anyway.

Because of the high wind, there's a lot of debris flying past including an old lady in a rocking chair, a saucepan and a cow or two—and suddenly you're knocked clean out of that window by a passing pig. Fortunately, you land on a ship which seems lucky until you happen to notice that it contains seventeen hideous pirates and a trained octopus. Maybe you could cope with seventeen hideous pirates and an *ordinary* octopus . . . but a *trained* octopus . . . Now that, in the language of James Stevenson, is Big Trouble.

James Stevenson is a New York reporter: "My life", he told us in a telephone interview from the States "is drab" (A New York reporter *drab?*). But his part-time activity is writing and illustrating children's books and that is where—as you'll see from the above quoted situation in one of his books—drabness (if it exists) goes out.

As well as reporter he is also a contributor of cartoons to The New Yorker and his text in his children's books shows that influence. It is laconic, sharpened to essentials . . . "a technique", he says. "learnt when captions have to be short, or ideally, don't exist at all". Listen to the opening of *Worse Than Willy!*

> "How's that new baby brother of yours?" said
> Grandpa.
> "Willy?" said Louie. "No fun".
> "Not cute", said Mary Ann.
> "All he can do is eat and sleep", said Louie.
> "Or cry", said Mary Ann.

Now that's life: straight from the shoulder. None of that "Isn't he sweet" business. New babies—as any child knows—just eat, sleep, cry and take all the attention.

James Stevenson's technique is so deft that you don't even notice you're turning the pages as you rollick through the zestful, muted stories. Often the stories are set in a frame, the frame being Grandpa. Mary Ann and Louie mildly grumble about this and that to Grandpa who recounts how much worse things were when *he* was a boy and how, mostly, things straighten out in the end.

James Stevenson's characters are allowed no self pity. Children and animals keep their dignity but always with a stoical "just wait and see" acceptance. Very often a situation is coped with in the only way a child can—by taking the sideways approach. So in *Yuck!* the snooty witches Dolores and Lavinia who are downright mean to that meek witch, Emma, (who only wanted to try a simple potion) get their come-uppance when Emma's friends, the animals, rally round with a series of tricks. The midget V the mighty approach—familiar to all from birth.

It's a cheer-up, things-could-be-worse attitude—perhaps something James Stevenson learnt from involvement with his own nine children—. . . .

Many of his stories are based on happenings familiar to children. Take *The Night After Christmas*. Ted and Annie—a bear and a doll—find themselves in adjacent dustbins. The conversation goes like this:

> "So you got thrown out, too?" said the doll. "Sure did . . . the kid who owned me got a space gun for Christmas."

And now arrives Chauncey, a brown dog, who knows a thing or two.

> "A word to the wise", says Chauncey. "They collect the rubbish here first thing in the morning."

So Ted and Annie climb aboard Chauncey and all—if not well—becomes supportable.

So the situations are built into comfortable stories, often in a cartoon format visually familiar to today's children. . . .

The constant in his children's stories is that he takes a situation immediately familiar to a child, then extends it—sometimes by comparing it to what might happen, sometimes through pure fantasy, sometimes by a child orientated victory—but his gentle moral never moralises. Always, help is at hand, whether it's Grandpa, a brown dog, an alligator, a frog and three mice or an odd-job man, Alf. His courageous characters swim gamely against the tide and comfortingly always find another shore.

> *Margaret Carter, "James Stevenson," in* Books for Your Children, *Vol 20, No. 3, Autumn-Winter, 1985, p. 25.*

BARBARA BADER

Stevenson the writer and cartoonist is familiar from the pages of *The New Yorker*, where he has congenially plied his trade since 1956, and from his picture books—an astonishing 30-odd since he took off with *"Could Be Worse!"* in 1977. Earlier Stevenson entries are stories with pictures; the subsequent ones are stories in pictures—briefly captioned pictures, akin to cartoons and comic strips in economy and suggestiveness (and often in form), yet eclectic and various in execution.

Stevenson the watercolorist turns up periodically on the cover of *The New Yorker*. But he may be found also, and increasingly, in the picture books. Like many a cartoonist before him, from Rowlandson to Lear to Steig and Low, Stevenson has an affinity for atmospheric landscape. And like many another purveyor of humor, he is prone to sadness: a quiet, pensive melancholy.

In the body of work, the several Stevenson picturebook worlds, there is no hierarchy. Rather, the execution suits the contents and the meaning—touched always with dramatic invention and Stevenson's almost uncanny gift for suspended animation. Throughout, an enlargement and a deepening has taken place.

"Could Be Worse!" and its exuberant successors could be set down as cartoon drawing with color washes. But over time we have seen Grandpa's outrageous yarns turn into sly, turnabout responses to Louie and Mary Ann's anxieties and discontents. Grandpa has become, in the comic strips that tell the tall tale, the mustachioed tyke of the children's imaginings—after shrinking to child size and donning a false mustache in *That Terrible Halloween Night*. (Reappearing in *We Can't Sleep*, he was mustachioed for good.) Stevenson came to distinguish pictorially between exterior and interior stories; he found in Uncle Wainwright a second, contrasting old gent (and a mustachioed babe with a topknot). In *There's Nothing to Do!*, their new outing, they are a duo—loop-de-looping through the air (a tornado's got them) in pursuit of two bowls of ice cream on the cover, cradled in wicker armchairs and leafy tendrils on the last, placid, porch-sitting page. A second major Stevenson world, of the displaced or dispossessed, is rendered in watercolor sketches, where background becomes foreground, in effect, and scenes of place, even more than characterization, set the mood and convey the feelings. This is the world of Howard, the wild duck stranded in New York for the winter, and of *The Night After Christmas*, a toy's-eye-view of city chill with Gogolesque dialogue that is, altogether, Stevenson's most despairing and jubilant work. . . .

When I Was Nine, Stevenson's memoir of a boyhood summer, is wholly watercolor: a sketchbook of impressions and single images, domestic scenes and personal belongings, without a single defining or enclosing line. What happens in the summer is that the family drives out west—with a natural mix of squabbles and pleasures and marvelous new sights. What happens visually is that Stevenson draws in watercolor: the northern sky alight or the desert's awesome edge or dog Jocko welcoming the party back, the artwork is spontaneous, animated, expressive.

The twentieth century has broken down boundaries, and hangs sketches along with finished paintings, satirical cartoons along with academic portraits. For Stevenson and his few peers, using their freedom to the full, boundaries don't exist.

> *Barbara Bader, "The Moods and Modes of James Stevenson," in a promotional piece for* When I Was Nine *by James Stevenson, Greenwillow Books, 1986.*

COLIN MILLS

[In *What's Under My Bed?* and *The Great Big Especially Beautiful Easter Egg*], Grandpa tells Mary Anne and Louie tales of his boyhood. He recounts his own fears of bedtime sights and sounds in *What's Under My Bed?* In *Easter Egg*, there's a fantastic story of his adventurous quest after the world's biggest egg. The flashing back and forth between the here-and-now and Grandpa's childhood is witty and dashing, building upon techniques the readers know well from TV and video. Six to eights enjoy the gentle teasing camaraderie between the young and the old. This writer/artist has a quirky, generous sense of humour.

Colin Mills, in a review of "What's Under My Bed?"
and "The Great Big Especially Beautiful Easter Egg,"
in Books for Keeps, No. 47, November, 1987, p. 19.

IF I OWNED A CANDY FACTORY (1968)

[If I Owned a Candy Factory *was written by James Walker Stevenson.*]

James Walker Stevenson was eight when he dreamed this impossible dream, as the ingenuous ending attests. His father, who drew the laconic illustrations, projects the contrast between diminuitive children and huge factory, between the multicolored splendor of the candy and the drabness of the world at large. Nothing to chew on but, like confectionery sugar, a fleeting satisfaction.

A review of "If I Owned a Candy Factory," in Kirkus
Service, Vol. XXXIV, No. 18, September 15, 1968,
p. 1045.

The artist's eight-year-old son originated the just-pretend idea for this slight picture book. The small hero imagines that if he had a candy factory he would present one friend with a railroad car full of gumdrops, another with a mountain of lollypops, and another with a string of licorice that extends across four pages. The spare simplicity and clean spacing of the color-washed line drawings keep this very slender story from being overly precious, but there is hardly enough here to make a book worth purchasing.

Nancy Young Orr, in a review of "If I Owned a
Candy Factory," in School Library Journal, Vol. 15,
No. 3, November, 1968, p. 81.

WALKER, THE WITCH, AND THE STRIPED FLYING SAUCER (1969)

Very timely is this picture story of a small boy's encounter with a witch, a long-established member of the space community and with a tenant of a flying saucer, a yet to be seen neighbor. Very timely and very funny, which won't surprise anyone who enjoyed James Stevenson's illustrations for that earlier funny picture book, *If I Owned a Candy Factory.*

A review of "Walker, the Witch, and the Striped
Flying Saucer," in Publishers Weekly, Vol. 196, No.
5, August 4, 1969, p. 49.

Whimsical, black-and-white, cartoon-like illustrations match the humorous tone of an equally whimsical story that may, however, be too understated for broad picture-book crowd appeal. Walker tells Jane the story of his encounter with a high-flying, bad-tempered witch and a cigar-smoking little man in a striped flying saucer. Walker accepts the man's invitation to do some flying, first in a car, then in a biplane, but in coming back to earth he finds that the witch has made the man and his saucer invisible. She does the same to the biplane, prompting a furious Walker to shout her own magic word—"Elbisivni!"—at her, causing her to disappear. Though no visible proof remains of witch or saucer man, Walker knows he hasn't dreamt the whole adventure because he finds a cigar in the field and hears the man's voice promising to return one day. He's further reassured by Jane, who responds to his admission of "Well, some parts of the story were truer than others," with "I believed a lot of it." Slight, humorous reading and viewing fare, with mild chuckle potential.

Jeraline Nerney, in a review of "Walker, the Witch,
and the Striped Flying Saucer," in School Library
Journal, Vol. 16, No. 4, December, 1969, p. 44.

This Americanised picture book will appeal to some children with a taste for the odd and the way-out. It has dull pictures and trite humour, which ape but have none of the genius of Dr. Seuss, and make it a rather expensive joke that goes off like a damp squib. . . .

As Walker says to his friend Jane at the end, "Well, Jane, did you believe my story". "Most of it", said Jane. Well sorry, but I did not and I doubt if many children will either.

J. Russell, in a review of "Walker, the Witch, and
the Striped Flying Saucer," in The Junior Bookshelf,
Vol. 35, No. 6, December, 1971, p. 367.

THE BEAR WHO HAD NO PLACE TO GO (1972)

Poor Ralph is a picture of bearish pooh-plexity as he sets off in his bicycle in search of a new home after being fired by the circus. A hitchhiker, Frank the rat, invites him to live in the woods ("said Ralph, 'What's the woods?'") and all is happy again until Ralph learns that his new friends Herb and Paul bear plan to sleep all winter. The animals hold a Big Woods Circus to convince Ralph to stay around and try the rural custom of hibernation—which he does—settling down happily in his baggy striped pajamas for a peaceful winter's snooze. The gentle gray-washed sketches make this simple parable of acceptance work, and Ralph's own endearing modesty should win him a home.

A review of "The Bear Who Had No Place to Go,"
in Kirkus Reviews, Vol. XL, No. 11, June 1, 1972,
p. 621.

[*The Bear Who Had No Place to Go* is] an easy, low-key, almost effortless performance by The New Yorker artist-writer, with softly shaded black-and-white drawings. Not classic but comfortable.

George A. Woods, "The Art of the Picture Book,"
in The New York Times, August 4, 1972, p. 29.

HERE COMES HERB'S HURRICANE! (1973)

After hearing a turtle reminisce about a hurricane, Herb, a rabbit, organizes a weather-watch among the animals. After a few false alarms, he is scorned by the community. His nephews and a beaver try to bail him out by faking a storm—but then a real hurricane strikes and Herb is vindicated. The dialogue is generally banal; the beginning is wordy and slow moving, with too many animals merely identified by name cluttering the text. Midway the plot picks up, but reluctant readers who might especially enjoy the fun would not be likely to stick that far. The well-meaning, easily hurt main character is short on appeal, as is this slapstick parody which does not equal the success of the noted cartoonist-author's *The Bear Who Had No Place To Go.*

Ruth M. McConnell, in a review of "Here Comes
Herb's Hurricane!" in School Library Journal, Vol.
20, No. 4, December, 1973, p. 51.

Stevenson's sketchy, expressive drawings of his animal community help to reinforce the mild, indulgent humor of his story about Herb, the rabbit who takes it upon himself to organize a hurricane alarm system although there are some who pooh-pooh his efforts on the grounds that he just wants to be running something. The system relies upon a lookout seagull doing three loop-the-loops, at which point a squirrel in the treetops drops a sunflower into the stream and a frog by the waterfall pulls a rope which rings Herb's bell. So it's no surprise that there are malfunctions and that Herb leaves home in disgrace after two false alarms. But as this is a likably goodnatured tale it's just as unsurprising when Herb's nephews frighten the community with a simulated hurricane in order to restore their uncle to general favor, and when—on top of all that commotion—a real rip-roaring storm does blow through and make Herb a hero. Unaffectedly breezy, affectionately bemused.

> *A review of "Here Comes Herb's Hurricane!" in* Kirkus Reviews, *Vol. XVI, No. 23, December 1, 1973, p. 1310.*

There's a debonair charm to the dialogue in this entertaining story about an animal community, and the brisk sketches have humor and vigor.... The story line is sturdy and needs no support, but it gets wonderful buttressing by the characterization: the perennial whiner who reiterates the fact that he never asks for sympathy, the hard-working beaver who dwells lovingly on how much harder he works than others do. Great fun, and a good story for reading aloud to children too young to read it independently. (pp. 150-51)

> *Zena Sutherland, in a review of "Here Comes Herb's Hurricane!" in* Bulletin of the Center for Children's Books, *Vol. 27, No. 9, May, 1974, pp. 150-51.*

"COULD BE WORSE!" (1977)

"At Grandpa's house things were always the same." That is, until he overhears his grandchildren's complaint and concocts a humdinger for them over breakfast. "Last night ... a large bird pulled me out of bed and took me for a long ride," he begins, and before he's through, he's been snowballed by a yeti, squished by a giant something-or-other, chased by a blob of marmalade, and he's hitched a ride on a sea turtle. Stevenson's scraggly, expressive pictures of the pajama-clad, thoroughly taken-aback old gent, and of the creatures who toss him about, make this a delightful flight of fancy and a skillfully paced read-aloud.

> *A review of "'Could Be Worse'," in* Kirkus Reviews, *Vol. XLV, No. 6, March 15, 1977, p. 282.*

One has only to look at the season's crop of new children's books to realize that grandparents are currently in vogue. But it is possible to produce an original and wonderfully integrated book on any subject—as the author-artist demonstrates in a brief text and in imaginatively designed, free-spirited watercolor paintings. To Mary Ann and Louie, Grandpa's life appears uneventful and monotonous; worse yet, his laconic response to the family's minor catastrophes is inevitably the same: "Could be worse." The children decide that "Grandpa never says anything.... because nothing interesting happens to him." But one morning the old man catches them off guard with a magnificently impossible tale of his wild adventures in exotic places.... The book, however, represents no mere flight of fancy, for the two children, having the last—and predictable—word, bring the story to a neatly grounded conclusion. (pp. 432-33)

> *Ethel L. Heins, in a review of "'Could Be Worse!'," in* The Horn Book Magazine, *Vol. LIII, No. 4, August, 1977, pp. 432-33.*

James Stevenson's *"Could Be Worse!"* could not, in fact, be better. Though the talk in his pictures has been freed from the encapsulating bubble, it is in essence the same and works as effectively.... James Stevenson's pictures of grandfather in the talons of a huge bird, grandfather hiding under an air-filled teacup at the bottom of the sea to avoid confrontation with a giant goldfish, and grandfather sailing back to bed on a mammoth paper dart, are stupendously funny.

> *Elaine Moss, "Begin at the Beginning," in* The Times Literary Supplement, *No. 3943, October 21, 1977, p. 1245.*

WILFRED THE RAT (1977)

Stooped, buck-toothed Wilfred is the picture of battered dejection when he arrives shivering at the closed-up amusement park; even in his dreams, he's "being chased again by big dogs." Then Wilfred meets squirrel Dwayne and chipmunk Rupert ("We hang around here") and, in them, finds his first friends. Dwayne and Rupert show Wilfred all the pleasures of the park, but come summer when the people are slated to return and his friends leave for safer quarters, Wilfred chooses to stay and watch the fun. On his own then, Wilfred is chased by the owner's dog on opening night, and his frantic but spectacular leap from the roller coaster earns him a job offer as "Daredevil Rat." But "it wouldn't be any fun being a star unless Dwayne and Rupert were around too," and so Wilfred joins his friends to wait in town until all three can return at summer's end. A winning choice, without a doubt—both for Wilfred and for the picture book audience who will take to this slack-bodied rat and delight in his good fortune.

> *A review of "Wilfred the Rat," in* Kirkus Reviews, *Vol. XLV, No. 13, July 1, 1977, p. 668.*

The author, who has a talent for stories about the lonely and friendless, such as *The Bear Who Had No Place to Go*, embellishes this thoroughly satisfactory story with casual, offhand dialogue and deceptively sophisticated pencil drawings, leaving not only Wilfred but the reader with a feeling of contentment.

> *Ann A. Flowers, in a review of "Wilfred the Rat," in* The Horn Book Magazine, *Vol. LIII, No. 6, December, 1977, pp. 656-57.*

"HELP!" YELLED MAXWELL (with Edwina Stevenson, 1978)

If animals and an occasional plant can aid the human heroes of old-time fairy tales, why not a fire hydrant, street lamp, gas pumps, and phone booths in a modern one? The Stevensons (father and daughter) have just such an assembly bustling about trying to help third-grade Maxwell save the town from washing away when rain swells the water in an old riverbed. Fortunately for the story, it turns out that these contentious, bumbling devices are no help at all, and in the end it's a small, dented oil can who gives Maxwell the much-needed confidence—and, gently prodding, the ideas—that do the trick: the can, held by Max, oils the old dam door's rusty crank, which Maxwell—bravely, precariously—then turns to open the dam. There's a sweet-sad parting at the end when the oil can goes down the river "to see what there is to see," and Maxwell and his dog Linda go home. But the authors' handling of the ego-boosting

From The Sea View Hotel, *written and illustrated by James Stevenson. Greenwillow Books, 1978. Copyright © 1978 by James Stevenson. All rights reserved. By permission of Greenwillow Books (A Division of William Morrow & Company, Inc.).*

function of the adventure is perfunctory, and even though Stevenson's drawings are as appealingly human as can be, it's awfully hard to get sentimental over an oil can.

> *A review of "'Help!' Yelled Maxwell," in* Kirkus Reviews, *Vol. XLVI, No. 4, February 15, 1978, p. 179.*

The story seems to be about Maxwell's struggles against his own absent-mindedness and inferiority complexes but due to the handling of the fantasy element, it is never quite clear whether he succeeds in saving the community or whether it is mostly done for him.

> *Craighton Hippenhammer, in a review of "'Help!' Yelled Maxwell," in* School Library Journal, *Vol. 24, No. 9, May, 1978, p. 71.*

THE WORST PERSON IN THE WORLD (1978)

The worst person in the world "lived all alone in a terrible mess . . . in an old house in a yard full of poison ivy." And when children in a field ask old Mr. Worst if he's seen their lost baseball—"'Certainly not,' he said, looking right at it. Then the worst person in the world meets the ugliest thing in the world (a sort of pastel-spotted, one-horned stegosaurus)— but Ugly, convinced that "if you've got a pleasing personality that's all that counts," follows the worst home, cleans the

place up, and decorates it for a children's party. The worst, fed up, orders Ugly, children, and party out and away . . . and then, alone in the usual but suddenly less satisfying gloom, reconsiders. A mean old character is always more interesting than a kindly one, and you can trust Stevenson to make the worst (as he frequently calls him) as grumpy, sour, and lonely as anyone could wish. He is also touching, and his inevitable reform is effected with wit, and without violating the old codger's established gruff manner.

> *A review of "The Worst Person in the World," in* Kirkus Reviews, *Vol. XLVI, No. 7, April 1, 1978, p. 368.*

When the worst person in the world (who's also one of the meanest) meets the ugliest creature in the world (who's also one of the nicest), we all know what happens. . . . The pictures are grand—Stevenson's soft comedy is delicious. But the text is carelessly written without cadence or style, and the plot is entirely predictable without the humor that the premise promises.

> *Marjorie Lewis, in a review of "The Worst Person in the World," in* School Library Journal, *Vol. 24, No. 9, May, 1978, p. 59.*

James Stevenson seems to be new to this country. He is a man to be reckoned with. . . . Mr. Stevenson's text is beautifully crisp and matched well to the page. His line-and-wash drawing is equally to the point. He is a little like an American Quentin

Blake, a little less funny but just as pertinent. A very nice book and a most promising debut. (p. 17)

> *M. Crouch, in a review of "The Worst Person in the World," in* The Junior Bookshelf, *Vol. 43, No. 1, February, 1979, pp. 16-17.*

THE SEA VIEW HOTEL (1978)

Wonderfully human animal characters, delightfully appointed Victorian settings, black-and-white comic strip format: an odd combination of elements, but Stevenson makes them seem to belong together in this charming depiction of a well-dressed little mouse's vacation with his parents at the leisurely Sea View Hotel. Popping with anticipation at first, Hubert is soon deflated to find that there are no other children at the hotel, that the creaky adult guests won't tolerate any activity above the tiptoe level, and—the final blow—that stinging jellyfish make even swimming impossible. But then Hubert meets Alf the caretaker, a nice old pipe-smoking dog, and through him discovers the ordinary delights of wild raspberries, swinging vines, stone skipping, night fishing. . . . From the hotel's gazebo for idling guests to the stars Alf sights from the fishing boat, every detail is so lovingly and accurately remembered that readers, like Hubert, will come to feel the charm of the Sea View Hotel. Then, just when they're settling into the pace—SWOOOOOOOSH! Hubert is carried off on an untended solo flight in Alf's homemade glider. A wild finale to the perfect vacation: it sure beats Disney World.

> *A review of "The Sea View Hotel," in* Kirkus Reviews, *Vol. XLVI, No. 16, August 15, 1978, p. 877.*

A story with simplicity, harmony, and ease in the telling plus pictures that have joy and warmth, all fused into the form of a comic book taken beyond its limits. . . . The characters, whose bodies in their turn-of-the-century clothing seem human, have heads of birds, turtles, dogs, or whatever suits their personality or Stevenson's whimsy. The relaxed cartoon drawings, black-and-white pen-and-ink with a wash, may come one to a double page, or four to a page, but usually somewhere in between. They seem filled with fresh air and light, as does this whole happy, gentle, and appealing book.

> *Mary B. Nickerson, in a review of "The Sea View Hotel," in* School Library Journal, *Vol. 25, No. 2, October, 1978, p. 139.*

The Sea View Hotel is . . . a virtuoso piece of drawing. . . . It is done in comic-strip style with lots of swiftly-drawn sketches, with a balloon text, showing the adventures of a family of mice on their seaside holiday. . . . The monochrome drawings are in the New Yorker tradition and so is much of the humour. It may please father just a little more than junior but there is something here for all. (pp. 320-21)

> *M. Crouch, in a review of "The Sea View Hotel," in* The Junior Bookshelf, *Vol. 43, No. 6, December, 1979, pp. 320-21.*

WINSTON, NEWTON, ELTON, AND ED (1978)

Sibling squabbling is a whole new show when it's performed by Stevenson's expressive, flipper-wielding walrus family. Winston, Newton, and Elton bicker, throw fish (their supper) at each other, lose the fish in the water, and blame each other when Mama steps in. Their mother supplies more fish on the

condition that they settle down and behave, and it seems that they do—but we leave them arguing about which one has been the most polite. There's another story about Ed, a stranded penguin, who writes snow messages for the birds and is rewarded with a whaleback ride home. Thin stories, but Stevenson's loose drawings make his characters appealingly laughable.

> *A review of "Winston, Newton, Elton, and Ed," in* Kirkus Reviews, *Vol. XLVI, No. 20, October 15, 1978, p. 1136.*

Giving walruses clever names like **Winston, Newton, Elton, and Ed** and making them the leading characters do little to relieve the boredom of this 20-page sibling feud by James Stevenson. Less trivial is the second chapter about penguins, but the package offers nothing new.

> *Kathy Coffey, in a review of "Winston, Newton, Elton, and Ed," in* School Library Journal, *Vol. 25, No. 4, December, 1978, p. 66.*

MONTY (1979)

An alligator who daily accommodates a little frog, duck, and rabbit by carrying them across the river on their way both to and from school? You might well question the arrangement, and Monty does also after too many weeks? months? of being prodded and rebuked by the unappreciative little scholars. ("Don't wobble so much, Monty!" "Let's see some speed, Monty!") Monty simply decides without warning to take a vacation, and after unsuccessfully trying to get across on four turtle backs and then a plank/springboard, the children no longer take the alligator for granted. The three learn their well-deserved lesson in loosely-sketched, lightly colored comic-strip frames that well suit the easy flow of the story; the expressive pictures and brisk lines ("Who wants to watch a duck think?" asks a disgruntled turtle at one point) amuse in themselves as they move things along.

> *A review of "Monty," in* Kirkus Reviews, *Vol. XLVII, No. 9, May 1, 1979, p. 516.*

This is a very entertaining story where plenty happens, and there is a nice understated moral. . . .

Stevenson's strip cartoon technique makes for very fast and lively reading, the pictures are full of life and expression, and who cares if it's about animals again: it's funny.

> *Virginia Makins, "Where Have All the Humans Gone?" in* The Times Literary Supplement, *No. 3319, January 18, 1980, p. 37.*

The greatest of all gifts is laughter. These books [which also include *Mister Magnolia* by Quentin Blake and *Gentleman Jim* by Raymond Briggs], by three undisputed masters of the art, are reminders that comic situations and grotesque characters are not enough; one must have style. (p. 166)

In this company James Stevenson's offering is more modest in scale and concept, but it too has a fine consistency. . . . The tale is told briefly in swift sketches and hilarious speech-balloons. Lovely.

> *M. Crouch, in a review of "Monty," in* The Junior Bookshelf, *Vol. 44, No. 4, August, 1980, pp. 166-67.*

FAST FRIENDS: TWO STORIES (1979)

The pleasures of friendship are celebrated in two short, easy-to-read stories accompanied by simple line drawings washed with soft pastel tones. The first story presents the plight of slow-moving Murray, a turtle whose inability to keep up with swifter species automatically stamps him as an outsider, until he discovers an abandoned skateboard. With the set of wheels he and a snail become instant celebrities, introducing the neighborhood to the wonders of racing, only to conclude that having learned "'what it's like to go fast,'" they "'can take it or leave it.'" The companion vignette features another turtle, Clem—who is equally friendless—as one of the central characters. Then one day Thomas, a migrating mouse, builds a house and shows Clem through his own hospitality what it takes to make friends. Showing the same kinds of animals in two stories with different names but with no physical differences in the drawings might possibly confuse young readers. But the author-illustrator evokes with dexterity the gentle humor of the situations. (pp. 530-31)

> *Mary M. Burns, in a review of "Fast Friends: Two Stories," in* The Horn Book Magazine, *Vol. LV, No. 5, October, 1979, pp. 530-31.*

Under the surface of two stories about small woodland creatures is the theme of friendship, what it needs and doesn't need to keep going. To this end, Stevenson makes his rather charming stories ring with true feelings. His characters tend to be low on ego, though many readers will commiserate with them and the stories make everyone feel better. . . . Action is appropriately ample, as is dialogue; the very low reading level is primarily a factor of brief, but not stiff, sentences. Stevenson adds his own unassuming art work.

> *Judith Goldberger, in a review of "Fast Friends: Two Stories," in* Booklist, *Vol. 76, No. 12, February 15, 1980, p. 838.*

HOWARD (1979)

Howard the duck lags behind and loses his southbound flock. His first solo flight lands him in a storm and strands him in Manhattan. Can a lone mallard make it in the Big Town? Lucky duck, he soon hooks up with a frog who takes him on a sewer sightseeing tour and three companionable mice left homeless by the Sanitation Department. They all sit out the cold in a condemned but plushly appointed theater entered through Howard's aerial reconnaissance and converted into a winter haven for strays. A wrecking ball breaks up the idyll but by then it's spring and the streets look so savory in Stevenson's soft water colors that Howard bids his returning flock goodbye. *New Yorker* cartoonist Stevenson bathes the city in a mellow light that makes it glow. The same goes for the up-tempo story alive with sheer high spirits.

> *Pamela D. Pollack, in a review of "Howard," in* School Library Journal, *Vol. 26, No. 4, December, 1979, p. 78.*

Line and watercolor drawings, softly colored and filled with wonderfully detailed scenes of New York City, illustrate a story that is told with verve and humor, and that has a surprise ending the lap audience (and their readers-aloud) should enjoy. . . . The illustrations are Stevenson at his best, but it's in the bland humor of the dialogue that the book's chief charm lies; for example, when Howard discovers the other ducks have gone,

he asks some rabbits where they went. "Up in the air." "I know that," says Howard. A rabbit points out, helpfully, "Then they turned left."

> *Zena Sutherland, in a review of "Howard," in* Bulletin of the Center for Children's Books, *Vol. 33, No. 6, February, 1980, p. 120.*

James Stevenson gives us a duck's-eye view of New York in *Howard*. . . . All the grimy grandeur of the city—particularly the Upper West Side—is captured in Mr. Stevenson's quick, gentle watercolors in a way that any tourist or native, child or adult, will enjoy. The story is perfunctory, but the breezy pictures make it all worthwhile.

> *Harold C. K. Rice, in a review of "Howard," in* The New York Times Book Review, *April 27, 1980, p. 49.*

THAT TERRIBLE HALLOWEEN NIGHT (1980)

The imperturbable Grampa from *"Could Be Worse!"* is back. He turns the tables on the kids and scores a scare with his recollections of "that terrible Halloween night" when he was about their age. The popeyed reactions of Mary Ann and Louie to his adventures in the strange old house (with a giant spider that runs off giggling; with a giant pumpkin that offers to turn him into same) will amp the fun for readers. The full-color cartoon illustrations are typically funny and imaginative. Stevenson manipulates color with craft: eerie, electric yellow and purple signal the moment of greatest intensity. (pp. 63-4)

> *Marilyn R. Singer, in a review of "That Terrible Halloween Night," in* School Library Journal, *Vol. 27, No. 1, September, 1980, pp. 63-4.*

Old Grandpa of *It Could Be Worse* tells Mary Ann and Louie another whopper, this time a hair-raising tale of yuck and monsters in a haunted house. The story of his childhood experience is drawn out of an ostensibly reluctant Grandpa, who has to explain why he is no longer frightened by such tame tricks as the children's Halloween antics. And he never does tell what finally happened: "It's too scary to tell you—but when I came out of that house, I was an old man. And I've been that old *ever since!*" What we do get from Grandpa's laconic telling and Stevenson's gleefully ghastly pictures is an inspired funny-scary distillation of haunted house lore. There's a bat-winged, fish-tailed, lobster-clawed, wide-mouthed, snaggle-toothed something that describes itself as "the worst parts of a lot of things"; and there's a cellar floor that's hard to walk on because it is "entirely frogs—very slippery. I kept getting caught in the cobwebs. Then I heard a horrible voice. . . ." A new high in shivers and Halloween delight—only a cool old codger like Grandpa could remain untransfixed.

> *A review of "That Terrible Halloween Night," in* Kirkus Reviews, *Vol. XLVIII, No. 17, September 1, 1980, p. 1160.*

It's fresh, it's amusing, and it's illustrated by appropriately eerie (but not really frightening) pictures; the story's told with brio, and listeners can enjoy the fact that Grandpa is telling a whopper, as well as enjoying the whopper itself. (p. 42)

> *Zena Sutherland, in a review of "That Terrible Halloween Night," in* Bulletin of the Center for Children's Books, *Vol. 34, No. 2, October, 1980, pp. 41-2.*

CLAMS CAN'T SING (1980)

Because of their certainty that "'clams can't do anything,'" the inhabitants of the seashore exclude Benny and Beatrice from their evening concert. But the two dauntless mollusks prove their neighbors wrong with their performance of "Symphony for Two Clams," a little-known occasional piece. Onomatopoeia is the stylistic technique in an easy-to-read, off-handedly humorous story which integrates sound effects into the illustrations as an accompaniment to the straightforward text. For instance, "The morning was full of noises at the beach" is followed by the words *quack, skeek, skwaawk, bzt-bzzzt, whoosh, chomp-chomp, splash*—all of which appear on a succeeding double-page spread illustration in association with the appropriate fauna. As well as providing amusement for beginning readers, the nonsense syllables also offer possibilities for orchestrating the book as a choral reading project for an entire class. (pp. 516-17)

> *Mary M. Burns, in a review of "Clams Can't Sing,"*
> *in* The Horn Book Magazine, *Vol. LVI, No. 5, October, 1980, pp. 516-17.*

You can count on even the least of Stevenson's picture stories for wit and wiggy humor tied to a sound, supportive base. This begins—to the deadpan announcement "The morning was full of noises at the beach"—with a free-wheeling chorus from crabs, ducks, gulls, and other small creatures, each contributing its ZIZZA-ZIZZA, BZT-BZT-BZT, SKWAWK, SKEEK, or CHAKA-CHAKA-CHAKA. Soon we're into a frenzy of performing art, with drumming and clacking (KA KA DAK KIK KIK) and klonking, and bird Liza teaching crab Clinton to dance. Only clams Benny and Beatrice are silent—and only Benny and Beatrice are not invited to perform at the night's concert. "Clams can't sing," lobster Foster explains. "Clams can't do anything." But Benny and Beatrice put their heads (or whatever) together, and as the concert ends they move in. They start with bubbles (OOSH! . . . OOSHA-FUSHA! . . . BA-LOOP! . . ."), then they get fancy, and though they can't take a bow as requested, they do dance (so they say) inside their shells, as the party goes on. Well, maybe you have to see it. In Stevenson's hands, it's a smacking putdown of the concept *can't,* and a zippy (that's ZIZZA-ZIP-ZOOEY) demonstration that having fun is the best defense.

> *A review of "Clams Can't Sing," in* Kirkus Reviews,
> *Vol. XLVIII, No. 20, October 15, 1980, p. 1356.*

Every word in James Stevenson's text counts, and there are lots of penned-in beach noises and a lesson in human (clam?) achievement to boot. Green and salmon washed cartoon sequences—a sea gull/horseshoe crab percussion act, a sandpiper/crab softshoe—catch the beach action and the humor of taking clams seriously.

> *Nancy Palmer, in a review of "Clams Can't Sing,"*
> *in* School Library Journal, *Vol. 27, No. 4, December, 1980, p. 66.*

THE WISH CARD RAN OUT! (1981)

Stevenson has hit his biggest jackpot since *Could Be Worse* with a perfect kids' spoof on credit cards. Charlie's birthday goes badly when he doesn't get a baseball glove; but a lost International Wish card fixes that—and a lot of other things, including his dog's ability to talk and his little brother's dis-

appearance. To get Billy back, Charlie goes to Wish Central, where the whole company has gone out of business except for Daphne the cleaning lady, who used to be a fairy godmother. She intervenes in the machines gone mad for an eventual happy ending, but meanwhile clever details are piling up in the storytelling and art departments. Each character has some quietly witty lines ("Well, maybe I could give you *two* wishes." / "Why not three?" / "I've cut back"), including a cockroach they meet at the IWC ("Jump on all the buttons at once!!" / "Brilliant idea, Chester!" / "Oh, you just have to have a knowledge of electronics"). Stevenson's zippy cartoon line work benefits from tasteful colors in a format that will appease youngsters' appetite for comic books without indulging their craving for junk art.

> *A review of "The Wish Card Ran Out!" in* Booklist,
> *Vol. 77, No. 12, February 15, 1981, p. 812.*

What happens when a big corporation takes over from those old-timey fairy godmothers and wishing wells proves just the nightmare one might anticipate, and Stevenson revs up his pace and patter to match the electronic menace. . . . Stevenson tells this zappier story in straight comic-strip format without supplementary narrative, and his pictures make delightful use of comic-strip conventions. But Stevenson keeps his colors soft and low-keyed, and he keeps one foot firmly planted in the old-timey non-technological world. (A computer might frizz out [Charlie's dog] Spalding with a mighty ZAP in one frame, then entangle the kids with a just-as-menacing GOTCHA! in another.) With lots of snappy lines, some of the best from

Howard woke up on a roof.
He looked over the edge.
He didn't see any ducks.

From Howard, *written and illustrated by James Stevenson. Greenwillow Books, 1980. Copyright © 1980 by James Stevenson. All rights reserved. By permission of Greenwillow Books (A Division of William Morrow & Company, Inc.).*

Spalding and [the giant cockroach] Chester, it's an inspired interface and a grand adventure.

> *A review of "The Wish Card Ran Out!" in* Kirkus Reviews, *Vol. XLIX, No. 6, March 15, 1981, p. 354.*

Fresh, funny, lively, and pithy—what more could the lap audience ask? Stevenson's lightly colored cartoon style drawings are just right for this fantasy spoof of credit cards, fairy godmothers, the computer society, and meaningless catch phrases. . . . Replete with action, wit, and humor.

> *Zena Sutherland, in a review of "The Wish Card Ran Out!" in* Bulletin of the Center for Children's Books, *Vol. 34, No. 11, July-August, 1981, p. 219.*

THE NIGHT AFTER CHRISTMAS (1981)

Like the plum pudding, James Stevenson arrives at least once a year to make things brighter and tastier. In his *The Night After Christmas*, a doll named Annie and a Teddy named Teddy sit discarded with the post-holiday garbage. A dog named Chauncey rescues them. He is sympathetic to Annie and Teddy but tells them that he cannot replace the children they belonged to. "I'm not much for games," he admits. "I run, bark, and wag my tail. That's about it." Modest as he is, Chauncey, like many a rumpled canine, is also a prince, and the solution he works out for Annie and Teddy will satisfy everyone. Whether writing or drawing, Mr. Stevenson understands perfectly the strength of a simple, understated line and a quiet laugh. Like Chauncey, he will win your heart and make it look as if he wasn't even trying. (pp. 57, 60)

> *Karla Kuskin, "The Art of Picture Books," in* The New York Times Book Review, *Novemeber 15, 1981, pp. 57, 60.*

A story about two discarded toys—a plump teddy bear and a ragged but still lovable doll—could easily degenerate into sentimentality. But the opening double-page spread quickly establishes the dry, reserved tone of the concisely told tale. . . . Balancing the simple story are the illustrations, drawn freely in charcoal and washed in warm tones; the watercolors evoke the emotion hinted at by the text, depicting the beauty of rows of brownstones through swirling snow, the coziness of Chauncey's basement haven, and the appealing demeanors of Annie and Teddy. (pp. 655-56)

> *Kate M. Flanagan, in a review of "The Night After Christmas," in* The Horn Book Magazine, *Vol. LVII, No. 6, December, 1981, pp. 655-56.*

James Stevenson's *Night After Christmas* . . . has real depth. . . . The brief text, chiefly dialogue, is pregnant with deeper implications, but not too difficult for a child who has first read with an adult, to grasp. There is a delightful laconic humour, and the characters contrast firmly with each other, in illustration as well as word: Annie's round-eyed gaze registers her stoic blunt pessimism. The cold and the snowstorm of the beginning are tangible, against the wide street backgrounds, and the large impressionistic interiors are full of odd detail, carried out in soft pencil and delicate wash—a thoughtful and attractive book.

> *M. Hobbs, in a review of "The Night After Christmas," in* The Junior Bookshelf, *Vol. 47, No. 1, February, 1983, p. 13.*

OLIVER, CLARENCE, AND VIOLET (1982)

Oliver, Clarence, and Violet, a beaver, a turtle, and a turkey, respectively, squabble as kids do and otherwise behave in a recognizably imperfect manner. This begins with Oliver pounding away at a secret project and the other two pretending they aren't curious. But Clarence tricks Oliver into confiding in him—Oliver is building a ship to go round the world—and soon the whole pond community has heard the news. And so, when Clarence and Violet are taken on for the voyage (Clarence providing sandwiches and Violet contributing the sail and the vessel's name, the *Violet II*), they have a time beating off the horde of animals who've been sold tickets by slimy Vince the frog. But at last the three are under way, with only a few small stowaways: First, "What's that stuff hanging from the yardarm," Oliver asks. "Looks like some old rags," says Violet—but it turns out to be Grover and Cheryl, a pair of bats. And later, as the boat seems to drag, Violet looks down over the stern. "Are there supposed to be green fingers attached to the rudder?" she asks Oliver—and thus they discover unpopular Vince, with his sickening smile, clinging to the rudder. Before a waterfall ends the voyage, two heroes have been made: first Vince, who goes over the falls while playing the hero, and then, more impressively, Oliver, who quickly fells a tree across the top of the falls to save his two nonswimming friends. Back at the pond there's a welcome-home party, but Stevenson doesn't end the adventure all sweetness and accord. Vince is still unlovable and unpopular, and the Swamp-Tones, a quintet of salamanders, are still such terrible singers that their party entertainment prompts the three principals to plan another voyage. This one is refreshing all the way.

> *A review of "Oliver, Clarence & Violet," in* Kirkus Reviews, *Vol. L, No. 6, March 15, 1982, p. 347.*

In a season of generally disappointing readers, one seizes on a new book by James Stevenson with especial enthusiasm. But this usually dependable author has not come up with an unqualified winner this time. *Oliver, Clarence & Violet* has a simple plot involving an animal that sets out to sail around the world, but the cast of characters is much too complicated. Bats named Grover and Cheryl fly through scenarios with a beaver, a turtle and a turkey (the title characters), along with a Kermit-like frog called Vince, while other animals, with names like JoAnne, Margaret, Edith and Waylon, wander in and out. One tries to keep it all straight, but it really isn't worth the effort.

> *Ann Haskell, "Something Easy to Read," in* The New York Times Book Review, *April 25, 1982, p. 42.*

[*Oliver, Clarence & Violet* provides] lots of laughs and some exciting moments in a book ideal for third-graders. The large print and the pencil-and-wash illustrations increase the book's suitability for young readers looking for longer texts. When Oliver and his personable crew arrive home after their abbreviated journey, readers will have the same readiness as the characters for another adventure—let's hope Stevenson will provide one.

> *Ilene Cooper, in a review of "Oliver, Clarence & Violet," in* Booklist, *Vol. 78, No. 20, June 15, 1982, p. 1370.*

WE CAN'T SLEEP (1982)

With a Gramps like Stevenson's spinning the yarns, who wouldn't try to wrangle a bedtime story? Here Louie and Mary Ann, though they can't agree on why they can't sleep ("It's too hot and quiet." "Too windy and noisy." "Too light." "Too dark." "Too lonely"), end up on Grandpa's lap—to hear about the time he had "that very same problem . . . many years ago. I was about your age." At this we see a little boy who needs a stool to reach the bathroom sink, with brown hair instead of Grandpa's sparse gray, but still equipped with the droopy mustache that he'll wear throughout the adventure. Like his yarns in *It Could Be Worse* and *That Terrible Halloween Night*, this is another flatly, laconically related whopper, in which Grandpa deals handily with ocean waves, sharks, an iceberg, a polar bear, and walruses—only to wind up on an island with smoke and fire and galumphing noises emerging from the jungle. ". . . The ground was shaking. Are you two getting sleepy?" asked Grandpa. "No!" said Louie and Mary Ann. "What was it?" "It was a huge dragon, breathing fire. He chased me into the ocean. All I could do was splash water at him." "I guess that didn't do any good," said Louie. "Yes, it did," said Grandpa. "It put his fire out. . . . But then. . . ." And so he continues, with more pop-up hazards and twitted expectation, until we see the children (and the dog) contentedly to sleep. A canny storyteller, that Gramps; and Stevenson's characteristic loose, free pictures reinforce the tone and the fun of the tongue-in-cheek, taken-for-granted wonders.

> *A review of "We Can't Sleep," in* Kirkus Reviews, *Vol. L, No. 17, September 1, 1982, p. 996.*

Stevenson's much-mustachioed Grandpa returns with another tall-tale spoof as antic as imagination itself. This time, pajamaed Louie and nightgowned Mary Ann can't sleep. . . . The solution is a round-the-world adventure involving sharks, polar bears, 6,000-pound walruses, fire-breathing dragons, etc. Improbably, all this lulls the two tykes to sleep—but who's going to argue verisimilitude at this point. Stevenson's deftly wacky watercolors provide the perfect offbeat accompaniment to this intergenerational romp.

> *Kristi L. Thomas, in a review of "We Can't Sleep," in* School Library Journal, *Vol. 29, No. 2, October, 1982, p. 146.*

"We can't sleep," announce Louie and Mary Ann to their grandpa, who acknowledges that he had that very same problem himself one time. His cure is a tale of that time—an account that starts out with a 50-mile uphill hike and escalates into a roller coaster of a whopper that has grandpa easing out of one tight squeeze only to be caught up in another. That's OK, except the run is too long and may leave some bedtime-bound tykes bored by their recognition of the story's pattern, strikingly similar to the adventure in the author's *Could Be Worse*. Others, however, might just relish the familiarity and find its larger-than-life movement just their cup of tea. In any case, Stevenson's quick-lined, full-color cartoons have an energy of their own and a literary jocularity that's easy to take. (pp. 373-74)

> *Denise M. Wilms, in a review of "We Can't Sleep," in* Booklist, *Vol. 79, No. 5, November 1, 1982, pp. 373-74.*

We Can't Sleep is a masterful blend of child psychology, tall tale humor, rhetorical understatement, and exuberant cartooning. . . . Stevenson cleverly depicts Grandpa during his childhood years with the same droll mustache that he wears as an adult. This is a delightful way to deepen the whimsical tone, even though the comical illustrations and the fantasy element in the exploits do this well enough already. . . .

As in the matter-of-fact text, the cartoons convey a balance between frenzy and a sense of aplomb. The line technique is so vigorous and spontaneous that the pictures seem to come freeflown from the tip of the pen. The colors are often applied in unconnected brush strokes that resemble lines, adding to the nervous activity within the illustration. Stevenson knows the exact amount of detail that will not interfere with the momentum of the composition, and when he discontinues a line, he is really maximizing the sense of structure and mood in a scene. This fine instinct for proportion and variation characterizes Stevenson both as an illustrator and a storyteller.

> *Donnarae MacCann and Olga Richard, in a review of "We Can't Sleep," in* Wilson Library Bulletin, *Vol. 57, No. 7, March, 1983, p. 591.*

BARBARA'S BIRTHDAY (1983)

Stevenson's pop-up beats most toy books and his own previous successes in intricacy, surprises and sheer fun. Barbara the mouse girl glumly anticipates a dull birthday, but a friend assures her that a veritable extravaganza is in preparation for the event. Paintings in marvelous spring colors are set in motion when pages are turned and tabs are pulled to show the promised attractions: 823 guests bearing gifts with the boxes spilling out the contents; a mountain of ice cream and a sky-scraper cake flown to the party by an army of birds; a maestro waving his baton as he conducts the symphony orchestra playing "Happy Birthday"; a big parade; fireworks and myriad other fantasies. Then the friend gives Barbara a little bouquet, and when she asks, "What about all that other stuff?" he says, "That's for next year." Still she has had the joy of imagining, along with all of the book's charmed young readers.

> *A review of "Barbara's Birthday," in* Publishers Weekly, *Vol. 223, No. 3, January 21, 1983, p. 84.*

A party in itself, full of pop-up and pull-tab surprises. . . . But this is not one of those staggering spectacles designed to impress; Stevenson aims more to delight than to astonish, and he goes at it with an air of playful innocence that's irresistible.

> *A review of "Barbara's Birthday," in* Kirkus Reviews, *Vol. LI, No. 4, February 15, 1983, p. 183.*

Barbara's Birthday is for fun. It is in fact a typical James Stevenson picture-book with the pop-ups as an added bonus. . . . Mr. Stevenson is one of my favourite comic artists and he is at his best here, simple, direct, full of lightly carried wisdom and observation.

> *M. Crouch, in a review of "Barbara's Birthday," in* The Junior Bookshelf, *Vol. 47, No. 5, October, 1983, p. 200.*

THE GREAT BIG ESPECIALLY BEAUTIFUL EASTER EGG (1983)

Stevenson uses an egg hunt as an excuse for some grandiose adventures. Two grandchildren ask their grandpa about his youthful egg hunts. In a visual flashback we see him with full black hair and mustache and short pants going off to find the egg of the book's title. Several adventures later he returns with one to give to his young girlfriend. And surprise! It's still there for the grandchildren to find behind a tree. Stevenson remains true to his loose watercolor style. His animated figures operate in, around and over a range of framing boxes that suggest comic strips. And the dialogue is found in such strips' typical verbal balloons. The cartoon-like composition helps maintain the frenetic action while reinforcing the make-believe. Lots of pinky purples for the spectacled cigar-smoking Easter Bunny, and a big brown bear with a solid sense of paranoia help give character to the adventure. The florid, hand-calligraphed title sets the appropriate mood for this lightweight bit of tongue-in-cheek. Grandpa may be balding and gray, but he sure can tell a tall tale or two.

> *Kenneth Marantz, in a review of ''The Great Big Especially Beautiful Easter Egg,''* in School Library Journal, *Vol. 29, No. 8, April, 1983, p. 107.*

When Mary Ann and Louie remind Grandpa that it is Easter again, Grandpa is persuaded to tell another story; happily for us, he still has a few tricks up his sleeve.... The sketchy drawings bubble with humor and with the amiable good nature of both man and beast. Grandpa's little Eton suit and bow tie remain remarkably tidy, as usual, throughout his preposterous experiences; but even more remarkable is the strong resemblance between the egg Grandpa found in the Frammistan Mountains and the one that Mary Ann and Louie find behind the tree in Grandpa's yard.

> *Ethel R. Twichell, in a review of ''The Great Big Especially Beautiful Easter Egg,''* in The Horn Book Magazine, *Vol. LIX, No. 4, August, 1983, p. 437.*

Lively wash and line strip-pictures contain most of the text in speech-balloons in a book just right for children shrewd enough to appreciate Grandpa's deadpan ingenuity as well as sharing the delight of his grandchildren in the desirable climax to a tall story.

> *Margery Fisher, in a review of ''The Great Big Especially Beautiful Easter Egg,''* in Growing Point, *Vol. 23, No. 2, July, 1984, p. 4295.*

GRANDPA'S GREAT CITY TOUR: AN ALPHABET BOOK (1983)

Like his stories Grandpa's tour of New York City is full of surprises. As the imperturbable gentleman leads his two young charges around the city—starting with a ride on Alligator Airlines—they observe an alphabet full of unusual sights. Playing the banjo, Grandpa sits on a sightseeing boat while overhead a buffalo, a bicyclist, and a bus cross a bridge. The park where the three stop for a picnic teems with things beginning with *P:* a panda, a pig, a parade, pears, pigeons, and a pelican. A citywide tour covers museums, the opera, the zoo, the ball park, and even the library as well as various spots in between. Every double-page spread invites repeated examination, and each perusal yields new discoveries; the freely painted watercolors swirl with movement and detail held in check by skillful composition. Under each letter the inclusions range from the obvious to the brain-teasing but always reflect the cartoonist's imagination and sense of fun.

> *Kate M. Flanagan, in a review of ''Grandpa's Great City Tour: An Alphabet Book,''* in The Horn Book Magazine, *Vol. LIX, No. 5, October, 1983, p. 567.*

James Stevenson features in his *Grandpa's Great City Tour* the irresistible old-boy character he has used in several of his in-spired tall tales. Mr. Stevenson's urbane sophistication and graphic dash make this alphabet a paean to megalopolitan pleasures and a treat for viewers of all ages. Wordless (except for signs and labels occurring in the illustrations), this work offers more letter objects per alphabet page than any single viewer is likely to discover alone. It's a bravura performance to please the entire family.

> *Selma G. Lanes, in a review of ''Grandpa's Great City Tour,''* in The New York Times Book Review, *October 9, 1983, p. 39.*

In the mode of Babar's *ABC*, Grandpa and Mary Anne and Louie do up the town (recognizably but not parochially New York) in alphabetical disorder.... There's hilarious method to some of the madness—Ee is a (Soho) Easter egg hunt—complete with elephant, eagle, and elk; Qq takes place in a library, where the Quiet is shattered by the Quack, Quack of ducks. A Stevenson spectacular, altogether: endlessly inventive, consistently expressive, and great-great fun.

> *A review of ''Grandpa's Great City Tour: An Alphabet Book,''* in Kirkus Reviews, Juvenile Issue, *Vol. LI, No. 21, November 1, 1983, p. J-187.*

WHAT'S UNDER MY BED? (1983)

In *What's Under My Bed?* Gramps confesses to the children Mary Ann and Louie that once he too was afraid of going to bed in his own grandparents' house. There were ghosts that turned out to be the wind, skeletons that were simply tree branches and a tidal wave of ''goblins, witches, spiders, giants . . . slitherers, creepers'' that sent little Grandpa into the comforting arms of his Grandma and Grandpa for that ultimate restorative, strawberry ice cream. Mr. Stevenson, as always, is a master of the difficult art of making things look easy. His story reads as if it were being spun just now and just for us.

> *Karla Kuskin, ''Picture a Ghost, a Moose or a Tin Soldier,''* in The New York Times Book Review, *November 13, 1983, p. 55.*

''It was awful! A creature with wild hair, no head, and a long tail was standing there.''

''But, Grandpa,'' said Mary Ann, ''wasn't that your shoes and your bathrobe and your hairbrush, just where you had left them?''

''Why, that's just what it was,'' said Grandpa.

Thus proceeds a confidence-inspiring exchange of roles by which Grandpa, eager to quell his visiting grandchildren's nighttime fears, gently elicits *their* assurances as he relates a ''scary nighttime'' ordeal he had when he was a boy. One by one his own bedtime imaginings are seen by the kids for what they really were, and laid to rest through a liberating commonsense analysis—everything from pirates fighting with swords (cats jumping on garbage cans), to wailing ghosts at the window (high winds whistling through the cracks).

Children will love this book's humor and cartoonlike watercolors. Mr. Stevenson's honest and compassionate treatment of bedtime fears represents a rational and sensitive approach to what can be a serious challenge for some children. Some books addressing this subject induce the very fears they seek to debunk. And parents will have to first consider their own children's responses in order to gauge the impact of this book's many nightmare images. Yet Mr. Stevenson's intent is certainly

From We Can't Sleep, *written and illustrated by James Stevenson. Greenwillow Books, 1982. Copyright © 1982 by James Stevenson. All rights reserved. By permission of Greenwillow Books (A Division of William Morrow & Company, Inc.).*

to liberate children from the meanderings of dark thoughts—and no doubt many children will derive just that benefit from it.

> *Darian J. Scott, "Grandpa Changes Roles with the Kids," in* The Christian Science Monitor, *January 6, 1984, p. B5.*

Two joyous 'Grandfather' picture-books, [*Granpa* by John Burningham and *What's Under My Bed?*], both revealing under the fun much understanding of the relationship that can exist between the very old and the very young, but one communicating its message more directly to young and old.

John Burningham is master of the happy cross-purposes that can build up in adult / child relationships. In *Granpa* there is, at a superficial glance, no narrative and little relevance in the apparently disconnected scraps of dialogue between child and grandparent. A closer look reveals the fine thread of story linking one opening with the next and the tender, moving association that underlies the funny drawing and the random scraps of text. . . .

What's Under My Bed? will, I think, have the same message for children and adults and speak equally clearly to both parties. When Grandpa puts Mary Ann and Louie to bed he leaves

them prey to all sorts of night fears. It is not long before they race downstairs to the comfort of his armchair. Grandpa indulges in a bit of typical adult garrulousness, in the course of which he exposes their fears and enables them to overcome them. It is all done with style, fun and with the surest of touches. James Stevenson's humour is the child's own. Who but he would think of Grandpa, in childhood, still wearing his walrus moustache?. . . A most satisfying book this, with fluent drawings and a finely economical text both directed to the same end.

> *M. Crouch, in a review of "What's Under My Bed?" in* The Junior Bookshelf, *Vol. 49, No. 1, February, 1985, p. 12.*

***WORSE THAN WILLY!* (1984)**

In this book we again meet one of Stevenson's favorite characters, Grandpa, who engages his two grandchildren in a conversation about their new baby brother, Willy. The two older kids feel terribly left out, since their parents seem to be lavishing all their attention on the baby. Grandpa commiserates and explains his own similar predicament, as a child being ignored because of his own "awful" baby brother, Wainwright—"Uncle Wainey"—when he appears on the scene and steals the show from Grandpa, getting him into trouble, breaking his toys, and generally making a pest out of himself. Soon Stevenson's quick illustrations and nimble wit have Grandpa blown out to sea in a storm to be taken aboard a galleon by "seventeen hideous pirates and a trained octopus." Just as the creature grabs him, who sould appear on the yardarm but baby Wainey, moustache and all, to trick the pirates and rescue Grandpa, carrying him back home on a contracting rubber band. The absurd implausibilities of the story are in total synch with Stevenson's cartoon graphics. But at the same time Stevenson is keenly aware of children's feelings, and he respects these injured feelings while he is helping his young readers to find their way out of these emotional impasses with releasing, healing laughter. Like Uncle Wainey, maybe their own baby brother will turn out fine in the end. "You never can tell about brothers," Wainey knowingly observes when he has joined Grandpa and the children on the porch for some lemonade. But you can tell about books. And at the end of this one I found myself savoring the kind, loving gesture of an adult (both Grandpa and Stevenson) who can find the right story to subtly speak to the child's heart, without preaching or condescending. (pp. 14-15)

> *John Cech, "Pretty Picture Books All in a Row,"* in Book World—The Washington Post, *May 13, 1984, pp. 1, 14-15.*

James Stevenson writes and illustrates witty, raucous books about children. And he knows there's nothing like a dose of hyperbole to cure what ails jealous siblings. In *Worse Than Willy!* Louie and Mary Ann are disgusted by their parents' fawning over their loathsome, useless baby brother, Willy. When they complain to their grandfather, it turns out he knows just what they're going through. "I'll be darned," he declares with dignified amazement, "sounds just like the way it was with *my* baby brother, Wainwright."

Now it's the children who are surprised. It can't be that nice, funny old Uncle Wainwright was once a ghastly little brother. So Grandpa describes the torments inflicted on him years ago by his whimsically mustachioed baby brother, Wainey. . . .

Louie and Mary Ann, powerfully impressed, have to agree that Wainey does sound "worse than Willy!" "Quite likely he was," Grandpa nods, lost in his memories, but adds, "Well, of course, there was the time he saved my life."

Here Mr. Stevenson's wacky adventure tale—half storybook and half cartoon strip—turns positively loony. It seems that a pig, blown past the boys' house during a ferocious storm, knocked young Grandpa out the window into a raging flood. Carried out to sea, he was rescued, if you could call it that, by 17 pirates and their trained octopus. It would spoil this very, very funny story's suspenseful ending to tell how Grandpa was rescued by the intrepid Wainey. Suffice it to say that the plot depends on Wainey's ingenious use of Great-Grandpa's red suspenders, a lot of bouncing and jeering and some very stupid pirates.

This is a terrific book for little children—good-humored, hysterically funny and true about sibling rivalry. Best of all, at a time in publishing history when young children's problems are too often treated with gloomy respect, it's nice to have a book with a sense of perspective. Not every important event in a child's life is permeated with melancholy, after all. Mr. Stevenson understands that this too shall pass, and that it'll pass a lot quicker if you make up a funny story about it.

> *Elizabeth Crow, in a review of "Worse than Willy!"* in The New York Times Book Review, *May 20, 1984, p. 28.*

Some of the finest humorous writing for children is in the tone of James Stevenson's Grandpa. . . . The wit is deadpan and droll, but the underlying sensibility is one of tender acceptance of the child's foibles. Stevenson . . . gives his young readers some credit for sophistication: Though the unstated theme of *Worse than Willy!* is the children's resentment of a new baby brother, he never stoops to glib reassurances or the usual head-patting condescension. Instead, a poker-faced Grandpa, his straw hat sitting on the end table beside his wicker chair on the porch, treats Louie and Mary Ann to a wild story about the antics of his own "awful" brother Wainey. And, most delicious of all, in the cartoonlike, irresistibly funny panel illustrations of Grandpa and Wainey in their infancy, we see them exactly as the listening children visualize them: junior editions of their grown selves, complete with a brush moustache tucked under the infant Grandpa's button nose.

> *Michele Landsberg, in a review of "Worse than Willy!" in her* Reading for the Love of It: Best Books for Young Readers, *Prentice Hall Press, 1987, p. 80.*

YUCK! (1984)

How to put witches to shame? Trust Stevenson for an artful, comfy deception. This exuberant new spoof features two of the most rapturously gruesome witches around—"Oh, it's foul, Lavinia!" "Stencheroo, Dolores!" They're also nasty, hateful, mean. They snap at the forest animals, explode in laughter at little witch Emma's timid request to make a potion too. "All I wanted to do," says Emma to the animals, "was . . . maybe one magic spell." The animals set to thinking. Emma strides forth with her own pot, spoon, and book of potions. And what do Lavinia and Doris see but a mooing duck, a quacking cow. Birds fly by upside down. ("Hey, what are you doing upside down, Dolores?") A rabbit passes, with an open umbrella— "Just in case it starts to rain frogs!" (Instantly.) What's gotten into them? "We're all under Emma's super spell." And when Lavinia and Dolores hear what's in Emma's potion, they take off with an enormous "YUCK" To the glee of Emma and friends, who go on slurping vegetable soup. Knockabout, tender, and hilarious.

> *A review of "Yuck!" in* Kirkus Reviews, Juvenile Issue, *Vol. LII, Nos. 10-17, September 1, 1984, p. J-66.*

If the ingredients for the author-artist's latest concoction—a couple of cackling witches and a good-tempered novice, some gruesome potions, an assortment of creatures, and a surprise ending—leave any doubt as to the book's appeal, the title alone would seem to guarantee an audience. . . . The very awfulness of descriptions such as "a gallon of snail slobber" in combination with the illustrations of green-complexioned witches should evoke some delighted shudders. In comic-strip style the complete text is contained within balloons. (pp. 584-85)

> *Karen Jameyson, in a review of "Yuck!" in* The Horn Book Magazine, *Vol. LX, No. 5, September-October, 1984, pp. 584-85.*

Stevenson's second Halloween story seems a little peaked after the rich inventiveness of his "Grandpa" tales. . . . The scribbled ink and watercolor illustrations, in concert with the text, suggest a hurry-up job, and the hand-lettered text, appearing largely in balloons, reinforces the feeling that *Yuck!* has closer ties to comic books than to literature. A one-trick treat for uncritical Stevenson fans.

> *Janet French, in a review of "Yuck!" in* School Library Journal, *Vol. 31, No. 4, December, 1984, p. 77.*

EMMA (1985)

Yes, Stevenson's game little witch Emma is back—with those horrible old witches, Dolores and Lavinia, to torment her. But Emma doesn't have two good friends, Botsford the cat and Rowland the owl, for nothing. After their combined efforts to launch Emma on a broom of her own only make her a laughing-stock, Lavinia and Dolores are awakened by the figure of a little Emma-like witch engaged in stunt-flying (actually, Roland in Emma's cape and pointy hat) and they're totally floored when, at Emma's instruction, her broom "flies" (thanks to some string-pulling by Botsford) up into a tree to sleep. It's an accolade of a kind to say that Emma & Co. are one-dimensional personalities with the repeat potential of comic-strip characters. Not as chilling-and-warming as *Yuck!*—but gratifying for the no-quarter war between the young / old forces.

> *A review of "Emma," in* Kirkus Reviews, *Juvenile Issue, Vol. LIII, No. 5, March 1, 1985, p. J-9.*

The exaggerated humor, obvious characterization, straightforward plot line, and "right over might" theme are well suited to the comic-book format, balloon-encased dialogue, agile line, and no-nonsense colors: Emma's curls are electric red, the witches' faces pea green. Like the Saturday afternoon movies of the thirties and forties, this book should enthrall a restless audience. And while it is an obvious alternative to ghouls and ghosties for Halloween, it is not limited to one season. (pp. 307-08)

> *Mary M. Burns, in a review of "Emma," in* The Horn Book Magazine, *Vol. LXI, No. 3, May-June, 1985, pp. 307-08.*

Children who have been teased by older, more proficient siblings or classmates will understand Emma's triumph in turning the tables on Dolores and Lavinia. . . . The pictures emphasize that this is a story for chuckles rather than chills. The night sky is pink and lavender, and the witches wear purple. Comic expressions and slapstick action underscored by boldly lettered *Thuds* and *Whaps* are the rule. One of the things for teachers to note is that all of the text occurs as dialogue within the cartoon balloons. An interesting thing to watch if children retell the story is how much of the action is retained in dialogue and how much is transformed into narrative.

> *Janet Hickman, in a review of "Emma," in* Language Arts, *Vol. 62, No. 6, October, 1985, p. 660.*

ARE WE ALMOST THERE? (1985)

Daddy and Mommy are planning to take Harry and Larry to spend a day at the beach—if they can stand the drive. The family is canine, but the goings-on are all too human. The puppies squabble and bicker until Daddy loses patience and parks in a truck stop for a nap. Harry and Larry realize that they have gone *too far* and become models of puppy behavior, fanning their sleeping Daddy (with gale force) so that his nap will be cool and refreshing; then, when he wakes up, they climb aboard in positively courtly fashion: "Would you care to join me in the back, Harry?" "Why, thank you, Larry. That would be most enjoyable." They have a great day at the beach—the best ever—and home at last, tired but happy, they are still muttering in their sleep "Are we almost there?" "Are we, Daddy?" They'll be just as bratty, and just as lovable, the next time. Each page is divided into cartoon panels, and the story is told entirely through dialogue balloons. Children may not appreciate this little gem, and it may be misused as a stuffy object lesson, but parents, or any other victims of travel with children, will surely find it quite irresistible.

> *Joan McGrath, in a review of "Are We Almost There?" in* School Library Journal, *Vol. 32, No. 2, October, 1985, p. 164.*

They may look like animals, Harry and Larry, but no child will be fooled; the two who squabble and squirm in the back seat are children testing their parents' patience and stamina on the long ride to the beach. Stevenson's flyaway drawings, in cartoon strip frames, have ebullience and humor, and the dialogue (in balloons) should evoke amused recognition reflexes from most members of the read-aloud audience. Stevenson also captures the feeling of joyous freedom children have at the seashore.

> *A review of "Are We Almost There?" in* Bulletin of the Center for Children's Books, *Vol. 39, No. 3, November, 1985, p. 58.*

The title is the joke—the plaint from the back seat of every family car on the way to every family holiday, vacation, party, or, in this case, day at the beach. James Stevenson . . . has an inimitable way of capturing familiar situations and turning them into books.

> *A review of "Are We Almost There?" in* The New York Times Book Review, *November 17, 1985, p. 45.*

THAT DREADFUL DAY (1985)

When his grandchildren come home complaining about their first day at school and contemplating lifelong truancy, Grandpa, from *Could Be Worse!*, tells of his own first school day, when a green-faced teacher with an abhorrence of squeaky chalk terrorized the class. The tale of Mr. Smeal, a cruel tyrant who delights in children's mistakes, but who is ultimately outwitted and expelled by his class, is amusingly illustrated; of particular note is Grandpa as a young boy sporting his usual mustache. Stevenson uses a comic book format; dialogue is in balloons in all capital letters. Narrative sequences are in standard print, and Grandpa's recollections are framed panels so as to avoid confusion between then and now. The dialogue balloons, often larger than the illustrations, tend to overpower the illustrations, giving the layout a cluttered look. While the idea is not very original—Grandpa has been more inventive in the past—it serves the purpose. Certain to chase away those first-day-of-school blues.

> *Lisa Castillo, in a review of "That Dreadful Day," in* School Library Journal, *Vol. 32, No. 3, November, 1985, p. 78.*

Old fans of the series of tales told by Grandpa will welcome this latest; new fans will probably be won by the story of

Suddenly the twister was gone.
Wainey and I fell down through the sky."

"Fortunately we landed in the
back seat of Grandpa's wagon.

From There's Nothing to Do! *written and illustrated by James Stevenson. Greenwillow Books, 1986. Copyright © 1986 by James Stevenson. All rights reserved. By permission of Greenwillow Books (A Division of William Morrow & Company, Inc.).*

Grandpa's first day of school. As always, his horror stories are designed to make his two grandchildren feel that theirs is the happier lot; as always, the pictures showing Grandpa as a boy endow him with his bristly little mustache (not yet whitened by age) and echo the zestful exaggeration of Grandpa's storytelling. Here Mary Ann and Louie, discouraged by their first day of school, are so struck by the awfulness of Grandpa's memories that they are encouraged by the contrast and decide the second day of school will be better. Message deftly accomplished.

> *A review of "That Dreadful Day," in* Bulletin of the Center for Children's Books, *Vol. 39, No. 5, January, 1986, p. 97.*

In a new addition to the endless saga of Grandpa's peculiar but instructive youthful adventures, we find Grandpa consoling Mary Ann and Louie about an unfortunate first day of school by detailing his own more unsettling introduction to the classroom. . . . A treat, as usual, by a master cartoonist with a clear understanding of the trials of childhood.

> *Ann A. Flowers, in a review of "That Dreadful Day," in* The Horn Book Magazine, *Vol. LXII, No. 1, January-February, 1986, p. 52.*

THERE'S NOTHING TO DO! (1986)

Because of the format—brief text plus many dialogue balloons—this story will be more successful for individual reading than for group reading. Louie and Mary Ann complain of boredom to Grandpa who, in his usual droll and understated way, reminisces about the time he and his brother Wainwright were bored while visiting their grandparents' farm. Stevenson's watercolor and ink cartoon-style illustrations perfectly capture the absurdity of the adventure, from the dust settling (fuf . . . fuf . . . fuf) to the cows yawning to the birds which "were so bored, they kept dozing off and falling out of the trees." This book reinforces Stevenson's reputation as an author who can provide inventive, original, exciting and truly funny books. A great complement to Spier's *Bored, Nothing to Do* (1978).

> *Ellen Fader, in a review of, "There's Nothing to Do!" in* School Library Journal, *Vol. 32, No. 8, April, 1986, p. 80.*

Stevenson is a gifted cartoonist whose facility for visual comedy is well matched by his sprightly deadpan repartee; the rather tenuous plot here is enough to string the chuckles together and keep the kids happy, but we may wonder if there aren't enough books about Grandpa now. (p. 933)

A review of "There's Nothing to Do!" in Kirkus Reviews, *Vol. LIV, No. 12, June 15, 1986, pp. 932-33.*

Most adults have plenty of reminiscences about the difficulties of the good old days to share with their grandchildren, and Grandpa is no exception. But his reminiscences are gorgeous extravaganzas, for he is a teller of tall tales rather than a nostalgia buff. This latest addition to his remembrances of time past equals its predecessors in frenetic pace, tongue-in-cheek humor, and zany situations. . . . Designed in a comic-strip format with balloon-encased conversations, onomatopoeic sound effects arranged like bold banners in the drawings, and an economical text to provide the unifying narrative, the book is carefully planned to create excitement through a satisfying series of images. True to the young child's idea of grownups as youngsters, Grandpa and Uncle Wainey appear in the flashbacks as miniaturized versions of their adult selves, with mustaches and darkened hair as a concession to youth. The characterization is deft and sure, created through marvelously expressive, agile lines; the setting and time are suggested through the sensitive and elegant use of the watercolor medium. A superb example of the cartoonist's work as art, the book is as aesthetically pleasing as it is fun. Who could ask for anything more?

Mary M. Burns, in a review of "There's Nothing to Do!" in The Horn Book Magazine, *Vol. LXII, No. 4, July-August, 1986, p. 444.*

WHEN I WAS NINE (1986)

Thinly washed watercolors in muted shades help to evoke a gently humorous recollection of childhood during the 1930s. In a quiet departure from his usual cartoonlike drawings and the wildly preposterous adventures in his recent picture books, the author-illustrator displays the same flair for the quickly sketched image and talent for capturing the telling gesture. He recalls the modest delights of his childhood—skating, baseball, and bicycling—and even his inability to master mathematics. He explains the way he printed a neighborhood newspaper and deftly pictures his difficulties in peddling it. But, clearly, the highlight of that particular year was the family trip out West with its panorama of new scenery and experiences and, above all, the purchase of his own large cowboy hat. Anecdotal and understated in its story line, the book will find a sympathetic audience of grandparents who have shared the same pleasures, yet a universal appeal exists in the brotherly squabbles, the adventures of a family trip, and in the welcome return home at the end of a long and glorious summer.

Ethel R. Twichell, in a review of "When I Was Nine," in The Horn Book Magazine, *Vol. LXII, No. 4, July-August, 1986, p. 445.*

Don't be fooled by the title—this book isn't just for third graders. It's a visit to a time when things were simpler but people were just the same. . . . A life like this, without television or Xerox machines, could seem impossibly exotic to today's children, but Stevenson throws in a comforting handful of things any child knows—visits to Grandma in the summer, a best friend who's only fun "about half the time." Stevenson's blobby watercolors in warm pastels, this time without his characteristic black holding lines, create a hazy, nostalgic atmo-

sphere. *When I Was Nine* is a book to think about and to savor; a special treat for children and their grandparents.

Lucy Young Clem, in a review of "When I Was Nine," in School Library Journal, *Vol. 32, No. 10, August, 1986, p. 88.*

Nostalgia is avoided, in Stevenson's reminiscences of his childhood, by the pervasive humor and the brisk pace. In fact, the writing is at time staccato, functioning as though it were captions; for example, there are three misty (very nice) watercolor pictures on a single page: the first shows two views of the author on a bicycle, the second a dog, the third a telephone, and the text reads: "I had a bicycle, and I knew where all the bumps were on the sidewalk. We had a dog named Jocko. Our telephone looked like this. Our number was 3348." While there are comments on a family vacation, most of the text is rather static.

Zena Sutherland, in a review of "When I Was Nine," in Bulletin of the Center for Children's Books, *Vol. 40, No. 1, September, 1986, p. 20.*

FRIED FEATHERS FOR THANKSGIVING (1986)

Stevenson has done several picture books distinguished by their dry wit, rambunctious action, and facile draftsmanship. Successive books seem to become more slapdash and scribbly; this one is strongly reminiscent of Saturday morning TV, although Stevenson's gift for conveying emotion with a few deft lines is undiminished. Children will be satisfied with the green-faced meanies' come-uppance. With a shortage of good Thanksgiving stories, this does fill a need.

A review of "Fried Feathers for Thanksgiving," in Kirkus Reviews, *Vol. LIV, No. 20, October 15, 1986, p. 1581.*

How the naive Emma, a model of generosity, manages with a little help from her buddies to score another victory over the green-faced, selfish duo is the chief organizational element of an inventive, good-humored look at the meaning of friendship. Executed in comic strip format, with the plot enhanced by balloon encased dialogue, the book is recognizably James Stevenson—not simply because of the design and style but because of the expressive, economical use of line to suggest characters and action and the sure sense of color as a complement to but not a substitute for draftsmanship. As lively and immediate in feeling as a series of instant photos, this Thanksgiving book can be served at any season.

Mary M. Burns, in a review of "Fried Feathers for Thanksgiving," in The Horn Book Magazine, *Vol. LXII, No. 6, November-December, 1986, p. 741.*

NO FRIENDS (1986)

This time Grandpa's storytelling helps ease Mary Ann and Louie through a move to a new neighborhood. As the two children complain that "It's lonely and awful! We have no friends!", Grandpa launches into the story of the time he and brother Wainey moved into a neighborhood that was cold and ugly and populated with bullies. Grandpa, of course, managed to make friends by the finish, as do Mary Ann and Louie. In the meantime Grandpa's experiences emerge as both instructive and entertaining. As with the previous Mary Ann and Louie books, Stevenson combines cartoon storytelling and straight narrative with the pictures energetically elaborating on the bare fact. The humor here is unstrained and largely successful; Stevenson's fans should find this right up their alley.

> Denise M. Wilms, in a review of "No Friends," in Booklist, Vol. 83, No. 3, October 1, 1986, p. 275.

Grandpa is back with another entertaining and comforting story.... In this exaggerated tale, the use of humor helps to erase the fear of meeting new people and emphasizes that children and grandpas alike have faced similar problems. Stevenson's zany cartoon-like pen and watercolor illustrations and the dialogue balloons befit the story's mood and are appealing to children. The format, however, lends itself to individual reading rather than group sharing. This book can be used with *The Berenstain Bears' Moving Day* (1981) and Delton's *Lee Henry's Best Friend* (1980). A delightful tale sure to drive away moving day qualms.

> Orvella Fields, in a review of "No Friends," in School Library Journal, Vol. 33, No. 3, November, 1986, p. 83.

Written in racy cartoon style, this tale romps along carrying the reader effortlessly with it.... The hilarious exploits are described and illustrated with wit and skill. In the end, Grandpa's clever therapy puts things in perspective and the book ends on an optimistic note.

Although some may decry the odd Americanism, these are essential to the story and it would be a pity to let them deprive children of this splendid reading experience.

> Maisie Roberts, in a review of "No Friends," in The School Librarian, Vol. 35, No. 3, August, 1987, p. 225.

HIGHER ON THE DOOR (1987)

Like the author's *When I Was Nine,* a nostalgic reminiscence about his childhood, this time outlining daily life in a small town.

Selecting things that were different (the iceman and coal truck, seeing someone off on an ocean liner), but more that are the same (bickering with an older brother, being afraid of a dozen things like tough kids, snakes, and the dark; knowing the neighbors), Stevenson presents a busy, interesting time when the worst thing that happened was the family dog being hit by a car (he got well in a few days). His impressionistic watercolor sketches are a perfect complement to the text—light, airy, with plenty of white space for the imagination to fill in and occasional drama in the huge dam, scary because it might collapse, and a marvelous steam train.

Quiet, but a visual treat, and one of Stevenson's more pleasant offerings.

> A review of "Higher on the Door," in Kirkus Reviews, Vol. LV, No. 2, January 15, 1987, p. 132-33.

Here Stevenson expands more fully on the themes he introduced in *When I Was Nine;* once more, there are none of his familiar black lines and scrawls, filled with puddles of watercolor. His people and landscapes have the simple forms of distant memory. With them he offers a friendly, quite gentle glimpse of his childhood, answering, perhaps, the youthful query "What was it like in the olden days?"...

The text is spare and given to understatement, consisting of amusing, on-the-mark observations about the pitfalls and proud moments of being a kid....

The vigor of the remembrance is in the paintings. The artist's strokes of color are unaffected and abstract; mere blots of paint represent children in one context and entire forests in another. There is humor and the tender irony of hindsight, especially in the last lines: "I asked, 'Can I go on an ocean liner?' 'When you get older,' my parents said.... I couldn't wait to get higher on the door." Stevenson touches on the color-filled moments of childhood that are at once particular and universal.

> A review of "Higher on the Door," in Publishers Weekly, Vol. 231, No. 2, January 16, 1987, p. 72.

James Stevenson as a real-life grandfather looks back and remembers his childhood. As in his previous book of reminiscences, *When I Was Nine,* the events of his life are quiet and nonspectacular. Their charm lies in the inherent wit of this artist-observer and his spare use of words and lines to capture the humor in simple situations.... The discipline of the cartoonist is seen in the complete economy of word and line to convey an idea or create an object. The watercolor drawings are almost optical illusions, as even negative space acquires shape and form. One knows that the dentist, who consists of a head, a row of buttons, and two arms and legs, needs to go on a diet. As always, Stevenson's humor is appealing to all ages. (pp. 335-36)

> Hanna B. Zeiger, in a review of "Higher on the Door," in The Horn Book Magazine, Vol. LXIII, No. 3, May-June, 1987, pp. 335-36.

The magic of James Stevenson is that he recaptures for those of us old enough now to be grandparents, were our children marrying instead of cohabiting, a time in this slum of a century when innocence did truly seem to prevail. The kingdom of *Higher on the Door* is the kingdom of memory, a wondrous place of ethnic, racial, social and economic homogeneity, where no canker ever blights the rose.

As he demonstrated in his charming *When I Was Nine,* Mr. Stevenson has perfect pitch for the concerns and vernacular of a young boy not yet assaulted by the insistent demands of adolescence. The time is the period between the two world wars, the wars we won. Reading *Higher on the Door*—the title refers to the way our parents marked off our growth on a doorjamb with each passing birthday—I was thrust back into those summers just before Pearl Harbor.

It was like a watercolor. My Aunt Kate pickled peaches and put up raspberry preserves and made rhubarb pies and filed recipes, which she called "receipts." My Uncle Gene took me to the depot (pronounced DEE-poh) so we could count the cars on the freight trains rumbling through—was it 97 or 101, and did the caboose count, and the engine and the coal car? The maid, Modelle Jackson, I thought an integral and integrated member of the family, and the world's wisdom was exchanged at Mario's Barber Shop, where Mario did not exactly deny nor exactly confirm that he was a distant cousin of Dario Lodigiani, a utility infielder for Connie Mack's Philadelphia A's, reason enough for a season to be a fan of the last-place Athletics.

In Mr. Stevenson's watercolors, childhood becomes as real as yesterday. The iceman delivered ice (I remember Mr. Dibble, Old Man Dibble behind his back, bent at the waist under the weight of the 50-pound blocks) and the coal truck came when the leaves began to turn so there would be heat for the winter. "There were a lot of things I couldn't do," Mr. Stevenson writes. "I couldn't make a loud whistle with two fingers." (I still can't, and I am still trying.)

When you took a train to New York City (always New York City, never just plain old New York), the seats on the train were "shiny woven wicker," and then you got there, and went to the top of the Empire State Building, it was so high you were sure you could see your house. Your brother's diary captured the daily rhythm: "Got up. Had breakfast. Went to school. Came home. Had supper. Went to bed." Of course there were things to be afraid of: "iodine on cuts" and, my particular favorite, "tough kids."

What James Stevenson does is forge a link between generations. "I have a grandson now," he writes. "That's how old I am. But sometimes I look back and remember. . . ." His memories are the color of sunlight.

> *John Gregory Dunne, in a review of "Higher on the Door," in* The New York Times Book Review, *September 20, 1987, p. 33.*

WILL YOU PLEASE FEED OUR CAT? (1987)

Mary Ann and Louie are back, to let Grandpa top their difficult situation yet again; this time they're taking care of the Murphy's dog, but when Grandpa and his brother Wainey, years ago when they were small boys, agreed to feed the neighbor's cat, they were trapped in a Herculean task.

So begins one of Stevenson's funnier tall tales. The two mustached tots are responsible for turtle, cat (well, a whole roomful of cats), parakeet, gerbils, hamster, rabbit—you name it. Escapes, rescues, and disasters are the order of the day. But when watering the greenhouse takes too long, Grandpa invents a remote control Rube Goldberg to handle his tasks from a distance, and after a final bit of mayhem, all returns to normal just in time for the neighbors' return.

Stevenson's expressive, comically suggestive line keeps the story rollicking along; the cartoon-balloon text is less distracting than in some of his recent books; visually, the illustrations take priority, as they should. Fun.

> *A review of "Will You Please Feed Our Cat?" in* Kirkus Reviews, *Vol. LV, No. 2, January 15, 1987, p. 133.*

This latest in Stevenson's series featuring Grandpa's exaggerated tales of his childhood is as irresistible and as ingenious as the others. . . . Stevenson combines the light fun of a comic strip format with a romp of a story and beautifully executed, lively drawings (he's a master of understatement in facial expressions and body stance). Because the humor operates on various levels, his formula keeps on working, and is as much fun for adults as it is for kids.

> *A review of "Will You Please Feed Our Cat?" in* Publishers Weekly, *Vol. 231, No. 8, February 27, 1987, p. 164.*

The parade of misfortunes gives James Stevenson plenty of scope for humour and movement in his illustrations. He uses muted colours, allowing Grandpa and Wainey to remain centre stage throughout, their animated antics recorded in witty caricatures and expressive reactions. A general tone of exuberance

energises the cartoons, buttressed by brief running captions and snappy 'balloons'—a robust romp of a book.

> *G. Bott, in a review of "Will You Please Feed Our Cat?" in* The Junior Bookshelf, *Vol. 52, No. 1, February, 1988, p. 26.*

HAPPY VALENTINE'S DAY, EMMA! (1987)

Having recovered from their Thanksgiving debacle (*Fried Feathers for Thanksgiving*), low-minded witches Dolores and Lavinia sally forth once again against their nemesis, young Emma.

As Valentine's Day approaches ("Oh, barf me out," groans Lavinia), the dastardly duo discover Emma cutting out paper hearts and decide to spoil her holiday. One box of chocolate worms and a hypoallergenic nosegay later, Emma and her friends Roland (owl) and Botsford (cat) are irritated enough to strike back; using rotten eggs, a fake giant rat's tail, a bucket of green drool, and a few other props, they concoct a fiendish and suitable revenge. There's nothing subtle about the ending, either; having sent out lots of valentines, Emma (if not the reader) is surprised when her woodland neighbors send a blizzard of them in return. The story's message is clear: Do as ye are done by. As usual in this series, the colorful, slapdash illustrations appear in panels, the hand-lettered but easily legible dialogue in balloons.

Stevenson's fans will welcome this newest encounter.

you'd run for safety!

From Higher on the Door, *written and illustrated by James Stevenson. Greenwillow Books, 1987. Copyright © 1987 by James Stevenson. All rights reserved. By permission of Greenwillow Books (A Division of William Morrow & Company, Inc.).*

A review of "Happy Valentine's Day, Emma!" in Kirkus Reviews, *Vol. LV, No. 15, August 1, 1987, p. 1164.*

The newest book about that endearing little witch Emma and her two nasty nemeses Dolores and Lavinia is the perfect choice for any child who has ever fantasized about seeking revenge for one wrong or another. . . . As tantalizing a brew as its three predecessors, children will delight in the humor, the down-to-earth language ("Oh, barf me out, Dolores!"), and the satisfying ending. The prolific Stevenson once again uses sketchily rendered line drawing bathed in watercolors. The familiar comic-strip format is also intact; the dialogue is completely enclosed in balloons. Although there's nothing new here, this formula has proven to be a sure-fire winner, not only at holiday time, but all year round.

Julie Corsaro, in a review of "Happy Valentine's Day, Emma!" in School Library Journal, *Vol. 34, No. 1, September, 1987, p. 171.*

NO NEED FOR MONTY (1987)

That immensely likable alligator from *Monty* is back, still reliably ferrying the children to school. One day, however, the grown-ups decide that "the Monty system" is too slow; surely they can come up with a faster one. As the weeks go by, each method they propose, from skyride to stilts, fails with more hilarity than the one before. Finally, a grinning Monty appears, and the children climb aboard what *they* knew all along was the best way to go to school—"the Monty way." As always, Stevenson's message—here, about the perils of innovation for its own sake—is delivered with an ample dose of humor. The pacing is sure and swift, and the dramatic failures of the grown-ups' deliciously pompous inventions are hilarious.

A review of "No Need for Monty," in Publishers Weekly, *Vol. 232, No. 9, August 28, 1987, p. 79.*

Stevenson's amusing story is written in his usual comic-strip format, but the boxes showing the action vary in size creating a more interesting layout. The softly colored illustrations are well conceived and suit the warm story well. Fans of Monty and his friends will give them a rousing "welcome back."

Ilene Cooper, in a review of "No Need for Monty," in Booklist, *Vol. 84, No. 5, November 1, 1987, p. 485.*

Stevenson presents a simple moral in an effective and humorous fashion. The underlying theme that grown-ups are not always right is subtly presented in a simple style. The text has a definite beginning, middle, and end that is hand printed in cartoon captions; illustrations are in watercolor and black line that sustain the drollness found in the text (note Monty's subdued smile). This is a remarkably effective picture book with definite child appeal that will be treasured, remembered, and enjoyed by young children. (pp. 77-8)

Bessie Egan, in a review of "No Need for Monty," in School Library Journal, *Vol. 34, No. 4, December, 1987, pp. 77-8.*

THE WORST PERSON IN THE WORLD AT CRAB BEACH (1988)

"Oh, no, not another nice day!" the worst person in the world exclaims, and heads off for a spot more to his liking. Cold, drizzly Crab Beach, he thinks, will be perfect: there are plenty of jellyfish and mosquitoes, and the food is unspeakably bad. But when Miriam and her son Cranston appear on the scene, their screechy accordion playing and unfailing rudeness are too much even for the worst person in the world, and his joy in the dreadful place fades. After they leave, however, he finds he misses them, and so he sets out for home. He isn't sorry to find the pair ensconced there already, tending his cactus garden and poison-ivy patch in his absence, and the three enjoy a companionable snack of dry crackers and prune juice. Stevenson's depiction of grouchiness personified makes for high comedy in this second tale about the curmudgeonly worst person, whose perverse criteria for enjoyment remain funny and surprising to the end. And because his loneliness is apparent, readers will end up rooting for just the sort of development as that odd friendship. The illustrations capture every sour expression and abound with funny details of the aptly named Crab Beach. (pp. 86-7)

A review of "The Worst Person in the World at Crab Beach," in Publishers Weekly, *Vol. 233, No. 6, February 12, 1988, pp. 86-7.*

Like the first book, this should amuse Stevenson's fans, since the entertaining cartoon drawings are augmented by some very nice forms-in-fog paintings, the irascible protagonist is a comic non-hero, and the relatively happy ending, after the return from Crab Beach, preserves the cantankerous attitude of *the worst.*

Zena Sutherland, in a review of "The Worst Person in the World at Crab Beach," in Bulletin of the Center for Children's Books, *Vol. 41, No. 7, March, 1988, p. 145.*

Put a frightful grump, a loudmouthed shrew, and a rude brat together in what must be the dreariest of all resort hotels, and a clash of zanies is the happy result. . . . While the reconciliation of the terrible threesome seems a little specious after their monumental battles, the worst's peace offering of prune juice and dry crackers seems a perfect solution. As always, Stevenson's scratchy, busy, lively cartoons bounce the story along at a rapid pace and make positively lovable the most misanthropic grouch since Ebenezer Scrooge. (pp. 196-97)

Ethel R. Twichell, in a review of "The Worst Person in the World at Crab Beach," in The Horn Book Magazine, *Vol. LXIV, No. 2, March-April, 1988, pp. 196-97.*

(Mary) Noel Streatfeild

1895-1986

English author of fiction, nonfiction, and picture books; playwright; scriptwriter; poet; and editor.

Streatfeild secured an enduring place among writers for children by creating warm family stories for middle graders which feature child professionals in the performing arts and sports fields. Credited with pioneering a new type of children's book—the career novel—at a time when Arthur Ransome's holiday adventures were popular, Streatfeild combined a retentive memory of how it felt to be the rebellious middle child in a vicarage family with well-researched information on such diverse backgrounds as the drama school, traveling circus, concert stage, athletic tournament, and movie set. She is chiefly remembered as the writer of *Ballet Shoes* (1936), the landmark portrayal of three adopted girls who are groomed for serious dancing careers, and for the ten subsequent books which, due to a marketing decision by her American publisher, all have titles ending with *Shoes* in the United States. Spirited stories about plucky children who represent a variety of specialized fields, the works depict both the difficulties and the rewards of their respective professions. Streatfeild's lively plots about likable, imperfect youngsters who overcome financial or personal difficulties through hard work and enthusiasm reflect both her understanding of children and her belief in them. Written in a concise style that enlivens narrative with witty dialogue and occasional sarcasm, the *Shoes* books stress individuality, the responsibilities of natural talent, perseverance in the face of adversity, and the importance of family solidarity. Although Streatfeild claimed that she wrote primarily for the enjoyment of her audience, her works are considered excellent character studies as well as valuable sources of information about the world of entertainment.

An actress for ten years as well as a popular author of adult novels, Streatfeild was prompted to write *Ballet Shoes* by her questions about the lives of child performers and her desire to create a book for young readers with fully realized characters, an attribute she saw lacking in juvenile books of the period. When the story appeared, it achieved immediate popularity among both children and adults and spawned many imitations, particularly in the 1950s. *Ballet Shoes* is currently lauded as a forerunner of the modern children's book. It is also considered notable for legitimizing show business as a setting for juvenile literature and for highlighting poor children as its characters. In her next book, *Tennis Shoes* (1937), Streatfeild created the lazy but proud Nicky Heath, whose outrageous behavior and championship talent are acknowledged to be autobiographical in spirit. *The Circus Is Coming* (1938), published in the United States as *Circus Shoes*, was widely acclaimed for its unromanticized documentation of circus life and for its depiction of the dedicated professional versus the amateur. With the exception of the early 1940s, when she was limited in research travel by the Second World War and often concentrated on adventure stories, Streatfeild continued to write *Shoes* books. She interspersed these consistently popular titles with amusing animal tales for younger children and occasional nonfiction such as the well-received *First Book of England* (1953) and *The Boy Pharaoh, Tutank-*

hamen (1972). In addition, Streatfeild wrote several plays for children, a book of verse, a popular series of radio dramas on the Bell and Grey families, two stories about the strongly independent orphan Margaret Thursday set at the turn of the century, and informational books for young adults on the ballet and opera.

Critics praise Streatfeild for her exceptional sensitivity to children and their interests, her ability to individualize whole casts of characters, her consistent accuracy, the shrewdness of her observations, and the direct, unpatronizing tone of her books. Although critics note a decline in her technical ability in her later works as well as a formulaic pattern in the *Shoes* stories, they agree that Streatfeild was the best writer of her kind, an author who informed, entertained, and inspired generations of young readers.

Ballet Shoes and *Tennis Shoes* were both runners-up for the Carnegie Medal in 1936 and 1937 respectively. In 1938 *The Circus Is Coming* won the Carnegie Medal. In 1983 Streatfeild was awarded the Order of the British Empire for her work as a writer of children's books.

(See also *Contemporary Literary Criticism*, Vol. 21; *Something about the Author*, Vols. 20, 48 [obituary]; and *Contemporary Authors*, Vols. 81-84, Vol. 120 [obituary].)

AUTHOR'S COMMENTARY

The *Junior Bookshelf's* invitation to me to write something either about my own three children's books, or my views on children's books generally, has made me think. My own children's books have a similarity in that they are all written round professional or semi-professional children and their careers. Now why? After a lot of probing in my mind and my childhood I think I have arrived at the reason.

I had a narrow childhood. We always knew the same sort of people, and never saw anyone outside our own little world. From the time I was a baby I was bored by the *milieu* in which I lived. I was convinced other people's lives were more interesting than my own, a theory which my grown-up experience has found to be perfectly true. This vague dissatisfaction crystallised when at quite an early age I was taken to see a troupe of child dancers called, I think, "Lila Field's Wonder Children." Those children excited me as hardly anything has excited me since. Who were they? Where did they live? Did they go to school?

As things turned out, my grown-up life threw me into contact with any number of professional children, and they interested me just as much as ever, which was lucky, for instead of spending my years on the stage only learning my own business I acquired a mass of knowledge about child professionals which has been a godsend ever since. In three or four straight plays in which I was playing there were child actors, there were several in a musical comedy with which I toured, and eighty in a pantomime that I played in. Like all people with a hobby I was dead to all decent feeling, and pryed and nosed into those children's lives and trainings until not one of my childhood's questions remained unanswered.

When in 1930 I gave up the stage and took to novel writing I naturally wrote of my great hobby; my first book was devoted to child professionals. In the same way when five years later I was asked to write a book for children it was automatically on the same subject.

That first book for children was enchanting to write. It was called *Ballet Shoes,* and it was just like giving a present from the grown-up me to the child me. I pictured, while I wrote it, myself and hundreds like me, leading rather circumscribed lives, and I attempted to open the stage door and show exactly what happened on the other side of it.

I suppose everybody has vague ideas floating about in their heads, which it takes some person or event to crystallise. In the back of my head was a loathing of inefficient training, and what I call "hop-skip-and-jump children," pushed forward by proud mothers to wobble on ill-trained points. This loathing came out on writing the book and made me combine the most efficient stage schools I knew in the one I drew in *Ballet Shoes,* and made me attempt to show what real training for the stage and the ballet means.

Of course, having once had a taste of blood, as it were, I could not stop, and my next book *Tennis Shoes* was another present from the grown-up to the child me. As a family we had been educated in a smattering sort of way, a little all round and side lines thrown in. I, for instance, was taught the violin, without a spark of music in my soul, merely because I had inordinately long fingers. An elder sister was a good artist and we all had extra drawing lessons in case we were too. The result was that I grew up as a very indifferent jack of all trades, and quite certainly master of none of them, with the obvious result that

from about the age of twelve onwards I had a quite appalling inferiority complex. Now I believe every child can be good at something if it specialises, and that the child who is good at something feels automatically that it has got a place in the world, and nothing to be ashamed of. I can remember now the emotion which stirred me at the luck of other girls, who rode really well, played some game above the average, were being properly trained for one of the arts, or did exquisite needlework. They seemed to me by their honest knowledge of one subject to be set free from the need to brag and pretend which overcame less fortunate people; they were competent on their one subject and did not care if they could not rise above the average in any other. *Tennis Shoes* was written crystallising this point of view. I never myself had the slightest hope of shining at a game, though amongst the rest of my education a smattering from a variety of coaches had been thrown in. I came into the juvenile tennis world quite open-minded as to what training for championship play did for you. I was charmed by what I found. Because they were specialising, the children seemed to me engagingly happy even when, as one or two confided to me, they knew they would never reach a first-class standard. On the other hand they were all children who were well above the standard of play accepted in their schools. I was used to watching children at bar practice, but I must say I was amazed at the amount of hard labour that tennis children get in, and was glad to see that their training enabled them to get the same breath-catching pleasure at watching technically well-played shots that child dancers get when watching a perfectly executed figure in a ballet.

When in Hollywood last year I met and studied most of the child film stars. (pp. 121-23)

When I was writing *The Circus is Coming* I was back with my first love, the professional stage child. For all that they live in caravans and work in a big-top, circus people are blood-brothers of music hall artistes. Enormous numbers in both professions are in the line of business that their family has been in for generations, or even (as in the case of the Lupinos) for hundreds of years. The result is that their children, although not yet working, are professional to their finger-tips. The circus is the place to see what specialised training means, it is there you can hear a child of as little as five or six express disgust at careless practice or a clumsy performance. Every child attached to the circus world has a remarkably clear view as to what perfection in their line could be, and though few, if any, artiste attains that perfection in his lifetime, they are all more than willing to work at it until they are in their coffins. Of course, given a fine summer, I suppose no child could have a happier life than travelling with a first-class circus. There are new towns every week, often twice a week, new schools, new places to explore. The children I knew were of all ages and nationalities, they were amusing and could chatter on any subject, of which only one that I ever found was serious, and no matter for light gossip, and that was methods of training and technical proficiency.

Of all the children that I have envied in my life, and I have envied many of them, I am not sure that the child of acrobats does not come first. How heavenly, I say, looking back to my own dull youth, to be one of them! What luck they have, I think, even now gazing at them with the awe with which I gazed at their prototypes when I was ten. (pp. 123-24)

Noel Streatfeild, "Myself and My Books," in The Junior Bookshelf, *Vol. 3, No. 3, May, 1939, pp. 121-24.*

GENERAL COMMENTARY

MARGERY FISHER

By far the most successful theatre stories for children are those which, with children as their subjects, can show rivalries and ambitions unaffected, as yet, by the awkward, sordid, bewildering adult world. Here Noel Streatfeild is outstanding. Her young actors, skaters and ballet pupils are infatuated by the theatre. They are ambitious, self-centered, as deeply obsessed by technique as any young aspirant for a jumping rosette. She even succeeds, sometimes, in conveying that intangible but unmistakable thing, star quality—in Posy, for instance, youngest of the three girls in **Ballet Shoes,** who, when the brilliant teacher falls ill, inquires at once what is to happen to her own career; or in Rachel in **Wintle's Wonders,** whose talents are discovered almost by accident, but whom you recognize at once as a dedicated dancer.

Though Noel Streatfeild knows her theatre as well as Pamela Brown does, she does not put it first. She has an insatiable curiosity about people, and especially about theatrical children, with their peculiar, hard-working, rigidly organized life; and she is curious, too, about the effects of publicity and performance on young people. Her books, for all the detail and skill of their backgrounds, are primarily studies in character. Mrs Wintle's dancing-school is the battlefield for her daughter Dulcie, a conceited little girl who wants the best parts in all the shows, and the two children, Rachel and Hilary, who are taken into the family and threaten to steal some of Dulcie's thunder. The same theme, of the poor and modest child coming to the fore, is brilliantly used in **Whiteboots,** in the rivalry of Harriet Johnson, daughter of a poor (but well-connected) green-grocer, and Lalla Moore, a well-to-do orphan whose aunt is pushing her into the limelight in the world of ice-skating. In all Noel Streatfeild's books we have portraits of the professional child, set off by the occasional brave souls who resist the dazzle of the footlights, like Petrova in **Ballet Shoes,** whose heart is in motor-engineering, or Hilary, in **Wintle's Wonders,** whose attitude is entirely refreshing, when she is offered a star part:

'What do you want me for? I won't be any good.'

The producer was thoroughly amused.

'I'm sorry if I've inconvenienced you. But there's a comic robin in this new children's play which I thought would suit you.'

'Has he anything to say?'

'No, it's all mime with a little dancing.'

Hilary gave in grudgingly.

'Well, I suppose I'll have to be him.'

The producer laughed.

'Don't you want to? Most children would jump at the chance, I thought I was doing you a good turn.'

'Well, you aren't. All I want to be is just an ordinary Wonder, and look what happens to me. My first engagement is to understudy Dulcie, which nobody could like, and now I've got to be a robin. Wouldn't you rather have somebody else? There are heaps of Wonders who'd be better than me.'

The producer gave Hilary's hair an affectionate rub.

'You're a card. But no, thank you, I'm sticking to you.'

The intrusion of such a robust point of view into the somewhat rarefied air of the theatre saves these stories, full of technical detail as they are, from becoming too specialized for the general reader. Noel Streatfeild has her feet firmly on the ground, and children who reread her books when they are older will bless her for this.

Theatrical children, of course, are not ordinary, and neither are circus children. In **The Circus Is Coming,** still perhaps Noel Streatfeild's most popular book, she emphasizes the oddity of circus characters by bringing into Cob's Circus a prim little hero and heroine, Peter and Santa, who have to shake down, after a suburban upbringing, in the heady atmosphere of sawdust and performance. (pp. 187-89)

> *Margery Fisher, "Fossils and Formulas," in her* Intent Upon Reading: A Critical Appraisal of Modern Fiction for Children, *1961. Reprint by Franklin Watts, Inc., 1962, pp. 187-89.*

BARBARA KER WILSON

Noel Streatfeild's outstanding characteristic as storyteller is the *rapport* she creates between her readers and herself. The children who read her books know that she cares about the story every bit as much as they do themselves; they have complete confidence in her ability to guide the fate of the characters they have got to know so well. She engenders in her writing a warmth and friendliness that extends both to her characters and her readers. This warmth, or 'heart' as Noel Streatfeild herself expresses it, springs partly from the immense care she takes in creating her characters, and also from her uninhibited approach to the child reader. She speaks to him directly, without preamble, treating him as an equal and assuming that he has the wit to understand exactly what she means to say. 'Of course,' she says to him in effect, 'you as a person of common-sense will realise that a given set of circumstances lead to a certain result.' (p. 30)

Noel Streatfeild likes children, has a good deal of contact with them in everyday life, and gets on well with them. She knows the audience for whom she writes her books, and is particularly sure of the ten to fourteen-year-olds for whom the main stream of her children's writing is intended. (pp. 30-1)

True simplicity is the hall-mark of the best children's authors. It extends to every feature of a story: narrative style, plot, characterisation . . . and it underlies all Noel Streatfeild's writing for children.

The narrative style in her children's books is unfussy, the train of thought practical. She is never vague; her narrative is filled with facts. For instance, she always tells her reader the exact ages of the children in the stories, what they look like, and where they live, and there is a careful time sequence throughout each story. From the start the reader knows where he is. . . . (p. 31)

Money matters, too, are worked out to the last penny. (p. 32)

Descriptive passages of a picturesque nature are infrequent and brief. Noel Streatfeild writes in short, logical sentences which make a very definite impression on the reader's mind; an impression which leaves no doubt that she is *telling* the story, actually talking to her reader. And this is the essence of Noel Streatfeild's manner of writing: it is verbal. The natural result of this is that children are aware of the storyteller's personality as they listen to her narrative, and so a particular feeling of affinity between author and reader is formed. Noel Streatfeild's dramatic training, her professional awareness of spoken tones and inflections, is surely responsible to a large extent for this verbal approach to writing narrative.

As part of her strict professional attitude towards writing, Noel Streatfeild is meticulous in the research which underlies her stories. This not only involves finding out all the relevant facts about a subject, but also—which is more difficult— absorbing the atmosphere, the climate, surrounding it. When she set out to write *The Circus is Coming,* Noel Streatfeild was as ignorant as Peter and Santa about circus life; and she knew nothing of either championship tennis or the ice-skating world before she wrote *Tennis Shoes* and *White Boots.* (pp. 32-3)

The extreme trouble Noel Streatfeild takes over the research for her children's books is an integral part of her character as a storyteller. Those of her stories which are concerned with professional training for a particular career are documentary in their accuracy. Look at dialogue such as this, where old Ben, Master of the Horse in Cob's Circus, is giving Peter a riding lesson:

> '... you want to turn your toes a bit out. That's particular important in high-school ridin', 'cause that means the 'oss'll feel the touch from your leg before he feels the spur, and same time your foot's right for usin' a spur.'

Or this description of Lalla's skating difficulties:

> For her inter-gold she had to do figures called change edge loops. Change edge loops needed the sort of skating which was not Lalla's. They needed control, and rhythm, both of which she had sometimes, but as well they needed immense concentration, and that was not a quality Lalla possessed when she was skating figures.

This sort of thing can never be written casually or vaguely: the author must know exactly what he is talking about. And Noel Streatfeild makes it her business to know.

Such conscientious research and passion for accuracy could result in dullness on the part of an inexperienced or a lesser writer. But 'dull' is the last adjective to apply to Noel Streatfeild's writing. A lively sense of comedy and gaiety runs throughout her children's stories. The most fun is derived from her keen sense of the ridiculous; in humour of situation. A good example is the rehearsal of Phoebe's pageant scene in *Party Frock,* with Partridge, the very correct butler, Mrs Miggs, an uninhibited charlady, and Miss Lipscombe, a vinegary spinster, neatly played off against each other in reciting Phoebe's doggerel rhymes. The humour of this situation is mingled, of course, with a certain caricaturing of the three characters involved. But when any of her important or 'serious' characters venture into ludicrous situations, Noel Streatfeild is careful not to detract from the reader's sympathy with them. In the tragi-comedy of the cat-swallowed goldfish in *The Bell Family* the reader feels a genuine sympathy with Andrew's distress and Ginny's anxiety, even while he laughs at the absurd situation.

In dialogue, the youngest members of the families often provide amusement by their use of difficult words, and in original mannerisms of speech, while 'below stairs' characters have some picturesque turns of phrase. A sort of light sarcasm often plays a part in the narrative—for instance, in a passage describing Santa's violin teacher in *The Circus is Coming:*

> 'Miss Fane liked pieces which she described as ''that dear little slumber song'' . . . Santa could never remember how her fingers went in the dear little slumber songs. . . .'

Thus Santa, the sympathetic character, is neatly juxtaposed to Miss Fane, the unsympathetic character.

Apart from the actual comedy in the stories, the whole of Noel Streatfeild's writing for children is imbued with an intrinsic good humour, which reassures the reader that all will be well in the end. There are serious and sad moments, but these are resolved and pass away. Tragedy may be mentioned, but it is never explored; the overall atmosphere is light-hearted. In *Curtain Up,* for example, the Forbes children are faced with the tragic news that their father is missing at sea, and they may therefore be orphans. This event, however plays its part only as a starting-off point of the story. It is not a dramatic peak in the narrative. The information is given and digested, and other happenings absorb the main attention of the characters and the reader. Again, if the overall atmosphere of *Ballet Shoes* were not light-hearted, the three Fossil children—and the reader—might well be led to spare much more than a passing thought for their parents. But as it is, we are skilfully led away from speculation on that score. The girls are orphans, this is an essential condition of the story, and once it has been swiftly established, it is merely taken for granted throughout the rest of the narrative.

Noel Streatfeild the storyteller emerges from behind her narrative as a benevolent personality whose aim is primarily to entertain her readers, and who knows that worthwhile and successful entertainment demands the utmost attention to detail. (pp. 36-9)

> *Barbara Ker Wilson, in her* Noel Streatfeild, *The Bodley Head, 1961, 63 p.*

MARCUS CROUCH

The most skilful, sincere and honest writer of [career books]— and she was much more besides—was Noel Streatfeild. Noel Streatfeild had turned to writing after a brief career on the stage, and her first book for children was a set of short plays *The Children's Matinee* [1934]. Before this, in an adult novel, *The Whicharts* [1931], were the seeds of her first important book, perhaps her best, for children. *Ballet Shoes* established her immediately as a major writer for children. A story about three orphan children adopted by an absent-minded professor, it showed a profound understanding of child behaviour and a rare concern for accuracy in the factual background. What gave the books its enduring quality was its warm, strong tenderness. The three Fossils were characters who exist in their own right. Noel Streatfeild was too wise and industrious to adopt the soft option of a sequel, but she could not prevent the Fossils creeping back into later stories. The recurrent theme of Noel Streatfeild's writing is the virtue and the necessity of hard work; it was implicit in *Ballet Shoes* and was the very heart of *The Circus is Coming* which won the Carnegie Medal in 1938. Nothing ever came easy to her heroes and heroines. She showed in precise detail the stages of progress towards success and the rewards, in terms of self-respect, of success. Hers were, almost in Victorian terms, 'moral' and 'success' stories, but the moral was not imposed on a story but came from the heart of the writer. (p. 79)

> *Marcus Crouch, ''Renaissance,'' in his* Treasure Seekers and Borrowers: Children's Books in Britain 1900-1960, *The Library Association, 1962, pp. 55-86.*

MARY CADOGAN AND PATRICIA CRAIG

Towards the end of the last century, the theatre began slowly to shed its loose-living associations. By the time of King Edward VII, children from all sections of society were encouraged to attend elocution and dancing classes, though in most cases these were expected merely to provide a gloss for their everyday behaviour. The small proportion of those who were being trained full-time at drama or ballet schools, in fact, were likely to be more serious and better-behaved than the majority who were not, since their careers—always a serious topic—had been decided on and had to be kept constantly in their minds. The well-chaperoned child star of impeccable propriety had been a feature of American film studios as far back as the early 1900s; but it was not until the 1920s in England that the middle-class images of model child and child actress or ballet dancer began to coalesce. Noel Streatfeild was the first children's author to express the theatre's increasing social respectability . . . in a book which is respectable also from a literary point of view; and *Ballet Shoes,* which came out in 1936, remains the best example of the type of fiction which began with it—the family story with a theatrical bias.

It is appropriate that this book should use conventions of the media which provide its subject matter. It is stagey in the obvious sense of being about the preparation for careers on the stage, and also in the sense of being contrived; but the contrivance is that of a fairy tale, which is appropriate both for a children's book and for the theatre. The limitations imposed by a theatrical form are made to work here as a valid part of the author's whole disciplined approach. In the theatre, for example, every line must be relevant, and it is from the strict relevance of Noel Streatfeild's expression that much of her humour derives, since the most direct conclusions (particularly when reached by a child) usually are also the wittiest. (pp. 286-87)

The title *Ballet Shoes* perhaps is not the most apt one for this book, since only one child—Posy—has ambitions to be a dancer; but it is to Posy's ambitions that everything in the end is subordinated, including the artistic integrity of the oldest child. Pauline, who is a better stage than film actress, signs a five-year contract to work in Hollywood so that she can pay for Posy's training in Czechoslovakia. In Posy, the economy of the author's method of presentation is seen at its most stringent. Posy not only has no characteristic which does not relate to her dancing, she has no existence outside of a ballet-school context. She is simply the most basic idea of a ballet dancer embodied, and for this reason the author cuts out the "sensitive", soul-searching, self-realizing process which so weakened the presentation of other theatrical or musical children (Kit Haverard, for instance, in Elfreda Vipont's *The Lark In The Morn*). Posy is ruthless, exhibitionist, and these qualities are suggested to be an effect of her startling ability. She remains, however, a charming fairy-tale figure. Noel Streatfeild often introduces a clichéd image or character trait only to give it an enlivening twist: here, the Russian child, Petrova, is the one who is *not* a dancer; "Madame" is there, imperial Russian to the soles of her dancer's feet, but she does not speak in the dreadful broken English common to most children's-book foreigners. . . . (pp. 287-88)

Not the least feature of the book's skilful construction is the character of Petrova Fossil; she is of a mechanical turn of mind, which provides a balance for the stage enthusiasm of the other two, without in the least upsetting the theatrical bias of the book as a whole. Petrova "thought the rehearsals a frightful bore, but she brought her handbook on aeroplanes with her, and when not wanted for the fairy scenes, or to work at one of the innumerable ballets, she would curl up in a corner, and study it".

Petrova's obsession with cars and aeroplanes is an offshoot of the short-lived adulation which, in the '20s and '30s, was accorded to women who made their mark as aviators, explorers, engineers: the glamour of these as professions for women was related to their apparent unsuitability, to the potent attractiveness of the exception which is held to prove the rule. Naturally women who succeeded in these fields were exceptional; so were men, for that matter, but in their case success did not have the additional spectacular quality of a dog on its hind legs, walking *well.* (p. 288)

With the three Fossils, however, Noel Streatfeild has managed to indicate a whole range of occupational possibilities open to girls; she even suggests that Petrova's ambition may be the most worthwhile:

> "Fancy," Petrova said, "me. You'd think I'd be the one to do nothing at all."
>
> Pauline shook her head. "I wouldn't. I've always thought you were the one that might. Film stars and dancers are nice things to be, but they aren't important."

What *was* important, to Noel Streatfeild and her readers, was an image of child stars—Wintle's, or Lila White's, or anyone else's, Wonders—which had fascinated the author since the time when, as a child, she had been taken to see a matinée on the pier at Eastbourne. Speculation about the origin and lives of the glittery, sequined little performers . . . provided the germ for many of her books; here own experience of drama school and as a repertory actress . . . ensured a background authenticity which imposes order even on the least realistic of her plots. *Ballet Shoes* consciously avoids realism in its treatment of character; *Tennis Shoes,* which followed it, contains as its star the first of her series of difficult, self-opinionated, prickly children who *are* real, in the sense that even in outline they are recognizable. (She was to perfect this type in Jane Winter in *The Painted Garden.*) Nicky Heath trains to be a tennis champion in secret; she cannot bear it to be known that she requires training. . . . (pp. 288-89)

Noel Streatfeild took something of a risk with Nicky Heath: readers at the time were not used to heroines who behaved in a way which was consistently opposed to the principles of team spirit, self-effacement, thoughtfulness for others, and so on. None of the other characters is strong enough to shift attention away from perverse Nicky. She is surrounded with siblings who are superficially more attractive; but these too are less than understanding in their treatment of their sister. Susan and Jim are twins, wrapped up in one another; David is the prototype for another character, this time a minor one, which Noel Streatfeild was to use as a recurrent motif: the eccentric toddler. (One, in *Party Frock,* 1946, prefaces every sentence with "My dear", so that he sounds like an old quean.) . . . The important point that *Tennis Shoes* makes is untypical: it is that "team spirit" is not conducive to individual achievement. Nicky comes out on top because of her perky, unsuppressible egotism; she has a self-assured disregard for conformist pressures which exasperates her sister. . . . Nicky's "unsporting" behaviour culminates in an incident which takes place when she is playing in a county junior championship match: she serves a double fault, flings down her tennis racket, and stamps her foot. Her family is outraged: "As one person they got up and walked out."

The lecture from her father which follows fails to subdue Nicky, who has won the match: "She helped herself to a piece of bread and butter. She took a bite. Then she grinned at her father. 'Miss N. Heath, the pocket star is very grieved. It won't occur again.'" This is the nearest she can come to admitting herself to be in the wrong—we are a long way here from the remorseful, reorientated outlook of the usual puffed-up child who has been made to see the awfulness of her behaviour. The whole book, in fact, is an argument for the special treatment of special people—in spite of the explicit denial of this which occurs on the last page:

> "Meringues! For all of us?" asked David anxiously.
> "Or just Nicky?" Annie snorted.
>
> "All of you, of course. . . . There's no favourites in this house."

Tennis Shoes was followed by *The Circus is Coming.* Again the background is meticulously observed; again, the two children who are its chief characters are treated fairly—so fairly, in fact, that they are not endowed with any special capabilities. Peter and Santa, brought up to be "a couple of ninnies" by a misguided aunt, have run away to join their uncle, Gus, who is a clown in a circus. Gus is off-hand, noncommittal about what he plans to do with them; they are hardly aware of the disruption which they have caused in his well-ordered existence. In the end, they are fitted out with training schemes: Peter prepares to be a groom, Santa a gymnast—but only because in that environment there is no place for anyone who does not work.

That principle can be shown to apply with equal force in a wider social context: almost all Noel Streatfeild's books are concerned with children who make the most of their abilities, in order to earn money or simply as a means of self-expression. (Her performing children may be of either sex, though usually they are girls; no distinction is made between girls' ambitions and boys', and unlike most other "career" stories, there is no reference in Noel Streatfeild to the matrimonial advantages of any profession. Even pretty girls of sixteen or so never consider that they may be other than self-supporting, and certainly no ambitious child sets an artificial limit to the duration of her chosen career.) Two exceptions are *The House in Cornwall,* an unmemorable adventure story involving a kidnapped prince, and the more successful wartime *Children of Primrose Lane,* in which a group of resourceful working-class London children capture a spy: the actual capture is effected by two girls who wrap him up in a rug and sit on him. If spies have to be caught this obviously is the way to do it: with panache, exuberance, and a dogged British determination. . . . (pp. 289-92)

The character of Millie Evans, the child horror in this book, is adjusted precisely to the requisite social level. Where the middle-class children of the other books are self-assertive and contrary, Millie is pert, self-satisfied, curled and frilled by the kind of mother who likes a good cry at the pictures. "Our Millie" whines if anyone speaks crossly to her. . . . (p. 292)

It is an index of Noel Streatfeild's skill that she can create awful children and proceed to make them likeable, without altering their characters in any radical way. (Incidentally the qualities which *make* Millie awful are precisely those which tend to be imposed on pretty little girls by adults who subscribe to the most conservative theory of femininity: coyness, sugary sweetness, flirtatiousness, an ability to simper and a habit of trading on their good looks. Millie can be as sensible as anyone, but because she *is* clever she has found out that in certain circumstances it pays off to appear silly.) Nicky, Millie and the others come off not simply because they are amusing or true-to-type; they are acceptable almost on their own terms.

(The qualification is necessary because their own terms *are* inflated: this is part of their awfulness.) Technically, this is achieved because their positive qualities are shown in action, not merely stated; on a realistic level because often they *do* have something to be conceited about; and morally, because the origins of their ill-adjustment are suggested. Jane Winter (*The Painted Garden*) suffers from acute resentment of the fact that her brother and sister are more obviously talented than she is: "She couldn't do anything, not anything at all, and she was the only plain Winter." When she is chosen to play the part of Mary in a film version of *The Secret Garden* she makes herself insufferable by lording it over everyone, on the set and off. She is not treated with the respect which she considers her due. . . . (p. 293)

Jane does not blossom into an accomplished actress. She has been considered suitable for this part only because of her natural resemblance to spoilt, cantankerous Mary at the beginning of Frances Hodgson Burnett's story; she can convey Mary's sulky aggressiveness with a minimum of acting. The transformation which is effected in Mary's nature is not repeated in Jane; the book's moral implications are more subtle than that. "Rachel had plenty of time to notice Jane and be surprised about her. 'How queer,' she thought, 'now she really is acting Mary and they're pleased with her, she's nicer instead of worse.'" It is, of course, the satisfaction which Jane gets from having done something well which makes her nicer; there is no suggestion that the niceness will remain. What she really craves is appreciation; this is a common, but not a "nice" trait. At its most tangible, vulgar and extravagant level, appreciation takes the form of orchids—"'Hundreds of them! Real, film star flowers.'" It is at the point when these are presented to Jane—incidentally, the end of the book—that her isolated acting success and her sense of personal worth can crystallize, to become something that is safely over, but which has had its effect. Jane's original ambition has been to train dogs; even here, there is no pandering to the readers' expectations of easy fulfilment. The boy who plays Dickon in the film, one of the few people whom Jane likes, presents her with a reed pipe like the one which he uses to tame wild animals. However, "To play pipes needs patience and a certain natural ability. Jane had neither." She makes no progress with her pipe playing, and obviously is in for a disillusionment when she tries it out on real animals. (pp. 293-94)

After *The Painted Garden* there is a slight but perceptible falling off in Noel Streatfeild's style. (Perhaps this was inevitable; *The Painted Garden* provided a standard which could not easily be maintained.) *White Boots* is a lightweight but competent tale of two young ice skaters: one has been brought up to be a champion—"'Pushed here in a pram, she was, by her nanny'"; the other builds herself up steadily by unostentatious hard work. The author's admirable restraint is still in evidence: there is no spectacular success for Harriet, merely one or two indications that she *may* do well. *White Boots* is less successful than some of the earlier books chiefly because its subject matter to a certain extent has had an influence on its treatment; the kind of light, superficial glamour which adheres to ice skating, ballroom dancing, circus or music-hall performances, certain types of water sports such as surfing, has crept into the writing of this book. The author's detachment has receded by several degrees, which makes for a lessening in the sharpness of outline. Even the name Lalla Moore is almost too authentic in this context for an ice-skating child: it is neither outrageously idiosyncratic, like Posy Fossil, nor determinedly unpretentious, like Jane Winter. It imparts to the book its own philistine connotations.

The encroaching vulgarity in Noel Streatfeild's books culminates in the sleeveless black plastic mini-dresses which are worn by Gemma (another unfortunate name, this time because it was unfashionable at the time when the character was conceived) Bow, an ex-film star, and her two cousins, during performances of the sub-pop group into which they have formed themselves. In the four Gemma books there is hardly a memorable episode: there is the usual near-fatal accident (near-fatal this time in terms of career, not life); the usual end-of-term play in which actress Gemma shines; the usual singing and ballet-dancing children; and a boring small boy whose only enthusiasm is for "swirling" tunes (perhaps it is because this word is *un*usual that it seems to be spattered all over the text). The Gemma books are propped up by their many references to contemporary facts of life: Headstone Comprehensive; kidney machines; television advertising; the children even speak occasionally in a diluted pop-world jargon: "'I don't need a room for my thing and Lydia does'". For this reason they may acquire a sociological interest. *Ballet Shoes* and certain other of Noel Streatfeild's better books, however, were not at any time considered out-of-date.

This is not to minimize the effect of their historical evocations, but simply to suggest that these are not detachable from the themes of the books. The victory atmosphere of *Party Frock,* the mood conjured up by the idea of a circus at Carlisle on a wet Saturday afternoon in the 1930s, have a mysteriously compelling cohering function. Perhaps the flashy, grease-paint ambience of a stage training academy needed to be balanced by a way of life as highly regulated as the Fossil sisters'. This, in its turn, is part of a wider orderliness which has all but disappeared, and this makes a similar theme more difficult to treat effectively in the 1960s, without a great deal of literary adjustment. (pp. 295-96)

> *Mary Cadogan and Patricia Craig, "New Vistas,"*
> *in their* You're a Brick, Angela! A New Look at
> Girls' Fiction from 1839-1975, *Victor Gollancz Ltd.,*
> *1976, pp. 286-308.*

BOB DIXON

In Noel Streatfeild's *Ballet Shoes,* the aptly-named Fossils (all orphans) are brought up in a family of the three-servant-poor category (the book was first published in 1936) and go to the Children's Academy of Dancing and Stage Training. It's run by 'Madame' Fidolia who's presented as gracious, talented and immediately inspiring respect. Obviously, however, she's a person sickeningly obsessed with her own self-importance. Petrova Fossil is the tomboy. She's interested in cars and other 'masculine' pursuits. In the book, there's a never-ending concentration on dress and a preoccupation, as in other Streatfeild books, with knickers. It's very important that all clothes should be respectable and just right for the occasion. (*Party Frock,* a lesser-known book, is expressly concerned, throughout, with the manufacturing of an occasion on which a young girl, during the second world war, can wear a frock and shoes sent to her from the USA.) *Ballet Shoes* also gives a good example of a feature very important in girls' fiction—we get the development of an in-group with its own special language and practices. Here, of course, the in-group is centred on ballet and there's an argument, lasting about two pages, between the girls about whether a certain dance sequence was a 'pas de chat' or a 'capriole'. Really, it's the ending that gives the game away. It's the dreams and fantasies this writer is after, as we leave

the Fossils headed for a glamorous future. Pauline's a success in films and accepts a Hollywood contract, Posy's to study ballet under a great 'maître' and Petrova's going in for flying and cars. At least, she's allowed to do this, which is a good thing but her object is to get the Fossil name into the history books and make it famous and in this she's clearly aligned with the others.

The Circus is Coming, by the same writer, begins with the sentence 'Peter and Santa were orphans.' In the last sentence of the first chapter, we are told that their guardian dies. They decide to run away to their Uncle Gus who works in a circus. Although Peter does all the planning and makes all the decisions, the efficient Uncle Gus, once they find him, does make it plain that some of the things they did were not very sensible. However, he puts it down to the fact that they were brought up by their Aunt Rebecca. Gus is by no means a stereotype. He can sew, darn, cook and look after himself in all respects. No doubt this, and many other positive features in Streatfeild's books, are due to the fact that she went to great trouble to get her details right. Her stories are always well-researched. (Blyton, for instance, wouldn't have known what this meant.) It's a pity that Streatfeild settled for the dreams. In this book, the children join the circus at the end.

Curtain Up is almost a sequel to *Ballet Shoes* but with the addition of a boy. Also, the family is in the two-servant-poor category (the book was first published in 1944). Their poverty is constantly stressed. In this story, the emphasis is on theatre so the reader is involved in the stage-training side of the 'Madame's' Academy. Of course, the glamour of the theatre is stressed and there's a seemingly endless preoccupation with clothes again. Petrova is now a ferry pilot and in correspondence with Mark, the boy in this book, who isn't happy at the Academy. Before going off to a boarding school as a step towards his ambition of joining the navy, he gives a revealing view: 'I think the Academy is all right for girls, it isn't all right for boys at all.'

In *Thursday's Child,* Streatfeild settles very firmly on some 'feminine' themes but doesn't seem to be so much at home until she turns to the glamour of the entertainment world towards the end. This change in focus, I think, is why the structure of the story—normally a strong point with this writer— has so many flaws. At several points, it's simply difficult to believe what you're being told. The themes are like the ones in girls' comics, only not so crude. Margaret Thursday is a foundling fostered in a family of the one-servant-poor category. (The book was first published in 1970.) In the first paragraph, the reader learns that Margaret sometimes forgets that skipping is 'a crime'. When, one year, her mysterious annuity fails to arrive, she has to be sent off to an orphanage where her first meal consists of stale bread, margarine, one ounce of cheese and a bottle of water. The Matron has the very best of food, we learn later, and rewards tell-tales with extra food. She sells the clothes the children bring with them and dresses her charges in dingy rags. This doesn't go down well with Margaret, who is no ordinary orphan, as she keeps on reminding us: 'I was found on a Thursday on the steps of the church with three of everything of the very best quality.' 'Everything', you must understand, means clothes. In this sub-Dickensian setting the agony is piled on. The Matron says of Margaret, 'She has a proud air, she must be humbled' and later, when Margaret has committed some small misdemeanour, Matron adds, 'It will take time before she is moulded to our shape' whereupon Margaret gets 'ten strokes' on each hand. Margaret cannot bear

Streatfeild family portrait taken about 1904.

the thought of the fine clothes she's brought with her being sold, so when she decides to run away, she has to find them and take them with her, including the 'drawers edged with lace'. Along with her two friends, Peter and Horatio, she escapes aboard a barge and is told that the bargewoman wears three pairs of flannel knickers in the winter. The three children suffer terribly pulling the canal barge in the rain. Meanwhile, the local aristocrats are sorting out the wicked Matron. Eventually, the three children join a travelling theatrical troupe and the two boys are given parts in a dramatised version of *Little Lord Fauntleroy*. Lavinia, who was put into service with the aristocrats while her two younger brothers, Margaret's friends, were sent to the orphanage, is discovered to be the grand-daughter of Lord Delaware. At the end, Margaret decides she'll become a famous actress. Again, the book has good points, not least the character of Margaret herself but it's a pity that this resourceful and determined girl can only escape from convention into dream. (pp. 13-16)

> Bob Dixon, *"Sexism: Birds in Gilded Cages,"* in his Catching Them Young: Sex, Race and Class in Children's Fiction, Vol. 1, *Pluto Press, 1977, pp. 1-41.*

ANGELA BULL

Ballet Shoes . . . begins very much as a bowdlerized version of [Noel's adult novel] *The Whicharts*, tidied, and moved a few runs up the social ladder. (p. 134)

The happiness awarded to the Fossils is total, and—in the terms of the book—deserved; that for the Whicharts is partial, and bittersweet. Noel is already demonstrating what was to be an important difference between her adult and her children's books. The former invariably settle for clear-eyed realism; the latter are allowed the comforts of romance.

Helped by her blotting paper memory, Noel set herself to re-capture, in *Ballet Shoes*, something of the thrill with which she had watched Lila Field's Little Wonders. She presents the theatre as it was in her teenage day-dreams. . . . The actors, producers and stage managers are kind and helpful, auditions are interesting experiences, talent is always recognized and never provokes jealousy, small rivalries are easily smoothed over. A haze of glamour is shed over everything, from Madame Fidolia with her cerise silk shawl and pink tights, to the spectacular production of *A Midsummer Night's Dream*. And beyond the Academy and theatre, the fantasy stretches outward, to include the house in the Cromwell Road, where the lodgers, like fairy godparents, give each Fossil sister the thing she most needs and wants—to Pauline an education in Shakespeare, to Petrova an introduction to machinery, to Posy a ballet training.

Just as in all the best fairy tales, romance is firmly anchored to reality. Pauline and Posy may be extraordinarily gifted, but they need food and clothes just as much as any other children; and with her own long experience of existing on a pittance,

Noel makes their financial problems almost as absorbing as their careers. . . . [The] stage careers of the Fossils are documented with complete technical accuracy.

Ballet Shoes was the warmest book Noel had written, full of fun, excitement and family affection; yet it was the book over which she had taken least trouble. 'The story poured off my pen, more or less telling itself,' she recalled. 'I distrusted what came easily, and so despised the book.' (pp. 135-36)

[When] theatre and ballet stories inspired by *Ballet Shoes* had multiplied beyond counting, its initial impact was forgotten, but in the context of 1936 it was extremely original.

In the mid 1930s the most acclaimed children's writer was Arthur Ransome. . . . A mass of stereotyped school and adventure stories padded out the children's book lists.

Ballet Shoes was different in both its setting and its outlook. Not one among the hundreds of fictitious schools had been a stage school; and the Cromwell Road house, with boarders crammed into every spare room, was quite unlike the spacious manor houses and vicarages inhabited by the general run of child characters. A central London background was in itself unusual. That the country was infinitely superior to the town was an article of faith with most children's writers, who aligned themselves with the popular 1930s cult of outdoor life. Arthur Ransome pre-eminently, but many other writers too, presented an idealized picture of country holiday life, filling the reader's mind with images of cloudless skies, ruffled water, and hedges rich with meadowsweet and wild roses, of campsites with kettles slung over the fire and sausages sizzling, of swimming, boating and caravanning, and sleeping under the stars. Very occasionally, on holiday, the Fossils dip into this world, but for them reality is the London Underground, or the Earl's Court Road with its motor showrooms.

If the setting of *Ballet Shoes* was original enough, the ethos was startlingly so. Most characters in contemporary children's books were firmly placed in the middle or upper classes at a time when such people had both ample leisure, and the money to enjoy it. With servants in every household, these story-book children have no practical chores to curtail their freedom. (pp. 138-39)

In such a society the question of earning one's living, as the Fossils are obliged to do, scarcely arises. This did not mean that hard work was in itself frowned upon; but children were expected to work only at certain permitted things, and in standard ways. Sport could be practised constantly, as long as it was amateur, not professional sport. Professionalism, carrying the taint of money, was no concern of young ladies and gentlemen. . . . So the kind of rigorous training provided by Madame Fidolia and her staff was quite new in fiction. Children in books managed on their own, and developed self-reliance without always running to grown-ups for help. The Swallows and Amazons learn to handle boats with no advice from sailing school instructors, and without even life jackets to save them if they make some terrible mistake. (pp. 139-40)

Within the limits of amateurism and self-sufficiency, children were allowed to excel, as long as it was clearly understood that prizes and rewards were quite unimportant. These were, of course, often won, but they were usually received with an approved offhandedness. Children who were too competitive in gymkhanas were condemned as pot-hunters. So both the pleasure with which Pauline and Posy naturally regard their successes, and the importance which they attach to them, were

a daring departure from tradition. Professionalism was made, for the first time, respectable.

Equally original, though here Mabel Cary [the children's book editor at Dent who asked Noel to write a theatre story for young readers] must take the credit, was the choice of the theatre as a subject, for longstanding puritan prejudice, and the exaltation of the amateur, had previously combined to make it unacceptable. Amateur theatricals and dancing had always been allowed in children's books. . . . But association with the professional theatre had always implied condemnation. (p. 140)

Noel did not at all realize what an innovation she had made. . . .

When serious criticism did begin, it was often said that Noel had initiated a new *genre,* the career novel. Of course no such intention had crossed Noel's mind as she dashed off *Ballet Shoes;* and the career books which proliferated particularly in the 1950s, with their emphasis on information—case histories, rather than stories, of young vets or social workers or hairdressers—bear little resemblance to anything Noel wrote. The difference lies in a confusion between careers and vocations. Noel's books were not meant, as most career novels were, to help readers make a rational decision about their future. They were stories of children discovering in themselves some strong vocation, and working with disciplined enthusiasm to achieve it. (p. 141)

The Fossils seemed exceedingly modern in 1936, but their special traits—the enthusiasm, the toughness, and the self-centredness, so characteristic of children—proved to be timeless and universal. They could belong equally to any period. Nearly fifty years after its publication, when *Ballet Shoes* had sold ten million copies, Noel was receiving letters almost identical with her original fan mail.

'Dear Noel Streatfeild,' wrote a child in 1937, 'I do want to tell you how much I like your book *Ballet Shoes.* It is one of the best books I have ever read.' The sentiments were to repeated over and over and over again. (pp. 142-43)

The thinking time, before she actually started a book, was always important to Noel. She needed to be completely familiar with her background, and to know her characters intimately. [As] she researched the story which she was to call *Tennis Shoes,* Noel thought deeply about what a junior tennis star would be like.

A starting point was Posy, a child who, seen from one angle, is ruthlessly self-centred, and a deplorable show-off, and, from another, so dedicated to her vocation that ordinary standards hardly apply to her. Such characteristics are also part of Nicky Heath, the heroine of *Tennis Shoes.* But Nicky is a more complex and interesting character than Posy, for, as Noel dug back into the past to revive memories of her tennis ambitions, she began also to remember attitudes and aspects of her own temperament which tallied remarkably with traits in Posy and Nicky. Always able to laugh at herself, she could now admit honestly that she must have been very tiresome, cocky and argumentative, but she could also understand why she had been so. The reason was that unshakeable conviction that she was special. It had taken years, and one long false trail, to discover where the specialness lay; but it had been there inside her, and no one had recognized it. Remembering it all so clearly, it now seemed right and appropriate to bestow just such a conviction on Nicky, giving her an arrogance which maddens her family, and for which the justification is only gradually revealed. Nicky is as close as Noel got to a self-portrait, drawn with subtlety and wit. She is difficult, assertive and conceited; she behaves as idiotically as Noel herself had sometimes done; but as a genius discovering herself she is totally convincing.

In choosing a heroine like Nicky, Noel took an enormous risk. Bumptious characters got short shrift in children's books, and Nicky does not even have Posy's romantic background to provide an excuse for her. She is no semi-orphan, clutching pink ballet shoes in the cradle, but a suburban doctor's daughter. In ninety-nine books out of a hundred Nicky would get her comeuppance, trounced in some dramatic competition like the pony book pot-hunters. Instead she is allowed the success she herself expects, and Noel's writing is so skilful that by the last tournament the reader is eagerly cheering her on.

The book centres on the contrast between two sisters, Susan and Nicky. Susan is the ideal heroine of the 1930s, modest, good-mannered, sporting, a natural conformer. She works hard at her tennis, reaches the final in her first tournament, and is praised by a discerning tennis correspondent. A brilliant future seems within her grasp. Yet all along it is clear to an alert reader that Susan lacks one vital element—a match-winning temperament. She is too self-conscious, too nice, and too unsure to have complete faith in herself.

While attention seems focused on Susan's high destiny, Noel is dropping tiny clues about her tiresome young sister, Nicky. Some apparently trivial juggling shows Nicky handling balls better than Susan. When Nicky begins to play tennis, 'it was odd how often, without any apparent effort on her part, her strokes came off'. Even her exasperating habit of arguing about everything shows an instinctive hunger for mastery, so deficient in Susan. Annie, the maid who understands Nicky, remarks— 'Funny kid, you are. You can do anything you put your mind to.' But what value is a maid's opinion, compared with a tennis correspondent's? Minor accidents prevent Nicky competing in tournaments, so that her progress goes unmeasured for a long time. Susan, who practices with her, is too immersed in her own game to notice Nicky's. When the crucial moment from Noel's childhood day-dreams arrives, and Nicky, not Susan, is picked for special coaching, the choice is both astonishing and absolutely right.

Tennis Shoes moves at the leisurely pace of the 1930s, creating a comfortable family atmosphere with holidays, plays and visits to the circus, as well as tennis. Noel wrote best when she could write expansively. Characters are introduced who would eventually become over-familiar in her stories, but who are now fresh and original—the ineffectual mother supported by her genteel dogsbody, Pinny; the tough, kind-hearted Cockney maid, Annie; the precocious small brother with a talent for singing; the adored family dog. D. L. Mays, a *Punch* cartoonist, captured them all in charmingly simple illustrations, full of period details of hats and deck chairs and penny slot machines. But leisurely days are only the background. The theme of the book is Noel's characteristic insistence on the highest professional standards, on Nicky working out her vocation, with toil and sweat and self-sacrifice. *Tennis Shoes* was always one of Noel's favourite books, and deserved to be. She handled her plot and characters with tremendous skill, and once again the reviews were warmly enthusiastic. (pp. 145-48)

Circus stories were nearly as rare as theatre stories. . . . [The] old-fashioned, traditional kind of circus . . . had ambled through the English countryside since the beginning of the nineteenth century. There were still such circuses on the roads, but Ber-

tram Mills circus, which Mabel Carey had contacted, was a very different affair.

It had been founded in 1920 when Bertram Mills, a former carriage builder and circus enthusiast, had been invited to revive the pre-war Christmas circus at Olympia. Having got a brilliant international show together, he was unwillng to disband it, so for most of the year he held it together with countrywide tours, returning to London for the Christmas season. By 1937 his circus was an enormous organization, with artistes recruited from all over the world, and standards of perfection which equalled or excelled anything Noel had seen in the theatre. (p. 149)

It was not easy [for Noel] to find the best way of using her material, and, in spite of the tour, she was aware of many gaps in her knowledge. Too many of her questions had been answered vaguely—'Oh, it's just our way,' or 'It's always done that way.' Lacking the sense of sure-footed familiarity which she would have liked, she decided she would have to write the book from an outsider's viewpoint. She would have two central characters, as ignorant as she had been, who would gradually learn about the circus.

Cob's circus, the imaginary setting for the book, is based on Bertram Mills', with its troupes of tent-hands and dancing girls, and performers from many countries. She packed the story with the intimate details she had learned about animal behaviour and personality, and about teamwork and professional dedication. She spotlights a handful of families—the Russian Petoffs, the German Schmidts, and the French Moulins—and shows how they work continually to improve their acts. The Schmidt children take everything, from making their beds to training their sea-lions, with the same grave solemnity, while Fifi Moulin, chic and self-possessed, has Posy's impersonal certainty about her own ability. Unrelenting effort is natural to them all; no one wastes time fooling around.

Into this austere world Noel introduces an orphan brother and sister, Peter and Santa. It is their misfortune that their Aunt Rebecca has brought them up exactly as a duchess, whose maid the aunt was, brought up her children. Improbable though this seems, it had actually happened to the beloved Grand-Nannie of Noel's childhood. Her mother had been the nursery maid in a castle, and had brought up her own offspring like the castle children. For Grand-Nannie, most of whose life was spent looking after children in big country houses, this had not mattered, but Noel must have wondered how a young girl, with Grand-Nannie's upbringing, would have fared in a harsher, less well-ordered *milieu*. Such speculation gave her the starting point for *The Circus is Coming*. When Aunt Rebecca dies, and the threat of separate orphanages hangs over Peter and Santa, they run away to find their only other relation, Uncle Gus, who is a clown in Cob's circus. The rest of the story shows how they adapt themselves painfully to circus life, and how the experience changes them.

If Noel took a gamble with Nicky in *Tennis Shoes,* she took an even bigger one with Peter and Santa, and the triumphant success of the book was the reward for her courage. Peter in particular is a most subtly developed character. In the opening chapters he appears molly-coddled and cissy, with a condescending manner which disguises from everyone, including Peter himself, his cool, resourceful brain. Through the folly of Aunt Rebecca's upbringing, he always gives the wrong impression. Gus, his uncle, takes an instant dislike to him, gibing at his assumptions of superiority, making sure Peter knows he has been nick-named Little Lord Fauntleroy, sneering at Peter's attempts to please him. These undeserved humiliations both swing the reader onto Peter's side, and open his own eyes to the image of himself he is presenting. Drawing on depths of courage and determination, which should have been apparent in his successful plan for running away, he sets himself to change his image; so that the boy who once primly refused to sit on a doorstep, ends by coping magnificently with a stable fire. Noel makes his progress absolutely convincing, demonstrating, as she did with Nicky, that heroes and heroines can be carved from the most unpromising materials.

Santa is more readily likeable, but there are setbacks and lessons for her as well. She too has tried to improve her image by boasting that she can play the violin, and the revelation of her ineptitude is as wounding as any of Peter's humiliations. The circus world is fiercely honest. No one makes false claims about themselves, and gay little Santa has to learn about seriousness of purpose and genuine achievement.

Some of the first reactions to *The Circus is Coming* missed the point Noel was making—that Peter and Santa have to be fitted, not just for ordinary life, but for the supremely demanding life of the circus. . . . But as a serious and successful writer, Noel felt justified in her unorthodox approach. She did not believe in easy heroism for her characters, or easy options for herself. Children's books were already full of readymade characters, tailored to fit run-of-the-mill day-dreams. She wanted to put forward something more challenging to the reader's intelligence.

Nothing shows this more clearly than her treatment of Gus. It was one of the traditions of children's fiction that, while fathers were a liability and best excluded, uncles could be picturesque, warm-hearted if occasionally hot-tempered, but basically full of good will. Like their counterparts, the scatty artistic aunts, they are ideal children's book guardians, providing the security of an adult presence without demanding any deep emotional commitment from their charges. Above all uncles, from the Bastables' 'poor Indian' to the Amazons' 'Captain Flint', are fun to have around.

Gus is very different, a complex character, unpredictable and hard to like. He is no well-disposed, fun-loving figure, but a touchy, self-sufficient man, with no wish to assume responsibility for two children who will only get in his way. He blames them for things which are admittedly irritating, but not really their fault—their expectations of special privileges, or their ignorance about their family. Even at the end of the book he does not understand them; it is they who have been obliged to make most of the adjustments. The relationship is dissected in an uncompromisingly adult way, untouched by easy sentiment, or any wish to make the reader comfortable. (pp. 150-53)

The Circus is Coming is highly original, the most penetrating, if not the most accessible, of Noel's children's books. (p. 153)

Of *The House in Cornwall* and *The Children of Primrose Lane*, Noel was to say—'I have only written two thrillers for children and they were both wartime books, because it was impossible at that time to travel around to get information for my usual type of book for children. Tied by her war work, Noel had lost the freedom she had needed in her research for *Tennis Shoes* and *The Circus is Coming,* but instead of looking round for interesting new material, she fell back on the clichés of the commonplace adventure story. Only a mixture of anxiety, utter fatigue, and the driving need to earn money quickly can explain why, after her penetrating analysis of the relations between children and grown-ups in *The Circus is Coming,* she suc-

cumbed, in *The House in Cornwall,* to the myth that a family of children could outwit a gang of criminals. (p. 177)

The Children of Primrose Lane, while an improvement on *The House in Cornwall,* falls far short of Noel's pre-war trio of children's books. Writing through the Blitz was a wearisome task. 'The spirit is willing to finish the children's book, the flesh is very laggard,' Noel wrote on 11 March 1941. The final result was a competent book which never quite catches fire. . . . Noel had no particular flair for a straight adventure story. Where the book succeeds is in the characterization of the children, especially Millie Evans, a pretty, quick-witted, bumptious child, a mixture of Flossie Elk and Nicky Heath, who, without any particular gifts, shares something of their star quality. Confidently, maddeningly, she is always one step ahead of the other children, and it is entirely characteristic of her talent for exploiting her own charm that, while all the children help to trap the spy, it is Millie's photograph alone which adorns the front pages of the newspapers. (pp. 178-79)

Noel received many letters from her readers asking for sequels to their favourite books. . . . Noel did not care for sequels, but somehow the Fossils had stayed stubbornly alive, and *Curtain Up* re-introduced them, if rather grudgingly and at second hand, as the donors of scholarships to Madame Fidolia's Academy. Noel was more interested in reviving the Academy itself, with its familiar staff. (p. 182)

But *Curtain Up* is also Noel's most detailed look at the serious theatre. The story centres on the theatrical clan of Warrens, from Grandmother, a once famous actress now struggling to keep up a pretence of stardom, through children and children-in-law in various branches of the profession, down to her five talented grandchildren. As the story begins, three of these, Sorrel, Mark and Holly, are setnt to live with their grandmother, and are plunged into the exciting, disturbing world of the stage. It is a bran-tub of a book, crowded with characters, and including, amongst the Warrens, an amusing gallery of theatrical types, with their speech and mannerisms acutely pinpointed. For a stagestruck child the kaleidoscopic scenes of auditions, rehearsals, first nights, performances and broadcasts make fascinating reading. The weakness of the book, which puts it well below Noel's highest level, is its central character, Sorrel.

Sorrel is a close copy of Susan Heath, the nice elder sister in *Tennis Shoes.* . . . Susan failed through her lack of star quality, and the same lack is clearly apparent in Sorrel. Noel tries to present her as a great actress of the future, the natural heir of the Warrens, and the account of her gradual discovery of what acting is all about, is convincingly done. But to the end, her personality remains colourless. The boldness of Noel's character drawing seems somehow to have evaporated.

Sorrel is continually compared with her unpleasant cousin Miranda, to Miranda's disadvantage. But the reader, who is expected to dislike Miranda, cannot fail to see that her determined egotism will get a good deal further in the theatre than Sorrel's gentleness. This confusion over the exact roles of the characters throws the whole book slightly out of gear. Noel does not seem quite in control. *Curtain Up* lacks shape too. Outline and movement are clouded; some characters remain undeveloped. Despite vivid moments it seems—not surprisingly—a tired book. (pp. 182-83)

Party Frock, actually published after the war, in 1946, is the best of Noel's children's books of this period, and as fine a piece of craftsmanship as she ever achieved. The story arises naturally from wartime conditions, specifically from the impossibility of finding a suitable occasion to wear a new dress. (pp. 183-84)

A close scrutiny of *Party Frock* reveals Noel's tremendous technical expertise. She manages a large cast and a complicated story with such ease that the very real difficulties are never apparent. A family of children decides to write a historical pageant, to give their cousin Selina an opportunity to wear her new party frock. Initially the children write brief scenes which illumine their own characters. One of them, bumptious Phoebe, chooses to be the child Anne Boleyn. Another, ballet-loving Sally, devises a masque to be danced in front of Queen Elizabeth I. The story then shows how each scene develops from its embryonic beginnings to its culmination in the hands of an experienced director, who transforms the original simplicity into a much more ambitious production which involves the whole village. From the lively opening chapter to the surprise ending, the story never flags. Characters are neatly pinned down; the vastness of the final structure is encapsulated in quick snatches of dialogue and cleverly selected details; and a whole colourful panorama is unfurled with masterly control.

Always in the background is the war, an English battlefield, full of everyday difficulties which have to be overcome. There is the problem of supplying all the costumes without clothing coupons, of keeping children clean when soap is rationed, of getting people together when buses are sporadic and often full. *Party Frock* aligns itself with the best wartime children's books, for the struggles it records are as compelling, and far more realistic, than any struggles with spies and secret agents. And, reflecting Noel's own attitude, everything American is spangled with glory, from the original parcel with its scarlet and green ribbons, to the beneficent Colonel who buys the Abbey where the pageant is staged, as a hostel for young American visitors, 'to keep alive for ever the bonds of friendship forged in these last years.' (pp. 184-85)

[*The Painted Garden* is] an ambitious enterprise which, in the end, disappoints through being overloaded with excessive adulation for everything American. Gone is the controlled narrative of *The Circus is Coming* and *Party Frock*. Instead, *The Painted Garden* sinks at times to a mere colourful travelogue with its lengthy descriptions of the Atlantic crossing and the trans-continental train journey, and its rhapsodizing over California. Well over a hundred pages must be read before the real theme of the book is reached—the story of how plain, contrary Jane Winter is spotted by a Hollywood director, and chosen by him for a part of Mary in a film of *The Secret Garden;* and how, through her difficulties with the part, and her contacts with the other film children, her prickly character is softened. . . .

[When] the Hollywood romance and fervid travel writing are stripped away, the disquieting truth that Noel was merely repeating old themes and old stories is laid bare. (p. 195)

A writer's imagination tends to run in grooves, but character drawing had been one of the great strengths of Noel's adult novels and early children's books. *The Painted Garden* was a respectable achievement by the standards of its day, but not by Noel's own standards. It is disappointing to find her shying away from the bold imaginative leaps she had once taken so confidently, and settling—perhaps through pressure of work and other commitments—for the well-known and well-tried. Just as she discovered children's books as a cause, her own seemed, paradoxically, to be declining. (p. 196)

Noel's popularity as a children's writer reached its peak in the 1950s. Her sales might not equal Enid Blyton's, but there was hardly a newspaper reference or library poll which did not place her in the first flight. Her success was helped by the wide age span of her readers. A decade later this had contracted to the seven to twelve age group, but teenagers in the early 1950s were fairly unsophisticated, and girls of fourteen and fifteen still read Noel's books.

Children's fiction of the time was tediously monochrome, with innumerable pony books and outdoor adventure stories, constant additions to the interminable seqences of writers like W. E. Johns and Elinor Brent-Dyer, and a scattering of worthy but pedestrian career stories. (p. 202)

Against this background Noel's books glowed. Other writers might imitate her stories of child professionals, but, lacking Noel's tough reality of characterization and genuine understanding of what working out a vocation meant, their actresses and ballerinas are merely pretty paper dolls, who demonstrate their genius by pirouetting compulsively in moonlit glades. Adventure stories Noel had wisely avoided since *The Children of Primrose Lane*. Instead, with *Party Frock* and the immensely popular new radio serial *The Bell Family,* she showed that ordinary life could be colourful and absorbing, its small incidents as much packed with drama and suspense as the most hectic inventions of the Blyton school. Unlike most of her contemporaries she wrote books without villains, yet she offered a firm scale of values, with a secure, loving family life as the highest of all. . . . A complete family interested her far more than the conventional story book children on the loose; and she was equally good at conveying the rubs of family life— shared bedrooms and handed-down clothes—and its simple pleasure of pets, holidays and Christmas.

Nothing increased Noel's fame more than the Bell family stories. They were broadcast in six-part serials on Children's Hour every year from 1949 to 1953, appeared in book form in 1954, were revived in a new setting for Children's Hour in 1955, and finally wound up in another book, *New Town,* in 1960. Television was still uncommon, and radio immensely influential. It was estimated that two million adults and four million children listened daily to Children's Hour in 1950—a vast audience for the Bells. (pp. 202-03)

The Bell Family was one of the most popular of all children's radio programmes, frequently voted top play of the year in Children's Hour Request Weeks. In weaving her stories about a poor clergyman's family in South London, Noel mixed several strands from her own past. The setting is clearly Deptford, grimy and overcrowded, but full of sterling characters. The poverty is that of Noel's childhood, where traumas over clothes can coincide with the employment of full-time domestic help. The morality is staunchly Victorian. High standards of manners, loyalty and unselfishness are displayed by everyone, giving the serials, even in the early 1950s, an old world charm which appealed as much to adults as to children. They are unashamedly stories about people who try to do the right things. (p. 203)

The Bell Family was successful because it presented a family who were idealized and yet credible—the sort of family every listener would like to belong to. It followed a simple formula of loosely connected stories, stemming from the temperaments and interests of the children, and their relationships with each other. (p. 204)

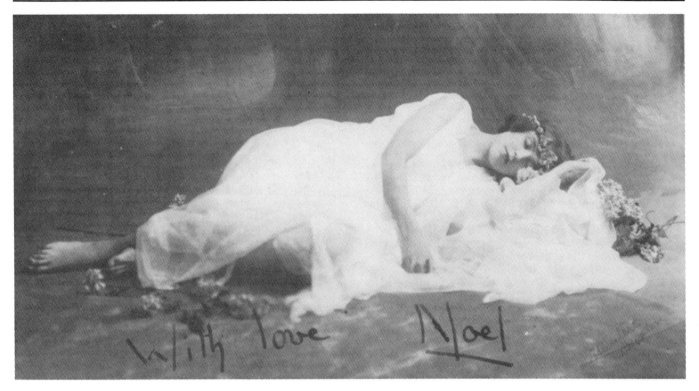

Streatfeild as Titania in the Doran Shakespeare Company's production of A Midsummer Night's Dream. *Courtesy of W. H. C. Streatfeild.*

Having covered theatre, ballet, films, tennis and the circus, Noel had been looking around for a new background. Children who sent her fan mail sometimes mentioned that they were taking part in ballets on ice, and, in an unguarded moment, Noel floated the idea of a skating book with her American editor, Bennet Cerf. To her consternation he seized it enthusiastically; and she found herself committed to a subject about which she knew nothing, and which demanded an enormous amount of research.

The preparation of *White Boots* demonstrates both Noel's thoroughness, and her close relations with her staff. People who worked for her always became linked by strong bonds of loyalty, caught up in her interests and pleasures. On this occasion, having decided that she was too old to learn to skate herself, she persuaded her secretary, June, to undertake a course of lessons, and report both on skating technique, and on all the happenings at an ice rink. Meanwhile Noel studied books on skating, and contacted an expert about the figures required for each graded test. With a background of knowledge, she began observing skaters in training; and when figures had been traced, 'I knelt on wet, cold ice, studying the tracings, trying to find out what made them faulty or otherwise. Then I began to fly high. I attended every stage of first the European and finally the World Championships. People were very kind. They sat by me for hours on end, explaining why one skater would get more marks for a figure than another. Finally I reached the grand state of being able to guess reasonably accurately exactly what marks a skater would get.' When the book was finished, Noel sent it for approval to a famous skating judge, before submitting it to the publishers.

Such exhaustive study gave Noel confidence, and confident *White Boots* certainly is, one of Noel's best books. After a rather shaky start, introducing the Johnson family who make

an improbable living by selling unwanted vegetables from a rich relation's estate, it develops into an enthralling account of the progress of two child skaters—Lalla Moore, orphan daughter of a famous ice champion, destined by her ambitious aunt to follow in her father's footsteps; and Harriet Johnson, who takes up skating first for her health, and then to be a companion and spur to Lalla. There is an almost Victorian contrast between rich, admired Lalla, who has everything except a happy family life, and delicate Harriet, 'all eyes, hair and legs', poor and shabby, but cradled in love.

The greatest triumph of *White Boots* is the character of Lalla. Charm is a difficult quality for a writer to convey, easy to assert, but hard to evoke, but Lalla has charm in abundance. At times cocky, at times self-pitying, she is always loveable and real. Her dashing style of skating conceals for a long time the horrible truth that she will never be good enough to reach the top. Gradually, while Harriet's skating improves, Lalla begins to fail her tests, and falls ill with nervous strain. As in *The Circus is Coming,* the climax of the book is not some breath-taking triumph, but the moment when Lalla has the courage to admit of those bogey skating figures—'I just couldn't do them. They were too difficult.'

White Boots contains many of Noel's favourite themes—the importance of family life; the lesson that hard work and determination are quite as essential to success as flair and personality; the varied opportunities within every field, so that Lalla can look forward to a thrilling future starring in ice shows while Harriet pursues her dedicated path towards the Olympic Games. Its richness of character and plot captivated readers and reviewers alike. (pp. 204-06)

Another of Noel's books to receive tremendous acclaim was *The Fearless Treasure,* a social history of England. When the suggestion for it came from the publishers, Michael Joseph, she was temporarily nonplussed. History had never appealed to her greatly. 'Odd to live outside your own period', she had observed when her friend, Theodora Newbold, was immersed in a course on the Victorian novelists; and, for a person of imagination, she was oddly indifferent to the romance of her ancestors—Elizabeth Fry, the Stuart regicide and royalist, and de Morville who had murdered Thomas à Becket. The present and future mattered to her, not the past. Unwilling though she was to refuse, Michael Joseph's idea seemed outside her sphere.

Then, by chance, she remembered how, on the Sussex Downs, her father had once found a flint arrowhead, and described to her the civilization of the man who had made it. 'As he talked . . . I saw the man's hut, I smelt his food cooking. Almost I saw him.' The memory gave her a shape for her book. Six children would journey back in time, and experience the daily lives of their ancestors in different generations. The plot mechanics are, in fact, clumsy; the conclusions about the greatness of England, though no doubt chiming with the mood of Coronation year, now seem sententious; but the feel of the past, which Noel conveys with apt details of sights, sounds and smells, is immediately convincing. Research and imagination dovetail into a whole. (p. 211)

Noel, after a run of excellent books, stumbled over *Wintle's Wonders* in 1957.

She had not written about professional theatre children since *Curtain Up*. The children who put on the pageant in *Party Frock* are amateurs in the hands of an experienced director. Jane, in *The Painted Garden,* steps into her film part by the mere accident of looking 'black doggish' at a lucky moment. But *Wintle's Wonders* is set again in a stage school, to which come orphaned cousins—pale, serious Rachel, and lively extrovert Hilary, for whom a splendid dancing future is prophesied. There was to be no repetition, however, of the ethos of *Curtain Up;* Mrs Wintle's Academy is very unlike Madame Fidolia's. Noel returned to the world of *The Whicharts* and *It Pays to be Good,* to a cheap, secondrate establishment, where children in cutely infantile outfits cartwheel and kick their way into pantomime troupes.

Noel imagines an interesting situation. Rachel has promised her dying mother that Hilary will prepare for an audition at the Royal Ballet School; but, to her dismay, Hilary is captivated by the Little Wonders' style of dancing, and only wants to tour seaside resorts with them. Unfortunately, instead of finding a proper solution, Noel muddles herself and her readers. Because Hilary has been labelled 'nice', she cannot be condemned outright for her choice of cartwheels and high kicks, yet Noel clearly despises them, surrounding them with all the attributes of conscious vulgarity. The result is a chaotically shifting viewpoint, left unresolved when attention switches to Rachel's discovery of her talents as an actress.

For the first time Noel's technical ability seems in decline. Climaxes are prepared, and then feebly slithered over. The once subtle dissection of character is lost, while incidents rattle past at breakneck speed. Noel almost seems afraid that she will lose the reader's attention if she does not keep up a rapid pace. There are too many echoes of *White Boots*. Rachel and Hilary are paler versions of Harriet and Lalla, surrounded by a similar cast of domineering aunt, well-meaning uncle, cosy nannie, and intellectual governess. (pp. 213-14)

Though [Noel] travelled so extensively, and particularly loved America, her favourite place of all was Ireland. (p. 231)

Noel saw Ireland as symbolizing magic and freedom. (p. 233)

Suppose, she thought, some children were taken away from their monochrome suburban existence, and exposed to the glorious anarchy of Ireland. What would happen to them?

This idea was the germ for *The Growing Summer,* the last of Noel's really outstanding children's books. It is a celebration of the enchantment of Ireland. The four Gareths, ordinary children with not a youthful ballerina or budding actress among them, are sent to County Cork, to spend an entire summer with their eccentric Great-aunt Dymphna. They find themselves in a ramshackle country house, festooned with cobwebs which Great-aunt Dymphna calls 'fairy lace', with an open garbage heap outside the back door, and a barn full of mildewed junk. Great-aunt Dymphna expects them—unskilled though they are—to cook for themselves, wash their own clothes and spread them on the fuchsia bushes to dry, and entertain themselves in the strange, planless, un-timetabled days which stretch dauntingly ahead. How the children grow and develop in response to the challenges of absolute liberty, and how Great-aunt Dymphna changes imperceptibly from something like a witch to a kind fairy godmother, is the theme of this entrancing, unusual book. Its charm is cumulative. At first the reader, like the children, is alarmed by a lifestyle that seems so odd, but no one can resist for long the persuasive delights of Irish pastimes and people, or the superstitions which Noel gleefully embroidered into still richer fantasies. And, as clearly as in *The Circus is Coming* and *White Boots,* Noel points her characteristic moral: children must not expect things to fall into their laps, but difficulties can be overcome, and the harder the effort, the greater the reward.

Noel too shows that she has learned something—how to cope successfully with a book of shifting viewpoints. Where *Curtain Up* and *Wintle's Wonders* were muddled, the changes of angle in *The Growing Summer* are brilliantly handled, giving the book a unique, prismatic quality. Are the children surviving well under ghastly conditions, or are they—as someone devastatingly puts it—'a hopelessly incompetent lot'? Is Great-aunt Dymphna right to scorn their suburban preoccupation with domesticity, or are they right to be alarmed by her chaotic ways? The Gareths expect to hear news of their parents by telegraph; Great-aunt Dymphna expects to hear it from the seagulls. Both methods of transmission seem equally effective. The children appear at first to be making all the concessions, but, in reality, Great-aunt Dymphna too is having to adjust to them. All the angles and attitudes are valid, all only partial. Life in a 'prehistoric fairyland' [as Noel called Ireland in an unpublished play] is a puzzling, stretching, growth-provoking experience.

Apart from an unnecessary sub-plot, *The Growing Summer* is a wonderfully rich and lively book, crammed with poetry, folklore and fun. It topped the children's bestseller lists, and the reviews were as enthusiastic as any Noel had had. (pp. 233-34)

All her best writing in the 1970s was linked to, or evolved from, recollections retained in her blotting paper memory. *Thursday's Child* . . . seems on the surface all breathless melodrama, with its story of Margaret Thursday, a late Victorian foundling baby, left in a church porch. When lack of money compels the elderly ladies who have adopted her to send her to a repressive orphanage, Margaret runs away, takes refuge on a canal boat, and ends in a travelling fairground theatre, captivating the audiences with her performances as Little Lord Fauntleroy. But between the crowding horrors and excitements are strewn numerous small memories from Noel's childhood.

She relives ancient agonies in Margaret's trials with her boots and orphanage clothes. The village where Margaret goes to school is very like Amberley, even to the old custom when the cruel orphanage matron is 'rough-music-ed'. The country house scenes, with their details of family prayers and servants' routines, are a recreation of Edwardian life at Chart's Edge. In the last chapters Noel seems to be drawing on memories of the Victorian nursery classic of fairground life, *A Peep behind the Scenes;* while the story which runs parallel to Margaret's adventures, about an orphan scullery maid who proves to be a Marquis's grand-daughter, is the very essence of late Victorian children's fiction, echoing Frances Hodgson Burnett's *A Little Princess,* and Mrs Moleworth's wilder flights of fancy. Above all, *Thursday's Child* brims with recollections of Margot Grey [a friend who overcame her illegitimacy to become a successful hotel manager]. The little girl of mysterious origins, full of courage and determination, is Noel's last tribute to a beloved friend.

Compared with Noel's best books, *Thursday's Child* is not so much a work of imagination as of fertile invention; indeed its very fertility gets in the way of a proper imaginative realization of events. The writing is hurried, the climaxes muffled. The leisurely control of the earlier books has given way to an anxious sense that on no account must the action be allowed to slow down. A loss of confidence seems to lurk behind the hectic pace.

These faults were not new. Glimpsed first in *Wintle's Wonders,* they were even more glaring in the four *Gemma* books published in the late 1960s, and recur in Noel's next story, the disappointing *Ballet Shoes for Anna.* They arose partly from Noel's awareness of the changing state of children's fiction, and her understandable fears that her own pre-eminence was under threat. After *The Growing Summer* reviews of her books became shorter and cooler. (pp. 236-37)

Now nearly eighty, Noel saw herself beginning to be patronized as a writer stuck in a groove, outstripped by younger writers with soaring reputations, and blamed for being out of touch with a new generation of readers. She was regarded, she complained, as 'a national monument', of great age and prestige, but little relevance to modern life—she, who had been considered a daring trend-setter. It was the price she had to pay for living and writing so long.

Children's books had changed vastly in her lifetime, while the number of experts on them had proliferated. To such critics, accustomed to the searching historical stories, fine-spun fantasies, and psychological dramas of the 1960s, Noel's recent books looked very ordinary. Her part in extending the frontiers of children's literature was often forgotten; her middle class outlook was noticed and condemned.

Stung by criticism, Noel fought back with one unassailable weapon—her continuing enormous sales. 'Naturally I write about the world and people I know best,' she explained in 1972. 'But I don't think children categorize, erect barriers in the way adults do. What could be more foreign to children today—even middle class children—than the world of *Ballet Shoes?* . . . (But) no child has ever written complaining about this. No, what they *all* want to know is what happens next.' Firmly she turned down suggestions that she might seek contemporary backgrounds for her stories. 'I can't write about industrial or working class families because I don't know them intimately, and unless you know how people will react in certain circumstances, you can't write about them.' Rounding on her critics, she frequently asserted that she did not believe children wanted to read about housing estates and downtown schools. She was sure they would far prefer the inside story of the Buckingham Palace nurseries.

Her actual popularity was immensely reassuring. Despite some unfavourable reviews, *Thursday's Child* was a bestseller for Christmas 1970, was shown on television in 1973, and repeated its success in paperback in 1974. Library polls of favourite authors throughout the 1970s show Noel continuing to score highly with the seven to eleven-year-olds; below Enid Blyton, but on a level with C. S. Lewis. Her long association with the Puffin Club kept her in touch with book-loving children, while, year after year, *Ballet Shoes* maintained its prime position among Puffin books. (pp. 237-38)

In 1972 Noel stunned her critics with a brilliant new book, *The Boy Pharaoh, Tutankhamen.* Timed to coincide with a British Museum exhibition of Tutankhamen's treasures, this was a book for both children and adults to enjoy. Noel, who had never cared much for history, suddenly, in her late seventies, produced a historical masterpiece. She had slaved over the research, building up a formidably convincing picture of everyday life in ancient Egypt; but it had been really hard. 'I think this was the toughest work we ever did,' she wrote on the title page of the copy she gave her secretary, still wincing at the memory of how the fourth chapter, on Tutankhamen's childhood, had had to be revised and rewritten eleven times. Yet, in the end, the impressive scholarship is carried lightly, the different angles of history and archaeology are perfectly integrated, and, by a justifiable use of imagination, the boy pharaoh and his cousin-wife, become totally believable people. Magnificently produced and illustrated, the book was another bestseller.

Still Noel did not rest; sheer professionalism carried her on. She edited five anthologies for Dent's in her old style, with linking commentaries; and she turned back to her memories of the war for another story, *When the Siren Wailed.* Unlike the Primrose Lane children, the central characters here were authentic Cockney children of the 1940s. There was no need now for pussy-footing hints about cream buns and tinned lobster to convey working class culture; the reader is introduced directly to a world of slums and searing poverty. The young Clarks are the sort of children Noel remembered from her Care Committee days, and she shows exactly how their home régime of treats, threats, and casual hours, hinders their adjustment when, evacuated to the country, they are billeted on a retired Colonel. Noel is scrupulously fair to both sides—to the Colonel who believes hot baths and regular letters home are essential to civilized living, and to the children who honestly cannot see the point of his evident peculiarities. Flawed in parts, *When the Siren Wailed* nevertheless gives an interesting picture of wartime ways and attitudes. (p. 239)

In 1976 she published her last two books of any value. *Gran-Nannie* is a memoir of the old nurse who had been loved by three generations of Streatfeilds. (p. 240)

Far to Go, also published in 1976, is a sequel to *Thursday's Child,* a slighter story, but remarkably well-plotted and coherent for a writer of eighty. And now it almost seemed as if writing were keeping her alive. *Meet the Maitlands* was planned as the first of a series of stories about the Maitland family, and even if it was only published on the strength of Noel Streatfeild's name, it still contains a few strong flashes of invention. (pp. 240-41)

Not many people can have lived to her great age, with such a record of successes, and incurred so little resentment and hostility. The memories of her friends were warm and affectionate. That she was occasionally pompous, and sometimes a little vain, were the worst things anyone could find to say about her. She sailed through her adult life, confident that people would like her—and they did.

For Christmas 1981 the members of the Puffin Club made her a special present. It was a 'loving tree', a ball of holly to which were tied many small, beautiful things which children had made and sent—miniature ballet shoes, violins, skates, apple boughs. She had given so much happiness to children, and this was their way of saying thank you. There was one advantage in being a national monument. She could be certain she would not be forgotten. (pp. 241-42)

> *Angela Bull, in her* Noel Streatfeild: A Biography, *Collins, 1984, 254 p.*

BRIGITTE WEEKS

Streatfeild was a formula writer of the very best kind: her books feel comfortingly familiar without being repetitive.

Despite their very British settings and what may now seem quaint ways, these books have not ceased to delight young readers and over the last few years have been reissued . . . in the United States for a whole new generation of readers. As a child, the Fossil girls were my friends, comforting evidence that nothing was impossible, even for kids. My daughter, veteran of today's lurid teen romances, discovered the primmer world of Streatfeild with equal enthusiasm. . . .

After several adult novels, *Ballet Shoes,* [Streatfeild's] first book for children (written at the age of 42), was an instant success, swiftly followed the next year by the popular *Tennis Shoes.* She went on to write a total of 11 books in the series known as *Shoes,* although, in fact, the matching titles were a marketing gimmick of her American publishers, which she disliked intensely. *Movie Shoes* for instance was originally published in England as *The Painted Garden* and *Dancing Shoes* as *Wintle's Wonders.*

Despite Streatfeild's annoyance at such crass brand-name marketing, these books do have a distinct identity, not exactly like a series, but as a familiar world with certain pieces firmly in place and characters that surface from time to time. (The grown-up Fossils have a habit of intervening as fairy godmothers in times of need.) Each one features a family of children triumphing over adversity with luck and the help of a few sympathetic adults.

Money is almost always in short supply. Love, loyalty and family solidarity are not. But parents are by no means the central adult figures in Streatfeild's families. Mothers are often talented, artistic but vague; fathers kind but shadowy. Polly Forum, mother of the child violinist Sebastian in *Traveling Shoes* is a typical example: "At first she meant to paint only for fun, but soon painting had such a hold on her that she was an artist first and a housewife second. If artists as a class could get awards for vagueness, Polly would have won first prize." Often, there just aren't any parents. The children in *Circus Shoes, Theater Shoes* and *Dancing Shoes* are conveniently and fairly painlessly orphaned to give space for their ingenuity and to plunge them into new lives.

Whether the children are alone or have parents too busy to worry about clean underwear, there is always a guardian angel. Generations of American children, who have envied the Brady Bunch's ubiquitous, patient, loyal Alice, will be delighted to find that almost every Shoes book has its Alice too. These loyal retainers in their sensible shoes are a magnificent bunch of doughty ladies. Nana, the anchor of the old house in the Cromwell Road that housed the Fossils never stood for any nonsense even from the fearsome Great Uncle Matthew. "Babies in my nurseries, sir," she said firmly, "never have had outlandish names, and they're not starting now," and that, of course, was that. Pauline, the first baby was called after Saint Paul, and not after a piece of rock. And there is Miss Purser, "Pursey," the retired nanny in *Dancing Shoes.* Without her, the orphaned Hilary and Rachel would have had a rough time indeed living with their Aunt Cora and enduring her vain and precocious daughter Dulcie. In *Movie Shoes,* it is the old family friend Miss Bean, "Peaseblossom," ("who had come to the house to give a hand when Rachel was born and had stayed on doing everything that nobody else wanted to do ever since") whose unexpected legacy pays for the Winters' trip to California.

Despite the lack of money, the patching and scrimping that routinely goes on in Streatfeild houses, there is always, fortunately, talent. Even the plainest and most uninspiring child has a gift. Petrova Fossil, the plain member of the family, who struggled with acting and dancing, is a whiz with engines and airplanes (quite revolutionary for 1936). Jane Winter can't really act despite her film success, but any wild animal trusts her. Motherly, overburdened and ignored Myra of the traveling Forum family turns out to have the best talent of all—making everyone happy.

There are simple messages spelled out in each of these 11 novels: money doesn't mean happiness; everyone has his own gifts and his own special place; pride goes before a fall; happiness comes in its own time and in its own way. Stated baldly, they sound priggish and old-fashioned, but Streatfeild's children are far from perfect, and their stories bring reassurance and support to their readers. Theirs is a world where the center holds.

Another ingredient essential to the charm of these books is the different background chosen for each family. From the circus, to movie studios, the theatre, the tennis court, the concert hall and the vicarage, each environment is created in minute, fascinating detail. Streatfeild knew that children, just like the readers of *People* magazine, want the inside dope. She once tried to pin down what it was in her books that appealed to so many children: "I'll tell you what children really like to know," she observed. "Not about themselves. They really like the inside story of Buckingham Palace nurseries, something like that." They want to know about stand-ins and warm-ups, how schoolwork is done between rehearsals, and whether Princess Di ever smacks Prince William's royal bottom. Streatfeild makes her readers feel they know the answers.

To compare Streatfeild to Judy Blume may seem incongruous, but Blume's popularity is based not just on her frankness about forbidden subjects, but on the fact that her readers know she is on their side, sympathetic to the problems of being at the bottom of society's power structure. Kids may be in trouble with the adult world but Blume—and Streatfeild—give them a fair hearing. Children from Los Angeles to London know when they are respected. And they like it.

> *Brigitte Weeks, "Noel Streatfeild's Writing Shoes,"* in Book World—The Washington Post, *November 9, 1986, p. 16.*

RICHARD PECK

[Noel Streatfeild died at ninety], leaving a body of work that changed the direction of children's books. Sir Bernard Miles, founder of the Mermaid Theatre, delivered her eulogy, for she had once been an actress, playing opposite John Gielgud in his first role. A dramatic character in her own right, Noel Streatfeild spent a half century mining this stage experience in books best known for their theatrical settings.

Yet she once told her fellow writer Rumer Godden that "what I always want in a book is a family." Her own family might have been astonished, for she was the classic young rebel: a clergyman's daughter with a mind of her own and an older sister too beautiful. . . .

The late-Victorian vicarage world recurs in her books: the unworldly father, the distracted mother, the painful publicity of being a clergyman's child, the shifting sibling allegiances, and, not least, the hand-me-down clothes. (p. 3)

The author's beginnings as an adult novelist served her well in children's books that diminished the usual patronizing piety and broke new ground in introducing the young to careers.

Most of her protagonists are girls marching without a backward glance into professional fields. None of them ever considers marriage and family, or the possibility of sexual prejudice in careers on and off the stage. She prefigures not so much the feminist movement as post-feminism. (pp. 3, 7)

Noel Steatfeild broke new ground for children's books by being who she was: a rebel with goals, a daughter of the vicarage who believed that children with personal discipline could achieve anything, a grande dame who maintained ties with the child within herself. Even her earliest work remains fresh for the young, achieving 1980s reader who may well be frustrated by schools and youth cultures moving at the pace of the least motivated. (p. 8)

> *Richard Peck, "Noel Streafeild," in* Dell Carousel, *Fall-Winter, 1988, pp. 3, 7-8.*

BALLET SHOES: A STORY OF THREE CHILDREN ON THE STAGE (1936)

One is frequently asked if there are any "really good new books—not school-stories—for girls." Here is one which can confidently be recommended for the nine to fourteen-year-old.

Miss Streatfeild has written about children in some of her novels for grown-ups. *Ballet Shoes* is a "novel of the theatre" about children and for children; and a most entertaining novel, too.

Pauline, Petrova and Posy Fossil are three adopted children who live in a large London house with a thoroughly human but impecunious guardian and an old-fashioned but endearing and practical Nannie. The household consists also of several kind and helpful tenants.

After a "nurseryhood" which is described with humour and real insight into the child mind, and *without* sentimentality, the three children, now somewhere round nine years old, find themselves unexpectedly at the Children's Academy of Dancing and Stage Training. Luckily they turn out to be successes, for money has to be earned somehow. They graduate from dancing-classes to stage work, and finally to film work; though none of them are geniuses. We leave them in their 'teens, and in very happy circumstances. Pauline is starting for Hollywood,

Posy is training for real ballet, and Petrova looks like realising her secret ambition to be a motor mechanic.

The book grips because it is sincere and perfectly possible. These events *might* happen to any child; these words could be spoken by every child. Pauline, Petrova and Posy are nice, unspoilt, naughty, natural children. They ought to be immensely popular, and so ought Miss Streatfeild, who will surely supply the need of many a grown-up this year and other years. Incidentally, her accounts of the training of child-dancers and actors—accurate in detail—are both interesting and amusing.

> *Lorna Lewis, a review of "Ballet Shoes," in* The Junior Bookshelf, *Vol. 1, No. 1, November, 1936, p. 33.*

It is greatly to Mrs. Streatfeild's credit that [Pauline, Petrova, and Posy Fossil] never become the precocious little prigs they might in clumsier hands. They laugh and play with a household of friendly boarders, and find the stage as exciting as their friends in the audience.

The author has made real a section of life too often distorted by fiction. By pointing out some of the things which make up stage magic, she has done a real service to the theater for its young audience. Her introduction in which she says the Fossils are real people and that Pauline is now in Hollywood makes the story even more exciting. If there is a young lady in your house who hates to practice, this charming book will save you a lot of coaxing.

> *Joan MacWillie, in a review of "Ballet Shoes," in* New York Herald Tribune Books, *July 4, 1937, p. 7.*

Parents who vaguely but hopefully dream that their children may grow up into fine actors and actresses should add Miss Streatfeild's admirable juvenile book to the family library at once, and place it on a low shelf well within reach of young hands. Few children with any sensitivity at all will be able to resist this little story about three orphans who tried their best to make good on the stage. . . .

Quite a few older people, especially those who relished the children in Hughes' *A High Wind in Jamaica,* will have an amusing evening with the book, too, for Miss Streatfeild is a master of dialogue, has as straight, natural style, and writes of the theatre as though she actually has some firsthand information about it. Let us hope that she turns her talents to a serious study of the adult life on the stage, for, unless *Ballet Shoes* is just a happy accident, such a book would be certain of an enthusiastic welcome.

> *A review of "Ballet Shoes," in* Theatre Arts Monthly, *Vol. XXI, No. 10, October, 1937, p. 825.*

Ballet Shoes contains the two chief elements for which, combined with her very individual style of writing, Noel Streatfeild has achieved distinction and popularity as a children's writer. First, the story involves the reader in the hopes, disappointments, and achievements of a *family*. Then, alongside the family interest, the reader is given a detailed picture of the professional training of children, in this case for the stage. (p. 23)

Apart from the fact that *Ballet Shoes* is an outstanding children's book, well written, entertaining, with an original theme, which well deserved its success, certain contributory factors played their part in this success. The book was published at a time when the concept of literature for children was beginning to change, after a long period of neglect. A few authors were producing notable stories for children. . . . But overall there was a dearth of books that would really interest and entertain young readers. (p. 24)

When she began writing *Ballet Shoes,* Noel Streatfeild herself was not aware of this state of affairs; she had been asked to write a children's story, and she simply carried out the task to the best of her ability as a writer, giving it the same care as she would an adult novel. She had no idea that this was rather an extraordinary thing to do at that time, when the average children's writer wrote with a patronising, or falsely simple, approach. It was no wonder that hosts of children seized upon *Ballet Shoes,* eagerly appreciative of the fresh attitude they found in it towards themselves as readers: that of equality with the author.

Another relevant factor that contributed towards the success of *Ballet Shoes* was the prevalent balletomania of the time. Going to the ballet was—and is still—an enormously popular recreation. Throughout the country, thousands of little girls attended their weekly dancing lessons, and dreamed of pirouetting in glory as a prima ballerina—and identified themselves with Posy Fossil. Although the story of *Ballet Shoes* is not exclusively concerned with the ballet, in following the career of Posy Fossil and in her choice of title Noel Streatfeild had hit upon a subject as popular as riding, which had already fostered the trend of the pony story. (pp. 24-5)

> *Barbara Ker Wilson, in her* Noel Streatfeild, *The Bodley Head, 1961, 63 p.*

Starting in 1937, Noel Streatfeild wrote a series known as the "shoes books," about children who compete, perform, or live in an unusual style. In the fourth and fifth grades I read them avidly. . . . The first of the books, *Ballet Shoes,* enveloped me. I entered the world of the three Fossils completely, sharing their classes, performances, and everyday routines. (p. 191)

The world the Fossils inhabit is very tidy and scheduled, governed by strict ideas of what is proper, with Nana, large and firm, acting as judge. Despite its financial precariousness, their world is secure. Everyday life is the focus of the story, and we enter their world through details. We know what the girls wear—practice clothes, audition clothes, everyday clothes. We know what they eat—rainy-day teas, sick-day suppers—and where they take their walks. We enter the school routine of classes, practices, rehearsals and the house routine of studies, walks, sewing, meals. With extra attention we participate in the special days: Christmas, with sugar pigs in each stocking; new jumpers to wear; a jigsaw puzzle for the afternoon; Father Christmas on the cake at tea; and a surprise tree, covered with frost, prepared by the two doctors. We share in the apprehension and excitement of performance day, which starts with breakfast in bed; later Pauline is allowed to ice the cakes for tea, and Petrova helps Mr. Simpson in the garage and receives her own mechanic's suit. Detail is the key—clear, precise, essential. It helps create the enjoyable combination of the incredible—three orphans collected by an old eccentric and left with his young niece in a big old house—with the concrete.

Just as the daily routine is fully described, the characters are thoroughly portrayed. In many ways *Ballet Shoes* is a celebration of individuality. Each of the three Fossils is distinct, with her own talents, tastes, and personality. In the course of the story, each one develops differently and discovers what gives her happiness. Pauline, the oldest, is the actress, classically pretty, with a flair for bringing a part to life. Posy, the youngest, is the dancer, a gifted ballerina. Red-haired and scatterbrained, she has inherited her mother's talent. Petrova, the middle child, is neither pretty nor talented in acting or dance. She is dark, thin, very bright, and interested in cars and planes. For Petrova, the Academy is something of a torture, and her special times of joy come each week when she goes to Mr. Simpson's garage to work on cars. Her dream is to be a flier, and she studies a flight manual during rehearsal breaks. Dancing becomes a routine, but acting remains an agony. Money is needed, however, so Petrova hides her discomfort and earns her share. The contributions and responsibilities of the children are taken seriously, and the money they earn is essential. But they remain children. Each has a temper and a sense of humor; each has her share of bad days, tantrums, stubborn streaks.

It is interesting to note that a book written forty years ago, presenting a tightly regimented world in which proper upbringing and a strong work ethic is stressed, seems so contemporary in the roles it depicts and encourages for women. Not only are the three girls all active and spunky, but with the exception of Mr. Simpson and the missing Gum, all the important adults in the story are women who work, who have responsibilities and skills, who make decisions, solve problems, and live independent lives. Furthermore, at the end of the book each of the three Fossils chooses a career: Pauline will act, Posy will dance, and Petrova will be a flier. Self-sufficiency is shown as essential, and independence taken for granted.

Although twenty years have passed since I first read *Ballet Shoes,* the Fossils do not seem to show their age. The author's clean, concise style is lively, and her characters are still believable. Individuality and independence are not out of fashion; indeed, in female characters they are much in demand. *Ballet Shoes* reminds me that such strong characters are not a recent invention. But unlike so many self-conscious, two-dimensional female protagonists, created to be positive models or images, the Fossils and the adults in their lives are natural, spontaneous, and very much alive. It is not their function to make a political statement; their job is to entertain and engage the reader. The *Ballet Shoes* performance is a four-star success. Where it has not been a long-running hit, a revival should be scheduled. (pp. 191-93)

> *Christine McDonnell, "A Second Look: 'Ballet Shoes'," in* The Horn Book Magazine, *Vol. LIV, No. 2, April, 1978, pp. 191-93.*

TENNIS SHOES (1937)

Tennis Shoes, like this author's previous book, *Ballet Shoes,* is a story of would-be child professionals. Miss Streatfeild brings a racy style, humour and a fair amount of interesting information about junior tennis tournaments, training and coaching.

There is a grandly exciting character in the juggling acrobatic cook who serves meals with an invariable "Whoop, whoop, coming over"—a relic of her circus days. The children themselves, however, do not come alive. Actually the steady round of training, the fierce concentration of star-standard tennis must have made their lives hardly worth living. Such a routine is heavy, especially for younger children such as the Nicky of the story. Yet the reader is asked to believe that these four were leading normal lives in normal family atmosphere.

The most unsatisfactory feature in a book which might have been excellent is the emphasis on publicity, on the applause rather than the game, so that the reader waits, not for the brilliant stroke nor the sustained effort, but for news of the reception and the remarks of the spectators. This is an insidious angle to present to young people and one with which the educational world is already having to contend, for the problem of the tournament-mad child is already in our schools.

Eleanor Graham, in a review of "Tennis Shoes," in The Junior Bookshelf, *Vol. 2, No. 1, October, 1937, p. 34.*

I do like a book that takes me into a family—one that I like—in the first chapter. Before it is over in this one I not only knew, but had determined to keep on knowing, this family in the suburb of Tulse Hill, from the doctor and his wife and four children under ten, no two in the least alike except that the top ones are twins, to Annie the cook who never quite gave up thinking of herself as a trapeze artist. . . .

The children keep on steadily learning, not only about tennis—the book is equal to a course of personal lessons—but about the right way to grow up in the right kind of family. You chuckle constantly over the unexpectedness of what the children do and the rightness with which they are handled. . . .

When an English writer of adult fiction writes for children he is likely to lose the condescension too often displayed by the English who write only for them, and give young folks stories that measure up, in technique and in interest, to anything offered their elders in the same field. A tennis fan of any age plunges through this story; like *Ballet Shoes* last year it will be read by any one in the family who gets a good look at the first page.

May Lemberton Becker, in a review of "Tennis Shoes," in New York Herald Tribune Books, *July 10, 1938, p. 6.*

[This] account of the making of a junior tennis champion is a better-built narrative than its predecessor, but it is a considerably smoother performance. Gratuitous whimsy is happily lacking and the characterization is quite as amusing.

Indeed, Miss Streatfeild's first claim to distinction lies in her witty and astute observance of human foibles as evinced in the young, and if the four Heath children were all red haired and all talented tennis players, it is easy enough to tell them apart, for each one is an individual in his or her own right. . . . The account of [Susan and Jim's] prowess is interesting and amusing when set off against their very English dread of being noticed, but it is Nicky, cheeky and arrogant, who really holds one's attention. . . .

It is unfair to tell who turned out to be the best player, and in any case the account of the children's training, the strict discipline in manners and character as well as technique, will hold the attention of any youngster who ever swung a racquet and for those less sportily inclined the clashes of temperament in the Heath household will furnish ample entertainment. Miss Streatfeild writes in a deceptively simple style which is as forthright as a schoolgirl's theme and as effective as a good fast serve.

Ellen Lewis Buell, in a review of "Tennis Shoes," in The New York Times Book Review, *July 10, 1938, p. 10.*

Streatfeild with Deptford children in 1942. Dee and Watson Ltd.

THE CIRCUS IS COMING   (1938; U.S. edition as *Circus Shoes*)

It seems ungenerous to qualify praise of this book that has so much in it that is new and lively and good. Yet it has one blemish that forces itself relentlessly on the attention of the reader, in spite of the goodness of the rest. This is the unconvincing picture of Peter, one of the two children who ran away from Battersea to their circus uncle; two children presented as an ordinary, nice, sensible boy and girl, handicapped only by horribly false standards induced by the shoddy and pretentious background. In effect the author says to her reader, "There, but for the grace of God go you!" And there I think she is wrong. Surely an ordinary boy at the age of twelve, escaping from the Behave-like-little-Lord-Bronedin atmosphere of the ex-lady's-maid-to-a-Duchess-Aunt would throw discipline to the winds and crash through any amount of early training before breakfast, so to speak. But even after an appreciable time in the new environment he does not forget to wear his gloves. He has to remember that he need not, and he doesn't seem to think it quite nice to do a real job of work out in the open. And when the circus girls call him Little Lord Fauntleroy (a jibe the reader cannot help echoing) he has to ask his sister what they mean!

The trouble is that the reader is thus prevented from identifying himself with the hero and so the temperature drops, crippling to some extent the really first class story of a summer's tenting with Cob's Circus.

There are rapid, lively pictures of the life. The men, the circus children and the animals all come to life under Miss Streatfeild's witty pen. The grown-up characters are a grand group of people, moving and speaking with completely convincing personalities, and even the animals appear as separate individuals, as distinct as we are ourselves in their tastes, and prejudices and whims.

I cannot but admire wholeheartedly the shrewd and generous powers of observation, the wit and understanding which Miss Streatfeild has brought to this story and which, but for that tiresome flaw in the character of Peter, would certainly have made it the outstanding book of the season. (pp. 95-7)

> *Eleanor Graham, in a review of "The Circus Is Coming," in* The Junior Bookshelf, *Vol. 3, No. 2, December, 1938, pp. 95-7.*

Partly because she makes her characters come to life and partly because she writes about what she has observed, Miss Streatfeild's circus book ranks among the best of those meant for children. It is the tale of two orphans who run away when threatened with separation, to find their uncle, an acrobat. Unlike many orphans of fiction they are not shining samples of perfection and a few lessons about life have to be thrown in with their education as new hands of the show. Avoiding all temptation to use lurid poster colours, Miss Streatfeild is very pleasantly matter-of-fact, even when she comes to a climax with the orphans stamping out a fire while everybody else is kept busy by a gale.

> *A review of "The Circus Is Coming," in* The Times Literary Supplement, *No. 1923, December 10, 1938, p. 788.*

The Circus is Coming appeals both to boys and girls, and to adults as well. . . . In her preface, Miss Streatfeild states that in spite of a summer "tenting" with Bertram Mills, she "doesn't know much about a circus" and she can only see what is under her nose. She does herself an injustice. She sees; she can make us see; but she does more. It is not just a panorama she spreads before us; it is a life she shows us. We begin to breathe circus air; we catch a glimpse of circus ideals and before long we feel that we, too, would like to shed our London habits with our London gloves and, like Peter and Santa, learn to play our parts in this strange but worth-while world. (pp. 125-27)

It is impossible to predict where Miss Streatfeild's talents will lead her next. After all, she has already had one play produced, so perhaps we may have plays for children as the next development. But whatever may lie in the future, we cannot but help remembering with gratitude the delightful worlds to which Miss Streatfeild has already introduced us, and not least among them that of Cob's Circus. (p. 127)

> *F. M. Exley, "Noel Streatfeild: Carnegie Medal Winner," in* The Junior Bookshelf, *Vol. 3, No. 3, May, 1939, pp. 125-27.*

Noel Streatfeild has the faculty of taking her readers backstage with an ease which gives them the feeling of first-hand experience whether it be in a dramatic school or the world of amateur tennis, and she adds the advantage of letting them see it through the eyes of children who are distinct personalities. In her new book she gives a special fillip of interest through the very inexperience of two young protagonists, for surely no two children were ever less prepared for tenting under the big

top than were Peter and Santa, who, at 12 and 11, had never even seen a circus. . . .

The gradual development of their characters is as amusing and interesting as is this account of that world compounded of glitter, hard work and loyalty which the author describes with a knowledge and understanding gained on tour with a real circus—a Summer well spent indeed, as a vivid and entertaining book testifies.

> *Ellen Lewis Buell, in a review of "Circus Shoes," in* The New York Times Book Review, *July 30, 1939, p. 10.*

Like all the best of Miss Streatfeild's books, *The Circus is Coming* is about work. (p. 14)

A moral tale, in fact. But how gay, how free from priggishness is Miss Streatfeild's treatment of her serious subject. She effectively points the contrast between the orphans and the circus children, all of whom approach their work with the single-minded devotion of the professional. The little world of the circus is brought vividly to life, its colour and glamour and the hard work that lies behind every performance. The characters are clearly realized; not only obviously colourful individuals like the old Groom, but also more complicated characters like Uncle Gus. It is characteristic of Miss Streatfeild that the only characters who do not ring true are the shallow unsympathetic people from Peter and Santa's world, and the story quickly turns its back on them.

The Circus is Coming is the result of hard thinking and hard writing. It represents the careful preparation, the rejection of easy solutions, which have made Miss Streatfeild one of the best loved but least prolific of writers. (pp. 14-15)

> *Marcus Crouch and Alec Ellis, in a review of "The Circus Is Coming," in* Chosen for Children: An Account of the Books Which Have Been Awarded the Library Association Carnegie Medal, 1936-1975, *edited by Marcus Crouch and Alec Ellis, third edition, The Library Association, 1977, pp. 14-15.*

***THE HOUSE IN CORNWALL*   (1940; U.S. edition as *The Secret of the Lodge*)**

This attractive, slender volume with its chequered cover, is frankly a thriller, and while it in no way bears comparison with such outstanding books from the same pen as *Ballet Shoes* and *The Circus is Coming,* it stands head and shoulders above its species. The setting is up-to-the-minute: a family of two brothers and sisters pay a visit to their uncle in Cornwall and find themselves right in the middle of a political intrigue, complete with servants in black uniform, a dictator and a kidnapped king. There follows a midnight visit to the prisoner which involves much crawling round bushes and climbing of drainpipes, a thrilling dash to London, a hand to hand fight and a rescue by aeroplane! All very impossible, of course, but most thrilling. At times the suspense is almost intolerable.

The characters of the children are clearly defined, and it is chiefly in this respect that the book scores over others of its type. However impossible the events, the children at least are real!

> *A review of "The House in Cornwall," in* The Junior Bookshelf, *Vol. 4, No. 4, July, 1940, p. 175.*

The ten to fourteen year old readers who enjoyed *Circus Shoes* and Noel Streatfeild's earlier books are due for a shock with this latest one—but it will not be one of disappointment, and Miss Streatfeild's audience will undoubtedly be enlarged by a considerable number of boys, since it pushes deeper into the fields of their interests than did any of the others. Indeed, this tale of a mystery which four children unravel in a remote mansion on the coast of Cornwall is every child's dream of triumph over villainous adults made as convincing as a billboard advertisement. . . .

[*The Secret of the Lodge* contains] action which will keep any reader galloping from page to page with suspense mixed with admiration for the courage and ingenuity which [the Chandler brothers and sisters] exhibited in their various ways.

Like all Miss Streatfeild's characters, these are real boys and girls, terse-spoken, given to family wranglings, but fiercely loyal, and much of the interest depends upon their individual reactions to crisis: John, level-headed and efficient, Sorrell and Wish, playing their own private games to overcome the timidity of which they were so much ashamed and growing truly brave under their bluffing; and Edward, a little too precocious and self-sufficient for his ten years, who adds, nevertheless, a special spice of humor. This is an intelligent and timely mystery-adventure story, which avoids the cheaply sensational in an entirely plausible manner.

> *Ellen Lewis Buell, "On Cornwall's Coast," in* The New York Times Book Review, *August 4, 1940, p. 9.*

[In Noel Streatfeild's romantic adventure, *The House in Cornwall*] four dauntless children rescue the nine-year-old King of Livia from sinister political kidnappers.

The elements which appealed to the first readers of the book in the early forties could still appeal to readers today, provided they did not expect much more than cardboard cutouts for characters. The saving grace of this predictable thriller is the humour which creeps in as Noel Streatfeild's shrewd understanding of children edges in to the improbable plot. The story leaps into life suddenly when the children work out a way for Sorrel to carry coffee to royal Rudi, to counteract the sleeping draughts administered by the wicked doctor, in a water-jug corked with a dirty sock belonging to Edward and wrapped in an old hot-water-bottle cover found in the wardrobe of Uncle Murdock's gloomy house. Edward is as proud of his ingenuity as he is critical of the cover:

> It's an awful thing, really, with a rabbit on it, but it's dark green and we can carry the rabbit inside where it won't show.

Touches like this make up for a wild climax when the children hold off a villain axing Rudi's door (Sorrel bites his hand) and another on a ladder outside the window (Edward smashes his hand with a brass bedknob) until the police and embassy officials land outside with reinforcements. (p. 106)

> *Margery Fisher, "Ruritania," in her* The Bright Face of Danger, *The Horn Book, Inc., 1986, pp. 81-108.*

THE CHILDREN OF PRIMROSE LANE   (1941; U.S. edition as *The Stranger in Primrose Lane*)

There were four houses in Primrose Lane, the first three occupied by the Brown, Evans, and Smith families respectively. Number four being vacant, the children were using it as a playhouse (calling it cryptically "Somewhere") until one day they found a strange man hiding there. Accidentally they divulged some military information to which the stranger reacted suspiciously. Realizing their guilt, the children then spent ingenious hours in preventing the German spy (for such he was) from using his knowledge. The scene is present-day London with its many problems, but at no time is a note of bitter hatred struck. The plot is concerned with a battle of wits and is worked out credibly along that line. As usual, there is humor and excellent characterization. This ranks next to *Ballet Shoes* as Miss Streatfeild's best book.

> *Marguerite Nahigian, in a review of "The Stranger in Primrose Lane," in* Library Journal, *Vol. 66, No. 19, November 1, 1941, p. 954.*

Miss Streatfeild always tells a good tale, always shows an acute understanding of what goes on in a child's mind, always gives us good characterization. She does all these things in her latest book and I believe children will be completely satisfied with it. But children accept many things without question for the sake of a story as a whole. In *The Children of Primrose Lane* they will accept the fact that a girl of thirteen and a girl of ten, albeit very fat, are capable of capturing a hefty German spy by throwing a blanket round him and then sitting on him. They will accept also as quite natural that the said spy hides in a house which, as soon as he gets into it, shows very evident signs of being inhabited—even a jug of fresh drinking water. In fact, the spy in the story offers quite a number of situations that will not bear analysis.

If we accept these situations as being admissible then we have an interesting story with a plot that is very well developed. The characterization is particularly good. But where on earth does Miss Streatfeild find such very clever children? But she disarms us by telling us they are very clever.

> *A review of "The Children of Primrose Lane," in* The Junior Bookshelf, *Vol. 5, No. 4, December, 1941, p. 161.*

HARLEQUINADE   (1943)

I have bracketed [*Henrietta the Faithful Hen* by Kathleen Hale and *Harlequinade*] because among the large number of picture books that have come my way this year these are the two that take pride of place. They are poles apart in their appeal but both are excellent. For me as a grown-up *Harlequinade* is favourite. Were I a child I should, without hesitation, choose *Henrietta*. . . .

Whereas *Henrietta* is a "picture" book, *Harlequinade* is better described as a "picture-story" book since the story is at least as important as [Clark Hutton's] pictures. Indeed the interest is primarily in the story. It is, briefly, the story of the development of the Harlequinade throughout the ages. But do not imagine it to be a dry-as-dust history. Under the skilful pen of Noel Streatfeild it has become an entertaining story and is a little gem, a loving tribute. The pictures . . . are superb. . . . Perhaps they will not be fully apprreciated except by grown-ups, and I for one am grateful to author and artist for a fine piece of collaboration. . . .

> *A review of "Harlequinade," in* The Junior Bookshelf, *Vol. 7, No. 3, November, 1943, p. 102.*

By now "harlequinade," which has been adopted for plays, poems and an autobiography, is one of the most popular of titles. What an actual harlequinade would have to call itself when published becomes a problem.

This new children's book . . . does justify its choice of name. It is about Harlequin, Columbine, Clown and Pantaloon, though it begins with the adventures of four circus children in billets. These little refugees find their way one foggy night into the red-plush parlour of a gracious old gentleman, spending his declining years at a feast of memories after a life well spent in spangles and triangles; indeed, the world's history to him is bound by the eternal triangle in the pattern of fleshings and tunic. The setting of his Victorian sitting room by firelight and lamplight is most apt for this guide to old-fashioned joys. Surely he must be a member of the Lupino family to care so zealously for every detail of his occupation's past! He speaks with a gentle delicacy that sets the heart aching for one more glimpse of old Christmastide gambols. Rich as the pictures are in mellow colour their quality is matched by the charm of the text.

> *"Harlequin Speaks," in* The Times Literary Supplement, *No. 2180, November 13, 1943, p. 551.*

CURTAIN UP (1944; U.S. edition as *Theater Shoes: or, Other People's Shoes*)

When Sorrel, Mark and Holly first went to live with their grandmother things looked very odd to them. For this grandmother was one of the great theatrical Warren family and she was determined that her grandchildren should all go on the stage. So she sent them to Madame Fidolia's Children's Academy of Dancing and Stage Training, where they immediately won scholarships. Noel Streatfeild, as may be expected, writes a most lively and entertaining story about the children's training and daily life in the Academy and about their meetings with their talented theatrical cousins, aunts and uncles. Sorrel, Mark and Holly are a nice trio. I was glad that Mark eventually got back to the ordinary preparatory school and so to the Navy as he wanted. Hannah, the children's devoted factotum, is a splendid character; the stagey grandmother and her ex-dresser-maid are more conventional types but good for a laugh. This is an enjoyable book for under-fourteens, with a real stage atmosphere.

> *A review of "Curtain Up," in* The Junior Bookshelf, *Vol. 9, No. 1, March, 1945, p. 31.*

The preceding *Shoes* stories lifted Miss Streatfeild into the first rank of contemporary children's authors. *Theater Shoes,* the best, lifts a book for children into general literature. We have novels for grown-ups about distinguished theatrical families and the working out of hereditary instinct in ways various and unexpected. Now for the first time we have a book for and about children, interesting them from the first and entertaining them till the last, which presents such a family, three generations at once on the stage, and holds the attention of any older reader interested in theatrical psychology.

> *A review of "Theater Shoes," in* New York Herald Tribune Weekly Book Review, *November 11, 1945, p. 28.*

PARTY FROCK (1946; U.S. edition as *Party Shoes*)

The Andrews are as nice and real a family as any created by Noel Streatfeild and that is saying a lot. The story begins with the arrival of the party frock from America and the children's reactions to such a surprise parcel. The question is: How to

have a party in war-time. From the idea of rather simple family theatricals a plan for a grand-scale pageant, including the neighbouring school of dancing, develops. It becomes a rapidly moving snowball which sweeps away all difficulties that lie in its way. One must accept certain improbabilities, and there are a good many here, and few children would have sat down under the monopolizing of their scheme by Philip (an R.A.F. officer) as the poor Andrews were forced to do. But Miss Streatfeild is always good and entertaining reading. . . . (pp. 188, 191)

> *A review of "Party Frock," in* The Junior Bookshelf, *Vol. 10, No. 4, December, 1946, pp. 188, 191.*

This story, set in an English village at the end of a long war, describes in detail the preparations for and many characters involved in giving a pageant. Details may become boring to many readers, although Streatfeild fans will undoubtedly enjoy it. The children are natural; with a more extended plot the story would have been an interesting one of postwar Britain.

> *Josephine E. Lynch, a review of "Party Shoes," in* Library Journal, *Vol. 72, No. 10, May 15, 1947, p. 818.*

THE PAINTED GARDEN: A STORY OF A HOLIDAY IN HOLLYWOOD (1949; U.S. edition as *Movie Shoes*)

One of the most engaging qualities about the children in Noel Streatfeild's stories is that they have their normal quota of human frailty. It is a debatable point if Jane, the central figure of this latest of the *Shoes* series, hasn't rather more than her share—but who wouldn't sympathize with a plain middle child, whose older sister and younger brother are extremely talented? Yet when the English Winters family went to California to visit, it was Jane's very contrariness, plus her love for animals, which won her a chance to play Mary in a film version of *The Secret Garden*. No sudden miracles are worked; Jane doesn't become all sweetness overnight, nor does she achieve an easy success. Therein lies the veracity of this story. Miss Streatfeild is as understanding of the nature of an "ordinary" child as she is of gifted youngsters.

Concomitant with Jane's problems are those of Rachel, who must continue her ballet lessons under difficult circumstances, and of young Tim, who solves the difficulties of piano practice in masterly fashion. One of Miss Streatfeild's best stories, this will please children of 8 to 12 and their parents by its restrained handling of the movie background.

> *Ellen Lewis Buell, "Plain Jane," in* The New York Times Book Review, *April 10, 1949, p. 26.*

From many angles this is the best of the popular "shoes" books for "middle-age" young American readers. Here the very, very English point of view takes a big, honest bump on the shores of this country. The author does not minimize the shock to her English family, and the many little differences; the way she shows them, through the eyes of this gay and intelligent family, is excellent. Also, one cannot commend too highly her Hollywood portrait, chiefly of the lives of child movie actors. . . .

Jane, who does not wear any shoes except her normal ones, is one of the most continuously horrid heroines ever invented. Always the plain, cross, middle child in her family, always jealous of her beautiful ballet sister and her talented pianist brother, she is catapulted into a movie through her passion for animals. Her director soon wishes he never had discovered her!

Children will believe in poor Jane, be glad that her sufferings do not reform her too much, and welcome her one saving grace—her ambition to be an animal trainer. They will enjoy all the adult characters too: the dreadful aunt who is such an unwilling hostess until two of them become famous, the grand martinet of the governess, "Peaseblossom," and the loving, helpful colored cook.

In spite of the fantastic luck which attends the varied talents of the Winter family, the underlying point of "earn it yourself" is shown to be what drives them on; that, plus such determined dreams as most youngsters have, but seldom carry through the hard road of practice. A jolly book.

> *Louise S. Bechtel, in a review of "Movie Shoes,"* in New York Herald Tribune Weekly Book Review, *April 17, 1949, p. 8.*

I find this quite the best thing Noel Streatfeild has yet done for children, richer even than **Ballet Shoes,** and that is saying something!

We all know her for a born storyteller with a touch of genius in writing about children. She is always good fun, gay, mischievous and—yes, warm-hearted.

Everyone knows some plain, difficult, undistinguished Jane like the heroine of this book. Practically everyone likes to know the inner workings of the Film world, and there can be few children who would not be thrilled to be picked out—even if it was only for a scowl—to play a part in a big film. (This was a film of *The Secret Garden*). In almost any hands these would go a long way to making a successful story, and while Noel Streatfeild's will certainly be very successful, these are only contributory factors. What counts at least as much is the quality she gives it by virtue of her own personality, her wide experience. Behind the exuberance, there is as much thought and skill as she would have given to a book for her adult readers. She writes in good faith, presenting her material at just the right level, understanding so well where inexperience will appreciate explanations, facts, a new point of view; satisfying but never teasing nor tantalising. I have never seen her writing to better effect than in the last few pages of her chapter on the Santa Fe Trail.

A characteristic which must carry her near the hearts of little girls is her uncommon knowledge of their private lives. Nice mothers know about them but not, as a rule, casual grown-ups; yet here is such a famous person as the author who has been an actress on the stage, who has film stars and ballet dancers and circus people as her friends, exposing them with a sympathetic but light hearted understanding which gives a special thrill to the fascination of the story of plain Jane's triumph. It would have been easy in this for Miss Streatfeild to sweep the reader emotionally off her feet and up to that gay sophisticated world of film stars, but that she resolutely avoids.

I wish she had made Tim a little older. He feels ten or eleven and at that, would have been more convincing as a pianist. The change would not have interfered materially with the family relationship as, instead of Jane's being middle between him and the pretty 12-year old sister who is going to be a ballet dancer, she would have been the plain youngest, still at a disadvantage beside the two budding geniuses. (And if such families are rare—well, the author must have some licence.) I was sorry about 'Peaseblossom' and felt the satire of that piece of characterisation had no real place here. The readers

will be perfectly aware of the mockery. For all the rest, however, Thank you, Miss Streatfeild! (pp. 158-59)

> *Eleanor Graham, in a review of "The Painted Garden,"* in The Junior Bookshelf, *Vol. 13, No. 3, October, 1949, pp. 158-59.*

WHITE BOOTS (1951; U.S. edition as *Skating Shoes*)

The sad thing about this new book of Noel Streatfeild's is that it does not ring true, and this is disappointing from the writer who made that strange story of the Fossils (in **Ballet Shoes**) so completely credible and satisfying. It is about two just ten-year olds: Lalla, rich but an orphan, cared for by an ambitious Aunt and a Nanny who has far less body to her than that delightful woman who looked after the Fossils—and Harriet whose family has come down in the world and now lives (parents and four children) in a shop that, by this account, would hardly have kept six hungry cats alive, let alone six humans. Harriet is given the run of a skating rink, *free* (as you are told rather often) because her doctor knew the owner. She had been ill for a long time and skating, which was no ambition of hers, struck the doctor as the best substitute for a holiday in the country. Lalla, child of a famous skater, is to be a great ice champion and goes to the same rink regularly for coaching and practise. The girls meet. The limelight hovers now on Lalla, now Harriet; but instead of showing them more strongly, the effect is weakening and one feels that the author was never quite certain what she meant to do with them. The characters are not consistent and I felt the basic realities were unreliable. (pp. 226-27)

> *Eleanor Graham, in a review of "White Boots,"* in The Junior Bookshelf, *Vol. 15, No. 5, November, 1951, pp. 226-27.*

The "shoes" this time are those of young professional skaters. Lalla, the rich little orphan, meets Harriet, at a rink. Their friendship changes both their lives. . . . The outcome for both girls, in regard to their skating, as well as their characters, is very clever.

English family home life, with Harriet's amusing family living over their strange shop, is well pictured, and girls will like the three different brothers. Lalla's aunt, with her snobbism and ambition, may be overdrawn, but someone like her must be behind every child star.

Miss Streatfeild writes so well that we welcome, for girls of about eleven to thirteen, whatever "shoes" she takes up. Her books are full of interesting characters, both young and old, of both quiet bits and emotional bits, which all add up to life in the round.

The talk here about professional skating is just enough to lure any girl who loves to skate, and to hint at the real drudgery that must be endured to be a star. New York City children can see girls like Lalla and Harriet at the Radio City rink, but their dreams and efforts go on in every village with a frozen pond.

> *A review of "Skating Shoes,"* in New York Herald Tribune Weekly Book Review, *November 11, 1951, p. 10.*

THE PICTURE STORY OF BRITAIN (1951)

In this excellent and sensible book Noel Streatfeild never talks down. She serves up hard facts about the United Kingdom from 55 B. C. to the present with a dressing of fascinating psychological data that makes the story easy to digest. Side by side with information concerning tradition, education, religion, the "most peculiar" money, government and industry are amusing tidbits. For instance: how the Welsh are trained not to be shy, why the English are calm and philosophical (it's the climate chiefly) and why the Scots think they need a better education than all the rest. . . .

It will be a learned parent (as well as child) who cannot glean from this slim but meaty volume some rich pickings not found in ordinary history or guide books.

> *Nancie Matthews, "Albion," in* The New York Times Book Review, *November 25, 1951, p. 52.*

An entertaining tour of Britain—tourist slanted—written by the British author of the popular "Shoe" series. This is infinitely more diverting than most of its ilk; the text bubbles along, soft pedalling the principle industries, playing up the romance of tradition, history, holiday-going sights which would intrigue the young American visitor. To be sure, an adult reader might cringe at a few blithe generalities, such as reference to the Cockney's "never failing sense of humor". However, this is a minor failing in a lively, deft and concise approach.

> *A review of "The Picture Story of Britain," in* Virginia Kirkus' Bookshop Service, *Vol. XIX, No. 23, December 1, 1951, p. 678.*

THE FEARLESS TREASURE: A STORY OF ENGLAND FROM THEN TO NOW (1953)

The idea of taking children through the door of history and introducing them to the past is by no means new, but Miss Streatfeild's manner of performing this miracle is unusual. Six children, their ages ranging from 11 to 13, from different parts of England and varying levels of society, are sent to stay with a mysterious Mr. Fosse, who enables them (at first with the aid of magic handkerchiefs and then by the use of their imaginations) to set foot in England at several different periods of her history. The sights, sounds and smells of the past are brought vividly to life, and in each historical 'picture' one of the children recognizes his or her ancestor. In this way, history becomes more real than it has ever been before for them, and they see the really important 'treasure' they have been looking for—"to be proud of their birthright, to think for themselves— to remember that they are free men, made in the likeness of God." Miss Streatfeild has evidently written this book with the idea of inspiring the new "young Elizabethans" with an ideal to live for, through an understanding of their past. I think she has succeeded in presenting the past very clearly and in giving children a sense of the continuity and importance of their heritage, and their need of sympathy and tolerance in the making of a new generation.

> *A review of "The Fearless Treasure," in* The Junior Bookshelf, *Vol. 17, No. 5, November, 1953, p. 243.*

Noel Streatfeild's tour de force, *The Fearless Treasure,* pursues ideas of inheritance and social obligation through various periods of British history. It is informative and brilliantly pictorial; but although the six children concerned are guided into the past through imagination, the boy or girl who reads the

book—and it is best for the over-twelves, I think—will find their interest caught rather than their emotions. (p. 127)

> *Margery Fisher, "Travellers in Time," in her* Intent Upon Reading: A Critical Appraisal of Modern Fiction for Children, *1961. Reprint by Franklin Watts, Inc., 1962, pp. 116-31.*

THE FIRST BOOK OF THE BALLET (1953)

This book is for girls and their parents who are fortunate enough to live not too far from a good teacher. It is the story of a ten-year-old girl who goes to the theatre, sees a ballet for the first time, and, like many other children under the same circumstances, thinks that she wants to become a ballerina. Only, she is in dead earnest, and we follow her through her first interview with the teacher, the beginning of her training, the development of her technique. The difficulties inherent to an artistic career, ballet especially, are not minimized by the author, who knows what she is talking about. . . .

In a book which acknowledges its debt to Arnold Haskell we are surprised to find no mention of Isadora Duncan, to whom, though not a ballerina in the academic sense, Mr. Haskell paid homage several years ago in his book *Balletomania*. Though Isadora's highly original contribution to the art of the dance may have had no influence on ballet directly, yet it awoke in many Americans a sense of beauty of movement, and no one interested in ballet, especially among Americans, should ignore her name.

Except for this one omission we find this first book on the ballet absorbing and distinguished in its simplicity. A must for all young devotees of the ballet.

> *Claire Huchet Bishop, in a review of "The First Book of the Ballet," in* The Saturday Review, *New York, Vol. XXXVII, No. 6, February 6, 1954, p. 43.*

The information is presented in a semi-fictionalized manner through the experiences of nine-year-old Anne who decides she wants to become a ballet dancer upon seeing her first ballet. In spite of the obviously contrived story there is enough information about choosing a school, some of the basic steps and exercises that must be learned, and some of the history of the ballet to give the book appeal for young ballet enthusiasts.

> *A review of "The First Book of the Ballet," in* Bulletin of the Children's Book Center, *Vol. VII, No. 9, May, 1954, p. 79.*

THE BELL FAMILY (1954; U.S. edition as *Family Shoes*)

Miss Streatfeild's story of the vicissitudes of the Bell family in their Rectory in South-East London is based on a radio serial which has held its place in Children's Hour for four years. While the rather picaresque plot certainly provides a happy mixture of grave and gay and a mirror in which many ordinary families may see themselves, there is no doubt that it does suffer more than slightly from its origin as a script for dramatic presentation. There is no faltering in incident or climax but here and there the grafting in of character to replace the effect of voice and intonation is apparent and may detract from the book's value for a perceptive child. But no amount of patching can destroy the essential lovableness of Ginnie, the adolescent perplexity of Paul, the mildness of Jane, the matter-of-factness of Angus and the timeless loyalty of Mrs. Gage.

A review of "The Bell Family," in The Junior Book-shelf, *Vol. 18, No. 4, October, 1954, p. 202.*

A London vicarage in the slums is the setting for Noel Streatfeild's latest *Shoes* book. From the very first page we are immediately in that house, sharing the Bells' fun and tribulations. . . . There are wisdom and humor here and a delightfully sane family feeling. In her other *Shoes* books the author introduced us to real boys and girls; now she has created a highly diverting family, each member a definite personality.

Mary Welsh, "Vicar of London," in The New York Times Book Review, *November 14, 1954, p. 32.*

The Bell Family revives, with brisk *élan* and with no little success, an older kind of children's story—the continuous family novel on a fairly credible level, involving, too, the good but neglected themes of being poor, having a conscience, and taking no small pleasure for granted. . . . If Virginia's common sense and drily entertaining manner are of no less interest than Jane's hopes of a dancing training and Paul's of studying medicine, this is a tribute to the author's quick ear for dialogue, and her attention to character—an unusual quality to-day.

"Home Days and Holidays," in The Times Literary Supplement, *No. 2755, November 19, 1954, p. v.*

WINTLE'S WONDERS (1957; U.S. edition as *Dancing Shoes*)

Miss Streatfeild has given us another gay and lively work peopled by a centre group of vivid personalities, while her intense interest in her subject gives detail and depth to the

Streatfeild with ballet shoes. Courtesy of W. H. C. Streatfeild.

whole scene. Mrs. Wintle has a dancing school whose "Wonders" feed the choruses of popular shows and pantomimes. Mrs. Wintle's own daughter, Dulcie, is the spoilt and conceited star of the school. Into this establishment come Rachel, Dulcie's cousin, and Hilary, Rachel's adopted sister, whose mother has died and left them homeless. Hilary becomes Dulcie's rival while Rachel, despised by nearly all because of her unprepossessing looks and general unattractiveness, eventually becomes a star to outshine the other two. Some of the characters are shadowy, some are caricatures by their exaggerated unpleasantness, but upon Rachel and Hilary, Uncle Tom, Mrs. Storm the governess, and Mrs. Purser the wardrobe mistress, Miss Streatfeild has lavished an intense sympathy and deep understanding so that the reader gains a real experience and something of the author's own insight into and perception of human nature. Miss Streatfeild seems here, however, to have patience with only her more likable characters. The villains of the piece are nearly always quite black and they are harsh and vague and less real because of that. The writing is excellent and the story spills out easily in an unhampered gay and chattering stream.

A review of "Wintle's Wonders," in The Junior Bookshelf, *Vol. 21, No. 6, December, 1957, p. 323.*

Girls of eleven or so who have their eye on the stage will be entranced with this story on the "ugly duckling" theme—the sad-eyed little girl who likes to read *The Wind in the Willows* while waiting for her dancing cousin in film studios and "snitches" the latter's contract from under her nose. There is, however, a good deal of common sense and some acidity in the account of the dancing academy with its troupes of little-girl dancers that will be relished by many a bouncing schoolgirl. Undoubtedly a popular book.

Phyllis Hostler, in a review of "Wintle's Wonders," in The School Librarian and School Library Review, *Vol. 9, No. 1, March, 1958, p. 72.*

Noel Streatfeild and Helen Dore Boylston are typical examples of writers who have selected the domestic scene for their books. In so doing, however, they have narrowed the background considerably.

These two writers were the pioneers of the "career" story and a whole flood of these stories flattered them in imitation. . . .

The imitators of Helen Boylston followed a somewhat stereotyped pattern. They usually had one heroine and the story traced her struggles, her set-backs and her inevitable and speedy rise to the top of the ladder of fame. The realism, the suspense, the adventure element, were still present in the shape of those setbacks, even if the reader knew all the time that they would be overcome.

Noel Streatfeild, on the other hand, with her first book for children, **Ballet Shoes**, was the forerunner of a different type of "career" story. Here the spotlight is widened in focus to take in not the single figure of the heroine but a group of children, their relationships and adventures, against the backcloth of the world of entertainment. The social background is the well-ordered family life of the British upper middle class. Miss Streatfeild is an excellent storyteller, holding the interest even when events are not particularly exciting. Her books are witty and humorous and her first-hand knowledge of the theatre makes the background of her stories very convincing. She has had many imitators, some of them very successful. . . .

With *Wintle's Wonders,* Noel Streatfeild's latest book, we return to the genuine world of child professionals, with dancing again the main theme. . . . The story is told with the skill which we have come to expect from Miss Streatfeild, the dialogue is lively and the interest is well held. Even so the book disappoints. Here is the same old story: the plain child with undiscovered talents, the same family retainer, or in this case an ex-children's nurse who "mothers" the children. Although the main characters are well drawn, clear-cut and individual, they seem to lack those essentially human qualities, that capacity for emotion, that vigour which distinguishes a memorable character. Reaction to tragedy is quite unmoving and typical of the restrained avoidance of emotional response common to this world of the upper middle class. The reactions of the children are those attributed to them by adults with a smattering of child psychology.

Thus, having set an excellent pattern with *Ballet Shoes,* Noel Streatfeild now seems content to join the ranks of her own imitators, using stock characters, stock scenes, stock coincidences. She does it with more skill than most but nevertheless fails to bring any greater depth or strength to this form of children's literature. Miss Streatfeild has stated that she writes about the theatre as the world she knows. No doubt she could present the same argument in favour of her upper-middle-class world. Nevertheless, it must be pointed out that she began writing about these two worlds twenty years ago. In that period of time one might expect any creative artist to widen the sphere of his own experience considerably. What would be thought, for instance, of a composer who, writing in the symphonic field, gave us precisely the same material in precisely the same pattern to-day as he did twenty years ago? There must be development of ideas as well as skills. Constant practice must improve the skills, but of what interest is craftsmanship alone? It is the material which counts, not so much the medium in which it is presented. Miss Streatfeild is too good a literary craftsman for her skill to be wasted on turning out replicas of her own early efforts. Children's reactions may change little from age to age, but the world in which they live, the very social structure in which they are brought up, has changed considerably in twenty years. The essential values do not change, but human assessment and acceptance of those values alter considerably with the changing order of life itself.

May one plead, therefore, with Miss Streatfeild, and indeed with all the writers of so-called "realistic" books, to descend from their inadvertent fantasy-adventure-realism to the actual world of reality, a world in which the way to the stars is never so easy as it would appear in books?

> *"Struggling towards the Stars," in* The Times Literary Supplement, *No. 2928, April 11, 1958, p. xix.*

THE FIRST BOOK OF ENGLAND (1958)

Wisely, Noel Streatfeild has not attempted in brief compass to give youngsters a tabloid history, but rather she has attempted—and in large measure succeeded—in conveying something of the feel of England and its people. From coronets to crumpets the England of homes and traditions comes across, engagingly, succinctly: her mores and points of view, her abbeys and institutions, her way of life and forms of government, her games and holidays and schools. And specifically her great figures in history and literature and the arts and the world scene, from Boadicea to Winston Churchill. A jolly goodwill builder, which is sorely needed.

> *A review of "The First Book of England," in* Virginia Kirkus' Service, *Vol. XXVI, No. 5, March 1, 1958, p. 183.*

A delightful formal introduction that manages to convey in a few pages the charm and variety of the country and its people. Simple concise chapters on government, schools, holidays, and the arts, with brief biographies of famous personages will be invaluable in answering school questions for 3rd and 4th grades. . . . Highly recommended. (pp. 45-6)

> *Carolyn W. Field, in a review of "The First Book of England," in* Junior Libraries, *an appendix to* Library Journal, *Vol. 4, No. 9, May, 1958, pp. 45-6.*

Acting on the sound principle that the best presents are those we should most like to receive, Miss Streatfeild offers in these cheerful chapters a vivid account of what she loves in her own country. For instance, from her own feeling for the ballet comes a description of people dancing through the streets and in and out of the cottages in a Cornish village on Flurry Day to celebrate spring's arrival. . . .

An attempt is made to perpetuate some popular but unfounded myths, such as the one about English taciturnity in trains, and the fascination of cricket still remains a mystery to the reader. But many solid facts are sprinkled about these pages, so that the book can be read for pleasure now and turned to again with profit when the school curriculum covers English history and geography.

> *Aileen Pippett, "Isle of Albion," in* The New York Times, *Section 7, May 4, 1958, p. 32.*

QUEEN VICTORIA (1958)

An informative and interesting life of Queen Victoria for readers in grades 4-7. This *Landmark Book* presents a realistic queen against the backdrop of political events and personages of her time. Writing is good and the text documented with well-selected contemporary writings, letters, etc. Best of all, Victoria appears as a woman, with human weaknesses as well as decisive strengths which do not detract from her dignity as a queen. Highly recommended.

> *Barbara M. Doh, in a review of "Queen Victoria," in* Junior Libraries, *an appendix to* Library Journal, *Vol. 5, No. 2, October, 1958, p. 160.*

[Noel Streatfeild] wrote a very pleasant introduction to her native land last spring, *The First Book of England,* and now has written a biography of Queen Victoria in the World Landmark Series which will hold young people's interest from beginning to end. It not only gives the outward facts of Victoria's life, without fictionalizing, but attempts to suggest the elements in her character and upbringing which influenced her as a queen, and by brief comments on her relations with Melbourne, Disraeli and Gladstone to make readers aware, if only in an elementary way, of the part played by the Crown in British government. Particularly valuable are the quotations from the magazines of the day, from the Queen's own diary and reminiscences, and from her letters and those of her Uncle Leopold. Girls old enough to remember seeing on television or in the movies the ceremonies of the coronation of Elizabeth II will be especially interested in the curiously lifeless account Victoria gives of hers. This is a book one might suggest to girls who have enjoyed the simpler, more romantic biography of Molly Costain Haycraft, to give a more rounded picture.

"An Artist, a Naturalist, a Poet and a Queen," in New York Herald Tribune Book Review, *November 2, 1958, p. 28.*

NEW TOWN: A STORY ABOUT THE BELL FAMILY (1960; U.S. edition as *New Shoes*)

A very English family story about the adjustment to a new situation. When Reverend Bell announced the move to a different parish, his four children received the news with varying degrees of dismay. Only when the Bishop appealed to the children to help the new parishioners get to know each other and to work for the town, did the Bell children begin to feel they had a role and a contribution to make. Elaborate plans for a town celebration (successfully executed) are described in the last several chapters: both the townsfolk and the Bells are happy. Family relationships are good, and there is a strong message of community responsibility and of friendship between adults and children. The children are quite precocious, but the author's deft humor and her consistency in portraying the children as distinctive personalities make the Bells credible.

A review of "New Shoes," in Bulletin of the Center for Children's Books, *Vol. XIII, No. 8, April, 1960, p. 139.*

Miss Streatfeild can write a masterly, sentimental tear-jerker of a story better than anyone, but *New Town* is by the doyenne of modern children's writers, not the magician who gave us, fresh and sweet with the dew on it, that exquisite story of the Fossil family so many years ago.

New Town is a story about the Bell family. It began as a Children's Hour serial, and bears the marks of its origin. The instalments are terribly tidy; the dialogue has that relentless brightness so characteristic of radio. It is very competent, exactly calculated, made to measure; uncommonly readable, too. It should be enormously popular. But how much better Miss Streatfeild can do! The hallmark of her best work is its accuracy, the first hand authenticity of the background detail. *New Town* is sketchy in the extreme. What an odd new town it is, in setting and in administration! It may be argued that without this oddness the story falls down; Miss Streatfeild, however, knows better than anyone that the good writer does not make his setting fit his plot.

A disconcerting feature of this book is the unconventional syntax and punctuation. Miss Streatfeild may feel that she can afford to write as she likes. Her readers however are of an age to learn to write themselves; they may well choose her as their stylistic model, and the style of *New Town* is not the key to success in the G.C.E.!

A review of "New Town," in The Junior Bookshelf, *Vol. 24, No. 3, July, 1960, p. 165.*

APPLE BOUGH (1962; U.S. edition as *Traveling Shoes*)

A new book by Noel Streatfeild is always something to which we look forward. Since the days of *Ballet Shoes* she has concerned herself with families where the children have marked talents for dancing, music, skating or acting, and where the parents take a prominent part in the working out of the story. The circus and the world of films have also been used as backgrounds, and the ordinary schoolchild with little or no talent in any of these directions, may well be fascinated for a time with the details of training for these professions. This story is no exception; David and Polly (the father and mother of the children) are musical and artistic; Sebastian, Wolfgang and Ethel are respectively highly talented as violinist, film star and ballerina—only Myra, the eldest, seems to have been left out when the fairies distributed their gifts. She, however, discovers that her grandfather's judgment of her character is correct—her talent is for "wisdom, and being a good sister," and it is through Myra that the family become united in the end, after years of travelling about the world with Sebastian on his musical tours (he is something of an infant Yehudi Menuhin). "Apple Bough" is the house that has always spelled "home" to them, and at last they come back to it, with helpful friends they have met during their travels.

The only drawback to Miss Streatfeild's stories, I find, is that they are beginning to get a little old-fashioned. We are still in the world where there are servants and governesses, and a cosy atmosphere pervades the relationship with grandparents (one set is called "Mumsdad" and "Mumsmum"). I suppose this cannot be helped if one is writing about the kind of family Miss Streatfeild obviously knows so well but it must be a closed world for many children of today. If the television authorities are looking for modern children's books to serialise, this author's books should prove fruitful ground; they have been popular on sound radio. Why not give them new life by introducing them to a wider world? (pp. 269-70)

A review of "Apple Bough," in The Junior Bookshelf, *Vol. 26, No. 5, November, 1962, pp. 269-70.*

Part of the reviewer's job is to separate the books that have life from those that only simulate it.

Alive without a doubt is Noel Streatfeild's *Apple Bough*. . . .

Some readers may be tempted into irritation against the mystique of child genius—perhaps enviously, for what stodgy children, for instance, *we* were! We should have found these children uppish in their absorption in their destinies; but the book explains reasonably that "in the Forums' world of artists, pretending you don't do something well when you do is considered affectation". And we can see that behind the Forums' dazzling achievement lies hard, precise work. . . .

Not all the book is equally alive: dear Miss Popple, for instance, is too self-forgetful in the Forum cause. There are other faults. The story is too long drawn out, and often carelessly written; but the carelessness is of something in a terrible hurry to live. The book is warm and bosomy, like a certain kind of mother; and, like that kind, it laughs a good deal, sometimes at not very good jokes; and sometimes its grammatical hairpins are coming down. But, oh yes! it's alive.

"The Good and the Dead: A Test of Quality for Teenagers," in The Times Literary Supplement, *No. 3169, November 23, 1962, p. 894.*

Once more Noel Streatfeild concerns herself with a family of artists and musicians, but there is none of the authentic feel of genius that came out in *Ballet Shoes*. If I believed, as I read, that Sebastian was an infant prodigy on the violin, it was because I was told, not because he really seemed to be; and the same applies to Ethel, the balletomane, and Wolfgang, who wants to write pop songs and ends up in films. Even Myra, who is ordinary and feels she ought not to be, is unconvincing as a character, partly because what she is like depends so much on her passion for the lost home, and this seems entirely unreal. Improbable successes, last-minute kind actions and a slight aura of sentimentality also put me against this book. Readable and competent but not vintage Streatfeild.

Margery Fisher, in a review of "Apple Bough," in
Growing Point, *Vol. 1, No. 8, March, 1963, p. 115.*

THE CHILDREN ON THE TOP FLOOR (1964)

Noel Streatfeild's public will be delighted with this book. Here are four very different children brought together in extraordinary circumstances, several kind and helpful adults and a lovable dog. The story is centred round television and gives a good deal of information about what happens behind the scenes.

One of the children is a persistent "career" child of the kind the author draws so well, and the three other children discover what they want to do before the story ends. At one time life promises to be hard for them but the threat is withdrawn at the last moment. Nothing sensational happens and the interest lies in the children's unusual background and their development as individuals.

The fantastic happening which opens the book has a wry and rather adult humour. Malcolm Master, a T.V. personality and a bachelor, rashly expresses a wish in his broadcast that he should wake up on Christmas morning to "the happy cries of children." His wish is fulfilled only too generously, for there are four babies on his doorstep next morning. As this is a story, there are no complications as to their background and parents, and he brings up the four children as his own.

As always with this author, there is warmth and understanding of children and the story is skilfully and smoothly told. (pp. 321-22)

A review of "The Children on the Top Floor," in
The Junior Bookshelf, *Vol. 28, No. 5, November, 1964, pp. 321-22.*

Twenty-seven years ago when there was no television but only books and the loneliness of long afternoons, I read **Ballet Shoes** by Noel Streatfeild. The memory of that book has persisted into afternoons that are not lonely enough, and into an age where, when we have mastered all our inventions, television may be the single one we continue to regret. Miss Streatfeild's new book, **The Children on the Top Floor,** is about two boys and two girls connected tangentially with television. The giant tube, whatever ills we may ascribe to it, has diminished neither the wonder of Miss Streatfeild's knowledge nor her story-telling gifts.

Don't be fooled by the jacket. **The Children on the Top Floor** is not about "the world of television." This novel, like **Ballet Shoes,** demonstrates, without platitudes or sanctimony, that to have a talent is to be blessed; that to love is to choose to give; that, as is evident to any child with proper parents, to be born is less satisfying than to be found on a doorstep and welcomed, on somewhat equal terms, into a world of adults more kith than kin.

Perhaps the incidents crowd in a bit toward the end of this tale, as life for children has lately become more eventful. But the 27 years which have changed me from a middle-aged child to a middle-aged woman have not, as this book makes clear, wearied Miss Streatfeild at all.

Carolyn Heilbrun, in a review of "The Children on the Top Floor," in The New York Times Book Review, *March 21, 1965, p. 26.*

ENJOYING OPERA (1966; U.S. edition as *The First Book of the Opera*)

Miss Streatfeild, with her good background knowledge of ballet and theatre, makes an excellent guide to the young opera-goer. Unfortunately, this book is so condensed that she has no chance to give more than the briefest information. To anyone of about 12 who is just beginning to be interested, this is a useful introduction, giving notes on the history and production of opera, brief biographies of composers and performers, and short accounts of some of the best-known stories. It was a happy thought to include modern operas which appeal to children, such as *The little sweep* and *Amahl and the night visitors.* . . . [School] and public libraries will . . . find it popular and handy.

A review of "Enjoying Opera," in The Junior Bookshelf, *Vol. 30, No. 5, October, 1966, p. 319.*

A clear, concise, and well-organized account of the opera, this covers how and where to enjoy opera, as well as brief mention of the history, types, important developments in the 19th and 20th centuries, and some mention of behind-scene involvement in production. More attention is given to "Some of the Best-known Operas" than to the afore-mentioned subjects. Unfortunately, the emphasis is purely European as shown by the great detail given to Britten's *Noah's Flood,* a work not commonly known in the United States. The same comment may be made about the list of "Opera on Records" compiled by Thomas Heinitz, the London correspondent of the *Saturday Review* "Recordings" section, which concludes this small volume. . . . Samachson's *The Fabulous World of Opera* remains a better, though longer and more difficult work on the subject.

Harriet B. Quimby, in a review of "The First Book of the Opera," in School Library Journal, *Vol. 13, January, 1967, p. 71.*

THE GROWING SUMMER (1966; U.S. edition as *The Magic Summer*)

Noel Streatfeild is an author who is a true master of her craft, and in **The Growing Summer** she has surely written a children's classic—not that children will define the book in those terms, they'll just enjoy it. A family of four children are sent to Ireland for the summer, because their mother has had to go abroad to nurse their father, who is desperately ill. They stay with their Great-Aunt Dymphna, an eccentric, rather mad old lady with no sense of time and a great appetite for poetry, in a huge, rambling house, rundown and full of cobwebs ("fairy lace," Aunt Dymphna calls them), with the furniture in disrepair. There they find opportunities to learn all sorts of things—practical things, like how to fish from a boat and how to cook; and also, in spite of themselves, they learn a new set of values. All this makes delightful reading, full of fun and tenderness, and with not a shred of moralising anywhere.

Ursula Robertshaw, "Bookworm's Banquet," in The Illustrated London News, *Vol. 249, No. 6644, December 3, 1966, p. 33.*

This is a charming book, and also an empty one. Something has gone very wrong.

What has gone wrong with **The Magic Summer** is its magic. The components are promising: a manor house in Ireland, a mad old aunt and four nieces and nephews who are bundled off to her for the summer. So far, so good. Aunt Dymphna is a jubilant soul who talks to seagulls and recites poetry—and her seaside eyrie in Cork is wonderfully dilapidated. A runaway boy appears and takes up secret residence in the house, giving us hope of suspense. Here the plot falters, and we are burdened with so many pages of the children's attempts to cook and clean, iron and launder, that we begin to think that the author is more interested in home economics than fiction. This, of course, is unfair. She is trying to contrast the youngsters' cautious practicality with Aunt Dymphna's unfettered love of life, and show how each child receives "a touch of the poet" by the end of summer. A worthy theme, but one—alas—which is drowned in dishwater.

> Barbara Wersba, in a review of "The Magic Summer," in The New York Times Book Review, May 14, 1967, p. 30.

[The Gareth children's] first impression of Miss Gareth is that she was more like an enormous bird than a great-aunt; with her flapping black cape and the nose that stuck out of her thin wrinkled old face just like a very hooked beak'. Her clothes are as unexpected as her abrupt, uncompromising manner and her individual way of driving the old black Austin in which the bewildered, weary children are bumped along to Reenmore—not quite there, in fact, for the house has no drive and they have to finish the journey stumbling across a field in pitch dark, carrying their luggage.

With such a beginning, it is hardly surprising that the Gareths regard their great-aunt as an ogress. Her preparation for their well-being consists mainly of clearing a couple of bedrooms in the enormous, neglected house and showing them the kitchen where, she tells them, they will find 'all they needed'. Since she never eats meat but subsists mainly on dubious concoctions from the hedgerows, the children would have had a still more uncomfortable time if they had not been helped out by Mrs O'Brien, who lives near by and comes to clean—and, as it turns out, to help them to develop a real respect and even affection for their eccentric hostess.

They begin to see the sense behind her refusal to cosset them and to learn a little, by watching and listening to her, about country matters and country lore.

Eccentricity is never allowed to become excessive in Noel Streatfeild's portrait of Miss Gareth. If the old woman changes the children radically, their visit has its effect on her too. It is clear to the perceptive reader that her abruptness hides a shy nature and her way of treating the children as rational equals is not only a compliment but also a reflection of the loneliness she never allows to overcome her spirit. (p. 127)

> Margery Fisher, "Great-Aunt Dymphna," in her Who's Who in Children's Books: A Treasury of the Familiar Characters of Childhood, Holt, Rinehart and Winston, 1975, pp. 124-27.

CALDICOTT PLACE (1967; U.S. edition as *The Family at Caldicott Place*)

Tim, the central character, is one of Miss Streatfeild's most attractive: he does the opposite to what the adults suggest, with excellent results. Though her old loves of stage and ballet reappear here, the author's chief theme is the adjusting to serious tragedy which can disrupt any family suddenly. Here father's car crash results in a head injury which temporarily makes him withdraw from life. The chauffeur of the other car

dies, and so, after a period in hospital where Tim visits her, does his wealthy mistress, first bequeathing to Tim, Caldicott Place, where his father can recover. The involuntary bad behaviour of the family under the stress of moving first into a cramped flat without treasured possessions and then into the vast unfamiliar mansion is sympathetically drawn. The solicitor's three rich wards who come as paying guests to pay for running the mansion, include a badly disturbed girl who also begins to adjust to society. Tim's faith brings about his father's cure in unorthodox manner. There are some delightful smaller characters like "Edup-when-pressed", so called through her mother's belief in her reluctance to work. The book is marred, however, by the scarcely veiled patronage towards suburbia at the beginning. (pp. 53-4)

> A review of "Caldicott Place," in The Junior Bookshelf, Vol. 32, No. 1, February, 1968, pp. 53-4.

Noel Streatfeild's characters are built on a simple principle, one dominant trait for each. The central figure of **Caldicott Place**, a small boy called Tim, has a certain bounce and independence which come to the fore when unexpectedly he is left a huge neglected mansion. The family are aghast when Tim, instead of agreeing to sell it, announces that he wants to keep it; but the idea of a holiday home for homeless children somehow grows and comes to fruition. So we get the familiar Streatfeild situation, a group of ill-assorted children—rich, spoilt Athene, timid Freddie who is heir to a great estate, the problem child Sophie; and from the assortment come the storms and calms of a highly skilled but somehow rather cold story. Readable though it is, up to the minute in social *mores*, I found myself thinking back wistfully to **White Boots** and **Ballet Shoes** and other stories from that early period when the Streatfeild boys and girls, still with one trait apiece, really came to life. (pp. 1091-92)

> Margery Fisher, in a review of "Caldicott Place," in Growing Point, Vol. 6, No. 9, April, 1968, pp. 1091-92.

THURSDAY'S CHILD (1970)

Noel Streatfeild's position in the children's book world is unique. She has had all the accolades: a Carnegie Medal, a Bodley Head Monograph [see excerpt dated 1961 in General Commentary], regular appearances in Puffins, large sales—in other words, both critical and popular esteem. Her first children's book, which has withstood the passage of time extraordinarily well, was published in 1936, the very year when the Carnegie Medal, that symbol of a new attitude towards literature for children, was first awarded. Miss Streatfeild herself has had a good deal to do with the changing attitude, and if, over this long span of time, her books have shown talent rather than genius, this does not trouble her child readers. It is we, the adults, who nowadays prefer fiction for children to be stronger and less predictable.

And Miss Streatfeild's subject-matter is easily despised. Her children belong mostly to the educated if impoverished middle classes and "the careers she writes about have tended rather to be the glamorous, wish-fulfilling kind", as John Rowe Townsend once observed rather chillingly. Even children have been known to express their preference for **The Growing Summer**, not because of splendidly eccentric Great-Aunt Dymphna but because no one in the family dances or plays the violin or even acts. (The cardboard boy film star is soon forgotten.)

At worst Noel Streatfeild can write very lazily indeed. One remembers a threadbare story in *Winter's Tales for Children 4*, and a paragraph in *The Painted Garden* which has the word "nice" five times. But mostly she is endlessly inventive, full of verve and real understanding of the surfaces of childhood. The stories are rich in documentary interest and entertainment, escapism of a most satisfying sort. She has managed, like her characters, to keep real feeling, deep emotion, at arm's length. Reading her attractive autobiography, *A Vicarage Family,* one begins to realize why.

Thursday's Child, Miss Streatfeild's new book, is farther away from reality than ever, in spite of the details of life on the canals and in a stock company. Set at the turn of the century, when she was herself a child, it has all the ingredients of a romantic fantasy. The foundling girl, who turns out to be a natural actress, and the orphans, who turn out to be the grandchildren of a marquess, run away together from an orphanage ruled over by a villainous matron. The characters are thinner than usual but the plot is excellently worked and it is really only when one compares the orphanage with Joan Aiken's in *The Wolves of Willoughby Chase* that one realizes what a pale shadow of the possibility this book is.

> *"Pennies from Heaven," in* The Times Literary Supplement, *No. 3583, October 30, 1970, p. 1263.*

Although the setting and situations are in the turn-of-the-century tradition of "orphan stories," the heroine is a remarkably contemporary character whose final decision to remain independent of her would-be benefactors is logical and consistent with a fully realized personality. A fresh and sprightly addition to a perennially popular genre.

> *Mary M. Burns, in a review of "Thursday's Child," in* The Horn Book Magazine, *Vol. XLVII, No. 3, June, 1971, p. 294.*

The story of Margaret's adventures more than bears out the old saying that 'Thursday's child has far to go'. Her exploits are only too believable, even to climbing out of a top window in the orphanage and legging a narrow-boat through a canal tunnel. The rigours of the orphanage are less terrible than they might have been for her, since she has firmly allied herself with the three Beresford children, who enter the place at the same time. When Lavinia Beresford goes into service at the local Big House, Margaret takes the responsibility for her younger brothers—Peter, who like Margaret is nearly eleven, and charming six-year-old Harotio; and when she finds that Peter has borrowed books (a necessity for him) from a private library, she impetuously decides they must all run away.... (pp. 199-200)

The adventures of the three children, working on a canal barge and in a travelling theatrical company, with the belated revelation of the true identity of the well-spoken Beresfords, make a rousing tale which owes its success less to its element of mystery, telling though that is, than to the character of Margaret. Margaret's behaviour is consistent throughout the story; her headlong mode of speech and her ingenuous self-confidence, her pride in the circumstances of her birth, make her so credible a heroine that it is no surprise when she declines to go to Ireland with the Beresfords to live with their newly-found grandfather Lord Delaware. 'I don't want to be anyone's daughter' is an unusual reaction but typical in her and, like the Earl, we can easily believe that she will, as she promises, make her name famous by her own efforts—'it might be as an ac-

tress'. With her trenchant manner, her courage in adversity, her quick wits, Margaret is perhaps the most attractive and vital of all Noel Streatfeild's heroines. The author has said herself that the character is based at least partly on a girl who, on a Channel crossing, had told her the story of her own highly independent life. It seems no accident that Margaret Thursday should find her true vocation while playing Little Lord Fauntleroy on the boards; there is more than a touch of Frances Hodgson Burnett's heroes and heroines in this engaging, spirited foundling of eighty years ago. (p. 200)

> *Margery Fisher, "Margaret Thursday," in her* Who's Who in Children's Books: A Treasury of the Familiar Characters of Childhood, *Holt, Rinehart and Winston, 1975, pp. 199-200.*

THE BOY PHARAOH: TUTANKHAMEN (1972)

Noel Streatfeild has produced for older juniors what should prove a useful and readable background for the current exhibition at the British Museum, *The Boy Pharaoh: Tutankhamen.* Three chapters of discursive general information on Ancient Egypt, tomb-building and the discovery of Tutankhamen's tomb up to the entry of the first chamber lead into a delightful biography of the boy Pharaoh, much more in Miss Streatfeild's usual flowing style: a perceptive and detailed reconstruction of a small boy's life in an Egyptian palace, with a charming picture of the affection between him and the sister he later married. The last chapters are an enthralling blow-by-blow account of the discovery, first of the treasures of the antechamber, then of the tomb and treasure.

> *"Tutankhamen," in* The Times Literary Supplement, *No. 3661, April 28, 1972, p. 492.*

BALLET SHOES FOR ANNA (1972)

Forty years on, and little girls still dream of becoming dancers, so there is room for an up-dated version of *Ballet Shoes.* Here is another romantic story, this time about three children who live a happy, nomadic life mostly in Turkey, living in a caravan with their English artist father and their Polish mother—until one hot day an earthquake engulfs parents, caravan and maternal grandparents while the three children are shopping in the next village. Sir William Hoogle, a distinguished archaeologist conveniently passing, rescues them and takes them to England to live with father's Uncle Cecil, a retired, childless bank manager in a neat new town, with a mousy wife and plastic gnomes in the garden. Here the fun begins, and at first it looks as if Miss Streatfeild is going to give a sharp and compassionate account of the confrontation between middle-aged respectability and three extraordinary children, half street-Arab, half Polish intensity; sadly, the chance is thrown away, the children are unbelievably resourceful and courageous, and there is no doubt at all that Anna will eventually find her fortune at world-famous old Madame Scarletti's studio....

Ballet Shoes . . . was a good deal tougher, and much more like life.

> *"Dancing Girl," in* The Times Literary Supplement, *No. 3692, December 8, 1972, p. 1490.*

This story is much more than a treat for balletomanes. Anna and two older brothers, Francisco and Gussie, are orphaned when their bohemian parents and refugee grandparents are killed in a Turkish earthquake. They are rescued by a distinguished traveller who delivers them to their only relatives, a severe retired bank manager and his timid wife who live within a garden full of plastic flowers in an English suburban house called Dunroamin.

The mastery with which both plot and characters develop provide twin joys. The picture which prevents the children being killed by the earthquake is ultimately their salvation; Gussie, faced with the task of transporting a plastic gnome in a pram, providentially discovers the local custom of penny for the guy. Even in her creation of the sour uncle Miss Streatfeild allows us sympathetic insight into his difficulty in coping with an influx of unexpected and unwanted children. (pp. 53-4)

> *R. Baines, in a review of ''Ballet Shoes for Anna,'' in* The Junior Bookshelf, *Vol. 37, No. 1, February, 1973, pp. 53-4.*

WHEN THE SIREN WAILED (1974; U.S. edition as When the Sirens Wailed)

[This] is the story of a Cockney family separated during the London blitz. Dad serves in the Navy, Mum gets a factory job, and the three Clark children are evacuated and are billeted with elderly Colonel Stranger and his housekeeper in a Dorset town. The children adapt well to the new and more rigorously disciplined way of life, but when the Colonel dies, they rebel against their second sponsor and run off to London to find their mother. Mum, bombed out and in a hospital, is happy to see them but sends them back to the country; the story ends happily when Dad returns, wounded, and they all are reunited and settle in a cottage left by the Colonel. Some of the terminology will be unfamiliar to readers (the wartime trains ''is something chronic,'' a woman complains) but can usually be understood because of the context. Streatfeild's style is lively and her descriptions colorful; the characters are well-drawn and the dialogue is excellent. While the problems and fortunes of the children should engage readers, it is the atmosphere of wartime England—both in London and in the country—that gives the book its strength.

> *Zena Sutherland, in a review of ''When the Sirens Wailed,'' in* Bulletin of the Center for Children's Books, *Vol. 30, No. 8, April, 1977, p. 133.*

[A] story of bombing and evacuation is Noel Streatfeild's *When the Siren Wailed.* Here . . . are the labelled children assembling at the station with gas mask and lunch pack bound for an unknown destination in the country, the tearful farewells at one end and the frosty welcome at the other. It is difficult to be fair to a novel which moves so complacently within national, sexual, and class stereotypes and which is as steeped in crass snobbery as this one. One example will have to suffice. The fine upstanding British Colonel Launcelot Stranger agrees to take in three cockney children, to prevent their being split up. He sends for his servant Martha and tells her: ''I will teach them absolute punctuality and table manners. . . . Will you see they understand they are to be in the dining-room at one o'clock exactly with, of course, washed hands?'' Chapter 6 is called ''Fitting In'' and here the three evacuees are made to observe a very strict and alien regimen, given sewing and gardening tasks as later they are given elocution lessons and taught the value of money. (p. 74)

> *David L. James, ''Recent World-War-II Fiction: A Survey,'' in* Children's literature in education, *No. 2, Summer, 1977, pp. 71-9.*

A YOUNG PERSON'S GUIDE TO BALLET (1975)

However young the reader of this 'guide', the interest can always be accompanied by awareness. I wish, therefore, that Noel Streatfeild had included more about appreciation in her otherwise excellent story of a boy and a girl learning to dance, for there are at least seven companies of varying quality regularly touring the provinces now. Her earnest desire to give, perhaps too much, purely factual information has led in several places to stilted and unnatural dialogue. Also it is difficult to believe that the children's parents (a doctor and a vet) would be hard-pressed to find the price of a theatre seat.

But these things aside, the book is sure to delight the many ballet enthusiasts among the children of today. It manages to include a potted history of ballet, something about technique, dancing in other countries, a few of the stories of the better-known ballets, and something about the lives of famous dancers past and present. It sensibly does not make light of the difficulties, hard work and disappointments which face the child bent on a dancing career, and by the end you really do care what happens to the children in the story.

> *B. J. Martin, in a review of ''A Young Person's Guide to the Ballet,'' in* The School Librarian, *Vol. 23, No. 3, September, 1975, p. 259.*

I wish when I were around nine or ten, someone had given me this book to read. Like all other children who dream of dancing, I was ripe for a book which viewed the ballet with wide-eyed wonder and common sense, one that could teach me about the art and make me see more clearly the work and problem sides of where my dreams would lead me.

A Young Person's Guide To Ballet is a down-to-earth introduction to what happens in a ballet class. The lively story of Anna and Peter's ballet studies between the ages of nine and twelve is interwoven with information on dance history, ballet stories and the current scene. The attitude toward technique inherent in the text is an unusually sound one. And because the treatment of the male ballet student is so realistic (not overly encouraged by anyone but his teacher), this is an excellent book for a boy.

The historical material is reliable (except for that one gaping error which changes Fanny Cerrito to Fanny Cenito), and a splendid collection of photos, litho and painting reproductions enhance the text. . . .

This book's great virtue is its attitude toward studying and pursuing a career in ballet, which is portrayed as both genuine and realistic. (These children do not become prodigies of The Royal at the book's finish.) There are, however, problems with some of the other attitudes of the text. This is a British book. And it is most definitely a ballet book. The comments on Isadora Duncan, Martha Graham (who is likened in approach to Isadora) and the view of modern dance are subtly pejorative. The contemporaries are depicted visually by an unrepresentative choice of pictures: Katherine Dunham in *Tropical Revue* (1940's) and Graham in *Xochitl* (1922).

As to the state of our ballet, the intimation in the text is that America is not quite classical, and our ballet is relegated to a nebish area the author calls ''American dancing.'' No American ballet dancers are shown or discussed. Ironically, though the author states that the old ballets such as *Spectre de la Rose, Petrouchka* and *The Dying Swan* are no longer seen, these works are currently in the repertoires of American dancers and American companies.

These biases should be pointed out to the young reader, and labeled as another possible viewpoint on the dance scene. But they are gentle enough that they need not deter you from buying and giving the book. It's charming nevertheless. I still wish I could have read it back when I was nine.

> *Heidi von Obenauer, in a review of "A Young Person's Guide to Ballet," in* Dance Magazine, *Vol. XLIX, No. 12, December, 1975, p. 94.*

Noel Streatfeild, who has made helpful contributions to dance literature in the past, has produced an unfortunate blend of fact and fiction called *A Young Person's Guide to Ballet.* Anna and Peter attend a ballet school in London where they learn the history of ballet as well as technique. The photographs are well chosen, the drawings are handsome and useful, and the information is accurate. But the unnecessary fictional frame seems merely to be the germ of another, less interesting book.

> *Amy Kellman, "For Very Young Dancers: A Quickstep through Recent Books," in* School Library Journal, *Vol. 24, No. 4, December, 1977, pp. 34-5.*

FAR TO GO (1976)

Far To Go takes up the adventures of foundling Margaret Thursday from the point at which *Thursday's Child* ended, with Margaret's independence finding expression in an acting career. Noel Streatfeild skilfully conveys the stringent professionalism of the serious theatrical child: she communicates the total involvement behind the scenes and on stage that can transform even the performances of "tawdry, seedy, bad actors" into something which compels belief. She is slightly less successful, however, in sustaining a sense of period atmosphere, despite her colourful evocations of fog-swathed streets and horse-drawn cabs.

The story is slight but well structured, and lively enough to ensure a wide appeal. Its brisk pace quickens to the excitement of chase and melodrama when Margaret is abducted by the now insane ex-matron of her old orphanage. She forces Margaret to "skivvy" for her in a filthy, rat-ridden hovel. Satisfyingly Margaret displays more fighting spirit than many authentic Victorian story-book heroines might have done in similar circumstances. Throughout *Far To Go* the robustness of Margaret Thursday has a modern rather than a Victorian flavour.

> *Mary Cadogan, "Victorian Melodrama," in* The Times Literary Supplement, *No. 3900, December 10, 1976, p. 1552.*

After forty years in the field Noel Streatfeild, incredibly, can still tell a story with the same glow and the same sturdy common-sense beneath the sparkle. . . .

The story is, appropriately enough, pure melodrama. This matters little, for Miss Streatfeild has always been able to turn dross into gold. The splendid heroine dominates the action and the well-drawn group of eccentrics who surround her. Surely a winner with children, both in its book form and in the television version which must surely follow.

> *M. Crouch, in a review of "Far to Go," in* The Junior Bookshelf, *Vol. 41, No. 2, April, 1977, p. 121.*

Laurence (Michael) Yep

1948-

American author of fiction.

Yep is a renowned Chinese-American writer of realistic fiction for children and young adults as well as a respected author of science fiction and fantasy. Drawing from his own search for cultural identity, he frequently portrays the view of an outsider in works which deal predominantly with alienation, the need for tolerance, and the importance of imagination. Noted for creating vivid, complex characters who rise above common assumptions of race, sex, and age, Yep presents universal themes—such as the conflict between generations and cultures—with humor, compassion, and well-researched backgrounds. Best known for his highly acclaimed *Dragonwings* (1975), which is based on a newspaper clipping about a Chinese immigrant who invented a successful flying machine a few years after the Wright brothers, Yep develops a convincing picture of eight-year-old Moon Shadow, who comes from China to join his kitemaker father in San Francisco around the time of the great earthquake. Yep continues his distinctive accounts of appealing Asian protagonists who discover both their unique individuality and traditional heritage in such coming-of-age books as *Child of the Owl* (1977), in which twelve-year-old Casey, the daughter of a compulsive gambler, is sent to live with her Chinese grandmother in San Francisco's Chinatown, and *Sea Glass* (1979), a partially autobiographical account of the struggles of twelve-year-old Craig Chin, who feels rejected by both his American peers and Chinese elders. Two quest-fantasies, *Dragon of the Lost Sea* (1982) and *Dragon Steel* (1985), not only chronicle the heroic adventures of Shimmer, a noble dragon, and her plucky young human friend, Thorn, but introduce a new approach to the dragon world rooted in Chinese mythology; Yep is also the author of a "Star Trek" novel, *Shadow Lord* (1985). A versatile writer, Yep breaks from his customary preoccupation with science fiction and Chinese-American themes in several books: two humorous Civil War tales which feature Mark Twain in his early journalistic career; a psychological novel focusing on two Caucasian teenagers and a suicidal mother; a murder mystery set in California's Silicon Valley; and a lively easy reader about a vampire squirrel.

Critics praise Yep for his memorable characterizations, sensitive development of relationships, humanity and wit, and the authenticity of his historical details of China and early California. Although reviewers note that a few of Yep's plots lose momentum, the majority of critics admire the broad range of his subject matter and treatments as well as his warm understanding of youth. Most observers recognize that Yep has made a significant contribution to children's literature through the success of his Asian-American perspective.

Yep has received many awards for his books. In 1976 *Dragonwings* was both a Newbery Honor Book and a *Boston Globe-Horn Book* Honor Book; it also won the International Reading Association Children's Book Award in the same year as well as the Lewis Carroll Shelf Award in 1979. *Child of the Owl* won the *Boston Globe-Horn Book* Award in 1977 and the Jane Addams Children's Book Award in 1978.

Photograph by Kathy Yep. Courtesy of Harper & Row, Publishers, Inc.

(See also *CLR*, Vol. 3; *Contemporary Literary Criticism*, Vol. 35; *Something about the Author*, Vol. 7; *Contemporary Authors New Revision Series*, Vol. 1; *Contemporary Authors*, Vols. 49-52; and *Dictionary of Literary Biography*, Vol. 52: *American Writers for Children since 1960: Fiction.*)

AUTHOR'S COMMENTARY

Probably the reason that much of my writing has found its way to a teenage audience is that I'm always pursuing the theme of being an outsider—an alien—and many teenagers feel they're aliens. As a Chinese child growing up in a black neighborhood, I served as the all-purpose Asian. When we played war, I was the Japanese who got killed; then when the Korean war came along, I was a North Korean communist. This sense of being the odd-one-out, is probably what made me relate to the Narnia and the Oz books. They were about loneliness and kids in alien societies learning to adjust to foreign cultures. I could understand these a lot better than the stories in our readers where every house had a front lawn and no one's front door was ever locked. When I went to high school, I really began to feel like an outsider. I lost my grammar school friends because they all went into basketball while I went into science fiction. Then every morning I would get on a bus and ride into Chinatown where I attended Catholic school. My family didn't speak Chinese so I was put in the dumbbell Chinese class. I resented that, but what I resented more was that all the dirty jokes and the snide remarks were told in Chinese so the Sisters wouldn't understand them. I couldn't understand them either.

At first it was only through science fiction that I could treat the theme of the outsider, but then I began to do historical fiction and finally contemporary fiction. *Sea Glass* is my most autobiographical novel, but I can't always write that close to home because it requires me to take a razor blade and cut through my defenses. I'm bleeding when I finish, and I have to take time off by writing fantasy or something only marginally related to my Chinese heritage such as *The Mark Twain Murders*. (pp. 426-27)

> *Laurence Yep, in an excerpt in* Literature for Today's Young Adults *by Alleen Pace Nilsen and Kenneth L. Donelson, second edition, Scott, Foresman and Company, 1985, pp. 426-27.*

GENERAL COMMENTARY

CHARLOTTE S. HUCK

While Asian-Americans have been portrayed in picture books for younger children, there are very few stories about them for middle-graders. . . . *The Child of the Owl*, written by Laurence Yep, is the fine story of a Chinese-American girl who finds herself and her roots when she goes to live with Paw Paw, her grandmother in Chinatown. When Barney, Casey's gambling father, winds up in the hospital after having been beaten and robbed of his one big win, he first sends Casey to live with her Uncle Phil and his family in suburbia. Casey doesn't get along with Uncle Phil's family and they are horrified by her, so she is sent to Chinatown. At first Casey doesn't like the place, the narrow streets and alleys, the Chinese schools. But Paw Paw tells her about Jeanie, the mother Casey never knew, about her true Chinese name, and the story of the family's owl charm. Gradually she comes to like it all and to realize that this place that was home to Paw Paw, Jeanie and Barney, is her home too. *Child of the Owl* is as contemporary as the rock music that Paw Paw enjoys and as traditional as the owl charm, but Casey and Paw Paw are true originals. This same author has written the sensitive novel of *Dragonwings*, a story that takes place in 1903 when an 8-year-old boy left China to join the father he had never seen in the strange country of America. This account of the courage and industry of the Chinese-American was a Newbery Honor Book. (pp. 438-39)

> *Charlotte S. Huck, "Contemporary Realistic Fiction," in her* Children's Literature in the Elementary School, *third edition, updated, Holt, Rinehart and Winston, 1979, pp. 388-463.*

SHARON WIGUTOFF

The conflict between parents and children, particularly at the onset of adolescence, is very real, as everyone who has lived through the experience knows. The need to establish one's separateness is a major preoccupation of nine-to-14 year-olds and, as such, deserves to be a primary theme in fiction for this age group. However, although parents are significant forces in children's lives, we noted over and over again the lack of depth in characterizations of parents. In most books, they are either invisible, shallow, lacking understanding, or preoccupied with their own lives. When they are presented as antagonists in relation to their children, we rarely gain insight into their thoughts and motivations. Adult authors of children's books have clearly

decided that young people do not want to read about parents or sympathize with them.

There are exceptions, of course. Laurence Yep, in two outstanding books, *Child of the Owl*, and *Sea Glass*, provides fathers who are complex characters, and as demanding of our interest as the younger protagonists. In the first book, Barney is a gambler, a loser who has to send his daughter to live with his mother when he can no longer care for her. Yet, he becomes sympathetic, as Yep lets us know that it was racial discrimination that interfered with Barney's ambitions. Similarly, Calvin Chin in *Sea Glass* is initially presented as an angry, frustrated man, driving his reluctant son to be a champion athlete. We learn later in the story the pressures placed on Calvin by his own father and by the realities of being part of a minority culture. (p. 8)

Educational research confirms that children from all backgrounds benefit from multicultural materials, including white children who need to rid themselves of what Eloise Greenfield terms "delusions that the whiteness of their skin makes them somehow special." Yet publishers of junior fiction have failed to seek out, encourage, *and publish* authors of diverse racial and ethnic backgrounds. Unfortunately, as long as our society is guided by what sells best rather than what is needed most, there is little likelihood that this will change unless economic pressure is applied. Ideally, if parents, teachers, and librarians demanded good multiethnic literature for young people, publishers would be forced to rethink their priorities. In reality, the adults who choose books for children do not always consider racial and ethnic diversity as a factor in selection. For those who do, information about good books has not always been accessible.

The job, then, for researchers and bibliographers is to help stimulate such a demand by informing people about the good multiethnic books that are available—and there are some fine ones. Yep's novels, *Sea Glass* and *Child of the Owl*, portray the painful conflicts that result from trying to maintain a sense of cultural identity in the midst of the dominant white culture. In *Sea Glass*, when Craig is both rejected by the white children in school and scolded by an older Chinese man for not knowing how to speak Chinese, he thinks:

> Funny, I'd always used the word "Americans" for whites, and "Chinese" for myself; but I guess Chinese really didn't apply to me. I was more like a white American than anything else, even if my skin was the wrong color. It was a shock. It was as if I wasn't anything anymore.
>
> (p. 16)

> *Sharon Wigutoff, "Junior Fiction: A Feminist Critique," in* The Lion and the Unicorn, *Vol. 5, 1981, pp. 4-18.*

MARLA DINCHAK

Laurence Yep is a frequently overlooked author of adolescent novels who deserves more attention. His four adolescent novels are sensitively told and beautifully written, speaking to problems young adolescents face today, particularly about the search for identity and the need for family relationships. His first novel was a science-fiction/fantasy, *Sweetwater*, and the other three were published at succeeding two-year intervals. *Dragonwings, Child of the Owl*, and *Sea Glass* are all set on the West Coast, and Yep's Chinese-American heritage can be seen in each of the young protagonists, for Yep puts himself and his own interests and background into his work. His work is based largely on his own experiences growing up in San Francisco's Chinatown and establishing his own personal identity in a dual culture. If a good author writes about what he knows, then Yep certainly is destined to be very good.

Yep's novels are aimed at younger adolescents, readers of average ability in the seventh through ninth grades. His protagonists are generally thirteen or fourteen years old, and boys and girls will both be able to identify with these realistic protagonists, strong young people who dare to be themselves. Craig Chin in *Sea Glass* has grown up in Chinatown, and when his family moves to Concepcion he finds it difficult to make "Westerner" friends. On the other hand, Casey in *Child of the Owl* has grown up in a Western society and finds adjustment to life in Chinatown difficult. Both face the problem of being the new kid but in reverse situations. Yep sensitively portrays feelings of rejection and loneliness early adolescents often feel. Young readers won't need to have experienced a physical uprooting to understand Casey and Craig's feelings of awkwardness and not belonging.

Most of Yep's novels for adolescents show his young protagonists in conflict with their parents. All being good, morally upright young people, the conflicts do not force them to choose between right and wrong but involve a searching for identity. Tyree, in *Sweetwater,* Yep's science-fiction/fantasy, pursues his study of music against his father's wishes. He doesn't want to contradict his father's wishes, but music is something in him which must be expressed, a creative drive needing an outlet. In *Sea Glass,* Craig rebels against his athlete father's wishes that he excel in sports, but an old uncle helps Craig see the contentment that can come from knowing and being himself. Both young men grow to understand their parents and themselves better as they mature. In *Child of the Owl* Casey's problems with her itinerant, gambler father are different but no less realistic than Tyree and Craig's conflicts. Casey's disillusionment when she realizes he has betrayed her is climactic and touching. The strength and maturity she has learned carry her through to a hopeful conclusion. Each protagonist matures gradually and realistically, showing strength and understanding which we, as adults, are continually trying to instill in youngsters today.

Possibly Yep's most interesting characters are taken from the pages of history. Moon Shadow, an eight year old Chinese boy, is the protagonist in *Dragonwings,* an historical novel set in turn-of-the-century San Francisco and based on a true account of a Chinese-American man who built and flew an airplane about the time of the Wright brothers. The story recreates the Chinese bachelor community of Chinatown, the great San Francisco earthquake, and the daring dream of a man to fly like a dragon. Yep's beautiful metaphors, symbolism, and figurative language help the reader understand and see life as it must have been in 1906 California. Through the eyes of a young Chinese boy, we see what a frightening and challenging place the Western world was. Chinese folklore, myths, and legends are interwoven so readers not only sympathize with Moon Shadow and the other Chinese but understand more of their culture and traditions. That is true of most of Yep's work, for he not only tells a story but bridges a cultural gap. Young readers learn much about another culture while enjoying his stories.

An outstanding feature of Yep's novels is his skillful use of language. Metaphors and figurative language create comparisons that make the stories and characters come alive. Symbolism is an integral part of his novels, and universal truths lend depth. In each story, an appropriate symbol is gradually explained to the young protagonist, generally by an older and wiser adult. As protagonists mature, they become more aware of the symbol and what it represents.Moon Shadow in *Dragonwings* sees the aeroplane his father builds as the symbol for the reach of humanity's imagination, the achievement of the impossible dream. In *Child of the Owl,* Casey comes to understand her own cultural heritage and dual identity through the little jade owl charm, symbol of her ancestor, the owl-woman. The ocean and a reef teeming with marine life become symbols to Craig which help him communicate with those he cares about in *Sea Glass.* As the young people become more aware of the symbols and their meanings, young readers also become more aware of symbolism and are introduced to an aspect of literature which may be new. Universal truths are presented to readers, and Yep tells them that it is not bad to be different, and they should be proud of who they are and where they come from. He shows readers the incredible scope of our imagination, and he shows that impossible dreams can come true. He reaffirms the importance of communication, and all of this is more understandable and believable because of symbolism.

Yep's four novels for adolescents are exceptionally good reading for junior high students, in and out of the classroom. Because of the range and variety in the novels, at least one of them should appeal to adolescents. Science fiction/fantasy fans will love *Sweetwater* with its exotic setting and action-filled, suspenseful story. Those who enjoy historical fiction will enjoy *Dragonwings.* Anyone who likes to read about female protagonists and their problems will identify with Casey in *Child of the Owl*; her male counterpart is Craig in *Sea Glass.* Both live in modern California and face problems other young people have.

While young people will enjoy these books just for their stories, Yep's novels are also well suited for classroom reading. The variety of themes and well-developed characters would make for interesting classroom study and discussions. Yep's skillful use of figurative language, symbolism, and other literary techniques make these books useful for teaching literary skills to junior high school students. While these aspects contribute to a well-written novel, the true test is whether adolescent readers enjoy the books. I'm confident young readers exposed to Yep's books will enjoy them. The future work of this young writer is something I, and my students, look forward to with great anticipation. (pp. 81-2)

> *Marla Dinchak, "Recommended: Laurence Yep," in* English Journal, *Vol. 71, No. 3, March, 1982, pp. 81-2.*

DONNA E. NORTON

Few highly recommended books for children represent an Asian American perspective. Folktales from several Asian countries . . . can help Asian American children and children from other ethnic backgrounds appreciate the traditional values and creative imagination of Asian peoples. The widest range of Asian American experiences in current children's literature is found in the works of Laurence Yep, who writes with sensitivity about Chinese Americans who, like himself, have lived in San Francisco, California. His characters overcome the stereotypes associated with literature about Asian Americans, and his stories integrate information about Chinese cultural heritage into the everyday lives of the people involved. (p. 531)

Yep's *Dragonwings,* set in 1903 San Francisco, is based on a true incident in which a Chinese-American built and flew an airplane. The characters are strong people who retain their values and respect for their heritage while adjusting to a new country. The "town of the Tang people" is eight-year-old Moon Shadow's destination when he leaves his mother in the Middle Kingdom (China). He is filled with conflicting emotions when he first meets his father in the country some call the "Land of the Demons," and others call the "Land of the Golden Mountain." The Tang men in San Francisco give Moon Shadow clothing and things for the body, but his father gives him a marvelous, shimmering kite shaped like a butterfly, a gift designed to stir the soul. Moon Shadow joins his father in his dream to build a flying machine. Motivated by the work of Orville and Wilbur Wright, Moon Shadow's father builds an airplane, names it *Dragonwings,* and soars off the cliffs overlooking San Francisco Bay. Having achieved his dream, he decides to return to work so his wife can join him in America.

In the process of the story, Moon Shadow learns that his stereotype of the white demons is not always accurate. When he and his father move away from the Tang men's protection, Moon Shadow meets and talks to his first demon. Instead of being ten feet tall, with blue skin, and a face covered with warts, she is a petite woman who is very friendly and considerate. As Moon Shadow and his father get to know this Anglo-Saxon woman and her family, they all gain respect for each other. When they share knowledge, the father concludes: "We see the same thing and yet find different truths."

Readers also discover that stereotypes about Chinese Americans are incorrect. This book is especially strong in its coverage of Chinese traditions and beliefs. For example, readers learn about the great respect Chinese Americans feel for the aged and the dead; family obligations do not end when a family member has retired or died. As Moon Shadow seeks to educate his white friend about the nature of dragons, readers discover traditional Chinese tales about a benevolent and wise dragon who is king among reptiles, emperor of animals. Readers realize the strong value of honor as they join the doubting Tang men who come to pull *Dragonwings* up the hill for its maiden voyage. They do not come to laugh at or applaud a heroic venture, but to share in their friend's perceived folly; if the Tang men laugh at Moon Shadow's father, they will laugh at a strong body of people who stand beside each other through times of adversity and honor. Children who read this story learn about the contributions and struggles of the Chinese Americans and the prejudice they still experience.

Other excellent books by Yep include *The Serpent's Children,* a story set in a time when China was battling both Manchu and British domination; *Child of the Owl,* in which young Casey discovers that she knows more about racehorses than about her own Chinese heritage; and *Sea Glass,* in which a boy deals with the unhappy experience of leaving Chinatown and learning to live in a non-Chinese community. The protagonists in all these books are distinct and believable individuals far from the conventional stereotypes about Asian people. (pp. 531-32)

> *Donna E. Norton, "Multiethnic Literature," in her* Through the Eyes of a Child: An Introduction to Children's Literature, *second edition, Merrill Publishing Company, 1987, pp. 500-61.*

SEA GLASS (1979)

During the last two decades, conflict between generations has been a dominant theme in children's litterature. In his fourth novel the author proves that the theme is not a cliché—given an original treatment in a well-structured story written with style and perception. Unlike *Dragonwings* or *Child of the Owl,* which explore ethnicity within a supportive community, the story of Craig Chin delineates the problems of a child searching for identity when caught between two cultures and seemingly rejected by both. Transplanted from San Francisco's Chinatown to small-town Concepcion when his father takes a job there, the overweight boy discovers that he is simultaneously denigrated by his occidental schoolmates as a fat Chinese "'Buddha Man'" and criticized by an elderly friend of the family for being "'like the white demons.'" To complicate matters further, Craig is bewildered by his cousins' indifference to their Chinese heritage and their lack of interest in his overtures of friendship. Most of all, the boy is hurt by his father's insistence that Craig follow in his footsteps and become a sports hero, despite an obvious ineptitude. Craig is constantly at odds with his father's methods of emulating the American lifestyle personified in Cousin Stanley—a "'real all-American boy,'" replete with trophies, straight A's, and friends. The gap is finally bridged through the wisdom of elderly Uncle Quail, a conservative recluse who had withdrawn to an isolated seacoast home because of the indignities heaped upon the early Chinese communities in California. But the old man is keenly aware of the tensions among Craig's family and offers the boy a more important perspective on life. Totally engaging, the first-person narrative is carefully but not self-consciously wrought.

> *Mary M. Burns, in a review of "Sea Glass," in* The Horn Book Magazine, *Vol. LV, No. 5, October, 1979, p. 542.*

The first-person narrative is sensitive and perceptive—a bit too so for a character Craig's age, and Yep's resolution of the boy's conflicts is too pat and easily won. But he skillfully packs a host of important themes (ethnicity, self-worth, family expectations, social status, etc.) into a winning, often moving story. He also makes distinct and complex characters out of stock types (wise old uncle, rebellious soulmate, hard-driving Dad). A worthy successor to *Child of the Owl* with wider appeal to both male and female junior high school readers.

> *Jack Forman, in a review of "Sea Glass," in* School Library Journal, *Vol. 26, No. 3, November, 1979, p. 95.*

Laurence Yep's *Sea Glass* is a thought-provoking book about an "average" child who, like most children, is not one of the superstar, trophy-toting, beautiful people. . . .

[The characters in the book] are a cast of "outcasts" in many ways. Though Craig's Dad excelled at all sports, he neve quite made it; he now attempts to make ends meet with a small grocery store. Uncle Quail is the "eccentric old man" that no one cares to associate with. Stanley and Sheila are two obviously Chinese cousins who strive to be "assimilated" Americans in order to fit in. Kenyon is the girl with the "frizzy red-gold hair" who tries to look like all the other girls (at least from the neck down) but really does stick out; her witty, caustic jokes insure her friendship with other kids. Somehow they, like Craig, are all people whose differences are sore points in their lives.

In dealing with questions of identity, Laurence Yep focuses on people's potential for being incredibly complex beings with much to offer once they acknowledge who they are. Craig becomes a pivotal point around which the characters either deal with their own identities or assume some other facade. Through the changes that occur for the different characters, Yep effectively counters many of the rigid race, sex and age biases that exist in other books. Craig's competitive, athletic father harbors a skill and love for growing plants. Uncle Quail, an elderly recluse, becomes Craig's swimming instructor with a perspective on life that is a constant stimulation for Craig. His mother is a pro at shooting baskets, and Kenyon, Craig's female "demon" friend, is an independent, abrasive yet sensitive person whose comments on racial identity help Craig understand his cousins.

Sea Glass brings into question the whole concept of "achievement and success." Craig is not a star, yet he is a full human being who strives only for those things that make sense. *Sea Glass* is highly recommended.

> *Donald Kao, in a review of "Sea Glass," in* Interracial Books for Children Bulletin, *Vol. 11, No. 6, 1980, p. 16.*

KIND HEARTS AND GENTLE MONSTERS (1982)

Charley, the narrator, is a sophomore at Loyola High School, and rather irritated by the hostility of some of his peers who had transferred to public school. He's more than irritated when he gets a poison pen chain letter that calls him a meddler, arrogant, and says, "to know him was to loathe him." He knows the girl who started it, and he goes to her house to confront her—and that's the start of a romance during which Charley discovers the reason for his girl's deserved reputation for being rancorous (a nagging neurotic mother) and also realizes that there can be a compromise between her emotional view of life and his logical, reasoned viewpoint. This has strong characters and a smooth writing style but its story line is not strong, and it is more a depiction of a situation than a development of a plot; Charley and his Chris do not so much change as improve their understanding of each other and themselves.

> *Zena Sutherland, in a review of "Kind Hearts and Gentle Monsters," in* Bulletin of the Center for Children's Books, *Vol. 35, No. 9, May, 1982, p. 180.*

In *Kind Hearts and Gentle Monsters* we see Chris loving her mother, yet not letting herself be consumed by her, and Charley adding another dimension to his life—that of caring for someone else. Weakened by a slow beginning, the story is nevertheless a moving portrayal of two teen-agers reaching out to one another, changing and growing up. Laurence Yep, who has written several fine novels about Chinese-Americans, has with this book broadened his scope successfully.

> *Colby Rodowsky, in a review of "Kind Hearts and Gentle Monsters," in* The New York Times Book Review, *May 23, 1982, p. 37.*

The author shows a fresh versatility in a story centering on two incisively characterized teenagers. . . . Actually a penetrating psychological novel, the book is written in a relaxed, contemporary style perfectly tuned to the thoughts and conversations of the bright, articulate protagonists.

> *Ethel L. Heins, in a review of "Kind Hearts and Gentle Monsters," in* The Horn Book Magazine, *Vol. LVIII, No. 3, June, 1982, p. 302.*

THE MARK TWAIN MURDERS (1982)

Laurence Yep has used actual events of Civil War San Francisco in *The Mark Twain Murders*. . . . In debt and haunted by the less-than-shining reputation that has followed him from Nevada, the young Mark Twain is working as a newspaper reporter, covering the murder of disreputable soldier Johnny Dougherty. Dougherty's 15-year-old stepson, the narrator, lives by his wits down at the docks and calls himself His Grace, Duke of Baywater. Twain and His Grace team up and become enmeshed in a conspiracy with Dougherty's murder just the tip of an insidious iceberg. Twain and His Grace eventually foil a plot by Confederate spies to rob the Mint, thereby prolonging the war and discrediting President Lincoln. The author has perfectly captured the tempo of old San Francisco with its marvelously salty characters. Rollicking reading—with Twain at the helm, readers can expect no less.

> *Drew Stevenson, in a review of "The Mark Twain Murders," in* School Library Journal, *Vol. 28, No. 9, May, 1982, p. 85.*

Some of [Twain's] self-confidence comes from his young friend, an aspect of the story that is not very convincing, as the adolescent who lives under a wharf lectures Twain on his behavior and attitudes. It is also not quite credible that the furious pace of the story is kept up for its three-day span. This has a modicum of historical interest, but it's far from the well-structured and smoothly written book that Yep's readers have come to expect.

> *Zena Sutherland, in a review of "The Mark Twain Murders," in* Bulletin of the Center for Children's Books, *Vol. 35, No. 11, July-August, 1982, p. 220.*

Mark Twain was an inept reporter in San Francisco during the Civil War. He was also a notorious liar who concocted elaborate hoaxes in an attempt to enhance his reputation as a reporter. Laurence Yep makes use of actual events from this time to create an amusing and entertaining novel. . . . The tale is replete with murder and mayhem and a touch of morality when Twain's reputation for lying confounds his efforts.

The book is short, punchy, and easy to read and should prove popular with middle and high school readers.

Yep writes with the same tongue-in-cheek style in this book as Twain does in his writing. It would be interesting to compare some of Twain's works to *The Mark Twain Murders*.

> *M. Jean Greenlaw, in a review of "The Mark Twain Murders," in* The ALAN Review, *Vol. 10, No. 3, Spring, 1983, p. 19.*

DRAGON OF THE LOST SEA (1982)

Shimmer the dragon discovers her archenemy Civet in an isolated village. In the company of Thorn, a boy she befriends, Shimmer sets out to destroy Civet, who is responsible for the destruction of the beautiful watery homeland of Shimmer and her dragon people. Most of Yep's story concerns Shimmer's pursuit of Civet, who proves a wily foe. Each of the three main characters is marked by a strong personality, so that dramatic tension stays high and general interaction between Shimmer and Thorn is lively. There is interesting character development, too, in the evolution of prickly, supercilious Shimmer's relationship with Thorn and in Yep's choice to turn the wily Civet into a victim as well as a villain. Shimmer's final choice not to destroy Civet represents a compassionate moral choice that gives the book substance above that of entertaining adventure.

Denise M. Wilms, in a review of "Dragon of the Lost Sea," in Booklist, Vol. 79, No. 3, October 1, 1982, p. 250.

There are magical and dangerous adventures, many of the characters and events based on Chinese myths, and the book shows Yep's versatility; this has the same fluent style as his realistic fiction, but it is beautifully adapted to the grand scope of high fantasy, it is deftly structured, and it's lightened by wry humor. (pp. 59-60)

Zena Sutherland, in a review of "Dragon of the Lost Sea," in Bulletin of the Center for Children's Books, Vol. 36, No. 3, November, 1982, pp. 59-60.

There is much to like about this book, but there's a stiffness of style that prevents the reader from getting as close to the two main characters, the Dragon of the title and the 13-year-old boy she reluctantly adopts and who accompanies her on her quest to reclaim her Lost Sea, as the author seems to have intended. It's as though Yep couldn't quite make up his mind between the conversational style more suited to the filling-out of personalities, and the lofty distant style more suited to the re-telling of old folk tales, on which . . . the book is somewhat based. Whatever its shortcomings, **Dragon** is a very readable story with some splendid bits of old legends and new imagination and general quest-adventure, and if the inconclusive ending means to suggest a sequel there should be plenty of young readers to cheer for volume two.

Robin McKinley, in a review of "Dragon of the Lost Sea," in Voice of Youth Advocates, Vol. 5, No. 6, February, 1983, p. 47.

LIAR, LIAR   (1983)

Sean Pierce is haunted by the "radar" eyes he saw on a Porsche owner who caught him and his friend Marsh Weiss in the act of deflating his tires. When brake failure involves the boys in an accident that is fatal to Marsh, Sean begins to wonder if it was an accident after all—or murder. His investigation leads him to a hot prospect, a ruthless business executive named Russ Towers, who just might hate young male drivers because one was responsible for the automobile deaths of his wife and daughter. When Sean tries to alert the police to Russ, his pleas fall on deaf ears because of his own past—four years previously Sean was involved in a burglary ring. No one else, friends or family, believes him either; all the while he is sure that it's only a matter of time before Russ, who knows Sean is after him, will try to silence him. Yep's fast-paced suspense story is weakened by forcing the issue of Sean's credibility. Still, the suspense is taut, and the conclusion, in which Sean and Towers battle it out, is worth waiting for. Dialogue is crisp, and Sean is a sympathetic victim who matures over the course of the story. This is effective escapist fare that should prove popular with junior high school audiences.

Denise M. Wilms, in a review of "Liar, Liar," in Booklist, Vol. 80, No. 2, September 15, 1983, p. 175.

In **Liar, Liar,** Laurence Yep sketches the contemporary scene in California's Silicon Valley with photorealistic detail. At the fore of this landscape are a father and son who have recently moved to the bedroom community of Almaden. Dad is a talented computer troubleshooter; Sean is the 16-year-old protagonist whose troubled history intrudes on his youthful efforts

to start afresh. Their lives, like their new house, seem at once empty and crowded by memories of past failures in their relationship. Nonetheless, this odd couple moves toward a workable partnership by the end of the story.

Mr. Yep's latest book, his ninth in the last decade, is primarily a mystery and not a novel about shaky family relationships. . . . The mystery plot, however, is not all that suspenseful, despite two well-paced and scary scenes (the fatal crash, the startling locked-house confrontation between Sean and the killer).

Carol Billman, in a review of "Liar, Liar," in The New York Times Book Review, November 6, 1983, p. 44.

The plot is contrived and difficult to accept. There is no particular reason for Sean's suspicions. Still, he convinces himself that Marsh was murdered and, sure enough . . . No surprises here. Everything falls into place neatly and predictably. The last three chapters provide the only suspense, and they could be effective in a booktalk. Overall, though, this is pretty flimsy.

Bill Erbes, in a review of "Liar, Liar," in Voice of Youth Advocates, Vol. 7, No. 1, April, 1984, p. 37.

THE SERPENT'S CHILDREN   (1984)

In a first-person account of Chinese peasant life, Cassia begins her story by describing her father's decision to go off and fight with the Manchu against the foreign devils who have brought opium into the Middle Kingdom. Although he and Mother have been active in the Work (the expulsion of the Manchu oppressors) they feel that they must unite against a common enemy. Cassia's mother dies, and the young girl rebels against her relatives' decisions, taking refuge in her home with little brother Foxfire until their wounded father returns. The rest of the story focuses on the generation gap between Father, an embittered political activist, and Foxfire, the dreamy youth who decides to go to America so that he can send money home to his nearly-starving father and sister. It is Cassia who bridges the gap, loyal to her father but pleading always for a reconciliation with Foxfire, remembering that they were of the Young clan, children of the serpent who must not fight each other. This is a powerful and vivid novel despite the fact that there are points at which the story sags because of slowed pace. The characters are strongly drawn, and the picture of the Chinese rural community convincing.

Zena Sutherland, in a review of "The Serpent's Children," in Bulletin of the Center for Children's Books, Vol. 37, No. 7, March, 1984, p. 138.

The Chinese American author, a strong storyteller who began his research seeking his "identity as a Chinese," brings considerable insight to the culture. Although the narrative occasionally seems thin and repetitive and the language sometimes belies the period, the story offers numerous vivid, engrossing episodes and a cogent view of social conditions in China in the nineteenth century. (p. 480)

Nancy C. Hammond, in a review of "The Serpent's Children," in The Horn Book Magazine, Vol. LX, No. 4, August, 1984, pp. 479-80.

With first-person narration, dialogue at times seems forced and unconvincingly explanatory, while general background is scanted. The book lacks an historic note or reference to nonfiction for this age group, such as Meltzer's *The Chinese Amer-*

icans. In spite of these faults, **The Serpent's Children** is well plotted and shows good characterization. An enjoyable story for children willing to do a little research on their own.

> *Ruth M. McConnell, in a review of "The Serpent's Children," in* School Library Journal, *Vol. 30, No. 10, August, 1984, p. 88.*

THE TOM SAWYER FIRES (1984)

His Grace, the duke of Baywater, the novel urchin who teamed up with errant reporter Mark Twain in **The Mark Twain Murders,** here narrates how he, Twain, and a San Francisco fireman named Tom Sawyer get caught up in uncovering who is responsible for a series of arson blazes in the city. The villain turns out to be the same nefarious Confederate major who masterminded the criminal scheme of the first book, and he gets a fatal comeuppance in a rather gory finish. This has a good deal of humorous repartee going on among the principal characters, but the story development doesn't seem as full as in the first book; scenes seem to whiz by before one has a concrete sense of what is happening and why. Local color is bright, however, and Yep's clever way with dialogue imbues his characters with a mischievous demeanor that is beguiling. Fans of the first book will enjoy this reprise despite its weaker execution.

> *Denise M. Wilms, in a review of "The Tom Sawyer Fires," in* Booklist, *Vol. 81, No. 3, October 1, 1984, p. 253.*

The names of the principals catch the reader's attention immediately. The Duke of Baywater is a teenage street urchin (evidently suggested by Twain's *The Prince and the Pauper*), who thinks he is of royal blood. He is street wise, and his name gives him a moral sense below which he will not stoop; hence, the respect his companions have for him. Tom Sawyer is a fireman (Twain evidently knew a man by that name in his California days and later used the name). . . . Mark Twain is an out-of-a-job journalist, living hand to mouth, on the prowl for a good story. . . .

The story is fast-paced, with near misses, intrigue, and diabolical cunning confronting the heroes. There are many humorous scenes, especially the one in which rival fire companies rush to the scene to up their ratings, somewhat in the manner of the Keystone Cops. But it is serious business too, as the three extricate themselves from impossible situations in the nick of time. . . .

There is added charm in the description of frontier San Francisco, where the populace is affected by the Civil War, though far from the scenes of battle, and is attempting to construct a respectable town; in the historical allusions and descriptions, the reader will be able to savor a bit of Americana. I have rated this book an A. It is evidently written for the 11-13 age readership.

> *Sr. Delphine Kolker, in a review of "The Tom Sawyer Fires," in* Best Sellers, *Vol. 44, No. 9, December, 1984, p. 360.*

There's some fact here and therefore some historical interest, but it's primarily a suspense story and, like its predecessor (and unlike Yep's other books) is overdone, stretched both in plot and characterization.

> *Zena Sutherland, in a review of "The Tom Sawyer Fires," in* Bulletin of the Center for Children's Books, *Vol. 38, No. 4, December, 1984, p. 76.*

SHADOW LORD (1985)

The latest Star Trek novel is a disappointment. Pairing Spock and Sulu for an adventure could have real possibilities. Here, however, Spock is used primarily for window dressing and Sulu's penchant for swords is given so much prominence that there seems little else. Except for a very few pages at beginning and end, this isn't really an ST story but just another sword-without-sorcery adventure.

The story lunges from violent action to philosophical discourse and back again. While the heroes are fleeing a murderous mob at their heels and reminding each other that they have to escape, they manage to stop and exchange conversation for the better part of two chapters.

Unless one is a dyed-in-the-wool ST fan, it would be best to avoid this one.

> *W. D. Stevens, "A Shadow of a Novel," in* Fantasy Review, *Vol. 8, No. 4, April, 1985, p. 30.*

Laurence Yep is known as a writer of young adult novels, many with Asian or Asian/American characters, many with a supernatural element. He has used these same elements in an excellent "Star Trek" novel, that pits Mr. Spock and Lt. Sulu against the political factions on a semi-barbaric world.

The central character is Vikram, the youngest member of a large and nasty family, who is returning to his ancestral planet after a prolonged stay at the Federation University. Like many young people, he must take up where his father left off, and try to correct many of the errors of going too far too fast. Yep shows both the good and bad sides of technological progress as Vikram fights against the palace factions and the peasant rebels. Spock's logic is useful, but Sulu, the intrepid swordsman, finds out a few things about being a Musketeer that he hadn't considered before!

Yep's writing is always interesting, often moving, and never dull. Prince Vikram and his people are well-depicted. . . . (pp. 195-96)

This is one novel that can be read by science fiction fans who are not necessarily Trekkers; moreover, non-SF fans will find in **Shadow Lord** as satisfactory a growing-up story as any that Yep has written. (p. 196)

> *Roberta Rogow, in a review of "Shadow Lord," in* Voice of Youth Advocates, *Vol. 8, No. 3, August, 1985, pp. 195-96.*

DRAGON STEEL (1985)

In a sequel to **Dragon of the Lost Sea** Shimmer (a dragon, centuries-old, who is an exiled princess of her clan and has magical powers) continues her story. While this second volume has the grand scale and fluent style of the first, it is less coherent in the development of a story line. Shimmer and the boy Thorn, who was an alternate narrator of the first book, continued their quest for restortion of Shimmer's homeland, acquiring a new companion, Indigo, in their undersea battle against the evil High King who would deny Shimmer her heritage.

> *Zena Sutherland, in a review of "Dragon Steel," in* Bulletin of the Center for Children's Books, *Vol. 38, No. 9, May, 1985, p. 178.*

Laurence Yep has woven factual details about marine life into a tale of dungeons, sea monsters, and mages in an underwater dragon kingdom.... The evolution of a caring relationship between the once haughty dragon and her supporters strengthens this sequel. A humorous counterpoint is provided by Yep's portrayal of Monkey, the devious magical being found in Buddhist legends, who can change the hairs of his tail into clouds of tiny replicas of himself to carry out his wishes. To Monkey's pledge of undying friendship, Shimmer responds, "That's just what I need on top of everything else. A personal curse." This segment of the quest ends with the boom of war drums heralding the start of conflict between the humans and the dragons. For readers who have enjoyed the dragon worlds created by Anne McCaffrey and Jane Yolen, which are rooted in Western tradition, Yep's dragon kingdom with its background of Chinese myths will be a welcome addition. (pp. 459-60)

> *Hanna B. Zeiger, in a review of "Dragon Steel," in* The Horn Book Magazine, *Vol. LXI, No. 4, July-August, 1985, pp. 459-60.*

This at times rousing fantasy continues the story begun in *Dragon of the Lost Sea*....

Not having read the first book in the series it took me some time to get oriented to the events, characters and the fact that a dragon is the story's narrator. Nevertheless, there is much to commend in this novel. Yep's conception of dragons as noble and heroic is an interesting departure from their villainous portrayal in much of western folklore and fantasy. The novel's fast pace, its exciting action sequences and Yep's fine treatment of Indigo's change from selfish egocentricism to a willingness to sacrifice herself for others, mark this as a tale sure to delight fantasy lovers.

> *Joel Taxel, in a review of "Dragon Steel," in* The ALAN Review, *Vol. 13, No. 1, Fall, 1985, p. 25.*

MOUNTAIN LIGHT (1985)

In *The Serpent's Children,* Yep introduced strong, self-reliant Cassia and her father, known as the Gallant, who are fighting with the Brotherhood to bring back the light and remove the Manchus' darkness from the Middle Kingdom. The story resumes as Cassia, the Gallant, and their companion, Tiny, meet up with Squeaky Lau, who had joined the Revolution as a lark, but has found his experience a demoralizing disaster. Squeaky has always been considered the village clown (a village which is the sworn enemy of Cassia's own); being a jester is a role which embarrasses Squeaky yet is also familiar and comfortable. As he and his three companions attempt the dangerous, sometimes desperate journey home, Squeaky struggles to bring forth the light that is in each person, as the Gallant urges, and to become a man in the process. Despite the strides he makes, and his growing love for Cassia, Squeaky eventually decides he must go to the land of the Golden Mountain—America— to make his fortune and complete the self-strengthening process

he has begun. Readers may find it difficult to understand the subtleties of Chinese society during the 1800s, but they should have no problem involving themselves in the fates and fortunes of Squeaky, Cassia, and Tiny, who is considered a Stranger in his own village because his family has lived there only three hundred years. This is a rich blend of action, moral lessons, and complex characterizations for advanced readers.

> *Ilene Cooper, in a review of "Mountain Light," in* Booklist, *Vol. 82, No. 2, September 15, 1985, p. 141.*

From Cassia, one of his colleagues in the Work, Squeaky learns that getting others to laugh could be an advantage in an argument. Cassia's cold, intense, serpent-like strength; hard, relentless logic; and affectionate nurturing provide the environment in which Squeaky lets out the light which is within him.... Yep's impressionistic writing succeeds because Squeaky becomes the vehicle through which Yep introduces much social comment into this telling of history. Readers learn as Squeaky learns. However, Yep's writing is not of the caliber found in *Dragonwings*. He has sprinkled in more dialogue and has failed to unravel his humanistic themes as carefully. *Mountain Light* is a companion book, rather than a sequel, to *The Serpent's Children* but it does not require the same intensity of engagement on the part of readers.

> *Shelley G. McNamara, in a review of "Mountain Light," in* School Library Journal, *Vol. 32, No. 5, January, 1986, p. 76.*

The China to America immigration of the 1800s is a historical framework that Yep has explored before in *Dragonwings* and provides valuable perspective on that segment of Chinese-American history. Squeaky and Cassia will appeal to adolescent readers who will sympathize with their feelings of isolation and indecision. Cassia is a strong female character who breaks the stereotype of the submissive Chinese female. This novel will be enjoyed by middle and high school readers who enjoy historical fiction.

> *Freya Zipperer, in a review of "Mountain Light," in* The ALAN Review, *Vol. 13, No. 3, Spring, 1986, p. 31.*

THE CURSE OF THE SQUIRREL (1987)

Howie and Willie are brothers, one a fearless hunting dog and the other a coward who, in the opening scene of the book, cowers in the chicken coop warning the other hounds away from a giant vampire squirrel named Shag. Shag is not only vicious, it turns out, but his bite transforms his victims into squirrels. The fantasy has some wildly inventive elements, but they're tumbled together too fast and furiously; Yep doesn't seem entirely comfortable with the abbreviated style and structure of easy-to-read books. Still, this beats most classroom practice materials, with just enough spoofy humor and slapstick action to hold it together.

> *Betsy Hearne, in a review of "The Curse of the Squirrel," in* Bulletin of the Center for Children's Books, *Vol. 41, No. 3, November, 1987, p. 60.*

[A] disappointing contribution from a noted chronicler, for older children, of the Chinese-American experience.... This is neither as scary nor as funny as it sets out to be, and its short sentences result in an annoyingly choppy style.

A review of "The Curse of the Squirrel," in Kirkus Reviews, *Vol. LV, No. 21, November 1, 1987, p. 1582.*

The tale is fast-paced and slapstick, with [a] crew of thoroughly enjoyable characters. It should be a good precursor to the "Bunnicula" series and others in which humor is derived from the mild-mannered becoming blood-thirsty.

Joanne Aswell, in a review of "The Curse of the Squirrel," in School Library Journal, *Vol. 34, No. 4, December, 1987, p. 76.*

Acknowledgments

The following is a listing of the copyright holders who have granted us permission to reprint material in this volume of *CLR*. Every effort has been made to trace copyright, but if omissions have been made, please let us know.

THE COPYRIGHTED EXCERPTS IN CLR, VOLUME 17, WERE REPRINTED FROM THE FOLLOWING PERIODICALS:

The ALAN Review, v. 10, Spring, 1983; v. 11, Fall, 1983; v. 11, Spring, 1984; v. 13, Fall, 1985; v. 13, Spring, 1986. All reprinted by permission of the publisher.

Appraisal: Science Books for Young People, v. 17, Spring-Summer, 1984. Copyright © 1984 by the Children's Science Book Review Committee. Reprinted by permission of the publisher.

Best Sellers, v. 41, November, 1981; v. 44, December, 1984. Copyright © 1981, 1984 Helen Dwight Reid Educational Foundation. Both reprinted by permission of the publisher.

Book Window, v. 8, Summer, 1981. © 1981 S.C.B.A. and contributors. Reprinted by permission of the publisher.

Book World—The Washington Post, May 1, 1977; February 12, 1978; November 12, 1978; June 10, 1979; May 10, 1981; May 13, 1984; November 9, 1986; December 14, 1986. © 1977, 1978, 1979, 1981, 1984, 1986, *The Washington Post.* All reprinted by permission of the publisher.

Booklist, v. 73, November 15, 1976; v. 76, September 15, 1979; v. 76, February 15, 1980; v. 76, April 15, 1980; v. 77, September 15, 1980; v. 77, February 15, 1981; v. 77, April 15, 1981; v. 77, May 1, 1981; v. 78, June 15, 1982; v. 78, August, 1982; v. 79, October 1, 1982; v. 79, November 1, 1982; v. 80, September 15, 1983; v. 80, July, 1984; v. 81, October 1, 1984; v. 81, March 15, 1985; v. 81, May 15, 1985; v. 82, September 15, 1985; v. 82, October 1, 1985; v. 82, December 1, 1985; v. 82, March 1, 1986; v. 82, April 1, 1986; v. 83, October 1, 1986; v. 84, November 1, 1987; v. 84, April 1, 1988. Copyright © 1976, 1979, 1980, 1981, 1982, 1983, 1984, 1985, 1986, 1987, 1988 by the American Library Association. All reprinted by permission of the publisher.

The Booklist, v. 70, December 1, 1973. Copyright © 1973 by the American Library Association. Reprinted by permission of the publisher.

The Booklist and Subscription Books Bulletin, v. 56, July 1, 1960. Copyright © 1960 by the American Library Association. Reprinted by permission of the publisher.

Books for Keeps, n. 47, November, 1987. © School Bookshop Association 1987. Reprinted by permission of the publisher.

Books for Young People, v. 1, April, 1987 for a review of "Jacob Two-Two and the Dinosaur" by Peter Carver. All rights reserved. Reprinted by permission of the publisher and the author.

Books for Your Children, v. 16, Spring, 1981; v. 20, Autumn-Winter, 1985. © *Books for Your Children* 1981, 1985. Both reprinted by permission of the publisher.

Bulletin of the Center for Children's Books, v. XIII, April, 1960; v. XIV, September, 1960; v. XIV, March, 1961; v. XV, October, 1961; v. 21, January, 1968; v. 23, November, 1969; v. 27, May, 1974; v. 29, December, 1975; v. 30, April, 1977; v. 33, October, 1979; v. 33, February, 1980; v. 34, September, 1980; v. 34, October, 1980; v. 34, February, 1981; v. 34, May, 1981; v. 34, July-August, 1981; v. 35, October, 1981; v. 35, May, 1982; v. 35, July-August, 1982; v. 36, October, 1982; v. 36, November, 1982; v. 36, December, 1982; v. 37, October, 1983; v. 37, March, 1984; v. 38, October, 1984; v. 38, December, 1984; v. 38, May, 1985; v. 39, November, 1985; v. 39, December, 1985; v. 39, January, 1986; v. 39, May, 1986; v. 40, September, 1986; v. 40, January, 1987; v. 40, May, 1987; v. 41, November, 1987; v. 41, March, 1988. Copyright © 1960, 1961, 1968, 1969, 1974, 1975, 1977, 1979, 1980, 1981, 1982, 1983, 1984, 1985, 1986, 1987, 1988 by The University of Chicago. All reprinted by permission of The University of Chicago Press.

Canadian Children's Literature: A Journal of Criticism and Review, v. 1, Autumn, 1975; n. 15 & 16, 1980; n. 49, 1988. All reprinted by permission of the publisher.

Canadian Literature, n. 6, Autumn, 1960 for "Wolf in the Snow, Part Two: The House Repossessed" by Warren Tallman; n. 78, Autumn, 1978 for "Writing Jacob Two-Two" by Mordecai Richler. Both reprinted by permission of the respective authors.

Catholic Library World, v. 47, April, 1976; v. 49, December, 1977. Both reprinted by permission of the publisher.

Children's Book Review Service, v. 7, December, 1978; v. 8, April, 1980; v. 8, Spring, 1980; v. 9, August, 1981; v. 15, August, 1987. Copyright © 1978, 1980, 1981, 1987 Children's Book Review Service Inc. All reprinted by permission of the publisher.

Children's Literature: Annual of the Modern Language Association Seminar on Children's Literature and The Children's Literature Association, v. 3, 1974; v. 6, 1977. © 1974, 1977 by Francelia Butler. All rights reserved. Both reprinted by permission of Francelia Butler./ v. 10, 1982; v. 12, 1984; v. 13, 1985. © 1982, 1984, 1985 by Francelia Butler. All rights reserved. All reprinted by permission of Yale University Press.

Children's Literature Association Quarterly, v. 10, Fall, 1985. © 1985 Children's Literature Association. Reprinted by permission of the publisher.

Children's literature in education, n. 22, Autumn, 1976; v. 8, Summer, 1977; v. 13, Spring, 1982; v. 19, Summer, 1988. © 1976, 1977, 1982, 1988, Agathon Press, Inc. All reprinted by permission of the publisher.

Choice, v. 18, October, 1980. Copyright © 1980 by American Library Association. Reprinted by permission of the publisher.

The Christian Science Monitor, May 3, 1978 for "Goofy, Growing Monster Eats Its Way to Fame" by Guernsey Le Pelley; January 6, 1984 for "Grandpa Changes Roles with the Kids" by Darian J. Scott; October 5, 1984 for "Mice and Monkeys, Dogs and Cats" by Darian J. Scott; May 3, 1985 for "Novels of Ouida Sebestyen Share Thread of Good" by Lyn Littlefield Hoopes. © 1978, 1984, 1985 The Christian Science Publishing Society. All rights reserved. All reprinted by permission of the respective authors.

CLA Journal, v. XI, June, 1968; v. XIII, September, 1969. Copyright, 1968, 1969 by The College Language Association. Both used by permission of The College Language Association.

Dance Magazine, v. XLIX, December, 1975. Copyright 1975 by Danad Publishing Company, Inc. Reprinted with the permission of Dance Magazine, Inc.

Dell Carousel, Fall-Winter, 1988. Reprinted by permission of Dell, a division of Bantam Doubleday, Dell Publishing Group, Inc.

Elementary English, v. XLVIII, February, 1971 for a review of "In the Night Kitchen" by Shelton L. Root, Jr. Copyright © 1971 by the National Council of Teachers of English. Reprinted by permission of the publisher and the Literary Estate of Shelton L. Root, Jr./ v. XLVIII, November, 1971. Copyright © 1971 by the National Council of Teachers of English. Reprinted by permission of the publisher.

English Journal, v. 71, March, 1982 for "Recommended: Laurence Yep" by Marla Dinchak. Copyright © 1982 by the National Council of Teachers of English. Reprinted by permission of the publisher and the author.

Fantasy Review, v. 8, April, 1985 for "A Shadow of a Novel" by W. D. Stevens. Copyright © 1985 by the author. Reprinted by permission of the author.

Growing Point, v. 1, March, 1963; v. 6, April, 1968; v. 15, January, 1977; v. 19, March, 1981; v. 21, July, 1982; v. 21, January, 1983; v. 23, July, 1984. All reprinted by permission of the publisher.

The Horn Book Magazine, v. XLVI, February, 1970; v. XLVI, December, 1970; v. XLVII, June, 1971; v. XLIX, December, 1973; v. LI, August, 1975; v. LII, June, 1976; v. LII, October, 1976; v. LIII, June, 1977; v. LIII, August, 1977; v. LIII, December, 1977; v. LIV, April, 1978; v. LIV, August, 1978; v. LV, October, 1978; v. LV, June, 1979; v. LV, October, 1979; v. LV, December, 1979; v. LVI, June, 1980; v. LIV, October, 1980; v. LVII, August, 1981; v. LVII, December, 1981; v. LVIII, February, 1982; v. LVIII, June, 1982; v. LVIII, August, 1982; v. LIX, August, 1983; v. LIX, October, 1983; v. LX, June, 1984; v. LX, August, 1984; v. LX, September-October, 1984; v. LXI, May-June, 1985; v. LXI, July-August, 1985; v. LXI, September-October, 1985; v. LXII, January-February, 1986; v. LXII, July-August, 1986; v. LXII, September-October, 1986; v. LXII, November-December, 1986; v. LXIII, May-June, 1987; v. LXIII, July-August, 1987; v. LXIV, March-April, 1988. Copyright, 1970, 1971, 1973, 1975, 1976, 1977, 1978, 1979, 1980, 1981, 1982, 1983, 1984, 1985, 1986, 1987, 1988, by The Horn Book, Inc., Boston. All rights reserved. All reprinted by permission of the publisher./ v. XXXIV, August, 1958. Copyright, 1958, renewed 1986 by The Horn Book, Inc., Boston. All rights reserved. Reprinted by permission of the publisher.

The Illustrated London News, v. 249, December 3, 1966. © 1966 The Illustrated London News & Sketch Ltd. Reprinted by permission of the publisher.

Instructor, v. LXXIII, March, 1964. Copyright © 1964 by Edgell Communications, Inc. Reprinted by permission of the publisher.

Interracial Books for Children Bulletin, v. 11, 1980; v. 16, 1985; v. 17, 1986. All reprinted by permission of the Council on Interracial Books for Children, 1841 Broadway, New York, NY 10023.

Journal of Canadian Fiction, v. III, Winter, 1974. Reprinted by permission from *Journal of Canadian Fiction,* 2050 Mackay St., Montreal, Quebec H3G 2J1, Canada.

Journal of Popular Culture, v. XII, Summer, 1978. Copyright © 1978 by Ray B. Browne. Reprinted by permission of the publisher.

The Junior Bookshelf, v. 24, July, 1960; v. 26, November, 1962; v. 28, November, 1964; v. 30, April, 1966; v. 30, October, 1966; v. 32, February, 1968; v. 34, August, 1970; v. 35, June, 1971; v. 35, December, 1971; v. 37, February, 1973; v. 41, April, 1977; v. 43, February, 1979; v. 43, December, 1979; v. 44, August, 1980; v. 47, February, 1983; v. 47, October, 1983; v. 49, February, 1985; v. 49, April, 1985; v. 52, February, 1988. All reprinted by permission of the publisher.

Junior Libraries, v. 7, September, 1960; v. 7, February 15, 1961. Copyright © 1960, 1961. Both reprinted from *Junior Libraries,* published by R. R. Bowker Co./ A Xerox Corporation, by permission.

Kirkus Reviews, v. XXXVII, May 1, 1969; v. XL, June 1, 1972; v. XVI, December 1, 1973; v. XLIII, May 15, 1975; v. XLV, March 15, 1977; v. XLV, July 1, 1977; v. XLVI, February 15, 1978; v. XLVI, March 15, 1978; v. XLVI, April 1, 1978; v. XLVI, August 1, 1978; v. XLVI, August 15, 1978; v. XLVI, October 15, 1978; v. XLVII, January 1, 1979; v. XLVII, May 1, 1979; v. XLVIII, September 1, 1980; v. XLVIII, October 15, 1980; v. XLIX, March 15, 1981; v. XLIX, May 15, 1981; v. XLIX, July 1, 1981; v. XLIX, October 1, 1981; v. L, January 1, 1982; v. L, March 15, 1982; v. L, September 1, 1982; v. LI, February 15, 1983; v. LIII, September 15, 1985; v. LIV, June 15, 1986; v. LIV, October 15, 1986; v. LV, January 15, 1987; v. LV, July 1, 1987; v. LV, August 1, 1987; v. LV, November 1, 1987; v. LVI, February 1, 1988. Copyright © 1969, 1972, 1973, 1975, 1977, 1978, 1979, 1980, 1981, 1982, 1983, 1985, 1986, 1987, 1988 The Kirkus Service, Inc. All rights reserved. All reprinted by permission of the publisher.

Kirkus Reviews, Juvenile Issue, v. LI, November 1, 1983; v. LII, September 1, 1984; v. LIII, March 1, 1985. Copyright © 1983, 1984, 1985 The Kirkus Service, Inc. All rights reserved. All reprinted by permission of the publisher.

Kirkus Service, v. XXXV, September 15, 1967; v. XXXVI, September 15, 1968. Copyright © 1967, 1968 The Kirkus Service, Inc. Both reprinted by permission of the publisher.

Ladies' Home Journal, v. LXXXVI, March, 1969. © copyright 1969, Meredith Corporation. All rights reserved. Reprinted by permission of the publisher.

Language Arts, v. 53, May, 1976 for a review of "Maurice Sendak's Really Rosie: Starring the Nutshell Kids" by Donald J. Bissett; v. 53, September, 1976 for a review of "Walking through the Dark" by Ruth M. Stein; v. 56, February, 1979 for a review of "Many Smokes, Many Moons: A Chronology of American Indian History through Indian Art" by Ruth M. Stein; v. 61, January, 1984 for a review of "The Vingananee and the Tree Toad: A Liberian Tale" by Ronald A. Jobe; v. 62, October, 1985 for a review of "Emma" by Janet Hickman; v. 63, February, 1986 for a review of "On Fire" by Janet Hickman. Copyright © 1976, 1979, 1984, 1985, 1986 by the National Council of Teachers of English. All reprinted by permission of the publisher and the respective authors./ v. 56, February, 1979. Copyright © 1979 by the National Council of Teachers of English. Reprinted by permission of the publisher.

Library Journal, v. 84, October 1, 1959 for a review of "The Apprenticeship of Duddy Kravitz" by Norbert Bernstein; v. 93, February 15, 1968 for a review of "Black Magic: A Pictorial History of the Negro in American Entertainment" by Edward Mapp. Copyright © 1959, 1968 by Reed Publishing, USA, Division of Reed Holdings, Inc. Both reprinted from *Library Journal,* published by R. R. Bowker, Co., Division of Reed Publishing, USA, by permission of the publisher and the respective authors./ v. 94, July, 1969. Copyright © 1969 by Reed Publishing, USA, Division of Reed Holdings, Inc. Reprinted from *Library Journal,* published by R. R. Bowker, Co., Division of Reed Publishing, USA, by permission of the publisher.

The Lion and the Unicorn, v. 1, Fall, 1977; v. 5, 1981. Copyright © 1977, 1981 *The Lion and the Unicorn.* Both reprinted by permission of the publisher.

Maclean's Magazine, v. 100, June 1, 1987. © 1987 by *Maclean's Magazine.* Reprinted by permission of the publisher.

The New Leader, v. XLIII, March 21, 1960. © 1960 by The American Labor Conference on International Affairs, Inc. Reprinted by permission of the publisher.

New York Herald Tribune Book Review, November 13, 1960. © 1960 I.H.T. Corporation. Reprinted by permission of the publisher.

New York Herald Tribune Books, March 3, 1929. Copyright 1929, renewed 1957 I.H.T. Corporation. Reprinted by permission of the publisher.

The New York Times, Section 7, May 4, 1958; June 1, 1968; August 4, 1972. Copyright © 1958, 1968, 1972 by The New York Times Company. All reprinted by permission of the publisher.

The New York Times Book Review, November 1, 1931; July 17, 1932; October 23, 1932; July 10, 1938; July 30, 1939; August 4, 1940; April 10, 1949; November 25, 1951; May 2, 1954; August 15, 1954; Part II, November 14, 1954. Copyright 1931, 1932, 1938, 1939, 1940, 1949, 1951, 1954 by The New York Times Company. All reprinted by permission of the publisher./ January 30, 1955; December 30, 1956; July 27, 1958; October 16, 1960; March 21, 1965; May 14, 1967; September 17, 1967; September 3, 1972; November 9, 1975; February 29, 1976; August 7, 1977; February 5, 1978; April 30, 1978; May 6, 1979; August 26, 1979; April 27, 1980; November 9, 1980; January 18, 1981; April 26, 1981; November 15, 1981; April 25, 1982; May 23, 1982; September 19, 1982; October 9, 1983; November 6, 1983; November 13, 1983; May 20, 1984; November 17, 1985; February 16, 1986; September 20, 1987. Copyright © 1955, 1956, 1958, 1960, 1965, 1967, 1972, 1975, 1976, 1977, 1978, 1979, 1980, 1981, 1982, 1983, 1984, 1985, 1986, 1987 by The New York Times Company. All reprinted by permission of the publisher.

The New York Times Magazine, June 7, 1970. Copyright © 1970 by The New York Times Company. Reprinted by permission of the publisher.

Parabola, v. VI, Fall, 1981 for "Too Many Sides to Count" by Lynda Sexson. Copyright © 1981 by the Society for the Study of Myth and Tradition. Reprinted by permission of the author.

PHYLON: The Atlanta University Review of Race and Culture, v. XIV, third quarter (September, 1953); v. XVI, third quarter (September, 1955). Copyright, 1953, renewed 1981; copyright, 1955, renewed 1983, by Atlanta University. Both reprinted by permission of *PHYLON.*

Publishers Weekly, v. 195, March 10, 1969; v. 196, August 4, 1969; v. 203, May 7, 1973; v. 207, June 2, 1975; v. 215, March 5, 1979; v. 215, March 26, 1979; v. 217, March 21, 1980; v. 220, September 25, 1981; v. 221, February 12, 1982; v. 222, September 17, 1982; v. 223, January 21, 1983; v. 224, September 23, 1983; v. 226, August 31, 1984. Copyright © 1969, 1973, 1975, 1979, 1980, 1981, 1982, 1983, 1984 by Xerox Corporation. All reprinted from *Publishers Weekly,* published by R. R. Bowker Company, a Xerox company, by permission./ v. 231, January 16, 1987; v. 231, February 27, 1987; v. 232, August 28, 1987; v. 233, February 12, 1988; v. 233, February 26, 1988. Copyright 1987, 1988 by Reed Publishing USA. All reprinted from *Publishers Weekly,* published by the Bowker Magazine Group of Cahners Publishing Co., a division of Reed Publishing USA.

Saturday Night, v. 90, July-August, 1975 for "Mordecai Richler's Subversive Accomplishment" by John Ayre. Copyright © 1975 by *Saturday Night.* Reprinted by permission of the author.

The School Librarian, v. 23, September, 1975; v. 33, June, 1985; v. 35, August, 1987. All reprinted by permission of the publisher.

School Library Journal, v. 12, November, 1965; v. 13, January, 1967; v. 14, October, 1967; v. 14, December, 1967; v. 14, February, 1968; v. 15, November, 1968; v. 16, September, 1969; v. 16, October, 1969; v. 16, December, 1969; v. 16, March, 1970; v. 16, April, 1970; v. 17, September, 1970; v. 19, September, 1972; v. 20, December, 1973; v. 20, April, 1974; v. 21, April, 1975; v. 22, December, 1975; v. 22, March, 1976; v. 22, April, 1976; v. 22, May, 1976; v. 23, October, 1976; v. 23, December, 1976; v. 23, April, 1977; v. 24, September, 1977; v. 24, December, 1977; v. 24, May, 1978; v. 25, September, 1978; v. 25, October, 1978; v. 25, December, 1978; v. 25, February, 1979; v. 25, May, 1979; v. 26, October, 1979; v. 26, November, 1979; v. 26, December, 1979; v. 26, May, 1980; v. 27, September, 1980; v. 27, October, 1980; v. 27, December, 1980; v. 27, January, 1981; v. 28, December, 1981; v. 28, May, 1982; v. 29, September, 1982; v. 29, October, 1982; v. 29, January, 1983; v. 29, April, 1983; v. 30, October, 1983; v. 30, December, 1983; v. 30, August, 1984; v. 31, December, 1984; v. 31, April, 1985; v. 31, May, 1985; v. 32, October, 1985; v. 32, November, 1985; v. 32, January, 1986; v. 32, April, 1986; v. 32, August, 1986; v. 33, November, 1986; v. 33, December, 1986; v. 33, June-July, 1987; v. 34, September, 1987; v. 34, October, 1987; v. 34, December, 1987; v. 35, May, 1988; v. 35, June-July, 1988. Copyright © 1965, 1967, 1968, 1969, 1970, 1972, 1973, 1974, 1975, 1976, 1977, 1978, 1979, 1980, 1981, 1982, 1983, 1984, 1985, 1986, 1987, 1988. All reprinted from *School Library Journal,* a Cahners/R. R. Bowker Publication, by permission.

Science Books & Films, v. XIII, September, 1977. Copyright 1977 by AAAS. Reprinted by permission of the publisher.

Signal, n. 51, September, 1986. Copyright © 1986 The Thimble Press. Reprinted by permission of The Thimble Press, Lockwood, Station Road, South Woodchester, Glos., GL5 5EQ, England.

Studies in the Literary Imagination, v. XVIII, Fall, 1985. Copyright 1985 Department of English, Georgia State University. Reprinted by permission of the publisher.

The Times Educational Supplement, n. 3361, November 21, 1980; n. 3477, February 18, 1983. © Times Newspapers Ltd. (London) 1980, 1983. Both reproduced from *The Times Educational Supplement* by permission.

The Times Literary Supplement, n. 3169, November 23, 1962; n. 3583, October 30, 1970; n. 3661, April 28, 1972; n. 3692, December 8, 1972; n. 3864, April 2, 1976; n. 3900, December 10, 1976; n. 3943, October 21, 1977; n. 3319, January 18, 1980; n. 4138, July 23, 1982. © Times Newspapers Ltd. (London) 1962, 1970, 1972, 1976, 1977, 1980, 1982. All reproduced from *The Times Literary Supplement* by permission.

Top of the News, v. XXII, April, 1966; v. 26, June, 1970. Copyright © 1966, 1970 by the American Library Association. Both reprinted by permission of the publisher.

Virginia Kirkus' Service, v. XXVIII, April 1, 1960; v. XXVIII, June 15, 1960; v. XXVIII, October 1, 1960. Copyright © 1960 Virginia Kirkus' Service, Inc. All reprinted by permission of the publisher.

Voice of Youth Advocates, v. 5, February, 1983; v. 6, April, 1983; v. 7, April, 1984; v. 8, August, 1985; v. 9, August & October, 1986; v. 10, June, 1987. Copyrighted 1983, 1984, 1985, 1986, 1987 by *Voice of Youth Advocates.* All reprinted by permission of the publisher.

The Washington Post District Weekly, February 16, 1984. © 1984, Washington Post Co. Reprinted by permission of the publisher.

Wilson Library Bulletin, v. 57, March, 1983. Copyright © 1983 by the H. W. Wilson Company. Reprinted by permission of the publisher.

Works in Progress, n. 3, 1971 for "Why I Write" by Mordecai Richler. Copyright © 1971 by The Literary Guild of America, Inc. All rights reserved. Reprinted by permission of the author.

The World of Children's Books, v. VI, 1981. © 1981 by Jon C. Stott. Reprinted by permission of the publisher.

THE COPYRIGHTED EXCERPTS IN CLR, VOLUME 17, WERE REPRINTED FROM THE FOLLOWING BOOKS:

Arbuthnot, May Hill. From *Children and Books*. Scott, Foresman, 1947. Copyright, 1947, renewed 1974 by Scott, Foresman and Company. Reprinted by permission of the publisher.

Arbuthnot, May Hill. From *Children and Books*. Third edition. Scott, Foresman, 1964. Copyright © 1964 by Scott, Foresman and Company. Reprinted by permission of the publisher.

Bader, Barbara. From *American Picturebooks from Noah's Ark to the Beast Within*. Macmillan, 1976. Copyright © 1976 by Barbara Bader. All rights reserved. Reprinted with permission of Macmillan Publishing Company.

Bader, Barbara. From "The Moods and Modes of James Stevenson," in a promotional piece for *When I Was Nine*. By James Stevenson. Greenwillow Books, 1986. Reprinted by permission of Barbara Bader.

Barksdale, Richard K. From *Langston Hughes: The Poet and His Critics*. American Library Association, 1977. Copyright © 1977 by the American Library Association. All rights reserved. Reprinted by permission of the publisher.

Beskow, Elsa. From an extract in *Illustrators of Children's Books: 1744-1945*. Bertha E. Mahony, Louise Payson Latimer, Beulah Folmsbee, eds. Horn Book, 1947. Copyright, 1947, renewed 1974 by The Horn Book, Inc. All rights reserved. Reprinted by permission of the publisher.

Bevan, A. R. From an introduction to *The Apprenticeship of Duddy Kravitz*. By Mordecai Richler. McClelland & Stewart, 1969. Reprinted by permission of the Literary Estate of A. R. Bevan.

Blount, Margaret. From *Animal Land: The Creatures of Children's Fiction*. William Morrow & Company, Inc., 1975. Copyright © 1974 by Margaret Ingle-Finch. Reprinted by permission of the author.

Brawley, Benjamin. From *The Negro Genius: A New Appraisal of the Achievement of the American Negro in Literature and the Fine Arts*. Dodd, Mead, 1937. Copyright, 1937 by Dodd, Mead & Company, Inc. Renewed 1965 by Thaddeus Gaylord. All rights reserved. Reprinted by permission of the publisher.

Broderick, Dorothy M. From *An Introduction to Children's Work in Public Libraries*. The H. W. Wilson Company, 1965. Copyright © 1965 by Dorothy M. Broderick. Reprinted by permission of the publisher.

Bull, Angela. From *Noel Streatfeild: A Biography*. Collins, 1984. © Angela Bull 1984. Reprinted by permission of the author. In Canada by William Collins Sons & Co. Ltd.

Cadogan, Mary, and Patricia Craig. From *You're a Brick Angela! A New Look at Girls' Fiction from 1839-1975*. Victor Gollancz Ltd., 1976. © Mary Cadogan and Patricia Craig 1976. Reprinted by permission of the authors.

Caldwell, Alma B. From an introduction to *Black Beauty: The Autobiography of a Horse*. By Anna Sewell. Winston, 1927. Copyright 1927, renewed 1955 by The John C. Winston Company. All rights reserved. Reprinted by permission of Henry Holt and Company, Inc.

Chitty, Susan. From *The Woman Who Wrote "Black Beauty:" A Life of Anna Sewell*. Hodder and Stoughton, 1971. Copyright © 1971 by Susan Chitty. All rights reserved. Reprinted by permission of Curtis Brown Ltd.

Cimino, Maria. From "Foreign Picture Books in a Children's Library," in *Illustrators of Children's Books: 1744-1945*. Bertha E. Mahony, Louise Payson Latimer, Beulah Folmsbee, eds. Horn Book, 1947. Copyright, 1947, renewed 1974 by The Horn Books, Inc. All rights reserved. Reprinted by permission of the publisher.

Crouch, Marcus. From *Treasure Seekers and Borrowers: Children's Books in Britain 1900-1960*. The Library Association, 1962. © Marcus Crouch, 1962. Reprinted by permission of the publisher.

Crouch, Marcus, and Alec Ellis. From a review of "The Circus Is Coming," in *Chosen for Children: An Account of the Books Which Have Been Awarded the Library Association Carnegie Medal, 1936-1975*. Edited by Marcus Crouch and Alec Ellis. Third edition. The Library Association, 1977. © Marcus Crouch and Alec Ellis, 1977. Reprinted by permission of the publisher.

Cullinan, Bernice E., with Mary K. Karrer and Arlene M. Pillar. From *Literature and the Child*. Harcourt Brace Jovanovich, 1981. Copyright © 1981 by Harcourt Brace Jovanovich, Inc. Reprinted by permission of the publisher.

Dixon, Bob. From *Catching Them Young: Sex, Race and Class in Children's Fiction, Vol. 1*. Pluto Press, 1977. Copyright © Pluto Press 1977. Reprinted by permission of the publisher.

Eaton, Anne Thaxter. From *Reading with Children*. The Viking Press, 1940. Copyright 1940, renewed © 1967 by Anne Thaxter Eaton. Reprinted by permission of Viking Penguin Inc.

Egoff, Sheila A. From *Thursday's Child: Trends and Patterns in Contemporary Children's Literature*. American Library Association, 1981. Copyright © 1981 by the American Library Association. All rights reserved. Reprinted by permission of the publisher.

Emanuel, James A. From *Langston Hughes.* Twayne, 1967. Copyright 1967 by Twayne Publishers. All rights reserved. Reprinted with the permission of Twayne Publishers, a division of G. K. Hall & Co., Boston.

Fisher, Margery. From *The Bright Face of Danger.* The Horn Book, Inc., 1986. Copyright © 1986 by Margery Fisher. All rights reserved. Reprinted by permission of the publisher.

Fisher, Margery. From *Intent Upon Reading: A Critical Appraisal of Modern Fiction for Children.* Brockhampton Press, 1961. Copyright © 1961 by Margery Fisher. Reprinted by permission of Hodder & Stoughton Children's Books.

Fisher, Margery. From *Who's Who in Children's Books: A Treasure of the Familiar Characters of Childhood.* Weidenfeld & Nicolson, 1975. Copyright © 1975 by Margery Fisher. All rights reserved. Reprinted by permission of the publisher.

Georgiou, Constantine. From *Children and Their Literature.* Prentice-Hall, 1969. © 1969 by Prentice-Hall, Inc. All rights reserved. Reprinted by permission of the author.

Highwater, Jamake. From *Anpao: An American Indian Odyssey.* J. B. Lippincott Company, 1977. Text copyright © 1977 by Jamake Highwater. All rights reserved. Reprinted by permission of Harper & Row, Publishers, Inc.

Highwater, Jamake. From *Many Smokes, Many Moons: A Chronology of American Indian History through Indian Art.* J. B. Lippincott Company, 1978. Copyright © 1978 by Jamake Highwater. All rights reserved. Reprinted by permission of Harper & Row, Publishers, Inc.

Highwater, Jamake. From an excerpt in *This Song Remembers: Self-Portraits of Native Americans in the Arts.* Edited by Jane B. Katz. Houghton Mifflin, 1980. Copyright © 1980 by Jane B. Katz. All rights reserved. Reprinted by permission of Houghton Mifflin Company.

Huck, Charlotte. S. From *Children's Literature in the Elementary School.* Third edition, updated. Holt, Rinehart and Winston, 1979. Copyright © 1961, 1968 by Holt, Rinehart and Winston, Inc. Copyright © 1976, 1979 by Charlotte S. Huck. All rights reserved. Reprinted by permission of the publisher.

Hürlimann, Bettina. From *Three Centuries of Children's Books in Europe.* Edited and translated by Brian W. Alderson. Oxford University Press, London, 1967. English translation © Oxford University Press, 1967. Reprinted by permission of Oxford University Press.

Lacy, Lyn Ellen. From *Art and Design in Children's Picture Books: An Analysis of Caldecott Award-Winning Illustrations.* American Library Association, 1986. Copyright © 1986 by the American Library Association. All rights reserved. Reprinted by permission of the publisher.

Landsberg, Michele. From *Michele Landsberg's Guide to Children's Books.* Penguin Books Canada Limited, 1986. Copyright © 1986, by Psammead Associates Ltd. All rights reserved. Reprinted by permission of the publisher.

Lanes, Selma G. From *The Art of Maurice Sendak.* Edited by Robert Morton. Harry N. Abrams, Inc., 1980. Text © 1980 Selma G. Lanes. All rights reserved. Reprinted by permission of the publisher.

Lukens, Rebecca J. From *A Critical Handbook of Children's Literature.* Second edition. Scott, Foresman, 1982. Copyright © 1982, 1976 Scott, Foresman and Company. All rights reserved. Reprinted by permission of the publisher.

MacCann, Donnarae, and Olga Richard. From a review of "The Art of Maurice Sendak," in *The First Steps: Best of the Early "ChLA Quarterly."* Edited by Patricia Dooley. ChLA, 1984. © ChLA Publications 1984. Reprinted by permission of the publisher.

Magee, William H. From "The Animal Story: A Challenge in Technique," in *Only Connect: Readings on Children's Literature.* Sheila Egoff, G. T. Stubbs, L. F. Ashley, eds. Second edition. Oxford University Press, Canadian Branch, 1980. © Oxford University Press (Canada) 1980. Reprinted by permission of the author.

Meltzer, Milton. From *Langston Hughes: A Biography.* Thomas Y. Crowell Company, 1968. Copyright © 1968 by Milton Meltzer. All rights reserved. Reprinted by permission of Harper & Row, Publishers, Inc.

Moss, Elaine. From *Picture Books for Young People 9-13.* Second edition. The Thimble Press, 1985. Copyright © 1981, 1985 Elaine Moss. Reprinted by permission of the publisher.

Naylor, Phyllis Reynolds. From *How I Came to Be a Writer.* Atheneum, 1978. Copyright © 1978, 1987 Phyllis Reynolds Naylor. All rights reserved. Reprinted with the permission of Atheneum Publishers, an imprint of Macmillan Publishing Company.

New, W. H. From *Articulating West: Essays on Purpose and Form in Modern Canadian Literature.* New Press, 1972. Copyright © 1972 W. H. New. All rights reserved. Reprinted by permission of the author.

Norton, Donna E. From *Through the Eyes of a Child: An Introduction to Children's Literature.* Second edition. Merrill, 1987. Copyright © 1987, 1983, by Merrill Publishing Company, Columbus, OH. All rights reserved. Reprinted by permission of the publisher.

Ørvig, Mary, and Nina Weibull. From "Children's Book Illustrations in Sweden: An Outline of Developments," in *Culture for Swedish Children.* By Mary Ørvig, Nina Weibull, and others. The Swedish Institute for Children's Books, 1981. © The Swedish Institute for Children's Books 1981. Reprinted by permission of the publisher.

Powers, Effie L. From an introduction to *The Dream Keeper and Other Poems.* By Langston Hughes. Knopf, 1932. Copyright 1932 by Alfred A. Knopf, Inc. Renewed 1960 by Langston Hughes. All rights reserved.

Sadker, Myra Pollack, and David Miller Sadker. From *Now Upon a Time: A Contemporary View of Children's Literature.* Harper & Row, 1977. Copyright © 1977 by Myra Pollack Sadker and David Miller Sadker. All rights reserved. Reprinted by permission of Harper & Row, Publishers, Inc.

Sebestyen, Ouida. From "On Being Published," in *Innocence & Experience: Essays & Conversations on Children's Literature.* Edited by Barbara Harrison and Gregory Maguire. Lothrop, Lee & Shepard Books, 1987. Copyright © 1987 by Barbara Harrison and Gregory Maguire. All rights reserved. Reprinted by permission of Lothrop, Lee & Shepard Books, a division of William Morrow and Company, Inc.

Sewell, Anna. From an excerpt in *The Woman Who Wrote "Black Beauty:" A Life of Anna Sewell.* By Susan Chitty. Hodder and Stoughton, 1971. Copyright © 1971 by Susan Chitty. All rights reserved. Reprinted by permission of Curtis Brown Ltd.

Sutherland, Zena, and May Hill Arbuthnot. From *Children and Books.* Seventh edition. Scott, Foresman, 1986. Copyright © 1986, 1981, 1977, 1972, 1964, 1957, 1947 Scott, Foresman and Company. All rights reserved. Reprinted by permission of the publisher.

Thwaite, Mary F. From *From Primer to Pleasure in Reading.* Revised edition. The Horn Book, Inc., 1972. Copyright © 1963 by Mary F. Thwaite. All rights reserved. Reprinted by permission of the publisher.

Townsend, John Rowe. From *Written for Children: An Outline of English-Language Children's Literature.* Third revised edition. J. B. Lippincott, 1987, Penguin Books, 1987. Copyright © 1965, 1974, 1983, 1987 by John Rowe Townsend. All rights reserved. Reprinted by permission of Harper & Row, Publishers, Inc. In Canada by Penguin Books Inc.

Toynbee, Mrs. From a letter in *The Women Who Wrote "Black Beauty:" A Life of Anna Sewell.* By Susan Chitty. Hodder and Stoughton, 1971. Copyright © 1971 by Susan Chitty. All rights reserved. Reprinted by permission of Curtis Brown Ltd.

Tucker, Nicholas. From *The Child and the Book: A Psychological and Literary Exploration.* Cambridge University Press, 1981. © Cambridge University Press 1981. Reprinted with the permission of the publisher.

Viguers, Ruth Hill. From "The Artist as Storyteller," in *A Critical History of Children's Literature.* By Cornelia Meigs and others, edited by Cornelia Meigs. Revised edition. Macmillan, 1969. Copyright 1953, 1969 by Macmillan Publishing Company. All rights reserved. Reprinted with permission of the publisher.

Wilson, Barbara Ker. From *Noel Streatfeild.* Bodley Head, 1961. © Barbara Ker Wilson 1961. Reprinted by permission of the author.

Wolfe, Leo. From "Maurice Sendak," in *Newbery and Caldecott Medal Books: 1956-1965.* Edited by Lee Kingman. Horn Book, 1965. Copyright © 1965 by The Horn Book, Inc. All rights reserved. Reprinted by permission of the publisher.

Yep, Laurence. From an excerpt in *Literature for Today's Young Adults.* By Alleen Pace Nilsen and Kenneth L. Donelson. Second edition. Scott, Foresman, 1985. Copyright © 1985, 1980 Scott, Foresman and Company. All rights reserved. Reprinted by permission of Laurence Yep.

CUMULATIVE INDEX TO AUTHORS

This index lists all author entries in *Children's Literature Review* and includes cross-references to them in other Gale sources. References in the index are identified as follows:

AITN: *Authors in the News,* Volumes 1-2
CA: *Contemporary Authors* (original series), Volumes 1-124
CANR: *Contemporary Authors New Revision Series,* Volumes 1-26
CAP: *Contemporary Authors Permanent Series,* Volumes 1-2
CA-R: *Contemporary Authors* (revised editions), Volumes 1-44
CDALB: *Concise Dictionary of American Literary Biography,* Volumes 1-3
CLC: *Contemporary Literary Criticism,* Volumes 1-52
CLR: *Children's Literature Review,* Volumes 1-17
DLB: *Dictionary of Literary Biography,* Volumes 1-76
DLB-DS: *Dictionary of Literary Biography Documentary Series,* Volumes 1-5
DLB-Y: *Dictionary of Literary Biography Yearbook,* Volumes 1980-1987
NCLC: *Nineteenth-Century Literature Criticism,* Volumes 1-21
SAAS: *Something about the Author Autobiography Series,* Volume 1-6
SATA: *Something about the Author,* Volumes 1-53
TCLC: *Twentieth-Century Literary Criticism,* Volumes 1-31
YABC: *Yesterday's Authors of Books for Children,* Volumes 1-2

CUMULATIVE INDEX TO NATIONALITIES

CUMULATIVE INDEX TO TITLES

Title Index

Title Index

Title Index